An Introduction to American Archaeology   Volume One: North and Middle America

Gordon R. Willey   *Peabody Museum, Harvard University*

An Introduction to American

VOLUME ONE   North and Middle America

Prentice-Hall, Inc.,   Englewood Cliffs, New Jersey

Archaeology

Prentice-Hall Anthropology Series   *David M. Schneider, Editor*

An Introduction to American Archaeology
Volume One: North and Middle America
Gordon R. Willey
© Copyright 1966 by Prentice-Hall, Inc.,
Englewood Cliffs, New Jersey.

Library of Congress Catalog No. 66-10096.
Printed in the United States of America.

Designed by Walter Behnke

Drawings by Avis Tulloch

Current printing (last digit):
11   10   9   8   7   6   5

C-47783

To the memory of William Duncan Strong (1899–1962)

This book has been written to introduce both the lay reader and the student to the broad field of American archaeology. The work is projected in two volumes: the present one, on North and Middle America, and a second, now in preparation, on South America.

It was written—and subsequently revised and re-written—in the period beginning in October of 1962 and ending in mid-year of 1965. I am indebted to the United States Fulbright Commission and to the authorities of Harvard University and Cambridge University for making it possible for me to have a year in residence in England, in 1962–1963, most of which time was spent on the preparation of this book. I am also indebted to Harvard University, its Peabody Museum and Department of Anthropology, and to the Bowditch Professorship which I hold for allowing me to continue and complete the work in 1963–1965.

The archaeological colleagues who have given me intellectual aid, guidance, and stimulation in the preparation of this volume have been so numerous that I hesitate to single any of them out by name. I have "picked their brains" with questions both direct and indirect for a good many years. This holds for both professional associates and students in the United States, Canada, Latin America, England and Europe, and Japan. I am deeply grateful to all of them and can only hope that my syntheses and interpretations offered here will not be a cause of dismay when and if they read them.

Those persons and institutions who have provided photographic illustrations are listed following the preface. I am very appreciative of their efforts on my behalf. Appropriate courtesy line citations also accompany individual pictures.

Preface

The drawings in the book are the work of Miss Avis Tulloch, except for maps and charts which were prepared by Ben Arrington, John Dunleavy, and the art staff of the Project Planning Department of Prentice-Hall under the direction of Walter Behnke. The manuscript was typed by Mrs. B. Leonard, of Cambridge, England, and Mrs. Maria von Mering Huggins, of Cambridge, Massachusetts. I am also indebted to the latter for her unfailing industry in helping me check the bibliography and in many other matters. I am grateful to my wife, Katharine W. Willey, for her numerous readings of the manuscript, and to her and to James J. Murray III of Prentice-Hall for constant encouragement and advice. I also wish to add a word of thanks to Mrs. Vera Timbanard for guiding the manuscript through the production process. Finally, the text has benefited from the editorial skill of Wilbur E. Mangas.

Gordon R. Willey

Acknowledgments

American Museum of Natural History
Amerind Foundation
Arizona State Museum
British Museum
Brooklyn Museum
Brown University Press
Cambridge Museum of Archaeology and Ethnology
Catalina Island Museum, California
Chicago Natural History Museum
Dartmouth College Museum
Denver Museum of Natural History
Dumbarton Oaks Pre-Columbian Collection, Washington, D.C.
Haffenreffer Museum, Bristol, Rhode Island
Instituto de Antropología e Historia, Mexico (National Museum of Mexico)
McGraw-Hill Book Co., New York
Museum of the American Indian, New York
Museum of Modern Art, New York
Museum für Völkerkunde und Vorgeschichte, Hamburg
National Geographic Society, Washington, D.C.
National Museum of Canada
Nebraska State Historical Society
New York State Museum and Science Service, Albany
Ohio State Museum

Peabody Museum, Harvard University
River Basin Surveys, Smithsonian Institution, Lincoln, Nebraska
Smithsonian Institution, Washington, D.C.
Texas Archaeological Salvage Project, University of Texas
United States National Park Service
University of Chicago Press
University of Pennsylvania Museum

G. A. Agogino	E. W. Haury
Raymond Baby	R. F. Heizer
Elizabeth Benson	Preston Holder
Ignacio Bernal	Henry Irwin
Charles Borden	Edward Jelks
W. R. Bullard, Jr.	Frederick Johnson
G. H. S. Bushnell	Marvin F. Kivett
D. S. Byers	John Krussow
W. W. Caldwell	W. D. Logan
John Champe	R. S. MacNeish
J. L. Coe	P. S. Martin
W. R. Coe, Jr.	S. H. Maule
L. S. Cressman	Clement Meighan
Adrian Digby	Nickolas Muray
C. C. Di Peso	G. I. Quimby
Frederick Dockstader	W. A. Ritchie
Wilson Duff	F. H. H. Roberts, Jr.
Dudley Easby	Emory Strong
G. F. Ekholm	Dee Ann Suhm
Colonel Fearing	John Thacher
E. N. Ferdon	J. E. S. Thompson
J. B. Griffin	Raymond Thompson
W. Haberland	G. T. Trewartha
Elmer Harp, Jr.	H. M. Wormington

Contents

An Introduction to American Archaeology   Volume One: North and Middle America

Archaeology as History

Intent and Outlook. The intent of this book is history—an introductory culture history of pre-Columbian America.

The methods that are used by the archaeologists impose rather severe limitations on such a history. To begin with, most of the pre-Columbian past is without contemporary written documents, and those few which do exist are imperfectly translated. This means that a great deal of the texture of history—the interplay of human personalities—is lost and that we will never be able to know how an ancient people felt about their world and themselves. In the main, the archaeologist is thrown back on material objects, those things which have survived the erosion of time or have left some sort of detectable trace, for his interpretations of the events of history. Inevitably this gives a technological slant to the story he has to tell. It should come as no surprise that archaeology frequently treats more effectively of man in his relationships to his natural environment than of other aspects of culture. These are the primary data of the discipline: the objects made by men and the ground they were left on or in. Then there is the perpetual dilemma of dealing with the minutely concrete, with the spear points and animal bones found at

Introduction

1

the hearth-side, and moving from this in a sweeping stride to the grand abstraction, to the ancient hunters following the herds over a hemisphere. Any generalizing history encounters these same difficulties, it is true, but for history reconstructed from archaeology the levels of inference that interpose themselves between fact and abstraction are more numerous and less well-documented. Finally, for a general work, such as this is intended to be, there is the important matter of selection. What data are to be presented and at the expense of what other data? It is with these problems and limitations that archaeological culture history is written. No easy solutions recommend themselves, but the task should be faced with caution rather than pessimism. Archaeology is the imaginative recapture of the past within the hard boundaries of the evidence, the steering between the Scylla of fantasy and the Charybdis of unrelieved fact; but unless we are willing to turn our backs on the vastly longer part of man's history on this globe— and on all of what happened in pre-Columbian America—it is our only recourse.

Inference and Analogy in Archaeology. Inference is the key or the methodological pivot of archaeology, for it is only through inference that inanimate objects are reassembled into the milieu of life. Inferences are drawn from analogies which rest on the premise that similar forms imply similar functions. There are two classes of analogy. General analogy is available to the archaeologist and the "man in the street" alike. It has a "common sense" basis which assumes an underlying affinity of all humankind. It is by such general analogy that the function of a spear point is read into a sharpened piece of flint or the uses of a cooking pot imputed to a fire-blackened vessel. Such humble analogies are not to be dismissed lightly, for they are fundamental to archaeological interpretation. They are most safely made in the universal realms of tools, weapons, the food quest, and shelter. But general analogies can be misleading. It is axiomatic in anthropology that cultures differ, and the same form, or approximate form, in two different cultures may not carry the same function or meaning. More reliable is specific historical analogy. These are the analogies which are projected within the limits of a specific historical or cultural tradition. Such analogies have been especially important for American archaeology, where the pre-Columbian past lies less than 500 years away and where in most regions some ethnohistoric records are available or aboriginal peoples and cultures are still extant. When it is possible to identify the archaeological remains of a given region with the ancestors of an Indian tribe found there in historic or modern times, a continuity from the present back into the past can be established. With this continuity the archaeologist operates within the confines of a tradition, and his chances of correctly inferring the function of archaeological objects or remains by analogy with historic or present uses and customs of the tribe in question are greatly improved. For instance, we understand the religious and mythological significance of certain subjects in pre-Columbian Maya art from Spanish ethnohistorical accounts of the sixteenth century, and can interpret the meanings and functions of prehistoric paintings and architectural features in the Southwestern Pueblo region from ethnohistorical and modern accounts of Pueblo Indian ceremonials. Despite its advantages, specific historical analogy is not infallible. Frequently, it is difficult to demonstrate a firm linkage between historic or modern peoples and archaeological periods; and even if this linkage can be established, cultures within the same historical tradition change through time and many of the objects or elements from the prehistoric past will have no meaning, or will not have the same meaning, even to those persons in direct line of cultural descent. The most unhappy New World example of this is the lack of any knowledge among present-day Maya Indians of the nature of the hieroglyphic writing of their forefathers.[1]

Methodology and Organization. In relating history, methodology should not intrude, and I shall try to keep special terminology at a minimum. The presentation is simple, and the concepts employed will emerge or be made clear in the course of it. The plan is to follow through the histories of the *major cultural traditions* of the Americas. By major cultural traditions I mean the principal native cultures or major cultural groupings as these can be discerned in geographical space and in chronological time.[2] In every instance these dimensions of space and time are appreciable. Each major cultural tradition is characterized by a definite patterning of subsistence practices, technology, and ecological adaptation. Each major cultural tradition also probably had a definite ideological pattern or world view. This can be demonstrated for some of them in their thematic

arts, evidences of religious practices, and intellectual pursuits. For others, however, particularly the earliest of the New World traditions, the data are inadequate to allow such reconstructions. From this brief definition it should be clear that major cultural traditions as conceived here are not culture types in the sense of hunting-gathering cultures as opposed to agricultural ones or "irrigation civilizations" as against "theocratic states." I am not classifying cultures by functional or developmental principles, but am describing them and tracing their discrete histories. A hunting-gathering or an agricultural economy, irrigation or a theocratic socio-political structure, are all, of course, highly important traits or conditions which, in specific cases, aid in the definition of major cultural traditions. But no one of them is, in itself, considered sufficient for defining a major cultural tradition. For example, as will be seen, several major cultural traditions have hunting-gathering subsistence economies and several others have agricultural economies. Other traits and trait patterings, however, distinguish among them.

This treatment is not a synthesis of New World culture history by stages.[3] Here the organization is primarily "vertical" rather than "horizontal." Our attention is on following the development of particular forms and patterns through time and in their unique interrelationships with one another rather than in seeing them laid out according to a broad, hemisphere-wide classification of types part functionally and only part historically derived. Any continental-wide appraisals, of a functional-developmental or an historical sort, are reserved for a concluding chapter.

The greatest difficulty in the present approach is, of course, determining the principal units, the major cultural traditions. This is a classic problem of culture history. What are the civilizations or the cultures of the world or any part of it? How many are there? How and where does one draw the boundaries to separate the complex intermeshings of histories? For cultures and civilizations do not grow up *in vacuo*. All the major New World cultural traditions which we will consider are in some way interrelated with other traditions, have been influenced by them, or have sprung, at least in part, from them. It would be idle to deny that a degree of arbitrariness and of subjectivity enters into the historian's or the archaeologist's judgment in his conceptions and separations, and my selections of the major pre-Columbian traditions carry elements of these qualities. It is unlikely that any two American archaeologists would agree on all the details of the lines of separation that might be said to diagram or to discriminate the most important New World culture growths. Knowledge of American archaeology is still too incomplete, and even if our knowledge were more complete authorities would differ on the criteria of selection according to their interests and points of view. At the same time, I think there would be considerable agreement on the major outlines, for these are, to all intents and purposes, the culture historical spheres or frames of reference for most archaeological discourse: the Desert Culture or cultural tradition of arid Western North America, the Big-Game Hunters of the Pleistocene grasslands of the Plains, the Archaic cultural tradition of Eastern North America, Southwestern culture, Mesoamerican[4] culture—to name only a few of the better known. It is this kind of entity that I purpose to make my primary unit of study.

The book is organized around this conception of major cultural traditions and the general chronological progression of history. The chapter on "The Early Americans" examines the earliest of the major cultural traditions, those of Pleistocene and early post-Pleistocene times. Then, chapters are arranged in a certain geographic order so that the Mesoamerican cultural tradition and culture area is dealt with first and is then followed by treatments of North American cultural traditions, both agricultural and non-agricultural. In following this scheme some of the earliest cultural traditions persist later than their Pleistocene and early post-Pleistocene beginnings and form a base for later traditions. The continuity of the narrative thus will be picked up or resumed in the appropriate geographical positions. In Volume 2 a similar plan of organization will be followed for South America.

As this organization implies, the reference frames of geographical culture areas and chronological scales for these areas are important adjuncts to the study of the major cultural traditions. The archaeological culture areas, as employed here, are extensions of the traditional ethnographic culture area concept. It is, however, much more difficult to delineate archaeological areas than those which are projected for a single ethnographic horizon, because archaeological culture boundaries change through time. Occasionally, such changes are drastic. Such phenomena usually coincide with the inception or introduction of a new major cultural tradition. A prime example would be the differentiation of the Southwest United States area from the nearby Great Basin area which partially surrounds it. At an early period the two areas were one, with the whole characterized by the Desert cultural tradition. Later, with the rise of village farming patterns and the beginnings of the Southwestern cultural tradition, the Southwest area came into existence. Often, however, the "hearts" or "cores" of culture areas remain relatively fixed, with only the borderlands expanding or retracting with the passage of time. Sometimes this is true even in spite of major cultural traditional shifts. Thus, the Eastern Woodlands of North America maintained an integrity as a culture area, as the homeland of the earlier Archaic tradition and of the two later traditions which succeeded it— apparently a testimony to the powerful conditioning factors of natural environment in culture development, at least under certain conditions. In sum, archaeological culture areas must be compromises which will embrace a significant cultural unity through a significant span of time. Those culture areas shown for North and Middle America in Fig. 1-1 are such approximations.[5] It should be noted, however, that these areas are most valid for the later or recent geological era rather than for the Pleistocene, and for that reason they are more pertinent to the later cultural traditions than to the earlier ones.

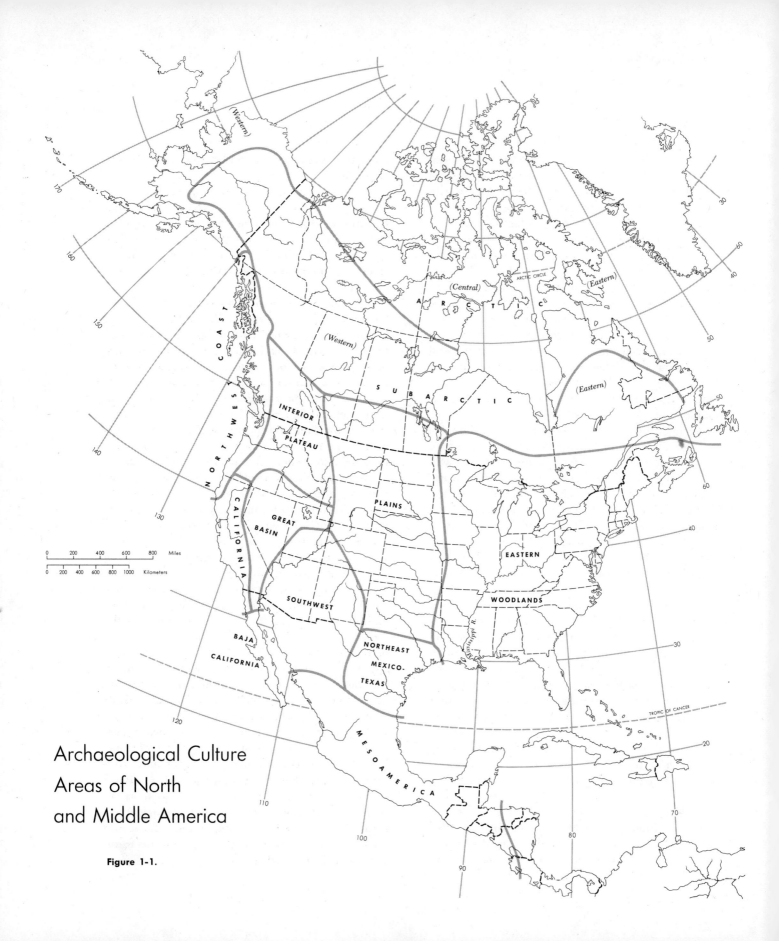

Archaeological Culture
Areas of North
and Middle America

Figure 1-1.

Each major cultural tradition, within the frame of the appropriate area or areas, will be discussed chronologically. The data of culture phases, as these are known from local and regional sequences, will be arranged by periods. These periods of area chronologies are defined in scales of absolute years. Although the dates assigned to periods are usually estimates, and the equating of culture phases on the same period level will most frequently be achieved through a comparison of the content of these phases, my intent is to approach correlations in absolute time insofar as possible. The means by which we can do this in American archaeology include, first and foremost, radiocarbon dates where these are available, and, to a much more restricted extent, dendrochronological readings and native calendars. Glottochronological reckonings and geological and archaeological estimates, or guesses, will be employed, failing more exact methods. It has been the custom to apply culturally descriptive, functional, or developmental nomenclature to periods in many American areas, and rather than to design new names or numbers for the periods of all these area chronologies which are established in monographic and other archaeological writings I have used the established terminology; however, it should be borne in mind that my usage is strictly in keeping with the definition of periods as horizontal time bands marked off on the chronological chart in years, centuries, or millennia.[6]

As already stated, the subject of this book is New World culture history. This includes not only the culture-historical integration of the data of archaeology in their appropriate contexts of association, geography, and chronology and the functions inferred from these data but also a consideration of explanation and cause. I shall be less concerned with process or a search for cultural "laws" than with at times attempting to explain why certain cultural traditions developed, or failed to develop, as they did. That process or "law" might be distilled from a cross-cultural or comparative examination of recurrent historical phenomena is, of course, possible; but this is not my purpose. The treatment is essentially historical and not comparative. From this it follows that although several types of cultural process may be evoked in attempting to explain culture change or growth in particular instances, I am not demonstrating or championing any one process, theory, or kind of explanation as a key to a comprehensive understanding of what went on in prehistoric America.

Scope and Detail. A word about the scope and detail of this history. Geographically, it embraces the Western Hemisphere, the Americas.[7] Chronologically, it begins with man's first appearance on these continents and continues up to the point at which native societies and cultures are replaced or transformed by European ones. As noted, analogies drawn between prehistoric cultures and historic or modern ones are a principal means of archaeological interpretation, and for this reason the line separating pre-Columbian from post-Columbian will be crossed to some slight degree as the occasions demand; however, our subject is essentially the archaeological past and not the ethnographic present. In making this distinction no single time line of archaeological-ethnographic division can be drawn for the whole New World. In this sense, the term "pre-Columbian" is a misnomer. Although West Indian aboriginal cultures were thoroughly shattered a few decades after the voyages of Columbus, those of other parts of the New World were spared for a longer time. In Mexico, Central America, and Peru the record of events passes from archaeology to colonial history somewhere in the sixteenth century. Elsewhere, in North America or in many parts of South America, this date line must be moved up to the seventeenth, eighteenth, or nineteenth centuries. And, in some inaccessible regions the story of native culture has, in effect, remained "archaeological" down to the twentieth century.

As to degrees of detail with which major cultural traditions and archaeological areas are treated, I have tried to strike a balance. Those for which a rich monographic and specialized bibliography is available tend to receive, on this count, more space than those for which data are few. At the same time, an attempt has been made not to let this consideration be completely overriding and to see that all the Americas are represented in this introduction. Throughout, the approach has been to sample rather than to treat completely and to inform the reader only with that substance of descriptive detail which will allow him to follow the narrative of history.

The Natural Setting of the Americas

The relationships of man to the land are a basic concern of human history. We will examine these relationships in diverse natural environments as we proceed with the archaeological story, but before doing this it will be well to have in mind the major patterns of physiography and climate that combine to produce these environments.[8]

Physiography. The New World land areas measure about 9000 miles from the Arctic to Cape Horn, and both continents are approximately 3000 miles across at their widest points. Thus, the territory involved is immense, covering one-quarter of the earth's habitable surface. All major climatic zones of the globe, except Antarctica, are spanned by the Americas, and even the most casual glance at a relief map will give an idea of the great variations in terrain.

The most impressive physiographic features of the hemisphere are the two western cordilleras which run the lengths of the continents like gigantic backbones. Appended to these are the main land masses, extending out to the east. Along the eastern sides of both continents are other, lesser mountain chains which also run north-south. Between these western and eastern mountain systems are vast central lowlands. The two Americas are joined by the narrow, twisting isthmus of southern Central America. East of this isthmus the Gulf of Mexico and the Caribbean Sea separate the main land areas of the two continents, but this separation seems only semi-complete, for the large and small islands of the Antilles dot the sea from Venezuela to Florida.

Geologists and geographers recognize several major physiographic divisions of these New World features. The great western cordillera of North America is composed of the Rocky Mountains on the east, the high intermontane plateaus and desert basins to the west of the Rockies, and the Pacific Mountains, still farther to the west. In Mexico, the Sierra Madre Mountains and the plateau country may be considered within the same general physiographic provinces as the Rockies and the northern intermontane lands. A high volcanic chain known as the Mesa Central marks the terminus of these systems. South of this the Sierra Madre del Sur of Mexico and the mountains of Chiapas, Guatemala, and Honduras are a part of another system which runs east-west and emerges in the Greater Antilles of the Caribbean.

In North America the eastern mountains are the Appalachians, an ancient eroded chain whose highest peaks are less than half as high as the tallest summits of the western cordillera. The plains or lowlands between the Appalachians and the Rockies include the glaciated peneplain of the Canadian Shield in the north, the Central Lowlands and the plains covered with glacial drift that lie to the south of the Shield, the Great Plains of the West, and the Mississippi Basin. Only the Ozark-Ouachita block of hills in Missouri and Arkansas breaks the vast sweep of these North American interior plains. East of the Appalachians a coastal plain, relatively narrow in the north but widening as it encircles the Gulf of Mexico, can be followed to the Peninsula of Yucatán.

The Andes are the western cordilleran chain in South America. Like their North American counterparts they are relatively young, high mountains. In the far south, the ocean has drowned many mountain valleys to produce a fiord coast, and, to the north, two parallel ranges run the length of Chile. Northwestern Argentina is a basin and range country and Bolivia has high intermontane plateaus. The cordillera narrows somewhat in Peru

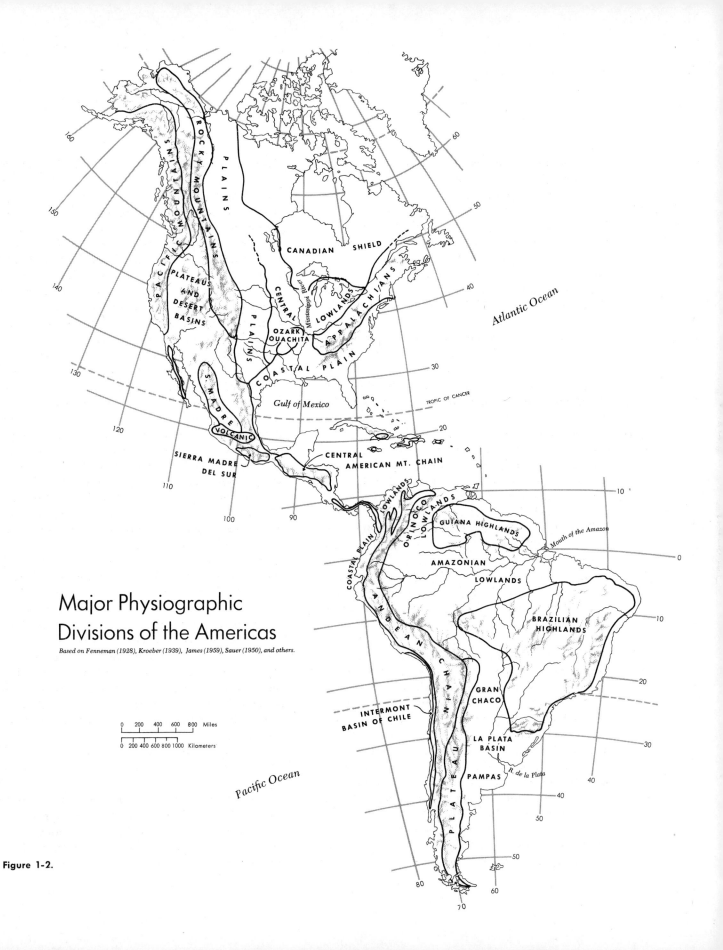

Major Physiographic Divisions of the Americas

Based on Fenneman (1928), Kroeber (1939), James (1959), Sauer (1950), and others.

Figure 1-2.

and Ecuador where there are, again, two more or less parallel ranges. In both these countries there are numerous intermontane basins. The Colombian Andes diverge to the north, passing into Panama and turning eastward along the Caribbean coast into Venezuela. A coastal strip of varying widths runs along the South American cordillera. In the south and up into Peru it is the narrowest kind of a ledge, but farther north, in Ecuador and Colombia, it widens to a true coastal plain.

The eastern highlands of South America are geologically old and deeply eroded. North of the Amazon they are known as the Guiana Highlands and, to the south of this river, as the Brazilian Highlands. The Brazilian Highlands extend up the Amazon for 2000 miles and for about the same distance down the South Atlantic coast. The coastal escarpment is steep and backs a very narrow coastal strip. Inland, the highlands drop off in elevation as one moves west over rugged ridge and valley topography. The South American central lowlands include the Amazon and Orinoco basins and the southern plains centering around the Plate, or La Plata, basin. These southern plains embrace the flats of the Gran Chaco, the alluvial lands of the Parana-Paraguay Rivers, and the Argentine Pampas. Farther to the south, in Patagonia, the land rises to form a plateau which flanks the southern Andes.

Climate. These patterns of physiography are one major element in the creation of the natural environmental zones in which man lived in the New World. Climate is another. Although conditioned by physiography, climate is determined primarily by latitude and by warm and cold air masses. Soils and vegetation tend to correlate closely with climate although they, too, are conditioned by physiography and geological understructure. Let us examine, rapidly, climatic zones, soils, and vegetation in the Americas.

Northern North America, from Greenland to Alaska, is crossed by polar tundra (ET), polar ice cap (EF), and subarctic, or Taiga (Dcf), zones.[9]

These zones overlie the Canadian Shield, northern Plains, and the northern portion of the western cordillera. The tundra is virtually treeless, the soils frozen. The subarctic supports coniferous trees although the soils are thin, infertile podzols. Below the subarctic, humid continental climatic belts cross southern Canada and the eastern United States. These are microthermal (Dbf, Daf), or relatively cold, in the north and mesothermal, or subtropical (Caf), in the south. These climates exhibit marked seasonal temperature changes. The vegetation cover is coniferous and deciduous forest which tends to thin out toward the west where trees are found only along the river courses that cut through the plains. The forest, prairie, and plains (chernozem) soils are all rich, and rainfall is sufficient for agriculture except along the western margins of the zones. Western North America generally has a dry climate. North of latitude 35 it can be described as "middle latitude semiarid or steppe (BSk)" type, whereas south of this line it is mainly "subtropical semiarid (BSh)" or "subtropical arid (BWh)". Vegetation varies from some bush and grass cover to complete desert conditions. Agriculture is either confined to oasis locations or is precariously subject to drought. The only exceptions to these semiarid or arid climates in western North America are the high mountains which, although having relatively low precipitation, are not properly classed as deserts or steppes by climatologists. The Pacific Coast of North America has a humid marine (Cb) climate in the north and a Mediterranean (Cs) climate in the south, which includes most of California. In the rainy north the soils are fertile and the land is covered with heavy forests; in the warmer, drier south the soils are poorer and scrub bush is the principal vegetation.

Most of the American tropics have rainy climates, either tropical rainforest (Af, Am) or tropical savanna (Aw). The exceptions are the high mountainous regions of Mesoamerica or the Andes and the Peruvian desert coast. The tropical rainforests consist of dense covers of broadleaf evergreen trees laced with vines and creepers. Their lateritic red soils are deep but low in mineral con-

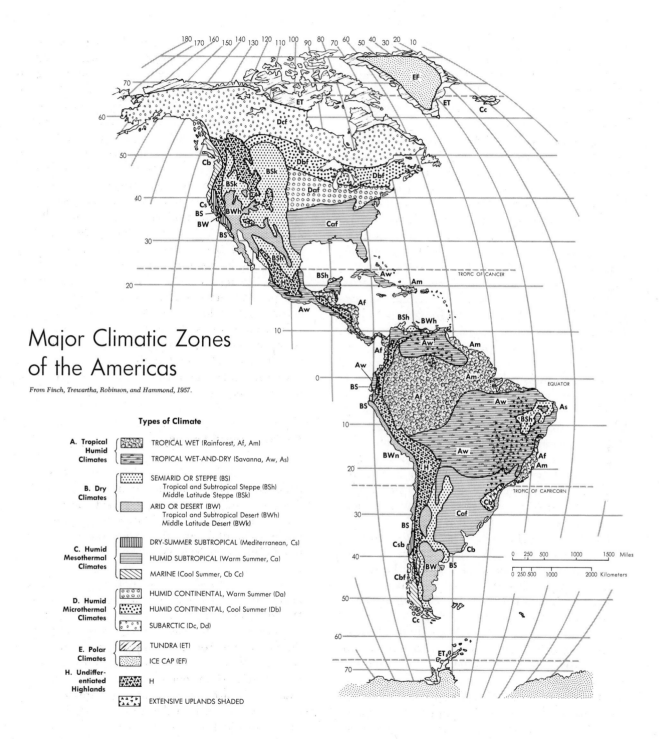

Major Climatic Zones
of the Americas

From Finch, Trewartha, Robinson, and Hammond, 1957.

Types of Climate

A. Tropical Humid Climates
- TROPICAL WET (Rainforest, Af, Am)
- TROPICAL WET-AND-DRY (Savanna, Aw, As)

B. Dry Climates
- SEMIARID OR STEPPE (BS)
  Tropical and Subtropical Steppe (BSh)
  Middle Latitude Steppe (BSk)
- ARID OR DESERT (BW)
  Tropical and Subtropical Desert (BWh)
  Middle Latitude Desert (BWk)

C. Humid Mesothermal Climates
- DRY-SUMMER SUBTROPICAL (Mediterranean, Cs)
- HUMID SUBTROPICAL (Warm Summer, Ca)
- MARINE (Cool Summer, Cb Cc)

D. Humid Microthermal Climates
- HUMID CONTINENTAL, Warm Summer (Da)
- HUMID CONTINENTAL, Cool Summer (Db)
- SUBARCTIC (Dc, Dd)

E. Polar Climates
- TUNDRA (ET)
- ICE CAP (EF)

H. Undifferentiated Highlands
- H
- EXTENSIVE UPLANDS SHADED

Figure 1-3.

tent due to leaching. Such soils may be cultivated in year-round growing seasons but they deteriorate rapidly. The tropical savanna zones have less rainfall, a marked wet-dry seasonal shift, and considerably less forest cover. Frequently, they are grasslands dotted with trees.

Dry climates occur in South America in scattered locations such as coastal Venezuela (BSh, BWh), northeastern Brazil (BSh), and coastal Peru and north Chile (BWn). In the latter region desert conditions in a tropical latitude are moderated by cool ocean currents. There is also a long north-south strip of semiarid or arid climate which extends from the Gran Chaco southward along the eastern edge of the Andes to Tierra del Fuego.

Andean climates (H), like those of the North American Rockies and Pacific mountains, are markedly affected by altitude. In general, these high-altitude climates become wetter and warmer and more suited for human habitation as one moves from south to north. In Colombia, for example, the elevations between 5000 and 10,000 feet are still heavily forested and shrouded in mists, and even above 10,000 feet wet paramos are suitable for potato-growing. Somewhat similar conditions prevail in Ecuador, but Peru is drier and colder at high altitudes, and Bolivia is more so. The uplands, or puna, of these countries are covered by grass or "tola heath" on which llama still graze. High-altitude crops, such as quinoa, oca, and potatoes, are grown here.

The Argentine Pampas, Uruguay, southern Paraguay, and southern Brazil lie in a humid subtropical (Caf) zone, much like that of the southeastern United States except for the native vegetation cover which is mainly grass rather than forest. Central Chile has a Mediterranean (Csb) climate much like that of California. Vegetation is largely thorny woodland, cactus, scrub bush, and grassland. South of the 37th parallel is a humid marine (Cbf, Cc) zone similar to the north Pacific coast of North America. Thick beech and conifer forests extend as far south as the 47th parallel, but beyond this point the forests diminish and give way to open country.

These conditions of climate and vegetation exist today, and they pertain, with some significant exceptions, to the Holocene, or Recent, geological era. One such exception, of importance to human life and culture, was the hot dry "climatic optimum," or Altithermal, of 5000 to 2500 B.C., at which time many regions now habitable were probably not so. Prior to the Recent era, the climatic conditions of the Pleistocene were undoubtedly significantly different from those we now know. At Wisconsin glacial maximum, ice sheets extended as far south as the Columbia River basin and the Ohio Valley, and other isolated glacial areas existed farther west and south in the Rocky Mountains, in Mexico, and in the South American Andes. During the various glacial maxima, and in the pluvial interstadials, climates were not only considerably colder than those of today but also vast areas to the south of the ice sheets in North America, which are now semiarid or arid, were then grasslands dotted with lakes and swamps. Elsewhere, colder and wetter conditions than those of the Recent era probably prevailed.

The New World Peoples

The New World aborigines are the American Indians and the closely related Eskimos. They are the people who occupied the two continents and the nearby islands when Columbus made his landfall, and their ancestors date back to remote times on New World soil.

Origins. The natives of America, back to their earliest appearances on the New World scene, are of the species *Homo sapiens,* or modern man. This basic finding means that man did not evolve from lower anthropoid forms in the New World. No living or fossil apes are known in the Western Hemisphere, as they are in the Old World, nor are more primitive examples of the genus *Homo* present in the Americas. It also means that man did not enter the Western Hemisphere until *Homo sapiens* had developed in and was fairly widespread throughout the Eastern Hemisphere, particularly northeastern Asia. From what is now known of man's biological evolution in the Old World, and of geological history and dating, it is unlikely that this entry of *Homo sapiens* into the New World antedated the Pleistocene third interglacial. Most physical anthropologists believe that America was peopled from northeastern Asia. Although not necessarily denying that some occasional trans-Pacific voyagers may have made their way from more central latitudes in Asia to the New World, the Bering Strait route of entry is considered as the single important one for the overwhelming majority of the immigrants. Finally, physical anthropologists agree that all the American Indians and the Eskimos have a strong Mongoloid racial cast or general resemblance.

Differences of opinion among physical anthropologists about the American Indian center around the significance of the physical variability within the New World populations. The late E. A. Hooton observed that although present-day Indian groups all exhibited a "Mongoloid wash" of features, including dark hair and eyes, medium-brown skin, and a relative absence of facial or body hair, these features represented a relatively late migration, or series of migrations, from Asia. The earlier American immigrants, according to him, were considerably less Mongoloid and could not, properly, be included in a Mongoloid race. To support these arguments, Hooton pointed to the Eskimo as being the most Mongoloid in appearance, with a smooth forehead, marked epicanthic eye-folds, a low-rooted and saddle-backed infantile nose, and a yellow skin. Farther south in North America, and presumably preceding the Eskimo as immigrants to the New World, American Indians were characterized by more receding, bony brows, boldly arched noses, and coppery skins. Still farther south, in Central and South America, were others with wavy hair, very dark skins, and short straight noses. These distributions suggested a series of separate migrations from Asia to the New World, with the earlier waves of immigration being non-Mongoloid in racial background. More specifically, Hooton

linked the early archaeological populations of the Southwestern United States with Old World Indo-Dravidian, Australian, and Ainu strains. Other anthropologists, while not identifying particular New World skeletal or living series as being representative of Old World non-Mongoloid types, admit the possibility of non-Mongoloid types in Asia in Pleistocene times as a potential pool for migrants to the Americas. J. B. Birdsell designates such groups as Negritos, Carpentarians ("primitive Veddoids"), and Amurians (Caucasoid prototypes of the Ainu); and, in his opinion, the American Indians had a dihybrid origin of Amurian-Mongoloid mixture. He also speculates that if man reached America as early as the third interglacial, he was more Amurian than Mongoloid.[10]

W. W. Howells tends to dissent from this argument for non-Mongoloid forbears of the American Indian with his suggestion that the earlier American Indians were descendants of a generalized Mongoloid stock which was present in Pleistocene times in northern Asia before the more specialized Mongoloids, such as the Chinese, had developed. He points out that present-day peoples bearing the nearest resemblances to the American Indians are to be found in those areas which are located around the fringes of the Old World Mongoloid stock; namely, in Indonesia, central Asia, and Tibet. Evidence for this generalized, American Indian-like Mongoloid type in Asia in early times is cited by T. D. Stewart, who compared the late Pleistocene Tzeyang and Liukiang crania of western and southern China with American Indian skulls from Florida and California and also indicated that the skulls from the Upper Cave at Choukoutien (late Pleistocene) resembled American Indian types.[11]

Variation: Sub-Races or Varieties. Whatever the racial origins of the American Indians and Eskimos in Asia, whether these be multiple following Hooton's interpretation, Mongoloid hybrids as in Birdsell's hypothesis, or Howells' unspecialized Mongoloids, considerable physical variation does exist among the aborigines of the New

World. A number of attempts have been made to describe this variation. R. B. Dixon made one of the first, followed by E. Von Eickstedt, J. Imbelloni, and by G. K. Neumann.[12] Underlying all these classifications of sub-races or varieties among the American Indians is the premise that each, or most, of the varieties can be attributed to a separate migration from the Old World. The most systematic and comprehensive classifications have been the Von Eickstedt and Imbelloni schemes. The two are similar, the Imbelloni plan being an extension and refinement of the former with special reference to the New World. Imbelloni set forth eleven major varieties based on stature, ruggedness of bone structure, cephalic and head height indices, nasal and facial indices, skin color, and hair color and form. Observations on living Indians predominated, but skeletal series also were considered. The eleven varieties were plotted on a hemisphere map and were assigned a chronological order of entry or migration into the New World. Some of these migrations were presumed to have come across the Bering Straits, others from more directly across the Pacific to South America.

Neither the Imbelloni nor the Von Eickstedt classification has been accepted generally by American physical anthropologists. M. T. Newman has summarized the criticisms leveled against them.[13] They are largely impressionistic and based on few metric data, they tend to be cross-cut by distributions of stature and head form, and they do not take *in situ* chronology into sufficient account. Nevertheless, as Newman admits, they do recapitulate to a degree some of the physical diversity which exists among the American aborigines.

A better documented and more finely scaled attempt is the one essayed by G. K. Neumann.[14] Neumann has used more carefully controlled metric data than were available to either Von Eickstedt or Imbelloni, and these data, from both the living and the dead, have been more exactly coordinated with archaeological and distribution information. Neumann has established eight varieties, but these pertained only to America north of Mexico, or, at least, the author did not attempt to

extend them farther. Like Imbelloni's types, the varieties have chronological significance but also some persistence through time. Thus, Neumann's Otamid variety, a rugged longhead with massive mandible, is identified with North American early man discoveries, with early Woodland cultures of Illinois, and with the historic populations of the Texas coast. Other varieties, such as the Iswanid and Ashiwid, are thought to be the peoples of the Archaic cultures of the southeastern United States and those of the Basketmaker culture of the Southwest, respectively. Neumann believes that all but one of his varieties represent separate migrations to the New World from northeast Asia, the two latest ones, the Deneid and Inuid, being the Athapascan and the Eskimo. These migrations began with the Otamid in late Pleistocene times and continued up to a relatively late prehistoric period with the Deneid and Inuid. In his hypothesis only the Lakotid, a North American Plains Indian type, first appeared in the Americas as a result of mixture among other varieties.

It remains to be seen how Neumann's classification will stand up as archaeological research makes new cranial and skeletal series available. One very definite conclusion does emerge from both the Imbelloni and Neumann studies. This is that the earliest American populations were dolichocephals and that the later ones, at least in certain large areas, were more mesocephalic or brachycephalic. This certainly suggests, although it does not prove, that man did emigrate from Asia to America at different times and in recognizably different sub-racial or varietal types.

Variation: Environmental Adaptation. An explanation other than that of a series of separate migrations from Asia has also been offered for the physical variability of the American Indian. This is that both stature and head form of New World populations have responded to environmental adaptation and change. The hypothesis has been set forth by M. T. Newman, who began by applying Bergmann's ecological rule to man. The essence of Bergmann's rule is that warm-blooded animals of a single, widely varying species will be larger in colder climates and smaller in warmer ones. This is a function of body heat retention or dissipation by respectively reducing or increasing radiating skin surface per unit of body mass. Plotting stature in New World man on a hemispheric scale, Newman observed close correlations between increased size and distance from the equatorial regions. He then examined archaeological skeletal series through time in given localities. The results of this study tended to confirm the former survey. That is, in Mesoamerica, the Southwest, and California the trends were toward a decrease in stature of several centimeters over time spans of a few centuries to a few millennia. Conversely, in the eastern United States and in the relatively cool upland climate of the southern sierras of Peru, marked-to-slight stature increases were tabulated. Since stature correlates closely with body size and body weight, it would appear that Bergmann's rule may well be operative in the examples given. In each case Newman selected archaeological sequences where strong cultural continuity minimized the possibility of replacement by invaders.

Changes in head form are not so readily explained by climatic adaptation. The trend, however, in a number of New World localities where archaeological and physical anthropological series are adequate to document it, is from dolichocephaly to brachycephaly or, at least to high mesocephaly. Thus, Newman noted a change of 5 to 6 cranial index points over a 5000 year span of Archaic to historic period Indians in the eastern United States and one of 2 to 3 index points in the 2000 year range of Basketmaker to historic Puebloans in the Southwestern United States. Similar changes also have been reported from Californian and some South American sequences. For much of the New World, however, inadequate cranial remains or data preclude an examination of the trend. As already mentioned, the adaptive nature of these changes is not apparent, and it is possible that they are conditioned by interbreeding between earlier local longheaded populations and later brachycephals; however, the archaeological

sequences in which the skeletal remains in question were found do not indicate that sudden population replacement or new infusions had occurred. It is, perhaps, worthwhile mentioning that this same trend through time, from long to roundheadedness, is also a general Old World trend and, possibly, a world-wide trend of a general evolutionary nature.

Newman concluded his arguments by stating that if man first spread to the Americas some 30,000 to 40,000 years ago, then much of the physical variation in the American Indian was formed in this hemisphere through adaptive change. Even if man did not arrive until 10,000 years ago, this would still have given ample time for changes of the kind which he sees in stature and head form. Moreover, Newman thinks it quite likely that "phenotypic alterations" other than those studied in stature and head form were also operative.[15]

These arguments bring us, again, to the question of how many migrations occurred between northeast Asia and America. Implicit in Newman's investigations is the idea that there were relatively few, at least of major proportions. The first of these migrations, or the first cluster of them, occurred in Pleistocene times. The people who crossed into the New World then were probably a fairly homogeneous biological unit. An examination of the early crania found in the Americas certainly suggests this. This list of early crania would include such finds as Brown's Valley Man (Minnesota), early Cochise Man (Arizona), Melbourne Man (Florida), Vero Man (Florida), Cerro Sota and Palli Aike crania (Straits of Magellan), the Confins and Lagoa Santa Men (eastern Brazil), the Punin calvarium (Ecuador), and Midland Man (Texas).[16] All these skulls are decidedly dolichocephalic or longheaded. Only Tepexpán Man (Mexico), of all the reasonably well-documented early human remains, is a high mesocephal.[17] After this Pleistocene migration, or migrations, to continue in the line of Newman's reasoning, variation in stature, head form, and presumably in other traits came about in the Americas through selective adaptations and genetic drift. At an appreciably later time, a second set of migrations occurred. These were responsible for bringing to northern North America the Athapascan and Eskimo peoples, both of a distinctly more Mongoloid cast than their predecessors on the New World scene. This course of argument for the long-time isolation and essential oneness of the bulk of the native New World populations is supported by blood-group data. These data indicate that most American Indians are separate from Asiatic Mongoloids except for occurrences of Group A in northern North America, where it is most reasonably explained as the result of the more recent immigrations from the other side of the Bering Strait.[18]

Summary. To sum up these similarities and differences in opinions, evidence from physical anthropology points to Asia, and to northern Asia, as the source for the peopling of the Americas. This same evidence, together with geological and archaeological findings indicate a late Pleistocene dating for the first entries of men into northern North America from across the Bering Strait. These first immigrants were *Homo sapiens* of a dolichocephalic, or longheaded, physical type. What appear to be their close relatives have been found in late Pleistocene, Upper Paleolithic contexts in Asia. They were less Mongoloid than later immigrants to the New World or than present-day Asiatics. The extent to which they may be categorized as Mongoloid, as archaic Caucasoid, or of some other race is debatable. Whether a series of subsequent migrations from northeastern Asia to the New World followed these earliest migrants is uncertain. American Indian populations, both of the ethnographic horizon and from archaeological levels, display a considerable diversity in stature, head form, facial contours, and skin color. This diversity may have resulted from such a series of migrations lasting through several millennia following the Pleistocene. On the other hand, these physical variations may have been produced by selective adaptations to a number of environmental circumstances and by genetic drift. About 5000 to 6000 years ago, some relatively late migrations

from northern Asia into northern North America did occur, and it was then that Athapascan Indians and Eskimos arrived in the New World.

Languages

Language, Race, and Culture. It is estimated that in 1492 some 2000 separate, mutually unintelligible languages were spoken in native America.[19] Language is one of the most persistent and slow-changing of culture patterns, which makes it particularly suited to historical investigation. No internal necessities are known which would cause race, language, and culture to predetermine one another, but there are numerous examples of historical adhesions between certain cultures and cultural traditions and certain languages. Such adhesions can be observed in the New World. For example, Eskimo language is associated with a more or less common Eskimo culture across several thousand miles of the Arctic Coast. Quite likely, this same Eskimo language has been spoken in this area as far back in time as we can trace a recognizable Eskimo culture in the archaeological sequences. Lacking a native written Eskimo language preserved on stone or ivory, we cannot prove this point, but it is quite probably valid. In the one New World instance where a pre-Columbian written language did exist, among the Maya of lowland Central America and southern Mexico, such an association of language and culture can be extended back into the past for over 1000 years. In spite of the fact that there are also many cases where language and culture do not coincide, where peoples of the same tongue will possess radically different cultures or where the same culture will be the property of peoples speaking two distinct languages, the links between language and culture are frequent enough in the Americas for the archaeologist to take cognizance of linguistic distributions and relationships.

Language Interrelationships and Classifications. Given the archaeologist's or culture historian's concern with language, a first and obvious question to ask is whether or not any American Indian languages are known to be related to any Old World languages. At present, no such relationships have ever been satisfactorily demonstrated,[20] although a number have been suggested. The late Edward Sapir is said to have believed that the Nadene speech of northwestern Canada may have had a common Old World origin with the Sinitic languages of Asia. Other linguists have claimed Eskimo affinities with Ural-Altaic and, somewhat more surprisingly, Hokan links with Malayo-Polynesian.[21] More recently, Morris Swadesh has indicated that the Wakashan languages of the Northwest Coast of North America have a distant genetic connection with the Asiatic Altai family.[22] In view of the rapid progress which has been made in recent years in linguistic studies, a progress which has seen the steady coalescence of American Indian languages and language groups into larger and larger interrelated clusters, it is a distinct possibility that Old World and New World languages will be proven related eventually even if all the former claims are not validated. Presumably, the fact that such relationships are not obvious is a testimony to the remoteness in time of the separation of the populations of the two hemispheres.

Within the Americas the relating of Indian languages into larger historical groupings of "language families" or "stocks" has been a central theme of linguistic research since the pioneer surveys and classifications of J. W. Powell of the Bureau of American Ethnology. In his classic study in 1891, Powell counted fifty-five language groups in America north of Mexico. Since that date the trend has been toward the coalescence of these groups into larger genetic clusters. Edward Sapir suggested that six language super-families or super-stocks might subsume all the native tongues of North and Central America. Subsequent research has tended to bear out his hypothesis, with some significant exceptions. A somewhat more conservative genetic classification proposed by Driver lists nineteen groups of historically related languages

for North and Central America. Viewing Central and South America, Greenberg has proposed drastic reductions of languages and language families into eight super-families. He also has designated sub-categories within some of these super-families.[23] The map on page 18 portrays the distributions of some of the more important of the language groups listed by Driver for North and Central America.

Before leaving the matter of linguistic groupings, one further hypothesis should be mentioned because of its interesting coincidence with the views of some of the physical anthropologists to which we have just referred. In outlining his major language groupings for South and Central America, Greenberg has suggested that all languages for these territories, together with all languages spoken in North America, with the exceptions of Nadene and Eskimo, probably relate to a single great genetic phylum, or group. Thus, Newman's idea of a single main migration of man from Asia to the New World in Pleistocene times, with no subsequent migrations until the arrivals of the Athapascans and other Nadene speakers and the Eskimo much later, may have linguistic support.

Glottochronology and the Reconstruction of "Proto-Languages." Of more particular interest to archaeologists, however, are some other developments in linguistics which, while relating to these very sweeping language classifications, are perhaps more applicable to immediate problems in culture history. The first of these is known as "lexico-statistical dating," or "glottochronology." To explain glottochronology it must be realized that in relating languages and dialects into larger groups of "families" or "super-families," grammar, phonology, and vocabulary have all played a part. Of these, grammatical structure has been thought to be most significant in tracing genetic relationships, as it is believed to be more resistant to borrowings and diffused influences than vocabulary; nevertheless, certain aspects of vocabulary also have been highly stable and of great value in establishing these relationships. Glottochronological studies

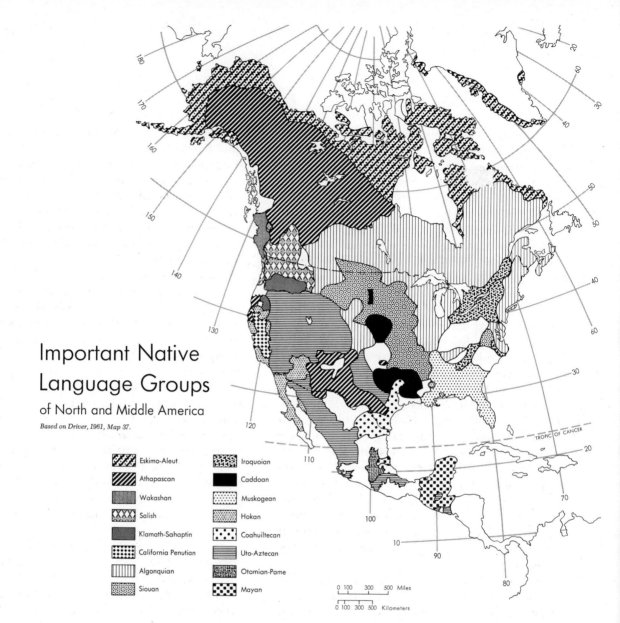

Important Native Language Groups
of North and Middle America

Based on Driver, 1961, Map 37.

Eskimo-Aleut	Iroquoian
Athapascan	Caddoan
Wakashan	Muskogean
Salish	Hokan
Klamath-Sahaptin	Coahuiltecan
California Penutian	Uto-Aztecan
Algonquian	Otomian-Pame
Siouan	Mayan

0 100 300 500 Miles

0 100 300 500 Kilometers

TROPIC OF CANCER

Figure 1-4.

of vocabulary have offered the linguists not only a means of demonstrating relationships but also, perhaps, of reckoning the time depth of these relationships. Utilizing a standardized list of about 200 words, including personal pronouns, names for parts of the human body, and other words selected for their slow rate of change, it has been claimed that when two societies speaking the same language separate from a parent body, and maintain this separation for 1000 years without subsequent contact, 80 per cent of the words of the standardized list or basic vocabulary will remain

unchanged whereas 20 per cent will no longer be related. This rate of change was determined from comparisons made mostly in Indo-European languages where documentation was available in written records and dates. Whether or not this same rate will apply to all languages the world over remains to be tested. Some linguists feel that such a constant rate is highly improbable, and that the results of glottochronology are to be viewed with extreme caution. Nevertheless, this attempt to probe back to those points where language families divided appears significant for prehistory.[24]

18

Closely allied to glottochronology is the reconstruction of "proto-languages." By studying the vocabularies, as well as the grammatical structures and phonologic patterns of related languages, linguists have synthesized a replica of the parent language from which the diverse daughter languages have sprung. Recently, this has been done for "Proto-Mixteca" and "Proto-Maya" parent languages in Mesoamerica.[25] After dating the parent language by glottochronological means, and analyzing its vocabulary, it may then be stated, for example, that a group speaking the "Proto-Maya" mother language in 2500 B.C. had words for "maize" or for "cotton cloth." The applicability of the method as an adjunct to archaeological research is, of course, obvious. Complications may arise, however. A rapid diffusion of a loan word from another and unrelated language to all the "daughter" languages under examination might result in this word being projected back into the reconstructed "proto-language;" however, it is likely that such circumstances usually would be detected by a linguist experienced in the languages of the area concerned. Again, as with glottochronology, the prospect is, at least, promising.

Culture Origins

Introduction. Much of New World aboriginal culture is an indigenous development; still, man did not enter the Western Hemisphere as a beast of nature, nor did he evolve here. He came as man, as *Homo sapiens,* and this means that he came with a cultural heritage. What was the nature of this original heritage? From where did it derive and when? Was such an original heritage supplemented by later accretions from outside the Americas? If so, from whence, and when? In a word, what were the relationships between the American continents and those earlier hearths of man and culture in the Old World?

These great questions are, to a very large extent, what American archaeology is about. They cannot be answered with any finality, but let us examine and summarize the main findings which bear on them. First, there are those findings which pertain to man's early entry on the American scene. They relate to Paleolithic horizons in Asia, and in the New World they are represented by archaeological discoveries in Pleistocene contexts or by widespread ethnographic traits which are assumed to be very ancient. It can be assumed that they result from migrations into the Western Hemisphere through the Bering Strait-Alaska region; however, within the Americas their geographical distribution is general. Second, another kind of evidence refers to those traits which belong to a later period, beginning, perhaps, in the early post-Pleistocene and continuing down to a thousand years ago. Significantly, most of these traits are grouped in northern and northwestern America, and it is believed they traveled to the New World either via the Bering Strait or some other north Pacific route. A third group of traits has a chronological range of from as early as 3000 B.C. up to the very late pre-Columbian centuries but a geographical distribution which centers in the tropical latitudes of the New World, suggesting a trans-Pacific entry.

The Paleolithic Level. There can be little question but that the first Paleolithic immigrants to the New World brought from Asia such basic skills as fire-making, flint-chipping, and at least a rude competence in procuring food, shelter, and clothing. It is difficult to go beyond this in depicting the heritage of the first Americans. Too many uncertainties exist concerning just when these first migrations occurred and in what kind of an Asian Paleolithic context they had their origin. We shall return to these questions in Chapter 2. It is, however, quite probable that the early migrants fashioned knives and scrapers of chipped flint and made projectile points and awls of bone. In addition, they may have been adept at making bifacially flaked stone projectile points, although this is a moot question. It is also possible, although not certain, that if they brought such stone projectile points with them from Asia, they came to the Americas already skilled in hunting the big mammals of the Pleistocene. They may, too, have used stone mortars, pestles, and milling stones for grinding seeds, and quite possibly they could weave baskets and mats, make cordage and devise carrying nets and bags, and produce sandals. All these items have a respectable antiquity in the New World, although they may not be as old as flint and bone tools. Similarly, a few objects of a non-utilitarian nature, such as paint pigments and shell ornaments, may also have been a part of the early migratory hunters' heritage.

The non-material culture that the early Americans brought with them from Asia is, of course, still more speculative, but, minimally, it must have included kin-group organization, beliefs in magic and the supernatural, and life-crises rites of the kinds that are still found among primitive peoples in the New World and the Old. The couvade and puberty ceremonies are probable examples. Even more specifically, some of the paraphernalia used in and related to these ceremonies must have had common origins in the Old World Paleolithic. An example would be the "bull-roarer," a paddle-like wooden object which is whirled in the air to produce a roaring noise and is used in ceremonies by native peoples in Melanesia, California, southern Brazil, and the South American Gran Chaco, to name but a few locations.[26] To call attention to the survival of such archaic elements in historic tribes is not to impute the status of Paleolithic culture to the tribes; but it does indicate that, in spite of change, evolution, and diffusion, certain small vestiges of very early practices have remained imbedded in later cultural contexts. The bull-roarer is not the only such trait. There are others which we will mention further along that may owe distribution to survival from this early level.

The Mesolithic Level and the Northern Boreal Sphere. The second clustering of evidence pertaining to Old World-New World contacts is, as we have remarked, later than the Paleolithic horizon and is northerly in geographical distribution. The earliest of these evidences found in the Arctic were chipped-flint tools and weapons of

a definite northeast Asian Mesolithic tradition.[27] A number of other Siberian traits, from the Lake Baikal and Lena River regions, were also shared with the Arctic, northwestern North America, and the Eastern Woodlands of the United States in this general chronological range of from about 4000 to 2000 B.C. Polished-stone adzes were among these, including a variety of forms of which the "beveled adze" is one. Others were the domesticated dog, "male" toggle harpoons, stone fish effigies, bone or antler spoons, and bone combs. Stone lamps for burning animal oils appeared in Eskimo or proto-Eskimo cultures at a slightly later date, and these were assuredly from Asia, as were the bow-and-arrow and pottery. Pottery began its diffusion eastward from the Baikal region around 3000 B.C., and apparently didn't arrive in eastern North America until 1000 B.C. A conoidal-base form, a fabric-impressed cord, cord-wrapped-paddle, or cord-wrapped-stick-impressed surface, and linear-stamping characterized this early Siberian pottery. Some of these decorative techniques and vessel-form traits are represented in the potteries of Alaska and of the Canadian Arctic coast. All of them are to be found in the early Woodland ceramic wares from the eastern United States—particularly from the northeastern part of that territory—where they date back to the first millennium B.C. and where their presence suggests a cultural connection, whether by diffusion or migration, with distant Siberia.

Although it does seem that Siberian and east Asiatic cultures were responsible for the spread of these various trait elements, including pottery, as far east and south as the Eastern Woodlands of North America, these distributions were not continuous. The greatest gap is in interior western and central Canada, between the Firth River on the northern Arctic coast and the Churchill River in northern Manitoba. Tolstoy emphasizes that such items as the adze and the harpoon probably began their diffusion eastward from Siberia at the same time as pottery, but that the former rapidly outstripped pottery in the rate at which they moved through the Arctic and Subarctic zones.

Asiatic influences on North America are also seen in a group of traits which are restricted to the north and northwest, and which are quite late. Many are ethnological, including the basketry hat and slat-armor of the Northwest Coast and the snowshoes and toboggan of the Subarctic. From Eskimo cultures come a variety of elements such as tubular bone-needle cases, the sinew-backed or reinforced bow, sleds and dog-traction, tailored clothing, and the occasional use of iron.[28]

The Question of Trans-Pacific Contacts. The third group of trait similarities between the Old and New Worlds suggests sporadic contacts by small parties of sea voyagers from across the Pacific. Although most anthropologists and archaeologists are willing to concede that the Paleolithic and Mesolithic migrations and diffusions from Asia did occur, and that evidences for these are indisputable in northern North America, they are less sanguine about both the possibilities and the importance of pre-Columbian trans-Pacific contacts. This hesitation has its historic setting in the sensationalism which has surrounded many of the claims for bringing higher civilization to the shores of the New World by "lost races" and other mysterious voyagers. Most of these claims have no basis in fact; however, through the years archaeologists and ethnologists have also compiled a long list of similarities, which do indeed exist, between the pre-Columbian cultures of the Americas and those of the Old World which lie on the opposite side of the Pacific. Quite probably, this list includes many items which were invented independently by the natives of the two hemispheres, but it also includes others which may have resulted from trans-Pacific contact. This statement represents an approximate consensus of present American opinion, and it is in marked contrast to views held a few decades ago. Thus, in 1928, R. B. Dixon remarked that to admit one instance of trans-Pacific contact between Asia and America was to lower the gates and admit them all and, thereby, to destroy forever the idea that the New World civilizations of Peru and Mexico were to any degree indigenous. But

Steward and Faron, writing in 1959, assume a quite different position. They readily admit the likelihood of several casual and accidental landings on the coasts of western South America by Asians or Oceanians and are of the opinion that certain common possessions held on both sides of the Pacific are proof of this. In spite of this, they feel that such borrowings were incidental to the growth of New World civilization, being "no more than superficial embellishments."[29]

Before commenting further on this, let us examine some of the elements and traits which are to be found on these lists of similarities or identities between American and Asiatic cultures and civilizations. Foremost among these in the minds of many students are cultivated plants. After all, plant species domesticated by man offer a specific kind of element which should be of great value in demonstrating culture contacts. Three plants are most frequently cited in this regard: cotton (*Gossypium* sp.), the sweet potato (*Ipomoea batatas*), and the gourd (*Lagenaria siceraria*).

The case for cotton as a trans-Pacific import of man rests on the following. Old World cotton, both wild and domesticated, has 13 large chromosomes. New World wild cotton (*Gossypium raimondii*) has 13 small chromosomes. American cultivated cotton (*G. barbadense*), with an antiquity going back to 3000 B.C. in preceramic shell midden deposits on the coast of Peru, has 26 chromosomes, 13 large and 13 small. Hawaiian wild cotton also has 13 large and 13 small chromosomes. These interesting facts have been interpreted as evidence that Old World cotton was brought to the Americas by man where it crossed with the native wild cotton plant to produce the 26-chromosome domesticate. Not all botanists will agree on this interpretation, however. P. C. Mangelsdorf asserts that it is an equally reasonable explanation that a 13-chromosome cotton of an Old World type was also present in the Americas in the wild state, as a result of ancient, pre-human plant distributions, and that the cross which resulted in the New World domesticate was between two New World wild species. Hutchinson, who originally proposed the trans-Pacific hypothesis for cotton, now admits this as an alternative interpretation. The case for the pre-Columbian transference of domesticated cotton from the Old to the New World by man is, thus, not proven. It remains only a possibility.[30]

The sweet potato is a pre-Columbian New World domesticate, and it was also cultivated in Melanesia and Polynesia during the European discovery and colonization of those islands. It may be of pre-Columbian date in these Old World localities, or it may have been introduced by the Europeans. If it is of pre-Columbian date in Oceania, an American rather than a Pacific origin seems more likely.

The gourd (*Lagenaria* sp.) was raised for its utility as a container. It is extremely ancient in the Old World and has also been found in America, as a probable domesticate, in the lower levels of cave deposits in Tamaulipas, Mexico, where it is dated by radiocarbon to between 7000 and 5000 B.C.[31] These dates would seem to put the gourd out of the range of trans-Pacific, or trans-Atlantic, travel, at least with man as the medium of transport. Since gourds float easily, and remain viable in the water for long periods, the *Lagenaria* may well have drifted across the oceans to the Americas during very early times.

Two other cultigens have also been considered by some as offering proof of pre-Columbian contact across the Pacific. The yam (*Dioscorea alata*) has a long and early history in Southeast Asia as a cultivated food plant, and in historic times it was a South American and West Indian crop. It may or may not be of pre-Columbian date in these latter regions. The other plant—maize (*Zea mays*)—is the most important of American Indian staples. Some years ago it was argued that with the absence of a wild pod ancestor in the New World, maize might be an Asiatic plant which was brought across the Pacific. Several southeast Asian grasses were known to be related to pod corn. This hypothesis seems most unlikely now with the recent geological finds of wild maize pollen dating to 80,000 years ago in the Valley of Mexico and the archaeological finds of pod corn, in a wild or very early state of domes-

tication, in Puebla, Mexico, where they are as old as the fifth millennium B.C.[32]

In sum, the evidence involving domesticated plants does not lend strong support to theories of pre-Columbian contact across either the Pacific or Atlantic oceans. An Asia-to-America transport of cotton and the yam is possible but not probable. The same is true of an America-to-Asia spread of the sweet potato. Overwhelming archaeological documentation supports the New World origin and entire pre-Columbian development of *Zea mays,* and the bottle gourd appears on an early post-Pleistocene level in both hemispheres.

What of other evidences of pre-Columbian "hands across the sea"? Nordenskiold addressed himself to the question a good many years ago, and he, more than anyone else, contributed to the list of traits which are shared by Asia and the New World. A complete review of his lists is beyond our purpose here, but Kroeber and others have analyzed and discussed many of the elements to which he called attention.[33] Some of them may be very ancient, possibly being survivals of a Paleolithic heritage about which we have spoken. The chewing of lime or ashes with some kind of a narcotic is such a trait. In southeast Asia the plant is betel-nut; in South America it is the coca leaf. Unfortunately, the material evidences for the lime-quid practice are of a kind rarely preserved, and its history in the world may never be plotted. In Peru, however, on the rainless coast, a small gourd filled with powdered lime (the kind of equipment used by present day Andean Indians addicted to coca-chewing) was found in a grave estimated to date at 2000 B.C.[34] While hardly of "Paleolithic horizon" date, the discovery does suggest considerable age for the trait in the Americas. The penis sheath or cover, known in both the South American tropical forests and in Oceania, is another such trait that could be an ancient survival rather than a later trans-Pacific transfer.

However, a number of other traits on the list are almost certainly too late—wherever in the world—to be considered as part of a Paleolithic heritage. This is especially true of metallurgy, involving the processes of "lost-wax" casting, welding, and alloying. The first record of this trait complex in the New World dates to the middle of the first millennium B.C. in Peru. Heine-Geldern has argued for a derivation from southeast Asia.[35] The methods and techniques are indeed complicated, and the argument cannot be dismissed lightly. Metallurgy, perhaps more than with any other trait or trait complex, poses the anthropologist's sorest dilemma. Were these methods and techniques invented separately in the Americas or were they not? As yet no long antecedent history of metalworking has been disclosed in the archaeology of the Peruvian area, although there are some indications that for a very few centuries cold hammering of metals preceded the other techniques. The question is posed and left. No satisfactory answer can yet be given. But if metallurgy was introduced to Peru from Asia in the fourth or fifth century B.C., it cannot be described as "a superficial embellishment" of native culture. It was too important in later pre-Columbian Peru to be so described.

What applies to metallurgy also applies to pottery. The ceramic craft in the New World has not usually been considered a trans-Pacific implant, although quite recently this idea has been suggested by Estrada, Evans, and Meggers, who compare the earliest pottery of the Ecuador coast, that of the Valdivia complex, with Japanese Jomon ware.[36] Radiocarbon dates for Valdivia are in the neighborhood of 3000 to 2500 B.C., fully consistent with the dating of late Jomon; and the similarities in vessel forms and decoration between the Valdivia and the Japanese ceramics are striking. Does Valdivia represent an early introduction of the idea of pottery into America from Asia?[37] Again, as with the metallurgical techniques, the question cannot be answered as yet; but if pottery was, indeed, so introduced, such an introduction was surely more than an embellishment of American native cultures.

Pottery and metallurgy, although basic inventions and of great importance in New World cultures, are not the only intriguing Asian-American culture trait similarities. Is the making of bark cloth or paper from tree bark the sort of process to be independently arrived at in two or more places? Bark cloth can be dated to 2000 B.C. in Peru.[38] Quite likely, it spread from there to the rest of South America, but did not come from across the Pacific. Tie-dyed cloth, the star-shaped macehead of stone, the blowgun, and the Panpipe are all pre-Columbian in Peru and elsewhere in the New World. They are also ancient in the Old World. Are their histories separate or related? In art motifs, Heine-Geldern compares the tiger in the Chou dynasty art of China with the feline in Peruvian Chavín art of the first millennium B.C.[39] Similarly, he points to Chou artistic elements in the "interlaced ribbon" motif of the Tajín style of Veracruz and to Han dynasty influences in the tripod cylinder jars of Teotihuacán and the tall pedestal-based bowls of the northern Andes and Central America.[40] Estrada and Meggers describe small pottery house models of a peculiarly Asiatic design found, along with pottery headrests, in an Ecuador coastal culture dating at about the beginning of the Christian era. Neither had prototypes in the local sequence or close parallels elsewhere in the Americas. Both had reasonable prototypical forms in Asia.[41]

These examples are widely scattered geographically and widely spaced chronologically, but this is not sufficient to rule out the possibilities of Asiatic origins.[42] Societies and cultures have a way of picking up oddments from other contexts and then firmly fixing them in new patterns of their own. To be sure, a highly subjective quality enters into the appraisal of these Asiatic-American trait comparisons, and what to one viewer appears as something so unique that its separate invention is unthinkable impresses another as comfortably within the bounds of the convergence of human ideas. Thus, to me, the Chavín and Tajín parallels to Chou art appear more likely as convergences, and I am inclined to think of them as incorporations of the elements of nature and simple geometric design into the integrated elaborations of styles which as wholes are quite different from one another. In contrast, the pottery headrests from Ecuador strike me as being related to Asian proto-types. In this case not only the similarity of form seems significant but also the total context. They appeared suddenly in a regional culture sequence in which they had no antecedents, they were associated with other new traits which also may have been imported, and they were found in a seacoast location which enhances the probability of their trans-Pacific arrival.

Summary. The origins of the New World cultures, insofar as Old World contacts and stimuli are concerned, is thus still very much a matter for debate and for the systematic marshaling of proofs. From an Old World Paleolithic level, man must have brought a minimum cultural heritage to the Americas, a heritage of flint-working, certain tools and weapons, clothing, ideas about social groupings, and the supernatural. Later, during the Siberian Mesolithic and Neolithic stages, a considerable number of technical traits probably diffused from western Siberia across that country into northern North America. In America some of these traits have been found in the Arctic, some in the Canadian and Pacific Northwest, and some in the Eastern Woodlands of the United States. They include such things as ground-stone tools, ivory implements, various weapons, ornaments, and pottery. Finally, a great many traits are duplicated in the areas of the American advanced civilizations and in the Asian and Oceanic areas which lie at about the same latitudes on the opposite side of the Pacific. These are traits of indubitable pre-Columbian date in the Americas, and most of them are equally old, or older, in Asia. Trans-Pacific voyages are offered to explain their presence, voyages which may have begun as early as 3000 B.C. and which continued until well into the first millennium A.D. The trait similarities involved are of different kinds, including food plants, technological inventions, artistic elements, and various oddments. Their distribution in the Americas in space and in time is rather wide and random, ranging from Peru to Mexico and over a span of several millennia. The same is true of them in Asia. Yet these facts cannot rule out the possibility that contacts did indeed occur. Most Americanists believe that the formation and the main courses of New World cultures and civilizations are indigenous. Most of them also feel that there is a very high probability that occasional trans-Pacific diffusions occured in pre-Columbian times but that the effects of such diffusions on American cultures were trivial. In general, these opinions appear well-founded, except the last. The triviality or significance would seem to depend on the elements diffused. The introduction of the idea of a headrest would probably have been of little consequence to the over-all development of New World cultures, but the introduction of the art of pottery-making or the craft of metal-casting would have had far-reaching and long-lasting consequences.

Footnotes

[1]See Willey (1953) for a consideration of analogy in archaeology; R. H. Thompson (1956, 1958); Ascher (1961).

[2]See Willey and Phillips (1958, pp. 34–39, 47–48) for a discussion of the concepts of "tradition", "full cultural tradition," and "culture." Cultural tradition as used here is the equivalent of either "full cultural tradition" or "culture" as these are defined by Willey and Phillips. I have preferred to use the term "cultural tradition" here, rather than "culture," to emphasize the long chronological persistence of the patterns concerned.

[3]See Willey and Phillips (1958) for an approach by "stages." Kubler (1962) has referred to the differences between the "vertical" and "horizontal" approaches.

[4]The term "Mesoamerica" is generally used by archaeologists and ethnologists to refer to the approximate southern two-thirds of Mexico and the

northern portions of Central America (see Chapter 3,)—essentially the same as "Middle America."

[5]See Wissler (1938) and Kroeber (1939) for treatments of this concept and compare the culture areas used here with those of Kroeber (1939, 1948); Driver and Massey (1957); Driver (1961).

[6]Willey and Phillips (1958, pp. 21–24) define "phase" as used herein. See Rowe (1962) for a discussion of archaeological periods and stages. Period, as I employ it here, follows his definition. See also Rouse (1955), with particular reference to "distributional correlation."

[7]The present volume is concerned with North and Middle America, the second with South America.

[8]This section is synthesized from Fenneman (1928); Kroeber (1939, pp. 182–201); Paterson (1960, pp. 1–15); James (1959, pp. 24–39); Sauer (1950); I. C. Russell (1927, p. 169); Trewartha, (1954); Finch, Trewartha, Robinson, and Hammond (1957).

[9]The abbreviations or climatic symbols refer to the Köppen system of classification, with modifications by Trewartha (1954).

[10]Hooton (1947, pp. 644–650); Birdsell (1951).

[11]Howells (1946, pp. 256–269); Stewart (1960).

[12]Dixon (1923); Von Eickstedt (1933–1934); Imbelloni (1958); G. K. Neumann (1952).

[13]M. T. Newman (1951).

[14]G. K. Neumann (1952).

[15]M. T. Newman (1953, 1962).

[16]Stewart (1953). See Stewart, pp. 77–90, in Wendorf, Krieger, Albritton, and Stewart (1955) for a description of the Midland skull.

[17]De Terra, Romero, and Stewart (1949).

[18]Stewart (1960). However, blood group A1 is found in Middle America and Andean South America in low frequencies (Newman, 1958).

[19]Driver (1961, p. 555). Refer also to Driver's account, pp. 555–586, and maps (pocket and no. 37) for a discussion of North and Central American Indian languages and their distributions. See also Driver and Massey (1957, pp. 169–172, map 1). For Mesoamerica consult J. A. Mason (1940); Frederick Johnson (1940); Mendizabal and Jimenez Moreno (1939). For South America, see Steward and Faron (1959, pp. 16–30); J. A. Mason (1950).

[20]Except the Eskimo, of course, whose language is the same in America and Siberia.

[21]Hoijer (1946).

[22]Swadesh (1960).

[23]Powell (1891); Driver (1961, p. 576, map 37); Greenberg (1960); Steward and Faron (1959, pp. 22–23).

[24]See Driver (1961, pp. 571–574) for a description of this method.

[25]Longacre and Millon (1961); McQuown (1964). For the Mesoamerican culture-historical reconstructions through linguistic analysis, see Swadesh (1964).

[26]Driver (1961, p. 411); Metraux (1946, p. 343); Lowie (1946 a, p. 390, 1946 b, p. 427, fig. 52c).

[27]Tolstoy (1958 a, b); MacNeish (1959 a).

[28]Tolstoy (1958 a, b); Kroeber (1948, pp. 782–783); Jenness (1940).

[29]Steward and Faron (1959, pp. 34–43); Dixon (1928).

[30]Hutchinson, Silow, and Stephens (1947); Hutchinson (1959); Steward and Faron (1959, p. 39); Mangelsdorf, MacNeish, and Willey (1964); Hutchinson (1962); C. E. Smith, Jr., and MacNeish (1964).

[31]MacNeish (1958 a, pp. 167, 192).

[32]Anderson and Stonor (1949). For early maize pollen see Bopp-Oeste (1961); for early maize from Puebla, Mexico, see MacNeish (1961, 1962 a); Mangelsdorf, MacNeish, and Galinat (1964).

[33]Nordenskiold (1912, 1921, 1931); Kroeber (1948, pp. 775–785). For a recent review of pre-Columbian America in the light of trans-Pacific contacts see Ekholm (1964).

[34]Engel (1957).

[35]Heine-Geldern (1953).

[36]Estrada, Evans, and Meggers (1962); Estrada and Evans (1963).

[37]Valdivia pottery is among the oldest of New World ceramic complexes. The only radiocarbon date for American pottery which is comparable to that of Valdivia is for the Puerto Hormigas complex of the Caribbean coast of Colombia, in the vicinity of 2900 B.C. (Reichel-Dolmatoff, 1961). Although by no means the same as Valdivia, Puerto Hormigas pottery is somewhat similar in its general simplicity and its incised and punctated decoration. In considering both Valdivia and Puerto Hormigas, as well as Monagrillo pottery of Panama (Willey and McGimsey, 1954), which also carries an early radiocarbon date (2100 B.C.) and which is typologically similar to the other two, the question may certainly be raised about pottery having been introduced or invented for the first time in the Americas in the Ecuador-Colombia-Panama regions, or what is sometimes called the "Intermediate area." These early pottery complexes of the Intermediate area are typologically quite distinct from the Woodland pottery of northeastern North America referred to in this chapter, which is believed to have been derived from Siberian Neolithic cultures by way of the Bering Strait.

[38]Bird, (1948).

[39]Heine-Geldern (1959 a).

[40]Heine-Geldern (1959 b, c).

[41]Estrada and Meggers (1961).

[42]The course of this discussion carries the implication of Asia-to-America as the direction of cultural flow. I think this the most likely direction for most elements discussed. For the America-to-Asia thesis see Heyerdahl (1952).

Pleistocene Glaciation and Chronology

During the Pleistocene geological epoch, ice caps and ice sheets covered vast areas of the Americas, both north and south. At the glacial maximum of the last major stage of the Pleistocene, the Wisconsin, a belt of unbroken ice ran across northern North America. Geologists, however, distinguish two main ice masses, a Cordilleran in the west and a Laurentide in the east. The Cordilleran ice centered in British Columbia and from there extended southward through the Cascade Mountains to the Columbia River valley. Beyond this point, in the Sierra Nevadas and the Yellowstone-Teton-Wind River country, were isolated highland glaciers. To the north, the Cordilleran glaciers covered the mountains of Alaska, the Aleutians, and the Brooks Range; but here lack of precipitation inhibited glacier growth, and there was little or no glaciation on the interior plains between the mountains. To the west and east in Canada the ice reached down the slopes of the western mountains to the Pacific Ocean and eastward down the Rockies to join the westward movement of the Laurentide ice. The northern border of the Laurentide ice also reached the Arctic, and its eastern edges touched the Atlantic Ocean. It extended south along a line running from northern

The Early Americans

New Jersey to the Ohio Valley and from there westward up the Missouri River. In Alberta and northeast British Columbia it coalesced with the Cordilleran glaciers. Isolated glaciers were also to be found in Mexico and in South America. The present-day masses capping the highest peaks in central Mexico and the Andes are the remnants of much larger Pleistocene formations. In the southern continent the ice caps and sheets were largest in the south, where they extended eastward onto the Patagonian plains.

In North America, in the areas south of the ice sheets, climates were cooler than those of today, and vegetation patterns differed. In the west, pollen cores from sediments of pluvial lakes indicate that tree lines stood much lower on mountain slopes; and in the east, spruce, larch, and northern pine forests grew at latitudes considerably farther south. As already mentioned, areas in the high plains and in the western basins which are now semi-arid or arid were then in lush grasses, swamps, and lakes. Presumably, similar climatic and vegetation differences existed in those parts of Middle and South America that were affected by glaciation.

Glacial stratigraphy in eastern North America reveals four Pleistocene stages separated by interglacial intervals. These are, in chronological order, from earliest to latest, and with the interglacial intervals indicated by parentheses: the Nebraskan (Aftonian), Kansan (Yarmouth), Illinoian (Sangamon), Wisconsin, and (Recent). It is with the Wisconsin, or final Pleistocene stage, that we are most concerned in the story of man in the Americas. The Wisconsin has been further subdivided, on the basis of Laurentide stratigraphy and the dating of terminal moraines in the Upper Mississippi and Great Lakes regions, into several substages separated by interstadial intervals. These substages, following most authorities, are, from earliest to latest; the Farmdale, Iowan, Tazewell, Cary, and Mankato. Some geologists would subdivide the Mankato or add another later glacial substage, the Valders. Others would also add an early substage, the Altonian, at the bottom of the Wisconsin sequence.

Radiocarbon determinations of organic specimens taken from within and under glacial drift provide a tentative scheme of dating for the Wisconsin substages. There are, however, some apparent contradictions among these radiocarbon dates as well as complicating factors in correlating glacial deposits with particular substages. One of the best dated landmarks in this glacial stratigraphy is the interstadial interval between the Mankato and Valders substages, the so-called Two Creeks interstadial. The Two Creeks recession of the glacial advances is placed at around 10,000 B.C. C. V. Haynes, Jr., has more specifically bracketed it between 10,300 and 9800 B.C. Earlier radiocarbon readings, on the Farmdale substage, the Farmdale-Iowan interstadial, the Iowan substage, and the Tazewell substage range from about 28,000 to 16,500 B.C. According to M. M. Leighton, the Wisconsin stage begins with the Farmdale substage, which marks the end of the Sangamon interglacial, at some time shortly before this earlier date. Frye and Willman, on the other hand, insert a pre-Farmdale Altonian substage and subsequent interstadial at the beginning of the Wisconsin sequence. They date the Altonian prior to 35,000 B.C., the extreme range of the radiocarbon determinations. Back of this point, it is estimated that the Altonian began or the Sangamon ended as long as 70,000 years ago. In accord with this downward extension of the dating of the beginnings of the Wisconsin, a major interstadial is inserted between what is here referred to as the Altonian and the Farmdale. Estimated dates for this interstadial reach back 30,000 to 40,000 years. The Wisconsin glacial sequence is summarized in Fig. 2-1. The accompanying approximate dates are estimated from radiocarbon determinations and from extrapolations from them.

Leighton terminates the Wisconsin stage with the end of the Valders advance, shortly after 9000 B.C. This is indicated in Fig. 2-1 by the solid horizontal line and (?). Haynes dates the Valders to a short (9800–9500 B.C.) period immediately following the Two Creeks interval and considers the two to three millennia following (9500–7000 B.C.) as the time of the Valders recession. Some authorities would describe an Anathermal climatic stage following the Valders and ranging from about 8000 or 7000 B.C. to the onset of the warm climates of the Altithermal, at about 5000 B.C. The minor Cochrane advance, within the Anathermal, is placed at about 6000 B.C. on the diagram. Some geologists assume that the beginning of the Altithermal at 5000 B.C. marks the line between the Wisconsin and the Recent. Frye and Willman, on the other hand, bring the Valders down to about 3000 B.C., at which point they close the Wisconsin. To a large extent these are differences in terminology; geologists generally recognize that since about

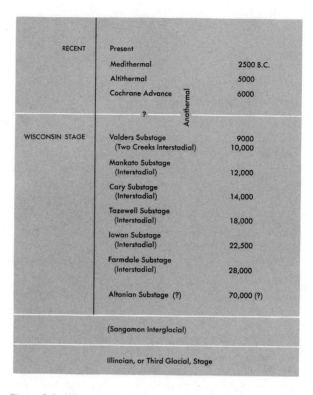

Figure 2-1. Wisconsin glacial sequence for North America with estimated dates.

8000 B.C. the glaciers have been on the wane and that this melting of the ice has continued down to the present, with a "climatic optimum," or warm period, lasting from about 5000 to 2500 B.C.[1] The climate of the Medithermal was essentially the climate we know today, although there have been slight local fluctuations within the last 4500 years that seemingly have affected both man and his culture.

The dating of Wisconsin stage glacial stratigraphy derives almost entirely from the Laurentide glacial formations; glacial sequences in western North America and elsewhere in the Western Hemisphere are less well-developed. Evidences of relatively dry and wet periods in geological columns in the North American High Plains, the Great

28

Basin, and the Southwest have been used, however, in attempts to relate such climatic changes to specific periods of glacial advances and retreats farther north. Thus, it has been argued that an arid, erosional interval on the High Plains correlates with the Two Creeks recession and that it was at this time that much of the Pleistocene fauna became extinct in that part of the continent. Attempts have also been made to coordinate glaciations in Middle and South America with European and North American sequences, and although these are still tentative, the continued advances in radiocarbon dating should eventually provide a means for establishing such long-distance correlations.

The foregoing is presented as the geological and the broad chronological background against which the early peopling of the New World and the early cultural traditions are to be considered.[2]

The Earliest Americans

The Earliest Definite Evidences. The oldest radiocarbon dates for archaeological discoveries which demonstrate, beyond any doubt, man's presence in the New World fall in the range of 10,000 to 9000 B.C. These dates and discoveries come from the High Plains of North America and from the southwestern United States. The prehistoric cultural traditions involved are characterized by bifacially flaked lanceolate projectile points which were used as spear tips in the pursuit of large game animals. Additional artifacts representative of these early cultures are a variety of unspecialized and specialized scrapers, choppers, knives, drills, and other chipped implements as well as occasional ground-stone, bone, and shell items that served useful or ornamental purposes.

In the Wisconsin glacial chronology the dating span of 10,000 to 9000 B.C. would fall in the Two Creeks interstadial or soon after, depending on the exact dating interpretation followed. Some authorities, such as C. V. Haynes, feel that these dates represent a true "floor" for man's appearance in the Americas. At the most, they would be willing to extend them back in time for only another millennium or so to take care of the arrivals in Alaska of the first immigrants from Asia and to allow for their movement southward to the western Plains.[3] According to this interpretation, the Asiatic cultural heritage of these earliest immigrants included certain technological skills and ideas, such as the knowledge of bifacially flaked points and the use of these points in hunting large Pleistocene herd animals.

The "Pre-Projectile Point Horizon" Hypothesis. Although the earliest radiocarbon dates on secure evidences of man's presence in the western hemisphere fall in the vicinity of 10,000 B.C., there are other signs that suggest that his arrival in the Americas was much earlier. In fact, he may have come over from Asia 30,000 or more years ago, in the middle or early Wisconsin ice age or, possibly, even during the Sangamon interglacial. The evidences for such an early appearance of man in the New World come from a great many localities in both North and South America. The artifactual materials in question are difficult to characterize in general terms. For the most part, they are crude, percussion-flaked tools—scrapers, flakes, pebble-choppers. Perhaps their most significant aspect is negative: the assemblages of tools with which we are concerned here do not include bifacially flaked projectile points or knives. The contexts in which these artifacts have been found include geological and Pleistocene faunal associations which, if acceptable as true associations, imply extreme antiquity. In several cases radiocarbon dates appear to support such antiquity. But by far most of these claims for an ancient American "pre-projectile point horizon" rest on typology alone. They are collections of implements found on the surface of the ground, but all the artifacts in a given collection are crude, simple forms, and projectile points are missing.

The earliest of the radiocarbon dates for these possibly very early finds of man in the Americas come from charcoal samples from two supposed hearths at Lewisville, in northeastern Texas. These samples were more than 38,000 years old. The geological and faunal associations implied an occupation by man at a time when the climate was considerably warmer than at present—either a major Wisconsin interstadial or the Sangamon interglacial. The faunal remains were abundant and included extinct peccary, bison, turtle, giant land tortoise (*Testudo* sp.), glyptodon, horse, camel, and mammoth. Three man-made artifacts are claimed to have been found in true association with the supposed hearths: a crude pebble-chopper, a hammerstone, and a flake scraper. However, the man-made nature of the hearths has been challenged; it is possible that they are no more than areas of ancient burned vegetation resulting from fires started by natural causes. The presence of the artifacts at the depths at which they were found may be explained by an accidental dragging down of superficial materials by the earth-moving equipment with which the site was excavated. The fact that a Clovis-type projectile point was also picked up in the excavations suggests a possible mixture of later materials with earlier geologic strata. Certainly such a point type is completely out of context for these geological strata and for 38,000 years ago. Thus as matters stand, the Lewisville finds are a possible but not a proven datum in the case for man in the Americas in early Wisconsin times.[4]

Friesenhahn Cave, in central Texas, is another debatable site. The strata of the cave contain the remains of a rich Wisconsin glacial fauna. Some cut-bone objects were found in association, and there has been some controversy whether these cuts resulted from the activities of men or carnivores. Chipped-stone objects also were included in the cave collections, and A. D. Krieger, who described these as plano-convex and, scraper-like, believes that they were true artifacts.[5] No radiocarbon dates have been established for Friesenhahn, however.

Other very early radiocarbon dates come from the California coast. On Santa Rose Island dwarf mammoth bones have been found in deep alluvium with what appear to be hearth areas, and a burned bone fragment from there has yielded a reading of more than 30,000 years. Only one specimen of what possibly is a crude chipped-stone implement has so far been found with any of these hearth or bone deposits.[6] A date of 19,500 B.C. comes from charcoal in what is possibly a buried occupation stratum near La Jolla, California.[7] A little to the south, at San Diego, claims for extremely old man-made artifacts have been made for the Texas Street site.[8] However, in all these instances there is either doubt whether or not the "hearths" in question were truly man-made or whether the flint objects involved were really human artifacts.

Another discovery with a series of early radiocarbon dates is the Tule Springs site in southern Nevada. This site appeared to have been a camp area on the edge of an ancient lake at a time when men and animals had been attracted to the valley by abundant water and lush vegetation, which no longer flourish there. The remains of a number of animals, including the camel (*Camelops hesternus*), bison (*Bison occidentalis*), horse (*Equus pacificus*), mammoth (*Parelphas columbi*), and ground sloth (*Nothrotherium shastense*) were found near what appeared to be blackened fire areas or charcoal lenses; and a quartzite scraper, two pointed bone implements, and an obsidian flake were discovered in these presumed "hearth" areas. The "hearths," bones, and artifacts were covered with several feet of lake-deposited silt and clay, interbedded with fine sand and gravel, and they were first discovered in an erosion channel which had cut through the valley floor. Radiocarbon dates on what appeared to be charcoal from the "hearths" were more than 23,800 and 28,000 years old.[9] But intensive excavations carried out at Tule Springs in the last two or three years have not supported the original claims. Laboratory analysis has shown, instead, that the dark, carbonaceous materials from the supposed "hearths," which had yielded the very early radiocarbon dates, may not have been entirely charcoal. Archaeologists in charge of these recent excavations have concluded that the earliest evidences of man cannot be placed before 11,000 B.C.[10]

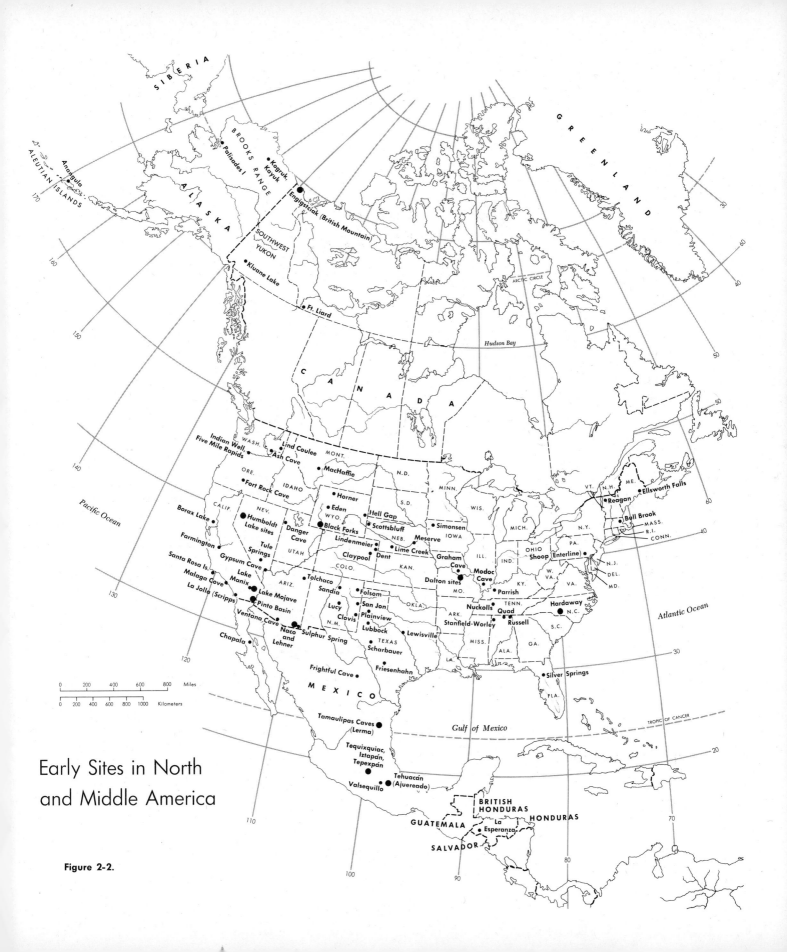

SIBERIA

GREENLAND

ALEUTIAN ISLANDS

Anangula

ALASKA

BROOKS RANGE

Palisades I

Kogruk, Kayuk

Engigstciak (British Mountain)

SOUTHWEST YUKON

Kluane Lake

Fr. Liard

CANADA

ARCTIC CIRCLE

Hudson Bay

Pacific Ocean

Atlantic Ocean

WASH.

Indian Well
Five Mile Rapids
Ash Cave

Lind Coulee

MONT.

MacHaffie

N.D.

ORE.

Fort Rock Cave

IDAHO

Horner

Eden

S.D.

MINN.

WIS.

VT. N.H. ME.

Ellsworth Falls

Reagan

Bell Brook

MASS.

Borax Lake

CALIF.

Humboldt Lake sites

NEV.

Danger Cave

Black Forks

WYO.

Hell Gap

Scottsbluff

Simonsen

IOWA

MICH.

N.Y.

R.I.
CONN.

40

Farmington

Tule Springs

UTAH

Lindenmeier

Dent

NEB.

Meserve

Lime Creek

PA.

Shoop

(Enterline)

OHIO

IND.

ILL.

N.J.

Santa Rosa Is.

Gypsum Cave

Lake Manix

Claypool

COLO.

Graham Cave

Modoc Cave

W. VA.

DEL.

MD.

Malaga Cove

La Jolla (Scripps)

Lake Mojave

Pinto Basin

ARIZ.

Tolchaco

Sandia

KAN.

MO.

Dalton sites

Parrish

KY.

VA.

Lucy

Folsom

Clovis

San Jon

Plainview

OKLA.

Nuckolls

TENN.

Quad

Russell

Hardaway

N.C.

Ventana Cave

N.M.

Naco and Lehner

Sulphur Spring

Lubbock

Lewisville

ARK.

Stanfield-Worley

S.C.

Chapala

Scharbauer

TEXAS

MISS.

ALA.

GA.

30

Frightful Cave

Friesenhahn

LA.

Silver Springs

FLA.

MEXICO

Gulf of Mexico

TROPIC OF CANCER

Tamaulipas Caves (Lerma)

Tequixquiac, Iztapán, Tepexpán

Tehuacán (Ajuereado)

Valsequillo

20

BRITISH HONDURAS

GUATEMALA

HONDURAS

La Esperanza

SALVADOR

Miles
0 200 400 600 800

Kilometers
0 200 400 600 800 1000

Early Sites in North and Middle America

Figure 2-2.

Early Sites
in South America

Figure 2-3.

In addition to these discoveries, a number of others suggest, by their typology, geological associations, or radiocarbon dates, extreme age. In western North America, assemblages of crude, heavy, chipped-stone tools, including bifacial choppers and other core implements, frequently have been found without associated projectile points, thin knives, or other delicately chipped artifacts; and it has been argued that these assemblages constitute, in effect, a "pre-projectile point horizon" in the New World. The collections gathered from the old shore lines of the Lake Chapala Basin, in Baja California,[11] the artifacts from Lake Manix and Coyote Gulch from the California desert,[12] the implements found in the Black Forks region of southwestern Wyoming,[13] the Tolchaco complex of northeastern Arizona,[14] and the Farmington complex of central California make up such a "horizon."[15] This is but a sampling from North America.[15a]

In Mexico, the Tequixquiac finds, including the carved llama sacrum and a number of crude stone and bone tools, are said to come from geological beds which may be mid-Wisconsin or older;[16] and a comparable dating is also suggested for the recent discoveries of artifacts at Valsequillo, in the State of Puebla.[17]

In Venezuela, crude flake and pebble tools were found with mastodon, glyptodon, and horse bones at Muaco, which radiocarbon methods date to 14,500 B.C.[18] The non-projectile point assemblage of tools of the Camare complex, from El Jobo region, and the similar artifacts found at El Manzanillo, both also in Venezuela may be ancient.[19] Farther south in South America various rough-stone tool complexes could well belong to a "pre-projectile point horizon." Among these are Viscachani I (Bolivia),[20] Ghatchi I (northern Chile),[21] Ampajango (northwestern Argentina),[22] Tandilense (Argentine Pampas),[23] Oliviense (Argentine Patagonia),[24] and Early Rio Chico (Tierra del Fuego).[25]

This, in brief, is the case, or a representative sampling of the case, for a "pre-projectile point horizon" and for man's presence in the New World between, let us say, 20,000 and 40,000 years ago.

Some of the evidence appears sounder than others. Lewisville and Friesenhahn certainly lend weight to the possibility of mid-Pleistocene man in America. Perhaps even more impressive, in my opinion, are the numerous instances of chipped-stone tool complexes whose typology and isolation from technologically more advanced implements suggests the possibility of great age. These have been found in all parts of the hemisphere, and the simplest way to explain them is to say that they represent a stage of cultural and technological development that had very ancient beginnings in the Americas —beginnings most likely derived from Middle Paleolithic chopper-chopping tool industries of eastern Asia. Krieger has argued the case for such a stage very persuasively.[26] Yet there are other explanations. Such complexes could, on occasion, represent no more than a partial sample of the full complement of artifacts possessed by the peoples who made them. Or they may represent technological regression from the more advanced standards of flint-working of the early projectile point complexes. As things stand now, the "pre-projectile point horizon" will not be demonstrated beyond reasonable doubt until a complex or assemblage of materials attributable to it are found stratigraphically beneath artifacts of the well-known, 10,000 to 12,000 year old, bifacially-flaked lanceolate or leaf-shaped point class, or failing this, until the crude, non-projectile point complexes are found in indisputable association with middle or early Pleistocene deposits and convincing radiocarbon datings. No amount of forceful argument, on the basis of present data, will change this situation.

Asia and America: Some Hypotheses. We are left with the possibilities that man entered the New World no earlier than 10,000 or 11,000 B.C.—perhaps in a Wisconsin interstadial contemporaneous with the Two Creeks interval—or that he was a much older inhabitant of this hemisphere, with his first arrival dating back 20,000 to 40,000 years ago. With these two possibilities in mind, what were the conditions in eastern Asia, with regard to human culture and to natural environment at these times, that would throw light on the question?

C. S. Chard has stated the case for man's entry into America from northeast Asia in mid-Pleistocene times or earlier.[27] He pointed out that the only Siberian and far eastern Asiatic Paleolithic cultures that were clearly old enough to have provided the cultural heritage for the early immigrants to the Americas were those with technological traditions relating to the relatively primitive Southeast Asian Chopper-Chopping Tool tradition to which we have already referred. These Asiatic chopping-tool industries lacked both bifacial blades and points and were, as their designation implies, characterized by rough core tools, choppers, and scrapers. Following Chard's hypothesis, it was this kind of technology which was carried early to the New World, and it was in the Americas, over a span of several thousand years, that the distinctive bifaced, lanceolate projectile point types were evolved independently of further Asiatic influence. No additional flint-working techniques were carried across the Bering Strait until Mesolithic or early Neolithic times in northern Asia. On the contrary, American-invented blade and point forms diffused back from North America to Asia in the early post-Pleistocene. At the time of his original statement Chard did not specify any Asiatic tool complex as being prototypical of the putative mid-Pleistocene complexes of the Americas, but in a later article he mentioned the Middle Paleolithic Fenho complex of North China as a possible source, pointing out similarities between it and the California Manix Lake choppers, handaxes, and flakes.[28]

If Chard's position is accepted, and the forebears of the American Indian did, indeed, enter the New World from Asia during a mid- or early Wisconsin glacial stage or even during the Sangamon interglacial that preceded the Wisconsin, these earliest explorers of the Americas must have had an extremely primitive and simple technology with which to face their environment. In fact, this argument has been used to rebut the claims for such an early migration in the Bering Strait region. If, however, the journey had been made during the warm Sangamon interglacial or a long Wisconsin interstadial, the climate would have been more favorable for a people with a simple technology. The objections to this theory are that in such a warm climate the sea level would have been higher and a dry land crossing of the Bering Strait would have been precluded. For it was only during times of Wisconsin glacial advance, when the sea level was low, that a wide land-bridge existed in the northeast Siberian-Alaskan regions. Chard is unimpressed with the arguments of technological inadequacy in the face of a severely cold Arctic climate, and has replied:

We were apt to forget that way back in the time of *Sinanthropus* (Lower Paleolithic) the population of Pacific northeast Asia was able to cope with a quite severe climate and to base their economy on the hunting of large and sometimes dangerous game animals with the aid of the most rudimentary technology imaginable.[29]

Setting aside the question of whether man could have traversed the Bering Strait region with a simple and unspecialized technology, a number of archaeologists have disagreed with Chard on the origins of bifacially flaked lanceolate and leaf-shaped projectile points in the New World. Rather than seeing them develop completely *de novo* from unspecialized flint-working beginnings in the New World, they would prefer hypotheses that relate them to Asiatic or Eurasiatic prototypes. This argument was first advanced by G. H. S. Bushnell and Charles MacBurney and has also been championed, although differently, by H. M. Wormington and E. N. Wilmsen.[30] It is based on the presence of bifacial blades or points in certain Paleolithic complexes of western and southwestern Siberia. These western complexes differ from those of the east in that they were affiliated with European Paleolithic cultures—Mousterian, Solutrean, and Magdalenian—and reflected the specialization to Pleistocene big-game hunting which was missing in the Asian Chopper-Chopping Tool tradition. Some disagreement exists about their age, and when they were first brought forward in the context of this argument Chard felt that they were too late and too remote geographically to have provided a prototype for New World developments of Mankato or Mankato-Cary age.[31] More recently, however, Rudenko's excavation of the Ust'-Kanskaia Cave site, in the Altai Mountains of southwestern Siberia, has disclosed an assemblage of tools under conditions which appear to date to the third interglacial.[32] Believed to be the earliest Siberian Paleolithic complex known, the artifacts reflected a Mousterian tradition and included, in addition to choppers, scrapers, and rough blades, retouched flake points, prismatic knives, a burin, and, significantly, a finely chipped, bifacial, leaf-shaped blade. In Wormington's hypothesis, the blade technology passed from southwestern Siberia to the east, to Lake Baikal, where it met and blended with the older resident Asian Chopper-Chopping Tool traditions. From Baikal, this fusion of traditions was then carried north to the mouth of the Lena River and from there eastward to the Bering Strait. Such events, she thinks, could have occurred as much as 20,000 years ago, sufficiently early for the complex to have entered the New World as the basis for the subsequent modifications that gave rise to the fluted and other lanceolate projectile points of the late Wisconsin stage.

Wilmsen's hypothesis is broadly similar to Wormington's, but he draws some apparently early American Arctic complexes into the argument. He points out that the Alaskan and northern Yukon

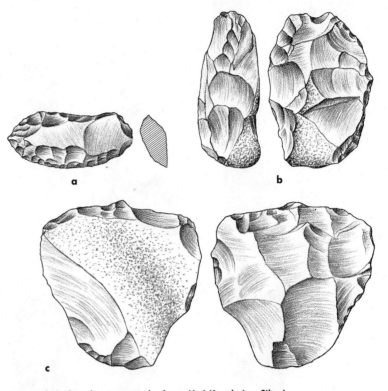

Figure 2-4. Rough stone tools from Ust'-Kanskaia, Siberia. a: Scraping tool. b: Chopping tool. c: Blade. Length of a, 7.4 cm. (After Rudenko, 1961.)

artifact assemblages of Kogruk and British Mountain shared such features as a Levallois-Mousterian percussion-flaking technique, large bulbar flakes resulting from this technique, and gravers, unifacial points, and crude bifaces made from flakes. These same features were, in turn, shared with the Siberian Buret-Malta complex from the central

Figure 2-5. Burin, points, and knives from Ust'-Kanskaia, Siberia. a: Burin. b: Bifacial leaf-shaped knife or point. c,d: Retouched flake points. e: Prismatic knife. Length of a, 6.7 cm. (After Rudenko, 1961.)

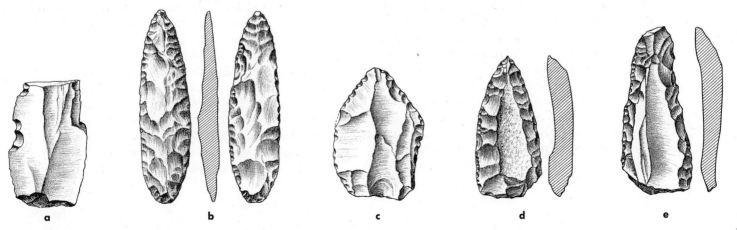

Figure 2-6. British Mountain flint artifacts. *a:* Uniface point struck from prepared discoidal core. *b,d,g,h:* Retouched flakes. *c:* End-of-blade scraper. *e:* Spokeshave-like implement on prepared flake. *f:* Pebble chopper. Length of *a,* 4.4 cm. (Courtesy National Museum of Canada; see also MacNeish, 1959 a.)

placed it in the range of 15,000 to 20,000 B.C.[33] Wilmsen favors such a dating and sees it as consistent with the presence of a Bering Strait land bridge between Asia and America during the period from 21,000 to 11,000 B.C. He sums up his hypothesis as follows:

. . . a group of hunting-oriented people, having developed efficient tools and social techniques to prey successfully upon the smaller units of the late Pleistocene megafauna, began expanding rather rapidly into areas favorable to this type of economy. Their tool-making technique was based on the Levallois-Mousterian flake tradition and developed into a flake-blade industry from which points effective in killing the smaller grazing animals evolved. Sometime during the period 21,000–11,000 B.C. these people crossed the Bering Strait, which was then crossable on foot, and became the first effective, if not the initial, inhabitants of the North American continent. Kogruk and British Mountain may or may not represent the earliest penetration, but they are certainly part of this same general movement and should, therefore, date within this period. These people spread eastward along the Alaskan foothill country, then southward, keeping to the foothills where, under the stimulus of a desire to include larger mammals in their regular diet, the incipient fluting technique which was part of their cultural equipment became the instrument which provided a highly effective tool for the realization of this end. This tool was the Clovis fluted point, which was so effective that it permitted its possessors to spread very rapidly over all of North America below the Mankato ice sheet.[34]

Chard has modified his views somewhat since his original statement; however, he holds to his position that the initial movement from Asia to America occurred about 40,000 years ago. Such a movement, according to his more recent statement, brought with it an "industrial tradition of choppers, bifaces, amorphous flakes and probably the Levallois-Mousterian technique." He concedes now the possibility of a second movement about 25,000 years ago which may have brought from central Siberia other Levallois-Mousterian elements, including a crude blade technique and "possibly the germ of bifacial flaking." But his opinion does

Siberian Lake Baikal region and from the Lena River valley. Presumably, although this is not a part of Wilmsen's thesis, the Levallois-Mousterian elements in Buret-Malta were derived from farther west, via complexes like that of Ust'-Kanskaia. A significant part of Wilmsen's argument is that the Malta assemblages included fluted flake tools —not points, apparently, but artifacts resembling burins. This crude or incipient fluting also characterized a few bifacial blades or points in the British Mountain complex. Neither British Mountain or Kogruk has been securely dated, but on stratigraphic and geological grounds they have been estimated to be as old as 6000 to 16,000 B.C. The date of the early culture of Buret-Malta has also been subject to debate, but recent opinion has

not seem to accomodate the picture of specialized hunters following the Pleistocene game across the Bering Strait land bridge.[35]

Summary. We have briefly presented a statement of the basic evidence of man's first appearances in the New World. Beyond reasonable doubt he was here by 10,000 B.C., and at this time we see him as a specialized hunter of big game, adept in the production of lanceolate flint points for this purpose. Similarly, we have summarized the arguments for man's presence in the Americas much earlier, as far back as 20,000 to 40,000 B.C. These facts and arguments have been regarded in the light of findings in Siberian Paleolithic archaeology. In considering these findings, we have outlined hypotheses concerning man's migrations from Asia across the Bering Strait, or the Bering land bridge of the Pleistocene. These hypotheses refer particularly to the idea that early, but nevertheless specialized, hunters came to America from Siberia and brought with them certain flint-working techniques, such as the fashioning of unifacial and bifacial points, which have their remote ancestry in the Eurasian Levallois-Mousterian tradition. Such events, it has been reasoned, transpired in the interval between the earliest estimates of man's presence in the Americas and the first definitely dated proof of his arrival—in other words, between about 20,000 and 10,000 B.C.

To this point I have not taken any clear stand on these arguments. The intention has been, rather, to offer to the reader a sketch of varied opinion along with the basic facts. By way of short summary, however, I present the following as my own views on these matters.

First, I think it likely that the "pre-projectile point horizon" is a reality and that man first crossed into America as far back as 40,000 to 20,000 B.C. I say this not so much because of the few excavated and disputed finds that suggest this but because of the numerous surface collection assemblages or complexes that have been found widely over the Americas and that present a typology that seems inconsistent with the American

specialized hunters. As Krieger has made clear, not all these complexes need be extremely ancient, but I think that some of them must be. In expressing this view I wish again to make it explicit that I do not believe that present evidence is adequate to support it beyond reasonable doubt.

Second, the hypothesis of a Levallois-Mousterian complex being carried to the New World from Siberia during the period of 20,000 to 10,000 B.C. strikes me as highly likely. I think that this is the best explanation for the presence of lanceolate and fluted blade forms in America and for the specialized hunting economy with which they are found in association. I see no essential conflict in postulating this as well as an earlier entry by less specialized flint-workers and hunters. The later arrivals could have superseded or merged with an earlier resident population. The earlier ways of life and stone industry would have been modified or replaced by the later patterns, being retained, perhaps, in marginal areas for a time.

The Big-Game Hunting Tradition

Definitions. The Big-Game Hunting tradition was primarily adapted to, and developed in, a grasslands environment of the late Pleistocene. Such an environment once existed on the North American Plains, and it is on the Plains that the principal discoveries relating to the tradition have been made. Additional significant finds have been made in the Arizona and New Mexico deserts, areas probably also once in grasslands, and in eastern North America. Plains-type environments formerly extended into parts of this latter area, and it is also believed that certain species of large Pleistocene mammals were adapted to those sections which remained forested.

It is with these areas that we will be concerned in this discussion of the tradition. Later in the chapter we will also take a look at certain finds in Middle and South America and in the Arctic which are related to the Big-Game Hunting tradition.

The designation "Big-Game Hunting tradition" is applied here to those early cultural complexes which were characterized by distinctive lanceolate projectile point types and other associated lithic, or stone, remains. The point types are the fluted Clovis, Folsom, and related forms; the single-shouldered Sandia; and the several types best classified as "Plano." All these points compose an historically related series. All were integral parts of complexes which reflected a way of life primarily dependent on killing large game animals, many of the species now extinct.

We have already mentioned that the earliest of these lanceolate points date back as far as 10,000 B.C. by radiocarbon determinations, and that there is a distinct possibility that they are several millennia older. This reckoning of a date earlier than 10,000 B.C. is based on derivations from Asiatic stone industries at a time between 20,000 and 10,000 B.C. and on the effective environmental adaptations which Big-Game Hunting tradition cultures display at the latter date. The eclipse of the Big-Game Hunting tradition began at about 8000 to 7000 B.C. with the onset of warmer, drier conditions; however, the old patterns showed remarkable tenacity in some regions, especially the

Plains, where modern herd animals (the bison) were hunted with Plano type points until 4000 B.C.

What I have called the Big-Game Hunting tradition is frequently referred to as the "Paleo-Indian tradition." I have not used this perfectly good term because in its general usage it usually gives a much wider reference, bracketing all early American hunters of the Pleistocene.[36] These other early hunters and early hunting cultures, such as those of Pacific North America, are treated separately farther along as distinct traditions. In applying the name Big-Game Hunter I am, of course, leading with an inference. This derives from the fact that a great many of the finds or sites which pertain to the tradition were no more than "kill" locations, where the mammoths or other large animals had been tracked down and slain. This undoubtedly has over-dramatized and perhaps over-emphasized this kind of activity in the lives of the people in question. Certainly their entire livelihood did not depend on the big Pleistocene animals of the hunt; there are, in fact, indications that smaller game and other edibles were taken or collected as opportunities arose. Still, the big-game pursuit is the most characteristic and diagnostic feature of the culture shared by these particular early Americans. There can be no question that it was an activity of great and, probably, primary importance. Viewed in the perspective of all of pre-Columbian New World history, it imparted a design, a style to their lives.

Clovis Fluted Points in the West. The earliest widespread projectile point type of the Big-Game Hunting tradition is known as the Clovis Fluted point. It was a large lanceolate form, usually measuring between 7 and 12 centimeters in length, although some were as short as 4 centimeters. The larger specimens were 3 to 4 centimeters wide near the base. Bases were concave and a fluting, or channeling, which was their most characteristic feature, extended from the base for one-quarter to one-half the length of the point. The edges near the base were ground down, apparently to keep them from cutting through the

Figure 2-7. Clovis projectile points. *a–c:* From Lehner site, Arizona. *d:* From Blackwater Draw site, New Mexico. Length of *a*, 8.5 cm. (*a*, after Wormington, 1957; *b,c*, after Haury, Sayles, and Wasley, 1959; *d*, courtesy G. A. Agogino.)

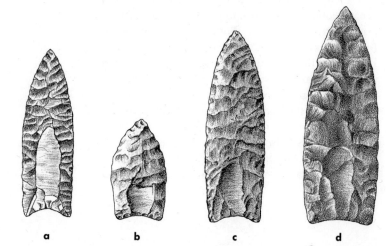

a   b   c   d

Figure 2-8. Clovis points from the Lehner site. (Courtesy Arizona State Museum.)

thongs which were used to help secure the point to the spear shaft. Clovis points were essentially percussion-flaked, only rarely revealing pressure retouching along the edges.

It is assumed that the Clovis points, as well as others of the Big-Game Hunting tradition, were used to tip spears but not arrows. All the early American projectile points are believed to have been too heavy and large for arrow tips. Spears must have been hurled or employed as thrusting, bayonet-like weapons. It is uncertain if the throwing-stick, or atlatl, which gave added propulsive force to a spear or dart, and which somewhat later was widely used in the Americas, was a part of the equipment of these early hunters or not. Prob-

ably the hunting tactics were to follow, wound, harass, and gradually kill the big animals, such as the mammoth. Favorite stalking grounds would have been—and do, indeed, seem to have been— shallow lakes and swamps where the great beasts could have become mired and rendered relatively helpless.

The name "Clovis" comes from a locality on the Llano Estacado, or "Staked Plain," of eastern New Mexico, between the towns of Clovis and Portales. Now arid and windswept, this district of the High Plains was covered by glacial lakes and ponds in the Pleistocene. Fossil animal bones and chipped-stone artifacts exposed in sandy basins or blow-outs led archaeologists to the region, where they found a stratigraphy in a location known as Blackwater Draw No. 1 (Fig. 2-2).[37] The basal layer was a gray sand stratum covering bedrock gravels. In earlier excavations, two Clovis Fluted points were found in this stratum along with the bones of a mammoth. Also associated in the gray sand layer were smaller points of the same general shape and with basal thinning but no true channeling, a scraper, a core, some retouched flakes, a hammerstone, and two tapering cylindrical bone shafts with beveled ends which may also have served as spear tips. More recent work has revealed still more Clovis points and other artifacts associated with the Clovis level of the site. Among the latter are a series of long prismatic flint blades made by an indirect percussion or punch method. These blades were apparently used as finished tools, with little or no retouching. F. E. Green, who has described them, believes that they are yet another trait leading back to Upper Paleolithic Siberian origins.[38]

The Clovis Blackwater Draw site was definitely a "kill" location. Camel, horse, and bison bones were found in the gray sand level of the Clovis point horizon, in addition to the mammoth remains. It may also have been a camp. E. H. Sellards has given the name "Llano Complex" to the earliest artifacts: points, scrapers, flakes, and bone bits.[39] To these we may add the punched blades. Recently, G. A. Agogino has described an artificially excavated pit or well on the site.[40] This feature may date from the Clovis or Llano Complex, and if so, gives us a little more information concerning the activities of the hunters who once lived there.

The gray sands of the Blackwater Draw are separated from overlying sterile brown sands by a disconformity, and the brown sands, again, show a disconformity with an overlying diatomaceous earth stratum. The latter contained Folsom Fluted points and Midland points—important projectile types of the Big-Game Hunting tradition which we will discuss farther along. These were associated with bison bones. This diatomaceous earth layer also reveals a disconformity with an overlying carbonaceous silt in which finely chipped Plano points of various types were discovered. These were formerly referred to as the Portales Complex, but recent stratigraphic excavations and analyses indicate this complex to be, instead, a series of complexes, typologically distinct and chronologically separable—Agate Basin, Cody, and Frederick, Agate Basin being the earliest.[41]

Mean radiocarbon dates on the full Blackwater Draw stratigraphy are 9220 B.C. for the Clovis point level; 8340 B.C. for the Folsom-Midland point level; and 7840 B.C. for the Agate Basin level. The subsequent Plano complexes have not been fully dated by radiocarbon, but by comparisons with other Plains localities, the Frederick level would date in the range of 6000 to 5000 B.C.

Clovis Fluted points have been found in association with mammoth remains at the Dent site, in Colorado, and there is a radiocarbon date on them of about 9200 B.C.[42] A comparable date is also available from the Clovis point and mammoth associations at Lehner, in southern Arizona.[43] In discussing the geographical distribution of Clovis points, Agogino and Rovner see a western concentration in the High Plains, the deserts of the Southwest, the Texas Panhandle, and the Texas Gulf Coast.[44] In the east, as we shall see, they have been found in the Mississippi, Ohio, Tennessee, and Cumberland valleys and along the Atlantic Coast from Florida to Nova Scotia. Their geo-

graphic center of origin is unknown. As is implicit in our discussions of Asiatic stimuli via Alaska and Canada, it is possible that the New World lanceolate points originated in the far north. As yet, however, there is no sound evidence to do more than suggest that the incipient idea of a fluted point was initiated there. As we have suggested, the early geological contexts for Clovis Fluted points in the southwestern High Plains, together with the reconstructed environment of that area, with its extensive grasslands, lakes, and abundant large herbivores, recommend it as a likely early center of the Clovis point and of the Big-Game Hunting tradition. If so, however, the idea must have spread rapidly, for insofar as we can tell now, the Clovis Fluted points found in eastern North America are just about as old (10,000–9000 B.C.) as they are in the High Plains. It is possible that climatic change accounted for the spread of early hunting populations from the western High Plains. Assuming that the Two Creeks interstadial—which is dated at about 10,000 to 9000 B.C.—was a time of dryness and desiccation preceding the Valders glacial advance, such conditions might have turned migratory hunters away from the drying Plains toward the east. This, however, is a speculation, and the validity of the idea cannot be tested until we know more about both climate and man in the Americas during the time of the Two Creeks interval and in the millennia immediately before.

Sandia Points. There is one other North American projectile form that may be as early as the Clovis Fluted point. This is the Sandia point. The Sandia points and the Sandia complex are named after Sandia Cave, which is located in the Sandia Mountains of central New Mexico—in the Southwest but near the border of the High Plains.

The limestone tunnel of the Sandia Cave is about 100 meters long and averages 3 meters in width. The uppermost levels of the cave are composed of wind-carried dusts and animal dung containing pottery and other artifacts of recent prehistoric cultures. Under this is a sterile stalagmitic layer which covers an occupation characterized by fluted Folsom type projectile points. Other artifacts taken from the stratum are small snub-nosed scrapers, small gravers, and unfluted lanceolate points which are probably Agate Basin and Plainview types. According to F. C. Hibben, the original excavator of the cave, this Folsom layer is underlain by a sterile stratum of yellow ocher; and beneath this water-deposited ocher stratum is the deepest and oldest evidence of man's use of the cave, the level of the Sandia projectile points.[45]

Nineteen Sandia points or point fragments were discovered in the lowest level. The Sandia points were percussion-flaked lanceolates, ranging from 6 to 9 centimeters in length, and one of their distinguishing characteristics was a slight shoulder at one side of the base. The Sandia "Type 1" points had a rather rounded outline, a bluntly pointed base, and were lenticular in cross-section. They frequently had use marks along one side, and it may be that they were actually knives rather than projectile points. The Sandia "Type 2" was a little more carefully made, had parallel sides, was diamond-shaped, (Fig. 2-9*a,b*), and had a straight or slightly concave base. The basal concavity on some points was the result of removing several small flakes, presumably to thin the base for insertion into the split end of a wooden spear or lance shaft. In one case, this concavity at the base had been extended as fluting up the sides of the point—in the manner of the fluting or channeling on the Clovis points and indicating a possible close relationship between the Clovis and Sandia forms. The nature of this relationship we can only speculate about; the Sandia fluting could be either the beginning of a trend or a vestigial remnant of a common practice so that, from a purely typological standpoint, Sandia points might be either earlier or later than Clovis points. Or they might, indeed, be a contemporaneous regional variant of the main Clovis development.

No reliable radiocarbon dates have yet been established on either the Folsom or Sandia level of the Sandia Cave, so chronology is best reckoned by cross-referencing with other finds. Elsewhere

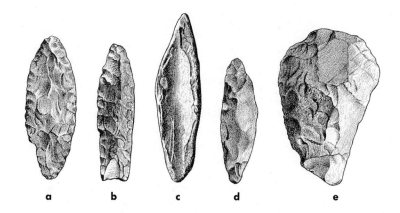

Figure 2-9. Sandia points and artifacts from Sandia Cave, New Mexico. *a:* Sandia Type 1. *b:* Sandia Type 2. *c:* Bone point. *d:* Crude chipped-stone leaf-shaped point. *e:* Snub-nosed scraper. Length of *a*, 7.4 cm. (After Hibben, 1941.)

we know that Folsom points have been dated by radiocarbon to between 9000 and 8000 B.C., or to the time of the Valders advance. This, presumably, should date the upper or Folsom level of the cave. If the ocher level correlates with the Mankato glacial advance, then the Sandia layer would be pre-Mankato, and by this reasoning, would be earlier than any Clovis or Llano complex finds now known.[46] However, the stratigraphy of Sandia Cave has been laid open to revision by recent investigations. According to G. A. Agogino, one of the recent investigators, there is strong suggestive evidence that Sandia points, while antedating the Folsom points, may originally have lain in the same geologic stratum with them and not in the layer below the yellow ocher. Redeposition to the layer in which they were reported found was probably the result of rodent activity which carried the artifacts through cracks and fissures into the sub-ocher layer. This reinterpretation would mean that the Sandia culture is approximately the same age as the Llano or Clovis complex.[47]

So far, Sandia points are well-documented from only one other station of which there is published record, the Lucy site near Sandia Cave. Today, the Lucy site is marked by a series of blow-outs along what was the shoreline of the former glacial Lake Estancia. Sandia points, including some that are fluted, have been found on the surface in these blow-outs, together with Clovis, Folsom, unfluted Folsom-like points, and mammoth and bison bones.[48] For the present, the Sandia point development is best considered an early offshoot of the more general line of the Big-Game Hunting tradition, and one which is known only from central New Mexico.

Figure 2-11. Folsom point and bison ribs *in situ*, Folsom, New Mexico. (Courtesy Peabody Museum, Harvard University.)

Folsom Fluted Points. Leaving the question of the Sandia points and their relationships to the Clovis Fluted forms, we know for certain that the Folsom Fluted point developed from the Clovis form, a development which occurred in a relatively circumscribed area of eastern New Mexico, eastern Colorado, eastern Wyoming, and the immediately adjoining territories of bordering states.

Figure 2-10. Folsom point. Length, 6.8 cm. (After Wormington, 1957.)

The Folsom point, usually smaller than the Clovis, also was more delicately made, with fine-edge retouch flaking. Widest at mid-section rather than near the base, it had a markedly concave base with ear-like projections. The flutes or channels marked both faces and extended for almost the entire length of the point. In brief, it appears as a more specialized version of the fluting idea. Its geographical distribution is more limited than that of the Clovis point, being confined largely to the North American High Plains. The Folsom point is an horizon marker in this area for the time period of the Valders advance and the latter part of the preceding Two Creeks interval. It takes its name from the Folsom site in New Mexico,[49] but the site best representing the Folsom complex, or perhaps culture phase, is Lindenmeier in northeastern Colorado.[50]

The Lindenmeier location is a vestigial valley cut through by an arroyo. Ash, animal-bone debris, and artifacts constitute an occupation stratum covered by 2 to 17 feet of alluvium. The site seems

Figure 2-12. Artifacts from the Lindenmeier site, Colorado. *a:* Ornamented bone disk. *b,c:* Folsom-type projectile points. *d:* Snub-nosed scraper. *e:* Side-scraper. Length of *b,* 4.1 cm. (After Roberts, 1939.)

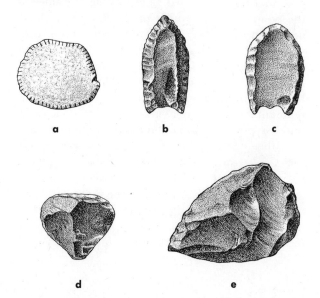

a   b   c

d   e

Figure 2-13. Folsom projectile points and knives from the Lindenmeier site. (Courtesy Smithsonian Institution.)

nosed" end-scrapers (Fig. 2-12*d*), small "thumb-nail" and "turtle-back" forms, and concave-edged scrapers sometimes called "spokeshaves." The weapons and tools were clearly an artifact assemblage of peoples dependent on the hunt and the utilization of animal skins. Bone implements were part of the complex, and, although the Lindenmeier findings are probably not fully representative because of the disintegration of bone materials, the awls, eyed needles, spatulas, and knives or "fleshers" all reflect the hunting preoccupation of the culture. Miscellaneous hammerstones and small rubbing stones were also found, the latter bearing remains of hematite pigments. A hematite bead, another stone bead, and three small bone disks with circumferential ticking or incising were the only obvious non-utilitarian items (Fig. 2-12*a*).[51]

A recent radiocarbon date for the Lindenmeier site is about 8800 B.C.,[52] which coincides with the geological context of the site occupation that is placed as beginning in the Two Creeks interstadial and continuing into the Valders pluvial. The associations of extinct bison, but not the mammoth, are, as already mentioned, significant. The upper levels of the Lindenmeier deposits, which correlate to the latter part of the Valders, contain Plano points. This recalls the upper stratigraphy at Black-water Draw (Clovis site), where the Plano points of the Agate Basin and other complexes succeeded Folsom types.

Other significant Folsom Fluted point finds include, to the north, the MacHaffie site, near Helena, Montana, the Brewster site in eastern Wyoming and, to the south, the Lubbock and Scharbauer sites in Texas. At MacHaffie, Folsom points and associated knives and scrapers were found, along with bison bones, in the lowest occupation stratum. Overlying this stratum were Plano parallel-flaked points of the Scottsbluff type.[53] At Lubbock, Folsom Fluted projectiles with radiocarbon dates of 7300 to 7800 B.C. were taken from contexts with the extinct *Bison antiquus*. In a lower stratum at the same site were bison, mammoth, tapir, and horse bones, but no points.[54]

The Scharbauer site, in west Texas, is famous

to consist of two parts, a "kill" marked by a heap of extinct bison bones and a camp some quarter of a mile distant. Besides the highly diagnostic fluted points, the chipped-stone artifacts from Lindenmeier included thin, unfluted projectiles all similarly shaped, knives showing channeling, other knives made from the channel flakes which had been struck from the characteristic points, leaf-shaped knives, core choppers, and a variety of scrapers. Among them were thick, "snub-

as the location of the early human remains of Midland Man.[55] The basal stratum at Scharbauer is a white lacustrine sand containing mammoth, camel, and bison bones, but, with the possible exception of a fragment of worked bone, no artifacts. Overlying the white sand was a gray sand stratum from which the human skeleton, that of a markedly dolichocephalic female, was taken. No diagnostic artifacts were associated with this stratum, although a few pieces of worked flint and the butt end of a possible Clovis point were found in this gray sand. Radiocarbon dates on the gray sand stratum are conflicting, but there can be little doubt that the human skeleton and the few miscellaneous artifacts were substantially pre-Folsom. Overlying the gray sand is an aeolian-deposited red sand, most likely laid down during the dry Two Creeks interval. On top of the red sand, in a soil indicative of a return to more moist conditions, archaeologists found Folsom Fluted points and a number of "unfluted Folsoms," or Midland type points, as they are now called. This occupation, which followed the marked dry period, would appear to correlate with the Valders advance of about 9000 B.C. The stratigraphy at Scharbauer is similar to that of the Clovis Blackwater Draw site, where brown wind-carried sands separate the earlier occupation from an overlying Folsom point stratum associated with diatomaceous earth.

In reconstructing the culture history of the Big-Game Hunters from the very few traces at his disposal, the archaeologist relies heavily on the study of former natural environments. These environments, and the changes that occurred in them through the millennia, are not only extremely important in cross-dating, as we have just seen, but they provide a better image of ancient cultures and societies as actual functioning entities rather than categories of chipped-stone types. An admirable reconstruction of a former landscape has been provided by Fred Wendorf and J. J. Hester as a background for the Folsom hunters of about 8000 B.C. From pollen analyses and invertebrate studies of old soils, the now dry Llanos Estacados of the High Plains are pictured as lush savannas interspersed with wooded valleys. Networks of streams linked ponds and marshes. On the edges of these waters animals were killed and butchered, as the locations of the "kill" sites attest. A mile or less away from the streams and ponds, on ridges and hills, were the hunters' camps, overlooking the watering places.[56] In such a manner we recreate the ancient surroundings of the American Big-Game Hunter: the camp, the hunting grounds, and the entire setting of the park-like grasslands of the late Pleistocene.

Plano Points. After the climax of the Folsom horizon, at about 8000 B.C. and after, many other types of projectile points appeared in the North American High Plains. These were all lanceolate forms, long and large. For the most part, they were characterized by excellent chipping techniques, usually fine pressure-flaking. Most archaeologists feel that these various Plano projectile points developed from the earlier fluted Clovis and Folsom forms and, perhaps, from the Sandia form. A. L. Bryan has distinguished two main groups within Plano, the Plainview and Parallel-flaked.[57] Under the Plainview group are those unfluted points which in general outline resemble the Clovis and Folsom Fluted types—the Plainview, Midland, Milnesand, and Meserve forms. The Parallel-flaked classification comprises such types as the Scottsbluff, Eden, Cody, Angostura or Frederick, and Agate Basin types.[58]

Figure 2-14. Lanceolate projectile point types. *a:* Midland. *b:* Plainview. *c:* Meserve. *d:* Milnesand. Length of *a,* 6.2 cm. (After Wormington, 1957.)

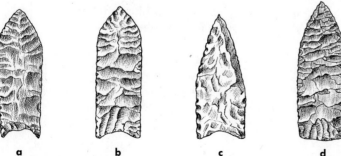

a   b   c   d

We have already pointed out that there were unfluted, Folsom-like points in the Folsom horizon at Sandia Cave, at Lindenmeier, and at Scharbauer. Some of these, and certainly the ones from Scharbauer, are Midland type points. In fact, the Midland point (Fig. 2-14a), is, to all intents, a point with a Folsom or Clovis shape and a blade too thin for channel-flaking. Both at Scharbauer and at the Hell Gap site[59] in Wyoming, the chronological position of the Midland point would appear to be equivalent to the Folsom horizon—or essentially between 9000 and 8000 B.C. But even earlier, in the Clovis horizon at Blackwater Draw, New Mexico, unfluted Clovis-like points were found in association with the true Colvis fluted forms. These data suggest that an unfluted point of a generalized Clovis-Folsom shape is as old as the fluted points. So in a sense, the prototypes of the later Plainview group of points were present much earlier.

The Plainview type (Fig. 2-14b) is similar to the Midland, but larger, heavier, thicker, and somewhat more roughly chipped. As with the fluted points, bases were concave, basal edges were smoothly ground, and the bases were thinned for hafting. Named after a site near the town of Plainview in northwest Texas, a large number of these points were found associated with a huge "kill" of bison. Radiocarbon dates of these finds span the

Figure 2-15. Projectile point series from the Hell Gap site, Wyoming. a,b: Midland. c–e: Agate Basin. f,g: Hell Gap. h,i: Alberta. j,k: Eden-Scottsbluff. l,m: Frederick. Length of a, 5 cm. (Courtesy Henry Irwin.)

period from about 7800 to 5100 B.C.[60] Plainview points are most common on the southern High Plains, but they also have been discovered as far north as the Canadian Plains and south into Mexico.

The Milnesand point is similar to the Plainview but had a straight rather than a concave base, marked basal beveling, and transverse parallel-flaking. The name comes from a site in New Mexico where the points were found in a bison-bone bed. Many of the points from the upper levels of the Blackwater Draw site are of Milnesand type and date to around 4200 to 4500 B.C.[61] The type has been found in Texas, in Iowa and Nebraska, and in Canada (Fig. 2-14d).

Meserve points were even more modified from the general Plainview outline. They had concave bases, slight basal flutings, and basal edge grinding; but whereas the lower sides were parallel, the upper sides converged to a long point (Fig. 2-14c). The opposite sides of this point were carefully chipped. The Meserve point is named for a find, in association with fossil bison, in Nebraska.[62] Meserve points in New Mexico have been dated as early as 4300 B.C.,[63] although they date much earlier elsewhere. In the Horne Rock Shelter, near Waco, Texas, Agogino reports a radiocarbon date

of 7320 B.C. on a Plainview-Meserve layer. The overlying cultural deposits in this case were of Texas Edwards Plateau Archaic affinities.[64] Also, at Graham Cave, in central Missouri—which takes us into the western fringes of the Eastern Woodlands area—they may go back to the seventh or eighth millennium B.C.[65]

There is no hard and fast typological separation between the points of the Plainview group and those of the Parallel-flaked group. For example, Plainview and Milnesand specimens exhibit careful parallel-flaking. The finest workmanship in parallel-flaking, however, was lavished on points which were, proportionately, long and slender and which had slightly tapering bases or, in some cases, slight shoulders. A. L. Bryan has suggested an origin for these points which is distinct from that of the Plainview group. Whereas the Plainview and related types appear to have derived from Clovis and Folsom Fluted points or from early unfluted forms similar to these, the Parallel-flaked group may have had its beginnings in the leaf-shaped points of the Old Cordilleran tradition.[66]

One of the earliest of the Parallel-flaked group of projectile points is the Agate Basin, which is best known from eastern Wyoming. In the sequence at the Hell Gap site, Agate Basin points follow the Midland type.[67] On the basis of geological and cultural stratigraphy—as well as some radiocarbon dates from higher levels in the site—the Agate Basin levels can be placed at about 8000 to 7000 B.C. The Agate Basin points were long and

Figure 2-16. Lanceolate projectile point types. a: Hell Gap. b,c,e: Agate Basin. d: Angostura. Length of a, 7.2 cm. (a,b, after Agogino, 1961; c–e, after Wormington, 1957.)

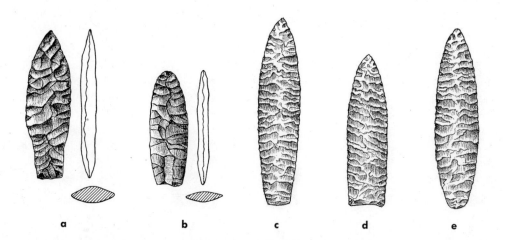

a   b   c   d   e

slender with slightly convex or almost parallel sides and with straight or convex bases. They exhibited fine horizontal parallel-flaking, and the lateral edges above the base were ground (Figs. 2-15c,d; 2-16b,c).

In the Hell Gap site, a Hell Gap type point (Fig. 2-15c,f) followed the Agate Basin type.[68] The Hell Gap points were lanceolate, but tapered abruptly to a straight or slightly rounded base. On some of the specimens this taper pinched in just below the maximum width of the blade to effect a vague shouldering and a stem process. In the same Hell Gap sequence a type known as the Alberta succeeded the Hell Gap form. The Alberta point was also a parallel-flaked lanceolate with a slight shouldering, a broad straight stem, and a straight base (Fig. 2-15g,h). Alberta points gave way to the Cody complex of Scottsbluff and Eden points and Cody knives. The Scottsbluff and Eden points —types well known in the Plains—were the most finely chipped projectiles of the entire Plano series. They were long in comparison to breadth, and characterized by transverse parallel or by collateral flaking (Fig. 2-15i,j). Like the Alberta form, which seems to be an earlier and somewhat less well-executed variant, they had slight shoulders and broad straight stems. At Hell Gap the Cody complex level carries a mean date of 6640 B.C. Finally, the uppermost Big-Game Hunting tradition level at the Hell Gap site featured a complex known as the Frederick. Hallmark of the Frederick complex was a long lanceolate point with a slightly concave base and oblique parallel-flaked surfaces.[69] Presumably, the Frederick complex immediately followed the Cody complex (Figs. 2-15k,l; 2-16d).

The importance of the Hell Gap site stratigraphy is emphasized by a comparison with the stratigraphy from Blackwater Draw, New Mexico. There, you will remember, the Clovis and Folsom levels were followed by Agate Basin, Cody, and Frederick complexes in that chronological order. Except for the absence of the Hell Gap and Alberta points, this succession parallels the Hell Gap stratigraphy; and, furthermore, the radiocarbon date for the Agate Basin level at Blackwater Draw

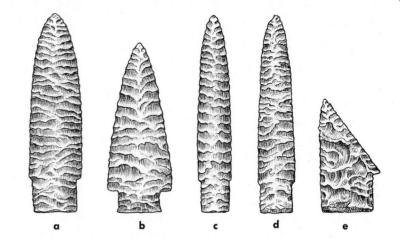

Figure 2-17. Lanceolate projectile point types. a: Scottsbluff Type I. b: Scottsbluff Type II. c: Eden Collateral-flaked point. d: Eden Transverse-flaked point. e: Cody knife. Length of a, 9.6 cm. (After Wormington, 1957.)

is 7840 B.C., conveniently in line with the estimates for Agate Basin occurrences in Wyoming.

A chronological and geographical sorting of the various projectile point types and culture complexes of the Plano series and of the centuries between about 8000 and 5000 B.C. remains to be done by Plains specialists. New results have come in from so many quarters in recent years—and are still coming in—that it is extremely difficult to synthesize what we do know about these later millennia of the Big-Game Hunting tradition on the High Plains. In general, it would seem that the parallel-flaked group of projectile points shared a northerly center of origin—in Wyoming and Montana. It may have arisen from Old Cordilleran beginnings, as A. L. Bryan has surmised; however, the earliest member of the long Hell Gap site sequence was a Midland point horizon, a point type that belongs with the Plainview rather than the parallel-flaked group.

Before leaving the Plains and these late Big-Game Hunting tradition complexes of the Plano projectile points, it might be well to take a closer look at one such complex. Perhaps the best known is the Cody complex, and a representative station is the Horner site, near Cody, Wyoming. Here Eden and Scottsbluff points were found together, the point types that archaeologists formerly referred to as "Yuma points." The context was an extensive butchering station for modern

47

bison and, perhaps, a habitation. A variety of artifacts other than the projectile points were recovered, including an asymmetrical stemmed knife, known as a Cody knife (Fig. 2-17*e*), and some scrapers, knives, perforators, choppers, pounders, and rubbing stones.[70] Significant, perhaps, was the latter item; rubbing or grinding stones were now beginning to appear.[71] Elsewhere in North America these implements were becoming even more important and widespread in the millennia between 8000 and 4000 B.C.

Fluted Points and Derived Forms in Eastern North America. So far we have followed the several strands of the Big-Game Hunting tradition in the High Plains of North America—possibly the hearth of the tradition, possibly not. But a very important branch of the story lies in eastern North America. Fluted points similar to those of the Plains and especially to the Clovis type have been found throughout much of the East. The northern distributional limits of these points was once thought to follow very closely the southern limits of what was the Valders ice advance. This line was believed to run from southern Maine across New York and southeastern Ontario, dipping southward around Lake Michigan, and turning northward again through central Wisconsin and southern Minnesota. In observing this situation, R. J. Mason stated: "these parallel distributions, one cultural, the other paleogeographic, virtually establish the contemporaneity of man and ice."[72] There can be little doubt of this contemporaneity; but, quite recently, D. S. Byers has reported Clovis points from geological contexts of Valders age at the Debert site in Nova Scotia.[73] This location is somewhat north of the presumed southern limit of the ice and poses the question of revisions of glacial phenomena and dating in the East or the possibility of Clovis points being used in the East in pre-Valders time. The question is of considerable interest, because it bears on the relative ages of fluted points in the High Plains and in the East, on their origins, and on the place of origin of the Big-Game Hunting tradition.

Many factors favor a High Plains origin for both the fluted point and for the Big-Game Hunting cultural tradition. The pattern of life seemed best adapted to the kind of environment which has been reconstructed for the High Plains in the late Pleistocene; the High Plains location lies along the most probable corridor for the southward movement of early man from Alaska to the rest of the Americas; and the most firmly documented findings fix the early presence of New World specialized hunters in the High Plains. Following this interpretation, we can argue that the early Big-Game Hunters spread to the East during the Two Creeks interstadial, a movement, perhaps, occasioned by the disappearance or decline of the mammoth on the open Plains in this drier geological interval. Some groups, of course, remained on the Plains and became the Folsom bison hunters and the later Plano hunters; but others, probably those who occupied more geographically marginal positions, moved east in continued pursuit of the mammoth. And, quite probably, the hunters drifting to the east were attracted still farther in this direction by the tree-browsing mastodon.

Such is one line of argument, possible but by no means demonstrated. Another possibility is that the Clovis hunters and their characteristic projectile point did, indeed, develop on the High Plains but that these hunters, successfully exploiting their new way of life, moved rapidly to the eastern part of the continent as well as spreading over the Plains. Still another counter-argument states that although hundreds of Clovis points have been found in the Plains, thousands have been recovered from the eastern United States. This is true, and if frequency or abundance is an indicator of geographical center of origin, then such an origin must be in the East, particularly in the drainages of the Ohio, Tennessee, and central Mississippi River valleys.[74] Unfortunately, most of the eastern fluted points have been surface finds, and there are few geological contexts, faunal associations, radiocarbon dates, or even cultural stratigraphies which throw much light on the problem of relative age as compared with fluted points in the West. The significance of the eastern fluted points has derived largely from their typology, which is similar or identical to the early projectile forms of the High Plains; however, there are some stratigraphic indications which imply considerable age relative to other archaeological cultures of the East.

Three of the best documented site assemblages of fluted points in the East come not from the Ohio-Cumberland region of the numerous casual surface finds but farther east, in Pennsylvania, Massachusetts, and Virginia. At the Shoop site in eastern Pennsylvania several hundred chert tools and a great many more fragments were found scattered over a plateau or low hilltop comprising about 20 acres. There is no geological stratigraphy in the thin top soil at the site, and no Pleistocene

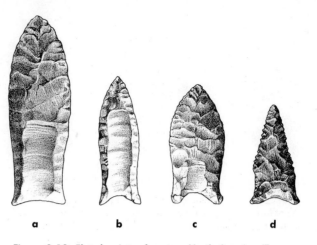

Figure 2-19. Fluted points of eastern North America (Tennessee). a: Clovis. b: Cumberland. c: Quad. d: Dalton. Length of a, 9.2 cm. (After Mason, 1962.)

fauna or radiocarbon dates testify to antiquity. The case for extreme age is typological but of undoubted merit. Most of the fluted points from Shoop are closer to the Clovis mode than to the Folsom, although a few resemble the Folsom in their outline and length of channel flaking. End- and side-scrapers and gravers made up the complex or industry which Witthoft, the investigator, has named the Enterline Chert industry.[75] The Bull Brook site, in northeastern Massachusetts, is located on a glacial terrace. Clovis type fluted points, together with gravers, drills, flake knives, snub-nosed end-scrapers, and side-scrapers were found in a number of small concentrations suggesting several separate shelters or hearths of a camp. Bull Brook radiocarbon dates strike a mean of about 7000 B.C.,[76] somewhat too late for an anticipated Valders or Two Creeks time. The third site is Williamson, in Virginia. It is a hilltop area of surface finds: fluted points, snub-nosed scrapers, and other implements which resemble the materials from the Shoop site.[77]

Although the fluted points at Shoop, Bull Brook, and Williamson sites, together with many found in the East in general, are of the Clovis form, or at least resemble that form fairly closely, a great many others differ significantly. The best known is the Cumberland Fluted point (Fig. 2-19b) which appeared predominantly in the Tennessee and Ohio Valley regions. This point was relatively long, like the Clovis, but frequently was widest near the mid-section and often bore long

Figure 2-18. Artifacts from the Shoop site, Pennsylvania (a–g), and the Bull Brook site, Massachusetts (h). a: Side-scraper. b: Flake knife. c: End-scraper. d: Unifacial graver. e: Burin-like tip. f–h: Clovis-type fluted points. Length of a, 4 cm. (a–g, after Witthoft, 1952; h, after Byers, 1954.)

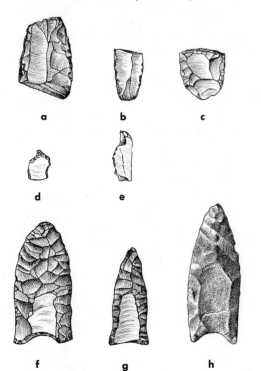

a   b   c   d

Figure 2-20. The earliest projectile points (*a,b*, Quad type) from the Hardaway site, North Carolina piedmont. Length of *a*, just under 4 cm. (Courtesy J. L. Coe; see also Coe, 1964.)

Folsom-like flutes. A definitive feature was the flare of the ends, or "ears," of the concave base. No reliable dates have yet been fixed for the Cumberland points, but by analogy with the trends in

Figure 2-21. Early Archaic projectile point types from the Hardaway site. *a–d*: Hardaway-Dalton. *e–i*: Palmer Corner-Notched. *j–l*: Kirk Serrated. *m*: Kirk Corner-Notched. Length of *a*, 5.8 cm. (Courtesy J. L. Coe; see also Coe, 1964.)

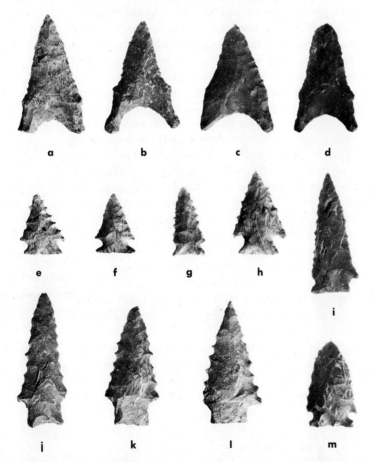

a   b   c   d

e   f   g   h

i

j   k   l   m

point-form modification on the Plains, from the partially fluted Clovis to the more fully fluted Folsom, it has been suggested that they are later than the true Clovis forms of the East.[78] Other possible Clovis-derived, and later, fluted points are the Dalton (Fig. 2-19*d*), named from Missouri but widely distributed in the Southeast,[79] the Quad[80] (Figs. 2-19*c*; 2-20), and Suwannee[81] from Alabama and Florida, the Hardaway (Fig. 2-21*a-d*) from North Carolina,[82] and Reagen from Vermont.[83] It seems likely that these several eastern varieties of the basic fluted form were local developments that occurred during the same millennia as the Folsom and post-Folsom Plano industries of the Plains. This thesis is suggested by a number of stratigraphies, such as at the Hardaway site, where Hardaway fish-tailed and slightly fluted points lay at the bottom of a long Archaic sequence,[84] or at the Stanfield-Worley Bluff Shelter, in northern Alabama, where the similar fish-tailed and semi-fluted Dalton points were found in the lowest levels underlying Archaic cultures.[85] The thesis is also suggested by the association of Cumberland points with those of the western Plainview and parallel-flaked groups of the Plano series in the Mississippi, Ohio, and Tennessee valleys and by the essentially complementary distributions of eastern and western late Big-Game Hunting tradition projectile types. For example, a number of Plano points have been found in the Great Lakes region and north of the Ohio River, but finds have been less frequent as one moves south, and they are missing entirely from the eastern Southeast, where Dalton, Suwannee, Cumberland, and related forms remain the dominant types.[86]

Summary. The Big-Game Hunting cultural tradition may have been derived independently from the cultural heritage of very ancient hunters and food-gatherers whose ancestors had come from Asia to America 20,000 to 40,000 years ago. Or, and to my mind more likely, it may have resulted from somewhat more recent arrivals of specialized hunters from Asia. Whatever these most remote beginnings, the distinctive lanceolate projectile points of the tradition—the weapon used to kill the large Pleistocene herd animals—appear to have been invented here, at least in their unique fluted forms. This invention, and the formation of the Big-Game Hunting pattern, had occurred by 10,000 B.C.

In my opinion, the primary center of development of the Big-Game Hunting tradition was the North American High Plains; but it is possible that such a development could have unfolded farther north, in Canada or Alaska or in the eastern United States. As far as we can now tell, Big-Game hunters, using Clovis Fluted projectile points, were in the East about as early as their presence can be definitely demonstrated in the High Plains.

As time passed, a number of regional adaptations changed the earlier Big-Game Hunting pattern. It is possible the first of these, in point of time, was the Folsom complex of the Plains, and the adaptations appear to be related to the shift from mammoth-hunting to bison-hunting. Other modifications of the Clovis tradition unfolded in the forested East, resulting in the Cumberland, Quad, and Dalton points and complexes. Back on the Plains the final expressions of the Big-Game Hunting way of life were the various Plano unfluted points. Some of these were carried East, especially in the northern part of the United States, and their distribution complements, and in part overlaps, that of the Cumberland and Dalton points. Gradually, the Big-Game Hunting tradition died out in the East and was replaced by another tradition, the Archaic. On the Plains the Big-Game Hunting tradition persisted longest, continuing to 5000 to 4000 B.C. In the West, in such places as southern Arizona, it appears to have been submerged in the expanding tradition of the Desert cultures.

Still farther west, in the Rocky Mountain valleys of western Montana and Idaho and on the Snake River Plain, it appears to have penetrated in a limited way, as, for instance, in the Lind Coulee in Washington.[87] But here it was replaced by less specialized hunting or hunting-collecting cultures. In the Great Basin and in California it seems never to have been established as a tradition, although some few vestiges of it have been found, usually as odd points in the contexts of other traditions. In Middle America and in South America, as we shall see farther along, there are indications of its presence, although under conditions which suggest a merger with elements of the other early American tradition, the Old Cordilleran.

The Old Cordilleran Tradition

The Concept. The most important fact to emerge from recent archaeological discoveries in the Pacific Northwest is that the dominant projectile point for the whole area, on an early time level, was a willow-leaf, bi-point form. This nicely chipped bifacial point is known as the Cascade type and is an index, or identifying feature, of what has been termed an Old Cordilleran complex, culture, or tradition. A few other elements are associated with this complex, including knives of a similar leaf-shaped form, oval knives, and

Figure 2-22. Cascade points of the Old Cordilleran tradition. Length of point at left, 5.7 cm. (After Butler, 1961.)

edge-ground cobbles. B. R. Butler, who has advanced the Old Cordilleran concept, has stated that the tool types composing the complex and the contexts of the finds reflect a relatively unspecialized hunting, fishing, and collecting way of life that was characteristic of much of the mountain and plateau country of Pacific North America.[88] He and R. S. MacNeish also have established a wide distribution of the Cascade or Cascade-like points, taking in considerable areas of Middle and South America and including situations and artifact complexes which are not particularly reminiscent of the Old Cordilleran complex as it existed in Washington or Oregon. The extent to which all these finds may constitute a culture complex awaits further study and clarification, but undoubtedly Butler has picked up a very important thread which should be of great help in unraveling early American culture history, particularly in the Pacific Northwest. Thus, although equating an "Old Cordilleran cultural tradition" with the better established Big-Game Hunting, Desert, and Archaic traditions may be premature, a number of reasons prompt the use of such an expository device and also prompt its presentation at this point in the story of the early Americans. First, the Old Cordilleran leaf-shaped Cascade point is sufficiently early to be contemporaneous with at least the latter stages of the Big-Game Hunting tradition; second, there are sound indications that the leaf-shaped point and the Old Cordilleran tradition were as early or earlier than the beginnings of the Desert tradition; and third, the leaf-shaped point was more widely distributed in South America than any other early New World point type, and such a distribution suggests not only extreme age but a significantly separate history.

There is also another, and somewhat more speculative, reason for believing that the Old Cordilleran tradition and the Cascade-type projectile point have very ancient roots. This is the logical argument and possibility that the simple willow-leaf point form was the basic prototype of all early American lanceolate points. If so, such points might constitute an horizon earlier than any of the fluted forms. As yet this proposition has not been demonstrated.[89] Even on logical grounds there are some objections to it. As Wilmsen says:

There is, however, no explanation of the technique involved in striking a flute from a pointed base, whereas Mason (1958: 7–16, Fig. 2) has carefully studied a large number of Clovis fluted points and has presented convincing evidence for an essentially straight-base striking platform for fluting (see also Witthoft 1952).[90]

Thus, the willow-leaf-shaped lanceolate point may not be the necessary forerunner of the fluted or channeled form. However, leaving this somewhat special argument aside, there is, as we shall see, considerable evidence for regarding the Old Cordilleran tradition and its leaf-shaped points as substantially early.

The Northwest. The original definition of the Old Cordilleran tradition is based on sites in the river valleys of the Cascade Mountains in Oregon and Washington. The Five Mile Rapids site, on the Oregon side of the Dalles Reservoir of the Columbia River, is the most important station. Here, at the bottom of a deep refuse accumulation, is an assemblage of leaf-shaped bipoints, bolas, burins,[91] and heavy cobble choppers. The level is dated by radiocarbon at about 7800 B.C., but L. S. Cressman, the excavator, estimates that this early culture phase was established in the Columbia Valley as early as 9000 B.C. Overlying later phases exhibit a trend toward a less nomadic existence, probably correlated with a growing dependence on fishing rather than land-hunting. Thus, the leaf-shaped points persist to 5700 B.C. but were accompanied by abundant salmon remains as well as bird and mammal bones.[92] Across the Columbia River from Five Mile Rapids, Butler has defined a phase which appears to be contempory with these, and the large collection of leaf-shaped bi-points found at this site, known as Indian Well, are the type series for the Cascade point. These points averaged about 6 centimeters in length, were relatively narrow, and either diamond-shaped or plano-convex in cross-section.[93]

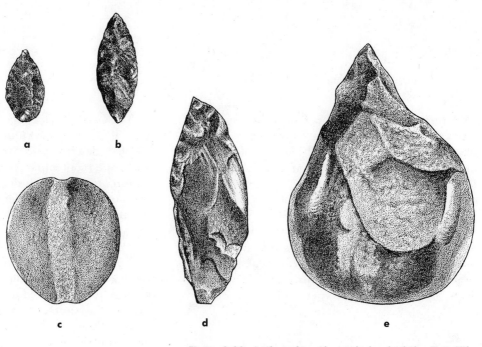

a   b

c   d   e

Figure 2-23. Artifacts from the early level of the Five Mile Rapids site, The Dalles, Oregon. a,b: Cascade or Old Cordilleran points. c: Grooved bola stone. d: Burin. e: Pebble chopper. Length of a, 2.7 cm. (After Cressman and others, 1960.)

To the north, in the Fraser River canyon, at the Yale site, on the edge of the British Columbia Plateau country, Old Cordilleran points were found in the lowest levels of a long stratigraphy and can be dated by radiocarbon to about 7000 B.C.[94]

To the east of the Cascade Mountains, at the interior plateau sites of Hat Creek, Oregon,[95] and Ash Cave, in southeastern Washington,[96] the leaf-shaped point appears to be as early as 7000 B.C. It also appeared this early in the northern Great Basin sites, in the lowest levels of Fort Rock Cave in the southeastern Oregon desert[97] and from a similar stratigraphic position in nearby Cougar Mountain Cave.[98] In both these caves the points were found with basketry, cordage, sandals, and notched points—all "classic" features of the Desert cultural tradition. The stratigraphy of these caves suggests, however, that the leaf-shaped point (and the Old Cordilleran tradition?) was then being replaced by projectile points and a general way of life more typical of this Desert tradition.

California. Southward, into California, the earliest archaeological cultures bore certain resemblances to the Old Cordilleran tradition —principally in the possession of leaf-shaped projectile points. This is true, for example, of the Lake Mojave complex,[99] of San Dieguito,[100] of the

Malaga Cove I phase, as represented at the bottommost level of a Pacific coastal shell midden,[101] and of the related Topanga I and II phases of the southern California foothills.[102] Krieger feels that these early California cultures should not be grouped with the Old Cordilleran tradition,[103] and it is true that, as complexes, they display differences. For one thing, they betray similarities to the cultures of the Desert tradition and reveal the beginnings of a specialization which leads into the much later cultures of the California area. Nevertheless, I am inclined to bring them into the discussion of early American cultures at this point, in a consideration of the Old Cordilleran tradition and its wider relationships.

The best known of these early California complexes is the Lake Mojave. The sites of the complex lie along old channels and salt "playas," or dry lakes, in the Mojave and Colorado deserts of southeastern California. This is an extremely arid region today, sustaining only a sparse scrub vegetation and reptiles and rodents. During the Altithermal, the area was even more forbidding; but earlier, under pluvial conditions, the lake beds were filled with water and the region was more suited to human habitation. The Lake Mojave phase dates to this pluvial period—to a time estimated at around 9000 to 7000 B.C.[104] The most diagnostic artifact, the Lake Mojave point (Fig. 2-24c), was lozenge-shaped, with a short blade and a long stem. Other artifacts found associated with this point along the old shorelines included Silver Lake points (a short triangular blade with a broad stem and rounded base, Fig. 2-24d), some leaf-shaped points similar to Old Cordilleran types, curious crescent-shaped chipped flints, crude choppers, drills, and a number of scrapers and scraper-planes.

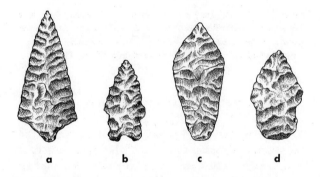

Figure 2-24. Projectile point types, southeastern California. *a:* Gypsum Cave. *b:* Pinto Basin. *c:* Lake Mojave. *d:* Silver Lake. Length of *a*, 6.7 cm. (After Wormington, 1957.)

In sum, the Lake Mojave complex appears to reflect a hunting, game-skinning, hide-treating culture. That fishing was a part of the economy seems reasonable, assuming the lakes were then present, but no fishing gear has come down to us in the remains. Nor are there any clues to such things as basketry and cordage, sandals or matting. These gaps in the record may be due only to lack of preservation of such perishable materials in open sites; on the other hand, the absence of basketry may reflect little concern with plant and seed-gathering, the traditional activities of the Desert cultures. Manos and milling stones were, significantly, scarce or absent.

The Lake Mojave phase, then, was certainly not typical of the Desert cultural tradition—a tradition we shall describe next. Nor was it closely affiliated with the contemporaneous Big-Game Hunting cultures to the East. It does exhibit some characteristics of the Old Cordilleran cultures of the Pacific Northwest, although admittedly it stands apart from them, too.

Some General Considerations. The concept of the Old Cordilleran tradition as here described, then, is linked to a relatively unspecialized artifact, a simple bifacially flaked leaf-shaped blade. These blades, usually percussion-chipped and sometimes retouched with pressure-flaking, were used as projectiles for spears or darts and probably also as knives. They were frequently associated with heavy chopping tools or edge-grinders, scraper-planes, and other cutting, scraping, and perforating implements which indicate a hunting culture. This description seems to fit the tradition in its earliest and purest known form as it is found in the Cascade country of the Northwest.

An alternative synthesis for the early cultures of the Northwest has been proposed by R. D. Daugherty, who would establish two traditions: an Old Cordilleran (or "Northwest Cordilleran," as he would prefer to call it) and an "Intermontane Western." The first would be restricted to the Cascades and the mountains of the west, and the second would embrace the Intermontane Plateau and Great Basin.[105] It is significant, however, that the early period of Daugherty's "Intermontane Western" tradition is essentially indistinguishable from Butler's Old Cordilleran. Both definitions refer to unspecialized hunting-collecting cultures, with local or regional emphasis depending on circumstances. The dominant projectile point was the leaf-shape, which later in its Intermontane and Great Basin lineages revealed some basic modifications. Basketry, matting, and netting were linked with the "Intermontane Western" tradition, but, only for sites in the semi-arid Great Basin country. In brief, the beginnings of the "Intermontane Western" tradition are the minimum Butler definitions of Old Cordilleran. What both archaeologists seem to be telling us is that the leaf-shaped projectile and an unspecialized hunting-collecting life prevailed in the Pacific Northwest in Anathermal times and that with the coming of Altithermal climates, more specialized regional adaptations developed.

Radiocarbon dating of the Old Cordilleran tradition yields a range of from about 9000 to 5000 B.C., with most of the dates grouped midway between these limits.[106] This is, of course, the period of the Anathermal and early Altithermal, with climates and fauna tending toward modern conditions. It was a time all over the Americas of settling into a variety of newly forming natural environmental niches. This undoubtedly explains why the Old Cordilleran tradition, as it is revealed to us, seemed always to be undergoing rapid modification or replacement. In the Cascades and Coastal Mountains, the modification and replacement emerged as the Northwest Coast tradition; in the Intermontane Plateau, the new pattern has been called the Northwest Riverine tradition;[107] south of the Plateau the replacement emerged as the Desert tradition, and in California, what I have designated as a California Coastal and Valley tradition arose.

In one sense, as E. T. Swanson has pointed out, the Old Cordilleran tradition never disappeared but continued in the leaf-shaped points and other chipped-stone tools which come down to historic times in certain parts of the Northwest.[108] In another sense, the old Anathermal way of life changed to such a degree in later prehistoric times that it is probably more useful to conceive of a new cultural entity or entities.

The Desert Tradition

The Concept. Gradually, over the past 30 years, archaeological and ethnographic research have revealed the significance and long persistence of the Desert pattern of life in western North America. In 1955, in an article by J. D.

Jennings and Edward Norbeck,[109] the concept finally was formulated and given clarity and focus. In particular, this article was an outgrowth of Jennings' excavations at the important site of Danger Cave, Utah, and in a monograph dealing with these excavations he has developed his ideas still further.[110] One of the most significant things about the Desert tradition is that it has persisted into historic times. As a result, it has been possible for archaeologists to project back from the ethnohistoric horizon many of the lifeways of the tribes of the desert to their ancient forbears. Thus, it is possible to say of the Desert culture, for prehistoric as well as historic times, that:

The effective social unit was small. An extended family—man, wife, or wives, children and children-in-law, some infants—numbering no more than 25 or 30 in all, would constitute a normal, year-round, grouping. . . . The pattern of life was a cyclic wandering, but it was not truly a nomadic one. The small groups moved regularly from place to place, from valley to upland, in search of the seasonal animal or plant resources which centuries of experience had taught them were to be had. . . . Under such conditions, the material possessions were few, utilitarian and durable or easily manufactured at need. . . . The twin hallmarks of the Desert culture were the basket and the flat milling stone. The orientation of the culture toward small seeds was well established by 7000 B.C., as these utensils testify. Supplementing vegetable foods, or perhaps of equal importance, was the hunt—virtually every animal of the desert fell prey to trap, snare and weapon.

We can evoke a substance of life from the archaeological findings of milling stones and baskets by referring to:

Vegetable foods used by the Northern Paiute in the 19th century, and deemed typical of the Desert culture, included acorns, piñons, nuts, various small grass seeds, cress, sunflower, burroweed, sego lily bulbs, bulrush rhizomes, berries of many kinds, and many roots. Nearly all of these were reduced to flour or paste upon the slab mill. Seeds were usually milled after they were parched with live coals in a flat basket. The embers were mixed with the seeds while the basket was shaken so as to keep the coals and seeds moving and still prevent the scorching or burning of the basket. The flour was often cooked, in a basket (by means of heated stones), into a mush or gruel. Meat foods were most often roasted. . . . In case of surplus, meat was dried and might even be pulverized and saved in a woven bag.[111]

The elements of the Desert cultural tradition, as these come to us through archaeology, include, of course, the milling stone and the basket, as well as a series of chipped-stone projectile points. For the most part, these points tended to be smaller and proportionately broader than the points of either the Big-Game Hunting or Old Cordilleran traditions. They definitely were used as tips for throwing-stick darts, weapons with which the men of the Desert hunted a modern fauna that on the average was smaller than the animals pursued by the Big-Game Hunters. For example, the bones of the larger animals found in Danger Cave represent modern species only: the mountain sheep, bison, deer, and antelope.[112] In general, the archaeological assemblages of the Desert tradition, and the reliable inferences which may be made about them, contrast sharply with what we know and can reconstruct about the Big-Game Hunting tradition. The distinctions are less definitive between the Desert and the Old Cordilleran traditions.

Utah. The earliest hearth, or center, of the Desert tradition is probably the Great Basin, a physiographic unit which includes eastern California, Nevada, western and northern Utah, southeastern Oregon, southern Idaho, and southwestern Wyoming. This is the most arid part of North America, and near its center, in western Utah, is the site of Danger Cave.[113] This cave was occupied by man shortly after the subsidence of the Pleistocene lake which had covered the locality of the Bonneville Salt Flats. According to radiocarbon dates, this first occupation occurred between 9500 and 9000 B.C., or during the Two Creeks interval which followed the Mankato advance.[114] The cave location is marked by fires and a few crude chipped-stone artifacts found on consolidated beach sands left in the cave by the retreating lake.

Interesting among the artifacts was a single leaf-shaped point.[115]

The Desert culture diagnostics to which we have already referred do not appear in this earliest cave stratum. They pertain, rather, to the overlying debris of what is termed "Zone II" and for which the radiocarbon dates range from about 8000 to 7000 B.C. In Zone II were found the slab milling stones; two examples of twined basketry; some bone awls; and several small, thick, corner-notched, side-notched, stemmed, and unstemmed chipped-stone points. In general, these various point types have been discovered throughout the successive and later cultural zones of the cave refuse. Core tools, including choppers and planes, were found from Zones II through V. A significant innovation in Zone V was a small triangular point, probably adapted to the bow-and-arrow. Zone V is believed to date from as late as the Christian era. The Desert tradition underwent a kind of florescence in Zone III. Coiled basketry techniques were added to twined varieties. A great many wooden objects were preserved in the dry dust of the cave from this and later periods, including foreshafts of darts and numerous skewers or wooden pins. Bone had been used to make not only a variety of implements but also tubes and what are probably game counters. Cordage, of hide or of vegetal fiber, was abundant. The principal vegetal fiber used in its manufacture was *Apocynum.* The chief material for baskets was the willow splint.

Other Utah caves have revealed Desert culture evidences, among them the Black Rock Cave No. 1 and Deadman Cave, both on the south shore of the Great Salt Lake.[116] In each, side-notched points were found above old lacustrine deposits. At Promontory Cave II, on the north side of the lake, a leaf-shaped point underlay stemmed types.[117]

Oregon. The southern Oregon caves containing Desert-type remains already have been mentioned. The lower levels at Fort Rock Cave, dated to about 7000 B.C., have yielded notched points similar to those from Danger Cave of the same date (Zone II); and the Cougar Mountain

Cave assemblages of points, milling stones, and basketry were clearly in this same general tradition.[118]

We shall return to the Desert culture in southeastern Oregon when we examine the tradition in its later chronological ranges (Chap. 6, especially for illustrations of Desert-type remains).

Nevada. The Humboldt Lake region of west central Nevada has furnished other and somewhat different manifestations of the Desert tradition. A number of sites, both cave and open, are located in the region, including the Leonard Rockshelter, Lovelock Cave, and Humboldt Cave. A long stratigraphy, with associated radiocarbon dates, unfolds in the Leonard shelter. The earliest occupation Heizer designated as the Humboldt culture. It is represented in bat-guano levels which overlie the old Lake Lahontan Pleistocene beach gravels of the cave floor. This guano was first deposited around 9200 B.C., and the process continued up until about 5000 B.C. It thus spans the usually accepted dates for the Anathermal and, as did the Danger Cave occupation, began even earlier. Humboldt culture artifacts from the cave included a bipointed leaf-shaped blade, some obsidian flakes, *Olivella* shell beads (indicative of contact with the Pacific Coast), some net cordage, and wooden atlatl darts. Radiocarbon readings on the actual wooden artifacts and the guano immediately surrounding them have spanned the period from 6800 to 5000 B.C. The obsidian flakes, however, came from deeper in the guano deposit and do indicate the presence of man, if only temporarily and casually, as early as about 9200 B.C. It is likely that the atlatl darts, shell beads, and other items were burial accompaniments, placed in the guano layers, although no human skeletal remains were found in association. What appears to be a related artifact assemblage has been termed the Granite Point culture or complex and consists of basalt core and heavy flake tools found in open sites along old beach lines. Apparently, the dating is the same—the Anathermal climatic stage—and Heizer thinks it likely that these rough stone tools

were manufactured by the same people who used the rockshelter and made the atlatl darts. A second level of the Leonard Rockshelter is defined by a Leonard culture, one which was in residence during the Altithermal. The only finds for this period have been an infant skeleton and carbonized twined basketry. Following a hiatus, the upper levels of the cave are characterized by the Lovelock culture, which is also well represented in other caves of the region. It dates from some point in the Medithermal and continues up until the historic Northern Paiute horizon.[119]

Before leaving Nevada in this survey of early Desert culture stations, mention should be made of Gypsum Cave, near Las Vegas.[120] It is distinguished from the caves just described, however, by its extinct faunal associations and by another projectile point form. In the lower levels of this cave were bones of ground sloth and camel along with man-made fireplaces, dart shafts, foreshafts of wood, basketry fragments, and a diamond-shaped point known as the Gypsum Cave type (Fig. 2-24*a*). It differs from the lozenge or diamond-shaped Lake Mojave point in that the blade was a much larger part of the whole than the opposite hafting end. The haft dwindled to a very small tapered stem. The radiocarbon dates for Gypsum Cave are 8500–6500 B.C. We will refer again to the Gypsum Cave projectile point in our discussion of the Desert tradition (Chap. 6).

Southeastern California. The Desert cultures of southeastern California which arose after 7000 B.C., are here considered part of the general Desert cultural tradition. They were, of course, somewhat different from the cultures of the Utah-Nevada Great Basin.[121] Yet the Pinto Basin phase,[122] which followed the Lake Mojave phase in southeastern California, was closer to the Desert tradition mode of life than the Mojave phase. Manos and milling stones were new additions to the complex. A diagnostic feature was the Pinto Basin projectile form, a triangular blade with narrow stem and an indented base (Fig. 2-24*b*). The Pinto Basin phase lasted until the first millennium B.C. or even later. The culture which replaced it remained in the food-collecting and hunting tradition of the Desert culture until well into the historic period,[123] modified only slightly by the addition of traits from the farming cultures of the southwestern United States.

Arizona and New Mexico. To the east, the Cochise culture of southern Arizona was another important manifestation of the Desert tradition. Its earliest phase, the Sulphur Spring, was characterized by percussion-flaked, leaf-shaped, stemmed, and barbed projectile points, along with simple manos and metates. The sites are open, so there are no evidences of basketry or other perishables. The surprising association with the Sulphur Spring phase, however, is the extinct fauna, including mammoth, horse, prong-horn antelope, dire wolf, and bison. Successive phases, the Chiricahua and the San Pedro, traced the traditional Desert line of chipped-stone hunting equipment and food-grinding tools up to the advent of agriculture and pottery and the transition from Desert to Southwestern tradition.[124] The radiocarbon dates for Cochise are consistent with Desert culture dating, the earliest ones being about 7350 to 6270 B.C. for Sulphur Spring. These dates are, however, somewhat out of line with the faunal assemblage. Apparently, the mammoth lingered on in southern Arizona to a relatively late period.[125]

The Cochise culture was related to the southern California Desert cultures, and a link is provided by what Haury has designated as the Amargosa and the Chiricahua-Amargosa II levels in the Ventana Cave site in southwestern Arizona.[126]

In New Mexico, at Bat Cave, the Chiricahua phase is represented by projectile points reminiscent of Pinto Basin and Gypsum Cave forms. It is in this same Chiricahua context of Bat Cave that a primitive maize, probably in its first stages of domestication, has been dated by radiocarbon to somewhere around 4000 to 3500 B.C.[127] Throughout much of the southwestern area remains similar to Cochise indicate a widespread Desert culture horizon which was antecedent to the later Southwestern farming cultures and which was, indeed, the base out of which that farming tradition developed.

The Problem of Origins. In appraising the place of the Desert cultural tradition in early America, let us return again to the "twin hallmarks" of the pattern, basketry and milling stones. Their earliest dated occurrences—and by inference the earliest dated appearances of seed-collecting and hunting societies—are in southern Oregon, northwestern Nevada, and western Utah at about 8000–7000 B.C. There is some question about Jenning's contention that the materials from the lowest Danger Cave level, which dates to 9500–9000 B.C., are part of the Desert tradition. Neither milling stones, basketry, nor the characteristic stemmed and notched projectiles were found in this basal zone. All such things belong to the second and overlying level of the cave. Similarly, in the Leonard Rockshelter in Nevada, the earliest stratum, dating to 9200 B.C., lacks the Desert diagnostics; again these appear in the succeeding level, which dates from 3000 to 5000 B.C. Are there, then, any traits or features of these earlier cave levels that supply a clue about pre- or proto-Desert cultures in the Great Basin?

Unfortunately, the collections from these earlier strata are extremely meager and difficult or impossible to identify in terms of cultural tradition. We have suggested that the leaf-shaped projectile from the bottom level of Danger Cave might indicate an affiliation with the Old Cordilleran tradition, and we have mentioned already that the early levels of Desert culture sites, such as the Oregon Fort Rock and Cougar Mountain Caves, contained the leaf-shaped points. Did the Old Cordilleran and Desert traditions have a common ancestry before 7000 or 8000 B.C., with the latter emerging as a specialization from the former?[128] Possibly the notched and stemmed forms evolved from the basic leaf shape as a Great Basin development; or another possibility is that such an evolution occurred farther north, in the Idaho Rockies, in what Swanson has called the "Bitterroot culture."

This "Bitterroot culture" is said by Swanson to replace the Mountain-Plains Big-Game Hunters in eastern Idaho and to have been adapted to modern game and characterized by side-notched points before 5000 B.C.[129]

Outside the Great Basin proper there are also some hints that the Desert and Old Cordilleran traditions shared a common ancestry. In Mexico, in Tamaulipas and in Puebla, the prevalent projectile point form prior to 7000 B.C. was the leaf-shaped Lerma, which was quite similar in outline to the Cascade point. Afterward, with the advent of an economy in which seed-grinding played an important part, the leaf-shaped point tended to give way to other forms.[130] In Frightful Cave, in Coahuila, the earliest complex, the Cienegas, contained a Desert-type assemblage of milling stones and perishables—baskets, sandals, atlatls, and shafts—and the associated projectile points were leaf-shaped. The radiocarbon dates for the Cienegas complex range from 6900 to 5300 B.C., or slightly after the time when a fully formed Desert culture existed in the Great Basin.[131] It seems quite possible that Cienegas, in its relatively remote northeast Mexican location, represents a marginal retention of an earlier projectile point type.

The relationships, chronological and otherwise, between the Desert tradition and the Big-Game Hunting tradition are more obscure than those between the Desert and Old Cordilleran traditions. This is particularly true with reference to the earlier time ranges and the time of origin of the Desert tradition. Later, Desert-type cultures definitely persisted after the Big-Game Hunting tradition had died out.

One difficulty in determining the relationships between the Desert and Big-Game Hunting traditions is that very few Big-Game Hunter finds have ever been made in the Great Basin. Elizabeth Campbell has reported some from near Tonopah, Nevada—small, Clovis-like points found with end- and side-scrapers and gravers on an old lake terrace. Their association with this terrace suggests a chronological position comparable to that of the very early Desert cultures.[132] A few other fluted points have come from California Desert sites, one, for instance, from Lake Mojave.[133]

Outside the Great Basin, fluted types have appeared associated with Desert point types at the Borax Lake site in northern California. C. W. Meighan believes that the former are intrusive to the site and locality, but whether or not they were brought in contemporaneously with the other artifacts remains uncertain.[134]

In Arizona, at Ventana Cave, an early cultural complex known as the Ventana reveals a slight hint of Big-Game Hunting influences preceding the Amargosa and Chiricahua-Amargosa complexes of the Desert type. The Ventana complex was associated with evidences of a pluvial period, including extinct horse and sloth bones. The most distinctive artifacts were two projectile points—one an "unfluted Folsom," the other a truncated leaf shape with slight corner notches.[135] Haury, who excavated Ventana Cave, felt that these points implied connections with the East and with the Big-Game Hunters, and his surmise seems reinforced by the more recent Naco and Lehner discoveries of Big-Game Hunting points only a little over 100 miles to the east in southeastern Arizona. Nevertheless, the evidence from the lowest Ventana level is very limited, and the two points are as conveniently assimilated to an Old Cordilleran as they are to a Big-Game Hunter pattern.[136]

In New Mexico, cave stratigraphies at Burnet, where a Clovis Fluted point was found below Desert culture remains,[137] and at Manzano, where a Sandia point underlay Gypsum Cave types,[138] favor the antecedent position of the Big-Game Hunters. Similar data also come from Lindenmeier, Colorado, where Roberts found Gypsum Cave points in a level overlying the Folsom complex.[139] All these localities, however, lie well to the east of the presumed Great Basin homeland of the Desert tradition, and relatively late, peripheral occurrences of the tradition might be expected here.

Summary. With the evidence now at hand, we can summarize the Desert cultural tradition somewhat as follows. It arose in the North American Great Basin and assumed a developed, recognizable form sometime between 8000 and 7000 B.C. Its prototypes are obscure, although there is reason to believe that the first occupants of the Great Basin caves, following the recession of the glacial lakes during the Two Creeks interval, were hunters similar to those of the Old Cordilleran tradition. This suggestion of the development of the Desert tradition out of an Old Cordilleran base receives more support both within and outside the Great Basin. The chronological relationships of the origin of the Desert and Big-Game Hunting traditions remain unsettled, for no conclusive stratigraphy bearing on the matter has been found within the Great Basin proper; but by general comparative dating, and viewing the whole of North America, the Big-Game Hunting tradition appears to have been the earlier of the two. The Desert tradition outlived the other, however, and during the Altithermal it spread at the expense of both the Big-Game Hunting and Old Cordilleran patterns.

The Archaic Tradition

Definition. The term "Archaic tradition" is used here to refer to those cultures of the eastern North American woodland and river valleys in which subsistence was based on small-game hunting, fishing, and wild-plant collecting. Like the other major cultural traditions we have been discussing, it is an abstraction synthesized from numerous archaeological assemblages of artifacts and site contexts. Archaeologists believe that these various components are historically interrelated in the same way that the components of the Big-Game Hunting, Old Cordilleran, and Desert components are interrelated into their respective traditions. The term "Archaic" is, thus, not used here as a culture stage of hemisphere-wide significance, as I have so used it before.[140]

The archaeological elements or traits which pertain to the Archaic tradition reflect a variety of regional adaptations to the quest for food and it is more difficult to construct a general description of the tradition than it is for any of those traditions already discussed. In its earlier stages it resembled and was in fact related to the Desert cultures. The projectile points were frequently stemmed, notched, or barbed broad-bladed forms, some of which bore close similarities to types found in western North America. From the middle stages on, milling and grinding stones came into frequent use. It was only during the middle-to-late stages of the Archaic that ground and polished stonework became the vogue for both utility and non-utility objects. Many of the polished-stone tool types related to woodworking and to the forest environment which was the fundamental milieu of the Archaic tradition. Characteristic artifacts included grooved axes, adzes, and gouges, as well as "bannerstone" and "boatstone" throwing-stick weights, plummets, pendants, and stone vessels. Bone was frequently carved and polished into ornaments and implements, typical examples being the hooks attached to the throwing-sticks. Settlement reflected either seasonal wandering from one kind of food-resource station to another or, in some instances, semi-permanent-to-permanent residence, with a definite trend toward increased sedentism. Quite likely, certain food plants, such as the sunflower and the jerusalem artichoke, were cultivated in the later stages of the Archaic tradition; but since few dry cave sites have been discovered the evidence for plants, as well as for the kinds of perishables that are found in Desert tradition sites, is usually missing.

The remains of Archaic cultures are found throughout eastern North America from the Gulf of Mexico north into southern and eastern Canada and from the Atlantic westward into the Plains. On the western border of the Plains they tend to merge with those of the Desert tradition.

Archaic-type cultures came into existence between 8000 and 7000 B.C., but it is not until nearer 5000 B.C. that the characteristic ground- and polished-stone artifacts become common. As with the Desert cultures, there is some continuity of the

Archaic tradition into historic times, especially of cultures on the margins of the Eastern Woodland area, in Canada, and on the Texas Gulf Coast, where native agriculture was impossible or impractical and where the later traditions of the east never became fully established. In these regions an Archaic-type tool inventory and subsistence did, indeed, continue down to the time of the first European explorers. The extent to which the non-material habits of the peoples of these cultures remained similar to those of much earlier times is, of course, unknown.

The Archaic cultures of eastern North America grew rich and complex in their later periods, much more so than is the case with the other early cultural traditions we have been reviewing. They provided a deep and influential matrix for later traditions in the area, and because of this we will return for another look at them in Chapter 5. Here we shall be more concerned with the possible origins of the Archaic, its earliest time ranges, and the place of the tradition with respect to its predecessors and/or contemporaries.

Hypotheses Concerning Origins. The most likely and best-supported hypothesis for the origin of the Archaic tradition of the east is that it developed out of the Big-Game Hunting tradition. This hypothesis assumes that the Big-Game Hunters, who first came into the area equipped with a Clovis technology, modified their technical culture and their subsistence pursuits to adapt to a woodland environment and to the climatic and faunal changes of the post-glacial era. The hypothesis is supported by several stratigraphies in the East. At Bull Brook, Massachusetts, Archaic artifacts overlie Clovis points.[141] In Alabama, the Southeastern fluted points—Quad and Suwannee—have been found below broad-bladed, notched points at the Flint Creek site;[142] and hints of a similar stratigraphy come from the Quad site in the same state.[143] In central Florida, at Silver Springs, Clovis and Suwannee points have been found below Archaic forms.[144] Besides this, the fish-tailed Dalton and Hardaway points—forms which are clearly derived

from the Clovis Fluted mode of point manufacture —underlay long Archaic sequences in Alabama[145] and in the piedmont of North Carolina (Fig. 2-21*a-d*).[146]

A second hypothesis would see the Archaic tradition of the east arising from an extremely ancient, simple, unspecialized lithic industry and subsistence adjustment. Such a lithic industry would have originated during a migration of man from Asia to the New World in the middle Pleistocene or earlier—some 20,000 to 40,000 years ago. In brief, this second hypothesis about the origins of the Archaic is grounded in the American "pre-projectile point horizon" hypothesis. A. L. Bryan has advanced this idea,[147] and John Witthoft[148] and D. S. Byers[149] have both called attention to a number of crude chipped-stone assemblages in the East which were found in circumstances that imply some antiquity. Witthoft refers to a series of crude quartzite tools, including choppers, adzes, and bifacial leaf-shaped blades or points, found along the eastern flanks of the Alleghenies and piedmont from New York to Georgia; Byers points specifically to the lower levels of the Prey site, in New England, and to the basal layer of refuse at Ellsworth Falls, Maine, as being possible proto-Archaic components. The artifacts recovered from Ellsworth

Figure 2-25. Kelley phase implements, Ellsworth Falls, Maine. *a:* Sinuous-edged implement. *b:* Large scraper. *c:* Knife. Length of *a,* 9.5 cm. (After Byers, 1959.)

a   b   c

Falls, of the Kelley phase, included such items as the percussion-flaked felsite scrapers, cores, hammerstones, and a large leaf-shaped knife. The Kelley phase has yielded no radiocarbon dates, but the overlying Archaic horizon, containing such markers as plummet stones, ground-stone adzes, and polished-slate spears, is placed at 2000 B.C. Another stratified site that appears to bear on the subject is Lake Springs, in the South Carolina piedmont. Here an horizon of quartzite points and other implements underlay a band of sterile sand, or sand without evidences of human occupation, and, above this, a late southeastern Archaic component.[150] The evidence for this second hypothesis is suggestive but not conclusive. The stratigraphies cited involve late Archaic assemblages overlying the rough, possibly very early, stone tools. At no place is there a long stratigraphic succession portraying a full Archaic developmental series. It may be that these crude industries of the eastern edge of the Eastern Woodlands were no more than early regional forms of the Archaic tradition in which the local populations were imitating the more advanced communities farther west and using materials which did not lend themselves to careful flaking as well as do flints or cherts.

A number of sites in the East show mixtures or associations of Big-Game Hunting and Archaic tradition artifacts, principally projectile points. Thus,

the Parrish site in Kentucky and the Nuckolls site in Tennessee have yielded collections of both lanceolate fluted and notched points. Are these true associations? Were the two kinds of points made and used by the same peoples? Lack of stratified deposits prevents any definite answers about these two sites.[151] But the question has an important bearing on the problem of Archaic tradition origins. Are we seeing, in these cases, a phase of transition from Big-Game Hunting to Archaic patterns—a time during which both kinds of points were in use; or are we observing the remains of prehistoric contact between Archaic peoples of the East and Big-Game Hunters and fluted point-makers from the Plains?

The questions arise again when we examine two other sites—both deeply stratified—in which Archaic and Big-Game Hunting projectile points have been found. The sites in question are Modoc Rock Shelter in southern Illinois and Graham Cave in central Missouri. In the Modoc shelter a long cultural sequence was preserved in 27 feet of refuse. The earliest radiocarbon dates from the bottom levels are in the neighborhood of 8000 B.C., and M. L. Fowler, who explored the shelter, defines a first period of occupancy as lasting from 8000 to 6000 B.C. No milling or mano stones and no ground- and polished-stone implements were found in this earliest Modoc phase. The projectile points were broad, concave-based lanceolate forms with side-notches just above the base, a well-known point shape associated with Archaic culture complexes elsewhere in the East, as in the Old Copper

Figure 2-26. A lanceolate and various stemmed points from Archaic cultural contexts in Modoc Cave, Illinois. Length of a, 7.2 cm. (a,b, after Fowler, 1959 b; c–e, after Fowler and Winter, 1956.)

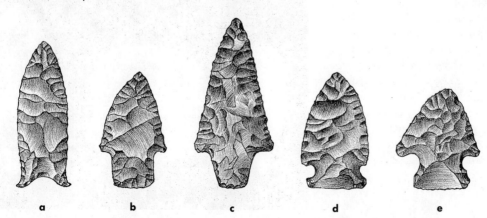

a   b   c   d   e

Culture of Wisconsin, although not so typical an Archaic point form as some which occurred in later Modoc levels. Scrapers and choppers, hammerstones, and bone awls completed the early period inventory. During the middle period, placed by radiocarbon at 6000 to 4000 B.C., the more typically Archaic broad, ovate-triangular bladed point with side notches or stem (Fig. 2-26) appeared with "standard" Archaic items as a polished bannerstone atlatl weight, a grooved axe (Fig. 2-27), and a

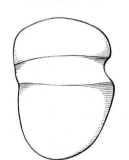

Figure 2-27. An Archaic tradition full-grooved axe from Modoc Cave. Length, 16 cm. (After Fowler, 1959 b.)

variety of grinding and nutting stones. It was in this middle level that the fish-tailed, basally fluted Dalton, or Dalton-Meserve, points showed up in the sequence. During the late period, after 4000 B.C., the Dalton-Meserve points disappeared, but the Archaic notched and stemmed varieties persisted. As a whole, during the late period there was an increase in ground- and polished-stone artifacts. Throughout all three periods subsistence seems to have remained much the same: deer, raccoon, opossum, birds, fish, freshwater mussels, and, by implication from the grinding artifacts, wild-vegetable foods.[152]

The lower levels of Graham Cave in Missouri also may date in the 8000 to 6000 B.C. range, although they contained a mixture of projectile types somewhat more like the middle levels at Modoc. That is, fluted points, including the Dalton type, and parallel-flaked lanceolates were found together with the Archaic stemmed and notched forms. Mortars and milling stones were also pres-

ent.[153] W. D. Logan, who excavated Graham Cave, interpreted the assemblage as transitional from Big-Game Hunting to Archaic. It could also be considered an Archaic culture influenced by Big-Game Hunters. If, in post-glacial times, a Plains type environment extended eastward into what later became forest country—and there is reason to believe that this did indeed happen in the region of what is now Iowa, Missouri, and Illinois—Plains hunters could very well have made contact with early Archaic peoples at such places as Modoc or Graham.

Elsewhere on the western periphery of the Woodlands other data tend to confirm the phenomenon of contact, association, or assimilation of Big-Game Hunting and Archaic cultures. Thus in the northwest, around the Great Lakes, the Plano complex, with its lanceolate parallel-flaked points was contemporaneous with the Archaic side-notched point types during the period from about 7000 to 4500 B.C.[154] In northeastern Oklahoma lanceolate points similar to the Plainview type have been found in the second of two sequent subphases of the Grove phase, but not the first. Both the Grove phases are characterized by stemmed and notched broad points, grinding stones, and mortars, and are clearly in the Archaic tradition.[155] Still farther west, and south, in Texas, Plainview points have been found in an otherwise Archaic context at Carrollton,[156] and Meserve points were associated with Archaic materials at the Jake Martin site.[157]

What conclusions may we draw from all of these data regarding Archaic origins?

To begin with, I do not think that these several associations of Big-Game Hunting projectile points with Archaic points invalidate the hypothesis that the Archaic cultures of the East developed out of an early Clovis point horizon. Wherever Clovis Fluted points have been found in stratigraphic relationships with Archaic materials in the Eastern Woodlands, the Clovis points are the earlier. The same applies to Cumberland and Suwannee fluted points, although these types have been discovered more frequently in surface and other ambiguous associations with Archaic types. Secondly, those cases involving association of Big-Game Hunter and Archaic projectile points—or even of the priority of Archaic forms to the former—take in the later fluted or semi-fluted modifications, such as the Dalton or Meserve types, or the unfluted Plainview or Plano forms. In other words, the Archaic associations are with Big-Game Hunting tradition types that for the most part date well after 8000 B.C. Furthermore, it is probably significant that most of these associations have come to light along the western margins of the Eastern Woodlands in proximity to the Plains and its late-surviving Big-Game Hunting cultures.

From these observations I would conclude that the East was at one time occupied by peoples of the Big-Game Hunting tradition, the makers and users of the Clovis Fluted point. Subsequently, this tradition changed to a more diversified subsistence pattern that was better adapted to the climatic conditions that followed the retreat of the Valders ice. In some instances these early Archaic, or proto-Archaic, groups appear to have hunted big game as circumstances afforded opportunities. For example, associations of man and mastodon have been reported from Ohio, Indiana, and Michigan, with radiocarbon dates from 7500 to 3500 B.C.[158] Steadily, though, the trend was moving away from such pursuits toward the intensive collecting of plants and shellfish and the hunting of smaller modern fauna that typified the Archaic tradition. During this time there was a local evolution of projectile point types in the East, beginning with modified fluted forms, such as Cumberland, Quad, Suwannee, and Dalton, and continuing with large stemmed and notched types. In the development of these latter types, contacts with the Desert tradition of the west were probably important, as the presence of Gypsum Cave or Pinto Basin-like forms in Archaic cultures of the east certainly indicate.[159] It seems most likely that these contacts came through the southern Plains. The Texas Archaic Balcones culture was a continuum which stretched from the Big Bend foci in the West, with their Gypsum and Pinto Basin-like projectile points

and milling stones, through the Edwards Plateau, into northeastern Texas, and from there to the Archaic Grove phase of Oklahoma, and so to the East. This could have been a route of diffusion in either direction with, perhaps, projectile point forms originating in the Desert tradition being carried eastward and ground- and polished-stone artifacts and techniques of the East diffusing back through Texas.[160]

Middle America

The finds of early man in Middle America resemble those from farther north, and it is obvious that relationships existed between some of the early cultural traditions we have been describing and the contemporary cultures of Mexico and Central America. As yet, however, the discoveries from Middle America are relatively few—by comparison with those from the United States—and archaeologists have been hesitant and less than unanimous about how to assess these discoveries. Because of this, the Middle American data are reviewed separately, although in the course of this review we will attempt to interpret them against the background of our information about North America. By Middle America we mean, here, the culture area of Mesoamerica (see Chapter 3), which is, essentially, the southern two-thirds of Mexico and the northern half of Central America, with the remaining northern part of Mexico.

Santa Isabel Iztapán. Perhaps the most spectacular as well as the most firmly documented finds pertaining to early man in Middle America are the discoveries from Santa Isabel Iztapán in the Valley of Mexico. These discoveries involve the bones of two imperial mammoths (*Mammuthus imperator*) found together with projectile points and other flint artifacts. The geological context of these finds was the Upper Becerra formation, a Pleistocene pluvial deposit which probably correlates, at least in part, with the Valders advance.[161]

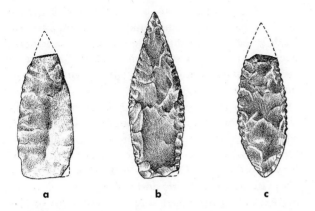

a   b   c

Figure 2-28. Points found with mammoths in central Mexico. a: Scottsbluff-like point. b: Angostura-like point. c: Leaf-shaped point. Length of b, 8.1 cm. (After Aveleyra Arroyo de Anda and Maldonado-Koerdell, 1953, and Aveleyra Arroyo de Anda, 1956.)

One of the projectile points found with the mammoths was reminiscent of the straight-based, almost imperceptibly stemmed Scottsbluff points (Fig. 2-28a) of the Plains; the flaking, however, was somewhat cruder than the fine parallel-flaking of the Eden-Scottsbluff types. A second point was lanceolate and suggested the Agate Basin or Angostura shape.[162] The third was a bipointed leaf-shaped projectile of the general Old Cordilleran type (Fig. 2-28b), and similar to the Lerma points of Tamaulipas, Mexico. On the face of it, then, the projectile point typology suggests both the Big-Game Hunting and Old Cordilleran traditions. The presence of prismatic knives was, however, more consistent with the former as was also the very context of the mammoth "kill" itself. A retouched flint blade, a bifacial knife, and several obsidian side-scrapers made up the artifact inventory.

The radiocarbon dates on the Upper Becerra formation of the Valley of Mexico range from about 14,000 to 7700 B.C., but it seems more likely that the Iztapán mammoths date near the upper end of this range. A date of 8000–7000 B.C. is consistent with what we know of the dates of both

Plano and Old Cordilleran points in the United States, but the association of these dates and artifacts with the mammoth appears out of line. Still, the mammoth may have survived this late in southern Arizona, as at the Sulphur Spring station of the early Cochise culture; and, if this is so, its late survival in central Mexico would be entirely possible.

The Valley of Mexico Upper Becerra formation also held the skeleton of "Tepexpán man," human physical remains of apparent late Pleistocene date but definitely of Indian type, and the artifacts of the "San Juan industry." This latter name pertains to a small collection of rather amorphous flint and bone artifacts that probably were contemporaneous with the Iztapán finds.[163] Lastly, the Tequixquiac finds, to which we referred briefly at the beginning of this chapter in the discussion of the possible pre-projectile point horizon, also came from the Upper Becerra formation, but from lower levels which may be considerably older than the Iztapán discoveries.

Lerma and Diablo. The Lerma phase was discovered in cave stratigraphy in the Sierra de Tamaulipas in the Mexican state of Tamaulipas. Tamaulipas is in the northeastern part of Mexico on the fringe of the Mesoamerican area. The typical artifact of Lerma, the Lerma point, is a laurel-leaf bipoint, such as the projectile found with one of the Iztapán mammoths. The economy of Lerma revolved chiefly around hunting, apparently modern fauna, including deer. No extinct animal remains have been found, but there is an associated radiocarbon date slightly in excess of 7000 B.C.[164] (Fig. 2-29d.)

The Tamaulipas caves have revealed the existence of a long developmental record succeeding the Lerma phase, and the cultural phases of this record will be described as a part of the Desert tradition farther along in this book (Chapter 3). Lerma, however, seemed much less oriented toward plant-collecting than these later Tamaulipas phases. To call it a part of the Old Cordilleran tradition, however, would distort that concept beyond its

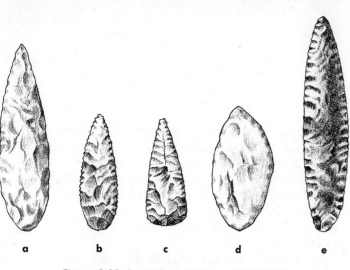

Figure 2-29. Projectile point types from Middle and South America. a: Ayampitín (Argentina). b,c, Lauricocha II (Peru). d: Lerma (Mexico). e: El Jobo (Venezuela). Length of a, 9.1 cm. (a, after Gonzalez, 1960; b,c, after Cardich, 1958; d, after MacNeish, 1958 a; e, after Rouse and Cruxent, 1963.)

present usefulness. The soundest conclusion we can make is that the Lerma phase was related to the Old Cordilleran tradition of the Pacific Northwest through its projectile point forms. This was a relationship somewhat similar to that which existed between the early cultures of southern California and the Old Cordilleran. There were links but the total content and the ecological setting of the culture was different.

Beneath the Lerma levels in the Tamaulipas caves was a phase or artifact complex which has been named Diablo by its discoverer, MacNeish.[165] According to MacNeish, the artifact assemblage included crude bifacial tools, such as choppers and ovoid blades, and end- and side-scrapers. No projectile points were found. MacNeish felt that the Diablo complex was ancient, definitely earlier than the 7000 B.C. date which marks the end of the Lerma phase, and probably much older. Its typology and presumed antiquity qualify it for admission to the ranks of the disputed pre-projectile point horizon finds.

Ajuereado. Ajuereado is the name of the phase that occupies the earliest position in the long Tehuacan sequence in southern Puebla, Mexico. As described by MacNeish, Ajuereado was a hunting culture very similar to Lerma.[166] It, too, was succeeded by phases of the Desert tradition.

Fluted Points. A few fluted points occasionally have been found in various parts of Middle America. Some have come from northern Mexico, including one from central Baja California,[167] two from Sonora,[168] one from Chihuahua,[169] one from Durango,[170] and one from Coahuila.[171] Going somewhat farther south, two were reported from near Lake Chapala, in Jalisco.[172] Most of these points belonged to the general Clovis type, or perhaps it would be better to say that they approach the Clovis style. They were lanceolate with an ovate blade and rather crude channeling extending only part way up the length of the blade. A point found in the Guatemala Highlands had the same general description.[173] Moving still farther south, out of the sphere of Mesoamerica and into Lower Central America, a fluted point was presumably found in Costa Rica[174] and two others in Panama.[175] The one non-Clovis exception among all these was the Chihuahua point, found not far from El Paso, Texas, and which is of the fully fluted Folsom type.

The full significance of these various point types is not clear. It may be that, eventually, such points will be found in the full contexts of Clovis complex or Llano complex sites in Middle America. The more likely possibility, however, is that they represent outlying influences, diffused or carried from the centers of Llano culture development in the North American High Plains, and that Clovis or Folsom complexes, comparable to those of the Plains or the North American Eastern Woodlands, did not spread south of the Rio Grande for any appreciable distance.

Summary. In upland Middle America, around the old Pleistocene lake beds of the Valley of Mexico, in the Sierra de Tamaulipas, and in the Tehuacan Valley of Puebla, there is sound evidence of the existence of early American hunters dating back to 7000 B.C. and before. In addition, scattered finds of fluted projectile points in northern Mexico indicate contacts of some sort with early peoples in the North American Great Plains. The traditional affiliations of these former inhabitants of the Mexican highlands are somewhat uncertain when we compare the Middle American finds with finds from the United States. The Iztapán mammoth discoveries from the Valley of Mexico are perhaps closest to what we have called the Big-Game Hunting tradition of the North American Plains. Actually, two of the projectile points found with the mammoths resembled most closely those which immediately post-dated the fluted point horizon of Texas, New Mexico, and Colorado. The third point was a leaf-shape which resembled the Cascade point of the Old Cordilleran tradition. These leaf-shaped points, on the basis of present evidence, were an important form in early Middle America. They characterized the Lerma phase of Tamaulipas and the Ajuereado phase of Puebla. As such, they appeared as the prototype for many of the projectile point types of the succeeding Desert tradition cultures of upland Middle America after 7000 B.C.

South America

A review of the evidence for early man in the South American continent is reserved for Volume 2; since, however, we have made brief mention of possible very early finds in South America in connection with our discussion of the pre-projectile point horizon, a word is in order now concerning some of the earliest definite proofs of man's presence in the southern half of the hemisphere.

One of these is the Chivateros I complex from the lower stratum of a stratified site in the Chillon Valley of the central coast of Peru. Two radiocarbon dates have placed the end of the Chivateros I occupation at about 8500 B.C. The complex of tools contained large flake scrapers and long bifaces, and these long bifaces were, apparently, heavy spear points. E. P. Lanning and T. C. Patterson,[176] who did the work at Chivateros, say that the assemblage was virtually identical to Camare in Venezuela and Ghatchi in Chile. You will recall that Krieger also considered Camare and

Ghatchi[177] as probable components of the early American pre-projectile point horizon. Lanning and Patterson, although believing that these complexes were among the oldest in South America, would assign them to a period no earlier than about 9000 to 8000 B.C.

The Chivateros I complex was succeeded by Chivateros II, which was distinguished by bipointed or leaf-shaped projectile points similar to those in North America that are considered the hallmark of the Old Cordilleran tradition. These same type points have been found at El Jobo in northwestern Venezuela and are most frequently referred to in South America as El Jobo points.[178] One problem that arises, however, is the typological identification of El Jobo leaf-shaped points as opposed to other leaf-shaped types which may be substantially later, among which are the Lauricocha II points from the Peruvian highlands[179], the Ayampitín points from northwestern Argentina,[180] and the leaf-shaped points from the Magellan III phase[181] and from Englefield Island[182] in the Strait of Magellan region.

The absolute and relative dating of the South American leaf-shaped projectile point complexes and the problem of their separation into earlier and later complexes is closely bound up with another early South American projectile type, the Magellan point. The Magellan point was a lanceolate with rounded shoulders and a tapered but basally flared stem shaped like a fishtail (Fig. 2-30). It is named for the region where J. B. Bird found it in the lowest occupation level of Fell's Cave, which dates to about 8700 B.C.,[183] along with extinct

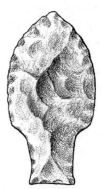

Figure 2-30. Magellan point, Strait of Magellan region. Length, 7.6 cm. (After Bird, 1946.)

horse and sloth remains. Magellan points and a complex similar to the associated Magellan I artifact assemblage have been found at Toldos in Patagonia;[184] and very similar points have been found far to the north, at El Inga in the highlands of Ecuador. The El Inga specimens were found in a context of gravers, drills, prismatic blades, end- and side-scrapers, and what may be fragments of Clovis points. Even if the identification of these fragments is incorrect, the El Inga points, as well as the Magellan points, are somewhat similar to the outline of the "waisted" and "eared" Clovis-derived Cumberland point of eastern North America. Furthermore, the fishtail bases of the El Inga points were slightly fluted. Bell and Mayer-Oakes, who excavated El Inga, are inclined to see the complex there as 1000 years or so earlier than Magellan I, but the radiocarbon dates for El Inga do not bear out their position.[185]

The Magellan point possibly derived from the North American Clovis point and from the Big-Game Hunting tradition. The occasional finds of fluted points in Mexico, Guatemala, and Panama may provide a link. Somewhere in Central America or northern South America the fluted form underwent modifications to become the fish-tailed form seen in El Inga and also in recent finds in Honduras.[186] Eventually, this form was diffused or carried as far south as the Strait of Magellan. The facts, however, are too few to make this more than a possibility. The evolution of the Magellan point from the Clovis point is tenuous, at best. Another complication is the absence—at least so far—of anything resembling the Magellan point in the long stretch between Ecuador and the Strait of Magellan. Are we, perhaps, dealing with two separate evolutions of fishtailed, and, eventually, stemmed points from an earlier, simpler, lanceolate form—say a leaf-shape?

We have, then, in South America two early projectile point types: the El Jobo leaf-shape and the Magellan fishtailed. These may be related, by direct diffusion or migration, to the North American Old Cordilleran and Big-Game Hunting traditions. Or both may be South American developments, evolving, perhaps, from an horizon of large bifaced points such as that of Chivateros I. In general, these points were made and used by hunting peoples who had a preference for land game. Some of the complexes we have mentioned, such as Englefield Island or Ayampitín, deviated somewhat from this land-hunting orientation toward, respectively, the sea and seed-collecting. In these two cases this may, however, reflect a general evolutionary trend toward a more diversified quest for food, since the Englefield and Ayampitín complexes possibly were later than some of the other complexes.[187]

One other early-man discovery—or series of discoveries—deserves mention, even in this quick glance at South America, if only to indicate that the eastern part of the continent was also occupied in the terminal Pleistocene. The Lagoa Santa cave finds from the State of Minas Gerais, Brazil, have long been known. The human crania from these caves displayed marked dolichocephalic, low-headed, prognathic features; but the physical type was, nevertheless, well within the range of living Indians, such as the Botocudo of Brazil. Various authorities have claimed that the Lagoa Santa skeletons came from associations with extinct fauna, including such species as the native horse, giant sloth, and mastodon; others feel that the human and animal bones were mixed by subsequent flooding of the caves.[188] A recent examination of the caves failed to substantiate the associations of man and Pleistocene fauna. W. R. Hurt has defined a complex of artifacts from the caves which he has called the Cerca Grande. Although no extinct faunal remains were found with these artifacts, two radiocarbon dates do indicate a considerable age for Cerca Grande: 7600 and 8350 B.C. The artifacts included bone and rather amorphous quartz projectile points, scrapers, hammerstones, and celts, the latter partially polished as well as chipped.[189]

The Arctic and Subarctic

It remains, now, in our survey of the early Americans, to take a closer look at those areas of the New World to which we referred in our opening discussions of "Asia and America"—the Arctic and Subarctic. If it was through these areas that the earliest immigrants to the New World made their journey—and it seems inevitable that they must have come this way—what traces of this movement are to be found? And what is the early culture history of these areas as it can be seen in the archaeological record?

British Mountain and Related Finds. If the early treks from Asia to America were made over land bridges that no longer exist—as we surmised earlier in this chapter—the campsites and remains left along the route are now covered by sea. Nevertheless, one would expect early man to have left some traces once he had arrived on what is now the Alaska mainland. H. B. Collins has suggested two routes for such migrations. One of these would have followed along the southern margin of the land connection which, in Wisconsin times, stretched from the Siberian Gulf of Anadyr to southwest Alaska. The other route would have been along the more northerly Arctic Slope which, on the present Alaska side, lies immediately to the north of the Brooks Range.[190] No early sites have been found within the path of the Alaska terminus of the southern route, but it is probably significant that what is now emerging as the earliest Arctic complex comes from locations which are on or lie relatively close to the presumed northern entry. This complex has been named the British Mountain, and R. S. MacNeish has recently conceived of it as an early Arctic technological and cultural tradition.[191]

The British Mountain complex was discovered at the Engigstciak site at the mouth of the Firth River on the Yukon Arctic Coast.[192] It is, thus, on the Arctic Slope and just east of the Alaska-Canada border. The flint artifacts (Fig. 2-6) did include disk-shaped cores and flakes struck from these cores. These flakes were also further worked to produce end- and side-scrapers; knives; "spoke-shaves," or notched flakes; serrated "saws"; crude unifacial projectile points; crude bifaces; what may be burins; and heavy pebble choppers. At Engigstciak the British Mountain artifacts were found associated with caribou and extinct bison bones and in contexts suggesting a warmer, wetter climate than now exists along the Arctic Slope. MacNeish estimates that the British Mountain complex was as early as 16,000 to 11,000 B.C. These dates may be much too early, for there are no sure reference points; but if British Mountain was that early it could well be one of the earliest, if not the earliest, projectile point complex in the New World, ancestral to the early hunting complexes farther south. MacNeish apparently sees the complex in this light and suggests its remote derivations in Asiatic Upper Paleolithic complexes such as the Buret-Malta of the Trans-Baikal area of Siberia.[193] MacNeish's thesis is similar to Wilmsen's, which we discussed earlier in this chapter.[194]

The Kogruk phase or complex at Anaktuvuk Pass, just above the Arctic Coast in the Brooks Range, is another member of the British Mountain tradition.[195] The range of tool and weapon types was similar, including unifacial points and bifaces, as well as some microblades. J. M. Campbell estimates its date to be 6000–8000 B.C. or older; and he, too, notes resemblances to far-off Buret-Malta.[196]

Still another early component possibly relating to British Mountain is the Palisades I group of artifacts which J. L. Giddings obtained from Cape Krusenstern on the Chukchi Sea. Here, the age inferences derived from the position of the remains on a high marine terrace, with later sites seriated on lower terraces, and from the marked weathering of the chert or chalcedony of which the implements were made. Many of them were axe-like choppers fashioned from beach pebbles; others were flaked cutting tools. A blade fragment also was included.[197]

Fluted Points. It is interesting that a few fluted points have been found in Alaska. Three were surface finds, all coming from the Brooks Range.[198] Another was from farther south, at Iyatayet, below the Seward Peninsula.[199] Most archaeologists have regarded these finds as stray, later occurrences, out of proper contexts and probably derived by diffusion from far to the south. C. V. Haynes, Jr., a geologist, has argued otherwise, believing that such Alaskan fluted forms represent the prototypes of the later Clovis Fluted points of the High Plains and the eastern North American Woodlands. If so, and since there was no fluted point tradition in the Old World, the fluting technique must have evolved somewhere in Alaska or in the now submerged Bering Strait land bridge region.[200] In this connection, one of the crude bifaces from the British Mountain level at the Engigstciak site bore a flute on one side.[201]

Old Cordilleran Leaf-Shaped Points. Bi-pointed lanceolate projectile points, similar to the Cascade points of the Pacific Northwest or to the Lerma points of Mexico, are more numerous in the Arctic and Subarctic than the fluted forms, and they have also been found in more satisfactory cultural contexts. In fact, MacNeish believes that the Cordilleran tradition prevailed over the western Subarctic and much of the Arctic between about 11,000 to 6500 B.C.; he relates these northern complexes directly to those of the Old Cordilleran tradition in the Northwest Coast and Interior Plateau areas. An important location in the Subarctic is Kluane Lake, in the southwest Yukon Territory. Most authorities feel that the environmental setting of the Kluane Lake complex was tundra and grasslands; today, however, the region is forested as the result of changing climatic conditions that began with the Altithermal or Hypsithermal interval. The Kluane Lake tool complex was that of a hunting people. Besides the leaf-shaped projectile points, it included scraping planes, blades struck from large conical cores, a burin type known as the "Ft. Liard," and pebble choppers. Related finds have come from near Ft. Liard, in the Mackenzie District of the Northwest Territories of Canada; and MacNeish also places the Kayuk complex of the Alaskan Brooks Range, and the Flint Creek complex of the Arctic Engigstciak site, in his Cordilleran tradition.[202]

In considering the wider relationships and origins of these Cordilleran leaf-shaped points in the far north the question immediately arises whether they were the result of a south-to-north back drift or diffusion from the Pacific Northwest or did they represent the progressive north-to-south movement of Asiatic immigrants or, at least, of culture traits? Our chronological control over New World finds is not yet sufficient to give us an answer. We should point out, however, that such Siberian complexes as the Afontova Gora, which succeeded Buret-Malta in the Trans-Baikal, have yielded bifacially flaked leaf-shaped points. Presumably, these would be sufficiently early to have served as the source or inspiration for the American Old Cordilleran forms.[203]

Plano Points. Another projectile point tradition—the Plano—was well-established in parts of the Arctic and western Subarctic. The Plano includes the lanceolate point forms found throughout the Plains. In the United States and southern Canada these points and their associated flint tool complexes date to early postglacial times, or from about 8000 to 4000 B.C. These points were developed in the North American Plains and were used to hunt buffalo. From there they must have been carried north into the central Subarctic where they were used against caribou as well as buffalo. Under present environmental conditions, none has been found far beyond the tree-line, although in earlier times they were probably used in tundra settings when these extended farther south. Besides the central Subarctic, their distribution included easterly portions of the Canadian Northwest Territories and extended as far west as the Brooks Range in Arctic Alaska.[204] They have not, however, been found to the east and north of the Great Lakes or east of Hudson Bay. MacNeish dates the Plano tradition—using the term to refer to a whole cultural complex rather than to a projectile point tradition alone—between 7000 and 2000 B.C.[205] The later date pertains to traces in eastern parts of the Northwest Territories.[206]

The Champagne complex of the southwest Yukon Territory, which has been dated around 6500–5500 B.C., was a type component of the Plano tradition in the Subarctic. Projectile points included a variety of the Agate Basin point, a type best known from the North American Plains. Some exhibited collateral or ripple flaking. Bone points, a variety of scrapers, ovoid bifaces, and "Ft. Liard burins" also were included in the complex. Other components of the complex are the Great Bear River and Artillery Lake sites, well to the east. To the north, moving from Subarctic to Arctic, Plano points have been recovered from both the Engigstciak and Anaktuvuk Pass sites. At Engigstciak the points were found in the Flint Creek complex, which MacNeish has grouped with the Cordilleran rather than with the Plano tradition. Apparently, here there was either a blending of both projectile point traditions, probably after 7000 B.C., or there is some stratigraphic confusion between presumably earlier (Cordilleran) and later (Plano) materials. The Plano points associated with Flint Creek included forms which resembled the Milnesand, Angostura, and Plainview types. These Flint Creek specimens were associated with bison and caribou bone refuse, with antler and bone leisters used in taking fish, and with scrapers, choppers, microblades, and burins.[207] At Anaktuvuk, in the Brooks Range, Campbell places the Kayuk complex in the Plano series, seeing no Cordilleran affiliations, and dates it to 5000 B.C. and after.[208]

The Anangula Finds. One other probable early complex, which was quite distinct from any of those we have just discussed, deserves mention. This is the Anangula material from a small island of that name, located near the larger island of Umnak in the Aleutian chain.[209] You will recall that before the last major glacial retreat of the Wisconsin, the Aleutian Islands were a part of the land bridge connecting Asia and Alaska. Perhaps the Anangula site was occupied at that time, although this is far from certain. The artifacts included a number of large blades—an unusual feature for the Arctic—some of which had been modified as scrapers. Burins, too, reportedly have been found. Irving tentatively classified Anangula as an "Aleutian Core and Blade Industry" and considered it quite apart from other Arctic or Subarctic traditions; however, he postulated no great age for the complex. Recently, however, three radiocarbon dates have been released on the artifact layer, and these range from 6500 to 5700 B.C. Black and Laughlin, the latter one of the excavators of the site, feel, however, that these dates may be too recent and suggest, by geological argument, that an age as early as 10,000 B.C. is possible.[210] If so, Anangula must mark an early way station in the spread of Asiatic flint-working techniques in the Americas.

Summary. In this brief survey of early evidences of man in the Arctic and Subarctic we have seen indications of an ancient Arctic hunting and flint-chipping complex, the British Mountain. It may be as old, or older, than any of the lithic complexes or early hunting traditions known from farther south in the New World, and it may have its derivations in the Siberian Paleolithic. The tool inventory of the British Mountain complex was rather unspecialized. Most of the projectile points, if indeed they were true projectile or spear tips, were crude and unifacial. A few implements, however, were bifaced, and some of these may have been points. One was partially fluted. A scattering of other fluted points of a generalized Clovis form have been found on the surface in other locations in the Arctic. Are these and the British Mountain assemblage of hunter's tools and weapons prototypes for the Big-Game Hunting tradition of the High Plains and the Eastern Woodlands? Or were they, instead, late and crude derivatives from the south? The questions can be posed but not yet answered.

In similar fashion, leaf-shaped projectile points

of the Arctic and Subarctic may mark the trail of diffusion and migration from Asia to northwestern North America and may be the forerunners of the Old Cordilleran tradition of the Pacific Northwest.

On the other hand, the presence of Plano projectile types in the far north and the Subarctic seems best explained as a spread of the later cultures of the Big-Game Hunting tradition northward in early post-glacial times.

The subsequent technological and cultural traditions of the Arctic and Subarctic are dealt with in Chapter 7. These are the Northwest Microblade and Arctic Small-Tool technical traditions which began, respectively, about 6000 and 4000 B.C. and which persisted variously for two, three, or four millennia. They were followed by the interior Denetasiro cultural tradition of the Athapascan Indians of the western Subarctic and by the well-known Eskimo cultural tradition of the entire Arctic. Also, in the eastern Subarctic, the Archaic cultural tradition of the Eastern Woodlands can be traced in its boreal aspects from a millennium or two B.C. until historic times.

Summary

Man's entry into the New World from Asia may have occurred during the middle or early Pleistocene, or even earlier, some 20,000 to 40,000 years ago. There is suggestive but not conclusive evidence to support this idea. Such early immigrants from Asia may have come equipped with a very simple stone-working technology, one that did not include the art of making bifacial blades or projectile points. This technique may have evolved here in the Americas from such early beginnings, or it may have been diffused or carried to the Americas from Siberian Levallois-Mousterian sources sometime after 20,000 B.C. Indeed, it may be that the people who brought the Levallois-Mousterian idea of making bifacial projectile points were the first immigrants to the New World.

Man's radiocarbon-dated presence in the Americas can be placed no earlier than about 10,000 B.C., the time of the last major Wisconsin interstadial preceding the Valders advance. By this time, however, he was a skilled and sophisticated hunter with a culture that we have termed the Big-Game Hunting tradition. The efficient, bifacially chipped, fluted Clovis point presumably had some centuries, or even millennia, of development and experimentation behind it. It seems highly likely, then, that although 10,000 B.C. is about as early as Big-Game Hunter campsites and "kills" have yet been dated by radiocarbon, the antecedents of the pattern are at least a few thousand years older than this in the Americas.

The other major cultural tradition in the New World which rivaled the Big-Game Hunting in age and general importance—at least as far as the North American continent is concerned—was the Old Cordilleran. Its hunting equipment was less specialized than the Clovis point, the characteristic projectile of the Old Cordilleran tradition being a simple bipointed or leaf-shaped form. In its general distribution the Old Cordilleran tradition, as the name implies, was western, along the Pacific and along the mountain chains, whereas the Big-Game Hunting tradition spread over the Plains and Eastern Woodlands.

The Big-Game Hunting tradition appears to have been the matrix culture for the Archaic tradition, which arose in the North American Eastern Woodlands at about 8000 B.C. The period from 8000 to 5000 B.C. was one of transition from the essentially hunting way of life of the old tradition to the more varied hunting-collecting-fishing, regionally adapted economies of the Archaic tradition. This transition can be traced in many ways, including the gradual modification of the Clovis Fluted projectile point form to such forms as the Cumberland and the Dalton and, then, the gradual replacement of these types by large stemmed forms that were typically Archaic. The appearance of numerous polished-stone implements and ornaments after 5000 B.C. marked the full establishment of the Archaic pattern. A significant factor in the change from a Big-Game Hunting to an Archaic way of life in the North American East was the climatic amelioration of the post-glacial era between 8000 and 5000 B.C.

Farther west, while the Big-Game Hunting-to-Archaic transformation was occurring in the East, the societies of the Plains were adapting to new kinds of herd game—the buffalo instead of the mammoth—and to other changes of climate and environment; but here the culture changes were less profound. The Big-Game Hunting tradition persisted during the Folsom horizon and the subsequent Plano developments; and, in fact, it cannot really be said to have come to an end until about 4000 B.C. when it began to be seriously modified by influences from the Archaic tradition of the East.

Figure 2-31. Chronological chart of early cultures and phases and their affiliations with major cultural traditions.

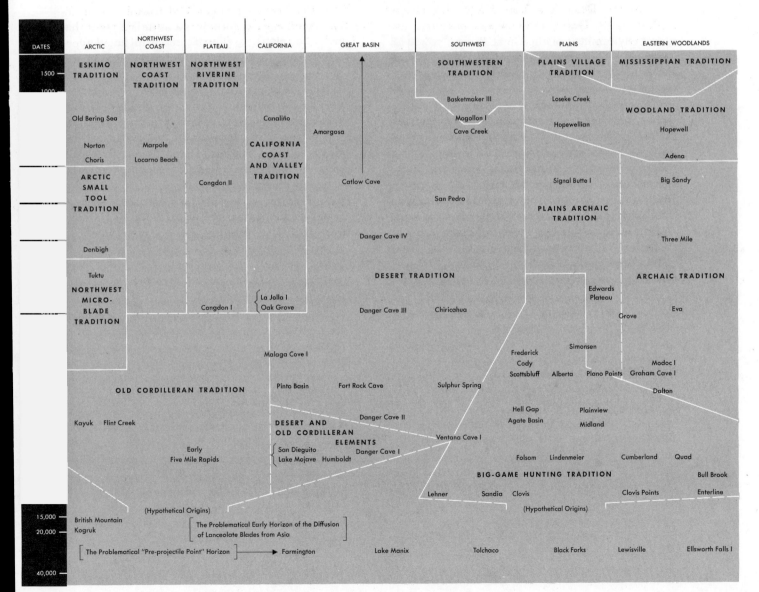

Moving still farther west, we see the Desert cultural tradition arising at more or less the same time as the Archaic tradition. The source of the Desert tradition, however, appears to have been the Old Cordilleran, although it was influenced to some extent by later Big-Game Hunting developments. For instance, the site of Ventana Cave in southern Arizona was influenced in its early occupation by both Old Cordilleran and Big-Game Hunting antecedents; and it is at Ventana Cave that we also see the early appearance of the cultures of the Desert tradition. Highly significant in shaping the Desert tradition was, of course, the desert environment of the Great Basin.

In the Pacific mountains and along the Pacific shore the Old Cordilleran tradition was the parent of the Northwest Coast tradition and the Northwest Riverine tradition of the Interior Plateau. These traditions, more specialized and regionally adapted than the Old Cordilleran culture, probably began as early as 5000 B.C., although firm evidence places them somewhat later. Similarly, in California the dominant early influence was, I believe, the Old Cordilleran tradition, with, however, significant contact with the Desert cultures.

In the Mesoamerican uplands we see terminal Pleistocene assemblages and animal "kill" sites that are reminiscent of both Big-Game Hunting and Old Cordilleran patterns. The cultural tradition that arose in these uplands after 7000 B.C. was the Desert pattern. Beyond Mesoamerica, in South America, we have taken only a quick glance. Man was present in the southern continent—perhaps at its southern extremities—as early as 9000–8000 B.C. He may also have been there much earlier, on a pre-projectile point horizon. The early hunting cultures of South America appear not to have used the fluted point—at least none has been found so far. Instead, the earliest principal type is a leaf-shape form which may indeed be derived from the North American Old Cordilleran tradition. Another early form was a fishtailed point that might be related to North American fluted types or could be a local South American development.

A look at the Arctic takes us back again to the problems of man's arrival from Asia. Actually, the evidence for his journey is extremely limited, but the search has only just begun. There are clues, such as the British Mountain and Kogruk complexes, and the scattered fluted points, that may point to an early migration of hunters who brought with them lanceolate points. Even if this is so, however, authorities generally are in agreement that the specialized fluted point of the Big-Game Hunting tradition was a North American invention. Later in the Arctic and Subarctic, hunting and technological traditions arose that owed their special artifact content to Asiatic diffusions.

Footnotes

[1]The reality of a dry Altithermal for the southwestern United States has been challenged (Martin Schoenwetter, and Arms, 1961) and rebutted (Antevs, 1962).

[2]This section is based on Flint (1957, pp. 302-327, 342, 426-429); Leighton (1960); Frye, Willman (1960); Haynes (1964); and A. L. Bryan (1962 ms. and personal communication, 1962-1963). I am especially indebted to the latter for our discussions of Wisconsin glacial stratigraphy and dating. My simplifications of these complex subjects do not necessarily represent his views. In this connection, Bryan has quite rightly emphasized the need for specific regional dating of climatic phenomena such as the Altithermal fluctuation (Bryan and Gruhn, 1964).

[3]Haynes (1964).

[4]Crook and Harris (1957, 1958); Krieger (1962, 1964). It is also possible that the Clovis point found at Lewisville was a "plant" by a prankster (Krieger, 1964). Heizer and Brooks (1965 ms.) do not believe that the "hearths" were man-made.

[5]Krieger (1964). For a consideration of the pre-projectile point horizon, the reader is referred to Krieger (1962, 1964), its leading protagonist.

[6]Orr (1956).

[7]Carter (1957); Krieger (1962).

[8]Carter (1957).

[9]Harrington and Simpson (1961).

[10]A. L. Bryan (1964); Shutler (1965).

[11]Arnold (1957).

[12]Simpson (1958, 1960, 1961, 1964).

[13]Renaud (1938, 1940).

[14]Bartlett (1943).

[15]Treganza (1952); Treganza and Heizer (1953).

[15a]Recent radiocarbon dates from two lower strata at Wilson Butte Cave, south-central Idaho, are approximately 12,500 and 13,000 B.C., (personal communication, Ruth Gruhn, 1965). They are associated with extinct fauna and stone and bone tools that may represent a sampling from a "pre-projectile point horizon" complex.

[16]Maldonado-Koerdell and Aveleyra (1949); Wormington (1957, pp. 199–200); Aveleyra (1962); Krieger (1964).

[17]A. L. Bryan (1962 ms.); Krieger (1964).

[18]Royo and Gomez (1960); Krieger (1964).

[19]Cruxent (1962); Krieger (1964).

[20]Krieger (1964).

[21]Le Paige (1958, 1960); Krieger (1964).

[22]Cigliano (1961).

[23]Menghin and Bormida (1950).

[24]Menghin (1952).

[25]Vignati (1927).

[26]Krieger (1964).

[27]Chard (1959 a, b).

[28]Chard (1963).

[29]Chard (1963).

[30]Bushnell and McBurney (1959); Wormington (1961 a); Wilmsen (1964).

[31]Chard (1963) now places Ust' Kanskaia at 35,000–30,000 B.C.

[32]Rudenko (1961).

[33]Chard (1963).

[34]Wilmsen (1964, pp. 341–342).

[35]Chard (1963).

[36]"Lithic" also has been used as the name for a general early American culture stage which includes the Big-Game Hunting as well as other patterns (Willey and Phillips, 1958). Here, however, we are concerned with lines of historical development rather than developmental stages, and the line of history we are trying to trace has been called the Big-Game Hunting tradition.

[37]Howard (1935 a, b); Cotter (1937, 1938); Sellards (1952); Wormington (1957, pp. 47–51); MacGowan and Hester (1962, pp. 151–154); Agogino and Rovner (1964). I am also indebted to G. A. Agogino for communications (1964, 1965) concerning his recent excavations at Blackwater Draw and for knowledge of as yet unpublished dates on this and other sites.

[38]Green (1963).

[39]Sellards (1952).

[40]Personal communication (1964).

[41]G. A. Agogino (personal communication, 1965).

[42]Agogino and Rovner (1964).

[43]Haury, Sayles, and Wasley (1959). See Haury (1953) for a discussion of the related Naco site.

[44]Agogino and Rovner (1964).

[45]Hibben (1941).

[46]Wormington (1957, pp. 85–89).

[47]Agogino (personal communication, 1965) believes the full sequence within this stratum was: Sandia, Folsom, Agate Basin, and Plainview, in that order.

[48]Roosa (1956).

[49]Figgins (1927).

[50]Roberts (1935a, 1936); Wormington (1957, pp. 31–39); Haynes and Agogino (1960).

[51]It is interesting to speculate if the small bone disks with circumferential ticking might not be "lunar count" markings of the kind Marshak (1964) has described and interpreted from the European Upper Paleolithic.

[52]This date, from Haynes and Agogino (1960), is given in approximate round figures and represents a median date. Most other radiocarbon dates in this book are so treated.

[53]Forbis and Sperry (1952).

[54]Sellards (1952); Wormington (1957). See also Krieger (1964, pp. 51–59) for a more extensive list of complexes which have yielded either Clovis or Folsom points.

[55]Wendorf, Krieger, Albritton, and Stewart (1955); Wendorf and Krieger (1959).

[56]Wendorf and Hester (1962).

[57]A. L. Bryan (1962 ms.)

[58]Most of the Plano point types are illustrated in this chapter.

[59]Henry Irwin (personal communication, 1965).

[60]Sellards, Evans, and Meade (1947); Wormington (1957, pp. 107–108); Wendorf and Krieger (1959); Krieger (1964).

[61]Wormington (1957, pp. 109–113).

[62]Schultz (1932); Wormington (1957, pp. 113–114).

[63]Steen (1959).

[64]Agogino (personal communication, 1965).

[65]Logan (1952); Wormington (1957, p. 65).

[66]A. L. Bryan (1962 ms.).

[67]The excavations at Hell Gap, Wyoming, that are being carried out by Agogino, Henry Irwin, and Cynthia Irwin-Williams. Geological studies have been made by C. V. Haynes, Jr. I am indebted to all these colleagues for information about that site. In addition, I have benefited from comment by H. M. Wormington.

[68]Agogino (1961) first thought that the Hell Gap points preceded the Agate Basin types; he has since revised this opinion.

[69]The Frederick point is the one formerly called Angostura by Wormington (1957, p. 139). In her opinion (personal communication, 1965) this type of point, which characterized the Frederick complex at Hell Gap, should be designated as the Frederick point whereas points formerly referred to as Angostura by Hughes (1949) and Wheeler (1954) should be classed as Agate Basin.

[70]For the Horner site see Howard, Satterthwaite, and Bache (1941). For further information on Scottsbluff points and on Plano points in general see Barbour and Schultz (1932); Wormington (1957, pp. 118–137); Schultz and Frankforter (1948); and Davis (1953).

[71]See Krieger (1964, pp. 59–65) for a discussion of the concept of a "Proto-archaic stage."

[72]R. J. Mason (1962, p. 235).

[73]D. S. Byers (personal communication, 1965).

[74]R. J. Mason (1962, fig. 1, pp. 234–235).

[75]Witthoft (1952).

[76]Byers (1954, 1955, 1959).

[77]McCary (1951); Wormington (1957, p. 71).

[78]R. J. Mason (1962, pp. 238–242).

[79]See Wormington (1957, pp. 113–114). The name derives from Missouri. The Dalton points were very similar to the more westerly distributed Meserve points. I am indebted to Stephen Williams for calling my attention to the chronological and developmental importance of the Dalton point in the southeastern United States.

[80]Soday (1954); Mason (1962).

[81]Goggin (1950); Neill (1958).

[82]J. L. Coe (1964).

[83]Ritchie (1953).

[84]J. L. Coe (1964).

[85]DeJarnette, Kurjack, and Cambron (1962).

[86]R. J. Mason (1962, fig. 8).

[87]Swanson (1961, 1962 a). Swanson has referred to these adaptations of the Big-Game Hunters to this environment as the "Mountain-Plains culture." See Daugherty (1956) for the Lind Coulee site.

[88]Butler (1961); see also MacNeish (1959 b).

[89]The "willow-leaf blade" hypothesis has been advanced by A. L. Bryan (1962 ms.).

[90]Wilmsen (1964).

[91]The presence of burins in early North American cultures has only come to light within the last few years. They occurred in Big-Game Hunting tradition contexts on the Texas plains at the time of the early fluted points as well as later (Epstein, 1963; Alexander, 1963) and, as stated, in Old Cordilleran contexts in the Pacific Northwest. They are, of course, also a feature of early and later complexes in the Arctic.

[92]Cressman and others (1960).

[93]Butler (1961).

[94]Borden (1960, 1961, personal communication, 1964).

[95]Shiner (1961).

[96]Butler (1961).

[97]Cressman and Krieger, (1940); Cressman, (1951); Wormington (1957, p. 184).

[98]A. L. Bryan (1962 ms.).

[99]Campbell and Campbell (1937); Amsden (1937).

[100]The term "San Dieguito" refers to an early culture of the southern Cali-fornia coast and mountains which is equated with the interior desert Playa, or Lake Mojave, culture. The sequence terminology for these southern California regions is confusing. It was originally established by M. J. Rogers (1929, 1939), but has since been revised by him (1958; see also Haury and others, 1950). In this work we shall use the term "Lake Mojave" for this horizon as it is found in the interior deserts (see this chapter and Chapter 6). For the coast the name San Dieguito is retained. The reader is referred, especially, to Warren and True (1961) and Heizer (1964) for further explanations of these cultures and the sequence terminology.

[101]Walker (1951).

[102]Treganza and Malamud (1950); Treganza and Bierman (1958). Meighan (1959 a) would place Topanga as early as 6000 B.C.; Heizer (1964) groups it with cultures dating between 5000 and 3000 B.C.

[103]Krieger (1964, p. 64).

[104]This is the dating followed here (see Bennyhoff, 1958). Wallace (1962) would prefer an estimate of 7000–5000 B.C. See Wallace (1962); Campbell and Campbell (1937); and Amsden (1937) for a description of the Lake Mojave phase.

[105]Daugherty (1962).

[106]Krieger (1964, pp. 55–57) mentions the early radiocarbon dates on Old Cordilleran complexes as ranging from 7500–10,000 B.C.

[107]Daugherty (1962).

[108]Swanson (1962 a).

[109]Jennings and Norbeck (1955).

[110]Jennings (1957); see Jennings (1964) for a most recent statement on the Desert culture.

[111]Jennings (1957, 1964).

[112]Jennings and Norbeck (1955).

[113]Jennings (1957); Bennyhoff (1958).

[114]This follows the geological chronology and terminology used in this chapter, in which Mankato and Valders are separated by the Two Creeks interval. Jennings (1957) makes no such separation and places a Two Creek interval as "pre-Mankato." This would correspond to "pre-Valders" in the present terminology. Haynes (1964), the geologist, places the Two Creeks interval between Mankato and Valders but dates it somewhat earlier, at 10,300–9800 B.C.

[115]This was called to my attention by A. L. Bryan.

[116]Steward (1937); Elmer Smith (1941, 1952).

[117]Steward (1937).

[118]Cressman and Krieger (1940); Cressman, (1951); Bryan (1962 ms.)

[119]Heizer (1951 a, b); Libby (1955); Wormington (1957, pp. 191–192).

[120]Harrington (1933); Wormington (1957, pp. 157–160).

[121]Wallace (1962) questions the inclusion of the California desert cultures in the Desert cultural tradition.

[122]See Campbell and Campbell (1935) for Pinto Basin. Bennyhoff (1958) and Meighan (1959) would begin Pinto Basin at about 7000–6000 B.C. Wallace (1962) would place it after 3000 B.C.

[123]Wallace (1962).

[124]A new phase, the Cazador, is now placed between Sulphur Springs and Chiricahua in the sequence. It has not yet been described in print, however.

[125]Sayles and Antevs (1941, 1955). Antev's geological opinion is that Sulphur Springs belongs in the pluvial. See also Wormington (1957, pp. 169–173).

[126]Haury and others (1950). In the terminology followed in this survey these Ventana Cave levels would be "Pinto Basin" or "Pinto-Gypsum." We have restricted the term "Amargosa" to a post–1000 B.C. complex. (See Chapter 6, footnote 22.)

[127]Mangelsdorf and Smith, (1949); Wormington (1957, pp. 173–175).

[128]Although not specifying these particular arguments, Krieger (1962) has suggested something like this.

[129]Swanson (1962 a). Name "Bit-terroot" derives from a local mountain range.

[130]MacNeish (1958 a, 1962 a).

[131]Taylor (1956, personal communication, 1963).

[132]Campbell (1949).

[133]Wormington (1957, p. 163).

[134]Harrington (1948); Meighan (1959 a).

[135]Haury and others (1950).

[136]Krieger (1964) surmises Plainview affinities for one of the lower Ventana

points. He also cites a recent radiocarbon date of 9300±1200 B.C.

[137]Howard (1935 a).

[138]Hibben (1941).

[139]Roberts (1940); Wormington (1957, p. 160).

[140]Willey and Phillips (1958).

[141]Editorial note by Byers in Fowler (1959 a).

[142]Cambron and Waters (1959).

[143]Cambron and Hulse (1960).

[144]Neill (1958).

[145]De Jarnette, Kurjack, and Cambron (1962).

[146]J. L. Coe (1964).

[147]A. L. Bryan (1962 ms.).

[148]Witthoft (1956).

[149]Byers (1959).

[150]Caldwell (1954).

[151]Wormington (1957, p. 66); R. J. Mason (1962, p. 241); Lewis and Kneberg (1958). Lewis and Kneberg (1959) doubt the contemporaneity of the lanceolate fluted and notched points at the Parrish site.

[152]Fowler (1959 a, b).

[153]Logan (1952).

[154]Quimby (1960).

[155]Baerreis (1959).

[156]Crook and Harris (1952); Baerreis (1959).

[157]Davis and Davis (1960).

[158]Stephen Williams (1957).

[159]For example, in the Flint Creek site, Alabama, or the North Carolina piedmont sites (see R. J. Mason, 1962; J. L. Coe, 1964).

[160]J. C. Kelley (1959).

[161]Aveleyra Arroyo de Anda and Maldonado-Koerdell (1953); Aveleyra Arroyo de Anda (1956).

[162]Wormington (1957, p. 95) ques-

tions this identification.

[163]De Terra, Romero, and Stewart (1949).

[164]MacNeish (1958 a).

[165]MacNeish (1958 a).

[166]MacNeish (1962 a).

[167]Aschmann (1952).

[168]Di Peso (1955).

[169]Aveleyra Arroyo de Anda (1961).

[170]Lorenzo (1953).

[171]Gonzalez Rul (1959).

[172]Lorenzo (1964).

[173]M. D. Coe (1960 b).

[174]Swauger and Mayer-Oakes (1952).

[175]Sander (1959).

[176]Patterson and Lanning (1964); personal communication, Patterson (1965).

[177]Krieger (1964).

[178]Cruxent and Rouse (1956).

[179]Cardich (1958, 1960); Lanning and Hammel (1961).

[180]Gonzalez (1960).

[181]Bird (1938, 1946); Lanning and Hammel (1961).

[182]Emperaire and Laming (1961).

[183]Bird (1938, 1946); Lanning and Hammel (1961).

[184]Menghin (1952).

[185]Bell (1960, 1963 ms.); Mayer-Oakes and Bell (1960).

[186]Bullen and Plowden (1963).

[187]Krieger (1964), for example, sees El Jobo as a part of a "Paleo-Indian stage," lacking, as it does, food-grinding implements. Ayampitín, on the other hand, he places with the succeeding "Protoarchaic stage."

[188]Man and Pleistocene faunal associations are claimed for the Lagoa Santa, Sumidoro, Confins, Lagoa Funda, and Pedro Leopoldo caves, all in the same

region. See Lacerda (1882); Mattos (1946); Walter (1948).

[189]Hurt (1956, 1960, 1964).

[190]Collins (1962).

[191]MacNeish (1964 a).

[192]MacNeish (1956, 1959 b).

[193]MacNeish (1964 a).

[194]Wilmsen (1964).

[195]MacNeish (1964 a).

[196]Campbell (1961).

[197]Giddings (1961).

[198]Solecki (1950, 1951).

[199]Giddings (1961).

[200]Haynes (1964).

[201]MacNeish (1959 b).

[202]MacNeish (1964 a).

[203]MacNeish (1964 a).

[204]An Angostura and an Agate Basin point were found near Fairbanks, Alaska, in possible association with mammoth and other Pleistocene animal bones (Rainey, 1939). Collins (1964) suggests that these might be related to an early north-to-south diffusion of these point types.

[205]MacNeish (1964 a). According to concepts followed in this book this "Plano tradition" of MacNeish's would merely be a part, or an extension, of the Big-Game Hunting major cultural tradition.

[206]Collins (1964) also calls attention to occurrences of Plano points in contexts of later cultures, as far west as the Bering Strait. Some of these may date to 2000–1000 B.C.

[207]MacNeish (1962 b, 1964 a).

[208]Campbell (1962). MacNeish (1964 a), however, lists another Brooks Range complex, the Nayuk, as being affiliated with the Plano point tradition.

[209]Laughlin and Marsh (1954, 1956).

[210]Black and Laughlin (1964).

Mesoamerica

Precursors and Foundations of the Mesoamerican Cultural Tradition

The Roots of the Mesoamerican Cultural Tradition. The Mesoamerican cultural tradition arose from established agricultural village life in southern Mexico and upper Central America about two millennia before the beginning of the Christian era. The tradition developed rapidly in the centuries which followed and spread over the cultural-geographical area which is called Mesoamerica. Farther away, in North and South America, a good many of the agricultural elements fundamental to the tradition became the vitalizing forces in other new traditions.

The roots of the Mesoamerican cultural tradition are imbedded in the North American Desert tradition. We have already seen how a Desert way of life, built around small-game hunting and wild-plant collecting, followed hunting of large game in the uplands of Mexico after around 7000 B.C. In Mesoamerica the period of the Desert cultures, from 7000 to 2000 B.C., the Food Collecting-Incipient Cultivation Period, was a time when societies of the area gradually developed a subsistence based on cultivated plants. At the close of this period we pass into the Mesoamerican cultural tradition and into the beginning of what is called its Preclassic Period.

The archaeological stratigraphic record for this period of Food Collecting-Incipient Cultivation unrolls in two principal regions: the mountains of Tamaulipas and the highlands of Puebla. In both of these places the long culture sequences have been derived from the excavations in deep, dry-cave habitation deposits.

Tamaulipas. The Tamaulipas mountains are semi-arid to wet-temperate, wooded, and with favorable natural potentialities for hunting, plant-collecting, and farming. Remains of Desert tradition food-collectors whose life was comparable to that of contemporary peoples of the North American Great Basin have been found in caves in the southwestern Sierra Madre Oriental and the Sierra de Tamaulipas.[1] The cultural materials from these two local sequences are quite similar and can be correlated to piece together a continuous story of several thousands of years of human occupation.

In the Sierra Madre sequence, the Infiernillo phase is the earliest, with radiocarbon dates from the seventh millennium B.C., and with an estimated span of from 7000 to 5000 B.C. Presumably, it followed soon after the Lerma phase hunters made their last appearance in the same region, but the subsistence adjustment was different. The Infiernillo people made twilled and plaited mats, rod-foundation baskets, and net bags, the baskets and bags being used to collect and store seeds and plants. Most of the vegetable foods found in the dry debris of the Infiernillo caves appear to be wild species, such as the agave, the opuntia, and the runner bean (*Phaseolus coccineus*), although some were probably domesticates, including the bottle gourd (*Lagenaria*), the chili pepper (*Capsicum annum* or *C. frutescens*), and the summer squash or pumpkin (*Cucurbita pepo*). The gourd was used as a container, the chili as condiment, the pumpkin for seed food. All three have a long history in the Mesoamerican tradition. The chipped-stone weapons and tools of the Infiernillo phase—diamond-shaped and tear-shaped projectile points for darts or spears, scraping-planes, and flake choppers or scrapers—indicate that the Infiernillo people hunted, although an analysis of the kitchen refuse suggests that game constituted only a minor part of their diet as compared with the wild plant foods. Snail-shell beads were the only objects taken from Infiernillo levels that do not appear to be strictly utilitarian.

The Early Ocampo phase of the Sierra Madre Oriental and the Nogales phase of the Sierra de Tamaulipas take up the story where Infiernillo leaves off and carry it to 3000 B.C. Slight changes occurred in projectile point forms; scrapers, choppers, and gouges were produced in greater variety. The basketry-netting-mat complex continued. Stone mortars and manos appeared for the first

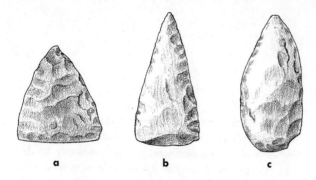

Figure 3-1. Projectile points of the Food Collecting-Incipient Cultivation Period, Tamaulipas, Mexico. *a:* Form characteristic of Late Nogales and La Perra phases (type: Tortugas Triangular). *b:* Form characteristic of Nogales through Almagre phases (type: Nogales Triangular). *c:* Form characteristic of Nogales through Almagre phases (type: Abasolo Round-base). Length of *a,* 4.7 cm. (Redrawn from MacNeish, 1958).

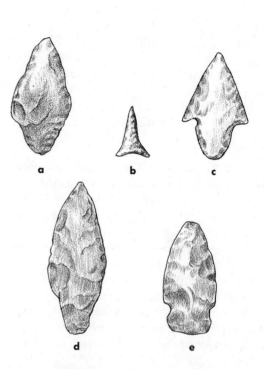

Figure 3-3. Projectile points of the pre-ceramic and ceramic phases, Tamaulipas, Mexico. *a:* Form of the La Perra and Almagre phases (both pre-ceramic) (type: Almagre Contracting-stemmed). *b:* Form of the Postclassic Period Los Angeles phase (ceramic), also characteristic of the post-1000 A.D. time range in Tamaulipas and northern Veracruz (type: Starr Concave). *c:* Form spanning Almagre (pre-ceramic) and early ceramic phases (type: Gary Stemmed). *d:* Almagre phase form (pre-ceramic) (type: Kent Stemmed). *e:* Form of the ceramic phases in Tamaulipas (type: Ensor Side-notched). Length of *a,* 5.7 cm. (Redrawn from MacNeish, 1958.)

time, and these food-grinding implements clearly reflect an even heavier dependence on plant foods than before. Perhaps as much as 70 to 80 per cent of subsistence came from wild plants, 5 to 8 per cent from domesticated plants, and only the remaining 12 to 15 per cent from hunting. Yellow and red beans (*Phaseolus vulgaris*) became a significant cultivated plant innovation at this time. Also, Ocampo pumpkins produced larger seeds than their Infiernillo predecessors and were clearly cultigens.

The Late Ocampo (Sierra Madre) and La Perra (Sierra de Tamaulipas) phases of the two Ta-

maulipas sequences date from 3000 to 2200 B.C. Maize (*Zea mays*) first appeared during this period in La Perra. It was a tiny, primitive corn, known in two varieties of the early Nal-tel race. Now, plant domesticates make up 10 to 15 per cent of the peoples' diet.

In the Flacco (Sierra Madre) and Almagre (Sierra de Tamaulipas) phases, from 2200 to 1800 B.C., agriculture increased to as much as 20 per cent of total subsistence at the expense of wild-plant collecting, which dropped to 65 per cent. The Bat Cave, or Chapalote, strain of maize came from

Figure 3-2. Chipped-stone tools of the Food Collecting-Incipient Cultivation Period, Tamaulipas, Mexico. *a:* Top and side views of large disk scraper of the Nogales-La Perra-Almagre phases. The type is also characteristic of the Abasolo and Repelo phases (see Chapter 5). *b:* Ovoid biface, found in the pre-ceramic and ceramic phases of interior Tamaulipas. Diameter of *a,* 7.3 cm. (Redrawn from MacNeish, 1958.)

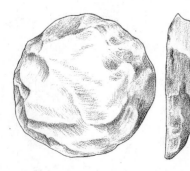

Flacco sites. Almagre settlements suggest that residency was more stable than in any other prior period. The sites in question, open and of considerable size, contained house remains that are correlated with Flacco cave site levels. Among the finds were coiled, twined, and twilled baskets and cotton cloth. Projectile points of these phases included stemmed and corner-notched forms.

The Guerra phase, in the Sierra Madre Oriental, developed out of the Flacco phase and is estimated to have lasted from 1800 to 1400 B.C. During this period the warty squash (*Cucurbita moschata*) made its first appearance and cultivated plants made up about 30 per cent of the diet, with wild plants accounting for 60 per cent and hunting, the remaining 10 per cent. There were no innovations in tools or textiles. Some primary flexed burials, covered with mats, were the first interments discovered in these Tamaulipas sequences. Baskets had been buried with the bodies. With the close of the Guerra phase the ancient Tamaulipans were nearing the threshold of established cultivation, a condition whereby sedentary village communities depended primarily on farming activities. Permanent village sites and pottery remains indicate that such a condition became established in the Sierra Madre region with the onset of the succeeding Mesa de Guaje phase.

Puebla. Tamaulipas, however, lies on the northeastern frontier of the Mesoamerican culture area, and there are many indications that it was peripheral to the southern centers of the Mesoamerican tradition. Had maize, for instance, been domesticated even earlier in southern Mexico or Guatemala? In searching for the answers to this and other questions, R. S. MacNeish, who investigated the Tamaulipas caves, discovered new rock shelter sites in the Tehuacán Valley of southern Puebla, a location that lies well within the perimeters of what might be considered the "core" or "heart" of Mesoamerica. Intensive and long-term excavations are now under way in the Tehuacán Valley under his direction, and, to date, several preliminary reports have been issued.[2] Although

these do not offer a full or final analysis of the remains, they reveal enough to indicate that this work will add considerably to our understanding of the growth of the Mesoamerican cultural tradition as well as of New World culture history as a whole.

The Tehuacán Valley is about 6000 feet above sea level. The valley floor is semi-arid and spotted with spiny scrub and cactus, but the surrounding mountain slopes, which receive more rain, support pine forests. A number of rock shelters have been found in hills in the lower, drier vegetation zone; and the plant and other remains from these caves, like those from Tamaulipas, fortunately are well preserved. We have mentioned already the earliest member of this long Tehuacán culture sequence— the Ajuereado phase with its Lerma leaf-shaped projectile points. Ajuereado was succeeded by a phase known as El Riego, which radiocarbon dating places at about 7000 to 5000 B.C.

El Riego appears to have developed gradually from the antecedent Ajuereado culture although its subsistence pattern was more dependent on the collection of wild seed plants. We have here considered it as a southern variant manifestation of the North American Desert cultural tradition. El Riego peoples were seasonally nomadic, like their predecessors, but populations were larger and the settlement pattern was different. Whereas all Ajuereado sites were small camps, El Riego sites are divided between small and large camp loca-

Figure 3-4. Stone metates and manos of the Food Collecting-Incipient Cultivation Period, Tehuacán Valley, Puebla. a: El Riego phase. b: Coxcatlán phase. c: Abejas phase. (After MacNeish, 1962.)

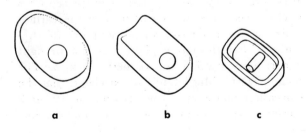

a   b   c

tions which, in the opinion of MacNeish, represent seasonally alternating "microband" and "macroband" communities in pursuit of wild plant harvests or game. El Riego peoples used bell-shaped pestles and mortars and crude metates and manos (Fig. 3-4a) in order to grind seed foods and made string nets, coiled baskets, and twined blankets of plant fibers. Animal bones were rare in the cave deposits, but dried wild grasses, maguey, agave, and opuntia cactus fruit were plentiful. Squash, probably *Cucurbita moschata* or *mixta,* may have been under domestication. In MacNeish's opinion, maize was probably one of the wild grasses collected by these peoples, although so far there is no direct evidence for this claim. Some burials were found in El Riego cave levels, and in the graves were baskets, nets, blankets, and what might be food remains. The bodies were found in pits in extended or flexed positions, and one appears to have been partially cremated. Circumstances surrounding a child burial suggest either cannibalism or special human sacrificial rites.

The Coxcatlán phase was a direct outgrowth of El Riego, and it, too, was essentially in the Desert food-collecting tradition, except that plant domestication had become a minor but significant element of the economy.[3] Settlements were somewhat larger than in El Riego and give the appearance of greater stability; however, a seasonal fluctuation between large and small camp locations seems still to have been in practice. Tiny ears of primitive, pod-like *Zea mays* were found early in this phase in a stratum of refuse dated by radiocarbon to about 5000 B.C. Other radiocarbon dates from Coxcatlán strata indicate a span for the entire phase of from 5200 to 3400 B.C. These early Coxcatlán maize cobs are, thus, the earliest yet known anywhere in the world, and their presence in Puebla over 2,000 years earlier than the earliest maize in Tamaulipas strongly supports the hypothesis that the maize plant was first brought under domestication in southern Mexico. The botanist P. C. Mangelsdorf has declared that the Coxcatlán maize was either a wild variety or a variety in the very initial stages of domestication.

Found together with these early Coxcatlán maize ears were remains of avocados, chili peppers, and gourds (*Lagenaria*). Later in the phase the Coxcatláns acquired amaranth, tepary beans, zapotes, and squash (*Cucurbita moschata*). Some plants, such as the squash, were domesticates; others may have been. Perhaps as a function of plant cultivation, site residence appears more stable in the Coxcatlán than in El Riego. MacNeish was led to make this conclusion because of the greater depth and abundance of the cave shelter refuse accumulations and from the fact that wild plants harvested in both fall and spring seasons were found associated in the same cave strata. The implications are that Coxcatlán man was remaining in the same place for the entire year, or at least for a large part of the year, to plant and tend his gardens, rather than following the pattern of seasonal wandering suggested for El Riego. A significant change in the artifact complex for Coxcatlán was the addition of both carefully made basin-shaped metates and stone bowls (Figs. 3-4b, 3-5b).

During the succeeding Abejas phase, 3400–2300 B.C., wild plants and seeds probably were still the main food supply, but the volume and variety of domesticated plants had increased. A hybrid maize, crossed with the wild grass, teosinte, appeared. Squash and amaranth were common, and

Figure 3-5. Stone vessels of the Food Collecting-Incipient Cultivation Period, Tehuacán Valley, Puebla. a: El Riego. b: Coxcatlán. c: Abejas. d: El Riego. e: Coxcatlán. (After MacNeish, 1962.)

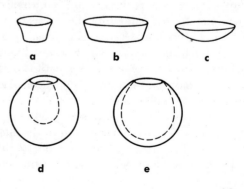

pumpkins (*Cucurbita pepo*) and common beans (*Phaseolus vulgaris*) had been introduced. Cotton was also widely used. Community size and stability had continued to increase, and among such communities were small pithouse villages that appear to have been year-around residences. Obsidian bladelets, struck from prepared polyhedral cores, made their first appearance. This common little implement was to become one of the most persistent of the Mesoamerican technological traditions. Many well-made stone bowls have been found, and although they definitely were not metates or mortars, they may have developed from such seed-grinding prototypes. Very interestingly, they assumed tecomate (seed-jar), hemispherical bowl, and flat-bottomed bowl forms—the same forms which were to appear in the pottery of the region a few centuries later.

Following Abejas, the Purron phase, dated from 2300 to 1500 B.C., is marked by further evidences of settled life in open-site villages, more hybrid maize, and pottery in the same vessel forms as the aforementioned stone bowls and ollas. It is at about this point in the sequence in the Tehuacán Valley where we may say that the Mesoamerican agricultural threshold was attained.

The Development of Mesoamerican Agriculture. These amazingly full records from the caves of Tamaulipas and Puebla tell us several important things about the origin of agriculture in Mesoamerica. First, it was a long, drawn-out process. Originally, the cultivation of food plants was trivial, perhaps no more than seeds being dropped accidentally near a camp site and the casual selection of new seeds for desultory planting. With the increasing heat and dryness of the Altithermal climatic era, after 5000 B.C., this casual, minimal cultivation seems to have been taken more seriously. It may have been that as the natural wild plant cover retreated before the increasing aridity, man became anxious about and conscious of plant growth and sought to aid, protect, and encourage it in whatever small favored localities were available. For whatever reasons, in the Mexican uplands

there was a gradual augmentation of plant cultivation from 5000 to 2500 B.C., a process marked by the appearance of more cultigens, their genetic improvement, an increase in the amount of plant refuse found in dwelling sites, and the development and improvement of tools for processing plant foods. Then, with the return to the cooler and more moist conditions of the Medithermal, after 2500 B.C., plant cultivation apparently "exploded". This "explosion" coincided with the appearance of hybridized strains of maize, and it is not unlikely that this hybridization followed in the wake of improved climatic conditions, with the attendant possibilities for the diffusion of plants from one locality to another.

This leads us to a second important finding about early agriculture. It appears to have sprung from multiple centers rather than from a single small one. Data are still scarce, with only the Tamaulipas and Puebla locations to rely on, but they suggest a pattern of diversity. For instance, maize appeared as early as 5000 B.C. in Puebla and was definitely domesticated within the next thousand years, probably within that same region. It did not appear in Tamaulipas, however, until 2500 B.C. The pumpkin (*Cucurbita pepo*), on the other hand, may have been cultivated in Tamaulipas as early as 7000 B.C., and definitely was by 5000 B.C.; but it did not show up in the Puebla sequence until 3000 B.C. The squash (probably *Cucurbita moschata*) was growing in Puebla as early as 6000 B.C., but was unknown in Tamaulipas until 2000 B.C. The bean (*Phaseolus vulgaris*), though, seems to have arrived considerably earlier in Tamaulipas, at least on present evidence, as did the bottle gourd (*Lagenaria*) and chili pepper (*Capsicum*). The Tamaulipas and Puebla regions are about 400 miles apart. This distance plus the chronological variations in the initial appearances of plants in the two sequences do, indeed, suggest that not all these plants were first cultivated in the same place. As Mesoamerican cultivation developed, one of the principal processes that probably brought it to the level of fully established agriculture was not only the interexchange of different plant species from one locality to another, but the hybridization resulting from crosses of local strains of the same species. Thus, it is quite possible that the domestication of maize began separately and more or less independently in a number of plant-collecting communities of southern Mexico in the fifth millennium B.C. and that the rapid progress in the genetic development of the species occurred later when small localized strains began to be crossed, particularly as the climate began to ameliorate after 2500 B.C.[4]

Still another important Mesoamerican discovery about agricultural origins is that they occurred in a cultural context of relative poverty. The Desert tradition life was hard. Those who followed it eked out an existence as best they could from whatever provender the countryside offered, unlike the peoples of the relatively rich food-collecting and hunting cultures, such as those of the contemporaneous Archaic tradition of eastern North America, for example. During the hot Altithermal, desert conditions worsened so that in a real sense, the slow rise of plant cultivation in the Mexican uplands was a hard-won victory of necessity. It was a response to a challenge that opened the way to a new and completely unforeseen kind of life: the life of the sedentary farmer.

The Puebla and Tamaulipas cave discoveries, when examined in conjunction with other American findings, throw some light on wider New World diffusions and origins of cultivated plants. Maize, as we implied, seems almost certainly to have been a southern Mesoamerican primary domesticate. As a primitive, relatively undeveloped cultigen it spread through the highlands of northern Mesoamerica and beyond, eventually reaching the southwestern United States.[5] Its diffusion southward on an incipient cultivation level has not been traced. Since maize is a highland grass, it is likely, though not certain, that as a primitive domesticate it was confined to upland environments. So far, only a very few archaeological sites of the period 7000 to 2000 B.C. have been reported from lowland regions in Mesoamerica, and these have not been favorably situated for the preservation of vegetal remains. A coastal shell-mound site at Islona de Chantuto, in Pacific Chiapas, is one such location. No radiocarbon dates are available, but its apparently pre-ceramic levels imply antiquity. Unfortunately, we can say little about the nature of the culture at this site, let alone the question of incipient cultivation.[6] It is distinctly possible, however, that various early food-collecting or fishing cultures did exist in Mesoamerica in the coastal plain lowlands, either of the Atlantic or the Pacific, and that they, too, figured in the development of early plant cultivation.[6a]

Later, as a successful hybridized cultigen, maize was carried as far as Peru by the middle of the second millennium B.C.,[7] and in the next 2000 years it became established throughout the Americas from southern Canada to northwestern Argentina.

The pumpkin (*Cucurbita pepo*) and the squashes (*C. moshcata* and *C. mixta*) are also primary Mesoamerican domesticates, as is the bean (*Phaseolus vulgaris*). They, too, were diffused to other parts of the Americas from this primary center. The chili pepper (*Capsicum frutescens* or *C. annum*) and the bottle gourd (*Lagenaria*) may or may not be primary Mesoamerican domesticates. As we have seen, they were very long in the area, but they are also ancient in Peru and their range as wild species extends from the southwestern United States to Brazil. Cotton (*Gossypium hirsutum*) appeared in Tamaulipas as early as 1700 B.C., and at about this same time in Puebla. This particular species may have been first domesticated in Mesoamerica; its relative (*Gossypium barbadense*), appeared even earlier in Peru, and the two are most likely separate domesticates. The amaranth (*Amaranthus*) is definitely Mesoamerican and, as we have seen, was as early as the Coxcatlán phase in Puebla. One species of tobacco (*Nicotiana rustica*) probably originated in Mesoamerica from whence it spread, at an early time, into the southeastern United States.

In addition to all these definite or probable primary Mesoamerican domesticates, significant imports were added to the complex somewhat later. The lima bean (*Phaseolus lunatus*) may have been one of these, brought or diffused from Peru; and the South American root crops, including the peanut (*Arachis hypogaea*), the sweet potato (*Ipomoea batatas*), and manioc (*Manihot esculenta*) most definitely were. Although all these root plants appeared relatively late in the pre-Columbian sequence in the Tamaulipas highland region, it is quite possible that they may have diffused from South to Middle America much earlier and were confined to lowland tropical regions during the Incipient Cultivation Period.[8]

The foundations of the Mesoamerican cultural tradition thus were laid in southern Mesoamerica by about 2000 B.C. through the genetic improvement of food plants and the assembling of the various species of domesticates, particularly those "core" elements such as maize, beans, squash, and the chili pepper. With this achievement we turn to the history of this new tradition.

The Mesoamerican Culture Sphere

The Mesoamerican culture sphere is the geographical-culture area of Mesoamerica, the cultural tradition which defines that area, and the period of time during which the tradition persisted. Let us review these dimensions briefly.

The Area. The Mesoamerican area extends from central Honduras and northwestern Costa Rica on the south northward through Mexico to the Rio Sota la Marina in Tamaulipas and the Rio Fuerte in Sinaloa on the north. (Fig. 3-6). The area exhibits great physiographic, climatic, and vegetational variation.[9] In the north are the semi-arid ranges of the Sierra Madre Occidental and Oriental, between which lies a high, desert plateau. To the south is the volcanic zone of central Mexico with its upland basins and remnants of old glacial lakes, such as the Valley of Mexico. Mountain and valley country continues through the Sierra del Sur, which runs from Jalisco southeastward through Oaxaca. Similarly, below the low-lying Isthmus of Tehuantepec, are the mountains, valleys, and basins of Chiapas and Guate-

mala. The Pacific coastal lands are relatively narrow plains which descend from mountains to sea, but on the other side of the continent the Atlantic coastal plain forms a relatively wide belt of low-lying savanna and tropical forest country.

The climate of Mesoamerica is in large part tropical, although temperature and rainfall are moderated by elevation. As a result, temperate-to-cool upland zones exist alongside hot and humid rain forests. In general, the north and west are dry, and in these directions the environment becomes progressively more desiccated, so aboriginal farming was limited to oasis valleys. The south and east, however, are areas of heavy precipitation and forest and savanna cover. Here, in pre-Columbian times as today, cultivation was by the swidden or slash-and-burn method. Different from both these extremes are the upland valleys and basins of central Mexico, the Sierra del Sur, and the highlands of Chiapas-Guatemala. In these regions there is adequate rainfall, relatively light vegetation cover, and deep and fertile soils. In these places intensive farming was practiced in ancient times and aboriginal populations were most numerous.

The Mesoamerican Cultural Tradition. The fundamental basis of the Mesoamerican cultural tradition—its agricultural village life—had developed by 2000 B.C. As time went on the tradition became richer and more elaborate, adding to itself new elements developed locally or imported. By about the beginning of the Christian era, the Mesoamerican tradition was essentially crystallized, although some important traits were assimilated later. Actually, for many traits it is difficult or impossible to say at just what point in time they became a part of the tradition, but for most it is probably safe to assume that they are older than their earliest secure archaeological documentation.

We have already described the vital agricultural complex of the Mesoamerican tradition insofar as the most important food plants are concerned. A number of others might be added to the list, however, including the cacao, or chocolate, bean, which was used to make a beverage and also as a

SONORA

CHIHUAHUA

TEXAS

COAHUILA

NUEVO
LEON

BAJA
CALIFORNIA

DURANGO

Gulf of Mexico

Mesoamerican Culture Area
and Subareas

(With slight revisions from Kirchhoff,)

SINALOA

ZACATECAS

⑩

TROPIC OF CANCER

Rio Soto La
Marina

SAN LUIS
POTOSÍ

TAMAULIPAS

⑨

Tampico
R. Panuco

NAYARIT

20

JALISCO

GUANAJUATO

QUER.

HIDALGO

YUCATÁN

COLIMA

MICHOACAN

Rio Balsas

VALLEY
OF MEXICO

⑧

TLAX.

MOR.

PUEBLA

VERACRUZ

QUINTANA
ROO

⑦

CAMPECHE

MICHOACAN

⑥

GUERRERO

⑤

OAXACA

④

TABASCO

②

BRITISH
HONDURAS

CHIAPAS

GUATEMALA

①

HONDURAS

③

Culture Subareas

1 The Maya Highlands
2 The Maya Lowlands
3 The Southern Periphery
4 Southern Veracruz-Tabasco
5 Oaxaca
6 Guerrero
7 Central Mexico
8 Central Veracruz
9 The Huasteca
10 The West and the Northern Frontier

100

EL
SALVADOR

NICARAGUA

Ulua R.

NICARAGUA

Lake
Nicaragua

– – – International Boundaries

········· Mexican State Boundaries

▬▬▬ Culture Subareas Boundaries

0   100   200 Miles

0   100   200 Kilometers

COSTA
RICA

10

Nicoya Peninsula

Figure 3-6.

90

PANAMA

kind of money, and a variety of fruits and vege-
tables, of which the tomato and the avocado were
particularly important. Besides the plants themselves, and undoubtedly very ancient, were planting, preparation, and storage techniques. Planting
in Mesoamerica was usually carried out by first
clearing the fields of bush and trees by chopping
and burning and by sowing the seeds with the aid
of a fire-hardened digging-stick. In some regions,
generally uplands tending to semi-aridity, intensive
techniques such as irrigation, terracing, and the
construction of artificial islands, or chinampas, in
lakes or marshes increased agricultural production,
although these methods probably do not go back
to the beginning of the tradition. After harvesting,
the crop was stored in pits or granaries. Maize was
prepared by boiling it in lime-water and grinding
it wet on a stone metate with a stone mano or

handstone. Tamales, tortillas or flat cakes, or a
thick gruel called pozole were then made from the
cornmeal paste.

The basis of Mesoamerican settlement was the
village, and Mesoamerican society rested on the
foundation of the nuclear, or extended, family
household, several of which made up such a village. These villages were organized into larger territorial units with leadership focused in ceremonial
centers or politico-religious capitals. This pattern
is very ancient and is area-wide. The individual
huts or houses were constructed of poles, wattle-
and-daub, and thatch-roofs. Ceremonial centers
were more elaborate, usually flat-topped pyramids
of earth and rubble or adobe. Some were faced
with limestone or tufa masonry blocks which had
been dressed with chipped- or ground-stone celts.
Masonry was frequently set in lime mortar. Later,

elaborate temples or palaces capped these pyramids. Stairs, balustrades, plinths, moldings, superstructural facades, and ornaments were all employed as architectural features, and sculptures in stone and stucco adorned buildings and pyramids.

Mesoamerican artisans were accomplished ceramists and lapidaries. Pottery, made without the fast-turning wheel, as was all New World pottery, embraced a great variety of shapes and decorative techniques. The modeled *incensario,* or incense burner, was a typical Mesoamerican form. Pottery figurines, both hand and mold-made, and usually representing the human female, also were characteristic. Fine textiles were woven of cotton and agave fiber, and paper was made from bark by pounding it with a grooved-stone beater. Metallurgy, with gold and copper, was one trait complex that was introduced to Mesoamerica in late prehistoric times from southern Central America. Most manufactures were ornaments, but in parts of western Mexico a number of copper utensils were made.

Religion, ritual and ceremony, were of first-order importance in ancient Mesoamerica, as the grand ceremonial architecture and religious sculpture and painting of the period attest. Hieroglyphic writing seems to have developed in a sacred context and appeared during the first millennium B.C. Calendars combined astronomical, mathematical, and astrological knowledge and lore with religious beliefs and rituals. Although these calendars were expressed variously in the different regions of Mesoamerica, a number of complex ideas were shared throughout the area. One of these was the division of the year into 18 months of 20 days each, plus 5 additional days. Another was a 260 day calendrical round based on a permutation of 20 day signs and 13 numbers. Deity concepts also were widely diffused, among them being a rain god and a feathered-serpent culture hero. Throughout most of Mesoamerica a complicated ritual game was played between two opposing teams with a rubber ball on a prepared court.

Sanctions and control in the higher echelons of Mesoamerican society were primarily religious, although as the state increased in size and power, secular and militaristic elements probably won a more important leadership role. Large territorial empires possibly arose as early as the beginning of the first millennium A.D.; certainly such political organizations existed in the centuries immediately before the Spanish Conquest. The Aztec empire, which is known from historic documentary as well as archaeological sources, held sway over a large portion of what is now Mexico and developed a class structure with a religious-military aristocracy at the top, a sort of "middle class" of soldiers, lesser officials, merchants, and artisans, and a broad base made up of the agricultural peasantry.[10]

Mesoamerican Subareas. These common bonds should not, however, obscure the significance of cultural diversity within the Mesoamerican culture tradition and the area it embraced. We will treat this matter in detail below, but we can begin by mentioning ethnic and linguistic diversity which is a clue to cultural regionalism.

As we have already indicated on the linguistic map (Fig. 1-4), several major language groups were represented within the Mesoamerican area.[11] Foremost were the Uto-Aztecans who, at the time of the Spanish Conquest, held much of west and northwest Mexico and had penetrated deep into central and southern Mesoamerica. The Mayans were another major group, their domain being largely in southern Mexico and Guatemala. In addition, there were the Otomians (central Mexico), the Tarascans (western Mexico), the Totonacans (Gulf Coast), and Mixtecans and Zapotecans (Oaxaca). Though there is no over-all, one-to-one correspondence between these language groups and cultures—for Mesoamerican ethnic, linguistic, and cultural boundaries had been disrupted, particularly in late pre-Columbian times, by wars and migrations—certain partial and significant correspondences did exist, and these are best summed up in a number of archaeological subareas which divide the larger Mesoamerican area. There are ten such subareas and they are outlined in Fig. 3-6.[12] See also Fig. 3-7 for tribal locations.

(1) *The Maya Highlands* (upland Guatemala and Chiapas and the bordering Pacific coasts) is and was the home of Maya-speaking peoples, the Uto-Aztecan-speaking Pipil, and other smaller groups.

(2) *The Maya Lowlands* (lowland Chiapas, most of Tabasco, lowland Guatemala, the Yucatán Peninsula, British Honduras, and a western fringe of Honduras) is and was the home of Maya-speaking tribes, the area in which the Classic Maya civilization, known for its arts, architecture, and hieroglyphic inscriptions, flowered.

(3) *The Southern Periphery* (most of western Honduras, Salvador, and the Pacific coastal strip of Nicaragua and northwestern Costa Rica) is a subarea occupied by diverse language groups at different times, including the Maya, the Uto-Aztecan Pipil, the Lenca, the Jicaque, and the Chorotega. In this subarea Mesoamerican culture shades off and interblends with lower Central American cultures.

(4) *Southern Veracruz-Tabasco* (the southern third of the former and the adjacent strip of the latter) was the homeland of the Olmec art style and related archaeological culture of the Preclassic

Figure 3-7.

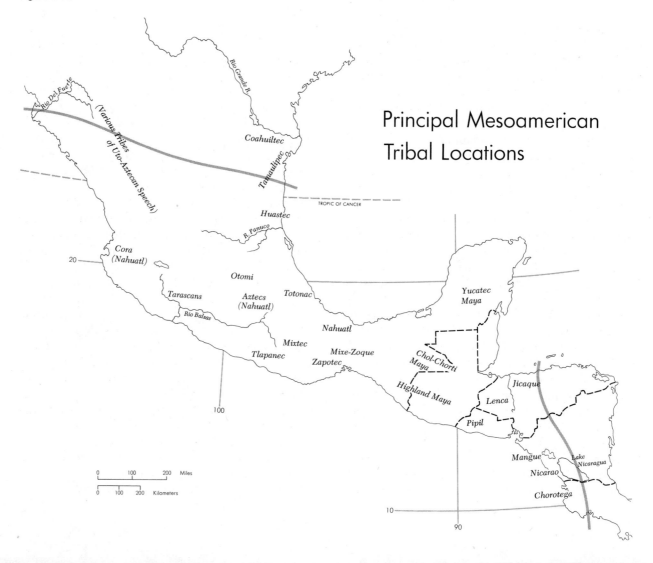

Principal Mesoamerican Tribal Locations

Period. The sixteenth-century inhabitants, presumably unrelated to this earlier archaeological culture, were Nahuatl (Uto-Aztecan), and Mixe-Zoquean tribes.

(5) *Oaxaca* (that Mexican state) was the homeland of the Zapotecs and the Mixtecs and the center of the Monte Albán civilization (Zapotecan).

(6) *Guerrero* (that Mexican state) has not been thoroughly studied by archaeologists, but local art styles suggest its long cultural independence and separation from other Mesoamerican subareas. Mixtec and Tlappanec were the principal languages spoken here in historic times.

(7) *Central Mexico* (the Valley of Mexico, eastern Estado de Mexico, southern Hidalgo, Tlaxcala, Puebla, and Morelos) was the seat of the great Teotihuacán civilization in earlier times and the bastion of Toltec and Aztec power in later centuries. Nahuatl (Uto-Aztecan) was the principal language of the Conquest period, but Otomian was also spoken on the northern edge.

(8) *Central Veracruz* (coast and interior of that state from Cerro de las Mesas to Tuxpán) is known for the archaeological Remojadas and Tajín art styles and for being the territory of the Totonac nation during the sixteenth century.

(9) *The Huasteca* (the coast and interior of northern Veracruz and southern Tamaulipas and including San Luis Potosí and part of Hidalgo) was the territory of the Maya-speaking Huastecs.

(10) *The West and the Northern Frontier* (embraces all of semi-arid and mountainous Mexico to the west and northwest of the Central subarea, extending to the Pacific Coast and the northern borders of Mesoamerica) is a subarea of relatively lower cultural contour than the others and it appears as definitely derivative of the main developments in the south and east. Most of the tribes were Uto-Aztecan-speaking.

Major Periods. Another way of segmenting the history of the Mesoamerican tradition is by major periods. The periods (Figs. 3-8, 3-9) we conceive as strictly horizontal time divisions, adhering to absolute dating insofar as this is possible.

They are not stages, although the names used for them and the dominant cultural characteristics of the periods have been used by other writers in stage as well as period concepts.[13] As we mention in the definitions of the periods given, the salient cultural characteristics of the periods do not always coincide with strictly horizontal time divisions. The absolute dating of the periods is keyed to the Maya Long Count native calendar and to the archaeological sequences dated by that calendar in the Maya Lowland subarea. The correlation of that calendar with the Christian calendar follows the 11.16.0.0.0, or Goodman-Martinez-Thompson, system.[14] This extension of the Maya native calendar to general Mesoamerican dating pertains, primarily, to the Classic Period, the time at which this calendar was in use. Postclassic Period dating estimates follow automatically from this. For periods earlier than the Classic, radiocarbon determinations are the main basis for absolute time estimates. Finally, as in any such archaeologically constructed area chronology, stratigraphy, and typological cross-dating have been employed in plotting the interrelationships of local, regional, and subareal sequences.

The five major periods which recapitulate man's residence in Mesoamerica are listed below. The first two antedate the Mesoamerican cultural tradition; the last three pertain to that tradition:

(1) *The Paleo-Indian Period (before 7000 B.C.).* This period pertains to those early complexes of the late Pleistocene which were characterized by hunting subsistence patterns.

(2) *The Food-Collecting-Incipient Cultivation Period (7000 to 2000 B.C.).* This period pertains to those Desert tradition cultures in which subsistence depended primarily on wild-plant collecting but which saw the beginning and spread of plant cultivation. Insofar as information is available, there were no other cultural traditions in the Mesoamerican area at this time.

(3) *The Preclassic Period (2000 B.C. to A.D. 300).* This period mainly embraces the beginnings and early development of the Mesoamerican cultural

tradition and its agricultural subsistence patterns. In certain regions, however, cultures of the generally earlier Desert tradition persisted for a few centuries after 2000 B.C. The period has been called variously "Archaic," "Formative," "Middle Cultures." We also follow here a tripartite division into Early Preclassic (2000–1000 B.C.), Middle Preclassic (1000–300 B.C.), and Late Preclassic (300 B.C.–A.D. 300). The latter half of the Late Preclassic is frequently called the "Protoclassic."

(4) *The Classic Period* (A.D. *300–900*). This period is derived from the span of the Maya Long Count calendar as rendered in the 11.16.0.0.0 correlation. It relates, particularly, to those civilizations in the

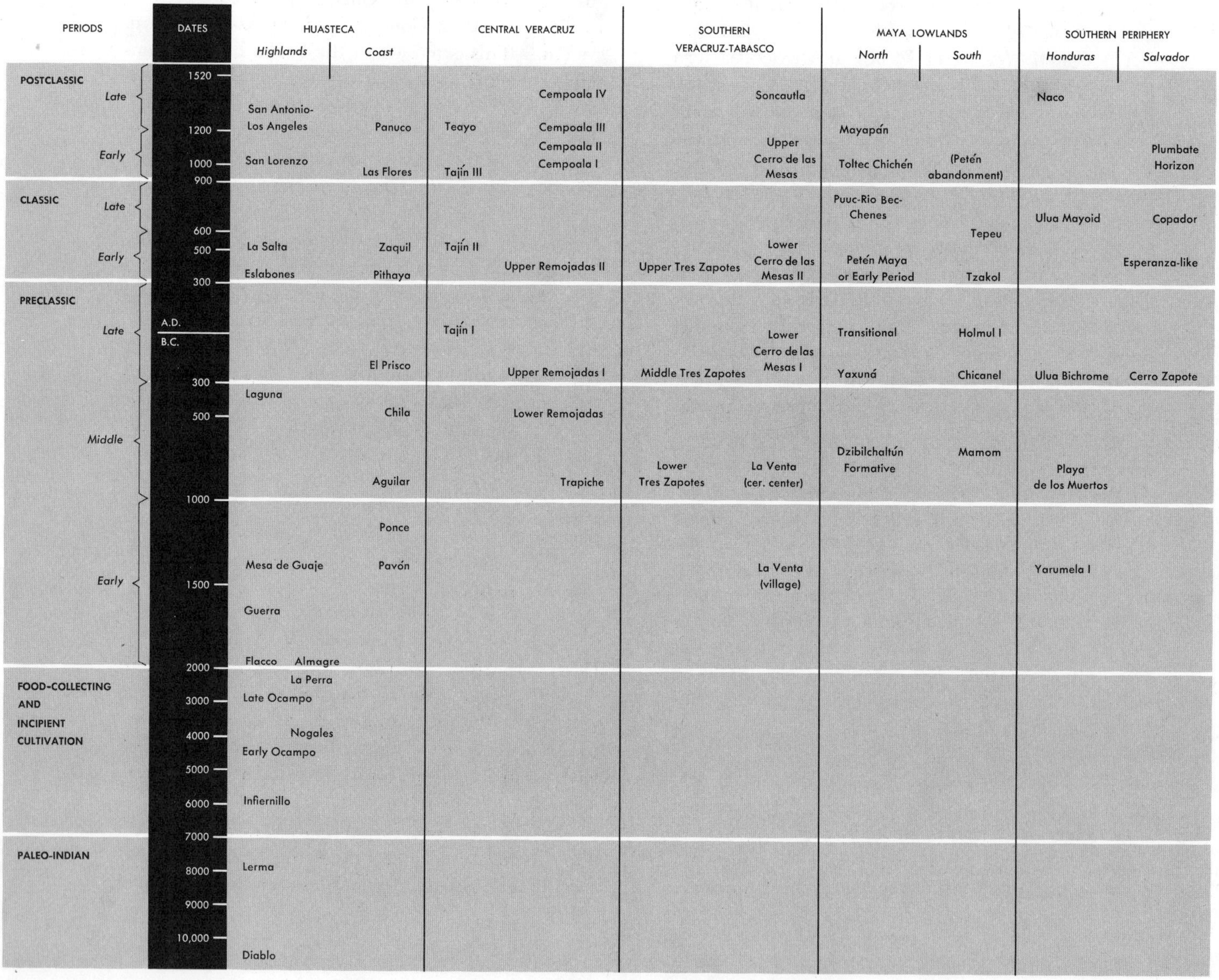

Figure 3-8. Mesoamerican chronological chart for Huasteca, Central Veracruz, Southern Veracruz-Tabasco, Maya Lowlands, and Southern Periphery subareas.

PERIODS		DATES	HUASTECA Highlands	HUASTECA Coast	CENTRAL VERACRUZ	SOUTHERN VERACRUZ-TABASCO		MAYA LOWLANDS North	MAYA LOWLANDS South	SOUTHERN PERIPHERY Honduras	SOUTHERN PERIPHERY Salvador
POSTCLASSIC	Late	1520	San Antonio-Los Angeles	Panuco	Cempoala IV / Teayo / Cempoala III	Soncautla		Mayapán		Naco	
	Early	1200 / 1000 / 900	San Lorenzo	Las Flores	Cempoala II / Cempoala I / Tajín III	Upper Cerro de las Mesas		Toltec Chichén	(Petén abandonment)		Plumbate Horizon
CLASSIC	Late	600						Puuc-Rio Bec-Chenes	Tepeu	Ulua Mayoid	Copador
	Early	500 / 300	La Salta / Eslabones	Zaquil / Pithaya	Tajín II / Upper Remojadas II	Upper Tres Zapotes	Lower Cerro de las Mesas II	Petén Maya or Early Period	Tzakol		Esperanza-like
PRECLASSIC	Late	A.D. / B.C.			Tajín I		Lower Cerro de las Mesas I	Transitional	Holmul I		
		300		El Prisco	Upper Remojadas I	Middle Tres Zapotes	Lower Cerro de las Mesas I	Yaxuná	Chicanel	Ulua Bichrome	Cerro Zapote
	Middle	500	Laguna	Chila	Lower Remojadas						
		1000		Aguilar	Trapiche	Lower Tres Zapotes	La Venta (cer. center)	Dzibilchaltún Formative	Mamom	Playa de los Muertos	
	Early			Ponce							
		1500	Mesa de Guaje	Pavón			La Venta (village)			Yarumela I	
			Guerra								
FOOD-COLLECTING AND INCIPIENT CULTIVATION		2000	Flacco Almagre								
		3000	La Perra / Late Ocampo								
		4000	Nogales / Early Ocampo								
		5000									
		6000	Infiernillo								
PALEO-INDIAN		7000 / 8000	Lerma								
		9000 / 10,000	Diablo								

central and southern parts of the Mesoamerican area which enjoyed an aesthetic, architectural, and intellectual flowering at this time, a development that does not appear to have characterized the contemporary cultures of the northern part of the area. A subdividing line between Early and Late Classic is conventionally set at A.D. 600.

(5) *The Postclassic Period* (A.D. *900–1520*). This period pertains principally to those civilizations which arose following the collapse of the Classic Period civilizations; this collapse, however, did not occur simultaneously throughout Mesoamerica, but began during the preceding Late Classic Period in central Mexico and not until later in the

Figure 3-9. Mesoamerican chronological chart for Northern Frontier and West, Central Mexico, Oaxaca, and Maya Highlands and Pacific slopes subareas.

PERIODS	DATES	NORTHERN FRONTIER AND WEST			CENTRAL MEXICO		OAXACA	MAYA HIGHLANDS AND PACIFIC SLOPES
		Durango	Colima	Michoacan	Valley of Mexico and Environs	Tehuacán		
POSTCLASSIC — Late	1520			Tarascan Empire	The Aztec Empire (Aztec IV) (Aztec III) (Aztec II)		M.A.V-Mitla	Chiapa XII — Chinautla
	1200	Calera						Chiapa XI — Tohil
POSTCLASSIC — Early	1000 / 900	Rio Tunal		Tarascan	Chichimec and Aztec Culture; Tula-Mazapán (Aztec I)		Monte Albán IV	
CLASSIC — Late	900	Las Joyas	Aztatlan		Coyotlatelco; Teotihuacán IV	Venta Salada	Monte Albán IIIB	Pamplona; Chiapa X — Amatle; Cotzumalhuapa
CLASSIC — Early	600 / 500	Ayala; Alta Vista	Chametla; Ortices	Delicias	Teotihuacán III		Monte Albán IIIA	Chiapa IX; Chiapa VIII — Esperanza; Aurora
PRECLASSIC — Late	300				Teotihuacán II		Monte Albán II	Chiapa VII; Chiapa VI — Santa Clara
	A.D. / B.C.				Teotihuacán I	Palo Seco		Chiapa V — Arenal; Izapa
PRECLASSIC — Middle	300 / 500		Chupícuaro		Cuicuilco-Ticomán		Monte Albán I	Chiapa IV — Miraflores; Providencia; Majadas; Chiapa III
	1000		El Opeño		Tlatilco; Middle Zacatenco	Santa Maria		Chiapa II — Las Charcas; Conchas
PRECLASSIC — Early	1500				Early Zacatenco; El Arbolillo I	Ajalpán		Arevalo; Chiapa I; Ocos
	2000					Purron		
FOOD-COLLECTING AND INCIPIENT CULTIVATION	2000							Islona de Chantuto
	3000					Abejas		Santa Marta
	4000							
	5000	Chalco				Coxcatlán		
	6000							
	7000					El Riego		
PALEO-INDIAN	8000							
	9000				Iztapán	Ajuereado		
	10,000							

Gulf of Mexico

TEXAS

BAJA CALIFORNIA

Mesoamerican
Archaeological Sites
and Regions

TROPIC OF CANCER

SIERRA MADRE OCCIDENTAL

SIERRA MADRE ORIENTAL

Rio del Fuerte

Rio Soto La Marina

R. Panuco

Rio Balsas

SIERRA MADRE DEL SUR

SIERRA DE OAXACA

SIERRA MADRE

GUATEMALA

BRITISH HONDURAS

HONDURAS

EL SALVADOR

Usuma R.

Archaeological Sites or Regions

1   Sierra Madre Oriental region
    of Tamaulipas
2   Sierra de Tamaulipas region
3   Tehuacán Valley
4   Islona de Chantuto
5   Chiapa de Corzo
6   Ocos
7   Kaminaljuyú
8   Tampico-Panuco region
9   Valley of Mexico
10 La Venta
11 Tres Zapotes
12 San Lorenzo
13 Monte Albán
14 Izapa
15 El Baúl
16 Uaxactún
17 Tikal
18 Altar de Sacrificios
19 Piedras Negras
20 Palenque
21 Yaxchilán
22 Benque Viejo
23 Lubaantún
24 Copan

25 Oxxkintok
26 Dzibilchaltún
27 Cobá
28 Uxmal
29 Tajín
30 Cerro de las Mesas
31 Cempoala
32 Remojadas
33 Tula
34 Mitla
35 Chichen Itzá
36 Mayapán
37 Tulum
38 Yarumela

39 Tamuin
40 Acapulco
41 Apatzingan region
42 Ixtlán region
43 Alta Vista de Chalchuites
44 Schroeder
45 Yaxuná
46 Zacualpa
47 Tazumal
48 Tzintzuntzan
49 Ortices
50 La Quemada
51 Rio Bec
52 Xpuhil

–––– International Boundaries
······· Mexican State Boundaries

0   100   200 Miles

0   100   200 Kilometers

southern part of the area. The date of A.D. 900 is derived from events in the Lowland Maya subarea.

The Preclassic Period: Crystallization of a Tradition

General Characteristics. The two millennia or more of the Preclassic Period, from 2000 B.C. to A.D. 300, were a time when the elements of the Mesoamerican cultural tradition were assembled and welded together. During the Early Preclassic (2000–1000 B.C.) we see forming the outlines of a "Neolithic" milieu of village agricultural subsistence, pottery-making, stone-grinding, and weaving. Beyond this it is uncertain what distinctive complexes of behavior had developed in other aspects of life; but in view of what was to take place in the centuries immediately following, it is likely that a fairly rich ceremonialism had already been conceived, even if it had not been immortalized in art and architecture. Such immortalization in stone was being practiced, however, in the Middle Preclassic (1000–300 B.C.), with the rise of the first of the Mesoamerican cultures that had some of the characteristics of civilization, the Olmec.

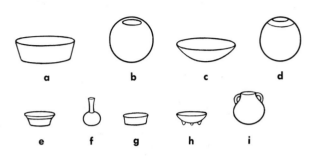

Figure 3-11. Preclassic Period pottery from Tehuacán Valley, Puebla. *a,b,c:* Purron phase. *d,e:* Ajalpán phase. *f-i:* Santa Maria phase. (After MacNeish, 1962.)

Olmec culture flowered around its brilliant ceremonial centers, and during the succeeding Late Preclassic Period (300 B.C.–A.D. 300) a number of other regional cultures, to some extent Olmec-derived, exhibited this same general form—the great ceremonial center, with its temples, palaces, arts, and intellectual attainments as the integrative focus of a society sustained by numerous outlying peasant villages.

The Early Preclassic. The beginnings of the Early Preclassic Period, as has been indicated, were at the "threshold" of Mesoamerican village agriculture, or, in other words, were concommitant with the beginnings of the Mesoamerican cultural tradition. The date we have set for this is, in round figures, about 2000 B.C. As we have already pointed out, in some parts of the Mesoamerican area this date would have to be advanced considerably. In other regions it might even be set back a few centuries. This last would seem to be the case with the Tehuacán Valley where, if we draw the line at the inception of the Purron phase, the date becomes 2300 B.C.

Purron (2300–1500 B.C.), we have seen, was characterized by a number of traits which signal significant culture changes. Some of these, such as pottery, appeared for the first time; others, including new hybrid maize and evidences of settled villages, made a slower, more gradual appearance on the scene, being traceable back into the latter

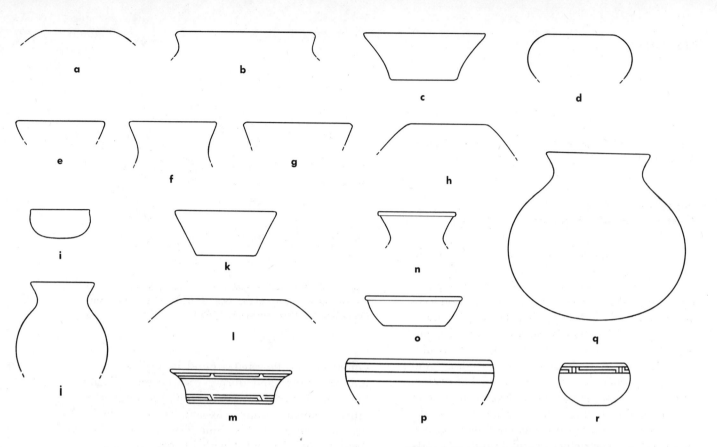

Figure 3-12. *Above:* Preclassic Period vessel form outlines, Tehuacán Valley, Mexico. *a–c:* Purron phase. *d–g:* Early Ajalpán phase. *h–k:* Late Ajalpán phase. *l–r:* Early Santa Maria phase. (Courtesy R. S. Peabody Foundation, Andover.)

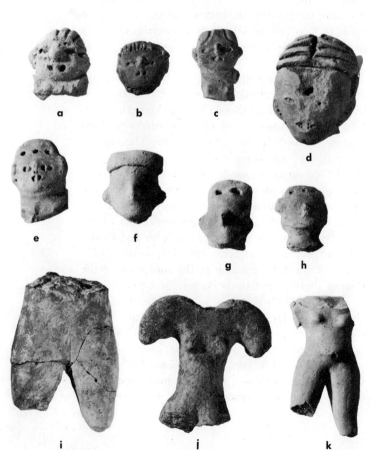

Figure 3-13. *Left:* Some figurines of the Ajalpán phase, Tehuacán Valley, Mexico. *a–e:* Early Ajalpán pottery figurine heads. *f–h:* Curious "no-face" or featureless Late Ajalpán figurines. *i,j:* Body portions of Early Ajalpán figurines. *k:* Body of "Venus style" Late Ajalpán figurine. (Courtesy R. S. Peabody Foundation, Andover.)

part of the antecedent Abejas phase. Even the new innovation of pottery shows ties with stone vessels of the local past. The ware was largely unslipped and undecorated. Vessel forms included some basic Mesoamerican shapes: the globular seed-bowl or tecomate, a similar globular bowl with an out-flared rim, hemispherical bowls, and flat-bottomed bowls with outflared rims (see the examples in Figs. 3-11*a–c*, 3-12*a–c*).

The Ajalpán phase of the Tehuacán sequence, dated at 1500 to 900 B.C. by MacNeish, falls largely

Figure 3-14. Early Santa Maria phase figurines, Tehuacán Valley, Mexico. Height of *a*, about 7.5 cm. (Courtesy R. S. Peabody Foundation, Andover.)

in our general Early Preclassic Period. By then the population had perhaps doubled or tripled what it was in Purron times. The tecomate bowl form was still the dominant vessel shape (Fig. 3-11*d*), but the vessel surfaces were decorated with zoned brushing, punctuations, and red washes or red-banded rims. New pottery types included black-fired bowls with interior incised lines (perhaps molcajetes for grinding chili peppers, a widespread Mesoamerican trait in later times) and some zoned rocker-stamped sherds. Unlike Purron, the Ajalpán ceramics resembled forms found elsewhere in Mesoamerica, and the Tehuacán complex appears to have been one member of a widespread Early Preclassic ceramic horizon. Pottery figurines also appeared in Ajalpán, and the succeed-

Figure 3-15. Large hollow pottery figurine, Late Ajalpán phase, Tehuacán Valley, Mexico. This specimen, painted in red and black, and, perhaps, representing a dwarf, stands 45 cm. high. (Courtesy R. S. Peabody Foundation, Andover.)

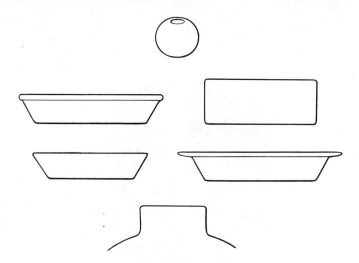

Figure 3-16. Early Preclassic vessel forms (Chiapa I phase) from Chiapa de Corzo, Chiapas, Mexico. (After Dixon, 1959.)

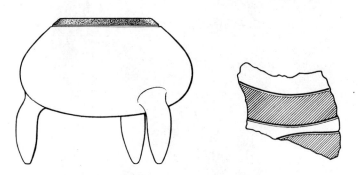

Figure 3-17. Ocos phase pottery, La Victoria, Pacific Guatemala. The banding is iridescent pigment painting. (After M. D. Coe, 1961.)

Figure 3-18. Ocos phase pottery and figurine, La Victoria, Pacific Guatemala. a: Shell-edge rocker-stamping. b: Plain rocker-stamping. c: Hand-made figurine. (After M. D. Coe, 1961.)

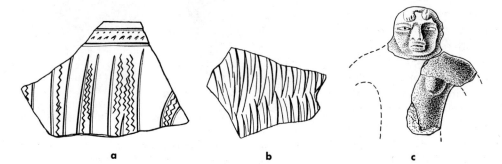

a   b   c

ing early Santa Maria phase—solid, handmade, human female effigies, again a first in this Tehuacán sequence for what was to become a Mesoamerican-wide Preclassic trait.[15]

The Ajalpán pottery complex was similar to that of the Chiapa I, or Cotorra, phase of the Grijalva Valley of Chiapas. Although technically in the Maya Highland subarea, the immediate locale of the Chiapa de Corzo site is the bottom of a tropical river gorge in the mountains. One of the longest culture sequences in Mesoamerica has been revealed here, and the Chiapa I phase is the first member of the stratigraphic column. Chiapa I pottery also featured the brushed, gouged, rocker-stamped or red-painted tecomate bowl as well as the typically Mesoamerican flat-bottomed bowl or pan form. Some Chiapa I ware was a white-slipped or red-and-white hard-fired pottery. Again, there were the small, hand-made, solid human female figurines. The phase is dated, stratigraphically and with the aid of radiocarbon, from 1500 to 1000 B.C., contemporaneous with Ajalpán.[16]

Presumably contemporary and typologically similar pottery complexes to those of Chiapa I and Ajalpán have been found farther south, at Ocos, on the Pacific coast of Guatemala,[17] and in the Arevalo phase of the Guatemalan Highlands.[18] In the opposite direction, the Pavon phase, at the base of the Huasteca culture sequence, at Tampico, on the Gulf Coast, also probably fits here, in the latter part of the Early Preclassic Period.[19]

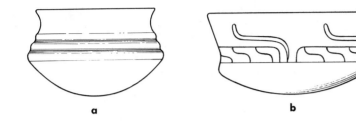
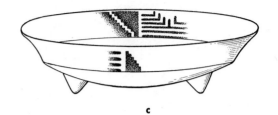

Figure 3-19. Preclassic pottery from the Valley of Mexico, the Zacatenco site. *a*: Bowl of thin black ware with a modeled or channeled decoration, Early Zacatenco phase. *b*: Bowl of incised black ware, Middle Zacatenco phase. *c*: Red-on-white tripod bowl, Middle Zacatenco phase. (After Vaillant, 1930.)

Somewhat more debatable is the placing of the earliest farming cultures of the Valley of Mexico on this same horizon.[20] The phases in question are El Arbolillo and the slightly later Early Zacatenco, both known from village refuse beds on the old shore lines of the now much shrunken Lake Texcoco. These sites cover several acres, and their depth indicates long, sedentary occupation. The refuse debris itself consisted of wattle-daub house wall fragments, impressions of maize leaves, deer bones, potsherds, and general detritus. The little hand-made female figurines were so abundant that they can hardly be interpreted as anything else than everyday household fetishes relating to human or agricultural fertility or both. Ceramics did not resemble the Chiapa I-Ajalpán horizon types, however, and included black wares with red pigments rubbed in incised or engraved lines, and tripod bowls.[21] Radiocarbon dates are somewhat contradictory for Early Zacatenco; some readings indicate an Early Preclassic position but others are later.[22] El Arbolillo and Early Zacatenco were probably this early, or if not, were certainly no later than the succeeding Middle Preclassic Period.

None of these Early Preclassic culture phases have yielded any clear evidence of ceremonial centers such as might be marked by sizable artificial mounds that could have been the bases for temples, palaces, or other politico-religious buildings. The most likely exception is the Arevalo phase of the Guatemalan Highlands, but here the question is clouded by some doubt if Arevalo was, indeed, this early. On the Guatemalan Pacific coast, platform mounds may be associated with the Ocos phase, although this association is not certain.

Elsewhere, for other phases we have listed, there are no such "special buildings" or mounds. Thus, we must conclude that the rise of the ceremonial center—at least as an aggregate of mounds or architectural features of size and consequence—was not a characteristic of the Early Preclassic Period in Mesoamerica.

The Middle Preclassic and the Olmec Style. The rise of the ceremonial center is a Middle Preclassic Period phenomenon, and the transi-

Figure 3-20. Preclassic pottery forms from the Valley of Mexico, the Zacatenco site. All Middle Zacatenco phase. (After Vaillant, 1930.)

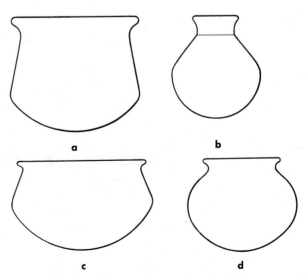

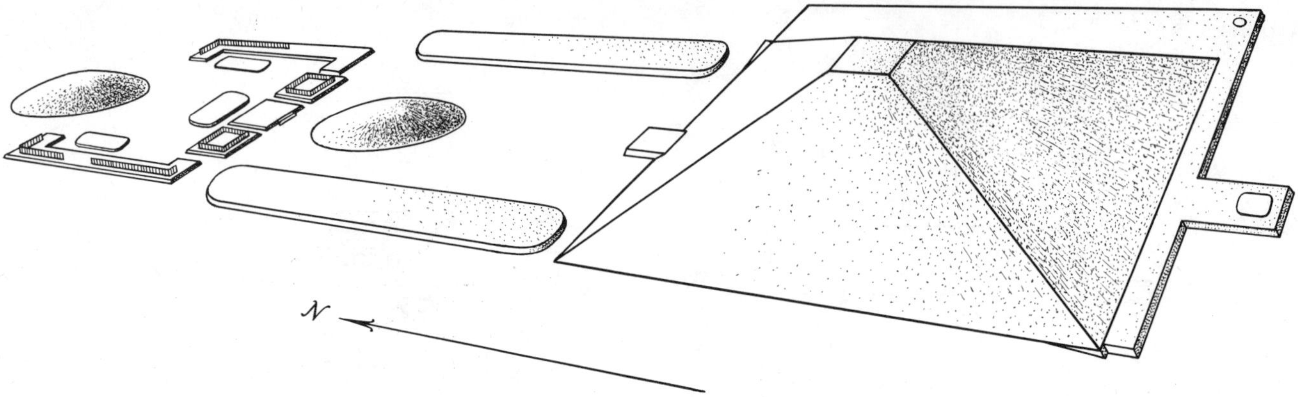

Figure 3-21. Plan of the ceremonial center of La Venta, Tabasco. (Redrawn from Drucker, Heizer, and Squier, 1959.)

tion which it marks—from the village as the social universe to the larger order of villages-and-center— is a significant turning point in Mesoamerican culture history and the shaping of the Mesoamerican tradition. The change probably occurred not long after 1000 B.C., and it seems that these ceremonial centers arose in response to population increase and out of a desire to maintain and symbolize kinship and religious unity. We can imagine the process as new village units splitting off from old ones. Some villages, probably the original ones, were revered as homes of leaders and became seats

Figure 3-22. Great head and stone column tomb at La Venta, Tabasco, Mexico. *Left:* Huge human head, Olmec style. *Right:* Tomb of pieces of columnar basalt (after excavation).

of religious and political authority. They were visited by pilgrims from the surrounding villages, shrines and temples were erected, and the priest-leaders were buried there. As resident leadership grew in size and power, its members and their retainers patronized the arts, crafts, and formal learning. In some instances, such centers became market places, and, eventually, some of them grew into cities.

The first great ceremonial centers of the Middle Preclassic Period—at least the ones that are, to date, known to the archaeologists—are in southern Mesoamerica. Perhaps the earliest of all is La Venta, in the Tabasco Lowlands not far from the coast of the Gulf of Mexico.[23] The La Venta ceremonial center is located on a small swamp island, a patch of land only a little over 5 square kilometers in size and even by generous computation unable to have supported more than 30 families in prehistoric times. The size of the ceremonial works, including its large stone monuments, implies a tributary population of considerable size, and there is little doubt that La Venta as a center drew on the efforts of the people of a sizable outlying region. Radiocarbon dates indicate that the buildings and monuments of the ceremonial center date from about 800 to 400 B.C. Four sequent subphases can be detected in the construction. The complex of the ceremonial mounds extends for over 2 kilometers on a north-south line. The most imposing feature was a rectangular earth mound 120 by 70 meters at the base and 32 meters high. Long low mounds bordered a carefully laid out rectangular plaza or court in front of the great mound, and another complex of walls and mounds lay at the other end of this plaza. The walls or bordering ridges of this second complex were made of adobe brick topped with upright basalt columns. Other features of the complex included another large terraced clay mound, smaller earth mounds, one of which covered a box-like structure made of basalt columns, and mosaic "pavements" of green serpentine blocks laid out in designs on the floors

Figure 3-24. Olmec figurine of a seated woman from La Venta, Tabasco. A small polished hematite mirror or ornament has been fastened to the breast. The figurine was carved from whitish, mottled jadeite and was found covered with red cinnabar powder. (After Drucker, 1952.)

Figure 3-23. Jadeite objects in the Olmec style. a: Celt with anthropomorphic jaguar face, about 16 cm. high. b: Two views of a human figurine, about 18 cm. high. (a, after Drucker, 1952; b, after Drucker, Heizer, and Squier, 1959.)

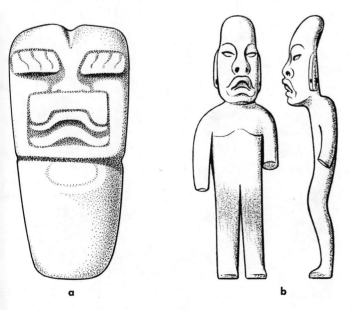

a   b

of deep pits. Rich dedicatory caches of jade celts, figurines, beads, and earplugs, and monumental stone sculptures such as stelae, altars, and huge human heads lie about the site. The labor involved in such undertakings seems astounding when we realize that there was no stone suitable for fashioning such monuments in the marshy flats around La Venta and that the nearest source is some 100 kilometers upstream. The largest stela at the La Venta ceremonial center has been estimated to weigh 50 tons.

La Venta appears to be a principal source for the first great Mesoamerican art style, the Olmec. Actually, the Olmec were a late prehistoric, early historic tribe of the region who probably had nothing to do with the ancient La Venta builders. Olmec art was sculptural, both full-round and relief, and was realistic in its portrayal of the natural and the supernatural. It tended to be uncluttered and free of adornment, had a slow, curvilinear rhythm of line, and adhered to a standard iconography. A were-jaguar, or anthropomorphized jaguar, was the central theme. These creatures were given an infantile or "baby-faced"

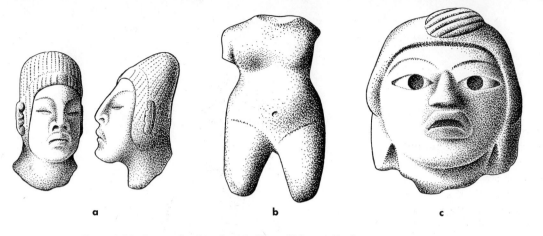

a   b   c

Figure 3-25. Pottery figurines from La Venta, Tabasco, Mexico.
a: Front and side views, Olmecoid style, 4.5 cm. high; b: 6 cm.
high; c: 9 cm. high. (All after Drucker, 1952.)

Figure 3-26. *Below, left:* Altar 5 at La Venta, Tabasco, Mexico,
a monumental sculpture in the Olmec style. The altar is about
1.5 meters high. (Redrawn from Stirling, 1943.)

Figure 3-27. *Below, right:* Altar 5, La Venta, south end of
sculpture (see Fig. 3-26). (Redrawn from Stirling, 1943.)

quality, with drooping lips and swollen, oblique
eyes. Subtle shades of this infantile "jaguarism"
infected human representations, ranging all the
way from only slightly snubbed noses and heavy,
down-turned mouths to fanged and snarling
demons. Some portrayals seem Negroid, as is the
case with the famous giant stone heads, others
more Mongoloid, and still others depicted an aqui-
line physical type.

Figure 3-28. Olmec style stone carvings. *a*: Reclining figure of a man carved in serpentine, reportedly from Puebla, Mexico. Length, 11.2 cm. *b*: "Yuguito" head or stylized skull from Tlatilco, Valley of Mexico. Height, 10.2 cm. *c*: Jadeite figure of a man, Mexico. Height, 23.9 cm. *d*: Front and back views of jadeite figure of a man, Mexico. Height, 8.5 cm. (Courtesy Dumbarton Oaks pre-Columbian Collection.)

a

b

c

d

Figure 3-29. Olmec or Olmecoid style stone carvings. a: Were-jaguar figure. Height, 9 cm. b: Fragment of jadeite vessel with human face in distinctly Olmec style. c: A seated, bearded man, not typically Olmec. The piece is probably an Olmec-derived Veracruz manufacture. Height, about 35 cm. All pieces are from southern Mexico. (a, Courtesy Museum für Völkerkunde und Vorgeschichte, Hamburg; b, courtesy British Museum; c, courtesy Cambridge Museum of Archaeology and Ethnology, England.)

Olmec monumental art was confined to a relatively few ceremonial center sites in the Southern Veracruz-Tabasco subarea of Mesoamerica, although discoveries also have been made at San Lorenzo, Tres Zapotes, Rio Chiquito, and Potrero Nuevo. The ethnic identification of the Olmec civilization remains a mystery. In speculating about this, M. D. Coe cites an old Nahuatl legend about a famous site or nation on the "eastern sea" by the name of Tamoanchán.[24] Perhaps significantly, the name is not Nahuatl but Maya. The

Maya language was spoken just to the east of Olmec territory, and another enclave of Maya-speakers, the Huastec, lived farther north on the Gulf Coast. Was all this Gulf coastal lowland once held by peoples of the Maya language family, before others, such as Nahua and Totonac, displaced them? And if so, were the creators of the Olmec civilization and art style Mayas? Another possibility is that the ancient Olmec were Mixe-

Zoque in speech, a language family still represented in the Veracruz-Tabasco subarea. Whoever they were, their contribution to the Mesoamerican cultural tradition and to the civilization of the whole area was enormous. For theirs was the first great art style and, probably, the first great Mesoamerican religion.[25]

Elements of Olmec style and iconography diffused widely throughout Mesoamerica during the Middle Preclassic Period. The spread of the style appears to have been from Southern Veracruz-Tabasco westward and northwestward across Puebla, Morelos, and Guerrero. From Guerrero southward, Olmec sculptures have been found in Oaxaca, Chiapas, the Pacific slopes of Guatemala, and Salvador. Some of these manifestations of the style were typical; others appeared to be slightly later derivations. Olmec influence is also apparent in small objects, such as figurines, jade ornaments, or in pottery. Because of the abundance of these remains in Guerrero, Miguel Covarrubias believed that Mesoamerican subarea to have been the original homeland of the Olmec style.[26] But although this is possible, there is as yet no hint that the Guerrero Olmec objects are older than La Venta and the great Olmec sculptures of Veracruz-Tabasco. Certainly insofar as the style is expressed in a monumental manner there can be little argument that it originated in the latter region.

One particularly outstanding non-monumental occurrence of Olmec influence was discovered in the Tlatilco phase of the Valley of Mexico. Tlatilco appears to follow, or perhaps to be intrusive into and in part contemporaneous with, the Early Zacatenco phase of the Valley. The Tlatilco Olmec-like figurines exhibited an amazing naturalism, totally unlike the rather stiff and stylized El Arbol-illo and Early Zacatenco types. Others, although realistic, were at the same time monstrous or allegorical, showing two-headed individuals and human or monstrous faces divided vertically into living and skeletal halves. Many Tlatilco ceramics in new and exotic vessel forms, hitherto unknown in Mesoamerica, have survived, such as stirrup-mouthed jars, tall-necked bottles, and animal and

Fig. 3-30. Preclassic pottery figurines from the Valley of Mexico. a,b: "Type D," or Tlatilco type. c,d: "Type C1," characteristic of Early Zacatenco phase. (Courtesy Cambridge Museum of Archaeology and Ethnology, England.)

Figure 3-31. Tlatilco pottery vessel. (Courtesy Cambridge Museum of Archaeology and Ethnology, England.)

fish effigies. Incised-zoned color and zoned rocker-stamping were typical decorative techniques, frequently applied to polished black wares.[27]

La Venta probably was destroyed in the latter part of the Middle Preclassic, for many of its finest monuments were intentionally defaced. In

any event, after about 400 B.C. it seems to have been used only as an occasional place of worship or as a shrine for votive offerings. Tres Zapotes, an Olmec site to the north of La Venta, then perhaps became the most important center of the Gulf Coast lowlands. Tres Zapotes was, during its earliest occupation, partly contemporaneous with La Venta, but it also flourished later.[28] In the Late Preclassic Period a stela was carved at Tres Zapotes with a bar-and-dot numerical date which is presumed to be in the same system as the later Long Count, or Initial Series dates, of the Classic Maya.[29] The Tres Zapotes date is, in fact, the earliest Long Count date known in Mesoamerica, falling in the seventh cycle, or baktun, of that system and being the equivalent of the Christian calendrical date of 31 B.C. Neither bar-and-dot numbers, evidence of the Long Count calendar, nor hieroglyphics have been found at La Venta or on monuments in any other ceremonial center of the full Olmec style; however, hieroglyphs appear occasionally on small Olmec jades, and these, together with the early Tres Zapotes inscribed stela,

Figure 3-32. Two Monte Albán stelae with glyphs and numbers, Monte Albán I phase. (After Caso, 1947.)

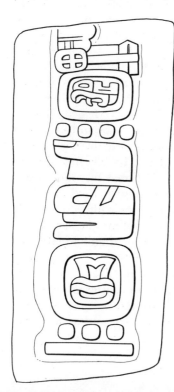
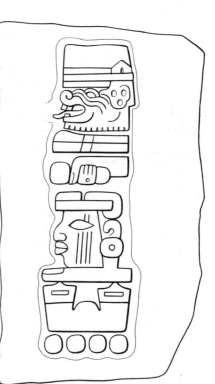

suggest that writing and the Long Count calendar were probably developing in the Middle Preclassic and quite likely were Olmec contributions to Mesoamerican and, particularly, to Maya culture.[30]

Monte Albán. Early Monte Albán of the highlands of central Oaxaca is an Olmec-derived or Olmec-influenced regional culture which appears to date from late in the Middle Preclassic Period and to have lasted through much of the Late Preclassic. The Monte Albán I phase, with its large, flat-topped mounds, has yielded evidences of monumental art, a system of hieroglyphics, numerals, and a calendar. The latter does not pertain, however, to the Long Count dating system but to the more common Mesoamerican 52-year cycle, or "calendar round." Notable is a series of Monte Albán monumental relief carvings on stone slabs known as the "Danzantes," or dancing figures. These carvings depicted nude, and probably sexually mutilated, dead men rather than "dancers," probably sacrificed captives. Their faces, in profile, are Olmec, with thick lips and flattened noses. Relief-modeled pottery incensarios

Figure 3-33. Monte Albán I and II phase glyphs. *a,b,d:* Day signs with numbers. Notice use of finger digits in *b* and *d*. *c,e:* Day signs without numbers. *f,g:* Other signs. (After Caso, 1947.)

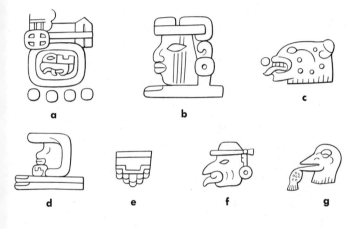

a   b   c   d   e   f   g

Figure 3-34. Two "Danzante" sculptures from Monte Albán, Oaxaca, Mexico, Monte Albán I phase. (After Caso, 1947.)

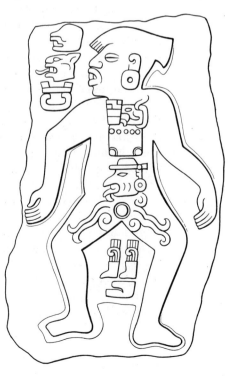

Figure 3-35. A Monte Albán I style urn. Notice Olmecoid mouth of figure. (After Caso and Bernal, 1952.)

Figure 3-36. Stela 1 at Izapa, Chiapas, Mexico. An anthropomorphic figure grasps a bowl or basket which rests on a small stand or altar. On the figure's back is a basket, or olla. (Redrawn from Stirling, 1943.)

with their anthropomorphized jaguar faces indicate another tie with the Olmec style.[31]

Chiapas-Guatemala. The Olmec-derived monumental art, rather similar to that of Tres Zapotes, also has been found in Chiapas and the Guatemalan Highlands. Izapa, a great ceremonial center of mounds, courts, and stone monuments in the Pacific coastal plain of Chiapas, has given its name to the art style found here. This style resembled both Olmec and the later Classic Maya sculpture of the lowlands. Its scenes and representations in the relief carvings were considerably more cluttered or full than the relatively chaste Olmec conceptions, but Olmec links are evident in the face of a deity which is a long-lipped or long-nosed metamorphosis of the man-jaguar. An Izapa style monument at the site of El Baúl, on the Pacific plain of Guatemala, carries a baktun 7 Long Count date in bar-and-dot numerals of A.D. 36.[32] Two other fine sculptures in the Izapán, or a very closely related style, have also come from Kaminaljuyú in the Guatemala City basin in the highlands. One of these bore not only a central figure, but also hieroglyphs and numbers which clearly related to the later hieroglyphs and calendrics of the Maya Lowlands and were prototypes of these.[33]

Figure 3-37. Preclassic vessel from Kaminaljuyú, Guatemalan Highlands. Black-brown incised ware, Miraflores phase. (After Shook and Kidder, 1952.)

Kaminaljuyú is one of the largest, and was certainly one of the most important, Preclassic and Classic ceremonial centers in southern Mesoamerica. We have already mentioned its occupation during the Arevalo phase in our survey of the Early Preclassic Period. The site zone then developed as a complex of hugh earth and adobe

mounds in the Middle and Late Preclassic Periods. Although monumental stone was relatively rare at the site, the two monuments referred to above date from the Late Preclassic Period. So does a particularly lavish tomb. This tomb had been constructed as a rectangular, stepped shaft into the summit of a large platform adobe mound. It contained the skeleton of a priest or dignitary. Hundreds of pottery and marble vessels and jades had been heaped around the body, and a wooden superstructure had been built over the grave before it was covered with additional levels of mound construction.[34]

Other Subareas. In the Maya Lowlands, ceremonial mound groups were constructed during the Late Preclassic, both in the Petén and to the north in Yucatán; but the later great Classic art style of the subarea had not yet emerged, or at least no evidence of it has yet been found. The tiger-face masks (see p. 129) on the stair balustrades of Temple E-VII-Sub mound at Uaxactún may mark the first important stirrings of this artistic

Figure 3-38. A Late Preclassic or Protoclassic Maya building at Uaxactún, Guatemala. *Left:* Temple E-VII-Sub shortly after excavation. This pyramid supported a wood and thatch superstructure, now destroyed. *Right:* A museum model of Temple E-VII-Sub, showing the superimposed pyramid of a later Classic Period building. This latter feature had been removed before the photo at left was taken. (Courtesy Peabody Museum, Harvard University.)

Figure 3-39. Late Preclassic or Protoclassic pottery from the Maya Lowlands. *Left:* Polished red jar of Chicanel phase or Late Preclassic Period, Tikal. *Right:* White-slipped spouted jar with incisions, Protoclassic Period, Holmul. (*Left,* courtesy University of Pennsylvania Museum; *right,* courtesy Peabody Museum, Harvard University.)

tradition, and it is likely that this structure belongs to the end of the Late Preclassic, or the Proto-classic, Period.[35] In brief, Maya civilization was still evolving during the Preclassic; its flowering would be one of the highlights of the succeeding Classic Period. Similarly, to the north in the Valley of Mexico, the Preclassic Period closed with the building of the ceremonial mound at Cuicuilco[36] and with the laying of the foundations of the mammoth ceremonial center and civilization of Teotihuacán.[37] But these events preceded the subsequent Classic Period greatness of that civilization.

Summary. It was during the Preclassic Period that the Mesoamerican cultural tradition achieved its distinctive pattern and this pattern, starting from a simple village agricultural design, grew steadily more complex. The village became but a component part of a larger social order integrated around the ceremonial center. More villages and more centers sprang up as population increased with the extension of agricultural subsistence to new lands. Religion developed in the

ceremonial centers in the sense that gods and pantheons were formalized, a regular priesthood arose, and religious beliefs found expression in architecture, art, the development of writing, mathematics, and the calendar. This codification of belief systems through art styles and through the medium of writing undoubtedly contributed greatly to welding small local societies into larger ones. The appearance and spread of the Olmec style in the Middle Preclassic, signaling as it must the creation and propagation of a religious system, suggests one of the most important means whereby a Mesoamerican traditional unity was fashioned relatively early. For agricultural subsistence alone does not describe the Mesoamerican cultural configuration. Agriculture was tremendously important. It supported life and large communities, but we cannot explain the Maya Long Count calendar or the civilization of Teotihuacán simply in terms of maize, beans, and squash. The most uniquely distinctive Mesoamerican features are not so much material as they are ideological, and it was this ideological realm—a kind of Mesoamerican world view—that even more than the technological side of life developed in the Preclassic Period. The result was that at the threshold of what we are calling the Classic Period, Mesoamerican society was mature—mature in its beliefs about man's relation to his gods and to other men. Similar pantheons of deities, derived from a common Olmec heritage, were worshipped throughout the area (or at least in its southern and central parts). Similar priest-aristocrats ruled their peasant farming populations from similar ceremonial centers. And they had done so for almost a thousand years. It is only in the light of this background that we may attempt to understand the civilizations of the Classic Period.

The Classic Period Civilizations: Teotihuacán

The Teotihuacán Site. Northeast of modern Mexico City, in a side pocket of the Valley of Mexico, lies one of the most impressive ruins of pre-Columbian America, Teotihuacán. It was the principal ceremonial center, and undoubtedly the political capital, of the civilization of the same name. Certainly, in the centuries of its heyday, the early half of the Classic Period, Teotihuacán was the greatest cultural and political force in all of Mesoamerica. Eric Wolf has pointed out that the Central Mexican subarea, with the Valley of Mexico as its heart, has long dominated the rest of Mexico and Mesoamerica and does so today.[38] This domination appears to have been established first with Teotihuacán. Prior to its ascendancy, the Valley of Mexico had lagged somewhat behind southern Mesoamerica in its cultural development. The Olmec lands of the Gulf Coast, Monte Albán in Oaxaca, the Izapa culture, and the Preclassic center of Kaminaljuyú in the Guatemalan Highlands all were more advanced in the civilized arts —ceremonial-center construction, sculpture, and painting. But during the closing centuries of the Preclassic, the peoples of the Valley of Mexico erected both the great ceremonial center of Cuicuilco and the first of the mound constructions at the northern edge of the site of Teotihuacán in a location designated as Ostoyahualco.[39] These Ostoyahualco, or Teotihuacán I,[40] ruins presaged the development of the Teotihuacán civilization that was to come. According to R. F. Millon, they cover 3 square miles and consist not only of plat-form ceremonial mounds, but of closely-packed, walled residential structures.[40a] Such a settlement approaches modern urban proportions, and it is this urban quality that is one of the outstanding features of Classic Period Teotihuacán that followed.

Classic Period Teotihuacán was constructed in the Teotihuacán II and III phases, and its ruins cover more than 7 square miles of either ceremonial mounds or wall-to-wall palaces and residences.[41] Two enormous flat-topped pyramids, a long and wide avenue or central concourse, and a huge walled enclosure with an interior pyramid are the main constructions at the site, and these appear to have been carefully laid out. The largest of the pyramids, known as the "Pyramid of the Sun," and quite possibly dedicated to that deity, is 64 meters high and 210 meters square at the base. Built of earth, adobes, and rubble, and faced with stones, it is one of the largest of native American structures. Pottery from within the fill of the pyramid dates the bulk of its construction as Teotihuacán II phase, although a small interior platform, later covered by the principal pyramid mass, was probably built during Teotihuacán I.[42] Severely plain, the pyramid was constructed in four great terraces with a wide stair rising on one side from ground level to summit. The surmounting temple building probably was of wood-frame construction for it has not survived.

Massive stone sculpture is relatively rare at Teotihuacán. Only a few examples of columnar stone statues exist, one of these being the Water-Goddess figure which was found in the plaza of the second largest pyramid, the Pyramid of the Moon. Another is a composite stela which is believed by Luis Aveleyra Arroyo de Anda to be a ballgame marker and is, in fact, the only evidence of the game at this relatively early time in the Valley of Mexico.[43] The finest examples of monumental sculpture are the carved heads of feathered serpents, and what may be Tlalocs, or rain gods, that are tenoned and mortised into the terrace facings of the pyramid that stands within the great rectangular enclosure to which we already have referred.

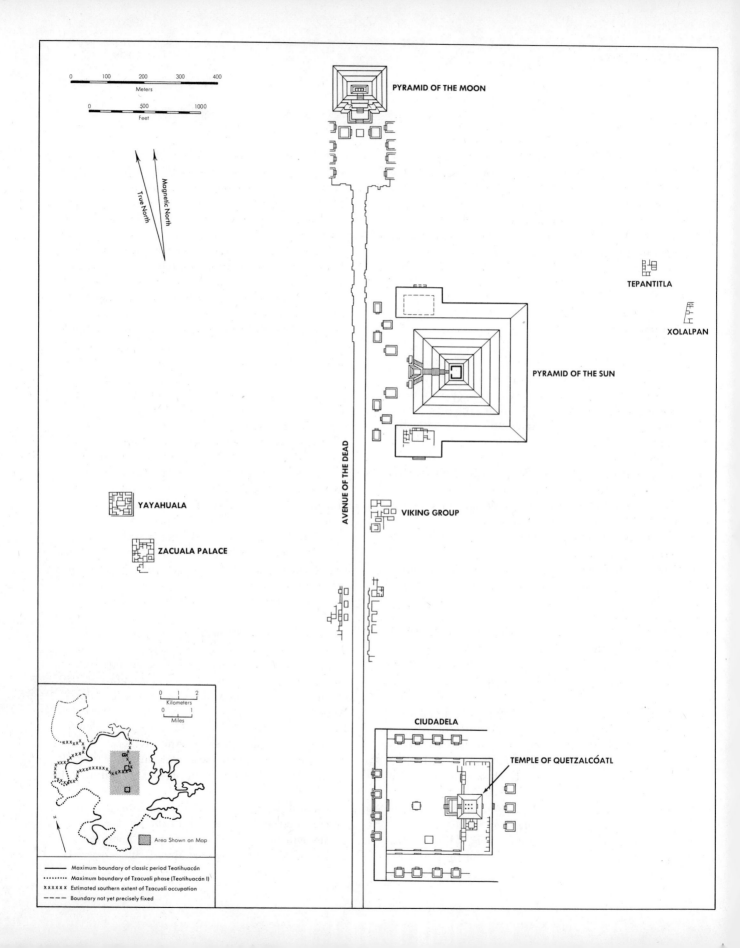

PYRAMID OF THE MOON

0 100 200 300 400
Meters

0   500   1000
Feet

Magnetic North

True North

TEPANTITLA

XOLALPAN

PYRAMID OF THE SUN

AVENUE OF THE DEAD

YAYAHUALA

ZACUALA PALACE

VIKING GROUP

CIUDADELA

TEMPLE OF QUETZALCÓATL

0 1 2
Kilometers

0   1
Miles

N

Area Shown on Map

————   Maximum boundary of classic period Teotihuacán
....   Maximum boundary of Tzacuali phase (Teotihuacán I)
xxxxxx   Estimated southern extent of Tzacuali occupation
– – – –   Boundary not yet precisely fixed

Figure 3-40. *Left:* Map of main ceremonial center of Teotihuacán, Valley of Mexico. Only principal buildings and certain other excavated structures are indicated. Such units as Tepantitla and Xolalpán are surrounded by many unexcavated ones; in fact, the area of the map is virtually a solid field of presumed "residential" units. See inset at lower left for relationship of this map to the total zone of Teotihuacán and for the respective sizes of the Teotihuacán I (Late Preclassic) and the total site occupation. (Redrawn and simplified from a map prepared by R. F. Millon, May 1964.)

Figure 3-43. Teotihuacán monumental sculpture, the so-called "Water Goddess." This figure stands over 3 meters high.

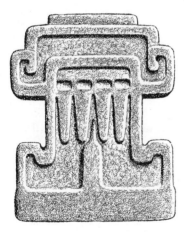

Figure 3-41. Monumental sculpture from Teotihuacán.

Figure 3-42. Teotihuacán monumental sculpture.

Figure 3-44. Detail of feathered serpent and Tlaloc (?) heads on Temple of Quetzalcóatl, Teotihuacán.

Figure 3-45. Wall painting from Teotihuacán, Tetitla section, Teotihuacán III phase, in various shades of red. (Courtesy Dumbarton Oaks pre-Columbian Collection.)

This enclosure, known as the Ciudadela, was possibly the principal or "royal" palace at Teotihuacán, and the pyramid standing within it is known as the Temple of Quetzalcóatl, or Temple of the Plumed Serpent.

Figure 3-46. Ground plans of a Xolalpán architectural assemblage at Teotihuacán, Valley of Mexico. *Left:* Plat map. *Right:* Artist's projection of same building. (After Linne, 1934.)

Some of the finest temple and palace art was rendered in mural painting rather than sculpture. One such painting in the building known as the "Temple of Agriculture" shows agricultural produce being apportioned among various deities. Other murals in palaces or courtyards of residences depict humans, gods, and animals in a naturalistic style.

Spreading out in all directions from the great pyramids and the heart of Teotihuacán are thousands of small constructions. Some of them, as in the Xolalpán section of the site, were designed as

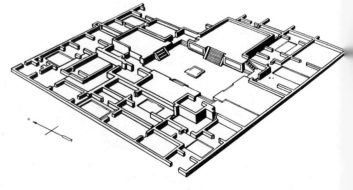

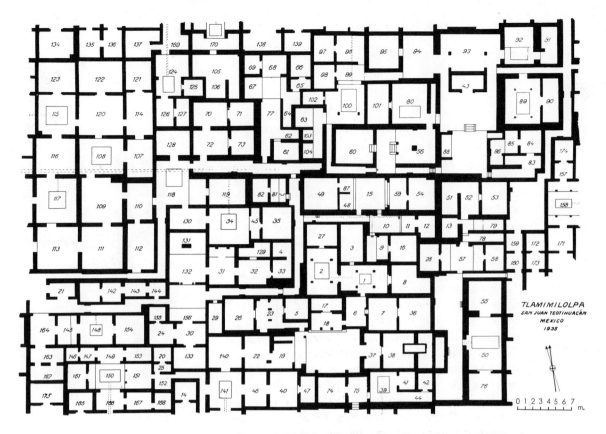

Figure 3-47. Ground plan of a Tlamimilolpa architectural assemblage at Teotihuacán, Valley of Mexico. (After Linne, 1942.)

Figure 3-48. A palace building at Teotihuacán, restored. The columns and porch-like feature are typical. (Courtesy Peabody Museum, Harvard University.)

courtyards with rooms arranged around a central sunken plaza in which an altar was often placed. In the Tlamimilolpa section of the site, massed conjoined rooms, rather than the courts, were the common pattern. The walls of these buildings were of rough unhewn stone and mud mortar with the surfaces covered with lime plaster. Walls were strengthened by wooden posts which also upheld roof beams. The function of these outlying buildings has not been determined. Some of the courtyards, particularly those with the wall paintings, seem rather elaborate for ordinary dwellings and might well have been palaces; but others, especially those of Tlamimilolpa, are such vast complexes of relatively small rooms that it seems likely that they were common domestic quarters.[44] Certainly the entire site of Teotihuacán, the great pyramids, the long concourse known sometimes as the "Avenue of the Dead," the Ciudadela and its enclosed temple, and the vast extension of courtyard-and-room complexes and other closely arranged apartments make the application of the term "city," by any definition, most appropriate.

The urban dimensions of the ruins of Teotihuacán imply a large population, both to build and
occupy it. Estimates have varied from 10,000 to
100,000 persons, and an intermediate figure seems
most likely. Since the immediate locale is rather
arid today, and has been dry for some time in the
past, archaeologists have argued that irrigation would have been necessary to have produced
the food to support such a population. No archaeological evidence of irrigation has been found so
far, but canal irrigation was utilized in later Postclassic times in the Valley of Mexico and may have
been practiced at Teotihuacán. Another possibility
is that small artificial islands constructed in Lake
Texcoco might have permitted intensive cultivation. Again, this technique traces to the Postclassic; but we have no definite proof of its being
employed during the Classic Period. However it
was done, the fact remains that Teotihuacán was
supported and that it was, indeed, a city.[45]

Teotihuacán Pottery and Manufactures.
Classic Period pottery at Teotihuacán reflected
past local Preclassic styles of the Valley of Mexico,
such as a red-on-buff tradition, but also featured
new wares and forms. Among the latter, appearing
in both Teotihuacán II and III phases, was Thin
Orange pottery, a useful descriptive term which
applies to a distinctive, thin-walled, fine-paste,
orange-fired ware that was usually used in annular-
based bowl or tall collared-jar shapes. Even more
distinctive was a Teotihuacán III style cylinder jar
with slab-shaped tripod legs and a knobbed lid.
This elegant shape was often decorated with carving or with painted layers of stucco applied after
the vessel was fired. The tripod cylinder jar was a
hallmark of Teotihuacán civilization and has been
found in such distant places as the Maya regions
of Guatemala, where it was traded and imitated
during the Early Classic Period. A tall, thin-necked
jar called a "florero," or "flower-jar," was another
typical Teotihuacán shape.

Figurines were common in both Classic Period
phases. Teotihuacán II examples were hand-made,
slit-eyed types which were not much different from

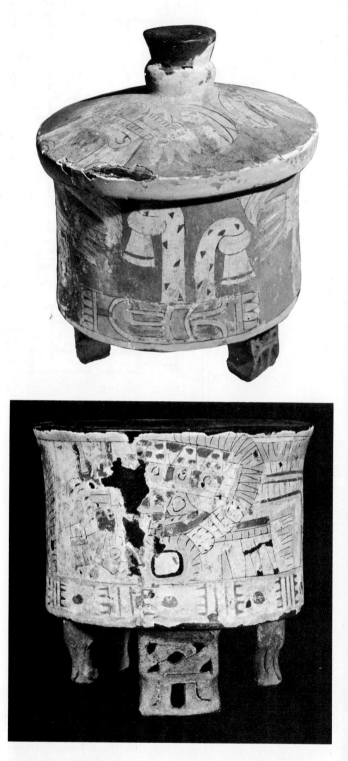

Figure 3-49. Teotihuacán III fresco-covered tripod cylinder
jars. The top specimen is about 20 cm. high; the other, about
14 cm. (Courtesy Dumbarton Oaks pre-Columbian Collection.)

Figure 3-50. *Above:* Teotihuacán pottery figurines. *a:* Teotihuacán II style. *b,d:* Typical Teotihuacán III mold-made "portrait-heads." *c:* Tlaloc head, mold-made, Teotihuacán III. *e:* Figurine mold. (Courtesy Cambridge Museum of Archaeology and Ethnology, England.)

Figure 3-51. *Left:* Teotihuacán III limestone mask. Height, about 25 cm. (Courtesy Dumbarton Oaks pre-Columbian Collection.)

some of their Preclassic prototypes. Teotihuacán III figurines are in a more distinctive mold-made tradition. They have a rather bland, naturalistic appearance and are sometimes called, inappropriately, "portrait heads." They resemble in style the life-size human faces or masks which were carved from onyx or other fine-grained stones and are also associated with Teotihuacán III.[46] (See Fig. 3-50*a,b,d.*)

115

The Influence of Teotihuacán. During the Early Classic Period, in the Teotihuacán III phase, prior to A.D. 600, Teotihuacán enjoyed its greatest splendor and influence. Undoubtedly, the Valley of Mexico was united under its leadership, with the large contemporary centers of Azcapotzalco and Portesuelo[47] as its tributaries and allies and the numerous smaller hamlets and villages in the valley providing additional support.[48] Beyond the Valley of Mexico, the great ceremonial center and the huge pyramid mound of Cholula reveal Teotihuacán influence, or else were constructed by a people with a similar culture.[49] Farther afield in Mesoamerica, it is not clear at just what geographical points Teotihuacán cultural and possibly political hegemony ceased and its ceramic and artistic elements persisted as mere evidences of influence or trade. Some archaeologists, such as A. V. Kidder, believe that Teotihuacán was a conquest state or an empire and that its influences were carried to such distant places as the Guatemalan Highlands by military might.[50] This thesis is supported at Kaminaljuyú in Guatemala by discoveries of Teotihuacán grave pottery and by the fact that the dominant temple pyramid architectural style of the Early Classic Period is fully Teotihuacán, with its tablero-talud architectural terraces (Figs. 3-52, 3-53). Some investigators have thought that in the Maya Lowlands Teotihuacán influence was exerted largely through pottery trade, but lately this opinion has been revised somewhat by the discovery of an Early Classic stela at Tikal which bears a Teotihuacán rather than a Maya style figure.[51] This stylistic intrusion into the very heart of Maya Classic ceremonial-center life would seem to indicate something more than casual trade relations. Although I would by no means interpret this as evidence of conquest, it is certainly testimony to the force and prestige of a civilization whose center lay 700 miles to the north.

The power and grandeur of Teotihuacán ended, suddenly, around A.D. 600, when the great city itself was destroyed, probably by northern barbarians who acculturated to a degree to Teotihuacán civilization and then destroyed it. The descendants of the conquerors lived for a time over the burned ruins of the former metropolis, but its great days were over. This event was the first of a chain of disturbances which brought down the several civilizations of the Mesoamerican Classic Period and opened the way for the rise of the later successor civilizations of the Postclassic. The next 200 or 300 years were an uneasy time in the Valley of Mexico. Hegemony, of a sort, probably passed to Cholula, in the neighboring valley, or to the smaller city of Azcapotzalco, in the Valley of Mexico on the opposite side of Lake Texcoco, where a Teotihuacán IV culture phase continued.[52] Subsequently, the next great power in Central Mexico arose at Tula, in Hidalgo, just north of the Valley, but the story of Tula and the Toltecs belongs to the Postclassic Period.

Ethnic Identification. Writing was practiced at Teotihuacán. A few glyphs have been found on pottery and in paintings. In style they suggest later Central Mexican picture writing rather than Maya hieroglyphs, and they indicate a knowledge of the ceremonial 260-day calendar but not the intricacies of the Maya Long Count. They do not furnish sufficient evidence on which to postulate that the ancient inhabitants of Teotihuacán spoke a Nahua language although this is a distinct possibility. There are, for instance, a number of similarities between Teotihuacán and Tula-Toltec ceramics and even iconography. The connection, however, may be rather indirect, merely reflecting a general Central Mexican heritage. The Totonacs and the Otomis have also been advanced as the descendants of the creators of Teotihuacán, but here, too, no sound proof exists. Like their great predecessors on the Mesoamerican scene, the Olmecs, the Teotihuácanos are to be identified only by their works.

The Classic Period Civilizations:
Lowland Maya

Introduction and Origins. The inception of the Classic Period in the Maya Lowlands is marked by hieroglyphic inscriptions, Long Count calendrical dates, a distinctive art style, certain ceramic types, and the corbeled masonry vault. The transition from Preclassic to Classic appears to have been gradual. During the Late Preclassic and Protoclassic centuries, ceremonial centers were constructed in the Maya Lowlands, and hieroglyphics and calendrics probably were known. Most likely, these were borrowed from the Olmec-Izapán tradition. Polychrome ceramics also appeared for the first time in the Protoclassic Period in such complexes as Holmul I. Perhaps the idea of polychrome painting came from the Guatemalan Highlands or from southern Central America; in any event, the style of the polychrome painting was typically of the Maya Lowland artistic tradition and seems to have developed locally. The corbeled vault, which is such an important feature of Lowland Maya architecture, appeared more or less simultaneously with these other traits and was also probably a local development. Thus, to understand the origin of Maya Lowland civilization is to see it neither as the import of a fully crystallized entity nor as a completely *sui generis* growth from the jungle plain. As Maya civilization it was assembled, formed, and set in the lowlands, but many of the elements that went into its development may be traced elsewhere.

Earliest discoveries indicate that the first settlers of the Maya Lowlands entered that subarea in Middle Preclassic times.[53] Quite likely these earliest immigrants spoke Mayan, and they may have come from the Maya Highlands or, possibly, from the adjoining Tabasco Lowlands. For several centuries they seem not to have been in the main currents of those Mesoamerican developments that were moving toward civilization, but toward the end of the Late Preclassic Period they were drawn into them. By A.D. 300 they had produced a brilliant and unique brand of Mesoamerican civilization.

Just where in the Maya Lowlands this civilization first crystallized is uncertain. Preclassic remains are found scattered throughout the area, and many of the later Classic ceremonial centers were built over earlier Preclassic and Protoclassic villages and mounds. The well-known centers of Uaxactún[54] and Tikal[55] in the northeastern Petén are such examples, as is Altar de Sacrificios[56] in the southwestern Petén, or Yaxuná[57] and Dzibilchaltún[58] far to the north in the Yucatán Peninsula. Among the greatest and oldest of the Classic Period centers, however, are those of the northeastern Petén—Tikal, Uaxactún, and such other important ruins as Nakum, Naranjo, Yaxhá, and Holmul. It may be that this area was a central hearth for the earliest spread of typically Lowland Maya writing, the Long Count calendar, art, architecture, and ceramics. Certainly during the Early Classic (A.D. 300–600) these elements of Maya civilization were diffused to, or colonized within, Maya-speaking communities of a Preclassic level of culture throughout the entire southern part of the Lowlands. For example, Classic architecture and hieroglyphics arose in the centers of the west, at Piedras Negras, Yaxchilán, Altar de Sacrificios, and Palenque on the Usumacinta drainage and in Chiapas. To the east, Maya civilization was established at Benque Viejo, Pusilha, and Lubaantún, all in British Honduras, and at Copán in Honduras. To the north, in the Yucatán Peninsula, such sites as Oxxkintok, Yaxuná, and Coba also fell under the influence of the Petén civilization. In Late Classic times, from A.D. 600 to 900, still more centers were constructed, and strong Maya influence extended all the way from the lower Usumacinta River in Tabasco at the northwest to the Ulua Valley in Honduras at the southeast.

Maya Sites and Settlement. The content of Maya Classic civilization is enormously rich and can be summarized here only in the

Figure 3-52. *Above, left:* Teotihuacán tablero-talud platforms after excavation and restoration.

Figure 3-53. *Above, right:* Cross-sectional diagram of tablero-talud architecture.

Figure 3-54. The temples of Tikal. *Left:* Two of the great temples rising above the rainforest jungle. *Right:* Temple I with terraces, stelae, and altars of the North Acropolis in the left foreground. (Courtesy University of Pennsylvania Museum.)

briefest fashion.[59] The ruins themselves are awe-inspiring in their magnificence and permanence. Abandoned for centuries, torn by tree roots and choked by jungle, they nevertheless retain the essence of their original purpose: to impress the beholder. They consist of large pyramidal mounds and platforms made of earth and rock fill, usually faced with cut limestone blocks set in lime mortar. Many of them are tremendously high and amaz-

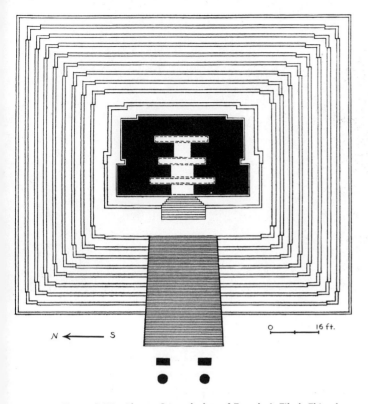

N ← S   0 ⊢─────┤ 16 ft.

Figure 3-55. *Above:* Ground plan of Temple I, Tikal. This plan shows the stepped, superimposed terraces of the pyramid; the stairs leading up the side of the pyramid to the summit platform; two stelae with associated altars at the foot of the stair; the massive masonry of the temple (in solid black); and the three, narrow, interconnected temple chambers. (After Tozzer, 1911.)

ingly steep. As examples, the great temple pyramids of Tikal rise tower-like to heights of over 60 meters above the plaza floors. The buildings which surmount the pyramids and platforms also were constructed of rubble fill and stone-block masonry. In some, as in the northern lowlands, the dressed-stone facings were no more than a veneer set in stucco. Walls of the buildings were thick and rooms were relatively narrow; roofs were vaulted with corbeled arches. Doors were usually small and windows very rare so that the interiors of those structures still intact are dark and cool. Small buildings, of from one to three rooms, placed on the tops of steep pyramids, likely were temples; longer and larger buildings, with many rooms, and set on lower, broader platforms, probably were palaces. The ball court, a Late Classic Period feature, was the other principal building type.

Figure 3-56. *Below:* Cross-section of Maya corbeled vaults. This particular construction is typical of northern Yucatán. *a:* Upper cornice. *b:* Medial cornice. *c:* Upper zone of building. *d:* Lower zone of building. *e:* Wooden lintels. *f:* Doorway to outer room. *g:* Doorway to inner room. *h:* Offset at spring of vault. *i:* Capstones to vault or false arch.

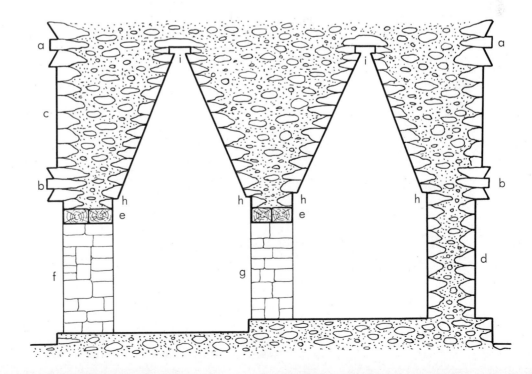

Figure 3-57. Classic Maya buildings and architectural features. *Above, left:* Temple of the Inscriptions at Palenque, Chiapas, Mexico. This structure covers a tomb which was built into the original ground level and was reached by a stairway descending through the floor. *Above, right:* Great corbeled arch at Labna, Yucatán, Mexico. *Facing page, left:* Hieroglyphic stairway at Copán, Honduras. *Right:* Ball court (restored) at Copán.

The basic plan of the Maya ceremonial centers, particularly in the southern lowlands, was a rectangular plaza enclosed on three or four sides by mounds. These plazas were often artificially dressed

Figure 3-58. Cross-sectional diagram of the Acropolis at Tikal, Guatemala. This drawing gives some idea of the numerous superimposed building levels and the deep accumulations of constructional fill that characterized great Mayan ceremonial centers of the Classic Period. (Courtesy University of Pennsylvania Museum.)

hilltops, as at Uaxactún, or terraced hillsides, as at Piedras Negras and Palenque. By successive layers of construction, the plaza unit gradually assumed the aspect of an acropolis, of which the famous "Main Group" at Tikal or the "Acropolis" of Copán are good examples. Carved stelae and altar stones were set up in the plazas, frequently at the feet of pyramid stairways. High above the plazas, the temples and palaces were ornamented with intricate roof-combs, flying facades, and carved and stucco-sculptured decoration.

The ceremonial centers were constructed and supported by sustaining populations of jungle farmers, but the archaeological record of this people is now only beginning to be set down. The ordinary Classic Maya dwellings were probably

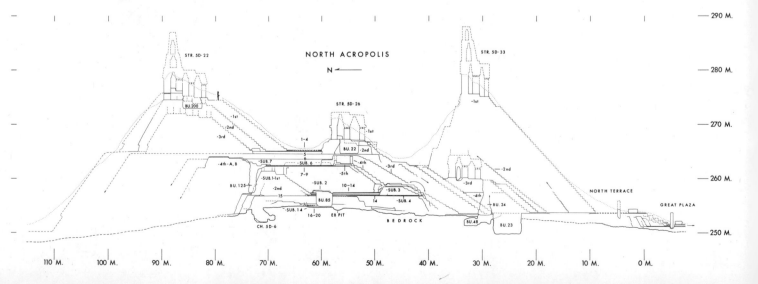

Figure 3-59. *Below:* The Maya ruin of Copán, Honduras. This site, with its courts, plazas, pyramids, platforms, stelae, and altars, is representative of Maya Classic Period ceremonial centers of the southern lowlands. (After Morley, 1920.)

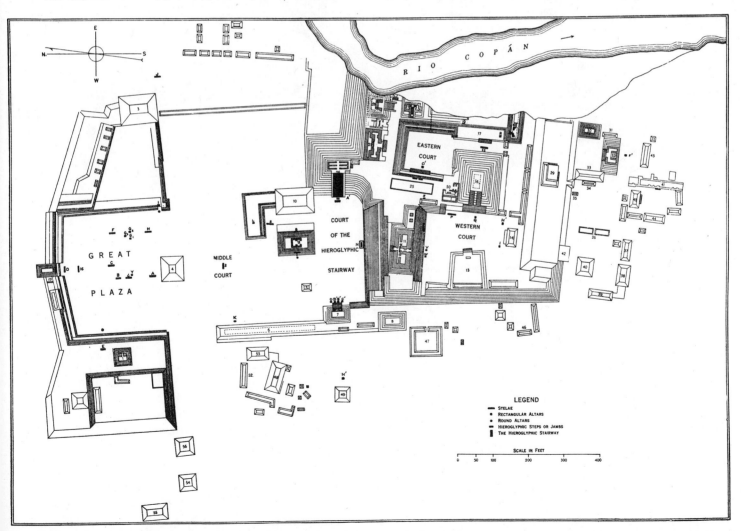

Figure 3-60. Prehistoric Maya house mounds and modern Maya houses. *Top, left:* House mounds at Barton Ramie, British Honduras. *Top, right:* Excavation of a house mound at Barton Ramie, showing interior stone-faced platforms and plaster floors. *Bottom, left* and *right:* Modern Maya houses with stone or pole walls and thatch roofs. Superstructures like these once stood on the platforms found in the house mounds. (*Top,* after Willey, Bullard, Glass, and Gifford, 1965; *bottom,* courtesy Peabody Museum, Harvard University.)

much like the wood, mud, and thatch huts of their historic or modern descendants, and such buildings have left little trace above ground. Fortunately, many of them were built on small platforms of earth or stone, and a number of these "house mounds" have been discovered and studied. These studies indicate that dwellings were not closely packed in and immediately around the ceremonial centers. Clusters of mounds have been found close to the main plazas and mounds of the centers, but equally large clusters were scattered along the river bottoms or around the edges of lakes and bajos (swamps) several kilometers removed from the ceremonial centers.[60] There are some debatable exceptions. Some archaeologists claim that Tikal in the Petén was truly urban in its proportions, as was Dzibilchaltún in northern Yucatán. But for the most part, the over-all settlement pattern of the Classic Maya was of scattered hamlets dotting

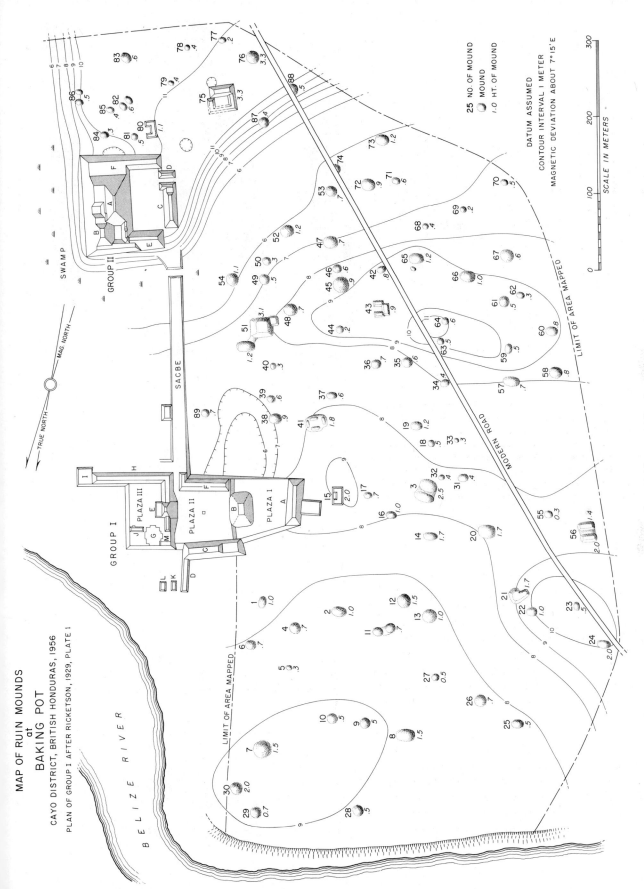

Figure 3-61. The Maya ceremonial center of Baking Pot, British Honduras, with surrounding house mounds. (After Willey, Bullard, Glass, and Gifford, 1965.)

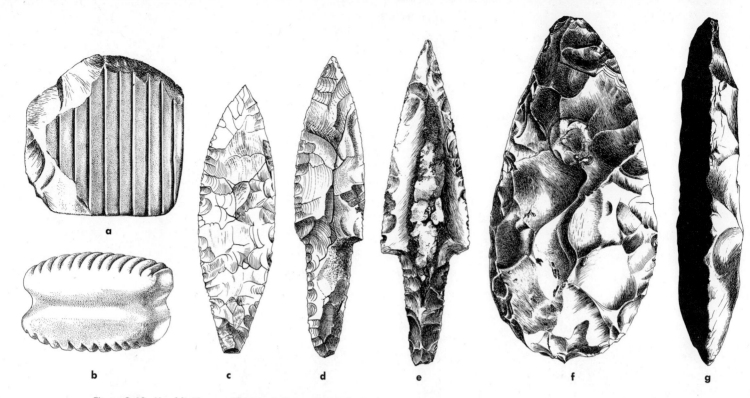

a b c d e f g

Figure 3-62. Humble Maya artifacts. *a.b:* Top and end views of a ground-stone bark-beater for making bark paper or cloth. *c:* Leaf-shaped chipped-stone projectile point. *d:* Long, stemmed projectile or spear point of chipped stone common to Maya Lowland Classic periods. *e:* Spear or dagger of chipped stone, unifacially flaked. *f,g:* Front and side views of the chipped-stone celt, the land-clearing implement of the jungle Maya. (After Willey, Bullard, Glass, and Gifford, 1965.)

most of the suitable farming land. Interspersed among these hamlets were minor ceremonial centers, and somewhat more distant from one another were the major centers with their elaborate architecture and monuments. Presumably, several hamlets coordinated their efforts to construct and maintain a minor ceremonial center, and in turn, the total populations tributary to such minor centers coalesced with other similar groups to support major centers.

Subsistence, Technology, and Crafts. The subsistence base of Maya society was simple. The Maya farmer cleared the jungle with stone tools and fire, planted his maize and bean crop, harvested the crop, and stored it. After two years of planting, a field was abandoned to the jungle and

another patch cleared; five years or so elapsed before the original plot was again used. Maya women ground the grain with metates and manos.

The extreme simplicity of Maya technological equipment contrasts sharply with the glories of the ceremonial center. Excavations in the centers and in the outlying hamlets have yielded only a few tool types. One of the most common implements is a chipped-stone celt about 15 centimeters long, 7 centimeters wide, 5 centimeters thick—bifacially chipped with blade at one end and

Figure 3-63. Maya basin metate and mano from a Late Classic Period level at Altar de Sacrificios, Guatemala. These implements, common to the Maya Lowlands, were used for corn-grinding.

Figure 3-64. Maya Early Classic pottery. a-c: Basal-flange bowls from Holmul, Guatemala. The polychrome bowl, b, and the black incised bowl, c, have scutate lids. d: A two-part effigy-censer from Tikal, Guatemala. e: Detail of polychrome vessel from Tikal, showing Teotihuacán-style Tlaloc face. f: Incised, slab-footed tripod cylinder jar with scutate lid, Tikal. (a-c, courtesy Peabody Museum, Harvard University; d-f, courtesy University of Pennsylvania Museum.)

pointed or blunted head, or poll, at the other. It may have been hafted either as an axe or as an adze and was the principal land-clearing tool and the principal cutting implement for dressing limestone blocks. In addition, numerous manos and metates for corn-grinding, projectile and lance points of flint, and little obsidian flake bladelets have been recovered. Although not abundant, grooved stone bark-beaters for making paper and polished stone celts were found in Maya sites.

In the minor arts and crafts the Maya were somewhat more spectacular than in their stone technology. Pottery was both painted and carved, and includes some of the finest decorated pieces of pre-Columbian America. Polychrome pottery usually was coated with an orange or buff slip, which

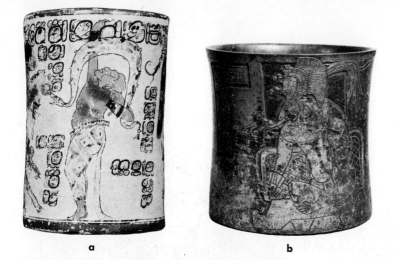

a   b

c

Figure 3-65. Maya Late Classic cylinder jars. a: Polychrome from Altar de Sacrificios, Guatemala. b: Carved slateware, Yucatán, Mexico. c: Polychrome from Nebaj, Alta Verapaz, Guatemala. (a, courtesy Peabody Museum, Harvard University; b, courtesy Dumbarton Oaks pre-Columbian Collection; c, courtesy British Museum.)

Pottery designs and the style in which they were rendered relate to, but by no means duplicate, the art of the great sculptures. Apparently, the great arts and the minor ones followed semi-separate traditions, and it is unlikely that they were practiced by the same individuals. Bowls, cylinder jars, and modeled incensarios were characteristic Maya

Figure 3-66. A Maya pottery figurine and a carved peccary skull. The figurine is from the Island of Jaina, Campeche, Mexico, and stands 41 cm. high; the skull (p. 127, *left*) was found at Copán, Honduras. Both date from the Late Classic Period. (Figurine, courtesy Dumbarton Oaks pre-Columbian Collection; skull, courtesy Peabody Museum, Harvard University.)

then was painted over with black-outlined designs of darker orange, red, white, or brown. Serpents, monkeys, birds, jaguars, humans, and grotesque beings were favorite decorative devices. Sometimes the pottery bore bands of glyphs, or pseudo-glyphs, arranged to form borders or decorative panels.

Figure 3-67. Maya jadeite carvings. *Left:* Small human figurine. *Right:* pendant. (Courtesy University of Pennsylvania Museum.)

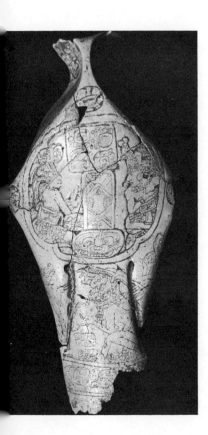

vessel forms. Many of our finest pottery specimens come from caches that often were interred with important persons who were buried in the mound tombs or beneath the plaza floors of the ceremonial centers. Less elaborate burials have been uncovered in the small houses. The versatile Maya craftsmen also fashioned pottery figurines, jadeite ear-plugs and beads, celt-shaped amulets, obsidian and flint "eccentric" forms often found in stelae caches, and also carvings of bone and shell (figurines, Fig. 3-67, *left;* pendants, Fig. 3-67, *right*). The Maya made bark paper for clothing and for books, or "codices." Cotton clothing also was worn. Gorgeous ceremonial costumes, as represented in murals or on painted pottery, appear to have been made of dyed textiles embellished with tropical bird feathers and jaguar pelts.

Art. Classic Maya great art is expressed in the media of full-round stone sculpture (as at Copán), in relief carvings in stone and on wooden lintels (as at Piedras Negras or Tikal), in stucco sculptures (Palenque), and in wall painting (Bonampak). Decoration was applied to roofcombs and facades of buildings, to room interiors, to cornices, moldings, and balustrades of buildings and mounds, and to free-standing stelae and

Figure 3-68. Classic Maya sculpture. *Above, left:* Stela B, Copán, Honduras, characteristic of the elaborate high-relief carving of that site. *Right:* A maize god bust, from Copán, a full-round sculpture. *Below, left:* Curious carved-stone monster figure from the building known as the "Reviewing Stand," Copán. *Right:* Stucco relief sculpture of a priest figure, Palenque, Chiapas, Mexico. (*Above, right* and *below, right,* courtesy British Museum; *below, left,* courtesy Peabody Museum, Harvard University.)

altars. A mask panel of mosaic carvings or stucco frequently adorned the exterior of structures. The panel bore a serpent head, highly stylized, and with various human, jaguar, and bird attributes and additions. Human figures of rulers, priests, soldiers, and captives sometimes were realistically portrayed. A great deal of Maya art also was bound up with god-representations and with hieroglyphic writing.

Religion. The religion of the ancient Mayas may be reconstructed from the monumental art of the ceremonial centers, from pre-Columbian

Figure 3-69. Maya wall paintings. *Left:* Treatment or torture of prisoners, from the interior wall of a building, Bonampak, Chiapas, Mexico. The original, brilliantly colored, dates from the Late Classic Period. The delineation of human figures was a high point in Maya art. *Right:* Rather crudely painted glyphs (?) and an Initial Series inscription painted on the wall of a tomb at Tikal, Early Classic Period. (*Left,* courtesy Peabody Museum, Harvard University; *right,* courtesy University of Pennsylvania Museum.)

Figure 3-70. Maya mask elements in architecture. *Left:* Stucco mask from pyramid of E-VII-Sub at Uaxactún, a structure dating from the Late Preclassic or Protoclassic Period. *Right:* Mosaic mask from a building at Labna, a structure dating from the Late Classic Period. (Courtesy Peabody Museum, Harvard University.)

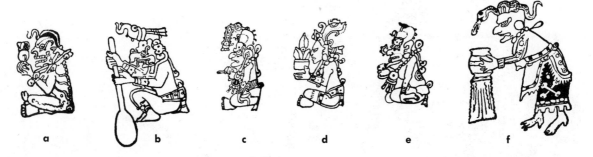

Figure 3-71. Some Maya gods of the codices. *a:* God A, death god. *b:* God B, Chac, or long-nosed god of Rain. *c:* God D, probably Itzamná. *d:* God E, the maize god. *e:* God G, the sun god. *f:* The goddess Ixchel. (Following Schellhas, 1904.)

manuscripts such as the Dresden Codex, from early native documents prepared by Spanish-educated Mayas, from sixteenth century accounts of Spanish priests, and from modern residues of the old religion which still exist in the context of local Catholic Christianity. Pervading the old Maya religion

was the idea of man's dependence on the gods. The gods, in their ordered universe, could be conciliated or won over, however, by prayer, fasting, and propitiation. Maya gods pertained primarily to time, to the cosmos, and to agriculture. They were often conceived of as coming in sets of four, or being, in effect, four beings in one, a concept related to the four cardinal directions. A powerful god, perhaps a sort of supreme deity, was designated as the "Long-nosed God" or, in the terminology of Paul Schellhas, "God B of the codices." This deity was represented as a man with a long, proboscis-like, pendant nose and a tongue (or teeth or fangs) hanging out in front or at the sides of the mouth. He was fashioned in contexts and with attributes of power and the natural elements, such as fire and rain. Frequently, he was associated with

Figure 3-72. The Maya gods in sculpture. *a:* The long-nosed god emerging from a serpent's jaws (Copán). *b:* The youthful head of the maize god emerges from a maize plant (Palenque). *c:* A small god figure emerges from a conch shell holding maize plant in which is the head of the maize god. (After Maudslay, 1889–1902.)

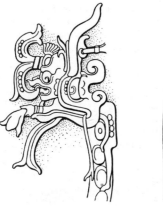

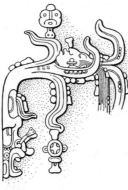

a   b   c

the serpent—arising from the serpent's open jaws or having the body of a serpent. This "God B" or "Long-nosed God" may have been the equivalent of Kukulcán, of the historic Mayas, and of the Central Mexican Quetzalcóatl. Perhaps another name for him was Itzamná, the lord of creation and the founder of civilization.[61]

Although "God B," Kukulcán, or Itzamná probably presided over the heavens and was the bringer of life-giving rain, the Maya pantheon included other rain gods as well, called Chacs. These gods also had snake-like attributes or associations, and they were usually conceived of in sets of four. Quite possibly they were older, simpler forms of the "God B" concept, or it may be that they were regarded as "assistants" or "workers" who were carrying out the will of the higher deity in providing rain.

Other deities included the maize god (Fig. 3-71d, 3-72b,c), a handsome young man who often appeared as an anthropomorphized ear of corn on a maize plant; "God G," the sun god (Fig. 3-71e), portrayed as a grotesque old man; "God A," (Fig. 3-71a) a skeletal "Lord of Death"; and another old man, "God D," (Fig. 3-71c), who may be the representation to be identified with Itzamná rather than God B; and the moon and maternity goddess, Ixchel (Fig. 3-71f).

Inasmuch as Maya hieroglyphic writing has not been completely translated, much of which they obviously have to tell us about the old Classic Period Maya religion remains unknown; and our understanding of Maya deities and supernatural beliefs has come to us through the medium of the late Postclassic and early historic Mexican-influenced Maya of Yucatán. Consequently, Maya religion as we reconstruct it may have been as much Central Mexican as it was Maya in its concepts and outlook. A real knowledge of a Maya pantheon of deities probably awaits translation of the hieroglyphs.

Religion, and the ceremonial centers, were undoubtedly directed by a highly organized priesthood, probably hereditary, at least in its top ranks. The high priests also presumably played a major

Figure 3-73. A Maya priest or dignitary treating with captives (?) from behind a god-mask, Yaxchilan. (After Maudslay, 1889–1902.)

role in government. Certainly they were custodians of the esoteric and scientific knowledge of the civilization. They were the astronomers, astrologers, and historians. They understood the hieroglyphic writing and manipulated the complex calendrical systems.

Hieroglyphics. The Maya hieroglyphs of the Classic Period compose the most advanced and complex system of embryonic writing of any Mesoamerican civilization. Glyphic texts were carved on the stelae or on temple walls and lintels, were modeled in stucco as building ornament,

Figure 3-74. Maya stela and hieroglyphs. *Above:* Stela 26, Tikal, Guatemala, an Early Classic Period monument. Only the feet of the priest dignitary still remain, but the hieroglyphic inscription on the side is beautifully preserved. *Below:* Detail of the inscription. (Courtesy University of Pennsylvania.)

and were incised on hand-sized objects such as jade, bone, or shell ornaments and painted on pottery and in books. The book specimens are unusually interesting. Three have come down *inter vivum* from early Conquest times. The best specimen, the Dresden Codex, is a screen-fold manuscript about 20 centimeters high and several meters long painted on lime-sized bark paper or cloth. According to J. E. S. Thompson, the Maya hieroglyphs combine simple phonetic and ideographic principles.[62] There was no alphabet, and no fully adequate key for their translation, which explains why only about 25 per cent of them have been translated. The glyphs themselves are fantastically grotesque— human, monster, or deity head forms for the most part. In context, affixes were appended to principal glyphic elements. In Thompson's opinion, Maya hieroglyphics treated wholly of time, astronomy, astrology, gods, and ceremonies. Proskouriakoff, on the other hand, feels that some texts dealt with more mundane matters of dynastic succession and other specific human historical events.[63]

Calendrics. The Classic Maya shared certain calendric notions and principles with other Mesoamerican peoples, but they were the outstanding elaborators in this intellectual field. They possessed the sacred 260-day calendar, the tzolkin, presumably an ancient Mesoamerican development. Its Aztec equivalent was the tonalpohualli. The 260-day calendar corresponds to no natural astronomical phenomena; it is, rather, a pure invention. It works on a permutation principle of 13 numbers and 20 day names which revolve about each other so that the same number and name recur in combination every 260 days. The tzolkin was closely allied to ritual and to divination. The Maya were also cognizant of the solar year of 365-plus days, which they had organized into 18 months of 20 days each plus a period of 5 extra days. The permutation of the 260-day tzolkin and the 365-day true year, rotating on each other cogwheel fashion—to use a figure of speech which surely would have been alien to the Maya mind— produced the calendar round, or 52-year cycle.

132

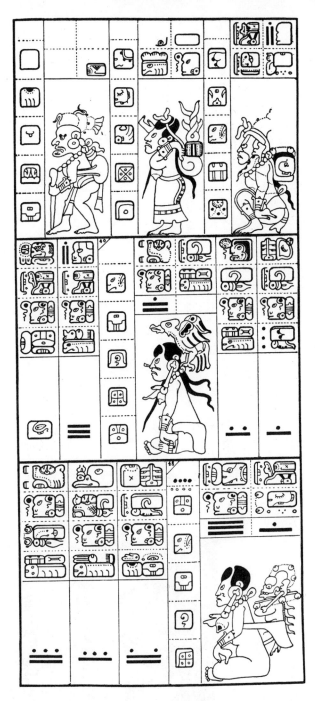

Figure 3-75. Above: Maya hieroglyphs, a page from the Dresden Codex. (After Gates, 1932.)

Figure 3-76. Top, right: Maya hieroglyphs, the day signs in the inscriptions. (After Morley, 1915.)

Figure 3-77. Bottom, right: Maya hieroglyphs, the day signs in the codices. (After Morley, 1915.)

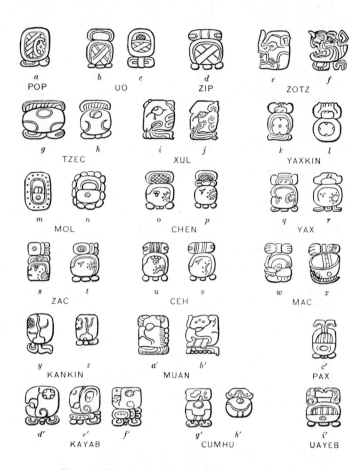

Figure 3-78. *Above, left:* Maya hieroglyphs, month signs in the inscriptions. (After Morley, 1915.)

Figure 3-79. *Above, right:* Initial Series date from Stela A at Copán, Honduras. The date, read from top to bottom, and left to right, begins, below the introducing Glyph, with the Baktun Glyph surmounted by the bar-and-dot coefficient for 9. To the right of this is the Katun Glyph and the number 14. Continuing below, in order, the reading is 19 Tuns, 8 Uinals, and 0 Kins. (After Morley, 1915, Plate 7 and pp. 169–170.)

That is, a complete cycle of all the variations of the day names and numbers of the tzolkin and the month names and day positions of the true year was run through in the least common multiple of 260 and 365, this being 18,980 days or 52 true years. Two other Maya calendars presuppose extremely careful and long-term astronomical observations and recordings. One of these, a lunar calendar, was based on the 29-and-a-fraction days between two successive new moons. The other, a

Venus calendar, integrated five 584-day revolutions of the planet Venus with eight 365-day solar years. The Dresden Codex dealt with both lunar and Venus calendars.

Most impressive of all as a feat of calendrics, and also most important for archaeological dating, is the Maya Long Count, or Initial Series, calendar. The Long Count calendar essentially involved counting days from a mythical starting point in the past. It was based on astronomical knowledge, place enumeration and notation, a concept of zero, and a counting system based on the number 20. Long Count inscriptions on stelae read from top down and from left to right. Hieroglyphs indicated the time period units of the system and bars, signifying 5, and dots, representing 1, served as numerals. The units of time, in descending order, were the baktun of 144,000 days, the katun of 7,200 days, the tun of 360 days, the uinal of 20 days, and the kin of 1 day—successive multiples of 20 except the tun, which was comprised of 18 uinals, apparently to approximate the true year. A Maya Long Count date, which we express as 9.14.19.8.0,

refers to a date which is $9 \times 144{,}000$ plus 14×7200 plus 19×360 plus 8×20 plus 0×1 days from the calendrical starting point in the past. This starting point in the past was fixed at 3113 B.C. in the Goodman-Martinez-Thompson correlation of Maya and Christian calendars, and approximately 260 years earlier than this date in the Spinden correlation.

The earliest Maya stela Long Count date is from Tikal. It falls in the twelfth katun of the eighth baktun (8.12.14.8.15) and has a Christian calendrical equivalent of A.D. 292 in the Good-

Figure 3-80. Maya stelae from Tikal, Guatemala. *Far left* (p. 134): The Initial Series inscription on Stela 29, the earliest stela date in the Maya Lowlands. Below the Introducing Glyph, the Baktun coefficient of 8 has been partially obliterated. The date reads as 8.12.14.8.15, or A.D. 292 in the Goodman-Martinez-Thompson correlation. *Left* (p. 135): A Teotihuacánoid Tlaloc-faced figure on Stela 32, Early Classic Period. *Center:* Ornate priest figure in Early Classic style, Stela 31. *Right:* Stela 22, Late Classic Period, with an Initial Series date of 9.17.0.0.0, or A.D. 771. (Courtesy University of Pennsylvania Museum.)

man-Martinez-Thompson correlation. The most recent Maya Long Count stela date is 10.3.0.0.0 or A.D. 889. These dates bracket the Maya Classic Period.

You will recall that in our discussion of the Preclassic Period we indicated that a few 7 baktun bar-and-dot dates were associated with non-Maya cultures of the latter part of that period. Thus, it would appear that the Maya did not invent this particular calendar but refined and developed it.

The correlation of Maya and Christian calendars is an extremely complex problem and has long been studied by archaeologists, epigraphers, astronomers, and mathematicians.[64] The great difficulty is that the Long Count system was discarded shortly after the Maya date 10.3.0.0.0. At the time of the Spanish entry into Yucatán, a Short Count calendar was in use, and some observations were made on this calendar by Bishop Diego de Landa. Specifically, Landa noticed the similarities between dates in the native calendar in use at that time and current Christian calendar dates. The problem that remained was to integrate the Maya Short Count of the sixteenth century with the earlier Long Count. This has been accomplished in several ways, but the two most satisfactory correlations are one which equates the Christian year 1539 with the katun ending 11.16.0.0.0, and another which equates the Christian year 1536 with the katun ending 12.9.0.0.0. The former, properly designated as the 11.16.0.0.0 correlation, is more frequently referred to as the Goodman-Martinez-Thompson correlation, as we have already mentioned. The 12.9.0.0.0 correlation is known as the Spinden correlation. To date, the question is still in doubt. Either eventually may be proved correct, or still another correlation may turn out to be the right one. Radiocarbon dates on wooden lintels and other specimens taken from Classic Maya sites have not been conclusive on this matter, but at the present time a series of carbon tests from Tikal strongly support the Goodman-Martinez-Thompson position.[65] We have followed this correlation which, by archaeological extension, is applied to all of Mesoamerican chronology.

Regional and Chronological Diversity. To think that Maya civilization was uniform—an impression forced by such a rapid survey—is grossly misleading. Each of the famed "cities," or centers, had its special quality: the grandeur of Tikal, the Athenian classicism of Copán, the distinctive architecture and pure beauty of Palenque. These characteristics savor of ethnocentrism, a belief on the part of the inhabitants that their particular "city-state" was superior to all others.

The city-state concept seems most appropriate to what we may reconstruct of the social and political structure of ancient Maya civilization. Each major civic-religious center thus would have exercised hegemony over subsidiary centers and supporting hamlets. Relationships with other major centers would have been maintained by the priests, so that hieroglyphics and calendrics were harmonized and similar deities were worshipped. Architectural and artistic patterns and vogues must have followed along these same pathways of intercommunication, but the similarities in these fields are less striking than in writing and time-counting. On the more mundane levels of ceramics and small artifacts, the site-to-site and region-to-region similarities are less apparent. The concept of "empire" has been evoked to explain the resemblance in the hierarchical aspects of culture throughout the Maya Lowlands, but a better example is probably something like the spread of Islam or early Christianity among peoples who already shared a common language and basic culture.

The most striking regional difference in Maya Lowland culture was between south and north. In the Early Classic Period, probably as a result of the relatively rapid spread of many Classic elements, the difference was not so pronounced. Later, however, divergent styles and traditions appeared in Yucatán. For example, Long Count calendrical dates were discarded in the north and hieroglyphic inscriptions became rare. In architecture, the late peninsular styles depended on concrete rubble and thin block veneer construction rather than heavy block masonry, and in these same styles there was less monumental naturalistic art and a greater emphasis on mosaic facade decoration and highly conventionalized designs. Southern pottery continued in a gloss ware and polychrome tradition, whereas in Yucatán "slate wares" (pottery with a well-fired, hard paste and a thick, non-glossy slip) became the vogue and ceramic decoration was mostly carved.

In the southern lowlands a number of chronological trends distinguish Early and Late Classic Maya culture. For example, in architecture the outstanding Early Classic buildings were temples of one to three rooms perched on the tops of high, steep pyramids. In the Late Classic, although such temples were still being built, the dominant architectural type was the larger, multi-roomed palace which was placed on a relatively wider and lower platform mound. Also, in the Early Classic the dedicatory stelae were small monuments bearing brief hieroglyphic inscriptions and dates. During the Late Classic, on the other hand, the stelae were larger and inscribed with longer texts and more complex dates. In sculptural art, too, the trend was from the relatively simple and chaste to the over-elaborate, with an increasing tendency to fill all space with decorative detail. In ceramics, the pottery of the Early Classic, known as Tzakol style, featured basal-flanged bowls with geometric or naturalistic band decorations of polychrome. Late Classic Tepeu style potters abandoned the basal-flanged bowl form and turned their talents instead to fashioning some of the finest decorated ware of the period—polychrome cylinder jars painted with life scenes of dignitaries, gods, or animals, and occasionally ringed with hieroglyphic bands. During the Tzakol, or Early Classic, ceramic phase, the Teotihuacán lidded tripod jar made its appearance. Pottery figurines, which were rare during the Classic, occurred much more frequently during the Late Classic. These late Classic specimens were mold-made, usually as hollow whistles in human and animal shapes.

These Early and Late Classic Periods are divided by a curious brief break which is recorded all through the southern lowlands and lasted from the Maya Long Count dates of 9.5.0.0.0 to 9.8.0.0.0, or over a span of between 40 to 60 years. Very few stelae were erected during this time, and ceremonial construction appears to have ceased. What actually happened or what caused this hiatus is a mystery, nor can we be certain that all centers in the south were affected. Possibly the fall of the Teotihuacán civilization at approximately this time may have been felt in distant Guatemala. At least we know that Teotihuacán influences disappeared from Maya centers in the lowlands following this break. Soon thereafter, however, the arts and architecture were resumed with new vigor, the Maya Long Count calendar was resurrected, and during the next 300 years Maya civilization reached its peak.

Then, at the close of the ninth century A.D., the construction of ceremonial centers, the carving of dated stelae, and other artistic endeavors ceased throughout the whole southern half of the Maya Lowlands and were never resumed. Archaeologists once considered this event as marking the end of what was known as the Maya "Old Empire" and assumed that at this time the populations of the south moved northward into Yucatán to found the so-called "New Empire" of the Puuc, Rio Bec, Chenes, and related sites. S. G. Morley was

Figure 3-81. The Palace at Sayil, Yucatán, magnificent example of Puuc style architecture. Notice both the doorway columns and the false columns or colonnettes.

Figure 3-82. The palace at Xpuhil, an architectural reconstruction of a building in the Rio Bec style. (After Proskouriakoff, 1946.)

an advocate of this view.[66] J. E. S. Thompson, on the other hand, holds that the flowering of the Puuc, Rio Bec, and Chenes centers was contemporaneous with the Late Classic Period in the south, and that these centers, too, were abandoned at the same time that the centers in the south were deserted.[67]

Quite recently, E. W. Andrews has claimed support for the Morley position in his excavations at Dzibilchaltún in northern Yucatán. According to Andrews, the new data indicate that the Puuc-Rio Bec-Chenes centers flourished after the close of the Tepeu ceramic phase and the southern Late Classic developments.[68] The controversy cannot be resolved on the basis of present information, but for now I am inclined to accept Thompson's[69] chronological alignment and to set the abandonment of such northern centers as Sayil, Kabah, and Uxmal as simultaneous with, or no more than a century later than, the desertion of the south. This interpretation is best accommodated to the 11.16.0.0.0 correlation of native and Christian calendars, whereas the Andrews interpretation is somewhat more compatible with the 12.9.0.0.0 correlation; however, either correlation can be made to fit with either relative dating alignment.

The Maya Decline. The causes of the rapid decline—or, possibly, two declines—of the ceremonial centers of Maya Classic civilization remain a mystery. Various theories have been proposed. Epidemic diseases, such as yellow fever or malaria, is one of these;[70] but both yellow fever and malaria are probably post-Columbian imports to America. Nor is there convincing evidence of sudden and violent natural catastrophes such as earthquakes or devastating droughts. Gradually worsening crop failures and food shortages seem somewhat more plausible. One such explanation regards slash-and-burn farming, with its constant cutting and burning of forest cover, as the villain. This method of land-clearing, so the argument goes, produced man-made savannas covered with tough grass that could not be tilled by native digging-stick methods.[71] But milpa practices have been used in Central America for several centuries in historic time and have not produced savanna lands. The latter, as they are interspersed through the forests of the Petén, appear to be natural rather than man-made.[72] According to a different theory, Classic Period population pressure made intensive farming, rather than the slash-and-burn method, necessary, which denuded the land of its finest top soils;[73] but intensive cultivation in the Petén or Yucatán is impossible today without fertilizers and probably was impossible in the past. A third hypothesis assumes that the tropical soils of the Maya Lowlands were, from the beginning, inadequate to support dense populations, that Maya civilization developed elsewhere and was brought to the Lowlands, and that its history there was one of slow but steady death.[74] Yet soil chemists tell us that Maya Lowlands soils are not inherently poor. Although not the best, they are by no means the worst for primitive cultivation.[75] Still a fourth hypothesis sees the rivers and lakes of the Petén gradually drying up and a general water shortage causing the abandonment.[76] But this could hardly have been the case, because such rivers as the Usumacinta or the Belize did not dry up, and Maya centers along the banks were deserted as well as the more centrally located Petén sites.

Figure 3-83. Maya architecture at Chichén Itzá and Uxmal, Yucatán. *Above, left:* View along one side of the great Maya-Toltec ball court at Chichén Itzá, showing stone ring in side wall and building at end of court. *Above, right:* The House of the Governors at Uxmal, showing a massive corbeled vault and a typical Puuc style mosaic frieze above the medial molding. *Below, left:* Another view of the House of the Governors, with the Adivino, or House of the Magician, on the pyramid in the distance. *Below, right:* The Monjas, or Nunnery, quadrangle, Uxmal. (Courtesy Peabody Museum.)

Figure 3-84. Maya-Toltec and Puuc style architecture at Chichén Itzá, Yucatán. *Top to bottom:* 1. The Temple of the Warriors and associated colonnade, a Toltec-influenced Maya building, partially restored. 2. The Castillo, a Toltec-influenced pyramid and surmounting temple with ascending stairs on all four sides; the pyramid face and temple have been restored. 3. The handsome Monjas, dating from the pre-Toltec occupation. 4. A close-up view of the Monjas; notice the Maya mask elements on the corner of the upper frieze and above the doorway on the left. (Courtesy Peabody Museum, Harvard University.)

Social and political factors provide a more plausible explanation of the Maya collapse. First, we know from a count of ceremonial centers and from house mound studies that population increased during the Classic, particularly in the last 300 years.[77] Even without climatic or climatic-agricultural disasters, a large and growing population was bound to have placed a burden on the productive capacities of both land and man. Second, while the population was expanding, wars and tribal dislocations were brewing all over Mesoamerica. These had started with the fall of Teotihuacán at the end of the sixth century A.D., and then seem to have rolled steadily southward. We know that the Maya Late Classic centers of both the Usumacinta Valley and Yucatán were under Mexican influences, and at Altar de Sacrificios a Late Classic Tepeu-like phase shows strong ceramic and figurine elements of Mexican style.[78] In this connection, Thompson has suggested that the adoption of Mexican militaristic attitudes and beliefs, and the infiltration of such things as the alien cult of human sacrifice into Maya religion, would have been enough to produce internal dissension between Maya priest-leaders and peasantry.[79] Finally, we know that Mexican peoples did invade both Yucatán and western cities such as Altar de Sacrificios.

We have in all these elements sufficient troubles to have brought about a crisis. If peasant confidence in the old aristocratic leadership was lost, it is not surprising that the old life in the centers—religion, ceremony, the arts, and intellectual life—disappeared for lack of support. During this dissolution, which occurred in less than 100 years, peasant populations could have continued to live for a time in the localities of the abandoned centers, and some archaeological evidence from Tikal[80] and from the Belize Valley[81] suggests that they did. But the intricate structure of Classic Maya society was broken up, and the old patterns of its theocratic civilization were drastically modified or destroyed.

Whatever the causes, the Maya decline remains the mystery of Mesoamerican archaeology.

Other Civilizations of the Classic Period

The Gulf Coast. We left the story of the Gulf Coast with the rise of the Olmec-derived styles and ceremonial centers of the Late Preclassic Period. Tres Zapotes and Cerro de las Mesas, both in southern Veracruz, were such centers; and both continued to be occupied throughout the Classic Period and later. The Classic Period phases at these two centers were under strong Teotihuacán influence, as the slab-footed tripod cylinder jars, candelero vessels, and style of the mold-made figurines attest. Cerro de las Mesas was undoubtedly a very important "capital," and among the stone monuments from the site are two stelae with bar-and-dot numerals and Long Count dates reading A.D. 468 and 533.[82]

The outstanding civilization of the Mexican Gulf coastal plain during the Classic Period was not, however, in the south but in the Central Veracruz subarea. This was the Classic Veracruz civilization and style, of which the principal ceremonial center is El Tajín, near Papantla. El Tajín lies in a small valley among low, jungle-covered hills into which its pyramids, platforms, palaces, and ball courts are packed closely. Most famous of these structures is the Temple of the Niches in which the six terrace faces of the pyramid are inset with 365 masonry niches. Tajín architecture utilized the corbeled vault and roof-comb inventions of the Lowland Maya and may have borrowed them from the region of the Puuc in Yucatán. Tajín was built and flourished largely in the Classic Period, particularly the Late Classic, but it also continued as an important center through the early part of the Postclassic Period, to perhaps as late as A.D. 1200.[83] Although Tajín has been linked with the Totonac nation by some ethnohistorians and archaeologists, this identification cannot be proved. History and archaeology do indeed converge on the Totonac but much later, on the Spanish Conquest horizon in the Postclassic site of Cempoala.

Figure 3-86. Temple of the Niches, Tajín, Veracruz, Mexico. (Courtesy Peabody Museum, Harvard University.)

The Classic Veracruz style, as represented at Tajín and elsewhere, exhibits Olmec and Izapán strains and was probably derived from these earlier Gulf Coast styles.[84] Serpents, jaguars, frogs, and humans were its central motifs, and these were set within very ornate and intricate interlaced ribbon-scrolls. In fact, the ornamental embellishment

Figure 3-87. *Below:* Slate mirror back, Veracruz style; reflecting surface set with pyrites. (Courtesy Dumbarton Oaks pre-Columbian Collection; photograph by Nickolas Muray.)

Figure 3-85. *Above:* Stela 6, from Cerro de las Mesas, Veracruz, Mexico. The Initial Series in the column at the left is read as 9.1.12.14.10 1 Oc 3 Uayeb. (Redrawn from Stirling, 1943.)

dominated the iconographic themes. Carvings in this style decorate architectural features at Tajín, but the art also was lavished on carved-stone mirror-backs, "yokes," "palmas," and "hachas." The yokes, palmas, and hachas probably represent stone replicas of wooden paraphernalia used in the ceremonial ballgame.[85] Yokes, which are large horseshoe-shaped affairs, were worn around the waist of the players as protective belts and the long, thin, paddle-shaped palmas were apparently fitted into the fronts of these belts. Just what function the hachas performed is less certain; perhaps they were court markers or scoring devices used in the game. These hachas, or "thin-stone heads" as they are sometimes called, are approximately life-sized human heads or faces in profile. They were widely traded in southern Mesoamerica over routes that extended far beyond the borders of Central Veracruz into the Isthmus of Tehuantepec and down the Pacific coast of Guatemala.[86]

It may well be that the Mesoamerican ballgame was invented in Veracruz or at least along the Gulf Coast. The region apparently is a natural habitat for rubber trees. The ball employed in the

Figure 3-88. Elaborately carved stone yokes, Classic Veracruz style, measuring about 40 cm. in length. (*Top,* courtesy Dumbarton Oaks pre-Columbian Collection; *bottom,* courtesy American Museum of Natural History.)

Figure 3-89. Classic Veracruz style sculpture. *a,b:* Obverse and reverse sides of two ornately carved palmate stones. *c:* Panel carving from the largest ball court at Tajín, Veracruz, Mexico. (After Proskouriakoff, 1954.)

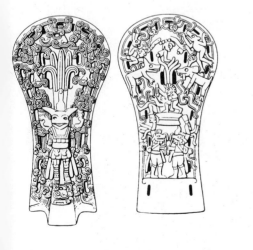

a   b   c

Figure 3-90. Thin stone heads, or "hachas," from Veracruz. The specimens are, respectively, about 18 and 35 cm. high. (*Left*, Courtesy British Museum; *right*, courtesy Dumbarton Oaks pre-Columbian Collection.)

Figure 3-91. "Smiling face" pottery head from Veracruz. (Courtesy American Museum of Natural History.)

game was made from rubber, and the game has a long history in Veracruz. Although the stone ball courts date only to the Classic Period, the yokes have been found in earlier contexts. A fragment of one, for example, came from a Middle Preclassic Period level at the Trapiche site in Central Veracruz.[87] Certainly from the Classic Period on the game was very popular in Veracruz. Seven ball courts were constructed at El Tajín alone.

Before leaving Veracruz, we should mention the so-called "smiling-heads," distinctive, hollow, mold-made figurines of men, women, ball players, and warriors characterized by smiling or grinning countenances. This type of figurine has long been associated with the Ranchito de las Animas collections,[88] and more recently it has been identified with the large and important site of Remojadas, near the city of Veracruz.[89] Here the heads are of

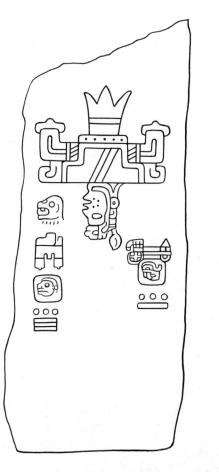

Figure 3-92. Monte Albán stela, Monte Albán II phase.
(After Caso, 1947.)

Preclassic origin, although the tradition reached its zenith in the Late Classic Period. Their distribution tends to be concentrated in the southern part of the subarea, south of Tajín. Like the builders of Tajín, the makers of these figurines have also been identified as Totonacs; but again, this represents only speculation.

Monte Albán. Contemporaneous with Classic Period Teotihuacán, the Maya, and Tajín was the great Oaxacan center of Monte Albán. Almost certainly, Monte Albán civilization was Zapotecan. The lines of stylistic continuity extend

unbroken from the historic Zapotec back to Classic Period phases and even into the underlying Preclassic levels at the site. These Preclassic levels, you will remember, are of the Monte Albán I phase, from which we described early hieroglyphs and numerals in our discussion of the Preclassic Period. Monte Albán II was a phase of the Protoclassic Period during which this presumably Zapotecan society shared in the general currents of ideas that were moving through southern Mesoamerica. Significant similarities existed, for instance, between the Monte Albán II ceramics and those of the Protoclassic Maya phases, such as Holmul I. In Monte Albán III, influences from Classic Teotihuacán are the most pronounced of any foreign styles, but the local civilization flowered essentially independently.

The Monte Albán site is located on a mountain spur which overlooks the fertile Valley of Oaxaca.[90] Its agricultural support undoubtedly came from numerous small sites in the valley bottomlands. Monte Albán seems primarily to have been a ceremonial or civic-religious center, but hundreds of small house platforms dot the slopes of the main hill on which the principal temples and palaces are situated, so that it is probably fair to say that the site was in process of becoming an urban center as well. The main buildings on the hill summit are extremely impressive. The entire hilltop has been leveled and dressed, creating a plaza that measures 300 by 200 meters, and this plaza is surrounded on four sides by platforms, pyramids, temples, and a ball court. In the center of the complex are three more large mounds. Construction is of fill and dressed-stone facings, and the general appearance of the mounds and buildings resembles Teotihuacán in the rather plain, severe lines that are broken only by tablero-talud type terraces and panels. There are at Monte Albán, however, some Classic Period stelae carved with figures and hieroglyphs. Classic Period tombs with either flat or corbeled vaults were placed in the terraces of platforms or under patios. Some of these tombs bear interior frescoes of gods, men, and hieroglyphic inscriptions.

Classic Period ceramics were primarily polished gray pieces, engraved and incised, and included spouted jars, cylinder jars, floreros, and candeleros. Particularly interesting are the intricately and heavily ornamented urns which were placed in graves.[91] This urn form originated in the earlier Preclassic phases at Monte Albán. Seated gods, hand-sculptured in clay, were modeled on the side of the urn. These representations depicted such deities as Cocijo, lord of the rain and alter ego of the Central Mexican Tlaloc, a maize god, and a feathered-serpent, or Quetzalcóatl counterpart. In

Figure 3-93. Monte Albán, with part of the Valley of Oaxaca in the background. (Courtesy Instituto Nacional de Antropología e Historia de Mexico.)

pottery, such shapes as the florero and candelero and the Thin Orange ware we have already described reveal Teotihuacán influences. That Monte Albán IIIA and Classic Teotihuacán were contemporaneous is also attested by the mingling of the two pottery styles at other sites, including Yucuñudahui in Oaxaca and Tehuacán in Puebla.[92]

The hieroglyphic and calendrical material from the Monte Albán Classic Period trace, as we mentioned, to the earlier Preclassic phases of the site. The early glyphs seem to have been day

Figure 3-94. A view over the main plaza of Monte Albán, Oaxaca, Mexico. (Courtesy Instituto Nacional de Antropología e Historia de Mexico.)

signs (tiger-like animals, monkey heads, serpents) accompanied by numbers and human- and bird-head glyphs. Another popular glyph form was a trapezoidal bar (interpreted as the symbol for "hill" or, perhaps, "ceremonial center" or "town") from which hung the inverted profile of a human head (Fig. 3-92). These were dated and contained other symbols, and Caso believes that they record the tale of a conquered city and its defeated king. The Monte Albán III inscriptions, which reflect the same tradition, were carved in stone and inscribed on modeled burial urns and on wall paintings in tombs. As with the Maya hieroglyphic system, very little else but calendrical information has been deciphered.[93]

The Monte Albán IIIB phase corresponds to the Late Classic Period, A.D. 600–900, during which the center continued to thrive. After the latter date it was abandoned except as a place of burial for Zapotecan or Mixtecan groups of the Postclassic Period.

The Guatemalan Highlands. The great center of Kaminaljuyú, in the Guatemalan Basin, although geographically farther from Central Mexico than Monte Albán, was more profoundly influenced by Teotihuacán, so much so that, as we mentioned, some investigators believe that the Guatemalan Highlands actually were conquered by a Teotihuacán group. This invasion may very well have been the blow which brought about the eclipse of the earlier Preclassic cultures of the Highlands, although the earlier of the two Early Classic Period phases at Kaminaljuyú, the Aurora, was more Mayan than Teotihuacán.[94] Not until the succeeding Esperanza phase did Teotihuacán

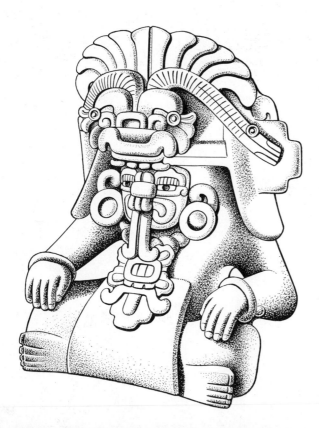

Figure 3-95. *Top:* A Monte Albán III phase tomb, with urn in niche above doorway. (Courtesy Instituto Nacional de Antropología e Historia de Mexico.)

Figure 3-96. *Bottom:* A Zapotecan or Monte Albán Classic style urn depicting the god Cocijo (god of rain and lightning). (After Boos, 1964.)

architectural and ceramic influences have their full effect. The Teotihuacán tablero-talud style of pyramid terracing was carried over to the Kaminaljuyú pyramids, and grave sites reveal an interesting mixture of Teotihuacán lidded jars and

Figure 3-97. A platform at Kaminaljuyú, Guatemala, showing tablero-talud type architecture. (After Kidder, Jennings, and Shook, 1946.)

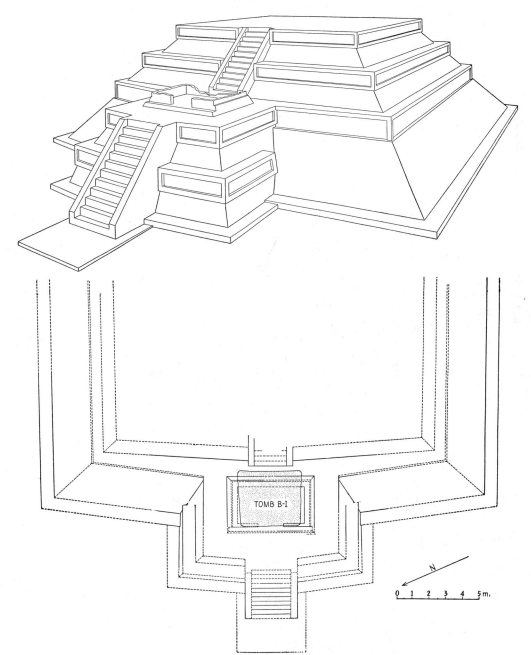

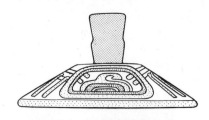

a

b

Lowland Maya polychrome vessels of the Early Classic Tzakol style. Whichever cultural strain was dominant in Esperanza—and it does seem to have been Teotihuacán—the Maya highlanders were being exposed to powerful influences from other regions of Mesoamerica.[95]

Esperanza temple mounds were made of adobe, occasional stone blocks, and adobe and lime mortar. Structures which once surmounted platform mounds were made of wood, so very little of the actual temples or palaces has survived. Burial practices of the earlier Preclassic Period still persisted. Graves were rectangular pits, and with the bodies of distinguished priests or rulers were buried sacrificial victims as well as a wealth of pottery and jade. A striking architectural feature of the Late Classic Amatle and Pamplona phases were huge basin-shaped, or "palangana," ball courts. Amatle and Pamplona ceramics were, of course, bare of Teotihuacán influences, which by this time had been cut off. In general, Amatle and Pamplona ware was rather drab, although some Lowland Maya Tepeu-style polychrome painted jars have been found as well as an early Plumbate-ware type called San Juan.[96]

Pacific Guatemala. On the Pacific Coast and coastal slopes of Guatemala, the Esperanza culture (or a culture similar to Esperanza) appears to have been limited to a small locality around Tiquisate. The architectural remains of the

Tiquisate phase bore a marked resemblance to those of Kaminaljuyú of the same period, and the Teotihuacán-influenced ceramics and the Petén-style polychromes were also similar to those of the great Guatemalan Highland site. Elsewhere, no Early Classic Period cultures have been identified. Late Classic, similar again to contemporaneous phases at Kaminaljuyú, is well represented on the coast by numerous ceremonial mound groups. It was in this Pacific Guatemalan Classic Period setting that the remarkable Santa Lucia Cotzumalhuapa sculptural style developed, which Thompson dated to Late Classic, associating its monuments with the San Juan Plumbate pottery which is regarded as a marker for the period.[97] The

Figure 3-101. Two sculptures in the Santa Lucia Cotzumalhuapa style.

Figure 3-98. (*Top, left*, p. 150) Cylindrical tripod jars from the Early Classic Period at Kaminaljuyú, Guatemala. The decoration is in painted stucco. *a:* A Mayoid motif in light green and dark red. *b:* A Teotihuacánoid motif in buff, light green, and dark red. (After Kidder, Jennings, and Shook, 1946.)

Figure 3-99. (*Bottom, left*, p. 150) Carved stone mirror back from the Early Classic Period, Kaminaljuyú, Guatemala, in the style of Classic Veracruz. (After Kidder, Jennings, and Shook, 1946.)

Figure 3-100. (*Right*, p. 150) A Santa Lucia Cotzumalhuapa style stela sculpture from Pacific Guatemala.

Cotzumalhuapa monuments were carved both in relief and full-round and depicted such subjects as men gazing upward at deities descending from the skies, human sacrifice, skulls, serpent heads, and a deity fashioned as a crab. Prominent, too, was a distinctive style of hieroglyphs, bordered in circular cartouches.[98] The style was more Mexican than Mayan, but its Mexican affinities are not easily recognizable. They are not Olmecan, Izapán, or of Monte Albán; neither are they typical of Teotihuacán or Toltec Tula, although perhaps closer to these. The Cotzumalhuapán style may have been the work of a Nahua-speaking tribe, such as the Pipil, who were believed to have migrated southward some time during the Late Classic Period. Descendants of the Pipil today live in the Guatemalan Highlands and Salvador. But recent excavations by Borhegyi and Parsons in the Cotzumalhuapa region have led them to question the Late Classic date assigned to the style by

Thompson and to suggest, instead, that the sculptures may belong to the Early Classic.[99] This would mean that an unknown Mexican peoples, other than from Teotihuacán, also invaded Guatemala during the Early Classic Period. Perhaps the scarcity of Teotihuacán-type Esperanza remains on the Pacific slopes in this period was occasioned by the presence of the groups responsible for the Cotzumalhuapán sculptures.

The Postclassic Period Civilizations

The Nature of the Postclassic. The city and civilization of Teotihuacán fell to the barbarian invaders around A.D. 600. During the next 300 years, the other Classic civilizations, which had remained more strictly regional in their influence, also collapsed, one by one, so the date A.D. 900 affords a convenient point at which to terminate the Classic Period for Mesoamerica as a whole and to inaugurate the Postclassic Period.

With the Postclassic Period, Mesoamerica broke with its past in the sense that old stylistic patterns, and undoubtedly religions and ideologies, were shattered. From region to region this dissolution was manifest in the destruction or abandonment of centers or cities: the burning of Teotihuacán, the forsaking of the Lowland Maya capitals, and the conversion of Monte Albán into a necropolis. This is not to say that the continuity of the Mesoamerican cultural tradition was destroyed. On the contrary, this heritage was passed on in all of its basic economic and technological elements and even in some of its ideological ones. The Postclassic brought more of a rearrangement of forms than a radically new content, and this rearrangement was fully a product of the troubled times. New ceremonial centers were built side-by-side with fortified sites. In some places they were one and the same. New gods were enshrined and old ones refurbished, but the emphasis was on violence, war, and militarism. To be sure, warfare was not unknown in the Preclassic and the Classic Periods, but the culture hero was the priest-intellectual and

Figure 3-102. Cotzumalhuapán hieroglyphs. (After Thompson, 1948.)

not the warrior. The latter came to the forefront in the Postclassic.

Chichimecs, Toltecs, and Tula. The dynamic force in these changes was the barbarian of the northern frontier. These "Chichimecs," to use a name later applied by the Aztecs to the "wild tribes" who had been their not too distant ancestors, were former peoples of the Desert cultural tradition—food-collectors, hunters, and incipient cultivators—who were becoming, or had very recently become, acculturated to the Mesoamerican tradition. It may be that drought and crop failure on the semi-arid northern frontier drove these tribesmen down onto the civilized populations of Central Mexico.[100] Or it may have been simply a matter of the "outlanders" finally developing to the point where they could successfully challenge the "soft" city dwellers. Whichever, they came southward. Some of them settled in the Valley of Mexico and the Central Mexican highlands; others probably pushed still farther south. Many or most of them were Nahua-speakers, and the migrations of the Nahua into southern Mesoamerica probably began at this time. But out of this welter of Chichimec invaders and migrations one group rose to power in the Early Postclassic Period, the group that became known as the Toltecs.

According to the semi-legendary histories handed down by the Aztec aristocracy after the Spanish Conquest, the Toltecs came into Central Mexico from the northwestern frontier and settled at Tula, Hidalgo, in the latter part of the tenth century. They were Nahua and Chichimecs, but they also assimilated other tribes who had had a longer history in the civilized Mesoamerican world.

Soon after the founding of Tula, according to the legend, factionalism arose between the followers of the king, Topíltzin, or Topíltzin Quetzalcóatl, and the adherents of a party who worshipped the god Tezcatlipoca. This story undoubtedly has some elements of truth. Topíltzin was a real ruler who either left or was driven out of Tula by his enemies around A.D. 987. But the tale

is also allegorical in describing a conflict in values and beliefs between the Feathered Serpent god, or Quetzalcóatl, with whom Topíltzin has become so firmly identified, and the evil Tezcatlipoca. The former represented the old civilized ways of peace while the latter was the symbol of war and death. That Tezcatlipoca should have triumphed was probably a poetic recognition of the trend of the times. In any event, Topíltzin Quetzalcóatl traveled south and east with his band, some say to immolate himself after he reached the Gulf Coast, or, as others believe, to set sail on the sea with the promise that he would later return. Or, perhaps, as certain Maya histories record, he was the Mexican king who with his followers subjugated Yucatán and founded a dynasty there. At Tula, during the two centuries that followed the ejection of Topíltzin, the Toltecs who remained under the tutelage of Tezcatlipoca became the leading military and political force in Central Mexico and Mesoamerica.[101]

The site of Tula, 60 kilometers north of the Valley of Mexico, is on a high promontory overlooking a river.[102] The location, unlike Teotihuacán, was selected for its defensive advantages. The main ceremonial or civic-religious zone of the site is only a little over a square kilometer in extent, but numerous plazas and mounds dotted over the nearby hills indicate a sizable resident population, although nowhere near so large as Teotihuacán. The main ceremonial plaza is flanked by two platform mounds. One of these was never fully excavated, but the other one was revealed as a terraced structure fronted by a colonnaded hall area and with a surmounting temple. The temple's interior is spacious; the roof was supported by wooden beams that had been placed across stone columns. These columns were typical of Tula. Each was made up of carved column drums which, when assembled, depicted Toltec warriors carrying atlatls, darts, and shields. An altar in the temple was supported by another kind of column, an atlantean figure bearing the supported element on his upraised hands and head (Fig. 3-104). A large capital-I shaped ball

Figure 3-103. Tula, Hidalgo. *Top, left:* The ball court. *Top, right:* Skull-and-cross-bones motif in terrace frieze. *Bottom:* General view of Mound B (after excavation and restoration) and Mound C (at right, after partial clearing and restoration). (Courtesy Instituto Nacional de Antropología e Historia, Mexico.)

court (Fig. 3-103, *top, left*) with stone marker rings set in the side walls, was near the temple pyramid, as was a second large but unexcavated ball court area. Characteristic decorative elements in the Tula friezes were warriors, jaguars, coyotes, eagles, skulls and crossbones, and feathered serpents (Figs.

3-103 *top, right,* 3-105). Curiously, in this setting bristling with the panoply of war, the foremost god represented was Quetzalcóatl, not the victorious Tezcatlipoca.

Earlier ceramics at Tula reflected a style known as Coyotlatelco. Coyotlatelco pottery antedated the rise of great Tula; in fact, the style was widespread in Central Mexico following the fall of Teotihuacán. Coyotlatelco featured red-and-buff painting, which derived from earlier Teotihuacán traditions. Later Tula ceramics, which are associated with its political rise, belong to a style called

a   b   c

Figure 3-104. Monuments at Tula. *a:* Atlantean figure (less than life size). *b:* Warrior (perhaps twice life-size). *c:* Chac Mool figure with broken head (about life size). (*a,c,* courtesy Instituto Nacional de Antropología e Historia, Mexico; *b,* courtesy J. E. S. Thompson.)

Mazapán, which developed out of the earlier Coyotlatelco. A distinctive Mazapán design element was a multiple, parallel wavy-line, usually painted on bowl interiors. Plumbate ware, a lead-ore glazed pottery and an Early Postclassic Period horizon marker for Mesoamerica, was an impor-

Figure 3-105. Frieze decorations at Tula. (Courtesy Instituto Nacional de Antropología e Historia, Mexico.)

Figure 3-106. Mazapán red-on-buff bowl. (Courtesy Cambridge Museum of Archaeology and Ethnology, England.)

Figure 3-107.

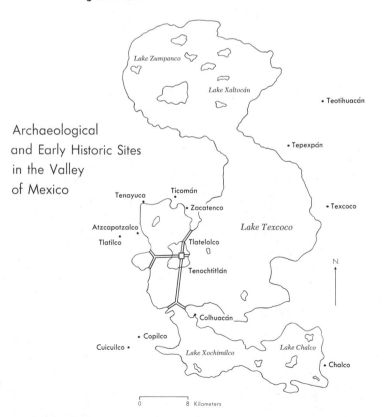

Archaeological and Early Historic Sites in the Valley of Mexico

Lake Zumpanco

Lake Xaltocán

• Teotihuacán

• Tepexpán

Tenayuca   Ticomán
• Zacatenco
Atzcapotzalco •   • Texcoco
Tlatilco •   Tlatelolco
                Lake Texcoco
        Tenochtitlán

                        N

        Colhuacán

• Copilco
Cuicuilco •   Lake Xochimilco   Lake Chalco
                            • Chalco

0   8 Kilometers

tant trade ware at Tula, probably brought in from Guatemala.[103]

The Aztecs and Tenochtitlán. Tula suffered the same fate as Teotihuacán—destruction by still other semi-civilized tribesmen from the northern frontier around A.D. 1160.[104] Central Mexico then was again rent by the warring rivalries of petty city-states, and from this competition the Aztecs emerged as the last great native power of Mesoamerica. With the Aztecs, archaeology merges fully with history. The picture and rebus writing of the Aztec manuscripts and the accounts of Bernal Diaz del Castillo and Bernardino Sahagún are sources as important as the monuments of Tenochtitlán which lie beneath the streets of modern Mexico City.[105]

We know that the Aztecs were among the last of the wild Chichimecs to enter the Valley of Mexico after the fall of Tula. For a time they were vassals to some of the more civilized city-states of the Valley, such as Colhuacán, and by the middle of the fourteenth century they had taken up residence on small islands in the marshy lake of Texcoco. They allied themselves with the Tepanecs, who ruled Azcapotzalco, but later turned on their allies and subjugated them in 1428. The great Moctezuma I, one of their earlier kings, then embarked on a policy of expansion and conquest beyond the Valley of Mexico, and one of his successors, Ahuitzotl (1486–1502), welded together an empire which reached from coast to coast and from the Valley of Mexico to Guatemala. The Aztecs, however, were never completely supreme in Mesoamerica, as the Incas were in Peru. The Tarascans, some of the Mixtecs, and even the Tlaxcalans, who were their near neighbors, held out against them—a circumstance that was to help the Spaniards bring about their downfall.

In one of the great moments of history, Cortez and his men finally beheld the Aztec city of Tenochtitlán after their march inland from Veracruz in 1519. Bernal Diaz del Castillo describes this confrontation of two worlds in simple but vivid prose. Within the lake of Texcoco and all

156

**Figure 3-108. Aztec gods as represented in the Codex Floren-
tino.** *Left:* Quetzalcóatl receiving an offering. *Right:* Huitzilo-
pochtli. (Courtesy Peabody Museum, Harvard University.)

around its edges were countless dwellings. Three
causeways led from the mainland to the island
center of the city, and a grid of canals laced the
metropolis. The lake and the canals were filled
with canoes and the whole scene was alive with
people. Estimates indicate that the full zone of
the city embraced 60,000 dwellings and 300,000
persons.

At the heart of Tenochtitlán was the great pyramid with its twin temples dedicated to Huitzil-
opochtli, the Aztec god of war, and to Tlaloc, god
of rain. Nearby were other lesser pyramids and
temples, and in the plaza stood the infamous
skull-rack with its grisly exhibit of the thousands
of human sacrifices to the nation's deities. The
whole of this central, sacred precinct was enclosed
by a wall, and just beyond the wall were the
palaces of the Aztec emperors, including that of
the tragic Moctezuma II, who was to face the
invaders bemused by the idea that the bearded
Cortez was Topíltzin Quetzalcóatl returned from
beyond the sea.

Along the streets and canals of Tenochtitlán
houses stood on stone-faced platforms. They resembled the dwellings of ancient Teotihuacán and
Tula in that the rooms for cooking, sleeping, eating, and storage were arranged around a central

Figure 3-109. Aztec stone sculpture. *Left,* Coatlicue, Aztec earth
and death goddess. *Right:* A Tlaloc figure. (*Left,* courtesy Museum of Modern Art and National Museum of Mexico.)

courtyard. The walls were of stone and adobe and roofs were formed of wooden beams and poles. The great palaces, although much larger and more elaborate, tended to follow the same plan. Most buildings were whitewashed and provided a glittering setting for the gaudily painted stucco-covered pyramids (Fig. 3-110, *left*). Although the main plaza and its pyramids were the grandest, other plazas and pyramids dotted the city. Each of 20 clans was said to have had its own plaza, temple, and market in its own part of the city; and these clan holdings were grouped, again, into four larger quarters, also with their own plaza ceremonial centers and markets.

Tenochtitlán stood on the least desirable portion of land (and water) in the Valley of Mexico, but the Aztecs may have chosen the site because it was the only location available and could be approached on foot only over the fortified causeways. The growth of the city and the eventual pattern that it took also was conditioned by chinampa farming, the method of cultivation whereby artificial gardens or plots of land are built up of water vegetation and lake bottom muck. The system is still practiced today in the Xochimilco section of the Valley of Mexico, so the technique is well known. Chinampa beds are prodigiously fertile. Their bumper yield, plus the relative ease with which foodstuffs could be moved by canoe over considerable distances, formed the economic basis of the city. One of the observations which the Spanish made about Tenochtitlán was that the houses in the outlying sections of the lake,

Figure 3-110. Aztec buildings as shown in the Codex Florentino. Top: A teocalli, or temple. Bottom: House. (Courtesy Peabody Museum, Harvard University.)

Figure 3-111. Modern chinampas, Valley of Mexico.

among the chinampas, tended to be simpler than those in the central sections of the city. These lake suburbs were, apparently, the dwellings of the farmers whose produce sustained the urban populace.

Tenochtitlán was a hive of activity for both merchants and artisans. Not only were merchants and the markets a part of the immediate life of the city, but some of the activities of the merchant group extended beyond the city to distant portions of the Aztec empire and to other nations. These merchants, *pochteca* as they were called, traveled widely on trading expeditions on behalf of the state and also served as emissaries and spies. The artisans of the city—potters, jewelers, featherworkers, and metal-workers—were craft specialists. Luxury articles for the aristocracy accounted for much of what they produced.[106]

Aztec social and political organization has been a matter of controversey among scholars, the point

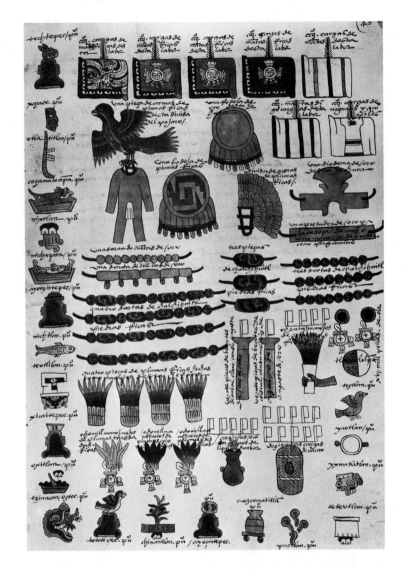

Figure 3-112. *Right:* An Aztec tribute list from the Codex Mendoza. (Courtesy British Museum.)

Figure 3-113. Aztec craftsmen and crafts as represented in the Codex Florentino. *Left:* A featherworker. *Center:* Metal-workers. *Right:* A finished gold ornament. (Notice similarity to Mixteca-Puebla ornaments shown in Fig. 3-122, *right.*) (Courtesy Peabody Museum, Harvard University.)

at issue being the extent to which it was a socially stratified despotism or a clan-based, tribal democracy. Although certain elements of a more primitive, clan-organized society were retained in Tenochtitlán, there can now be little doubt that the Aztec state was a rigidly class-structured system. The emperor was selected from a single royal lineage by a council of senior nobles, high priests, and warriors. His status was semi-divine, and he was treated with great reverence. His top administrators were chosen from others of the royal house, and the emperor and these councilors held great private lands and received the revenue from them.

Figure 3-114. *Left:* The Spanish Conquest through Aztec eyes from the Codex Florentino. *Top:* Moctezuma receives word of the arrival of the Spaniards on the east coast. *Bottom:* The Indian woman, Marina, acts as an interpreter for Cortez. (Courtesy Peabody Museum, Harvard University.)

Figure 3-115. Pottery of the Aztec Period, Central Mexico. *a,b:* Mixteca-Puebla ware. *c:* Painted and scored Aztec grater bowl. (Courtesy Cambridge Museum of Archaeology and Ethnology, England.)

a

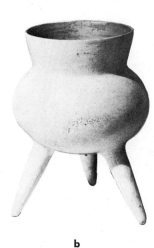

b

c

Commoners gave allegiance to clans, or *calpulli*, of which there were said to be 20; and these *calpulli* appear to have occupied designated sections of the city, each, as we have said, with its own temple and market. Farming lands were clan-owned and each family was assigned certain portions, but within the clans certain aristocratic families held more land and exerted more authority than others. Toward the bottom of the social scale were serfs or bondsmen who worked on the private lands of the high nobility and who were probably peoples subjected by the Aztecs. Below this stratum, still, were slaves who were prisoners of war or had been sold into bondage. The system suggests an adaptation of a more "democratic" pattern of a Chichimec group to the ways of Mesoamerican urban civilization.

Less directly tied to agriculture and land service were soldiers, bureaucrats, merchants, and artisans. War was a highly honorable profession and afforded the best avenue of social advancement to the successful. There were special military orders, or "knighthoods," for the select, such as those of the "eagle" or the "jaguar." Merchants, too, could attain status and wealth through service to the state. Similar opportunities were offered to the higher levels of the bureaucracy and priesthood; beneath these stations were lesser officials and priests and artisans.[107]

The foregoing summary is ethnographical and ethnohistorical rather than archaeological but the continuity from the Early Postclassic Period and from the Toltecs to the Late Postclassic Period empire of the Aztecs can be traced in the archaeological record as well. A series of black-on-orange pottery types are associated with those archaeological culture phases which represent the various competing city-states of the Valley of Mexico after the fall of Tula and prior to the rise of the Aztecs. This black-on-orange pottery tradition, which had its origins in the red-on-buff wares of Teotihuacán and Tula, continued on through the period of the Aztecs.[108] It, together with a myriad of other things, including the pyramids of Tenochtitlán and its great urban zone, was the final expression

Figure 3-116. Aztec stone sculpture representing the god Quetzalcóatl.

of traditions with deep roots in the Central Mexican and Mesoamerican past.

The Toltec and Aztec story is not the only one of the Postclassic Period, but since these two civilizations were the most powerful of their time in the Mesoamerican area, it was fitting to examine them first and at greater length. Let us now turn briefly to what was going on elsewhere at the same time.

Figure 3-117. Aztec stone sculpture. *Left:* Teocalli, a stone carved as a replica of a temple platform with Aztec calendar stone at top. *Right:* Coiled serpent figure. (*Right*, courtesy Dumbarton Oaks pre-Columbian Collection.)

Figure 3-118. *Right:* Aztec jadeite skull; height, 7.1 cm. (Courtesy Dumbarton Oaks pre-Columbian Collection.)

Figure 3-119. The Spanish Conquest through Aztec eyes, from the Codex Florentino. *Left:* A Spaniard uses gunpowder against an Indian. *Right:* Indians unhorse and kill a Spaniard. (Courtesy Peabody Museum, Harvard University.)

Figure 3-120. The Spanish Conquest through Aztec eyes, from the Codex Florentino. *Left:* The Spaniards cross the causeway to attack Tenochtitlán. *Right:* The Spaniards fire the temple at Tlaltelolco. (Courtesy Peabody Museum, Harvard University.)

Figure 3-121. Veracruz pottery of the Postclassic Period. *Left:* Vessels from Isla de Sacrificios; the specimen at the right is a Tohil Plumbate jar. *Right:* Cerro Montoso polychrome. (*Left,* courtesy British Museum; *right,* courtesy Museum für Völkerkunde und Vorgeschichte, Hamburg.)

The Totonacs. In Central Veracruz the center of Tajín continued to thrive after the collapse at Teotihuacán and lasted into the Early Postclassic Period, as is evident from Plumbate and Fine Orange trade wares found in the uppermost occupation phase of that site.[109] When it was abandoned, Cempoala, near modern Veracruz, became the major Gulf Coast center, and this town was inhabited by the Totonacs. The ruins of Cempoala, which date from Early to Late Postclassic, consist of a great central enclosure and four subsidiary enclosures within which are

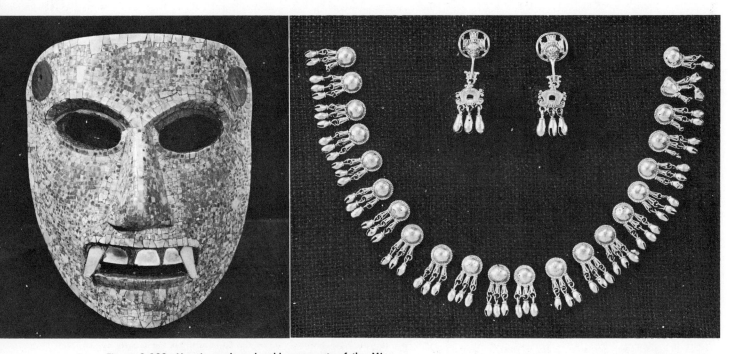

Figure 3-122. Mosaic mask and gold ornaments of the Mixteca-Puebla culture. *Left:* Mask of wood, turquoise, mother-of-pearl, and pink shell, purportedly from vicinity of Tilantongo, Oaxaca, Mexico. Height, 15.3 cm. *Right:* Cast gold necklace and ear ornaments. Length of earring, 6.1 cm. (Courtesy Dumbarton Oaks pre-Columbian Collection.)

mounds and plazas. When Cortez passed through on his way to the Aztec capital, it was described as a city of 30,000 people.[110] South of the Totonacs, in the region of Cerro de las Mesas, Tres Zapotes, and La Venta, the chronicler Sahagún has described a sixteenth-century tribe, the "Olmecas." These were the wealthy people of the rubber country who possessed jade, gold, jaguar skins, cacao, feathers, and cotton cloth. Their linguistic affiliation is uncertain, and their name, as applied to the old great Preclassic style, has no significance in linking those ancient remains with this ethnohistoric people.[111]

Zapotecs and Mixtecs. During the Postclassic Period two nations struggled for control of Oaxaca—the Zapotecs, whose ancestors had held the site of Monte Albán for centuries, and the Mixtecs, who were expanding eastward and southward from the Mixteca Alta of northwestern Oaxaca. Monte Albán had been abandoned as a great center at the close of the IIIB phase of that site's history, and the "Monte Albán IV" phase is represented by burials that date from the Toltec horizon. In "Monte Albán V," the Mixtecs took over the sacred city, or its ruins, and re-used old Zapotecan tombs for burying their great dead. The most famous of these burials, "tomb 7," contained nine males—probably a dignitary with immolated retainers—accompanied by a richness of gold and silver ornaments, copper objects, lapidary work, and animal bones carved with hieroglyphic and calendric inscriptions (see Fig. 3-122, *right,* for comparable goldwork). The characteristic ceramics of "Monte Albán V" were black wares, of local tradition, plus the brightly painted Mixteca-Puebla polychromes (Fig. 3-115a) from the vicinity of Postclassic Cholula.[112]

About 40 kilometers southeast of Monte Albán is the famous center of Mitla, which probably was constructed in the Early Postclassic Period but continued as an important religious and political center through the Late Postclassic as well. The architectural style of Mitla derived from Zapotec traditions and, according to native histories retold by Spanish chroniclers, it was the residence of the high priest of the Zapotecs. The principal buildings were arranged in groups of four around paved plazas. Made of rubble and concrete, they were faced with cut stone and stone mosaic reliefs. The ceilings of these buildings were flat rather than vaulted. Cruciform tombs under the plazas at the front of some of the buildings bore interior wall mosaics similar in their geometric designs to the building facades. Frescoes on interior walls of the temples or palaces were painted in a style quite different from that of the rigidly geometric mosaic reliefs, being more reminiscent of the Mixteca-Puebla polychrome designs and Aztec codices.[113]

Mixtec genealogies have been traced back to the seventh century A.D. The early Mixtec dynasties were centered in Tilantongo. Mixtec invasions of the Valley of Oaxaca and Monte Albán date to the fourteenth century or the Late Postclassic Period, and the Aztecs began their campaigns in Oaxaca about 100 years later. They defeated the Mixtecs in the northwest, but the Mixtecs and Zapotecs were never fully subdued and continued their resistance against the Aztec state up until the time of the arrival of the Spaniards.[114]

The Maya of the Postclassic Period. At the southern end of Mesoamerica, the close of the Classic Period coincided with the abandonment of the great ceremonial centers of the Petén and the southern lowlands and with the appearance in northern Yucatán of Toltec influences at Chichén Itzá. Chichén Itzá was an important ceremonial center in Late Classic times, built in an architectural style similar to the Puuc (Fig. 3-84, *bottom*). In the tenth century A.D. it was invaded, probably

Figure 3-123. Mitla, Oaxaca, Mexico. *Left:* Facade of a palace showing typical mosaic panels. *Right:* Detail of mosaic friezes.

by Mexican Toltecs. In fact, this invasion has been correlated with the migration legends of Topíltzin Quetzalcóatl from Toltec Tula. Certainly the architecture and art of Chichén Itzá during this Chichén-Toltec phase was similar in many details to Tula, and the scenes in the reliefs and paintings of Chichén depicted Mexican warriors defeating, capturing, and receiving obeisance from the Mayas.[115]

The great days of Chichén continued until the thirteenth century, and during this time the Castillo, the Temple of the Warriors, the Colonnade, and the huge ball court were constructed (Figs. 3-83 *top, left,* 3-84, *top, left and right,* 3-124). The last three of these structures have reasonably close counterparts at Tula. In architecture the Toltecs introduced such elements to the Maya as doorway columns in the form of serpents; atlantean or caryatid figures as stone columnar supports; reclining male figures holding a basin in the stomach, or "chac-mools"; colonnades as adjuncts to buildings; feather-serpent balustrade ornamentations; and wall reliefs of lines of warriors or prowling jaguars. An adaptation of Mayan to Mexican architectural traditions was the combination of vaulted roofing and column supports in the Temple of the Warriors.[116]

Figure 3-124. Maya-Toltec sculpture at Chichén Itzá, Yucatán. *Top:* The Temple of the Warriors with Toltec-inspired Chac Mool figure and serpent column in foreground and at right, and Puuc style mosaic masks in wall panels at left. *Bottom:* Sculptured frieze of jaguars in Toltec style, Temple of the Warriors. (Courtesy Peabody Museum, Harvard University.)

Figure 3-125. Sacrificial scene from sculptures of Upper Temple of the Jaguars, Chichén Itzá, Yucatán. (After Tozzer, 1957.)

Figure 3-126. Maya and Toltec depicted on gold breastplates from the Sacred Cenote, Chichén Itzá, Yucatán, Mexico. *Left:* A Tula-Toltec eagle attacking a Maya. *Right:* A Tula-Toltec warrior in action. The designs on these plates were raised in relief by reverse hammering. (After Tozzer, 1957.)

That the earliest resident population of Chichén Itzá and vicinity was not completely replaced by the conquering Toltecs is inferred from the bulk of the pottery taken from the site, which was the ancient Yucatecan "slate ware," although mingled with Plumbate and Fine Orange trade wares.[117] The hieroglyphs, too, at Chichén Itzá are in the Maya style, and if they are regarded as symbols of the language spoken at that time, they signify a continuity of the Maya heritage and peoples in spite of the superimposition of Toltec hierarchical elements.

The rise of the city of Mayapán, after the decline of Chichén Itzá, is interpreted as a sign of Maya resurgence in northern Yucatán. Mayapán was the most important center of the northern lowlands during the Late Postclassic Period and was the seat of a family related to the Itzás of Chichen—the Cocoms. The Cocoms centralized governmental power at Mayapán, and all the head chiefs of the various territories of the realm purportedly were forced to reside there, perhaps to guarantee their allegiance to the ruling house. Mayapán was a walled, urban clustering of houses grouped around a central ceremonial center. The walled enclosure embraced an area of 2 by 3 kilo-

meters, and archaeologists have counted 2100 household unit foundations within this area. Some 12,000 persons are estimated to have lived there.[118] This kind of an urban formation, within a defense wall, is found only in the Late Postclassic Period in the Maya Lowlands. Besides Mayapán, Tulúm, on the east coast of the Peninsula of Yucatán, is the only other well-known example.[119] It may be that the idea of both an urban aggregate and its fortification were Mexican imports to the Maya country.

Mayapán fell in the fifteenth century in the midst of civil wars, and no other Maya city rose to take its place as the leading political center of the lowland Postclassic Maya. When the Spanish entered the country early in the sixteenth century, Yucatán was divided into numerous small warring chieftainships.

In the Guatemalan Highlands, a number of important ceremonial centers were constructed during the Early Postclassic period, some of which, such as Zaculeu, show Toltec or Mexican architectural influence (Fig. 3-127). At the site of Zacualpa the Tohil Postclassic phase appears to be derived from earlier Classic Period occupation of the same site, but it also shows Toltec influence.[120] This Tohil phase gave its name to the Mesoamerican Early Postclassic trade ware, Tohil Plumbate. This curious glazed pottery, of a gray or orange-fired color, frequently was fashioned in pear-shaped jar forms with pedestal bases or in jars or ollas modified as animal effigies.[121] The Early Postclassic centers were, as a rule, located on hillspurs overlooking valley bottoms, which suggests that defense considerations may have been a factor in choosing a site; however, it is not until the Late Postclassic that the Guatemalan Highland sites were definitely fortified as well as strategically located. To the northwest, however, in the Grijalva Basin of Chiapas, hilltop refuge or fortified sites appeared earlier, some of them dating from the Late Classic Period.[122]

The Frontiers of Mesoamerican Civilization

The Marginal Subareas of Mesoamerica. In the Classic Period, the great civilizations of Mesoamerica flourished within a zone embracing Central Mexico, the central and southern Gulf Coast, Oaxaca, and Central America down to the Salvadoran and Honduran borders. Beyond this nucleus, but still within the orbit of the Meso-american area and culture, were territories whose prehistory can be equated with that of the nucleus, in time if not in kind. In these subareas, the irradiations from the centers of civilization fade gradually as one moves outward toward the peripheries of the Mesoamerican area. That this gradual disappearance may have been, in part, a factor of time lag is suggested by the increasingly "civilized" aspects of these peripheral territories as we proceed through time into the Postclassic Period. The differences between these "frontiers" and the Mesoamerican nucleus mostly involve intensity and elaboration of pattern. Sites were not so large,

architecture was not so imposing, the great arts not so refined or sophisticated, calendrics and writing not so developed. These marginal or "frontier" subareas lay on the southern, northeastern, western, and northwestern borders of the Mesoamerican area. They were, respectively, the ones we have designated as: *The Southern Periphery, The Huasteca, Guerrero,* and *The West and the Northern Frontier.*

The Southern Periphery. On the southern periphery, the Preclassic Period cultures of the Ulua River Valley, Lake Yojoa, and Yarumela, in Honduras, and those of Salvador relate quite clearly to Mesoamerica. In the Ulua-Yojoa region, these Preclassic cultures are overlaid by the Ulua Maya ceramics, which were inspired by Late Classic Maya polychromes, probably out of such southeastern Maya centers as Copán and Quirigua. A similar sequence occurs in western Salvador with the Late Classic pottery type, Copador ware, linking the Classic levels at the Tazumal site with those of Copán. Court arrangements of stucco-covered mounds were a part of the Maya complex both in Honduras and Salvador. These southern manifestations of Maya civilization were completely derivative. The Postclassic Period cultures of Salvador were probably related to the Nahua-speaking Pipil, as represented by the Cihuatán phase, in the western and central parts of that country, or, possibly, by the Lower Lempa complex to the east. In Honduras, the Classic Period

Figure 3-127. Toltec or Mexican influence in the architecture of the Postclassic Period, Zaculeu, Guatemalan Highlands.

Maya horizon was followed by a local ceramic complex which seems to center in the northeastern part of that country and may be the remains of the linguistically independent Jicaque or Lenca. Influences from Lower Central America, as opposed to Mesoamerica, are especially strong in the late northeast Honduras complex.[123]

Those other regions of the southern periphery subarea—Pacific Nicaragua and the Nicoya Peninsula of northwestern Costa Rica—are much less a part of the Mesoamerican sphere than western Honduras and Salvador. In Costa Rica, recent excavations have disclosed pottery levels which appear to be chronologically equivalent to the Mesoamerican Late Preclassic Period, and the typology of these levels suggests that they may have been Mesoamerican derived. The same can be said of Pacific Nicaraguan collections. Succeeding levels in Costa Rica-Nicaragua were markedly different from Mesoamerican Classic Period ceramics, however; and it is only in the very last centuries before the Spanish Conquest that definite Mesoamerican stylistic influences in the Costa Rican-Nicaraguan pottery suggest that these regions should be considered a part of the Mesoamerican world. These late-period pottery types were not of Mayan origin so much as they were Central Mexican, and it is likely that they related to the presence in Nicaragua-Costa Rica of Nahua-speaking tribes such as the Bagaces, Nicarao, and Nahuatlato, who probably were late immigrants from Mesoamerica. It is from these immigrants that sixteenth-century ethnographic accounts recorded such distinctive Mesoamericana as folded-screen books, deities and calendars with Mexican overtones, and the use of the cacao bean as a medium of exchange.[124]

In general, the archaeological picture on the southern frontier of Mesoamerica is complex because the influences flowing from Mesoamerica were interblended with strains of the alien cultures of Lower Central America.[125] No geographical break separates the two.

The Huasteca. The Huasteca subarea of Mesoamerica is a frontier which faces northward on the "low" culture area of northern Tamaulipas and the Texas coast. Hunting and collecting tribes occupied these desert lands up through historic times and served as a buffer between Mesoamerica and the agricultural societies farther north and east in the Mississippi Valley. The archaeological picture thus reveals Mesoamerican culture tapering off into the Tamaulipas deserts rather than the complex interpenetration of influences that occurred on the Mesoamerican southern frontier. The Huasteca was named for the Maya-speaking Huastecs who occupied the subarea in the sixteenth century and who probably had held it for many centuries. The absence of characteristic Maya archaeological traits of the Classic or Postclassic Periods suggests that the Huastecs became separated from the other Mayas before A.D. 300, and the glottochronological evidence on the split of Yucatec from Huastec Maya places it at about 1400 B.C.[126] This date would fall in the Early Preclassic Period and, perhaps, it is significant that Early Preclassic pottery from the Huasteca is not unlike Early Preclassic Guatemalan Highland and Pacific Coastal wares.

A long stratigraphic sequence on the Panuco River in the southern part of the Huasteca begins in the latter part of the Early Preclassic and runs through to the Aztec conquest.[127] We know that in the Late Preclassic phases of El Prisco and Tancol small ceremonial mounds were being constructed. Throughout the Classic and Postclassic Periods the Huastecs were, as might be expected, influenced primarily by Central Mexico and Central Veracruz via the Huastecan coast and thence inland to the mountainous part of the subarea. Both Teotihuacán and Tajín traits appear in the Huasteca, mainly in ceramics and figurines. Although ceremonial centers were constructed in Huasteca, no particularly large or elaborate sites have been discovered, and monumental stone sculpture was an alien art form during the Classic Period. The cultural climax of the Huasteca actually occurred in the Early Postclassic Period and is expressed in such major sites as Las Flores and Tamuin, the latter being particularly well known for its painted

Figure 3-128. Huasteca Postclassic Period stone sculpture. An apotheosis of a chieftain. (Courtesy Brooklyn Museum.)

frescoes.[128] Huastec monumental sculptures also date from this period. These pieces were stone statues of priests or kings carved with a death image of the individual on the reverse side.[129] The style reflected Toltec influence, and the god Quetzalcóatl was the dominant Huastec deity of the time. During the Late Postclassic a unique black-on-white pottery style became the hallmark of the Huastecs (Panuco phase), and this ware was traded north to the wild tribes, some of whom carried it as far as southern Texas.[130] Another late Huasteca item is the carved shell gorget or ear ornament (Fig. 3-130). These are rendered in a distinctive style, and it has often been speculated that they may have been traded northward along the Gulf Coast and that they may have served as the stimuli for the shell carving and the Southern Cult art of the late pre-Columbian cultures of the Southeastern United States. The Postclassic flowering of the coastal Huasteca did not, however, penetrate to the interior. In the Sierra de Tamaulipas and the eastern Sierra Madre mountains, the earlier Classic Period appears to have been an optimum time of cultural development, with some

Figure 3-129. Panuco phase black-on-white spouted pot with basket-handle. (Courtesy British Museum.)

MESOAMERICA

Figure 3-130. Huasteca shell disk, possibly an ear ornament, showing combined cut-out and engraving techniques. (After Beyer, 1933.)

decline in population and a shift away from fully established village agriculture in the Postclassic.[131]

Guerrero. The Guerrero subarea is one of the least explored of the Mesoamerican area and, as might be anticipated from its geographical location, its cultures were probably less marginal to the main stream of Mesoamerican developments than those farther north. Archaeological sequences go back to the Preclassic Period and, judging from the abundance of Olmec-style stone figurines that have been recovered, quite probably to the Middle Preclassic.[132] A stratigraphy of the coast, near Acapulco, reveals a Preclassic-to-Classic ceramic series, and Teotihuacán cylinder jars and Thin Orange ware constitute a part of the Tambuco II phase of that series. Additional Teotihuacán Classic Period influence shines through in the very fine stylized stone masks of Guerrero.[133] A local Guerrero style of small-object stone carving, the Mezcala, centered in the upper

Balsas River drainage in the central part of the state and appears to have elements of both Olmec and Teotihuacán styles. Unfortunately, the history of this style is very obscure.[134] Large mound, plaza, and ball court sites have been found in Guerrero, but it is not clear if these structures date from Classic times or later.[135] During the late prehistoric centuries, Mixteca-Puebla influences infiltrated

Figure 3-131. Mezcala style figurine of carved stone, presumably from Guerrero, Mexico. (Courtesy Museum für Völkerkunde und Vorgeschichte, Hamburg.)

Figure 3-132. Chupicuaro style Preclassic pottery figurine, Chupicuaro, Guanajuato, Mexico. (Courtesy Cambridge Museum of Archaeology and Ethnology, England.)

Guerrero and, still later, we know that the Aztecs occupied parts of the subarea.

The West and the North. In the west and the northern Frontier subarea, Preclassic Period cultures existed in Estado de Mexico, Michoacan, and Guanajuato,[136] the best examples being the Chumbicuaro phase of the Apatzingán region of Michoacan,[137] the shaft tombs of El Opeño, also in Michoacan,[138] and the Early Chupicuaro phase of Guanajuato.[139] Some investigators claim Olmec affinities for El Opeño, and the pottery and figurines of Chupicuaro relate quite obviously to the Late Preclassic cultures of the Valley of Mexico. For farther north and west, no definite evidence of Preclassic levels have come to light, but we agree with Covarrubias that the modeled life-form pottery of Colima and Jalisco are suggestive of Pre-

classic patterns in the Valley of Mexico, even though they may have been later in these western regions.

The succeeding Classic and Postclassic Period cultures were developed from these earlier local foundations, stimulated by contacts and influences from the east and the south. In Michoacan, the sequence at the site of Tzintzuntzán begins on a Classic Period time level, as indicated by ceramic remains which bear traces of the Teotihuacán style; however, the construction of T-shaped platform mounds, which were used as bases for temples and as places of burial, appear to be Postclassic. The Postclassic cultures have been identified with the Tarascan nation, and Tzintzuntzán was their capital. The Tarascans were the most powerful nation in the West in historic times, and they successfully withstood the Aztec empire. They, too, were empire-builders and expanded from their original homeland in the lake country of Michoacan to encompass most of that state plus Jalisco and Colima. Their culture was rooted in the earlier traditions of the West. For instance, the dominant pottery style was negative-painted, or resist-painted, a mode of decoration which had a long history in the region. The Tarascans were also superb metallurgists. Quite probably, metallurgy was introduced into Mesoamerica mainly by way of the west coast of Mexico, where it had been

Figure 3-133. Tiny copper "money axe" from western Mexico. (Courtesy Peabody Museum, Harvard University, and Dudley Easby.)

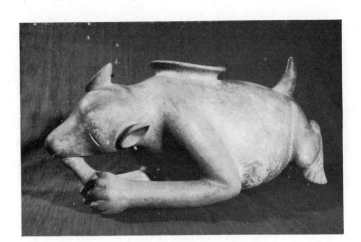

Figure 3-134. Colima dog vessels. Specimen on left, about 30 cm. high. (*Left*, courtesy British Museum; *right*, courtesy Colonel Fearing.)

Figure 3-135. Pottery figurines from Nayarit, Mexico. *Left:* Small (length 11 cm.), solid figure representing a human bound (?) to a bed-like frame. *Right:* Large (such vessels averaged 30–45 cm. in height), hollow figure of a warrior. (*Left*, courtesy Cambridge Museum of Archaeology and Ethnology, England; *right*, courtesy Colonel Fearing.)

brought by sea from Peru and Ecuador; and the Tarascans were among the earliest peoples to develop and employ the techniques of casting, gilding, soldering, alloying, and smelting. Ornaments were made of gold, and copper was used for implements as well as ornaments. Among the copper products were axes, fishhooks, tweezers, bells, rattles, rings, bracelets, functional axes, and tiny axe-like pieces that are believed to have been used as money.[140]

Colima, Jalisco, and Nayarit were centers where there developed an amazing style of life-modeled pottery that is now housed largely in private collections. This pottery is best represented from the earliest known period in these states and frequently has been found in deep-shaft tombs. In Colima, this modeled pottery has been assigned to the Ortices phase which is cross-dated to Teotihuacán Classic by means of Thin Orange trade ware in the graves.[141] Ortices-modeled pottery encompassed a variety of forms—men, women, warriors, prisoners, plants, and animals. The large, hollow figurines reflect a tasteful naturalism, most frequently in a highly polished red pottery. Smaller, solid figurines also depict various life scenes. Similar but distinct regional styles of this modeling have been discovered at Jalisco and Nayarit, and an Ixtlán style of figurine from southern Nayarit is interesting for its exaggeration and caricature (Fig. 3-135).[142] Mounds and copper implements were common features of these regions.[143] Both seem to have developed during the Classic-to-Postclassic Period transition.

Figure 3-136. The great fortified site of La Quemada, Zacatecas. *Left:* The citadel-like aspect of the ruin from a distance. *Center:* The colonnade, in the lower portion of the site. *Right:* A courtyard arrangement containing platform mound and small altar-like feature.

In the far northwest, two cultures appeared during Classic Period times—the Chalchihuites of the interior and the Chametla-Aztatlán of the coast. Traces of the Chalchihuites have been found in the states of Zacatecas and Durango, where such ceremonial centers as Alta Vista de Chalchihuites, Schroeder, and La Quemada must have been first established either by migrants from the south or by local Chichimec populations who were adapting rapidly to the Classic Period civilizations. Both the Alta Vista and Ayala phases of the Chalchihuites continuum date to before A.D. 900. J. C. Kelley has described their hilltop pyramids, Teotihuacán-type courtyard arrangements of residences, stone masonry walls, and stone columns.[144] It is unclear, however, if the largest ceremonial site in the northwest was raised this early. This site is La Quemada, impressive with its pyramids, huge colonnaded court, and sizable residential area within a hilltop fortress.[145] Quite possibly, La Quemada, at least in its most spectacular architectural features, dates to the Early Postclassic or Tula Toltec horizon.[146] Ceramics of the Chalchihuites culture, from Classic to Postclassic times, were polished, engraved, and red-on-buff types that relate to the potteries of Teotihuacán and Tula.[147]

The Chametla-Aztatlán culture phases[148] of the northern Nayarit and Sinaloa coasts can be cross-dated with those of the Chalchihuites sequence. The roots of Chametla-Aztatlán, however, sprang not from Chalchihuites but from a common source. Diffusions or migrations out of Mesoamerican Classic cultures appear to have spread northward along two lines: coastal and inland. The two branches may have separated somewhere in the vicinity of Lake Chapala on the borders of Michoacan and Jalisco.[149] On the coast, Mixteca-Puebla influences, from Puebla and northern Oaxaca, were an important strain in these diffusions, particularly in the Postclassic Period.[150]

It was through these Chalchihuites and Chametla-Aztatlán cultures that many of the elements of the Mesoamerican cultural tradition were carried northward to the oasis valleys of Arizona and New Mexico where they enriched the developing Southwestern tradition. It is also a virtual certainty that earlier Northwest Mexican cultures remain to be discovered and that these will prove to be the connecting links between Mesoamerica and the earliest pottery-making, sedentary village communities in the Southwest.[151]

Epilogue

In 1521 Cortez destroyed Tenochtitlán and the Aztec state. Soon afterward, the other Postclassic Period civilizations fell to the Spaniards, so that by the mid-sixteenth century Mesoamerica had, indeed, become "New Spain." Although many elements of the old native patterns continued after the Spanish Conquest, including the agricultural complex, items of technology, and many elements of religious belief, the Mesoamerican tradition, as an integrated cultural tradition, did not survive. Changes during pre-Columbian

174

times had given the tradition new content or new direction, but none of these—not even the drastic upheavals which closed the Classic Period—had obliterated its values in the way that the European Conquest did. After the Conquest, only fragments survived, and the Indian began the slow and painful task of reassembling these fragments into the mestizo societies and cultures of today.

Footnotes

[1]MacNeish (1958 a).

[2]MacNeish (1961, 1962 a).

[3]Because of this MacNeish (1964 b) is disinclined to see it continued as a part of the Desert tradition.

[4]Mangelsdorf, MacNeish, and Willey (1964).

[5]C. E. Smith (1950).

[6]Drucker (1948); Lorenzo (1955).

[6a]C. F. Brush (1965) has recently reported pottery with a radiocarbon date of 2440 B.C. from shell middens on the Guerrero coast. The ceramic-bearing layers occur immediately above a pre-ceramic occupation. Significantly, this early plain Guerrero pottery, designated as "Pox ware," is very similar to the earliest pottery (Purron phase) of the Tehuacán sequence. Whether plant, including maize, cultivation was present on the Guerrero coast at this time is, as yet, unknown.

[7]Ishida and others (1960); Willey (1962 a).

[8]Mangelsdorf, MacNeish, and Willey (1964). On the problem of New World agricultural origins the reader may also consult Mangelsdorf, MacNeish, and Galinat (1964); Mangelsdorf and Smith (1949); Mangelsdorf and Reeves (1959); Sauer (1952, 1959); Willey (1960 a, b).

[9]Kirchhoff (1943) proposes approximately this same area; see also Wolf (1959); Willey (1962 b); M. D. Coe (1962 a).

[10]For discussions of Mesoamerican culture as a whole see Kirchhoff (1943); Wolf (1959); Willey, Ekholm, and Millon (1964); M. D. Coe (1962 a, 1963); Armillas (1964); Wauchope (1964).

[11]For Mesoamerican language groups see F. Johnson (1940); Mendizabal and Jimenez Moreno, (1939).

[12]These subareas follow the breakdown given in Willey, Ekholm, and Millon (1964).

[13]For general area chronologies and/or stage arrangements see C. L. Hay and others (editors) (1940); Armillas (1948 a, 1964); Wauchope (1950, 1964); Caso (1953 a); Ekholm (1958); M. D. Coe (1962 a, 1963); Pina Chan (1963); Willey, Ekholm, and Millon (1964). This is only a sampling.

[14]For discussion of Maya-Christian calendrical correlations see p. 136.

[15]MacNeish (1961, 1962 a).

[16]Dixon (1959); MacNeish (personal communication, 1962); Lowe (1959 a, b, 1962 a, b).

[17]M. D. Coe (1961). Ocos pottery, significantly, bears a very close resemblance to Chorrera phase wares of the Ecuador coast (M. D. Coe, 1960).

[18]Shook (1951); Shook (personal communication, 1960) now places Arevalo as earlier than Las Charcas and at the bottom of the Kaminaljuyú column.

[19]Robert Squier (personal communication, 1965) informs me that Early Preclassic ceramic levels have now been found at La Venta, Tabasco, on the southern Gulf Coast.

[20]Usually El Arbolillo and Early Zacatenco are considered as Early Preclassic (cf. Pina Chan, 1955, for example). M. D. Coe (1962 a), however, feels they are somewhat later.

[21]Vaillant (1930, 1935, 1941).

[22]Compare, for instance, C-196 (1360 B.C.) (Libby, 1955) with M-662 (500 B.C.) (Crane and Griffin, 1958 a)—both dates on Early Zacatenco.

[23]Drucker (1952); Drucker, Heizer, and Squier (1959); Drucker and Heizer (1960); Heizer (1959); M. D. Coe (1962 a, 1963).

[24]M. D. Coe (1962 a).

[25]Willey (1962 a).

[26]Covarrubias (1957).

[27]Porter (1953); Piña Chan (1958); M. D. Coe (1962 a).

[28]Drucker (1943 a).

[29]Stirling (1940).

[30]M. D. Coe (1957) has argued for the integration of this and other Cycle 7 dates in the Maya "Long Count" system; Thompson (1941) has stated a different view. The "Long Count" system and other Maya calendrical features are discussed on pp. 132–136.

[31]Caso (1938); Caso and Bernal (1952).

[32]Stirling (1943); Thompson (1948); M. D. Coe (1962 a).

[33]Specimens in the National Museum, Guatemala City. S. B. Miles (1962 ms.) analyzes these various Chiapas and Guatemalan sculptural styles.

[34]See Kidder, Jennings, and Shook (1946) for a general discussion of Kaminaljuyú, and Shook and Kidder (1952) for tomb in question.

[35]Ricketson and Ricketson (1937).

[36]Cummings (1933); Heizer and Bennyhoff (1958).

[37]Armillas (1950); Millon (1957 a, 1960).

[38]Wolf (1959).

[39]Millon (1961).

[40]Two terminologies exist for the Teotihuacán sequence. That of Vaillant (1941) is numbered while Armillas (1950) uses names. These may be paired as follows: Teotihuacán I (Tzacualli); Teotihuacán II (Miccaotli); Teotihuacán III (Xolalpán and Tlamimilolpa); and Teotihuacán IV (Ahuitzotla-Amantla). Teotihuacán I pertains to the Protoclassic Period. Teotihuacán II and III

are the Classic Period city. Armillas' Xolalpán and Tlamimilolpa may be sequent phases, or contemporaneous sectors of the site. Teotihuacán IV is not represented in the Teotihuacán site zone but at the site of Azcapotzalco on the northwestern side of Lake Texcoco. A recent analysis of the periods and dating of Teotihuacán is to be found in Jimenez Moreno (1959).

[40a]Millon (personal communication, 1964–65).

[41]There are numerous descriptions of the ruins of Teotihuacán. Among these are Vaillant (1941); Marquina (1951); Armillas (1950); M. D. Coe (1962 a). Linne's excavations (1934, 1942) are also very important. Rene Millon (1964) is now engaged in preparing a detailed map of the site.

[42]The date of the construction of the great Pyramid of the Sun has been much debated. Recently, Millon (1960) and Millon and his associates (Millon and Bennyhoff, 1961; Millon and Drewitt, 1961) have argued that it is a Teotihuacán I structure; but still more recent ceramic analyses of R. E. Smith (personal communication, 1965) indicate that it was built in Teotihuacán II times.

[43]Aveleyra Arroyo de Anda (1963).

[44]Linne's work (1934, 1942) revealed these residential patterns.

[45]Millon (1954, 1957 b); Wolf and Palerm (1955); M. D. Coe (1964).

[46]Teotihuacán ceramics and artifacts are discussed by Armillas (1944); Vaillant (1941); Tolstoy (1958 c).

[47]Portesuelo was excavated by the late G. W. Brainerd; the collections are now being prepared for publication by H. B. Nicholson (Nicholson and Hicks, 1961).

[48]See Mayer-Oaks (1959) for a discussion of one of these tributary small villages.

[49]Noguera (1941); M. D. Coe (1962 a).

[50]Kidder, Jennings, and Shook (1946, pp. 254–256); see also Lathrap (1957).

[51]W. R. Coe (1962, 1963).

[52]Vaillant (1938).

[53]The earliest evidences of occupation in the lowlands appear to be the Xe phase, at the bottom of the Altar de Sacrificios column, southwestern Petén. Xe antedates Mamom of Uaxactún and has cross-ties with the Chiapa III phase of Chiapa de Corzo. The general time level is thought to be the Middle Preclassic Period (current research of Peabody Museum, Harvard, at Altar de Sacrificios).

[54]Ricketson and Ricketson (1937); A. L. Smith (1950).

[55]W. R. Coe (1962, 1963).

[56]Willey and others (1960); Willey and Smith (1963).

[57]Brainerd (1951, 1958).

[58]Andrews (1960, 1961).

[59]Archaeological monographs on the Maya Lowlands are numerous. Several general summary books are also available. Among these are Morley (1946); Morley and Brainerd (1956); Thompson (1954); Brainerd (1954).

[60]Bullard (1960); Willey, Bullard, Glass, and Gifford (1965).

[61]See Schellhas (1904) for an analysis of deities in the Maya pre-Columbian manuscripts.

[62]Thompson (1950).

[63]Proskouriakoff (1960, 1961).

[64]See Thompson (1935) for a survey of the problem.

[65]Satterthwaite and Ralph (1960).

[66]Morley (1946).

[67]Thompson (1945, 1954).

[68]Andrews (1960).

[69]This is also the interpretation favored by G. W. Brainerd.

[70]Spinden (1928, p. 148).

[71]Morley (1946, pp. 67–72).

[72]Recent soil and pollen analyses from old *bajos,* or lake beds, indicate, if anything, that some grassland or savanna conditions might have been more suitable for agriculture than forests. According to Cowgill and Hutchinson (1963), farming may have first started in the Petén in grasslands at about 800 B.C. These grassland conditions, they believe, prevailed until about A.D. 700 when a somewhat drier climate produced or accompanied the development of the present forests over much of the region.

[73]Ricketson and Ricketson (1937, pp. 10–13).

[74]Meggers (1954).

[75]U. M. Cowgill (1961).

[76]Mentioned along with other possibilities by G. L. Cowgill (1964).

[77]Willey, Bullard, Glass, and Gifford (1965).

[78]Current researches at Altar de Sacrificios, Peabody Museum, Harvard University.

[79]Thompson (1954).

[80]W. R. Coe (1962, 1963).

[81]Willey, Bullard, Glass, and Gifford (1965).

[82]Stirling (1943); Drucker (1943 b).

[83]For Tajín, see E. S. Spinden (1933); García Payon (1943, 1949 a, 1954) and numerous other accounts, Du Solier (1945); Proskouriakoff (1954).

[84]Proskouriakoff (1954); Covarrubias (1957, pp. 171–195).

[85]Ekholm (1946, 1949); M. D. Coe (1962 a). See Blom (1932) for a general account of the ballgame as played by the Maya and others.

[86]Covarrubias (1957).

[87]García Payon (1950).

[88]Strebel (1885–1889).

[89]Medellin Zenil (1960).

[90]Caso (1938); Linne (1938).

[91]Caso and Bernal (1952).

[92]Bernal (1949 a, b, 1958 a); Caso (1938); Noguera (1940, 1945).

[93]Caso (1947).

[94]Berlin (1952).

[95]Kidder, Jennings, and Shook (1946).

[96]Kidder, Jennings, and Shook (1946).

[97]Thompson (1948).

[98]Thompson (1948).

[99]Lee A. Parsons (personal communication, 1962).

[100]Both Wolf (1959) and M. D. Coe (1962 a) advance this hypothesis of a fluctuating ecological frontier of Mesoamerican agriculture as an important factor in the culture history of the area.

[101]Jimenez Moreno (1954–1955, 1959).

[102]For archaeological Tula see Dutton (1955); Acosta (1956).

[103]Tolstoy (1958).

[104]Jimenez Moreno (1954–1955, 1959).

[105]Diaz del Castillo (1908–1916); Cortez (1908); Sahagún (1829–1830).

[106]In addition to contemporary references cited in the preceding footnote, see modern summaries in Vaillant (1941);

Caso (1953 b); Bernal (1959); Peterson (1959); M. D. Coe (1962 a).

[107]See Bandelier (1878, 1880); Vaillant (1941); Caso (1953 b); Monzon (1949); Prescott (1843); Peterson (1959, pp. 85ff.); M. D. Coe (1962 a).

[108]Griffin and Espejo (1950).

[109]García Payon (1943, 1949 a, 1954); Du Solier (1945); Bernal and Davalos (1953, chart on endpaper).

[110]García Payon (1949 b, c); Covarrubias (1957, p. 197); Marquina (1951); Krickeberg (1956).

[111]Sahagún (1829–1830, Bustamente (editor), Vol. 3, Book 10, Chapter 31); Jimenez Moreno (1942); Covarrubias (1957, pp. 50–83).

[112]Caso (1941, pp. 56–60); Bernal (1958 b, 1964).

[113]On Mitla, see Caso (1941); Linne (1938); Spinden (1928, pp. 163–165).

[114]Noguera (1946); Dahlgren (1954); Covarrubias (1957, pp. 293–311).

[115]Most Maya archaeologists believe Chichén Itzá to have been invaded by Tula Toltecs, as stated here; but George Kubler (1961) takes the opposite view and sees a movement of peoples from Chichén north to Central Mexico to found Tula. However, in holding this opinion, Kubler admits to the Mexican-Maya blend of Chichén Itzá culture and would explain this as resulting from contacts along the Tabasco-Maya frontier just prior to the founding of Chichén Itzá. For a counter-argument to Kubler's see Ruz (1962).

[116]Numerous works exist on the archaeology and history of Chichén Itzá. A major summary is given by Tozzer (1957). See also Thompson (1945); Lothrop (1952); Bishop Landa's contemporary sixteenth-century account (Tozzer, 1941).

[117]Brainerd (1958).

[118]Pollock, Roys, Proskouriakoff, and A. L. Smith (1962).

[119]Lothrop (1924); Sanders (1955, 1960).

[120]Wauchope (1948). See also Dutton and Hobbs (1943); Shook and Proskouriakoff (1956); A. L. Smith (1955).

[121]Shephard (1948).

[122]Robert M. Adams (1961).

[123]For Honduras see Strong, Kidder, and Paul (1938); Strong (1948); Canby (1951); Stone (1941, 1957); Epstein (1959). For Salvador see Lothrop (1927, 1939); Longyear (1944); Boggs (1944); Haberland (1958, 1960); W. R. Coe (1955).

[124]Lothrop (1926, two vols.); Haberland (1959, 1963 a, b); M. D. Coe (1962 b); Baudez (1962, 1963); M. D. Coe and Baudez (1961); Baudez and M. D. Coe (1962); Norweb (1964).

[125]Lower Central America will be treated in Volume 2 of this work.

[126]Swadesh and others (1954).

[127]MacNeish (1954 a); Ekholm (1944).

[128]Marquina (1951, pp. 412–422); Ekholm (1944, pp. 373–391).

[129]Covarrubias (1957, pls. 45, 46, pp. 200–203).

[130]Covarrubias (1957, pl. 47); Staub (1920, pls. 7, 8, fig. 9); J. A. Mason (1937).

[131]MacNeish (1958 a).

[132]Covarrubias (1957, pp. 110–113) believed that the Olmec style originated in Guerrero.

[133]Ekholm (1948).

[134]M. D. Coe (1962 a). There is also some opinion among Mexican archaeologists that the Mezcala style is as old, or older, than Olmec.

[135]Armillas (1948 b).

[136]For a general archaeological summary of the West and the Northern Frontier see Lister (1955).

[137]Isabel Kelly (1947).

[138]Noguera (1939).

[139]Porter (1956).

[140]For Tarascan and "Pre-Tarascan" see Rubin de la Borbolla (1948); Moedano (1941).

[141]Isabel Kelly (1949, pp. 194–195). Covarrubias (1957, pp. 88–89) tends to feel that Ortices may be of Preclassic date.

[142]Covarrubias (1957, pp. 89–91). E. W. Gifford (1950, pp. 199–205, 237–238) places Ixtlán large figurines in his Early Ixtlán Period which he correlates with Early Chametla, to the north, and, following Ekholm (1942), with Late Teotihuacán. However, recent radiocarbon dates from deep shaft tombs at Ezatlán, Jalisco—associated with pottery figurines closely related to the Ixtlán style—fall in the Early Teotihuacán time range (A.D. 250) or even earlier (Furst, 1965). For illustrations of Ixtlán figurines see Gifford (1950, pls. 2-10), and also Lumholtz (1902, Vol. 2, pls. 1–5).

[143]Meighan (1959 b).

[144]J. C. Kelley (1956); see also Lister and Howard (1955).

[145]J. C. Kelley (1956); Lister and Howard (1955); Batres (1903); Marquina, (1951).

[146]Available radiocarbon dates for La Quemada are inconclusive. They range from about A.D. 740 to 1170, with a plus-or-minus range of error of 200 years (Crane and Griffin, 1958 b).

[147]J. C. Kelley (1956); Kelley and Winters (1960).

[148]See Ekholm (1942, pp. 124–132). Sauer and Brand (1932) first defined an "Aztatlán area." See J. C. Kelley and Winters (1960) for chronological organization of culture and its cross-ties. See also Isabel Kelly (1938).

[149]Lister and Howard (1955).

[150]Ekholm (1942, pp. 125–132).

[151]Di Peso (1963).

The Southwest Area

Geography and Environment. The Southwest culture area, as it can be defined most usefully for archaeological considerations, centers on the states of Arizona and New Mexico (Fig. 4-1). Its western boundary follows along the Colorado River Valley and curves eastward to include an edge of Nevada. The northern boundary can be drawn to embrace the southern two-thirds of Utah and western and southwestern Colorado. On the east, most of eastern New Mexico may be included together with a portion of western Texas. In Mexico the line can be drawn to include the State of Sonora and most of the State of Chihuahua. Native agriculture is one of the definitive characteristics of the area. To the west, north, and east the adjacent areas were essentially nonagricultural. Only to the south, where it touches upon Mesoamerica, is the Southwest bounded by an area of native farmers, and its cultural history, as we shall see, is closely related to this earlier Mesoamerican hearth of agriculture.[1]

In general, the climate of the Southwest is dry and like most of western North America it has grown more desiccated since the glacial era, reaching a peak during the Altithermal, from about 5000 to 2500 B.C. Since then, modern conditions

The North American Southwest

have prevailed with epicycles of erosion and valley sedimentation. There also has been some volcanic activity in the area, but only in very restricted regions. Elevation, of course, is and has been a major factor in modifying modern climatic conditions and vegetation, so that the original inhabitants lived amidst a considerable range of terrain, climate, and flora and fauna. Throughout, however, the rainfall pattern tends to divide into a relatively long winter season of intermittent rains, or mountain snows, and a short season of summer thundershowers. These periods are separated by marked dry seasons.

The Subareas. Four major cultural subareas may be distinguished in the Southwest (Fig. 4-1), and these correspond in large degree to natural environmental conditions.[2] The first of these is the Mogollon, which takes its name from its location in the Mogollon Mountains which run diagonally from north-central Arizona southeastward into New Mexico. From southwestern New Mexico, the subarea probably should be extended down into the Sierra Madre Occidental of Chihuahua. It is, in general, an environment of mountains and valleys, covered with dry grasslands in places and coniferous forests in others. The climate is mild.

The second of these subareas is the Anasazi of the high plateau country of northern Arizona, the southern edge of Utah, southwestern Colorado, and most of northern New Mexico. "Anasazi" is a term which refers to the prehistoric-to-historic Basketmaker-Pueblo cultural continuum. Parts of the Anasazi plateaus are deserts, parts are covered with coniferous forests, and the terrain is dissected with deep river arroyos and canyons. The climate is mild to cold.

The third subarea is the Hohokam, the desert of central and southern Arizona and adjacent Mexican Sonora. The Hohokam is much lower than either the Mogollon or Anasazi subareas, is less rainy, and is intensely hot during the summer. In climatic-vegetational terms it can be described as "succulent desert" country, which means that there is some scrub bush cover and that water resources are more plentiful than in extreme desert regions. The name "Hohokam" refers to the native prehistoric cultures of the subarea.

A fourth subarea is designated as the Patayan, also a prehistoric cultural term. The Patayan centers in the Colorado River Valley in a desert environment that, except for the Colorado River floods, is more severe than the Hohokam subarea. The Indians here practiced farming in the flood plains of the Colorado. The subarea extends from the river delta north to southern Nevada, for a distance of 100 miles or more eastward into Arizona, and for an even greater distance into southern California and Baja California. These wider

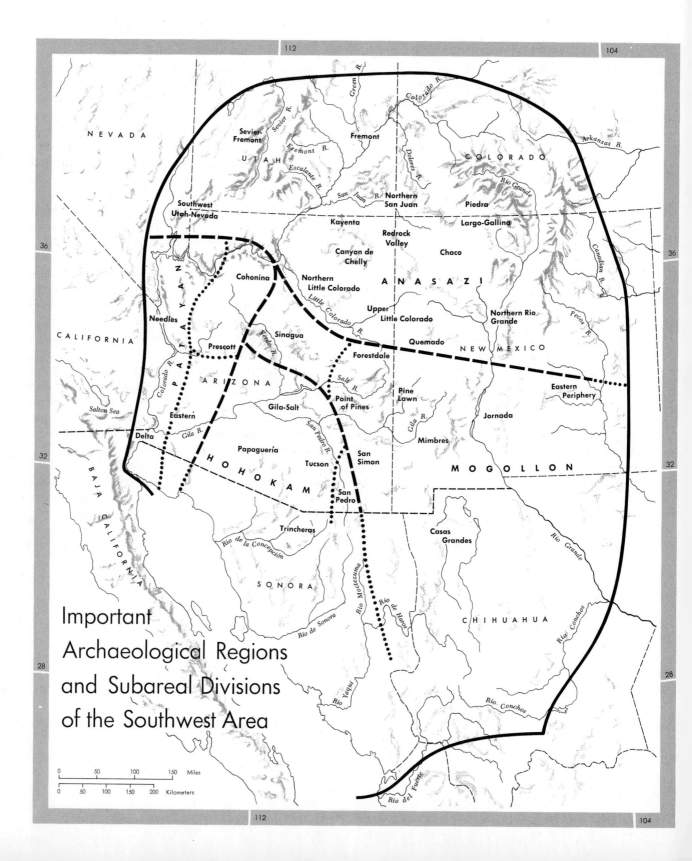

Important
Archaeological Regions
and Subareal Divisions
of the Southwest Area

boundaries are vaguely defined, and they have fluctuated through time. Essentially, however, the subarea is the intensely hot valley of the lower Colorado and the bordering desert.

Archaeological-Ethnological Continuities. The prehistoric archaeological cultures of the Southwest can be related to descendant historic and modern Indian cultures of the area. This continuity is most easily demonstrated in the Anasazi subarea where the present Pueblo Indians still live on the sites and in the towns of their ancestors. Among these Pueblos are the Hopi and Zuñi in the west and the Rio Grande towns of the east. Some of the western Pueblos, such as the Hopi, are affiliated with the Uto-Aztecan language family, and on the Rio Grande the Tano are also considered by linguists as being related to this speech family. The languages of the Zuñi and the eastern Keresan Pueblos are, on the other hand, classed as independent or unaffiliated.

Another apparent continuity of prehistoric-to-historic is seen in the Patayan subarea where the historic and modern Yuma-speaking Indians of the Colorado River, including the Yuma proper, the Havasupai, Yavapai, and Walapai are believed to be the descendants of the prehistoric Patayan.

In the southern Arizona desert, the relationship of the present-day Pima and Papago farmers to the ancient Hohokam peoples is less certain but nevertheless probable. The Pima and Papago, together with several tribes who live to the south and east of them, extending down into Mesoamerica, speak Uto-Aztecan.

It is still less certain what happened to the prehistoric Mogollon Indians and who their modern

relatives may be. Some of the Mogollon may have merged with Anasazi peoples to the north, others possibly joined with Hohokam groups to become the historic Sobaipuri of the San Pedro Valley of southern Arizona, and still others may have gone farther south to settle in Chihuahua.

There are two other significant ethnic groups in Southwestern culture history. The Paiutes and related tribes held the northern peripheral country of Utah. These northernmost Uto-Aztecans had followed largely in the ancient Desert cultural tradition of food-collecting and hunting, but for a brief period in prehistoric times they probably practiced Southwestern Anasazi agricultural techniques.

More important in their effects on the Southwestern farming cultures were the Athapascan-speaking Navajo and Apache, who invaded the Southwest area in the late prehistoric period. Their cultural tradition was, at first, markedly different from that of the local sedentary tribes of the Anasazi or Hohokam. Gradually, the Navajo and Apache became somewhat acculturated, although they always maintained their separateness. The territory they occupied was virtually area-wide; in effect, they surrounded and engulfed the older resident farmers. Although their archaeological remains have been identified in some few parts of the Southwest, most of our information about them comes from ethnographic sources.[3]

The Emergence of the Southwestern Tradition

The Desert Tradition and the Beginnings of Agriculture. The Southwestern cultural tradition, like that of Mesoamerica, had its roots in the Desert food-collecting pattern of western North America. You will recall that the tradition had its beginnings as early as 7000 B.C. or before, that its most likely hearth was the Great Basin country of Utah and Nevada, and that it was established in the Southwest before 5000 B.C. as the Cochise culture. Southwestern culture arose from this

Figure 4-1. (*Left*, p. 180) The solid lines indicate the subarea divisions. Broken lines set off those regions which are affiliated with neighboring subareas. A broken line also separates the Hohokam and the Mogollon in northern Mexico, because some authorities regard all Southwestern culture in Sonora and Chihuahua as Mogollon, others see stronger Hohokam influences in Sonora, and still others see it as Patayan (Hakataya).

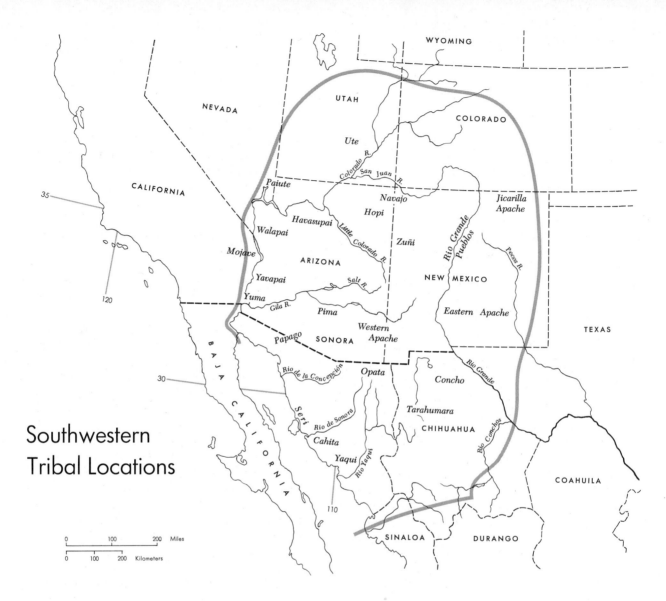

Southwestern Tribal Locations

Figure 4-2.

Cochise base at about the beginning of the Christian era. It appeared as a culmination of a series of events which had begun long before—the introduction of cultivated food plants from Mesoamerica, a gradual increase in community population size, more settled living, and, finally, the introduction of pottery.

The earliest Southwestern domesticated plants were, like those of Mesoamerica, extremely primitive cultigens. As time went on, however, these strains were improved by selection and by crossing with new varieties from Mesoamerica. This development was, in fact, comparable and related to what had gone on in the Mesoamerican area during the Incipient Cultivation Period except that the Southwest lagged behind by a millennium or more. The first indications of Southwestern village-sized population aggregates and village-site stability appeared late in the Cochise culture, associated with these incipient agricultural activities, and including such things as food-storage pits, more and better milling stones for seed foods, and, ultimately, pithouse dwelling structures. Finally, to cap these signs of sedentary life, pottery and pottery figurines appeared, and it was at this point in the sequence that the Cochise, Desert-type culture gave way to the Southwestern cultural tradition.

The Cochise-to-Mogollon Transition. All these trends and events—the shift from hunting-collecting to farming and from the Desert tradition to a Southwestern tradition—can be traced in all four Southwest subareas. So far, they are least well known in the Anasazi country. Even here, however, there are some evidences. As early as 1943 Kirk Bryan and J. H. Toulouse described a San Jose complex of chipped-stone tools that was found without ceramic associations.[4] More recently, Cynthia Irwin-Williams has undertaken excavations at a series of sites in northern New Mexico which show an unbroken cultural development from pre-ceramic levels of the second millennium B.C. up to the ceramic phases of the Anasazi. Although this work has not yet been fully reported, such pre-ceramic complexes show similarities to the Cochise culture of the South.[5]

In the Patayan subarea an Amargosa Desert culture underlies the pottery-using, farming cultures of a Southwestern type;[6] and in the Hohokam, the transition from Desert to Southwestern patterns has been partly traced in the upper levels of the stratigraphy in Ventana Cave.[7]

It is, however, in the Mogollon subarea that the story is revealed in greatest detail. Here, in southeastern Arizona, the Chiricahua period of the Cochise dates from 5000 to 2000 B.C.[8] Chiricahua was replaced by the San Pedro Cochise, which lasted from 2000 B.C. to approximately the beginning of the Christian era. This San Pedro period ends with the aforementioned appearance of pottery and the beginnings of the Mogollon variety of Southwestern culture.[9] It is with these last 2000 years, and particularly with the last three or four centuries of that time span, that we are now most concerned. In focusing our attention on them, we turn to several archaeological sites in the Mogollon Arizona-New Mexico border country, among them Bat Cave.

The dry deposits of Bat Cave in the Pine Lawn region of west-central New Mexico have yielded the earliest Southwestern finds of maize. This earliest corn was primitive and undeveloped, similar to the early tropical flint corn of Mesoamerica from which it was derived. It was found in a cultural context of the Chiricahua Period of Cochise, and it is dated by radiocarbon to between 2000 and 3000 B.C.[10] The cave stratigraphy in its upper levels revealed genetic improvement of the maize, probably the result of other and later introductions of hybridized maize strains from Mexico. Not far from Bat Cave, and still within the Mogollon subarea, maize pollen has been dated from soil deposits in the Point of Pines region in eastern Arizona to the second millennium B.C.[11] Still other maize specimens have been discovered in the Tularosa and Cordova Caves in the Pine Lawn region of New Mexico. Here the dating is somewhat later, pertaining to the last centuries of the pre-Christian era.[12] All these earliest appearances of Southwestern maize cluster within a radius of 100 miles and all the localities in question are in wooded upland valleys 6000 feet or more high. As the Southwestern archaeologist, E. W. Haury, has pointed out, this is the kind of terrain and environment in which the early Mesoamerican maize first appeared in Puebla and Tamaulipas. Taken together, this distribution in the Southwest, the environmental settings, and the relative proximity to the Mexican sierras suggest an early diffusion of the cultivated maize plant from Mesoamerica up the Cordilleran spine of north Mexico into the Mogollon subarea of the Southwest.[13] Quite probably diffusing with the earliest maize was the squash or pumpkin (*Cucurbita sp.?*) and the gourd (*Lagenaria*); later, at a date estimated by Haury as about 1000 B.C., the red kidney bean (*Phaseolus vulgaris*) was brought into the Arizona-New Mexico mountains along with improved maize varieties.

Very likely, the Mogollon mountains thereafter served as a dispersal center for these and other domesticated plants for the rest of the Southwest. This statement may be an oversimplification for, as we shall see, the early diffusion of agricultural plants through the area was complex and has not yet been fully traced in the archaeological record;

but what is important for our present discussion is that the earliest known maize, squash, and beans from the Southwest were found in the Mogollon territory in a late Cochise setting, and it is here that early settled village life with pithouse architecture and pottery was also established.

Settled village life is first known from Cave Creek in the San Simon region of southeastern Arizona. This region is an open-site location; and depth of refuse, storage pits, numerous basin-shaped metates for corn-grinding, and shallow pithouse structures leave little doubt of permanent

or year-round habitation. The houses had shallow excavated floors, timber and earth roofs, and lateral passage entrances, all features very similar to the later Mogollon houses of the Penasco phase of the same region. Estimates date them to about 300 B.C.[14]

The Tularosa and Cordova Caves in the Pine Lawn region just across the state line from Point of Pines in New Mexico document the Cochise-to-Mogollon transition in great detail, and because of the dry-cave preservation offer an unusually full inventory of late Cochise culture.[15] Maize, beans, squashes, gourds, and a variety of wild plants, including yucca pods, cacti, black walnuts, acorns, grass seeds, and sunflower seeds (some domesticated), were all found in the pre-pottery levels and carried over into the succeeding pottery-bearing strata of the Pine Lawn phase of the Mogollon culture. "Perishable" artifactual items bridging the transition included sandals, flexible cradles, netted carrying bags, wooden fire drill hearths, coiled and twined baskets, unfired basketry-impressed pottery, leather bags, reed flutes, wooden dice, and atlatls and darts. The same types of chipped-stone projectile points, knives, scrapers, choppers, ground-stone metates, manos, and various hammers and abraders have been taken from both the Cochise and Mogollon levels, as well as bone tools and ornaments and shell beads and bracelets.

In fact, the essential diagnostic of the Pine Lawn phase levels of the Tularosa and Cordova Caves is pottery. The particular pottery types are known as Alma Plain, Alma Rough, and San Francisco Red; and these types, which appeared here in a region of the Mogollon subarea at about 100 B.C., seem to be the earliest of the Southwest.[16] All were undecorated, although the San Francisco Red type was red-slipped. Vessel forms were simple and included hemispherical bowls and globular jars with or without necks. The ware was usually fired to a brown color, and, in some types, was polished or smoothed with a pebble.

The source of this early Mogollon pottery is generally believed to be Mesoamerica, but to

date, the specific Pine Lawn types have been found only as far south as northwestern Chihuahua.[17] Going farther south into Mesoamerica proper, resemblances to Pine Lawn and other Mogollon types are of a general rather than specific nature. Red and brown monochrome wares have been identified in Preclassic Period levels in the Valley of Mexico but the vessel forms of these monochrome types are not similar to those of the early Mogollon ceramics. In Zacatecas, Durango, and Sinaloa, the most likely points of Mesoamerican contact with the Southwest, none of the known pottery complexes are early enough to indicate suitable origins for the Alma and San Francisco types. They date from the Classic and Postclassic rather than the Preclassic Period. Nevertheless, it is probably significant that plain brown and red

Figure 4-4. *Top, right:* Manos and metates from the Mogollon subarea. *a,b,d:* Manos from pre-pottery and early pottery levels of Tularosa Cave, New Mexico. *c:* Mano associated with early pottery levels in same cave; *e:* Basin-shaped metate, Pine Lawn (early pottery) phase, SU site, New Mexico. *f:* Metate fragment from Tularosa Cave. (Courtesy Chicago Natural History Museum.)

Figure 4-5. *Below:* Early Mogollon plain wares. *a,c:* San Francisco Red, Pine Lawn phase. *a* is from Tularosa Cave; *c* is from the SU site. *b:* Alma Neck-Banded, a type that persisted from the Georgetown through the Three Circle phase. This specimen is from the Three Circle occupation at the Turkey Foot Ridge ruin, New Mexico. (Courtesy Chicago Natural History Museum.)

wares in simple bowl and jar forms were quite common on this northwest Mesoamerican frontier, even though they appeared in relatively late time levels. They are characteristic of a complex known as Huatabampo, which extended northward from Sinaloa into coastal Sonora;[18] and inland, on the eastern side of the Sierra Madre Occidental, pottery of this kind was found in association with a culture known as Loma San Gabriel from Zacatecas north to southern Chihuahua.[19] It seems likely, therefore, that earlier, but similar, ceramic horizons eventually will be discovered in these Mesoamerican frontier regions which will reveal the sources of the early Mogollon pottery.

The Southwestern Tradition. The succeeding 500 years, from 100 B.C. to A.D. 400, saw the establishment of successful village agriculture in the Mogollon, Anasazi, and Hohokam subareas, but in attempting to characterize the Southwestern cultural tradition at its inception, we must admit that for the period of the establishment and spread of village agriculture this tradition was not highly distinctive. Nor was it uniform in its details throughout the area. The essentials of the pattern—cultivated plants, pottery-making, and the pithouse village—were spreading and being adapted to various local conditions; but the arrangements and elaborations of these fundamentals were distinct from region to region and, particularly, from subarea to subarea. The maize-squash-bean complex had been derived from Mesoamerica in a succession of introductions which lasted over a period of 2000 years. The metate-mano means of corn-grinding had been evolved from the earlier local Desert cultures. Pottery and pottery figurines were most probably of Mesoamerican inspiration. The only really distinctive traits of this 100 B.C.—A.D. 400 period were the semi-subterranean pithouse and the larger, special, village ceremonial chamber which is patterned on the pit-dwelling model. The origins of the pithouse are obscure; but most probably it is an ancient North American concept derived from Asia, although when and how remain unknown.

Thus, at its threshold the Southwestern cultural tradition consisted of small village societies in the process of creating a new way of life by synthesizing Mesoamerican and Desert tradition elements.

Only after A.D. 400 did the Southwestern cultural tradition develop distinctive qualities along its several subareal and regional lines. Especially after A.D. 1000 a number of general characteristics emerged.[20]

To begin with, the Southwest became an area of dense and sedentary populations when viewed in the context of the surrounding parts of America north of Mexico. The earliest Southwestern villages were composed of pithouses, which later gave way to surface structures of jacal, adobe, or masonry. The latter, as time went on, were arranged in planned apartment-house fashion. Specialized religious structures, as we have mentioned, date from earliest times and continued as a prominent feature of the Southwestern tradition. They usually were semi-subterranean chambers, although there were significant regional and chronological exceptions.

Southwestern agriculture grew more important throughout the earlier and middle periods of the tradition. The farmers irrigated, trapped silt, flooded their lands, and, of course, depended on rainfall to grow their crops. Produce was stored in special pits or in granaries. In addition to agriculture, however, hunting and plant-collecting always remained of some economic importance. The only domesticated animals were the turkey and the dog.

All indications, from archaeology and from ethnohistory, are that Southwestern society was non-stratified or weakly stratified, unlike Mesoamerican society of the Classic or Postclassic Periods or the native cultures of the southeastern United States. Southwestern society was, however, so organized that community projects such as irrigation works and the raising of great kivas and other ceremonial buildings could be carried out effectively. Community projects probably were religiously sanctioned and under the direction of religious leaders. Militarism was not a significant institution, nor are there signs that human sacrifice or the taking of human trophies in war were important. No evidence for a sumptuous or spectacular "cult of the dead" has been found, although artifacts were generally placed in graves.

Typical artifacts of the Southwestern tradition include small, carefully flaked, notched projectile points suitable for use as arrow tips. The bow-and-arrow began to replace the atlatl and dart during the early centuries of the tradition and later completely displaced them. A trough-shaped metate was widely used for maize and seed-grinding. Ground-stone axes were grooved, and a hafted stone maul was used as a heavy pounding implement. Bone tools were common. Marine shells, brought from the Pacific Coast or from the Gulf of California, and turquoise were prized as ornamental materials. Basketry, both coiled and twilled, and textiles made from wild fibers, fur, feathers, and eventually, cotton continued their earlier Desert culture prototypes. Tobacco was smoked in tubular pipes and cane cigarettes. Although Southwestern pottery shows considerable subareal and regional variation in techniques of manufacture, vessel forms, and decoration, it is significant that throughout the area bichrome and polychrome painting was the preferred method of decoration. The one exception was corrugated ware, in which the vessel coils were not fully obliterated during manufacturing. Relatively crude, hand-made pottery figurines have been found throughout the area.

Southwestern Chronology. The above outlines the origins of Southwestern native culture and is a gross delineation of its form and content. With this background, let us consider next some of its specific lines of growth and development as these have been traced by archaeologists within the framework of the major cultural subareas of the Southwest. These major subareas are, as we have indicated: (1) the Mogollon of the mountainous basin and range country of southeastern Arizona and southwestern New Mexico; (2) the Anasazi of the northern plateaus; (3) the

Hohokam of the southern Arizona desert; and (4) the Patayan of the lower Colorado River. Within each subarea an archaeological chronology has been developed, and in our earlier discussions of the emergence of the Southwestern cultural tradition we have referred to the earlier periods of these chronologies. Before examining the culture history of these subareas further, let us set down briefly these chronologies and their apparent correlations with one another (Fig. 4-6).[21]

The most fully developed and accurately controlled is the Anasazi chronology.[22] It rests on a solid foundation of archaeological stratigraphy and tree-ring dates, and its earliest period, known as Basketmaker II, is believed to have spanned the centuries from about 100 B.C. until A.D. 400. This is the period to which we have just referred in our summary of the first appearances of sedentary villages, agriculture, and pithouse construction. No formal Basketmaker I Period was designated for the Anasazi subarea; the period was, in fact, a hypothetical construct based on the possibility that earlier evidences of Indian occupation would be found there. San Jose and related Cochise-like phases, recently discovered, actually constitute a kind of Basketmaker I. The Basketmaker III Period, which follows Basketmaker II, is estimated to have lasted from A.D. 400–700 and was followed by the Pueblo periods, I through IV, round dates for which are given in the chronological diagram (Fig. 4-6). The terminal period, Pueblo IV, extends from A.D. 1300 to 1700, continuing some 150 years beyond the first Spanish entry into the Southwest. During this time, native Anasazi culture continued more or less unaffected by European influences.[23] Although referred to as a "chronology" by most archaeologists, and referred to as such here, this Anasazi sequence is, in many of its applications, more of a series of stages than of periods. Each of the main divisions is characterized by certain broad cultural traits, and these traits do not always appear perfectly synchronized throughout all regions of the subarea, particularly when we turn to events in the heart of the subarea, in the San Juan or Chaco regions, and with analogous events in more peripheral regions. In these cases a definite time lag can be observed in the radiation of traits from the central zones outward. Nevertheless, the Anasazi stages do closely approximate periods, even if they do not correspond to exact time horizons in all parts of the subarea; and they are the most effective divisions to use in talking about culture events, content, and change through time.

The chronology for the Mogollon subarea is less securely tied to calendar dates than that of the Anasazi, and it is less widely used or referred to in archaeological writings. The dating is based, variously, on radiocarbon, tree rings, and cross-referencing to the Anasazi sequence. The period divisions are numbered from Mogollon 1 through 5. Mogollon 1 refers to the span between 100 B.C. and A.D. 400, and in the correlation presented here is, thus, fully contemporary with Anasazi Basketmaker II Period.[24] Further correlations with the Anasazi sequence are indicated on the chart (Fig. 4-6). The final period, Mogollon 5, ranges

Figure 4-6. Southwest area chronology chart. The vertical range of the earlier periods (prior to 100 B.C.) has been foreshortened.

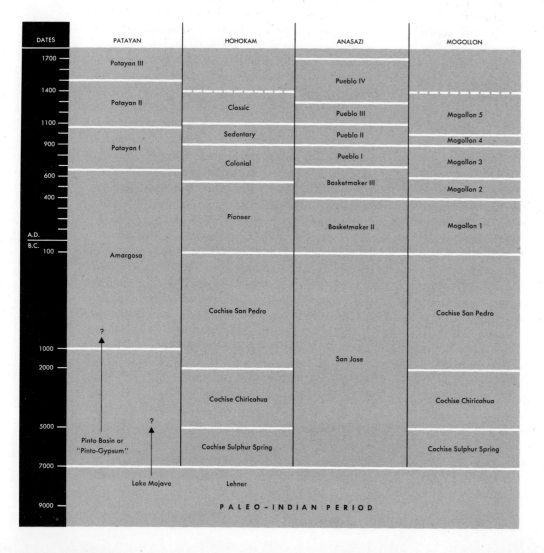

from A.D. 1000 to an indefinite upper limit. Mogollon culture withered after the fourteenth century and little is known of it in late prehistoric and early historic times.

The Hohokam chronology lacks tree-ring dates and is coordinated with that of the Anasazi and the Mogollon by cross-finds and other means of cultural cross-referencing.[25] The correlation of its four major periods, Pioneer, Colonial, Sedentary, and Classic, is indicated on the chart (Fig. 4-6). As with the Mogollon, there is a definite fading of Hohokam culture after A.D. 1400, at which time, for practical archaeological purposes, the Classic Period may be said to end.

The Patayan chronology follows the presentation of M. J. Rogers, with some slight modifications.[26] Its three periods have been dated largely by ceramic cross-finds of Anasazi and Hohokam phases (Fig. 4-6).

Mogollon

The Mogollon subarea occupies the southeastern part of the larger Southwest area. As we have already mentioned, it centers in the mountains of southeastern Arizona and southwestern New Mexico. From here its northern border lies somewhere between the upper tributaries of the Salt River and those of the Little Colorado farther north; but this border cannot be sharply drawn, especially for the later prehistoric periods, and there is considerable interblending with the Anasazi cultures of the plateau. Similarly, the San Pedro River Valley on the west is a zone of interpenetration between Mogollon and Hohokam. To the east, Mogollon culture fades out into the Llanos Estacados of eastern New Mexico and west Texas, and southward its extension into Chihuahua is, as yet, little known.

Within the Mogollon subarea are a number of regional divisions, each displaying a variety of Mogollon culture. Some of these we have already mentioned in dealing with the earliest appearances of Southwestern culture—for instance, the San Simon and Pine Lawn regions. The locations of these several regions are shown on the map (Fig. 4-1). These regions were not immutable, and like any geographical measure of culture characteristics, they changed through time. They are, however, useful points of reference, and it is within these regions that archaeologists have outlined sequences of culture phases.[27]

The Correlation of Mogollon Phases. Certain disagreement exists among archaeologists on the correlation of these Mogollon phases from one region to another and on the wider correlations of the Mogollon chronology with those of the Anasazi and Hohokam. Thus, Wheat sees the Pine Lawn phase of that region as beginning before the Christian era and definitely being a part of the Mogollon 1 Period, which ended in A.D. 400[28] (Fig. 4-6). Bullard, on the other hand, is inclined to merge Pine Lawn with the succeeding Georgetown phase, and to place Georgetown-Pine Lawn, together with the early Penasco phase of the San Simon region, as just after A.D. 400.[29] Placing it in a broader frame of reference, Wheat equates these early Mogollon phases with the Anasazi Basketmaker II Period, whereas Bullard is inclined to correlate them with Basketmaker III. These questions of subarea chronological correlations cannot be settled because of the scarcity of dendrochronological (tree rings) and radiocarbon dates. They are, however, important questions because they relate to the relative dating of such traits as pottery, agriculture, and pithouses and to their initial introductions and spread in the Southwest as a whole. Without involving ourselves in the specific arguments about Mogollon-Anasazi correlations, we shall follow the interpretation which favors the idea that ceramics and agriculture are older in the Mogollon subarea than in the Anasazi and that they diffused from the Mogollon northward. The history of the semi-subterranean dwelling or pithouse is less clear. At the present writing, with the pre-ceramic late Cochise pithouses of San Simon and of Mogollon 1 considered earlier than the earliest known Basketmaker II sites, the priority even in this trait seems to be with the Mogollon; but its origins, at least in its forms with which we are concerned here, may very well be Southwestern and, possibly, northern Southwestern.

Settlement and Architecture. Mogollon archaeological sites, as already indicated, represent sedentary villages and hamlets.[30] These consist of groups of houses. From Mogollon 1 through 4 these structures were pithouses; later, in Mogollon 5, they were built above ground. The pithouse villages tended to be relatively small, averaging, perhaps, 20 houses. The small hamlets that developed during the same periods consisted of two or three houses and, occasionally, individual isolated houses were built.[31] The Mogollon 5 villages were generally larger. Wendorf describes some in the Pine Lawn region that consisted of several units of pueblo or apartment-type surface dwellings with each unit incorporating 10 to 20 rooms. In the same region, and a little later, there were communities of well over 100 apartment-cluster

rooms.[32] Similarly, in the south, in the Mimbres region, the Swarts ruin consists of 125 late-period above-ground pueblo-style rooms, and in the same river valley are other contemporaneous villages even larger.[33]

As a general rule, the earlier Mogollon sites were located on high ground—ridges, bluffs, or mesas—possibly for defensive reasons, although no artificial defense works have been found. More probably, drainage and other considerations were the deciding factors in the placing of villages. Later sites were frequently in river valleys, either on natural terraces or sometimes even closer to the stream.[34]

No patterned arrangement can be detected in earlier Mogollon villages. Houses were simply dotted about randomly, although there is a tendency for their entrances to face in an easterly direction. Larger buildings, found within villages and presumed to have fulfilled some kind of community or ceremonial function, were sometimes, but not always, located more or less at the center of the cluster of dwellings.[35] For Period 5, Reed has pointed out that the pueblo, or apartment-like clusters of rooms, quite often faced inward on plazas or courtyards so that the whole gives some impression of planning, although the arrangement of rooms, one to another, was rather haphazard.[36]

The pithouses of the Mogollon 1 and 2 Periods were predominantly circular or oval. Through

Figure 4-7. Reconstruction of a Mogollon (Pine Lawn phase) pithouse, Pithouse J, SU site, New Mexico. Diameter, 6.65 m. No fire-pit or deflector stone was found. A number of pits were dug in the floor and one contained a stone mortar. The roof was supported by a large central post and 20 smaller ones. (Courtesy Chicago Natural History Museum; see Martin, 1943.)

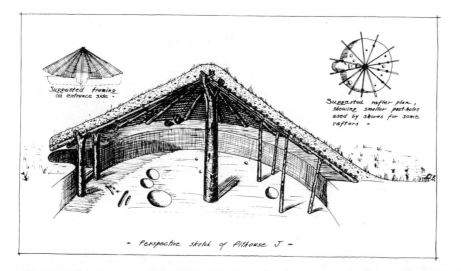

Suggested framing on entrance side.

Suggested rafter plan, showing smaller post-holes used by shores for some rafters.

- Perspective sketch of Pithouse J -

time, there was a trend, into the later periods, toward a rectangular form; and in some regions D-shaped or bean-shaped houses seem to represent transitional steps in this direction. The pithouses varied considerably in size, although an average floor area for all periods and regions would be about 17 square meters, not including the space taken up by benches, entryways, or antechambers. In the Pine Lawn region, for instance, there is some evidence that later houses were smaller than earlier ones, and some authorities have speculated that this change may reflect a shift from extended to nuclear family living. This trend, however, does not hold for other regions, such as the San Simon, where a gradual size increase seems to have occurred, or for still others, where no particular trend can be followed. Depth of the houses also varied. Some were less than a half meter below the surrounding ground surface, others well over a meter. Earlier houses were probably somewhat more shallow than later ones and, regionally, those of the south tend to be shallow.

The Mogollon pithouses were roofed with timbers over which smaller sticks were laid; the

Figure 4-8. Mogollon pithouses and a burial of the Pine Lawn phase. *Top, left*: Pithouse F at SU site, New Mexico. Larger diameter, 6.25 m. Fire-pit present, but no deflector stone. Ten small support posts, 4 storage pits. (See Martin and Rinaldo, 1939.) *Top, right*: Pithouse A at SU site, 10.4 m. in diameter. (See Martin and Rinaldo, 1940.) Its unusual size suggests a community or kiva structure. *Bottom, left*: Museum reconstruction of a Pine Lawn phase pithouse village. *Bottom, right*: Burial found under the floor of a Pine Lawn phase pithouse, SU site. The only grave goods are the shell bracelets. (Courtesy Chicago Natural History Museum.)

whole then was covered with earth and stones. These roofs were constructed and supported in several ways. The earliest method shunned interior post supports. Instead, the principal timbers were conically propped or were laid horizontally on low walls built on the ground surface beside the pit. Later on, a large, central, interior post was used to form the main support for a conical roof; four main corner posts sustained a flat roof; more than four peripheral posts were employed to hold up either a flat or a dome-shaped cribbed roof; and, in Mogollon 3 times and later, a distinctive gabled roof appeared, supported by three main center posts arranged in a row on the long axis of the house.

Early Mogollon pithouses had very short entrance passages or else none, but in later periods these entrances became the rule. Antechambers or vestibules were relatively rare. Wheat, nevertheless, feels that although rare, their few occurrences indicate their chronological priority in early Mogollon and a subsequent diffusion northward to the Anasazi. Bullard, on the other hand, emphasizes that antechambers were confined to northern Mogollon pithouses and, with his different chronological alignment of Anasazi and Mogollon periods, argues for diffusion in the opposite direction. Most Mogollon pithouses did not have benches or banquettes, which were ledges or offsets in the pithouse walls that served as resting places for the sloping sidepoles of the roof. The bench trait, which was characteristic of the Forestdale region only, was probably imported from the Anasazi subarea, where it was common. Similarly, those other pithouse embellishments, the ventilator shafts and the deflecting stones or walls which shielded the fire from air currents were most likely borrowed from the Anasazi and were built into Mogollon houses only in the northern regions. In Mogollon houses the fire-pit generally was about half-way between the center of the floor area and the entry.[37]

The Mogollon people stored food, and perhaps other goods, in bell-shaped pits located outside the houses and also in bins, wall niches, and sub-floor pits within the houses. These interior pits are a particular feature of the Mogollon 1 Period Pine Lawn phase of the Pine Lawn region.[38]

The above descriptions apply to the Mogollon houses and buildings of Period 1 through 4. Period 5, as we have said, marked a transition to above-ground forms, a transition undoubtedly influenced by Anasazi architecture. Intermediate house types of this transition in the Mimbres region were still semi-subterranean, with walls of masonry supporting the roofs. Often these were contiguous or apartment-type houses. The lower levels of the Swarts ruin, placed in the Mangus phase, would be representative of this transition.[39] Farther north, in the Pine Lawn region, above-ground jacal structures may have bridged the change-over from pithouses to masonry pueblos. The fully developed pueblo-style architecture of the latter part of Mogollon Period 5 was usually constructed of stone and mud masonry walls. In the Swarts ruin, river boulders were laid up in a large amount of adobe. Rooms were rectangular and roofed with beams that were supported primarily by the masonry walls. Interior walls were plastered with mud and floors were made of puddled adobe. Storage bins, stone-lined fireplaces, wall niches, and shelves and benches were constructed inside the rooms. Doorways were built only in partitions between rooms and not on the pueblo exterior. Entrance from the outside was, apparently, through the roof.

Special large houses or buildings were constructed in all Mogollon regions except San Simon. Because of their size, which averaged about three times the floor space of ordinary houses, they were probably used for non-domestic and ceremonial functions.

These large buildings, like the common dwellings of the earlier periods, varied considerably in shape. Some were roundish, others D-shaped, some bean-shaped, and some quadrilateral. Most of them contained fire-pits or hearths, and in some were floor pits similar to household storage pits. In later Mogollon periods, the ceremonial buildings in the Mimbres region were quadrilateral and had masonry walls. A curious special feature for both early and late chambers was a deep patterning of floor grooves. These grooves may be the impressions of interior log-linings or partitions, or, as has been suggested, they may mark the spots where hollow-log foot drums were placed.[40]

Burial. The Mogollon peoples disposed of their dead principally by primary burial. Bodies were buried either between or within individual houses (Fig. 4-8, *bottom, right*). When buried within, the bodies were actually placed in the

structures after they had been abandoned as living quarters, although there are some instances where graves were sealed over with clay, implying continued use of the house. In the pueblo sites of Period 5, bodies were placed both outside and inside rooms and often beneath the floors of rooms which remained in use. In general, throughout

Figure 4-9. The Swarts ruin, Mimbres Valley, New Mexico. The dots indicate the positions of burials found under room floors and in surrounding ground. (After Cosgrove and Cosgrove, 1932.)

the Mogollon, graves were simple pits, and bodies were placed in them in flexed or sitting positions.[41] Cremation was occasionally practiced. This custom was followed in late Cochise times and it never completely disappeared.[42] A variety of objects were placed in the graves with the dead, growing more abundant as the periods passed. Besides pottery, which dates to as early as the Circle Prairie phase (either Mogollon Period 1 or 2), grave goods

Figure 4-10. Mogollon-Anasazi pottery of the Tularosa phase (Mogollon 5 Period). Black-on-white pitchers and bowls. (Courtesy Chicago Natural History Museum.)

included shell and turquoise beads, bone talismen or ornaments, shell bracelets, and chipped-stone projectile points. Some idea of the perishable gear which went into the graves comes from the dry cave burials of Tularosa where Mogollon 1 Period interments were found with grass beds, rush mats, string and antelope-hide garments, and a stick-and-feather object (prayer-stick?).[43]

Ceramics and Artifacts. We have mentioned the earliest Mogollon pottery—and, presumably, the earliest pottery known in the Southwest—as being in a brown and polished red-ware tradition; the diagnostic types are of the Alma and San Francisco Red series (see Fig. 4-5), found widely throughout the subarea in Mogollon Period 1.[44] The first modifying trends in the early Mogollon period ceramics included increased surface polishing and the various techniques of texturing, including incising, brushing, scoring, and neckbanding. Surface corrugating, as a modification of the vessel construction coils, was not practiced at the beginning of the period, although most Mogollon pottery appears to have been made by coiling and scraping rather than by lump-modeling and paddle-and-anvil techniques. In general, during the earliest periods, the Mogollon pottery complex tends to be somewhat more elaborate in the southern and eastern regions of the subarea. It is here that most of the vessel forms have been found, including hemispherical bowls, sub-globular or seed-bowls, bowls with flaring rims, slender bottles, and small-necked jars. To the north, the complex is simpler.

Painted pottery decoration characterized Mogollon 2, a red-banded painting on brown surfaces most frequently involving the interiors of bowls and utilizing pendant triangles and other rectilinear designs. The Mogollon 3 red-on-brown painting revealed a refinement of line and a greater variety of rectilinear designs; but the period is most noted for the first appearance of white-slipped pottery, as exemplified by the type Three Circle red-on-white. At this period, also, the Mogollon red-on-brown wares were diffused eastward to the

194

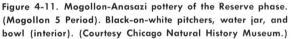

Figure 4-11. Mogollon-Anasazi pottery of the Reserve phase. (Mogollon 5 Period). Black-on-white pitchers, water jar, and bowl (interior). (Courtesy Chicago Natural History Museum.)

Rio Grande, or Jornada, region. In Mogollon 4, the Mimbres black-on-white types developed, apparently from the Three Circle red-on-white and, in general, the northern part of the Mogollon fell under the influence of the black-on-white pottery tradition of the Anasazi. The Tularosa (Fig. 4-10) and Reserve phase (Fig. 4-11) wares of the Mogollon 5 are good examples. In some parts of the south, however, such as the San Simon region, white-slipped pottery never gained a foothold and the red-on-brown tradition continued.[45]

Mogollon 5 is famous for the Mimbres classic black-on-white type of that region, some of it in both jar and bowl forms. Some of the designs were derived from the earlier Mogollon periods[46] and

were highly complex arrangements of triangles, frets, scrolls, and zigzags carried out in hachure and solid black alternating with white areas. More interesting, however, was a distinctive and charming style of stylized life-form painting which was usually expressed on open-bowl interior backgrounds. Frogs, rabbits, insects, birds, fish, deer, mountain sheep, and humans were all portrayed in an exceedingly lively manner despite the basically rectilinear quality of the style. In originality and execution, the Mimbres painted pottery was

195

Figure 4-12. Mimbres style pottery. *Top, left:* Insects. *Right:* Man and bear. *Bottom, left:* Geometric arrangement. *Right:* Rabbit. Two of the vessels show the basal "kill" holes. (Courtesy Peabody Museum, Harvard University.)

probably the outstanding aesthetic product of the Southwest.[47]

Mogollon artifact traditions began, at least for many types, in the Cochise culture, and this continuity we have already referred to in discussing the Tularosa and Cordova Caves of the Pine Lawn region. Perhaps because of the ancient seed-grinding basis of the Cochise economy and the abundance of heavy ground-stone implements in the early levels, Mogollon is particularly characterized by metates, manos, mortars, and pestles (Figs. 4-4, 4-13). Simple basin and slab metates were the most common early forms, undoubtedly inherited from the Cochise. These were irregular flat slabs

with an uneven development of a basin. The form continued through all Mogollon periods and has been found throughout the subarea; however, it tended to give way to basin-trough and trough shapes. Some of these trough forms were closed at one end; others were full troughs with both ends open. The full trough first appeared in Mogollon 3 and by Period 5 it was the most popular form. Another ground-stone artifact type which can be traced back to Cochise origins is a stone maul encircled with a full, nearly-full, or three-quarter hafting groove. Grooved-stone axes also have been found in Mogollon sites, but they did not become a standard item in the culture until Period 5. Both the full and three-quarter-grooved varieties have been uncovered. Mogollon peoples manufactured a great many other ground-stone items, including paint palettes, stone dishes, and tubular and truncated-conical stone smoking pipes.[48] Similar pipes were also made of fired clay.[49]

Figure 4-13. Mortar and pestle of the Pine Lawn phase, SU site, New Mexico. (Courtesy Chicago Natural History Museum.)

The typical Mogollon chipped-stone projectile point was either small or medium sized. It was triangular or ovate-triangular and had diagonal notches at the corners of the base.[50] This type was more common in the early periods, and in Mogollon 5 was partially replaced by narrow, small, triangular, side-notched points which frequently had serrated edges.[51] Mogollon chipped-stone assemblages also include knives, drills, scrapers, and chopping implements.

A great many awls were made of bone, utilizing deer and other mammal bones as well as large bird bones. Flakers, for working chipped stone, were made of bone or antler. Bone needles, pins, fleshing tools, and bone tubes also have been found at Mogollon sites. All these tools appear to have

been widely distributed throughout the Mogollon periods. Bone was also used for making small engraved or plain disks or rectangles or cubes—all perhaps used as gaming pieces, dice or counters—and for making small disk beads. Beads, bracelets, and pendants also were made of shell and ground stone. Such ornamental items became more common during the later periods but have been found throughout Mogollon regional sequences.[52]

Basketry, sandals, and artifacts of wood have been taken and described from the Tularosa and Cordova Caves in tracing the Cochise-to-Mogollon transition. There is a large inventory of such things, and for the Mogollon, we may add, among other elements, fur-and-feather blankets and cotton clothing. Cotton appeared in Mogollon Period 3 and later. In general, coiled basketry began to give way to twilled, and wickerwork sandals to plaited ones, during Period 3. Also at this time the bow-and-arrow (although dating as early as the pre-ceramic levels) replaced the atlatl and dart as the principal weapon.[53]

Mogollon Society. We have confined ourselves thus far to the material aspects of Mogollon culture. What can archaeologists say about the non-material ones? Settlement patterns and architectural forms offer a basis for inference in this regard by analogy with what we know of historic towns, villages, and societies. In this case, the analogies are drawn from the western Pueblo peoples—the Hopi, Zuñi, and others—whose cultural antecedents we believe were Mogollon as well as Anasazi.[54] These historic and modern communities were autonomous towns under the civil and religious leadership of democratically selected elders. Class differences were non-existent or at a minimum. Society was structured along matrilineal clan lines, and this structure is reflected in the apartment-type architecture with its matrilocal residence, and in the kivas, or ceremonial chambers. Fred Wendorf, an archaeologist who has worked in the Mogollon subarea, has suggested an evolution of Mogollon society and settlements which led to such a condition. First, during the

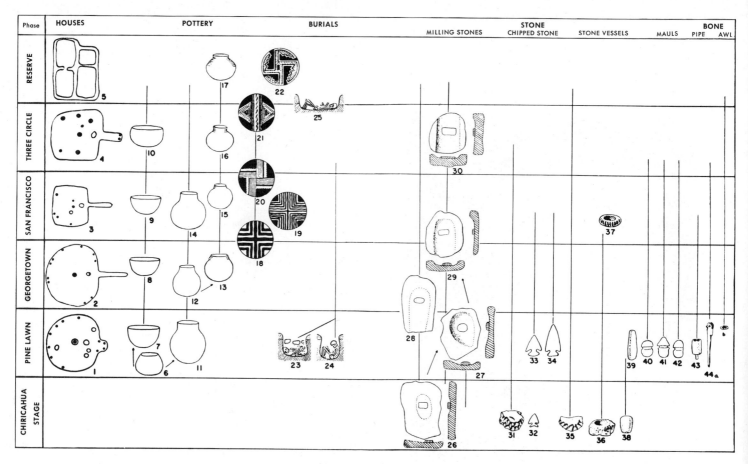

Figure 4-14. The development of Mogollon culture from its Chiricahua (Cochise) base. (After Martin, Rinaldo, and Antevs, 1949.)

earlier periods, the small villages of 20 or so pit-houses and an associated ceremonial building were the sites of lineage or extended family units. Later, during the Mogollon Period 5, these units came together to form clusterings of above-ground apartment-type dwellings in which each architectural unit of 10 to 20 rooms represented such a kin unit. Still later, the large consolidated pueblo-type towns developed; and these large towns, with their blocks of kin unit apartment rooms and their several kivas, were the final prehistoric prototypes leading to the historic western Pueblos.[55] Such an hypothesis accommodates the facts of archaeology and ethnology in a simple and logical fashion. Although some of its details, such as the matrilineality of the clan units, cannot be proved, the general reconstruction seems quite sound.

Summary. From an over-all perspective, the Mogollon line of development of the Southwestern cultural tradition appears less specialized than either the Anasazi or Hohokam lines. It has been our thesis that the essentials of Southwestern culture were first implanted in the Mogollon subarea and that they spread from there to the other two subareas. In spite of these earlier beginnings in farming and in ceramics, the Mogollon seems to have lost its leadership in Southwestern cultural development relatively early. Agriculture was never as firmly established as it was on the Anasazi plateau or in the Hohokam desert. In fact, in one regional sequence there is evidence of a possible relapse to more dependence on hunting and plant-collecting for a time, after the initial establishment of village farming in the Mogollon 1 Period.[56] This may have been a purely local phenomenon, but it is probably symptomatic of the nature of the subsistence adjustment in this

198

subarea as opposed to the others. In both the Anasazi and the Hohokam, natural environmental conditions made the initial establishment of farming more difficult than in the Mogollon. Also, plant and game resources were much rarer in the Anasazi and Hohokam than in the Mogollon. Perhaps these latter factors led to a more rapid agricultural specialization in the Anasazi and Hohokam.

Later in its history, the Mogollon was strongly influenced by both the Anasazi and the Hohokam, examples being the Anasazi influence in pueblo-style architecture and the black-on-white tradition of pottery decoration. Let us examine the Anasazi line of Southwestern development next.

Anasazi

The Anasazi[57] cultural subarea of the northern plateaus centers in those regions of the San Juan and Little Colorado drainages which cluster around the four corners of Arizona, New Mexico, Utah, and Colorado (Fig. 4-1). It also includes the northern Rio Grande region on the east, a region which remained culturally barren compared with the old Anasazi heartland until the later prehistoric periods. Definitely peripheral in distance and in cultural development are the Fremont and Sevier-Fremont regions of western Colorado and Utah and the eastern edges of New Mexico and western Texas.

Basketmaker II Sites. Anasazi culture is first revealed in sites of the Basketmaker II Period (ca. 100 B.C.–A.D. 400). These are the caves and rare open villages which are believed to be contemporaneous with the Mogollon 1 and Pioneer Hohokam Period villages of the south. Although a transition between earlier Cochise-like cultures and Basketmaker II has recently been reported by archaeologists digging in northern New Mexico, the details of this discovery have not yet been released.[58] Such a transition presumably would occupy the chronological niche of Basketmaker I

which was left open for such an eventuality in the Pecos chronology.

The earliest Basketmaker II sites which have been firmly dated—by tree-ring samples (and relatively, by overlying Basketmaker III Period remains)—are in the northern San Juan region near the city of Durango, Colorado.[59] One is an open site known as the Talus Slope Village, already referred to briefly in our account of the emergence of the Southwestern tradition, and the others are nearby rock shelters. They span a period from A.D. 46 to 330.

The Durango sites lie at the far northern border of the Southwestern plateau, and beyond are the Rocky Mountains. The locality is, and was, bountiful in wild game, including deer, elk, mountain sheep, rabbits, squirrels, other small animals, and water fowl. It is seasonally cold, but there is an adequate short growing season for maize and the river bottoms are arable. The sites in question occupy a high slope of the Animas River, a northern tributary of the San Juan. On this slope two small artificial terraces had been cut out to provide level ground for building houses. The floors of 35 houses were found on these terraces, many of them superimposed over others; at least nine, however, were occupied simultaneously. The individual house floors were roughly circular in outline and they measured from 2.5 to 9 meters in diameter, with most of them approximating the smaller figure. They were clay-lined and had a saucer-like appearance. The houses actually were only slightly subterranean and much shallower than the later Basketmaker III pithouses. They were walled with a curious wood-and-mud mortar masonry of which the bottom course was made up of a series of large logs laid horizontally on the ground at the edge of the saucer-like concavity of the floor. Smaller log chunks and mud were stacked on these foundations, probably to about head height. The roof supports rested on the tops of the walls. Entrance must have been through a small side door, without a passage entryway. The buildings were heated by placing large hot stones in a small central heating-pit. Besides these heating-pits, the only other distinctive feature of the Talus Slope Village houses were floor cists for storage. Some of these were bottle-shaped; others were more open and stone-lined and frequently were covered with dome-shaped "bee-hive" tops that stood above the surface of the house floor. These bee-hive tops were made of clay and were often decorated with punched and incised designs that were made to represent animal tracks and clawmarks.

The Talus Slope Village site is supplemented by finds from contemporaneous rock shelters nearby. Similar houses were built within these shelters, although these structures tended to be less substantial, and in some instances were so constructed as to utilize the natural backs or sides of the shelters as a wall side to the house. Domesticated plant remains were found in these dry-shelter deposits, including maize (*Zea mays*) and squash (probably *Cucurbita moschata*). Among the wild food plants were amaranth (*Amaranthus* sp.), sunflower seeds (*Helianthus annuus*), and tansy mustard seeds

Figure 4-15. Cedar bark bag (*left*) and fiber sandal, Basketmaker II Period. (Courtesy Peabody Museum, Harvard University.)

(*Descurainia* sp.). The economy was obviously varied, with hunting, wild-plant collecting, and domestication all contributing to the support of the village.[60]

The Durango maize was genetically more advanced than the earliest Mogollon maize from Bat Cave and Tularosa Cave. Its predominant racial strain is known as the "Hohokam-Basketmaker." For some time archaeologists and botanists thought that this Hohokam-Basketmaker maize was the earliest of the Anasazi subarea, but the Durango maize cobs were mixed with three other racial strains: the "Mexican," "Eastern," and "Tropical Flint." It is perhaps significant that the early primitive Bat Cave and Tularosa corn was most closely related to the Tropical Flint complex maize and that Hohokam-Basketmaker maize probably did not appear in the Bat Cave sequence until about 300 B.C.[61] Possibly, a blending of the two strains first occurred in the Mogollon before their diffusion farther northward; or, possibly, the strains were blended in the Anasazi country. To date, however, the "Mexican" and "Eastern" strains are not represented in the finds of early Mogollon maize, and the route or routes by which they reached the Anasazi remain a mystery. All four of these maize races ultimately originated in Mexico.

The people and the culture of the Durango Basketmaker II sites relate closely to the "classic" Basketmaker II discoveries which were made almost a half-century ago by Kidder, Guernsey, and others in the San Juan and Little Colorado drainages to the west.[62] Basketmaker peoples were of average American Indian stature with smallish, high-vaulted crania of meso-to-dolichocephalic form,[63] the physical type referred to by George Neumann as the "Ashiwid" and by Seltzer as the "Southwestern Plateau type."[64] A series of skeletons of this general description were found in graves at the Durango sites. The flexed bodies had been buried directly in or near the dwellings, occasionally in old cists, and were dressed in sandals, loincloths, string aprons, and robes of hides or fur and feathers, accompanied by baskets, bark bags, and various weapons, tools, and cere-

Figure 4-16. Basketmaker II fur-string robe and string aprons. (Courtesy Peabody Museum, Harvard University.)

Figure 4-17. A Basketmaker II carrying basket from Marsh Pass, Arizona. (Courtesy Peabody Museum, Harvard University.)

monial objects of wood and bone. Some sandals were woven from tule reeds, some from yucca, and others were made of leather; garments with fur-and-feather strips were wound on yucca fiber cordage; and baskets were made by coiling and stitching together several rod-and-bundle splints. The bodies were also adorned with shell, bone, and stone beads and other ornaments.[65] No fired clay vessels accompanied the burials or have been found at the Durango sites. This absence of pottery is, of course, characteristic of Basketmaker II Period cultures, although fragments of what may have been unfired clay containers and an unfired figurine have been found at Durango.

Typical Durango projectile points were medium-sized and corner-notched. The Durango metates were horse-shoe shaped—that is, one end had a tapered opening more like some of the Mogollon forms than the Cochise shapes, which were always closed basins. Tubular stone pipes have been found along with a profusion of bone implements and ornaments such as notched animal scapulae and ribs that were probably used for separating yucca fibers, the basis of cordage and textiles. Little bone "gaming disks" are another interesting item. These usually have been found in sets, and in other Basketmaker caves have sometimes been recovered in hide bags. They were rectangular or circular and usually with bore incised lines. In some instances they may have been fastened to stone or wooden bases with pitch.[66]

These cultural traits obviously resemble the late Cochise-early Mogollon complexes of the south. Morris and Burgh have compared the Durango sites with three early, and presumably contemporaneous, Mogollon complexes: the Penasco, Hilltop, and Pine Lawn.[67] They point out the strong resemblances in house type, to which we can add the rather distinctive tubular "cloud-blower" stone pipe, the medium-sized corner-notched point, and the horse-shoe (Durango) or basin-trough (Mogollon) metate. Also significant are the many general parallels—simple, flexed burial form; coiled basketry; sandals; atlatls; yucca-fiber garments; *Olivella* shell beads; and many more. The

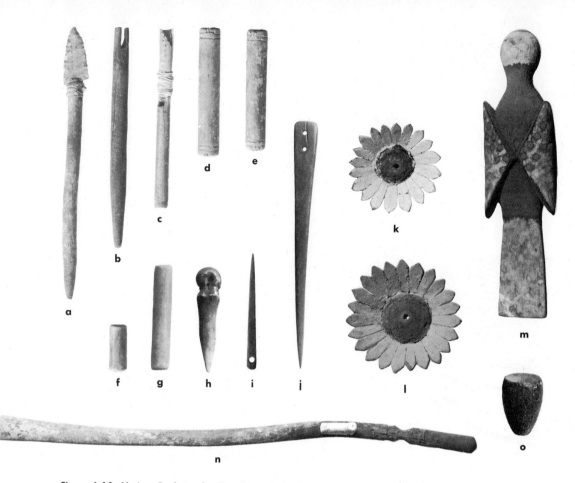

Figure 4-18. Various Basketmaker II artifacts of wood and bone. *a:* Wooden foreshaft armed with chipped-stone point. *b:* Wooden foreshaft. *c:* Cane flute. *d-g:* Gaming sticks. *h:* Bone awl. *i:* Bone needle. *j:* Bone awl or pin. *k,l:* Wooden sunflowers. *m:* Wooden bird. *n:* Atlatl. *o:* Wooden cone. (Courtesy Peabody Museum, Harvard University.)

Figure 4-19. Stone-lined cist filled with maize cobs from a cave near Marsh Pass, Arizona, Basketmaker II Period. (Courtesy Peabody Museum, Harvard University.)

striking difference is, of course, the absence of pottery in Basketmaker II. That the northerners were on the threshold of this introduction or discovery is attested by the appearance of the craft in the succeeding Basketmaker III Period.

Basketmaker III Sites. The Basketmaker III Period (ca. A.D. 400–700) represents a definite material advance over Basketmaker II. Farming was more firmly established, with the bean (*Phaseolus vulgaris*) now being a part of the Anasazi crop complex.[68] Basketmaker III sites were larger. In the Quemado region, for instance, estimates indicate that two Basketmaker III villages embraced over 50 pithouses apiece.[69] Basketmaker III pithouses were improvements over their type II prototypes, and ceremonial chambers, or kivas, were constructed in the villages, and pottery, as we know, made its first appearance. Although some archaeologists once suggested that type III pottery possibly had developed from Basket-

202

maker II unfired clay vessels, a more likely explanation for its introduction is by diffusion from
the Mogollon cultures to the south.[70] The pottery
was made by coiling and was usually fired to a
gray or gray-white color. A plain type, known as
Lino Gray, is diagnostic of the period, as are the
associated Lino Black-on-gray and La Plata Black-
on-white types.[71] Decoration was usually confined
to the interiors of open bowls, and designs took
the form of rectilinear elements of triangles, steps,
panels, and zigzags. Some authorities see a resemblance between these designs and the designs that
were painted on coiled basketry of the preceding
Basketmaker II Period. An additional decorative
element on Basketmaker III pottery was an imper-
manent, fugitive red pigment applied after firing.

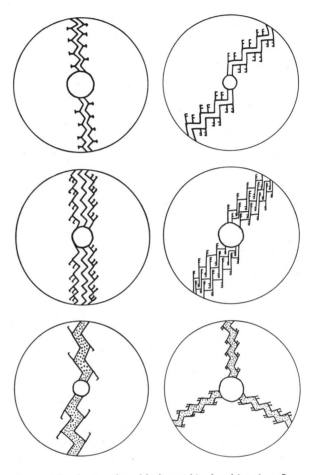

Figure 4-20. Vessel shapes (non-culinary) of the Basketmaker
III Period, from Shabik'eshchee, New Mexico. (After Roberts,
1929.)

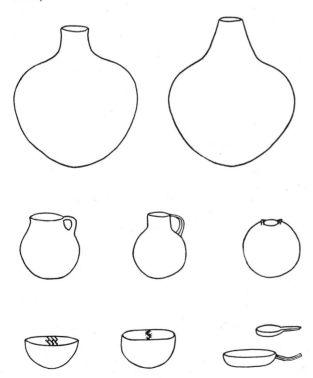

Figure 4-21. Designs from black-on-white bowl interiors, Basketmaker III Period, from Shabik'eshchee, New Mexico. (After
Roberts, 1929.)

In addition to pottery, other Basketmaker III innovations included the fully open-ended trough
metate as a household feature and, toward the end
of the period, the bow-and-arrow, the polished
grooved axe, cotton cloth, and the domesticated
turkey.[72]

The village of Shabik'eshchee in the Chaco
region of New Mexico is one of the best known
and most thoroughly excavated Basketmaker III
sites.[73] A total of 18 pit-dwellings, a large kiva,
a "courtyard," 48 storage bins, and two refuse

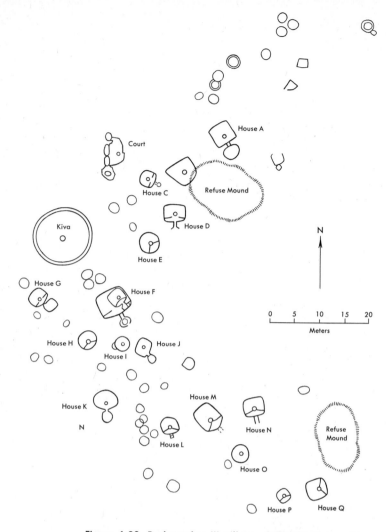

Figure 4-22. Basketmaker III village of Shabik'eshchee, New Mexico. The small circles are storage pits. (Redrawn from Roberts, 1929.)

diameter from slightly over 3 to almost 7 meters. They are circular, oval, and rectangular in outline, and the chronology of the site indicates that the rectangular form grew increasingly popular. The sides of the excavated walls of the pithouses had been either lined with large stone slabs or coated with mud plaster. The roofs were supported by four posts set in the floor at some distance from the corners, or approximate corners, of the pits. Presumably, cross beams topped these four posts, and these cross beams were covered with the poles of a flat roof. The upper walls of the house were formed by leaning poles and sticks from the cross beams to the ground surface outside the pit excavation. The debris found in the excavations indicates that all of the wooden superstructure was coated with a mixture of mud, twigs,

Figure 4-23. Plan of a pithouse in Shabik'eshchee Village, Chaco Canyon, New Mexico. a: Antechamber. b: Passage. c: Support posts. d: Deflector. e: Fire-pit. f: Sipapu. (After Roberts, 1929.)

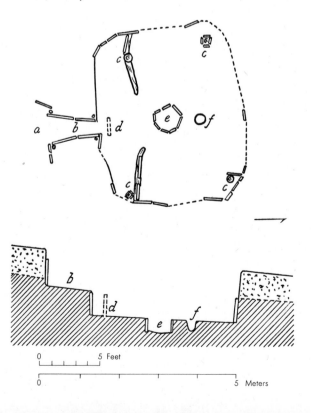

heaps compose the ruins. Stratigraphic evidence detected in the excavations indicates a double occupancy, with an intervening hiatus or abandonment, so the full living community at any one time would not have been more than nine households. Thus, Shabik'eshchee was relatively small for a Basketmaker III village. No plan of arrangement can be detected; the houses are scattered about, with storage bins clustered between houses. The whole describes a sort of rough crescent shape, and the large kiva lies at the edge of the community near the center of the crescent.

The Shabik'eshchee houses average between .60 and .90 of a meter in depth and vary in

and bark. The houses were entered through semi-subterranean passages which were usually located on the south or southeast side. Some of these passages terminated in small semi-subterranean antechambers. Within the main chamber was a centrally located fire basin, and these basins were screened against the rush of cold air from the entrance passage by upright stone slab deflectors. Near the fire basin was a small circular hole in the prepared floor, thought to be, by analogy with present-day Pueblo kivas, the sipapu, or the mythical place where ancestors emerged from the underworld to the surface of the earth.

Although bin-like compartments of stone slabs were placed along the interior walls of some of the houses, the principal storage facilities seem to have been the outside bins. They were made like the pithouses, although smaller, being circular, about 1.50 meter in diameter, and less than 1 meter in depth. They were usually lined with stone slabs or mud plaster and were covered with conical or dome-shaped roofs of poles, wattle, and daub. Presumably, entry was gained through these roofs.

The kiva at Shabik'eshchee was a circular pit-structure, a little over 12 meters in diameter. Its walls were carefully faced with stone slabs, and a low encircling bench had been built up around the interior base of the wall with smaller facing slabs and rock and adobe fill. The roof was supported, as in the houses, by four corner posts. There was no side entrance, only a side ventilating shaft; apparently the kiva was entered through the smoke-hole in the roof. The fire basin was centrally located and protected from the currents of the ventilating shaft by a deflecting stone.

The courtyard was not a central plaza or formally arranged feature but a stone-outlined and paved area covered with plaster which abutted against a row of four storage bins. It was slightly less than 6 by 3 meters in extent. Two fire basins were in the courtyard and two metates were found within it, which led Roberts to surmise that it was used as an outdoor eating and cooking place.

Only fourteen burials were found in the general village area at Shabik'eshchee. Abandoned bins had not been used as tombs. The standard position of the body was flexed, on the back, head to west, and face to north. Only three graves contained mortuary offerings, although perishable items such as basketry probably had been placed in the others.

Pueblo I and II Sites. Pueblo I (ca. A.D. 700–900) is best known as the period of transition from pithouse to above-ground, apartment-type architecture. J. O. Brew has argued that this transition was a gradual, local Anasazi development, pointing out that the previous Basketmaker III storage rooms and cists:

. . . which were close together in small groups, anyhow, were brought even closer together in a single structure of contiguous rooms, and characteristic Pueblo architecture was well on its way.[74]

This transitional nature of the Pueblo I Period is nicely illustrated by several sites.[75] Thus, Kiatuthlanna, in the upper Little Colorado region of eastern Arizona, is an example of the very early Pueblo I pattern. Here, the pithouse was still the principal form of residence, but the individual dwellings were grouped into small clusters of from three to six houses. The total village area was composed of four such clusters. Near each cluster were above-ground structures of jacal. Some of these may also have been dwellings, but most of them were probably storage rooms.[76] What looks like a more advanced stage of the transition is displayed in the Piedra region of Colorado. Again, the village was composed of several unit groups of houses, but here each unit was made up of above-ground jacal dwellings and storage rooms rather than pithouses. Most of the jacal buildings stood singly, although close together within each group, and some of them were actually contiguous, their walls common. Within each group there was a tendency for all buildings to be arranged in an arc or row. With at least one unit group was an associated single pithouse, probably a ceremonial

Figure 4-24. Basketmaker III pithouse, Quemada region, New Mexico. This pithouse was rectangular with rounded corners and measured 6 m. across. It had 4 main post supports, wall posts on the benches, a fireplace, a partition wall of upright stone slabs (one of which was a deflector), two heating pits filled with burned rocks, and other features. (After Bullard, 1962, Structure 203.)

chamber.[77] Site 13, Alkali Ridge in Utah (northern San Juan region), carries the transition still farther. This large village contained four habitation units, each consisting of from 30 to 50 above-ground and fully contiguous rooms. The dwellings were of a type of jacal construction, made of adobe, small rock, and wooden posts. The rooms which were used for both storage and dwelling purposes, were arranged in long, irregular arcs, with the openings of the arcs on the south or southeast. Within each arc opening, in a sort of small plaza area, were pithouses, from two to four to a plaza, apparently the ceremonial chambers for the respective units.[78]

It is, thus, perfectly feasible to bring Pueblo I architecture and settlement out of Basketmaker III without postulating the advent of a new people into the Anasazi subarea. This latter interpretation was favored for a time because it appeared to be reinforced by evidence from physical anthropology. Long-headed Basketmaker populations presumably had been overrun by broad-headed Puebloans. But more careful analyses of the human cranial material has not borne out this assumption.[79] For one thing, the dichotomy between long-heads and round-heads was confused by artificial lambdoidal cranial deformation, a culture trait which does, indeed, appear for the first time in Pueblo I. For another, it has now been made clear that the presumed earlier Basketmaker phys-

Figure 4-25. Site 13, Alkali Ridge, Utah, Scattered buildings (except where marked as kivas) are pithouses, dating to Basketmaker III times. The compound surface rooms are variously constructed (adobe, jacal) and date from Basketmaker III to Pueblo I. The kivas and the "coursed-masonry building" (so marked) are Pueblo II-III. (Redrawn from Brew, 1946.)

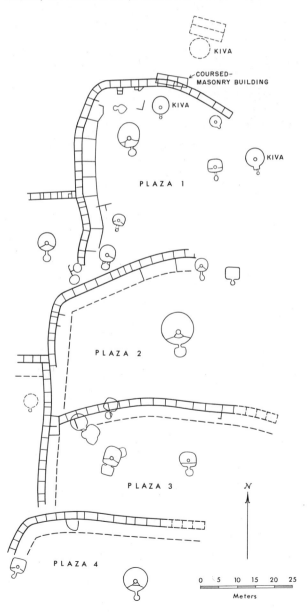

ical type, the one designated by Seltzer as the "Southwestern Plateau type," continues with relatively slight modifications to the historic and modern periods. Measurements on undeformed crania do indicate a slight tendency toward broadheadedness beginning at about Pueblo I times and continuing through the Anasazi sequence, but the extent of the trend is really from a low mesocephalic to a high mesocephalic index. The causes of such a trend might be the addition of new peoples of a differing physical type entering the Southwest in small numbers and gradually being absorbed into the resident Southwestern Plateau populations, or the causes may be in slow "genetic drift" of the kind M. T. Newman has postulated (see Chap. 2, pp. 14-15). What does seem to be certain, however, is that there was never a sudden heavy influx of a markedly brachycephalic group into the Anasazi country.

During the Pueblo II Period (ca. A.D. 900-1100) several changes in settlement and architecture occurred. None of these represents a sharp and perfectly synchronized innovation for the entire Anasazi subarea; in fact, in many instances the old and the new exist side by side.[80] But all are worth mentioning as general trends. First, settlement became dispersed. The large villages of late Basketmaker III and Pueblo I tended to give way to small, scattered, single-habitation-unit communities consisting of a solitary apartment structure of a few rooms together with a nearby kiva. Presumably, these were unilineal kinship settlements, although in some instances they were so small as to suggest quarters for only an extended family at the most.[81] Another change or trend saw jacal-type walls replaced by walls of coursed-stone masonry. In yet a third, the four floor posts that supported the roofs of the kivas gave way to wall benches and pilaster supports.

Two small sites in the Alkali Ridge locality exemplify these various Pueblo II changes and features. Site 9 contains the definite remains of two small, single-room, rectangular buildings, one of which may have had two other rooms attached to it. The wall foundations revealed small posts

packed with adobe and small rock jacal construction. A few meters to the southeast of these above-
ground jacal buildings was a circular, subterranean
kiva with the typical fire-pit, ventilator shaft,
deflector, and sipapu hole. This kiva appears to
have had four floor posts supporting the roof.[82]
In everything except its small size, this single-unit-
habitation site contrasts with Alkali Ridge No. 7.
At Alkali Ridge No. 7 were two conjoined, coursed-
stone masonry, rectangular rooms. The associated kiva, also a short distance to the south of
the above-ground building, and identified by its
fire-pit, ventilator, deflector, and sipapu, exemplified the "newer" style, with a wall bench and
six masonry pilasters rising from this bench to
support the roof.[83]

Pueblo III and IV Sites. Pueblo III
Period, defined, as it usually is, by the widespread
presence of large apartment-type pueblo villages
or towns, dates from about A.D. 1000–1100 to the
closing decades of the thirteenth century (ca. A.D.
1275–1300), when the northern portion of the
plateau country was abandoned by the Anasazi
peoples. Three regions—the Chaco, the Northern
San Juan, and the Kayenta—contain outstanding
examples of Pueblo III towns and architecture.[84]
In all regions the small Pueblo II unit-type houses
scattered about the countryside housed part of the
total population, but large towns also sprang up.
In the Chaco Canyon there are twelve of these
towns, of which Pueblo Bonito is the largest. This
ruin, situated on the valley floor with its back to
the towering cliffs of the mesa, is a huge, planned
architectural complex.[85] It is D-shaped, with its
curving side to the north and toward the cliff face.
Its straight side, which was the front of the complex, faces south and toward the river. As one
faces this front side, the room constructions rise
terrace-fashion like some great amphitheater to
a height of four stories. In the center of the D is a
huge open court, and the rooms of the lower terrace which open on this court are a single story
high. A single line of rooms, one story high, con-
nects the two ends of the arc of the "amphitheater"

Figure 4-26. *Above: Anasazi kiva architecture. A masonry
deflector and ventilator shaft, Alkali Ridge, Utah. (Courtesy
Peabody Museum, Harvard University.)*

Figure 4-27. *(Top, p. 209) Pueblo Bonito, Chaco Canyon, New
Mexico. The rectangular units are living quarters, the circular
ones, kivas. (After Judd, 1964.)*

Figure 4-28. *(Bottom, p. 209) Pueblo Bonito, Chaco Canyon,
New Mexico. A view taken from north rim of canyon. The
D-shaped layout of the pueblo is in the foreground. In the
background is the ravine of the river and, farther away, the
south canyon rim. (Courtesy 1921 National Geographic
Society.)*

and forms the straight side of the D and the front
wall of the courtyard. The total structure measures about 160 meters (east-west) by 100 meters
(north-south) and covers an area of 3 acres. There
are over 800 apartment rooms. Tree-ring dates
show that the first construction was started in what
are generally considered Pueblo II times, A.D. 919.
The total complex was not completed until A.D.

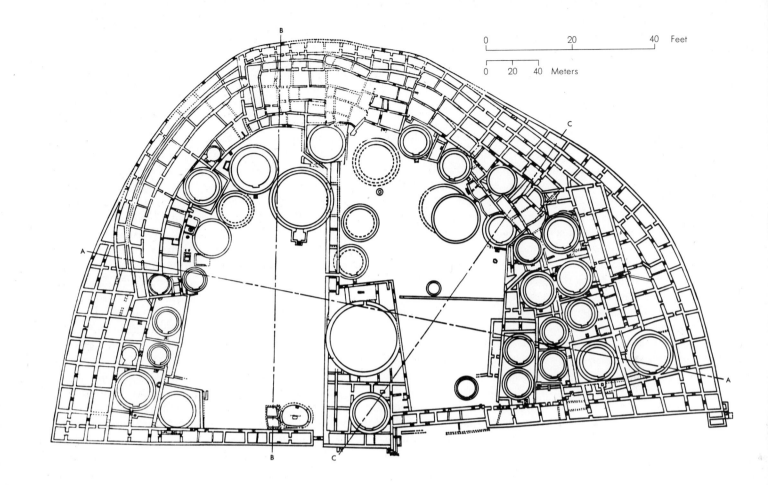

1067. It is estimated that in its heyday Pueblo Bonito housed about 1200 persons.

Several large subterranean circular kivas are located in the Pueblo Bonito courtyard, the largest being almost 20 meters in diameter. These large kivas are believed to have served community functions while smaller circular kivas, built within the apartment mass of rectangular rooms at various points, may have continued to be the ceremonial chambers of kinship units or clans that had been brought together to form the town.

The masonry of Pueblo Bonito and other Chaco Canyon ruins is mostly of coursed stone, which is used as a facing to cover interior cores of rock and adobe rubble. Both sides of the walls were veneered with stone blocks. In one type, laminate sandstone of more or less uniform thickness was set with a minimum of mud mortar. In another, the veneer was made up of alternate bandings of large, semi-dressed sandstone blocks and thinner blocks or spallings. In still a third type of wall construction, thin sandstone slabs and spalls were layered between very thick bands of adobe mortar.

Most of the rooms of Pueblo Bonito, presumably used for habitation or storage, are rather

large-sized, averaging, perhaps, 4 by 5 meters. They were roofed with cross-beams laid over the wall tops, atop which were laid cross poles covered with woven mats and splints and a coating of adobe. These roofs were sufficiently sturdy to support the floors of the rooms above, and some of them are still intact today. Walls of the rooms were coated with adobe plaster. Rooms in outer tiers contained doors and windows facing toward the general direction of the courtyard, and these appear to have been living quarters. Interior rooms without such apertures were probably used for storage. Courtyard or roof terrace space adjoining the rooms was usually reserved for corn-grinding and cooking.

The absence of doors and windows opening to the outside of the compound is as noticeable at Pueblo Bonito as it is in other Pueblo III ruins. Some apertures had been made at one time, but these were sealed up, including even a front main gate on the south side. Entrance here, apparently, was over the wall by ladder. These obviously defensive features of Pueblo Bonito, and of other of the large Pueblo III towns, tend to support the explanation of warlike invasions for both the establishment of large towns and for their abandonment at the close of the period. The Athapascans, who probably were invading the northern borders of the Southwest at about this time, may have been the causal agents. This explanation is not fully satisfactory, however, for a hunting-collecting people, which the Athapascans must have been at this time, would have been few in number and probably not a match for most of the relatively populous Anasazi farming communities. Thus, while the appearance of the Athapascan might have been important in bringing small, isolated unit habitations together to form the concentrated towns of Pueblo III, it is less likely that these newcomers were responsible for their subsequent abandonment. Ralph Linton has suggested inter-Puebloan warfare as a more likely cause of disruption and abandonment.[86] Others have felt that increasing aridity, a lowering of the water table, and, especially, a severe and long

Figure 4-29. Pueblo Bonito. Section of excavated pueblo, showing apartment quarters and circular kivas. (Courtesy 1921 National Geographic Society.)

drought which is recorded in the tree-ring growths between A.D. 1276 and 1299 were the chief reasons for the late thirteenth-century desertion of the northern plateau country.[87] The question of cause remains open. What archaeologists can be sure of, however, is that late Pueblo III times were troubled ones—as attested by defensive architecture, burned villages, and mutilated and unburied skeletons—and that they were also years of marked drought.

The Mesa Verde locality in the northern San Juan region is also known for its Pueblo ruins, of which the most famous is Cliff Palace.[88] It, too, is a terraced masonry multi-roomed building, but it has been constructed within a great natural niche in a sandstone cliff overhang. The complex totals over 200 rooms and has 23 incorporated kivas. The kivas are mostly small and circular with an encircling bench and the standard six masonry pilaster supports rising from the bench to sustain the roof. In other words, this is the dominant Pueblo III kiva type which first came into being in the preceding Pueblo II Period, as at Alkali Ridge. The Mesa Verde masonry differs from that of Chaco Canyon in having no rubble core walls and in being made of roughly dressed stone rather than tabular blocks. An odd and distinctive feature of Mesa Verde architecture are the towers. These towers sometimes were part of a compound, as at Cliff Palace, or sometimes were isolated from other buildings. We are not certain whether they were defensive features or, perhaps, ceremonial buildings or primitive observatories. Large "cliff-dwelling" pueblos are also found in the Kayenta region of northeastern Arizona. Betatakin and Keet Seel are two of the best known.[89]

Although Anasazi architecture and masonry seem to have originated and evolved locally, in the simple above-ground buildings of Pueblo I and II, some of the features of Pueblo III possibly were Mesoamerican inspired. The towers, particularly the circular ones, are one such Mesoamerican parallel, as are architectural colonnades in some of the larger Chaco Canyon buildings. A more general trait similarity is the typically Mesoamer-ican rubble-core masonry.[90] Such a diffusion from Mesoamerica, if it did occur, left no continuous geographic trail, for these architectural features were missing from the southern part of the Southwest at this time.

Pueblo IV (ca. A.D. 1300–1700) is sometimes called the "Regressive Pueblo Period,"[91] but perhaps "retractive" would be a better term. There was no general cultural decline, but the former trend toward assembling the population into fewer and larger towns increased and the total subarea of Anasazi occupation shrank. The northern regions were abandoned during the late years of the thirteenth century, leaving the Anasazi concentrated on the Little Colorado and the northern Rio Grande. It was in these locations that the Spaniards found the Pueblo Indians in the sixteenth century. The Pueblo IV towns were even larger than those of Pueblo III. Built of stone masonry blocks and adobe, they too were multistoried, terraced, planned apartment-house units grouped on or around plazas. The principal sites in the west are the Hopi and Zuñi towns, some of which are still occupied today. In the east, the largest was Pecos at the headwaters of the Pecos River on the eastern edge of the Northern Rio Grande region. Begun in late Pueblo III times, it continued as an important center until early in the nineteenth century.[92]

Anasazi periods are based primarily on the forms of settlement and architecture, and we have forged ahead of other culture aspects in so describing these periods following Basketmaker III. What of other changes in Anasazi development?

Trends. In the important matter of subsistence, it is likely that the Anasazi gradually grew increasingly dependent on farming and relied less on hunting and collecting and that they were able to increase agricultural production by various means of water control. We cannot say if more land was actually cultivated and total populations were larger in later times; but as the population congregated in the towns during the Pueblo III Period, larger water reserves and the control of

Figure 4-30. (P. 212) Anasazi cliff pueblos. *Top:* The "White House" in Canyon de Chelly, Arizona. *Bottom:* Cliff Palace, Mesa Verde, Colorado. (*Top,* courtesy Peabody Museum, Harvard University; *bottom,* courtesy 1921 National Geographic Society.)

Figure 4-31. *Below:* The pueblo of Rito de los Frijoles, near Santa Fe, New Mexico. This view shows the circular layout of dwelling units and the kivas in the central court area. (Courtesy 1921 National Geographic Society.)

Figure 4-32. Pueblo I pottery. *Left:* Neck-banded jar. *Right:* Kana-a black-on-white seed bowl. (Courtesy Peabody Museum, Harvard University.)

utilization of water must have become necessary.[93] In the Anasazi country improved control and utilization was effected by constructing terraces or check dams to retain rain and flood waters in the arroyos and by building stream diversion dams and irrigation canals. Irrigation techniques are especially well exemplified at the Mesa Verde sites, where one canal is as much as four miles long,[94] and in the Hopi towns, where such features are both prehistoric and modern.[95] Although difficult to pinpoint, these agricultural features probably date from Pueblo III times and later.[96]

To turn from subsistence to manufactures, we first see that the patterns of ceramic change from Pueblo I through IV involved an elaboration of the black-on-white painted tradition and an increasing regional diversity of styles and types. In Pueblo I the white ground color of the black-on-white vessels became a true slip rather than the pseudo-slip smoothing of Basketmaker III. The only exception to the black-on-white tradition during the Pueblo I Period was the oddly divergent red-fired type, Abajo Red-on-orange, which is encountered in the western part of the Northern San Juan region, as at Alkali Ridge.[97] The decorative painting of all these Pueblo I types was applied in geometric and rectilinear design elements: zigzags, parallel, parallel-stepped, and wavy lines, solid and dotted triangles, volutes, interlocking frets, checkers, and concentric elements. An horizon

Figure 4-33. A Kiatuthlanna black-on-white pitcher, Pueblo I Period. (Courtesy Cambridge Museum of Archaeology and Ethnology, England.)

marker for the period is "neck-banding"—not obliterating the coil strips on jar necks[98] of unpainted culinary ware (Fig. 4-32, *left*).

Before moving on from Pueblo I pottery, this is probably the most appropriate place to note the infusion into Southwestern pottery traditions of a curious series of new vessel forms, including duck-shaped and bird-shaped pots, slender-necked and double-necked bottles, bottles or jars with tri-lobed bodies, and stirrup-mouthed and ring-bodied jars. Appearing at the close of Basketmaker III and the beginnings of Pueblo I, these specimens are "exotics" which stand in sharp contrast to the rather simple vessels forms which had preceded them. It is difficult to explain them as the fruits of diffusion from Mexico, because they do not first appear in the southern part of the Southwest; but instead were found earliest in the northeastern edge of the Anasazi subarea in the Piedra and San Juan regions. Most of them were rather crudely modeled and resembled Middle Mississippian pottery from the Arkansas-Missouri region rather than Mesoamerican types. Consequently, and because of where they were first discovered, some researchers believed that the Mississippi Valley may have been their source and that immigrants coming from the east carried these pottery traits to the Anasazi by way of the Arkansas, Canadian, Red, or Cimarron River valleys. Such forms, however, are not known to be as early as Pueblo I (A.D. 700–900) in the eastern United States. It thus remains a possibility that they were local Anasazi inventions and, perhaps, that they were diffused from west to east.[99]

A ceramic marker for Pueblo II is spiral-coiling, as opposed to the ring-coil manufacture of vessels and the semi-obliteration and annealing of the coils by indentations that we have noticed previously. This corrugated ware, as it is called, was typical of much of the culinary pottery of both Pueblo II and III. In painting, black-on-white

Figure 4-34. Pueblo I and Pueblo II pottery. *a:* Gray ware duck jar, Pueblo I. *b,c:* Mancos black-on-white, Pueblo II. (Courtesy Peabody Museum, Harvard University.)

a   b   c

types remained dominant. A tendency for very broad-lined, bold decoration intruded at times, but, for the most part, designs continued in the same geometric traditions as before.[100]

By Pueblo III, the Anasazi ceramic complex attained its climax. Excellent black-on-white styles

Figure 4-35. Pueblo II pottery types from Alkali Mesa, Utah. *Top:* Tusayan polychrome (black-and-red-on-orange). *Bottom:* Corrugated ware. (Courtesy Peabody Museum, Harvard University.)

were produced in the Chaco, Mesa Verde, and Kayenta localities, and at Kayenta a black-red-and-white-on-orange polychrome was fashioned. Polychromes were also made in the Hopi country. As before, the main design motifs were the complicated arrangements of triangles, frets, bands, and spirals executed in solid colors or in hachure alternating with the plain backgrounds. A few stylized life motifs appeared as minor elements. A typical range of Pueblo III vessel forms for the painted wares would include handled pitchers and flat-bottomed mugs, flat-globular "seed-bowls," ladles, open bowls, and some effigy forms. In brief, it represents a similar, but fuller, assortment of the preceding Pueblo periods. The principal developments of Pueblo IV were the replacement of corrugated wares by plain culinary pots, the flourishing of the handsome red-and-black-on-yellow Sikyatki polychrome of the Hopi towns, and the rise in the Rio Grande region of black-on-tan "biscuit wares" and native lead-ore glaze paints.[101]

Baskets continued to be made from the close of Basketmaker III times throughout the Pueblo sequence until they were largely superseded by pottery containers. A twilled technique partially replaced the old coiled method of fabrication. Cotton, which first appeared at the end of Basketmaker III, became more popular later on and was used in weaving blankets and all articles of clothing. Anasazi sandals reflect chronological change through modifications in their toe styles. Thus, Basketmaker II sandals were square-toed; those of Basketmaker III had scalloped-toes; in Pueblo I and II round-toes were the vogue; and in Pueblo III and IV a notched-toe variety was most common. The principal change in chipped-stone implements was the steady increase of small projectile points at the expense of large ones, apparently correlated with the increasing popularity of the bow-and-arrow over the atlatl and dart. The earliest small point was slender and had either pronounced flaring barbs or basal notches set diagonally to the axis of the blade. These were replaced in Pueblo III times by small triangular

Figure 4-36. Black-on-white Anasazi pottery from Pueblo Bonito, New Mexico. *a:* Pueblo II water jar. *b,c:* Interior views of Pueblo III bowls. *d,e:* A distinctive type of Chaco Canyon jar, Pueblo III. *f:* Duck pot of the same general kind that appeared for the first time in Pueblo I (this specimen probably Pueblo II). *g,h,i:* Pueblo II pitchers. (Courtesy 1921 National Geographic Society.)

points with basal side-notches set at right angles to the blade axis.[102] In ground stone, the full-grooved axe became more common, and in the grinding and polishing of small stones for ornaments the finest workmanship—particularly in turquoise—belongs to Pueblo III–IV.[103]

Throughout the Anasazi sequence there was little change in the manner of burial or disposal of the dead. Primary, flexed inhumation remained the rule, and bodies were placed in refuse heaps, under abandoned house floors, and at random in village areas. The principal cemeteries for such large towns as Pueblo Bonito or Cliff Palace have never been found. Cremation was occasionally practiced, as at Mesa Verde, but there is no evidence to suggest that it was ever the general mortuary practice. Perhaps the only trend is that Pueblo III burials tend to have more grave accompaniments in the way of pottery and jewelry than those of the earlier periods.[104]

216

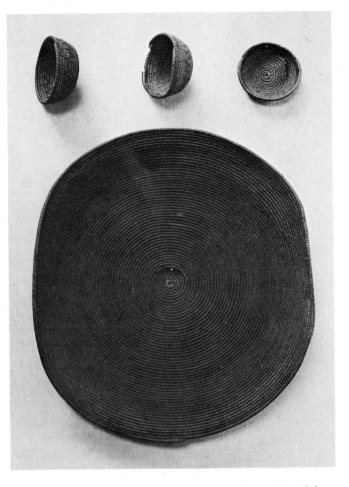

Figure 4-37. Coiled baskets of Basketmaker III Period from Broken Roof Cave, Arizona. (Courtesy Peabody Museum, Harvard University.)

forms to such a degree that their total culture in the twentieth century has been severely modified by the Europeans but is still intact. It is from this cultural persistence that we have some idea of what the nonmaterial life of pre-Columbian times may have been like.

In political, religious, and social matters it seems unlikely that the societies of the Anasazi Pueblo Periods were ever organized on a multi-

Figure 4-38. Scallop-toed Basketmaker III sandals from Arizona. (Courtesy Peabody Museum, Harvard University.)

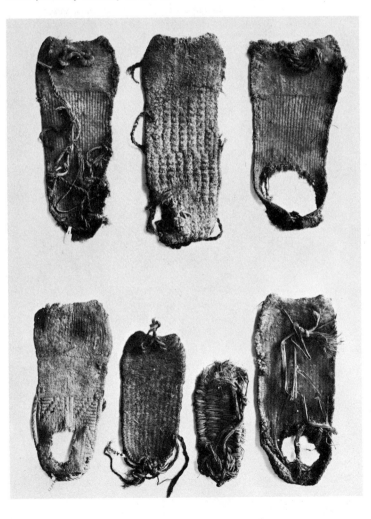

European Contacts. The Spanish Conquistadores discovered the Pueblo IV Period towns in the mid-sixteenth century, Coronado's major expedition passing through the Zuñi country and visiting the Rio Grande in 1540–1542. Colonization and Catholic missionary activities did not begin, however, until some decades later. In 1680 the Pueblos revolted and threw out their European rulers, and Spanish control was not restored until 1692. From then on, through Spanish, Mexican, and United States sovereignty, these Puebloan descendants of the Anasazi have followed a course of more or less passive resistance to the European world. Yielding and accomodating at those points where forced to, they have nevertheless maintained their native political, social, and religious

Figure 4-39. Chipped-stone points and drills, Pueblo I and II Periods, Alkali Mesa, Utah. (Courtesy Peabody Museum, Harvard University.)

Figure 4-40. Latter nineteenth-century photo of the Pueblo of Taos, New Mexico. (Courtesy Peabody Museum, Harvard University.)

town basis. Although there was such a multi-town organization for a brief time at the beginning of the rebellion of 1680, this confederacy was ephemeral. Today, Pueblo political organization is decidedly local. Leadership resides with elders

who are the heads of the various religious or politico-religious fraternities in each pueblo. Such leadership tends to remain in the same lineages and clans, but it is in no way a means by which individuals may consolidate aristocratic privileges in the total society. The various fraternities are concerned with such things as rain-making ceremonies, curing, and matters of social control. At one time, military defense was under the direction of one such fraternity in each town. The combined heads of the fraternal organizations make up a supreme town council to decide on important legislation and to exercise judicial functions.[105] As you might surmise, the tenor of Pueblo political, social, and religious life, which is set, in effect, in the kiva meetings of the religious fraternities, is extremely conservative and even secretive. Some of this conservatism may be an inheritance from the Anasazi past, but European pressures for change in recent centuries, also have probably helped form such attitudes.[106]

Largo-Gallina. Beyond the central Anasazi regions in which we have been following the story of Basketmaker-Pueblo development are other regions which are distinctly marginal in their divergence from the characteristic traits and trends. The closest geographically of all of these is a region in north central New Mexico which we will refer to as the Largo-Gallina (Fig. 4-1). An early phase in this region, the Rosa, is contemporaneous with Pueblo I Period, as its pithouses and above-ground adobe storage chambers indicate; but it differs from typical Anasazi cultures of the time in its fortified or stockaded villages and its crude, plain pottery.[107] Later, in the same general region, although in separate localities, the Largo[108] and Gallina[109] phases, which date from Pueblo III times, were probably local outgrowths of the Rosa phase. They assimilated new Anasazi traits, such as black-on-white pottery and stone masonry, but diverged from "core" Anasazi in a number of ways. Foremost among these was a plain utility ware which was paddle-and-anvil smoothed rather than scraped and which was further distinguished

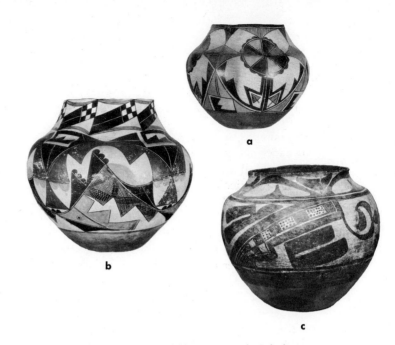

Figure 4-41. Historic Period Pueblo pottery. *a,b:* Polychrome vessels from Acoma. *c:* Vessel from Santa Ana. (Courtesy Peabody Museum, Harvard University.)

by deep, pointed-bottom vessel forms. It suggests, in a general way, the ceramic patterns of the eastern United States. Elbow-shaped pottery pipes, which were also a Largo-Gallina trait, also hint at eastern contacts. No specific ties with an Eastern Woodland or a Plains Woodland complex can be made, however, and it may be that this Largo-Gallina pottery represents early Athapascan influences on the northern borders of the Southwest, although this is by no means certain.[110] That the Rosa and the Largo-Gallina people were, indeed, "frontiersmen," and subject to attack from enemies, who were possibly northern and eastern

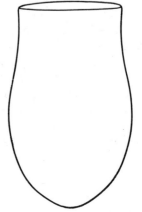

Figure 4-42. Typical Largo-Gallina vessel form. (Drawn from Mera, 1938.)

semi-nomads, is implied in the Rosa wooden-post stockades and in the extremely massive and thick-walled dwelling constructions of the later phases. Gallina, particularly, is known for its huge, stone-walled, tower-like dwellings.

The Northern and Eastern Peripheries. Farther to the north and west is the territory sometimes referred to *en toto* as the "Northern Periphery." Three regional subdivisions of this territory are indicated: a Fremont region, which includes western Colorado and eastern Utah north of the San Juan drainage; a southwest Utah-Nevada region, to the north of the Colorado River in northwestern Arizona and including adjacent edges of Utah and Nevada; and a Sevier-Fremont region, which takes in much of western Utah. As early as Basketmaker III times, a Desert culture in these regions was beginning to settle into a sedentary existence, probably as a result of diffusions from the Anasazi proper. Maize was grown and some pottery was manufactured. During Pueblo I and II times, the architecture of these northern peripheral regions reflected Anasazi influences, albeit belatedly. Thus, although both pithouse and above-ground stone and adobe architecture were practiced, the pit-dwellings continued to be used after they had gone out of fashion in the south, and they also retained such archaic features as side-passage entrances after the Anasazi had discarded them. These semi-subterranean structures were dwellings, not ceremonial chambers, for the kiva appears not to have entered the northern peripheral cultures. The pottery of the north was cruder and plainer than the southern variety. Plain black and gray wares in round-bottom jar forms, some with handles, were most typical. Some black-on-gray pottery was painted locally; black-on-whites, however, probably appeared only as a result of trade with the Northern San Juan region. The north developed certain specializations of its own. Among these was an elaboration of clay figurines, a trait derived from Anasazi Basketmaker cultures but which had tended to pass out of vogue in the south. Rock paintings

and petroglyphs were other distinctive developments. At about the beginning of Pueblo III times, most of these northern peripheral cultures disappeared. Quite possibly many of the people withdrew farther south, for whatever reason. Those who remained probably followed a simpler type of existence, more like the earlier Desert culture. Some of these holdouts may have been the ancestors of the Utes and Paiutes of the historic horizon.[111]

On the east, the Northern Rio Grande region, including the headwaters of the Pecos River, is not the easternmost fringe of Anasazi culture. Influences, although considerably thinned and diluted, extend into the Texas Panhandle. Here, a marginal agricultural complex, known as the Antelope Creek phase, developed along the Canadian River drainage in late prehistoric times. It is associated with pueblo-style stone masonry dwellings, although it is otherwise non-Anasazi and non-Southwestern.[112]

Hohokam

The Hohokam[113] and the Anasazi are strikingly different. Ancient Hohokam communities kept to desert valleys; farming depended on intensive irrigation of the desert; architecture was of semi-perishable wattle-and-daub or massive adobe without stone; and ceramics were paddle-and-anvil smoothed, red-fired, and painted a red-on-buff. During its earlier periods Hohokam shared many traits with Mogollon and later was strongly influenced by Anasazi culture and Anasazi migrants, although never to the same extent as Mogollon.

The Hohokam subarea is southern Arizona, and the culture is best known from what we shall call the Gila-Salt region which lies along the courses of those streams above their confluence. Another, and closely related, region is the Tucson, in the vicinity of that city and along the Santa Cruz River. To the west is the more divergent cultural subdivision of the Papaguería, the country of the present-day Papago reservation which lies south of the Gila, west of the Tucson region, east of the town of Ajo, and north of the international boundary. Two other regions are still more marginal to the Hohokam proper. One is the San Pedro River Valley to the east of Tucson. Here, Hohokam and Mogollon blended. Southward, in Sonora, is the Trincheras region, little known but probably an intermediate link between the Papaguería Hohokam and the Sinaloa cultures of Mesoamerica.[114] The stratigraphy of Ventana Cave in the Papaguería region implies that Hohokam beginnings lie in western Cochise culture. The upper levels show a transition from San Pedro hunting into early farming and pottery-using communities around the beginning of the Christian era, a transition accompanied by many continuities in lithic types from Cochise to Hohokam levels. There are also some indications that the Papaguería was not the first firm Southwestern setting of these transforming elements, that they had been diffused to this relatively inhospitable part of the southern Arizona desert from the Gila-Salt or Tucson regions.[115]

If we follow the hypothesis presented earlier in this chapter, these more centrally situated regions of the Hohokam had, in turn, received maize and the idea of pottery from the early Mogollon peoples who lived still farther east. It is possible, however, that Hohokam and Mogollon were separately stimulated to village farming and ceramic production by independent diffusions from Mesoamerica.[116]

Placing the beginnings of the Hohokam at around 100 B.C. is an estimate that is based on cross-referencing with the Mogollon radiocarbon dates, various late Cochise dates, and by reckonings from cross-ties between Hohokam and Anasazi higher up in the time scale.[117]

Snaketown and the Early Hohokam Sequence. The development of Hohokam culture through the Pioneer, Colonial, and Sedentary Periods is best reviewed from the excavations of the large site of Snaketown in the lower Gila Valley.[118] The ruins are today a mile from the present course of the river. Surrounding everything is the semi-arid desert—sand, mesquite, and salt bush. This was the land farmed by the Hohokam and is, today, farmed by the modern Pima Indians, their probable descendants. This cultivation was and is today carried out by means of irrigation canals. In aboriginal times, however, and in fact up until 100 to 75 years ago, there was more vegetation cover and more annual run-off into the rivers and streams than today. The generally more arid character of the area today has resulted not from any major climatic fluctuation but from the cutting of timber in the nearby mountains and from overgrazing—both activities of late European occupancy. In brief, when the Hohokam were thriving on the lower Gila, their environment was more favorable for cultivation, as well as for wild-seed-gathering and hunting, than it is at present.

The Pioneer Period (ca. 100 B.C.–A.D. 500) saw the pattern of Hohokam culture established in the Gila-Salt region. The earliest houses, those of the Vahki phase, were unusually large (over 8 meters in diameter), square, jacal and wattle-daub structures with central post supports and narrow passage entrances. One of them is a shallow pit-structure, but not a true pithouse, the other a surface building. Their size suggests that they were either multi-family dwellings or, possibly, were used for community ceremonial purposes. This style of jacal architecture continued for several hundred years in the Hohokam, later developing a trend toward smaller, single-family houses. During late Pioneer and early Colonial times, the house outline changed from squarish to oblong and in early Sedentary times became oval. With these changes, the main roof supports shifted from their four corner locations to a central position in a line down the long axis of the floor. Smaller wall posts served as secondary roof supports. Passage entrances continued to be used throughout the sequence, and the floor level of these and of the houses was usually excavated below the level of the surrounding ground; however, the designation "pithouse" remains inappropriate. Fire-pits were placed just inside the entrance passages. No particular plan is evident in the village layout, nor are there indications that Snaketown was selected as a potentially defensible location.

The canal irrigation works, which were the Hohokam lifelines, were first constructed in the Pioneer Period; indeed, it is difficult to understand how village habitation on any scale would have been possible in this desert environment without them.[119] The canals composed a huge system and represented thousands of man-hours of concentrated and coordinated labor. That more than a single village often benefited from the same canal proves their wide territorial cooperative basis. One canal section traced at Snaketown, along the edge of the upper terrace of the valley, had its point of divergence from the Gila River some 10 miles upstream from the site, and this particular canal is by no means the longest in the region. Measuring from crest-to-crest of the earth embankments thrown up on both sides of the channel, the main canals averaged about 10 meters in width. The canal systems were maintained and expanded in the Gila-Salt region after the abandonment of Snaketown and were probably most extensive during the Classic Period (ca. A.D. 1200–1400).

The Hohokam red-on-buff pottery tradition was firmly set in Pioneer times. The earliest Vahki phase pottery, a monochrome red or brown ware, closely resembled the early Mogollon; but a red-on-gray and the characteristic red-on-buff painted

Figure 4-44. Pioneer Period Hohokam jar, Vahki Plain. Diameter, 25 cm. (Courtesy Arizona State Museum; see also Gladwin and others, 1937.)

styles appeared during the later Pioneer phases. From Pioneer to Colonial Periods the red-on-buff design elements tended to become smaller, finer, and to combine small stylized life elements with geometric ones. These trends continued into the Sedentary Period (ca. A.D. 900–1200), which also was characterized by tightly integrated design layouts of interlocking scrolls and keys. These give an impression of negative design, although the technique of application was positive painting. More and more vessel forms appeared from the Pioneer through the Sedentary Periods, especially during the Sedentary, when legged and effigy vessels and trays joined bowl and jar forms. The Sedentary Period also marked the first appearance of the typical Gila olla, or jar form, a roughly globular vessel with a constricted orifice and a very low shoulder angle.

Pottery figurines date to the earliest Pioneer Period phases. In general, these figurines resemble

Figure 4-43. Hohokam house floor plan, Snaketown, Arizona (Sacaton phase, Sedentary Period). (Courtesy Arizona State Museum; see also Gladwin and others, 1937.)

Figure 4-45. *Above:* Hohokam red-on-buff pottery. *Left:* An olla of Sacaton red-on-buff, Sedentary Period, diameter, 34 cm. *Right:* A bowl of Santa Cruz red-on-buff, Colonial Period, diameter, 40 cm. (Courtesy Arizona State Museum; see also Gladwin and others, 1937.)

Figure 4-46. *Right:* Hohokam effigy vessels of the Sacaton phase (Sedentary Period). *a:* Animal. *b,c:* Birds. *d,e:* Fish. *f,g:* Shells. Length of *d*, 14 cm. (Courtesy Arizona State Museum; see also Gladwin and others, 1937.)

a   b

c

d

e

f   g

those from Preclassic central Mexico, although they tend to be cruder. All were handmade and most were human representations, probably females. During the shift from Pioneer to Colonial, figurine facial features were somewhat more carefully modeled; and in the Santa Cruz phase of the Colonial Period, heads and bodies were made separately and a "coffee-bean" eye, suggestive of Mesoamerican figurines, came into vogue. In the Sedentary Period separate heads of clay may have been attached to bodies of textiles or fibers. In this last connection, cotton textiles dating from the Sedentary Period were found at Snaketown, but cotton probably was grown and used in weaving by the Hohokam earlier than this. As a domesticate it was diffused to the Southwest from Mexico, and the textile techniques employed were also Meso-

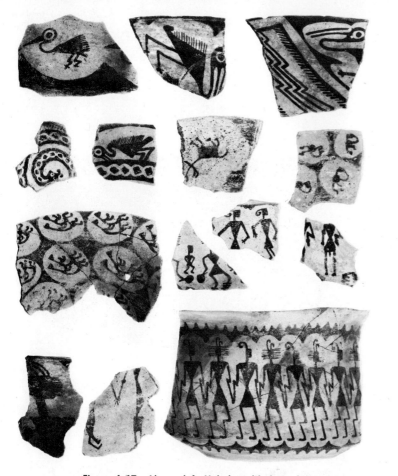

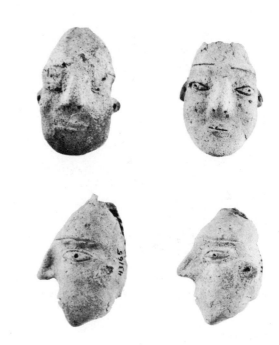

Figure 4-47. *Above, left:* Hohokam life-form designs. Sacaton red-on-buff pottery (Sedentary Period). Length of sherd at lower right, 30 cm. (Courtesy Arizona State Museum; see also Gladwin and others, 1937.)

Figure 4-48. *Above, right:* Hohokam pottery figurine heads from Snaketown, Arizona. (Courtesy Arizona State Museum.)

american-derived. This cotton-cloth complex was passed from the Hohokam on to the Anasazi subarea.

Other typical Hohokam manufactures which had their beginnings in the Pioneer Period included nicely carved stone paint palettes, stone beads, ornaments, ear-plugs, nose-buttons, stone vessels with lizard and other animal figures in relief, and a great variety of shell ornaments. These crafts were undoubtedly stimulated by Mesoamerican influences and trade in similar or related goods. For example, associated with the above were obvi-

ous trade items—finely worked mosaic plaques or mirrors inlaid with iron pyrite crystals. The various skills and crafts in stone and shell reached their peak of development in the Sedentary Period. This was especially true of the shellwork, which included objects ornamented by a sophisticated acid-etching process.

Starting in the Pioneer Period and continuing throughout the sequence, the Hohokam disposed of their dead through cremation. Bodies were burned in pits. Sometimes the remains were left in the pits, grave furniture was added, and the pits were covered with earth and gravel. Or the ashes and burned bone might be transported to another burial place, sometimes within a pottery vessel.

Not all characteristic Hohokam traits had appeared as early as the Pioneer Period. For instance, we cannot definitely identify any of the Pioneer Period house structures as ceremonial buildings. Only the two large Vahki-phase houses suggest that they may have been used for ceremonies. The Mogollon and Anasazi pithouse village with one larger and special structure does not seem to have been the early Hohokam pattern. Other types of community or ceremonial structures, of Meso-american derivation, appeared later. Early in the Colonial Period (ca. A.D. 500–900) a ball court was constructed at Snaketown, and this court was enlarged and continued in use throughout that period. It was made by excavating a playing floor which was enclosed by clay embankments. The two long embankments ran east-west and curved slightly inward at their ends. These open ends were enclosed by other semi-circular embankments. The total east-west length of the constructions, including the semi-circular end-enclosures, was 120 meters, and the maximum north-south measurement was 33 meters. The size of the actual playing floor was 56 by 19 meters. Two stones were placed in the center ends of the court, presumably as markers, and a third stone was found aligned with these in the center of the court. It is estimated that the side embankments were originally as much as 6 meters high. Thus, the Snaketown ball court was a public work of some magnitude, comparing favorably in size, as well as in form, to the Meso-american courts. The discovery of a preserved rubber ball in a Hohokam site also suggests that a game similar to the one played in Mesoamerica on such courts was a part of Hohokam custom and ceremony. Later Hohokam courts were smaller,

a
b
c
d
e

Figure 4-49. *Top, right:* Hohokam stone palettes, Santa Cruz phase (Colonial Period). *a:* Lizard motif on borders. *b,c:* Lizard outline of paint basin. *d:* Horned toad with basin in back. *e:* Human effiity. Length of *a*, 23 cm. (Courtesy Arizona State Museum; see also Gladwin and others, 1937.)

Figure 4-50. *Bottom, right:* Hohokam stone vessels. *Left:* Small incised bowl typical of Santa Cruz (Colonial Period) and Sacaton (Sedentary Period) phases. Diameter, about 7 cm. *Right:* Flat-based vessel with two opposing human figures, Santa Cruz phase (Colonial Period). Diameter, about 51 cm. (Courtesy Arizona State Museum; see also Gladwin and others, 1937.)

Figure 4-51. Hohokam shellwork. A horned toad etched with wax and acid on the back of a *Cardium* shell. Diameter, 10.2 cm. (Courtesy Arizona State Museum; see also Gladwin and others, 1937.)

Figure 4-52. A Hohokam ball court at Snaketown, Arizona. *Left:* Court prior to excavation. The long axis lay on a line running 15 degrees north of west. The earthen embankments in the photograph were about 60 m. long, 33 m. apart, and 2.5 m. above ground level. Semi-circular ridges, not readily apparent, joined the ends of the embankments. The total length of the court, including the areas within the end-ridges, was 120 m. *Right:* The same court (but looking in opposite direction) after excavation. (Courtesy Arizona State Museum; see also Gladwin and others, 1937.)

were oriented north-south rather than east-west, and lacked the semi-circular "end-zone" embankment features. These date from the Sedentary and Classic Periods. One has been excavated at Snaketown and there are others at several Hohokam sites, including Casa Grande.

The other Hohokam ceremonial architectural feature of Mesoamerican complexion was the platform mound. Such mounds were relatively small and made of earth and adobe. Several have been identified from the Gila, Salt, and Santa Cruz drainages, most of them probably relatively recent. Lately, an excellent example of a platform mound has been excavated at the Gatlin site near Gila Bend, Arizona.[120] It was made of earth and had been built in six stages represented by successive lateral and superimposed additions to a central platform structure. The summit and sloping sides of each stage of the mound had been finished off with caliche and adobe plaster. The Stage I mound was approximately rectangular in outline and measured 10 by 5 meters and a little over 1 meter in height. By the close of Stage VI, the final mound was rectangular, 29 by 22 meters across base and 3 meters high. At various stages in the construction, smaller ancillary platforms or mounds had been built contiguous to, or connected with, the main mound. There were no traces of superstructures on the main platform at most stage levels. They probably had been obliterated, but a rectangular post-mold pattern of a pole and wattle-

daub building on the platform top of Stage IV could be made out. This building, or "temple," had an interior hearth and a raised clay dais or altar-like feature. The probable ceremonial or religious nature of the Gatlin mound is implied by its structural similarity to Mesoamerican platform mounds and by the discovery, nearby, of a large cremation area. Burned human bones and ashes, accompanied by offerings of projectile points and copper bells, were found in this "cemetery." The entire mound and cremation complex at the Gatlin site dates by ceramic inclusions and associations to the Sacaton phase of the early Sedentary Period.

The copper bells at the Gatlin site cremations correlate with the first appearance of similar bells in the Sacaton phase at Snaketown. All these bells were of the "tinkler" type, with suspension eyelets, slotted bases, and pebble or nodule rattles inside the resonator. They all were made by the "lost-wax," or *cire perdue*, method of copper casting, and, since they are similar to bells from western and northwestern Mexico, it seems likely that they were imported to the Southwest from Mesoamerica. Although such bells are most frequently associated with the Hohokam culture, after the Sedentary Period, they were also carried farther north and have been found occasionally in late Anasazi contexts.[121]

The most common Hohokam projectile type during the Pioneer Period was the large, heavy, stemmed dart point. Long, very slender, stemmed and barbed points, suitable for arrow tips, appeared during the Colonial Period; and in the Sedentary Period and later, the dominant type was the small, finely chipped triangular point with the lateral side-notches, the same type, in fact, that characterized late Anasazi phases. These occur in vast numbers, especially as offerings with cremations. Instances of 400 or 500 with one cremation are known.

Other evidence, however, would seem to indicate that hunting was of less economic importance among the Hohokam than plant cultivation. The agricultural dependence, which is of course dram-atized by the great irrigation works, is further highlighted by the abundance of metate, mano, mortar-and-pestle seed-grinding stones. The earlier Hohokam metates, although technically of the "trough" type in that they were open at both ends, were thick and had a somewhat basin-like grinding concavity. Later Hohokam types were thinner and had the rectangular sides and concavity of the true trough form. This evolution of the metate suggests that the earlier ones were derived from the basin type of the Cochise culture. Hohokam axes were characteristically three-quarter-grooved. They first appeared during the Snaketown phase of the late Pioneer Period, and continued throughout the sequence.

The Classic Period. The Hohokam Classic Period (ca. A.D. 1200–1400) was a time of cultural innovation in the Gila-Salt region.[122] These changes are not apparent at the Snaketown

Figure 4-53. Hohokam three-quarter grooved axes of the ridged variety, Pioneer and Colonial Periods. Length of specimen *left*, about 16.5 cm. (Courtesy Arizona State Museum; see also Gladwin and others, 1937.)

site but do shine forth from two imposing ruins in the lower Gila and Salt drainages, Los Muertos[123] and Casa Grande.[124] The innovations touched architectural styles and pottery, as well as other arts, and the source of these new features is identified with the arrival of Anasazi peoples known as the Salado groups.

The Salado came south from the Little Colorado and the Tonto Basin, and there are signs that they actually moved into the same sites and communities with the Hohokam.[125] The two societies, with their distinctive brands of Southwestern culture, lived side by side in apparent peace for more than a century. The Salado produced a red, black, and white polychrome ware, and they buried their dead, without cremation, under the floors of houses. Salado architecture was above-ground, of caliche-adobe, and arranged in rectangular enclosures or compounds. Within these walled compounds were both single and apartment-type houses and, in some of them, multi-storied "Great Houses." The walls of these "Great Houses" were extraordinarily massive. At Casa Grande, the principal structure of this type had walls over a meter thick; the walls of the largest building at Los Muertos were over 2 meters thick. The Casa Grande main building, much of which still stands in the dry desert atmosphere, was built as a rectangular four-storied edifice which originally had over a dozen rooms.

Meanwhile, the canal systems of the Hohokam continued to flourish and were expanded in the Classic Period. Ball courts were still constructed, and the Hohokam segments of the villages went on making their red-on-buff pottery as before.

It seems likely that the walled compounds and thick-walled "Great Houses" of the Classic Period were built for security purposes. The enemies may have been Athapascan Apache or some of the Hohokam who never established a peaceful accommodation to their neighbors. In this regard, we should mention that the Papaguería Hohokam, in their more inhospitable environment, had lagged behind the other Hohokam regions and never assimilated the architectural and ceramic traits of

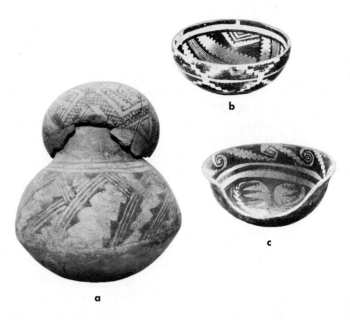

Figure 4-54. Classic Period Hohokam pottery. *a*: Casa Grande red-on-buff. *b,c*: Tonto polychrome. (After Haury, 1945.)

the Salado.[126] Perhaps they were hostile to the Gila-Salt tribes during the Classic Period. Whatever forces were at work, the Salado, and possibly some of the Hohokam, abandoned the Gila-Salt and Tucson regions after A.D. 1400. Whether they went back north to Anasazi country or eastward and southward to join with Mogollon groups is unknown. Quite probably, however, some Hohokam stayed on in the southern Arizona deserts, and their descendants were the Pima of the river valleys and the Papago of the Papaguería, whom the Spaniards met in the early sixteenth century. If so, their culture, and particularly that of the once thriving river-valley Hohokam, with their well-organized irrigation system, had suffered a severe material decline prior to the coming of the Europeans.[127]

Patayan, or Hakataya

In the sixteenth century when the Spaniards came into the lower Colorado River Valley, they found it occupied by Yuman peoples who farmed on the alluvial flood plains of that great stream and during flood times went into the surrounding desert mountains to hunt and forage in small parties. These Yumans were very warlike, and they fought constantly among themselves and farther afield with the Pima-Papago and the Athapascans. Although ethnologists have since found that they had developed a complex and formal mythology expressed through songs and shamanistic dreams, their material culture was, and is still, less impressive than that of their southwestern neighbors.[128] We should mention that the paucity of the archaeological remains in this lower Colorado River country is, perhaps, not altogether because of the material poverty of the former inhabitants but that it is probably due, in part, to the fact that centuries of seasonal flooding of the river have buried many of the prehistoric sites under many feet of silt. In spite of all these conditions, there is, nevertheless, an archaeological record in this subarea of the Southwest, and it is a record significantly different from the Mogollon, Anasazi, or Hohokam.

Figure 4-55. Casa Grande, Arizona. The "Great House" as it looked at the end of the nineteenth century.

Archaeologists have been divided over whether or not the prehistoric cultures of this subarea should be designated as Yuman. They have also been divided in their opinions as to just what territory the subarea should embrace and just what sites and archaeological complexes should be included. That peoples of Yuman speech—the ancestors, in fact, of the present Yuma, Cocopah, Maricopa, Havasupai, Mojave, and Walapai—have occupied the lower Colorado Valley and its adjacent regions for the last 1500 or 2000 years is quite probable. Some archaeological continuities support such an assumption, as do the linguistic distributions. Still, it cannot be proven, and it is, indeed, rather unlikely, that all archaeological complexes similar to those of the lower Colorado River regions are the remains of peoples of Yuman linguistic affiliation. Because of this, it has been the opinion of some authorities that a non-ethnic and non-linguistic term would be more appropriate for the archaeological cultures involved. Two such terms have been proposed: Patayan and Hakataya. I shall not attempt in this survey to follow all the arguments and reasoning of the proponents of these two terms. In brief, the name "Patayan" was first given wide currency in 1945 by H. S. Colton, who objected to M. R. Rogers' use of the designation "Yuman" in an archaeological context.[129] Its meaning is analogous to that of Anasazi or Mogollon; it is simply a Yuman word for the "old people" or "ancient ones." Subsequently, A. H. Schroeder, in consultation with other Southwestern colleagues, has offered the term "Hakataya," a Yuman word for the Colorado River.[130] The reasons for this change, according to Schroeder, were that the concept could be meaningfully extended to take in more geographically widespread units than originally had been incorporated under Colton's Patayan label. Moreover, use of the Patayan name and concept had led to certain inconsistencies and confusions in archaeological writing on the subject.

For this presentation we will use the term "Patayan," and we will apply it in the general sense of a major subtradition of the Southwest, as did

Colton. Our geographical limits follow his (Fig. 4-1). The subarea as defined here lies along the Colorado River from its delta north to beyond Needles. On the east it extends into Arizona but stops at about Gila Bend, in the south. Farther north are two marginal regions which, in both cases, show definite cultural blendings with other Southwestern cultures: the Cohonina and the Prescott. Schroeder would extend his Hakataya geographical concept still farther east to include all of Arizona north of the Gila and west and south of the Mogollon rim. To the west, we have drawn our line to include only the immediate drainage west of the Colorado River. It is, of course, true that Patayan, or Hakataya, influence spread farther west than this, going well into the Mojave Desert of southern California and into northern Baja California in late prehistoric and protohistoric times. Schroeder acknowledges this in his extension of a Hakataya area or Southwestern subarea as far west as the Pacific Coast Range of California. In our presentation we have, however, left this southeastern California desert country within the Great Basin area, noting only its late period affiliations with Patayan.[131]

Before turning to Patayan, or Hakataya, we should indicate that the antecedent culture of the subarea is a branch of the Desert tradition. It is either the Amargosa culture, as defined by M. J. Rogers from the Mojave Desert region of the Great Basin, or a culture which shares certain traits with Amargosa but overlies it and forms a transition into Patayan.[132] The dwellings of this late Amargosa or transitional culture were flimsy pole-and-brush structures of which only the circular or oval stone foundations remain. They were not pithouses although some of them had slightly basin-like floors. Cooking was done outside in roasting pits filled with cobblestones. Mortars and pestles or crude slab metates were used to grind seeds. The dead were disposed of by cremation. Into this relatively simple Desert culture base were added, by diffusion from Mexico, maize farming, a simple brown-ware pottery made by a paddle-anvil method, the trough metate, and jacal-walled houses. With these additions Patayan culture came into being.

A three-period Yuman sequence has been advanced by Rogers, and we will here apply it to the Patayan terminology.[133] The beginning date of Patayan I, which is marked by the appearance of the first pottery, remains obscure. We have set it at about A.D. 600 and have so marked it on the chronology chart.[134] However, Schroeder feels that the earliest Patayan, or Hakataya, pottery was, in effect, none other than the plain red and brown wares of the Hohokam Pioneer Period (ca. 100 B.C.– A.D. 600). In other words, it is his opinion that Pioneer Hohokam should really be called Pioneer Hakataya, that the earliest farming and pottery-making culture of the southern Arizona desert and Gila Basin was the Hakataya, or Patayan, and that a distinctive Hohokam pattern did not come into being until the diffusion of more complex elements from Mexico made this possible in the Hohokam Pioneer Period. According to this interpretation, then, a Patayan I Period would have begun at around 100 B.C. on the middle Gila River.[135]

Leaving this argument aside, however, the earliest Patayan I pottery, as it is found along the lower Colorado River from the delta up to the vicinity of the town of Blythe, has features which set it apart from Pioneer Hohokam. These include basket-molding of vessels, notched rims, and a peculiarly sharp-angled high shoulder on a large water jar, which is known as a "Colorado shoulder."

Throughout its history, however, Patayan pottery was influenced by both Hohokam and Anasazi. In the south this influence is particularly clear with reference to the Hohokam Papagueria phases which are geographically adjacent. To the north, Basketmaker III and Pueblo I vessels have been found in Patayan I sites; and the Patayan I wares —the small-mouthed olla, the crude incised and punctated decoration, the fugitive-red wash covered vessels—are similar to Anasazi.

Patayan II (ca. A.D. 1050–1500), as it is identified by pottery, was much more widely distributed than Patayan I. From the delta it reached north to southern Nevada; to the east, up the Gila River almost as far as Gila Bend; and, westerly, to as far as the southeastern California deserts. In Patayan II ceramics, the "Colorado shoulder" water jar, notched rims, and burnished red wares had disappeared, to be replaced by hemispherical bowls with deeper and slightly collared bowls, large trays, stucco-finished pottery, and frequent red-on-buff painting. These changes were particularly evident in the south and probably reflect increased contact with the Hohokam. Farther north, in a belt running from northwest Arizona to the Mojave Desert, the markers for the Patayan II horizon are a series of characteristic brown wares. Other Patayan II changes took the form of a more careful rectangular shaping of metates and manos and the use of Pacific, as well as Gulf of California, shells for jewelry. With Patayan II comes the first definite evidence of cremation. It may have been practiced earlier, in Patayan I, although there is no proof for it then. With the Patayan peoples, unlike the Hohokam, the ashes were not collected after cremation and buried with grave goods, but instead were, apparently, scattered.

After A.D. 1500, Patayan culture, in its Period III, can be traced from ethnohistory as well as archaeology, and is at this time associated with Yuman peoples. Changes from II to III were relatively minor, the most significant being in the area occupied. The Mojave Basin was abandoned, but there was a more than compensatory expansion eastward into Arizona and west and south into southern California and Baja California.

The Athapascans

Athapascan people and Athapascan culture do not have, relatively speaking, a long history in the Southwest area. No Athapascan sub-area can be designated. Instead, traces of the Athapascans and their culture are found widely throughout the area, as though they have flowed through and around the older resident peoples and cultures; and insofar as we can reconstruct their past, this seems to be what happened.

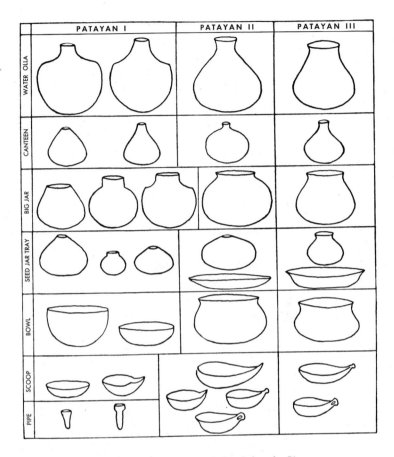

Figure 4-56. Common pottery forms of the Colorado River Patayan culture. (Redrawn from M. J. Rogers, 1945.)

Athapascan is the name for a language family which is sometimes considered a part of the larger linguistic superstock of the Na-Dene. The Na-Dene peoples are found mainly in northwestern North America, and the largest geographic block of Athapascan-speaking Indians are in interior Alaska and the Canadian northwest. The other principal Athapascan block is the one with which we are concerned here. It consists of seven main tribes who live, or recently lived, in the Southwest and the bordering Plains to the east. These seven tribes are: (1) the Navajo, who occupy the old Anasazi country of northern Arizona and northern New Mexico, except for the Pueblo islands; (2) the Western Apache, who are in Arizona between the Navajo and the Pima and Yuman peoples to the west and south; (3) the Chiricahua Apache, in the old Mogollon country of southeastern Arizona and southwestern New Mexico; (4) the Jicarilla Apache, in northeastern New Mexico and adjacent states; and (5,6,7) the Mescalero, Lipan, and Kiowa Apache, who are to be found in eastern New Mexico, western and southern Texas, and Oklahoma.

The earliest secure archaeological evidence for the presence of the ancestors of the Apache and Navajo in the Southwest comes from the early sixteenth century, from the Chacra Mesa and Gobernador localities of northern New Mexico.[136] These localities are a part of the larger Largo-Gallina region which we have already mentioned in connection with the appearance of alien traits on the northern border of the Anasazi subarea in earlier prehistoric times. You will recall that the pottery of the Pueblo III Period of this region included large pointed-bottom utility jars of a distinctly non-Southwestern type. These pointed-bottom vessels have been described variously as being related to the Woodland tradition of eastern North America or to a pointed-bottom pottery tradition of the northern Great Basin. It has also been suggested that pottery of this kind was introduced into the northern margin of the Anasazi country by Athapascans who, perhaps, were at first a threat to Puebloans living there and who later drove them out. It may be that in the Largo and Gallina phases of the period from A.D. 1000–1300, Pueblos and invaders intermarried, and the new ceramic traits were introduced in this manner to societies which were essentially of the Pueblo pattern. In general, this hypothesis accords with the discovery in the nearby Colorado Rockies of some circular, dry-laid masonry houses which are reminiscent of the Navajo hogan, together with crude, pointed-bottom pottery.[137] These Colorado sites may mark the route of Athapascans on their way to the Southwest in Pueblo III times. They are estimated to date to about A.D. 1100. Still, this hypothesis has been countered with arguments denying the Athapascan affiliations of either the Colorado stone houses and pottery or the Largo-

Gallina pointed-bottom ceramics. Perhaps the Utes or some other group were responsible.[138] Athapascans may not have entered the Southwest until nearer A.D. 1500, when their presence can be definitely demonstrated; and they may have come from the western Plains rather than by way of the Rockies. J. J. Hester inclines toward this view, and he has suggested that a culture similar to that of the protohistoric Dismal River phase of western Nebraska and Kansas and eastern Colorado may be the prototype of Southwestern Athapascan culture.[139] If so, then the pre-Southwestern Athapascans may have been at least partial farmers, for the Dismal River people practiced a little corn agriculture in addition to buffalo-hunting. Such an interpretation would mean that the Athapascans assimilated agriculture, to some small degree, before they came into contact with the Pueblos. On the other hand, a Plains tribe of apparent Apache affiliation, the Querecho, whom Coronado encountered on his expedition of 1541, had an economy based entirely on migratory bison-hunting, so it is possible that the Athapascans were, indeed, non-agricultural before settling near the Pueblos.

From this it is clear that the pre-A.D. 1500 history of the Southwestern Athapascans is as yet unrevealed. It is possible that they were in the Largo-Gallina region during Pueblo III times, living in a hostile or semi-hostile state vis-à-vis the Anasazi peoples. In fact, it is just possible that they were present even earlier, at the time of the Pueblo I Rosa phase, before A.D. 900, and that the threat of their presence was responsible for the fortified sites of that phase (see p. 219). In very remote times the Athapascans probably participated in the cultural tradition known as the Denetasiro (see Chap. 7), which archaeologists have traced to the very distant western Subarctic, the territory generally believed to be the original American homeland of Athapascan-speaking peoples.[139a] Leaving aside these speculative histories and reconstructions, we can only know for certain that the Athapascans were in the northern Southwest by about A.D. 1500. After this time they accepted much from the resident Indians, and their acculturation to Southwestern culture, and particularly to the Pueblo modes of it, continued through the historic centuries. This acculturation is most marked in those regions where Pueblo-Athapascan contacts have been closest and where the natural environment has most readily permitted the hunting-collecting Athapascans to adapt to agricultural life. Thus, the Navajo and Western Apache are more like the Pueblos than the Mescalero Apache are, with the Mescalero presumably retaining more features of the original culture which was carried to the Southwest by the Athapascans.

Archaeological research into Southwestern Athapascan problems has been much less intensive than the work directed toward Anasazi, Hohokam, or Mogollon remains, and most of it has been since 1940. In this brief time, however, work in the Navajo country in northeastern Arizona and northwestern New Mexico has led to the establishment of a systematic chronology. The earliest Navajo archaeological phase, the Dinetah, is dated from about A.D. 1500 to approximately A.D. 1696. This terminal date marked the end of the Pueblo Revolt against the Spanish and the consequent movement of Pueblo peoples and influences northward into the upper San Juan, Gobernador, and Largo localities. With this movement the Navajo Dinetah phase culture was markedly modified by Pueblo ceramic traits, such as polychrome pottery, and by Pueblo-style architecture. The Gobernador phase succeeds the Dinetah phase in the eastern Navajo country. It began and ended slightly earlier in the upper San Juan, Gobernador, and Largo localities (A.D. 1696–1775) than it did in the Big Bead and Chaco localities (A.D. 1739–1800) which are farther to the west. The Cabezon phase, which is best known from Big Bead Mesa, lasts from the late eighteenth century until the conquest and concentration of the Navajos by Kit Carson in 1863.[140]

The Dinetah phase shows evidence of corn and beans agriculture, but architecture was limited to the construction of forked-stick hogans or crude rock shelters. Pottery was either a pointed-bottom utility ware or a black-on-white Pueblo trade ware. During the Gobernador phase polychromes were made locally, a great variety of Pueblo trade wares appeared, and architectural innovations and changes such as pueblitos, or small stone-walled pueblos; stone-masonry hogans; cribbed-log hogans; and stone-masonry towers and fortified sites were introduced. Horses, sheep, and cattle were also acquired from the Spanish. The Cabezon phase was marked by a decline in such Pueblo architectural features as the pueblito dwellings and towers, by an increase in the economic importance of sheep-herding, and by stylistic changes in the trade wares received from the Pueblos.

We can get another view of Navajo archaeological culture by examining Keur's excavations at Big Bead Mesa, New Mexico.[141] The houses or hogans at the site were dated by dendrochronology to A.D. 1745–1820, overlapping between the Gobernador and Cabezon phases. This was an era of intermittent Navajo-Pueblo alliances and hostilities, following the Pueblo Revolt. The village consisted of 95 hogan structures, some sweat-houses, a stone-wall fortification, several caches, and refuse dumps. The hogans were of the forked-stick and stone-walled types. The former (in which some timbers were found preserved, were circular, 2 to 5 meters in diameter, and were constructed by interlocking several forked poles at the top to form a crude dome-like framework. The principal posts were placed at the north, west, and south, with two doorway posts facing east. Shorter poles were then laid from the circular floor margin to rest on the interlocked crotches at the top. Stone-walled hogans, the second type, were usually circular and had basal walls of boulders or sandstone block masonry. Forked-roof timbers were then rested on these bases. The masonry trait was undoubtedly Puebloan, but the hogan form, and especially the completely wooden structure, was an Athapascan contribution.

Maize remains were found in site refuse and bones of game animals and of sheep and horses were plentiful. Pottery was predominantly of the pointed-bottom utility ware, but there were Ana-sazi intrusives in the form of sherds from the historic Zuñi, Acoma, and Laguna Pueblos. A Navajo-manufactured, but Pueblo-inspired, poly-chrome style was also represented. Distinctly Nav-ajo were the sweat-houses, cleared areas marked with old fireplaces that were dance grounds, and soft pieces of sandstone that were pulverized to make the colors which the Navajos used in creating their ceremonial sandpaintings. These last were recovered from caches where they had been stored.

The non-material life of the Athapascans dif-fered from that of the Pueblos in basic social organ-ization and religion. The primary social unit of the Athapascans was the extended matrilocal fam-ily. These families lived in encampments. Clusters of encampments formed local groups and local groups, in turn, gathered together for war and for religious ceremonies. This kind of organization best describes the Eastern Apaches, the Mescalero and Chiricahua, who were hunting peoples and who, as has been said, probably retained more of their old pre-Southwestern ways than the Navajos and Western Apaches. With the Navajo and West-ern Apaches, social organization and settlement was modified. Matrilocal clans were developed in imitation of the Pueblos, and villages became more permanent, as at the Big Bead Mesa site. The old Athapascan religion centered in curing ceremonies, rather than rain-making, and was directed by shamans, rather than priests. Curing remained the paramount theme, but the Navajos and Western Apaches borrowed many symbolic features of the Pueblo rain ceremonies—for example—such as masks, and incorporated them in their medicine rites.[142]

The Navajos and Apaches have survived vigor-ously to the present. They have turned primarily to sheep-herding for subsistence. Their adjustment to Western civilization, although somewhat different from that of their ancient enemies and neighbors, the Pueblos, has also been selective and has ena-bled them to keep intact many of their native ways.[143]

Observations on Internal Relationships

We have presented Southwestern archaeology in the frames of reference of its prin-cipal subareas and cultural subtraditions, including among the latter the Athapascan cultural develop-ment insofar as this pertains to the Southwest. In so doing, we have made reference at several points to the blendings and mergers of these various sub-traditional lines. These phenomena of fusion and interrelationships are equally important parts of the Southwestern story, and they deserve some-what more attention than we have given them. In this section we want to review those instances of cultural interpenetration and synthesis, which we have touched on in passing, and also to describe briefly some others which we have not mentioned. It is particularly in reference to some of these last that important differences of interpretation have been raised among Southwestern archaeologists.

Cohonina and Prescott. Archaeological remains in the Cohonina and Prescott regions reflect the blendings of Patayan with other South-western cultures. The Cohonina region (Fig. 4-1) lies at the edge of the Colorado Plateau in north-western Arizona.[144] The principal drainage is Cata-ract Creek, which flows north into the Grand Canyon of the Colorado. The environmental set-ting is that of the Anasazi, a semi-arid plateau terrain. In historic times the Yuman Havasupai held the region, but whether the principal pre-historic inhabitants were Yumans or some other group will probably never be known. Cohonina pottery is paddle-and-anvil smoothed and other-wise like Patayan. Cremation, with scattering of ashes, another Patayan custom, can be inferred from evidence thus far gathered. Pithouses were more reminiscent of Anasazi. The Cohonina occu-pation lasted from the seventh to the twelfth centu-ries, with the population reaching its peak between A.D. 900–1100. After A.D. 1200 the Cohonina cul-tural continuity seems to have been broken, perhaps by an abandonment of the area which carried over until the appearance of the Havasupai.

The Prescott region is about 100 miles south of the Cohonina.[145] Prescott pottery also resembled Patayan types. Inhumation, however, was the mode of disposal of the dead, and other elements of the culture were very much like Anasazi.

Sinagua and Salado. The Sinagua culture centered in the Flagstaff and Verde Valley regions of north-central and central Arizona, mountain and valley country lying at the north end of the Mogollon Rim and just below it.[146] Its earliest appearance dates from A.D. 500–700 in the vicinity of Flagstaff. Wheat has felt that this early Sinagua phase was Mogollon-derived, but Schroeder has challenged this interpretation, seeing in such traits as the paddle-anvil manufactured plain brown pottery a basic Hakatayan or Patayan affinity.[147] Schroeder also has pointed to jacal houses and unshaped oval metates as Hakatayan-derived, contrasting these to the contemporary Mogollon deep pithouses and basin and slab metates. According to Schroeder, the Sinagua culture continued in the Hakatayan or Patayan pattern in the succeeding A.D. 700–1070 period, although during this time the idea of a circular great kiva appears to have diffused into the region from the Anasazi subarea. Following this period, in Schroeder's interpretation, two new groups moved into the Sinagua region, one coming from the Hohokam, the other from Anasazi country. The old resident Sinaguas and the newcomers lived side-by-side for several decades, and the result was a cultural fusion, the Elden phase, which is the best known manifestation of the region. This Elden brand of Sinagua culture was carried south sometime after A.D. 1125, to become established in the Verde Valley. It was also at about this time that such Hohokam traits as the ball court spread as far north as Flagstaff and that Pueblo architectural styles were adopted in the Verde Valley. Early in the fourteenth century the Flagstaff locality was relinquished by the Sinaguas, although they continued to occupy the Verde Valley for another century.

We have already mentioned Anasazi influence as a major force in culture change in the instance of a Salado invasion of the Gila-Salt region Hohokam sites after A.D. 1100. There can be no doubt of the actual movement of alien peoples, who brought with them new settlement and architectural modes as well as ceramics and artifacts, and established communities adjacent to or actually within earlier Hohokam villages. In fact, this process of site-unit intrusion with social units of different cultures living apparently peacefully side by side was characteristic of the Southwest during the late prehistoric periods.[148] It corresponds to what seems to have happened in the Sinagua region after A.D. 1070. In the case of the Salado intrusion into the Hohokam there are, however, different opinions as to who the invaders were and where they came from. According to the original Salado hypothesis, they moved south from the basin of the Tonto River, a northern tributary of the Salt River lying to the east of the Verde Valley. Schroeder, on the other hand, would bring them from the Sinagua settlements in the Verde Valley.[149]

The San Pedro Valley: Mogollon, Hohokam, and Ootam. Farther south in Arizona, the San Pedro Valley, west of Tucson, is a region of cultural blending between Mogollon and Hohokam. One interpretation of this blending—and the interpretation alluded to earlier in this chapter—is that the region is simply a zone of "overlap" between these two cultures. C. C. Di Peso, however, holds another view.[150] From his work in the San Pedro, he has come to see Hohokam and Mogollon in a quite different light. He believes that early Hohokam and early Mogollon represent a single culture, which he calls the Ootam. The bearers of this Ootam culture were the old local population of southern Arizona and adjacent southern New Mexico, associated with the pre-ceramic late Cochise culture. They were also the remote ancestors of the Pima-Papago. Their "low-level stable culture" of early pithouse-village farmers and pottery-makers was then radically modified by an invasion of peoples from Mexico—the Hohokam. They arrived during the Colonial Period which, incidentally, Di Peso would place later than other authorities, after A.D. 900. These Hohokam dominated and settled among the Ootam and transformed their culture with such new techniques as intensive irrigation, new pottery modes, more elaborate shell and stone-carving, copper bells, and the ballgame.

There is a similarity between this hypothesis and Schroeder's for the essential identity of Pioneer Hohokam and early Hakatayan culture. What both Di Peso and Schroeder are arguing is that the old Desert tradition populations of the Southwest, whether Cochise or Amargosa, were first turned away from their ancient pattern of life by a diffusion from Mesoamerica which introduced pottery and a form of domesticated maize that made farming economically practical. Whether these early influences entered the Southwest first in what later became Mogollon, Hohokam, or Patayan territory is uncertain. Perhaps such diffusion was accomplished more or less simultaneously in all three of these subareas. But, in any event, it was not until some time afterwards that the new diffusions from Mexico transformed the Hohokam line of development into something quite different from what had heretofore existed in the Southwest—into a culture, in fact, that was as much Mesoamerican as it was Southwestern.[151]

In this chapter we have not followed this interpretation, although we have brought it to your attention. Our interpretation has been closer to that of Haury, who considers early Hohokam, Mogollon, and Patayan as separate but related entities. The really crucial difference, however, between the Di Peso-Schroeder and Haury reconstructions is that Di Peso and Schroeder believe that the Mexican traits in Colonial and Sedentary Period Hohokam were introduced by a migration of peoples rather than by more indirect means of diffusion. On this question, for reasons given farther along, we favor Haury's interpretation.

Mimbres and Casas Grandes. We have already alluded to Anasazi influence in the Mimbres region of the Mogollon subarea in our dis-

cussions of the Mogollon late periods in southwestern New Mexico. This Pueblo influence was carried still farther south by Anasazi-Mogollon peoples. The best known example is the large site of Casas Grandes in northern Chihuahua, where multi-roomed and multi-storied Pueblo buildings were constructed after A.D. 1300. And at this same Casas Grandes site, in conjunction with the Pueblo architecture, are other traits which show strong influences from Mesoamerica to the south. This brings us to a good transition point for our review of the relationships of Mesoamerica and the Southwest.

Observations on External Relationships

Mesoamerica and the Southwest. We have referred repeatedly to the importance of Mesoamerica in the development of the Southwest. Let us try to draw together the principal elements and events of this relationship. To begin with, a primitive maize was cultivated in the Southwest between 3000 and 2000 B.C. This maize may have been a local wild variety or the seeds may have been actually imported from Mexico, but in either case the stimulus for the domestication of the plant was derived from Mesoamerica, where such domestication goes back several millennia earlier. Maize was improved through selection, hybridization, the importation of new hybrid varieties from Mesoamerica, or through all of these techniques, so that by a few centuries before the beginning of the Christian era it was a major economic element of Southwestern culture. Beans and squashes were also added to the cultivated plant complex, and by a few centuries after the time of Christ this complex was known throughout the Southwest area. Pottery and figurines also were manifest at about the beginning of the Christian era, appearing first, insofar as we can tell, in the same Mogollon regions where agriculture was introduced. This early Mogollon red and brown pottery apparently was another Mesoamerican import, although its source cannot be pinned down any more exactly. The most likely possibility is that it came from

236

early and as yet undiscovered horizons in the Sierra Madre Occidental.

A second wave, or series of waves, of Mesoamerican diffusion carried new Mesoamerican traits and trait complexes to the Southwest. These traits began to appear in the Hohokam Colonial Period, at about A.D. 500–700, and they continued until about 1200–1300. They included the red-on-buff painting of pottery with specific designs such as bulls-eyes, swastikas, and stylized small animals. New pottery vessel forms developed. Platform temple mounds of earth and adobe, ball courts and the ballgame, mosaic pyrites mirrors, carved-stone figures reminiscent of "Chac-Mool," cast copper bells, and cotton spinning and weaving all bespeak Mesoamerica. Some of these traits, of course, were of a general Mesoamerican nature; but others, particularly the red-on-buff pottery, point to the contemporaneous Classic and Postclassic cultures of northwestern Mexico. They were introduced primarily into the Hohokam subarea. It is this group of traits that Di Peso believes to have been introduced by the invading and conquering Hohokam peoples, and it is this same group of traits that have also been interpreted as being carried by diffusion without an accompanying migration. The fact that they do not all appear at the same time, but seem to grow by accretion, argues against the migration hypothesis. It is possible that the canal irrigation ideas were also brought into the Hohokam from Mesoamerica during this time period, although this is less certain, and earlier introduction or independent invention seems more likely. Other traits of possible Mexican derivation, which may be considered with this second wave, included those architectural features found far to the north in the Anasazi homeland— architectural colonnades, round tower-like structures, and rubble-core masonry.

The two most likely Mesoamerican sources for these traits of the second wave were the Chalchihuites and the Chametla-Aztatlan cultures of northwestern Mexico.[152] The Chalchihuites culture is known from sites in the mountain valleys of Zacatecas and Durango. Platform mounds, ball courts, colonnades, and red-on-buff pottery were among its characteristics, and the culture is believed to have been firmly established in this part of Mexico before A.D. 900. To the south, Chalchihuites was related to the Classic and Postclassic cultures of the Valley of Mexico, but Chalchihuites also shared traits with the Chametla-Aztatlan continuity of the Nayarit-Sinaloa coast. Here, too, red-on-buff ceramics, platform temple mounds, and a copper-working tradition which included cast copper bells like those of the Southwest have been found. Similarities between Chametla-Aztatlan and Chalchihuites appear to have resulted partly from exchange between the two regions and partly from common sources of ancestry in central and western Mexico. Chametla-Aztatlan, however, probably drew more on Oaxacan and Mixtec traditions than did Chalchihuites, and it is likely that metalwork diffused northward up the Mexican coast from Oaxaca and, perhaps, ball courts as well. Furthermore, Oaxaca and Guerrero are the regions in Mesoamerica where water-supply systems were, apparently, earliest, and it is possible that Hohokam irrigation had its remote inspirations here.

The northwestern frontier cultures of Mesoamerica were, however, separated from those better known regions of the Southwest by a considerable span of territory, both on the coast and inland; and it is these geographically intervening regions and their native cultures that were probably the connecting links between Chalchihuites and Chametla-Aztatlan to the south and Mogollon and Hohokam in the north. We have stated before that these regions probably were more Southwestern than Mesoamerican. What were they and what do we know of them? In the interior, in southern Chihuahua, is the Loma San Gabriel phase, only cursorily described. The pottery is plain red or plain buff, and there are some crude stone masonry buildings. North of the Loma San Gabriel is a phase or phases known as Bravo Valley-Upper Conchos. The sites are in a drainage that flows north and northeast into the Rio Grande. Its ceramics are Southwestern, as is its pithouse form of dwelling.[153] Continuing still farther

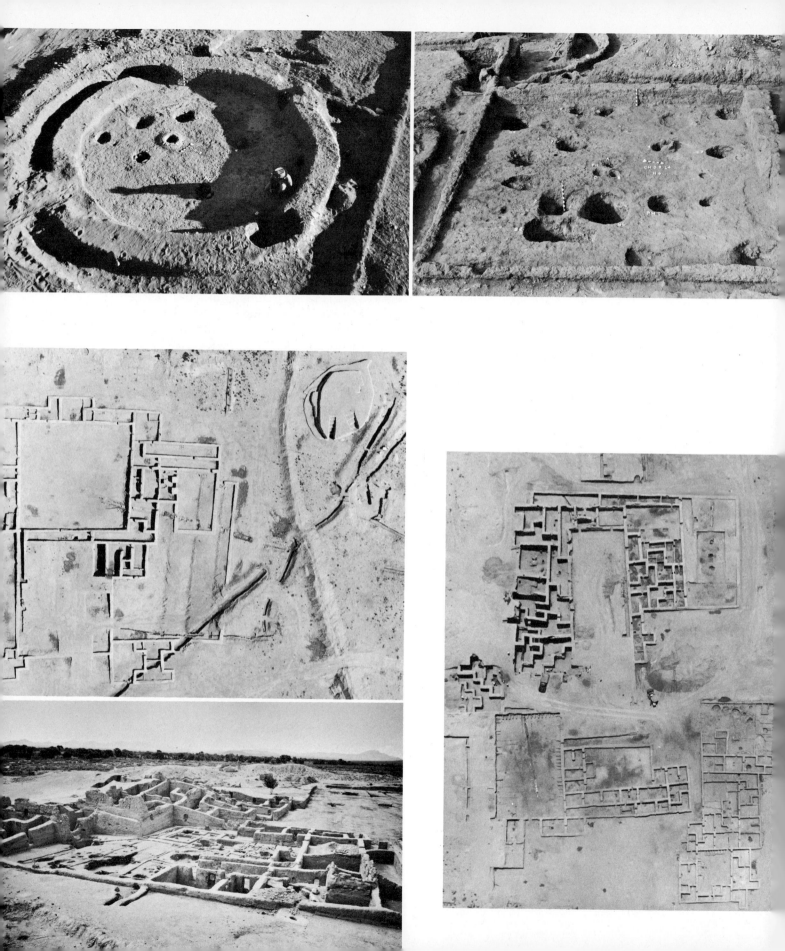

north, we find the Chihuahua or Casas Grandes culture. The Casas Grandes site is located less than 100 miles south of the New Mexican border. Di Peso's recent excavations there have defined three sequent phases—the earliest, the Viejo Period, before A.D. 1000, with pithouses and Mogollon pottery;[154] a middle phase, the Medio Period, essentially Southwestern, with adobe house compounds; and a third phase, Tardio Period, startlingly Mesoamerican, with platform mounds, a capital-I-shaped ball court, spindle-whorls, and copper bells. The dwelling units of this last phase, however, were the multi-roomed and multi-storied Anasazi-like buildings and the pottery was the unique Casas Grandes polychrome.[155] The third phase dates to after A.D. 1300. It was, in fact, the town presumed to have been built by the late emigrants from the Mimbres region to the north, although assuredly under strong Mexican acculturation. It would seem, thereby, to be too late to mark the passage of similar Mexican elements north to Colonial and Sedentary Period Hohokam sites. Moreover, the Casas Grandes culture probably lay too far to the east to have served as the conveyor of ideas and elements into the Hohokam.

Figure 4-57. (*Top*, p. 238) House floors at Casas Grandes, Chihuahua. *Left:* a Viejo (Early) Period community house. The fire-pit is marked by a raised clay ridge, and the door is at lower right. *Right:* Medio (Middle) Period rectangular surface structure. Most of the pits fix the position of sub-floor burials. (Courtesy Amerind Foundation.)

Figure 4-58. (*Left*, p. 238) Architecture at Casa Grandes, Chihuahua. *Top:* Aerial view of Medio Period house cluster construction. In the upper right corner is a stepped, truncated, bird-shaped mound. *Bottom:* Ground view of Tardio Period multi-storied adobe dwelling. (Courtesy Amerind Foundation.)

Figure 4-59. (*Right*, p. 238) Aerial view of Casas Grandes, Chihuahua, Mexico, during excavation. The architectural unit at the top dates from the Tardio (Late) Period; units below belong to the Medio (Middle) Period. Notice the more complex room forms in the Tardio unit. (Courtesy Amerind Foundation.)

Figure 4-60. Copper bell cast in the form of a turtle, from Casas Grandes, Chihuahua, Tardio Period. (Courtesy Amerind Foundation.)

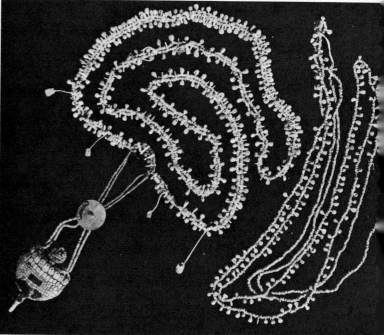

Figure 4-61. *Above:* Tardio Period necklaces from Casas Grandes, Chihuahua. *Left:* Copper bells and copper bell necklace. *Right:* Restored *Spondylus* shell necklace with turquoise, copper, and pyrite pendant. (Courtesy Amerind Foundation.)

Figure 4-62. *Right:* Typical olla of Casas Grandes polychrome from the Tardio Period. (Courtesy British Museum.)

Directly south of the Hohokam country is the region of the Trincheras culture, which we have mentioned briefly as being a possible southern outlier of the Hohokam. Its northern range reaches up to the international border. On the south, at least in the coast section, it meets the Huatabampo complex, and below the Huatabampo is the Chametla-Aztatlan region. Huatabampo is known only from its red and brown pottery. Trincheras is associated with a polychrome pottery style, a red-on-buff

Figure 4-63. Tardio Period pottery from Casas Grandes, Chihuahua. *Left:* Red-on-brown storage vessel with mammary appendages. *Right:* Playas Red vessel filled with turquoise beads, an offering found in a reservoir. (Courtesy Amerind Foundation.)

pottery somewhat in the manner of Hohokam, what appear to be stone-and-mud dwellings or defense works on hilltop locations, and hillside rainwater run-off cultivation terraces.[156]

From this rapid summary of Mesoamerican-Southwestern relationships, we get the impression that the crucially located intermediate cultures—Bravo Valley-Upper Conchos, Casa Grandes, Huatabampo, and Trincheras—may have been too late to have been the conductors for early cultural stimuli between the two major areas. This is obviously true for the basic agricultural and ceramic diffusions, and it may be true for much that spread in what we have referred to as the "second wave" of Mesoamerican traits that reached the Southwest proper. Yet some of these traits of the second group have been recognized in the geographical zone of the intermediate regions, albeit in a somewhat haphazard pattern of time and space distribution. Thus, it is very likely that continued archaeological investigation in Chihuahua and Sonora will clarify the situation. Probably, however, these intermediate regions will present something of a lower cultural contour than either the northernmost fully fledged Mesoamerican complex or the Gila-Salt River Valley Hohokam developments.

The Southwest and Other North American Areas. Less remains to be said here concerning the three other areas which surrounded the Southwest.[157] To the west, the Southwestern tradition appears to have given more than it assimilated, and this giving was through the medium of the Patayan. In the archaeological record, western imports are confined largely to marine shells.

On the north, the northern Anasazi peripheral cultures were forming and in existence from Basketmaker III through Pueblo II times, after which they withdrew. These cultures influenced the Utes and Paiutes. After the Anasazi withdrawal, Utes and Paiutes, following a simpler form of life, encroached on what had been Southwestern territory to some extent, but their inroads were never as significant as those of the Athapascans, who also invaded from a northerly direction. In the strictly archaeological record, the pointed-bottom utility pottery, with whatever ethnic groups it may have been identified, was the principal northern influence on the Southwest.

We have already mentioned a possible ceramic stimulus from the East invading the San Juan region in Pueblo I times. Certain diffusions into Texas from the Southwest also have been traced, and Krieger has demonstrated that it is possible to associate cross-finds between the relatively late prehistoric Caddoan cultures of the East and the contemporaneous cultures of the Southwest through the medium of geographically intermediate complexes of that state. We know, too, that Plains tribes traded and warred with the easternmost large Pueblos, such as Pecos; and in historic times, it was from the general direction of the Southwest that the Plains Indian obtained the horse. But all these contacts were brief and came relatively late. In general, the agricultural Southwest and the agricultural Eastern Woodlands were effectively separated from each other by the southern Plains in which the aborigines were non-farmers or, at best, marginal farmers.

Footnotes

[1]For various area delimitations of the Southwest see Haury (1962); Driver (1961, map 2); Jennings and Reed (1956, fig. 1 and pp. 63–64); Gladwin (1957); Reed (1964); Kroeber (1939, pp. 32–48). The definition given here is "expanded" rather than "contracted." It includes western, northern and eastern peripheries which are sometimes excluded. For the concepts of a Southwestern area proper and a "Greater Southwest," see Kirchhoff (1954) and Haury (1962).

[2]See Haury (1962). M. J. Rogers (1945) should also be consulted with reference to the Patayan subarea.

[3]See Reed (1954, 1962) for summary statements of prehistoric-to-historic events. See also Gladwin (1957, pp. 301 ff.); Haury (1962); and Kroeber (1939, pp. 32–48).

[4]K. Bryan and Toulouse (1943); see also Agogino (1960).

[5]Report at 1965 meeting of Society for American Archaeology, Urbana, Illinois.

[6]M. J. Rogers (1945).

[7]Haury and others (1950).

[8]Haury (1962).

[9]The Cochise chronological divisions (Sulphur Spring, Chiricahua, and San Pedro) are, like the chronological divisions of Anasazi culture, more properly considered as *stages* rather than *periods*. Thus, in the east, in New Mexico, the Chiricahua stage is believed to last until the beginning of the Mogollon culture, running concurrently with the San Pedro stage farther to the west (Wheat, 1955, p. 36).

[10]Mangelsdorf and Smith (1949). The radiocarbon dates on the earliest maize in the cave are not fully consistent, but this dating is a reasonable and relatively conservative estimate based on the radiocarbon determinations.

[11]Haury (1962).

[12]The radiocarbon dates are from about 300 to 150 B.C. Martin and others (1952, p. 483).

[13]Haury (1962); Mangelsdorf and Lister (1956).

[14]Sayles (1945); Haury (1962).

[15]Martin and others (1952). See also Wheat (1955, pp. 189–193) for a further discussion of the Cochise-to-Mogollon transition.

[16]The date is based on a radiocarbon reading of about 150 B.C. Martin and others (1952, p. 483). Bullard (1962, pp. 77–79) questions the undisturbed nature of the stratigraphy of the cave and suggests that the dates may apply to pre-ceramic deposits rather than to the Pine Lawn phase.

[17]Lister (1955, p. 168); Jennings and Reed (1956, pp. 79–81); see also this chapter, p. 239.

[18]Ekholm (1942, pp. 74–77).

[19]Kelley (1953); see also Riley and Winters (1963).

[20]This is based on Jennings and Reed (1956, pp. 88–89). See also Martin and Rinaldo (1951) for a discussion of the concept of a "Southwestern Co-Tradition" and Rouse (1954) and Wheat (1954 a) for a further discussion and critiques of this concept.

[21]As of the present writing, two general area-wide chronologies have been presented for the Southwest as a whole, synthesizing the three subareal sequences: Martin and Rinaldo (1951) and Daifuku (1952). These schemes have not been widely accepted, however, and I have not used their particular taxonomies in this brief summary statement.

[22]This is frequently referred to as the Pecos chronology or the "Pecos Classification," after an archaeological conference of 1927 at which it was first propounded by A. V. Kidder. Roberts (1935 b, 1937).

[23]A Pueblo V Period is also added to the sequence. It refers to the "historic and modern pueblos." A revision of the Pecos classification has been proposed by Roberts (1935 b) and it is frequently

used instead. In the Roberts revision the hypothetical Basketmaker I is dropped, and Basketmaker II is simply called "Basketmaker." The term "Modified Basketmaker" replaces old Basketmaker III. Pueblo I and II are lumped as "Developmental Pueblo." "Great Pueblo" is advanced as an alternative title to Pueblo III. "Regressive Pueblo" replaces Pueblo IV, and "Historic Pueblo" replaces Pueblo V.

[24]This Mogollon chronology follows most closely that of Wheat (1954 a, 1955, fig. 12).

[25]The correlation of the Hohokam sequence with those of Anasazi and Mogollon that is presented here is closest to that of Wheat (1955). Consult, however, Bullard (1962) for a thorough discussion of the problem and for presentations of other correlations (cf. p. 89).

[26]M. J. Rogers (1945). Rogers uses the terms Yuman I, II, and III, which have here been changed to Patayan I, II, and III.

[27]This device of a region is, in general, based on the concept of an "archaeological region" as given in Willey and Phillips (1958, pp. 19–20). For the Southwest application, it follows most closely the terminology and usage of Bullard (1962, see especially fig. 25). For the Southwest, Wheat (1955, see especially fig. 1) follows a dendritic culture classification scheme and employs units similar to the archaeological regions, which he calls "branches." Theoretically, however, these are quite different concepts; the *region* deals with geographic entities characterized by culture forms whereas the *branch* refers to the culture forms themselves.

Both Bullard (1962) and Wheat (1955) have been followed in devising the particular Mogollon regions to which we refer here. Bullard's regions are based primarily on village layout and architectural traits while Wheat's divisions are presumed to be founded on more inclusive cultural criteria. A number of specific differences obtain. Bullard divides Mimbres and Pine Lawn whereas Wheat does not. Wheat includes a Cibola unit, which is not designated by Bullard, who apparently divides it between Pine Lawn and the Anasazi Quemado region. Wheat includes Jornada and Eastern Peripheral regions; Bullard is not concerned with this eastern margin of the Mogollon.

It will be obvious in consulting our Fig. 4-1 as to how we have adjusted these differences.

[28]Wheat (1954 a, fig. 1).

[29]Bullard (1962, fig. 27).

[30]All authors (Wheat, Bullard, Martin, Haury, etc., as cited here) agree on the evidence of stability and duration of occupation for Mogollon villages.

[31]Bullard (1962, pp. 109–110).

[32]Wendorf (1956).

[33]Cosgrove and Cosgrove (1932, pp. 6–7).

[34]Wheat (1955, pp. 34–35); Wendorf (1956); Cosgrove and Cosgrove (1932).

[35]Wheat (1955, p. 35); Bullard (1962, pp. 109–110).

[36]Reed (1956).

[37]For descriptions and discussions of Mogollon pithouse architecture and Mogollon-Anasazi relations see Wheat (1955, pp. 35–56, 208–213); Bullard (1962, pp. 111–173, 186–188).

[38]Wheat (1955, pp. 62–65); Bullard (1962, pp. 170–178).

[39]Cosgrove and Cosgrove (1932); Wheat (1955, pp. 52–53).

[40]Wheat (1955, pp. 56–62).

[41]Wheat (1955, pp. 66–71); Cosgrove and Cosgrove (1932, pp. 23–29).

[42]Haury (1957).

[43]Martin and others (1952).

[44]Sayles (1945); Haury and Sayles, (1947); Haury (1936 a, 1936 b); Wheat, (1954 b); Martin (1940, 1943); Martin and Rinaldo (1947); Nesbitt (1938); Martin and others (1952). These principal early Mogollon pottery stations are San Simon, Bluff, Mogollon Village, Harris, Crooked Ridge, SU, Starkweather, Tularosa, and Cordova.

[45]Largely from Wheat (1955, pp. 73–109); see also Bullard (1962, p. 70).

[46]Martin and Rinaldo (1950 a).

[47]Cosgrove and Cosgrove (1932); Bradfield (1931).

[48]See summary in Wheat (1955, pp. 110–126); Cosgrove and Cosgrove (1932, pp. 31–46).

[49]Wheat (1955, pp. 104–105).

[50]Wheat (1955, pp. 127–138, fig. 9, e, f, particularly for principal projectile point types).

[51]Cosgrove (1932, pp. 48, pl. 50, particularly).

[52]Wheat (1955, pp. 138–149); see also other Mogollon monographs cited here.

[53]Wheat (1955, pp. 149–154); Martin and others (1952).

[54]Wheat (1955, pp. 158–159).

[55]Wendorf (1956), based on the northern or "Tularosa Mogollon" region. Other authors have treated this general subject of settlement, house, and social organization of the Mogollon (Martin and Rinaldo, 1950 b; Wheat, 1955, pp. 158–159).

[56]Martin and others (1952, pp. 461–79, 486, 498–500). See also Wheat's comments (1955, pp. 156–157).

[57]"Anasazi" is a Navajo word, taken over by the archaeologists, which means "ancient ones" or "ancient enemy" and refers to the builders of the Pueblos.

[58]C. Irwin-Williams (as reported orally in 1965).

[59]Morris and Burgh (1954, pp. 3–52, 80–86).

[60]Jones and Fonner (1954).

[61]Jones and Fonner (1954, pp. 106–115). The presence of Hohokam-Basketmaker maize in the upper levels of Bat Cave, around 300 B.C., is an hypothesis that is offered by Jones and Fonner and, as they make clear, they have not directly examined the specimens in question (see especially p. 113).

[62]The "classic" Basketmaker II sites which Morris and Burgh (1954, pp. 53, 74–79) use for their comparisons with the Durango material are: Cave du Pont (Nusbaum, 1922); White Dog Cave (Guernsey and Kidder, 1921); Kinboko Caves I and II (Kidder and Guernsey, 1919); Sayodneechee Burial Cave (Kidder and Guernsey, 1919); Broken Roof Cave (Guernsey, 1931); Rock Point Site 1 (Morss, 1927).

[63]Snow and Sanders (1954).

[64]Neumann (1952); see also this book, Chapter 1, p. 14; Seltzer (1944).

[65]Morris and Burgh (1954, pp. 25–26, 41, 64–72).

[66]Morris and Burgh (1954, pp. 53–64).

[67]Morris and Burgh (1954, pp. 80–86).

[68]Wheat (1955, p. 207).

[69]Bullard (1962, p. 102).

[70]Morris (1927); Jennings and Reed (1956, pp. 78–79).

[71]Roberts (1935 b, p. 12); Bullard (1962, p. 55).

[72]The exact first appearances of these traits are not known. Some writers (see Roberts, 1935 b) tend to place them as early Pueblo I; others (Jennings and Reed, 1956) as late Basketmaker III.

[73]Roberts (1929). The summary is based on this monograph.

[74]Brew (1946, p. 291); see also Bullard (1962, pp. 100–102).

[75]Bullard (1962, pp. 102–108).

[76]Roberts (1931).

[77]Roberts (1930).

[78]Brew (1946, pp. 152–202). This site is the type manifestation of what Brew has called the Abajo phase.

[79]See Brew for a full discussion of this (1946, pp. 67–73). See also Seltzer (1944).

[80]Brew (1946, p. 224 and entire chapter, pp. 215–226).

[81]Bullard (1962, p. 105).

[82]Brew (1946, pp. 136–138).

[83]Brew (1946, pp. 131–135).

[84]Wormington (1961 b, pp. 84–101).

[85]Judd (1954).

[86]Linton (1944); Wormington (1961 b, pp. 79–84).

[87]Bryan (1941); Hack (1941).

[88]Kidder (1924); see also Wormington (1961 b, pp. 91–96).

[89]Kidder (1924); Wormington (1961 b, 99–101).

[90]Ferdon (1955).

[91]Roberts (1935 b).

[92]Kidder (1924, 1931).

[93]Haury (1956, pp. 4–5).

[94]Brew (1946).

[95]Hack (1941).

[96]Woodbury (1961, p. 37) treats of similar arroyo terrace and slit-trap features from the Mogollon Point of Pines region and concludes that they probably all date after A.D. 1000.

[97]Whether this type is related to Mogollon or Hohokam red or buff ware traditions is uncertain. See Brew's lengthy discussion of this problem (1946, pp. 291–294).

[98]Roberts (1935 b).

[99]See Jennings and Reed (1956, pp. 82–86).

[100]Bullard (1962, p. 55).

[101]Wormington (1961 b, p. 112); Kidder (1931); Kidder and Shepard (1936).

[102]Jennings and Reed (1956, p. 99); see also Judd's comments (1954) on the projectile point sequence at Pueblo Bonito.

[103]See Roberts (1935 b); McGregor (1941); Wormington (1961 b). All deal with general trends of change.

[104]Roberts (1935 b); McGregor (1941); Wormington (1961 b).

[105]For general statement see Driver (1961, pp. 337–338).

[106]Jennings and Reed (1956, p. 115). Some works in Pueblo ethnology include: Stevenson (1904); Hough (1951); Cushing (1920); Parsons (1930, 1939).

[107]Hall (1944 a).

[108]Mera (1938).

[109]Hibben (1938); see also Wormington (1961 b, pp. 102–105) for a summary discussion of Largo-Gallina.

[110]Jennings and Reed (1956, p. 102).

[111]Wormington (1955). See also Jennings and Reed (1956, pp. 102–104).

[112]Krieger (1946, 1947).

[113]A Pima word for "the old people" or "those who have gone."

[114]See Haury and others (1950, pp. 546–548 and p. 16, fig. 2) for these suggestions of regional divisions. A. E. Johnson (1963) includes the Trincheras as a part of the Papaguería development, placing both in a "Desert" as opposed to a "River" Hohokam. Schroeder (1964) strongly opposes the "Desert" Hohokam concept, apparently seeing cultures such as Papaguería and Trincheras as a part of his Hakatayan or expanded Patayan tradition.

[115]Haury and others (1950, pp. 341 ff.).

[116]Schroeder (1965) argues that Mesoamerican agriculture first took root in the Middle Gila region and spread to the Mogollon from there.

[117]For Hohokam chronology see Haury and others (1950); Gladwin and others (1937); Gladwin (1948, 1957); Wheat (1954 a, 1955); Bullard (1962, pp. 88–93). Hohokam chronology is by no means firmly established as to absolute dating or as to its cross-dating with either Mogollon or Anasazi. I have used a chronology here which, in general, follows Haury and Wheat.

[118]Recapitulation here of Hohokam archaeology from Pioneer through Sedentary Periods follows largely the Snaketown monograph (Gladwin and others, 1937).

[119]Recent excavations at Snaketown, Arizona (1964–1965) have given evidence of canal building in the Pioneer Period (report of W. W. Wasley, Society for American Archaeology Meetings, Urbana, Illinois, 1965).

[120]Wasley (1960).

[121]Wormington (1961 b, p. 137).

[122]See Wormington (1961 b, pp. 137–144) for a summary of the Hohokam Classic Period.

[123]Haury (1945).

[124]Gladwin (1928).

[125]Schroeder (1947, 1963 a) believes the "Salado" influence was actually Sinaguan and from the Verde Valley.

[126]See Haury and others (1950, pp. 6ff.) for a summary of the Papagueria Hohokam; see also Wormington (1961 b, p. 142–144).

[127]Basic works in Pima and Papago ethnology include Russell (1908); Underhill (1939); Beals (1934); Ezell (1961).

[128]Basic works in Yuman ethnography include Forde (1931) and Spier (1936).

[129]See Colton (1945) and M. J. Rogers (1945) for a presentation of these two points of view.

[130]Schroeder (1957).

[131]See particularly Rogers (1945); Colton (1945); and Schroeder (1957). Consult also Jennings and Reed (1956, p. 91); Colton (1939); and Wormington (1961 b, pp. 167–168).

[132]Rogers (1945) seems to indicate that the Amargosa culture was succeeded by another which was essentially Patayan except that it lacked the pottery and agriculture of his Yuman I (or Patayan I) Period. This late preceramic culture appears to be the same as what W. J. Wallace (1962) (see also Chapter VI) considers as a late Amargosa phase.

[133]Rogers (1945).

[134]Rogers (1945) gives estimates of A.D. 800–900, referring primarily to Colorado River manifestations. Schwartz (1956) dates the Cohonina variant of Patayan to A.D. 600–700.

135Schroeder (1963 a). This, in a sense, returns to the earlier opinions of Gladwin (Gladwin, W. and H. S., 1930) and Kroeber (1939, p. 42) who felt that prehistoric Yuman or Patayan pottery was only a derivative of Hohokam.

136Hester (1962); Hall (1944 b).

137Huscher, B. H. and H. A. (1942, 1943).

138Hester (1962).

139Hester (1962). The Dismal River culture and its Apachean affiliations are treated by Gunnerson (1960).

139aThe date of the separation of the Apachean (Apaches and Navajos) from northern or Subarctic Athapascans has been estimated by glottochronology at A.D. 700–1000 (Hymes, 1957).

140Hester (1962).

141Keur (1941).

142Vogt (1961).

143Vogt (1961).

144Colton (1939); Jennings and Reed (1956, p. 91); Schwartz (1956).

145Colton (1939); Wormington (1961 b, p. 168); Jennings and Reed (1956, p. 91).

146Colton (1946); Gladwin (1943); Jennings and Reed (1956, p. 91); Wheat (1955, pp. 203–204); Schroeder (1963 b).

147Schroeder (1963 b).

148Haury has documented an excellent example of this sort of site unit intrusion in the Mogollon Point of Pines region (Haury, 1958).

149Schroeder (1963 a).

150Di Peso and others (1956).

151E. K. Reed has long leaned toward this view. See Reed (1963) and Riley and Winters (1963).

152See A. S. Johnson (1958); Kelley and Winters (1960); Kelley (1960).

153J. C. Kelley (1953, 1956); J. C. Kelley and Shackelford, (1954).

154Di Peso (1963). You will recall that Lister (1955, p. 168) also found Mogollon pottery in Chihuahua.

155Di Peso (1963).

156A. E. Johnson (1963).

157These relationships have been reviewed in detail in Jennings and Reed (1956, pp. 91–110).

Eastern North America, unlike either Mesoamerica or the Southwest, is not a single culture area made coherent by a unifying cultural tradition. As considered in this chapter, the East refers to all of the vast territory from the Rocky Mountains to the Atlantic and from southern Canada to northeastern Mexico and the Gulf of Mexico. This is a convenient presentation for an introductory survey of American archaeology, but it is also more than this. As Kroeber has recognized, most of the East does have a general unity of culture traits and natural environment.[1] It is a kind of superculture area, distinguishable from the lands to the west, north, and south. For these discussions, however, the East will be divided into more conventional culture areas. The two largest of these are the Eastern Woodlands and the Plains. These two areas are not easily and sharply separable in either culture or landscape. They share common cultural traditions and the histories of these traditions are interrelated. A third, and smaller, area will also be considered here: Northeast Mexico-Texas. The Northeast Mexico-Texas area stands both environmentally and culturally somewhat apart from the Eastern Woodlands and the Plains, and relatively little is known of its archaeology. The geographical position of the Northeast Mexico-Texas area lends it a special importance, however, for it lies midway between the other parts of the East and Mesoamerica.

Eastern North America

5

The Eastern Woodlands Area

The Natural Area. The Eastern Woodlands culture area, as here defined, includes all of the North American continent from southern Canada to the Gulf of Mexico.[2] It is rather arbitrarily divided from the Plains by a line drawn through the western portions of Minnesota, Iowa, and Missouri and the eastern edges of Oklahoma and Texas. As its name implies, it is, or was, an area of forests. Pines dot the coastal plains and cypress and gum trees, the river bottoms. The Appalachian and Ozark-Ouachita Highlands bear oak and oak-pine stands; the Ohio Valley and the northern Middle West are regions of deciduous trees; and as one goes northward deciduous hardwoods are mixed with conifers in New England and Canada. From Illinois, where they are interspersed with wooded river valleys, prairie grasslands stretch westward. Throughout, the soils are generally good, except for rocky localities in New England, the Appalachians, or the Ozarks, and some southern swamplands, such as the Florida Everglades. Numerous rivers and streams lace the area, and the alluvial riverbottom soils are unusually fertile. The climate is temperate, with a range from cold, in the north, to sub-tropical, in the south, and the rainfall is generally adequate for plant cultivation. The presence of deer, small game, fish, shellfish, nuts, and wild seed and root foods afforded an ample diet for human groups prior to cultivation.

The Cultural Traditions. The four cultural traditions of the Eastern Woodlands are: (1) the Big-Game Hunting; (2) the Archaic; (3) the Woodland; and (4) the Mississippian.[3]

We have expressed the opinion that the Big-Game Hunting tradition was a pattern of life that probably arose on the North American Plains and spread from there to the Eastern Woodlands (see Chap. 2).

The Archaic tradition, which succeeded the Big-Game Hunting tradition, appears to have evolved locally in the early post-Pleistocene, its economic foundations based on hunting, fishing, shell-fishing, and plant-collecting. It is the first major pattern to distinguish the Eastern Woodlands as a culture area and had a profound formative influence on the later traditions of the area, both in elements of technology and, apparently, ceremonialism. The tradition was characterized by large and broad-bladed dart points and ground- and polished-stone tools and ornaments.

The Woodland tradition appeared in the East around 1000 B.C. Although its roots are in the Archaic, it displayed new elements: Woodland pottery, ceramic figurines, mortuary mounds and

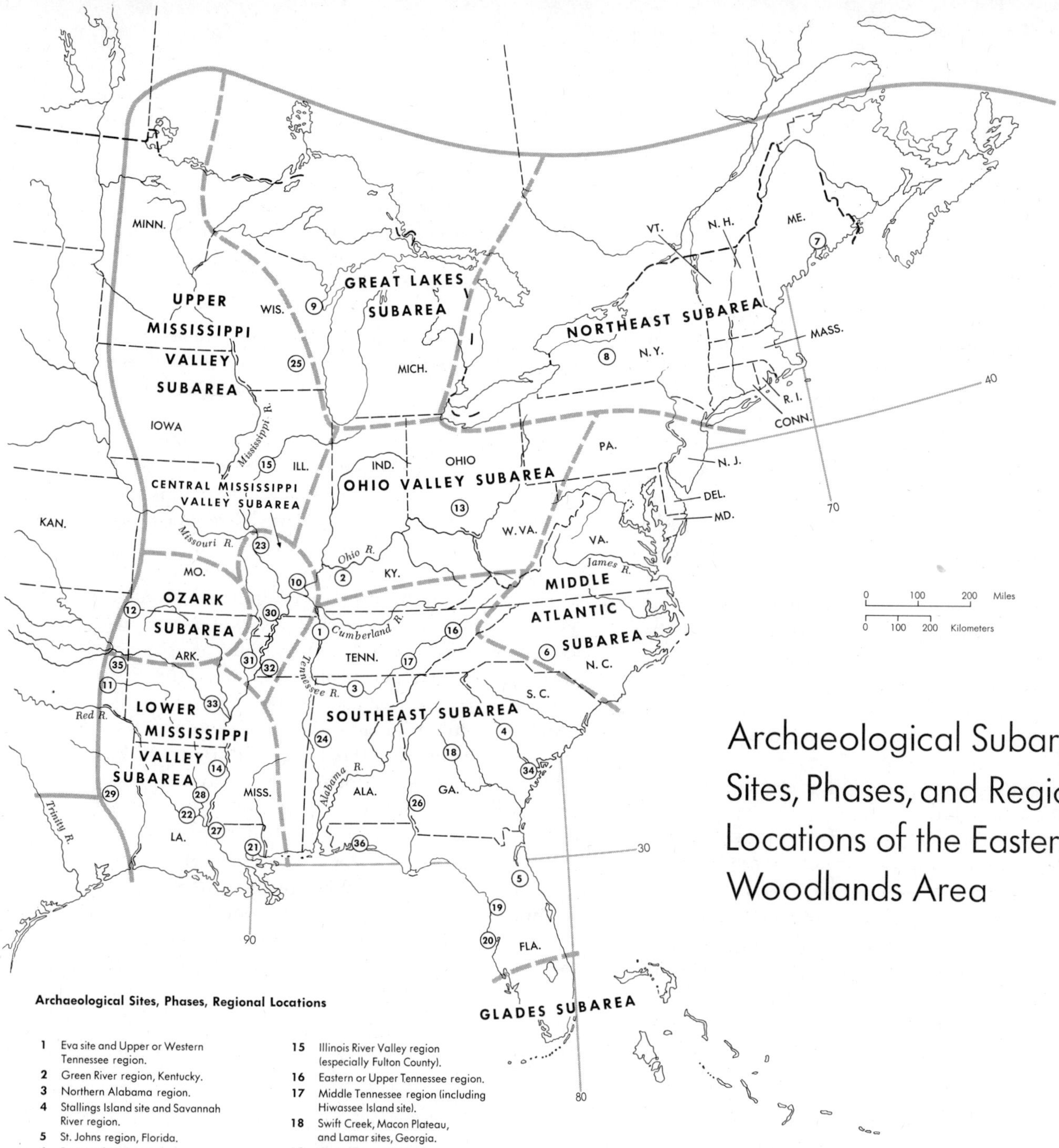

Archaeological Subareas, Sites, Phases, and Regional Locations of the Eastern Woodlands Area

MINN.

WIS.

MICH.

IOWA

UPPER MISSISSIPPI VALLEY SUBAREA

GREAT LAKES SUBAREA

NORTHEAST SUBAREA

VT.   N. H.   ME.

N.Y.

MASS.

R.I.   CONN.

KAN.

MO.

ILL.   IND.   OHIO

CENTRAL MISSISSIPPI VALLEY SUBAREA

OHIO VALLEY SUBAREA

PA.

N. J.

W. VA.

VA.

DEL.

MD.

Mississippi R.

Missouri R.

Ohio R.

KY.

MIDDLE ATLANTIC SUBAREA

N. C.

James R.

OZARK SUBAREA

ARK.

TENN.

Cumberland R.

Tennessee R.

LOWER MISSISSIPPI VALLEY SUBAREA

Red R.

MISS.

ALA.

GA.

S. C.

SOUTHEAST SUBAREA

Alabama R.

Trinity R.

LA.

FLA.

GLADES SUBAREA

40

70

30

80

90

| 0 | 100 | 200 | Miles |
| 0 | 100 | 200 | Kilometers |

Archaeological Sites, Phases, Regional Locations

1 Eva site and Upper or Western Tennessee region.
2 Green River region, Kentucky.
3 Northern Alabama region.
4 Stallings Island site and Savannah River region.
5 St. Johns region, Florida.
6 Region of Piedmont Sequence.
7 Ellsworth Falls site, Maine.
8 Lamoka and later phases, New York.
9 Oconto site, Wisconsin.
10 Faulkner, Baumer, and Kincaid sites, Illinois.
11 Fourche Maline site, Oklahoma.
12 Grove phase and Ozark Bluff Dweller sites, Arkansas-Oklahoma.
13 Adena and Hopewell centers, Ohio.
14 Poverty Point, Louisiana.

15 Illinois River Valley region (especially Fulton County).
16 Eastern or Upper Tennessee region.
17 Middle Tennessee region (including Hiwassee Island site).
18 Swift Creek, Macon Plateau, and Lamar sites, Georgia.
19 Crystal River site, Florida.
20 Weeden Island site, Florida.
21 Tchefuncte site, Louisiana.
22 Marksville site, Louisiana.
23 Cahokia site, Illinois.
24 Moundville site, Alabama.
25 Aztalan site, Wisconsin.
26 Kolomoki site, Georgia.
27 Coles Creek phase, Louisiana-Mississippi.
28 Troyville site, Louisiana.

29 Davis site, Texas.
30 New Madrid phase, Missouri.
31 Parkin phase, Arkansas.
32 Walls phase, Tennessee.
33 Menard phase, Arkansas.
34 Irene site, Georgia.
35 Spiro site, Oklahoma.
36 Ft. Walton site, Florida.

Figure 5-1.

earthworks, and plant cultivation (including maize). The places and times of origin of these new elements are debatable, and we will turn to these questions farther along, but we do know the tradition had its synthesis within the Eastern Woodlands area. The most intensive expressions of the tradition were in the Ohio and Mississippi valleys, and from these two drainages it appears to have fanned outward, replacing or modifying the cultures of the Archaic tradition.

During the latter half of the first millennium A.D., the fourth tradition, the Mississippian, appeared somewhere in the lower and central Mississippi Valley regions. This tradition derived in part from Archaic and Woodland heritages, but, again, there are significant innovations: the intensification of maize agriculture, the development of large permanent villages and towns, the construction of platform mounds to serve as bases for temples or palace-type buildings, and the arrangement of these mounds around rectangular open plazas. Mesoamerican strains in all these developments are obvious, and links with that area are also suggested by new pottery vessel forms and decorative techniques. Mississippian culture spread in all directions from its early river centers, so that by A.D. 1400 its influences were found throughout much of the Eastern Woodlands area.

Chronology. These four cultural traditions of the Eastern Woodlands are chronologically sequent, but they also overlap, as we can see by projecting them against an area chronology (Figs. 5-2, 5-3). The chronology is divided into periods: the Paleo-Indian,[4] Archaic, Burial Mound, and Temple Mound.[5] It is important to bear in mind the distinction between the concepts of traditions and periods. The former are cultural patterns persisting through time. The latter are intended as horizontal time bands.

The Paleo-Indian Period, the earliest, dates from before 8000 B.C. It need not concern us here. It was the time of the Big-Game Hunting tradition in the Eastern Woodlands, with which we have already dealt (Chap. 2).

The Archaic Period is set at 8000 to 1000 B.C. and is divided into three subperiods: Early (8000–5000 B.C.); Middle (5000–2000 B.C.); and Late (2000–1000 B.C.). The Early Archaic was the time of transition between the Big-Game Hunting and Archaic cultural traditions. The latter was replacing the former, but elements of both traditions mingled in the area during this period. During the Middle and Late Archaic subperiods, only the Archaic tradition appears to have survived.

The Burial Mound Period, which lasted from 1000 B.C. to A.D. 700, succeeded the Archaic Period. Its two subperiods, Burial Mound I and Burial Mound II, lasted from 1000 to 300 B.C. and from 300 B.C. to A.D. 700, respectively. The former was another time of transition, in this instance between the cultures of the Archaic tradition and those of the Woodland tradition. During the Burial Mound II subperiod, the area was largely dominated by the Woodland tradition, although some marginal Archaic tradition cultures still survived.

The Temple Mound Period dates from A.D. 700 to 1700. It saw the first establishment of the Mississippian cultural tradition in the Eastern Woodlands area and the beginnings of the spread of this tradition throughout the area. These events characterized the Temple Mound I subperiod (A.D. 700–1200). In Temple Mound II (A.D. 1200–1700), the Mississippian tradition had spread widely, and its impact on the older resident Woodland tradition cultures resulted in numerous regional fusions of the two traditions. In some subareas and regions, Woodland cultures, not radically modified by the new influences, continued through both Temple Mound I and II Periods.[6]

The absolute dates assigned to the several periods and their divisions are broad estimates, as is obvious. They are based on radiocarbon determinations and extensions of these findings by archaeological cross-datings. The dates of the Eastern Woodland area chronology are less reliable than those of the North American Southwest, particularly of the Anasazi subarea with its dendrochronological dates. The dates given here to the

Eastern Woodlands area tend to be *early* rather than *late* approximations, especially the termination date of 1000 B.C. for the Archaic Period, which expresses the first appearance of the Woodland tradition. At this time, according to some authorities, Archaic tradition cultures were still flourishing in essentially unmodified form in various places in the East.[7]

Our manner of presenting the culture history of the Eastern Woodlands will differ somewhat from the way we traced the culture histories of Mesoamerica and the North American Southwest. For Mesoamerica we traced a single cultural tradition on an area-wide basis with an area chronology as the main structure of exposition. In the Southwest, we examined a single cultural tradition in its four principal subareas with four separate subareal chronologies as the frames of reference.

Figure 5-2. Chronological chart for the Eastern Woodlands area, I, including the Ozarks, Lower Mississippi Valley, Southeast, and Middle Atlantic subareas. Regional sequences, cultures, and phases include only selected ones, primarily those mentioned in the text.

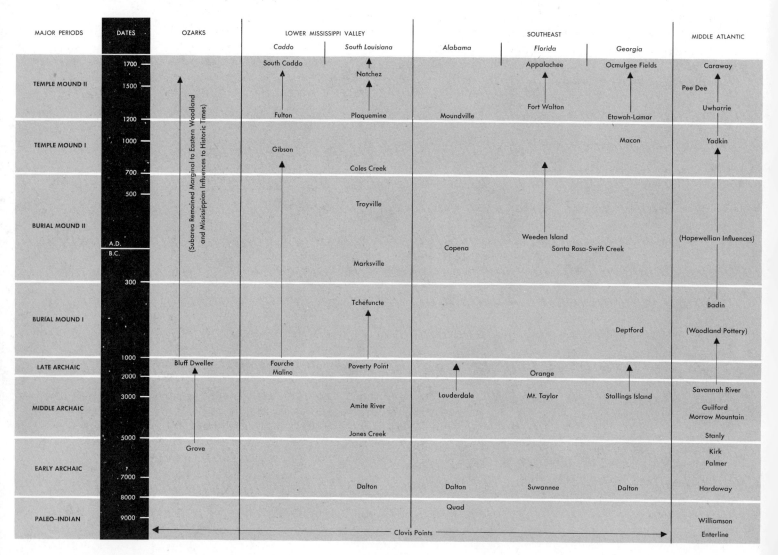

Three major cultural traditions command our attention in the Eastern Woodlands, and these traditions cannot be separated one from another on a subareal basis. We can comprehend their histories more readily in a frame of organization that emphasizes chronology rather than geography. Such an area chronology for the Eastern Woodlands is given in Figs. 5-2, 5-3. The periods are the ones just listed. The several columns represent subareas[8] of the Eastern Woodlands, with selected regional and local culture phases.

Ethnography. The Temple Mound II Period of the archaeological chronology for the Eastern Woodlands area persisted beyond the time of the first European incursions into the area. These came, to the Southeastern and lower Mississippi subareas, in the early half of the sixteenth

Figure 5-3. Chronological chart for the Eastern Woodlands area, II, including the Upper Mississippi Valley, Great Lakes, Central Mississippi Valley, Southeast (Tennessee), Ohio Valley, and Northeast subareas. Regional sequences, cultures, and phases include only selected ones, primarily those mentioned in the text.

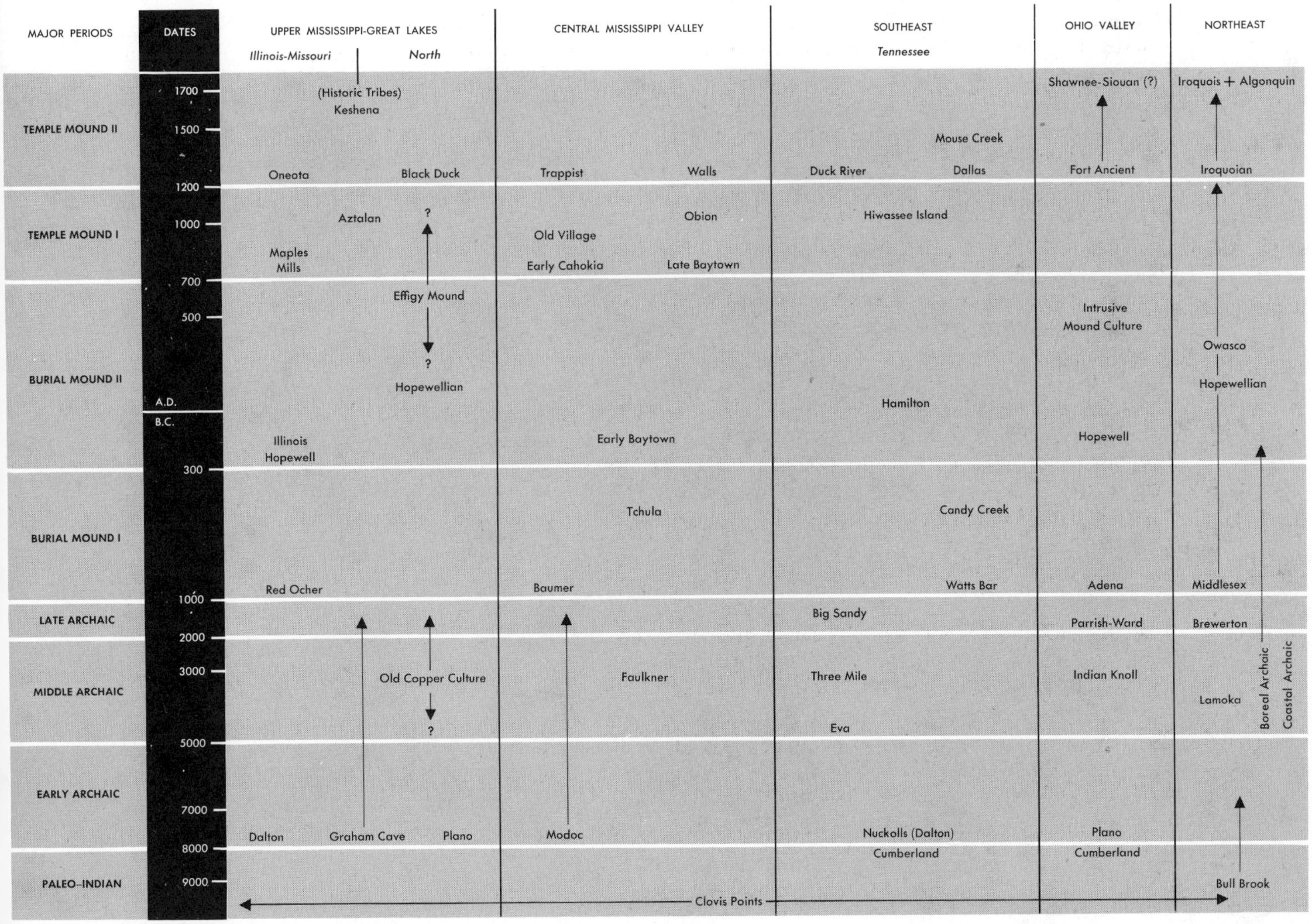

MAJOR PERIODS	DATES	UPPER MISSISSIPPI-GREAT LAKES (Illinois-Missouri)	(North)	CENTRAL MISSISSIPPI VALLEY		SOUTHEAST (Tennessee)		OHIO VALLEY	NORTHEAST
TEMPLE MOUND II	1700	(Historic Tribes) Keshena						Shawnee-Siouan (?)	Iroquois + Algonquin
	1500						Mouse Creek		
	1200	Oneota	Black Duck	Trappist	Walls	Duck River	Dallas	Fort Ancient	Iroquoian
TEMPLE MOUND I	1000	Aztalan ?		Old Village	Obion	Hiwassee Island			
		Maples Mills							
	700			Early Cahokia	Late Baytown				
	500		Effigy Mound ?					Intrusive Mound Culture	Owasco
BURIAL MOUND II			Hopewellian			Hamilton			Hopewellian
	A.D. / B.C.	Illinois Hopewell		Early Baytown				Hopewell	
BURIAL MOUND I	300			Tchula		Candy Creek			
	1000	Red Ocher		Baumer			Watts Bar	Adena	Middlesex
LATE ARCHAIC						Big Sandy			
	2000							Parrish-Ward	Brewerton
MIDDLE ARCHAIC	3000	Old Copper Culture		Faulkner		Three Mile		Indian Knoll	Lamoka
	5000	?				Eva			
EARLY ARCHAIC	7000								
	8000	Dalton	Graham Cave	Plano	Modoc	Nuckolls (Dalton)		Plano	
PALEO-INDIAN						Cumberland		Cumberland	
	9000								Bull Brook

(Northeast: Boreal Archaic / Coastal Archaic)

←————————————————— Clovis Points —————————————————→

century, the most famous being the expedition of Hernando de Soto in 1539–1542. Insofar as we can tell from the archaeological record, these early forays of the Spanish had little effect upon the Indians and their cultures. Appreciable culture change or culture disintegration did not come for another 100 years or more. Actually, no single date line can be selected at which to terminate a proto-historic upward extension of the Temple Mound II Period; A.D. 1700 is meaningful approximation for the eastern seaboard and the lower Southeastern regions. By this time, the native societies of Florida had been transformed by the influence of the Spanish missions, and the English colonies along the Atlantic Coast had disrupted many of the indigenous tribes and pushed them toward the interior. Still, even at this date, aboriginal customs retained their vigor; the famous early French accounts of Natchez funeral ceremonies and social class systems date from 1699; and farther to the north and the west, native cultures, although indirectly affected through trade, were not seriously disturbed.

There is a rather respectable body of information about most of the ethnic groups of this later, proto-historic part of the Temple Mound II Period. With a few doubtful exceptions, they can be grouped into five principal language families: Algonquian, Siouan, Iroquoian, Caddoan, and Muskogean. Algonquians are represented by Northeastern and Middle Atlantic tribes, such as the Abnaki, Mahican, Delaware, and Powhatan, and by the Ojibwa, Menomini, Miami, and Illinois from the Great Lakes and upper Mississippi Valley areas. (see map, Fig. 5-4). A few eastern Siouan and probable Siouan affiliates occupied the Middle Atlantic and Southeastern subareas, including the Tutelo, Catawba, and Yuchi; but the major Siouan distribution, including the Quapaw, Osage, and Missouri, and the various tribes of the Plains, was in the West, at least in early historic times. The Iroquois held the country around Lakes Erie and Ontario and their linguistic relatives, the Cherokee, that of the highlands of North Carolina, and adjacent portions of Tennessee and

of Georgia. The Caddoan-speaking groups were concentrated in the Plains area, although the Caddo tribe itself ranged the Eastern Woodlands area in the region of the Arkansas, Louisiana, and Texas border. Virtually the entire Southeast belonged to the Muskogean tribes: Creek, Choctaw, and Chickasaw, and their neighbors and probable linguistic kinsmen, the Timucua, Calusa, Natchez, Tunica, Chitimacha, and Atakapa.[9] In general, the archaeological cultures of the late pre-Columbian and proto-historic centuries can be attributed to the ancestors of the particular tribal groups that lived in the regions or localities concerned. There are, of course, exceptions, and a good deal of archaeological controversy in the Eastern Woodlands area has revolved around specific matters of archaeologic-ethnic identifications. We will refer to such points farther along.

Continuities of the Archaic Tradition

Introductory Comment. No one place, region, or subarea of the Eastern Woodlands can be pointed to as the center from which the Archaic cultural tradition spread to the rest of the area. The origins of the tradition are uncertain. We examined these beginnings in Chapter 2, and put forward two hypotheses—one tracing the rise of the Archaic from an ancient, unspecialized, hunting-gathering tradition of the Eastern Woodlands, the other favoring a derivation from the Big-Game Hunting tradition. We favor the latter hypothesis. These hypotheses are concerned, of course, with what we have defined as the Early Archaic Period (8000–5000 B.C.). It is later, in the Middle Archaic Period (5000–2000), that the tradition began taking on its distinctive form. At this time it is possible, even probable, that many of the elements of the Archaic tradition, especially certain of its polished-stone artifacts and the domesticated dog, were diffused to it from the northern boreal zones of North America and, ultimately, from the Old World. This projection presents still another hypothesis of origins; however, the

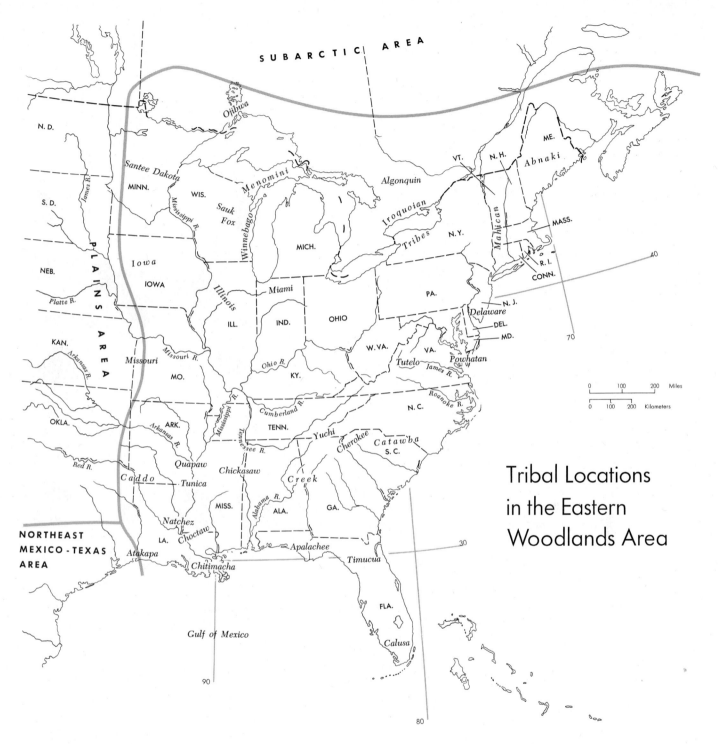

SUBARCTIC AREA

N. D.

Ojibwa

MINN.

Santee Dakota

WIS.

Sauk
Fox

Menomini

MICH.

Algonquin

Iroquoian

Tribes

VT.
N. H.
ME.

Abnaki

N. Y.

MASS.

Mahican

R. I.
CONN.

40

S. D.

James R.

NEB.

Iowa

IOWA

Illinois

Miami

Platte R.

ILL.

IND.

OHIO

PA.

N. J.

Delaware

DEL.

MD.

70

KAN.

Arkansas R.

Missouri

MO.

Missouri R.

Ohio R.

KY.

W. VA.

VA.

Tutelo

James R.

Powhatan

OKLA.

Red R.

ARK.

Arkansas R.

Mississippi R.

Cumberland R.

TENN.

Roanoke R.

N. C.

Caddo

Tunica

Quapaw

Chickasaw

Tennessee R.

Yuchi

Cherokee

Catawba

S. C.

Creek

Natchez

MISS.

Alabama R.

ALA.

GA.

Choctaw

LA.

Atakapa

Apalachee

Timucua

30

NORTHEAST
MEXICO-TEXAS
AREA

Chitimacha

FLA.

Gulf of Mexico

Calusa

90

80

PLAINS AREA

0   100   200   Miles
0   100   200   Kilometers

Tribal Locations
in the Eastern
Woodlands Area

Figure 5-4.

253

routes of such a diffusion are unclear, and it is uncertain if the elements in question appeared earlier in the northern subareas and regions of the East, as they would have if they had been carried from Asia. Thus in searching for a geographical point at which to begin discussions of the continuities of the Archaic tradition in the Middle and Late Archaic Periods, evidence for origins or first introductions is of little guidance. Choice of a starting place is arbitrary, influenced in part by the length and fullness of the particular archaeological record.

The Southeast. Some of the fullest archaeological records for the Archaic come from the deep shell midden sites of the Southeastern and Ohio Valley subareas, among them being several on the lower Tennessee River in Tennessee. These refuse heaps, composed largely of freshwater mussels, represent the accumulated living detritus of small village communities who occupied these locations over several millennia. This occupation was probably of a recurrent, seasonal sort, with the community (a kin-unit?) moving elsewhere for a part of each year but returning to the river location at the favorable time for gathering shellfish. At the time of occupancy, under Altithermal climatic conditions, the river was shallow and sluggish and the mussels could be gathered easily. Along the river were the forests which provided additional subsistence in the forms of nuts, berries, roots, seeds, and game. Faunal remains in the Tennessee shell mounds indicate that deer, elk, bear, fox, wolf, squirrel, raccoon, opossum, beaver, otter, fish, and turkey and other birds roamed the area.[10] Such were the main food resources of the Archaic peoples of the Southeast. It is also probable that they supplemented these wild foods by cultivating on a small scale such plant species as sunflower and goosefoot (*Chenopodium*); however, the earliest dates for such domesticates fall at the very end of the Archaic Period or at the beginning of the succeeding Burial Mound I Period.[11]

Radiocarbon dates from these lower Tennessee sites begin shortly before 5000 B.C., span the

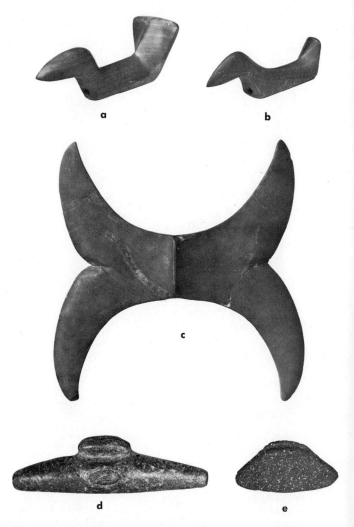

Figure 5-5. "Problematical" polished-stone objects, typical of the Archaic tradition and Period in the Eastern Woodlands. All probably were used as throwing-stick or atlatl weights. *a,b*: Birdstones from Indiana, about 13 to 14 cm. long. *c*: Fine specimen of a winged bannerstone from Indiana; diameter, about 14 cm. *d,e,*: Boatstones from Alabama, with the excavated surfaces turned down; length of longest, 12 cm. (Courtesy Museum of the American Indian, Heye Foundation.)

Middle and Late Archaic Periods, and continue even later. The cultural story is one of slow, gradual change, with occasional innovations. One of the largest and deepest middens is the Eva site, located on a small tributary of the Tennessee. Three sequent phases are represented. The earliest of these is the Eva phase, dating to the earlier half of the Middle Archaic Period.

The hunting, fishing, and other food-gathering habits of the Eva-phase people are revealed in artifacts as well as general debris. The common chipped-stone projectile points are the large, generally long, basal-notched or straight-stemmed types which were attached to darts and thrown with the aid of an atlatl or throwing-stick. Ground- and polished-stone weights, of winged or cylindrical styles, were hafted onto the atlatl shafts through a longitudinally drilled hole. Other dart points were made of antler. Game was butchered and hides scraped, dressed, and sewn with large chipped knives, scrapers, and drills and bone awls

and bodkins. Bone fishhooks attest to that activity, as do fish bones in the refuse. Rough mortars, nut-stones, and hammerstones were used to grind or break seed and nut foods. Ornaments of the Eva phase include bird-bone beads, perforated animal canine teeth, and simple stone pendants. The dead were buried in a flexed position in small round graves, occasionally with artifacts. Dog skeletons have been discovered in the same graves with humans, and also in separate graves. These finds are the first evidence of this domesticated animal in the Eastern Woodlands and perhaps in North America.[12] The Eva people themselves were mesocranic to dolichocranic, and it is presumed that they are a part of the early North American physical type that Neumann called Iswanid.[13] Although it is generally true that the populations associated with the Archaic cultural tradition tended toward long-headedness, we shall see farther along that some brachycranic individuals were present in the Middle and Late Archaic Periods.

The Three Mile phase succeeded the Eva phase in the stratification of the Eva site. Estimates indicate that it lasted from 3500 to 1200 B.C., or from the latter part of the Middle Archaic through the Late Archaic Period. Characterizing the phase was a shift from basal-notched to side-notched projectile points, the appearance of chipped-flint adzes, and more polished-stone forms—i.e., the prismoidal or bannerstone-type atlatl weights and cylindrical or bell-shaped pestles. Antler atlatl hooks and copper beads were other new features. Pottery, however, had not yet appeared, although it is the marker element for the Late Archaic Period (2000–1000 B.C.) farther south.[14]

The final Archaic phase on the lower Tennessee was the Big Sandy, which persisted into the Burial Mound I Period (1000–300 B.C.) and is associated with the increased precipitation of the Medithermal climatic era. Heavier rainfall widened and deepened the rivers and made the mussels less accessible. They vanished from the diet, and from the midden sites. Otherwise life seems to have followed much the same pattern. The only other

Figure 5-6. Some Archaic Period projectile points from the Eva site in western Tennessee. a,b: Forms characteristic of the 6000–4000 B.C. time range, or the close of the Early Archaic and the beginning of the Middle Archaic Periods. c,d: Forms characteristic of the 4000–1000 B.C. time range, or the Middle and Late Archaic Periods. e: Form characteristic of the Middle Archaic Period. Length of a, 9.8 cm. (Redrawn from Lewis and Kneberg, 1961.)

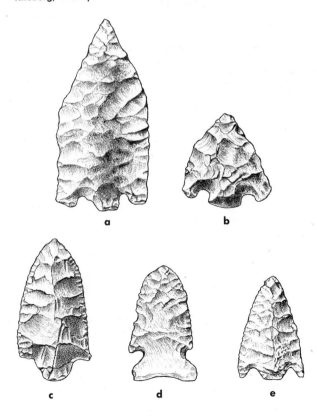

a   b

c   d   e

new developments were tubular stone pipes, grooved axes, celts, and oblong and expanded-center bar-gorgets. All these items were made of polished stone. In chipped stone, the earlier basal-notched or side-notched projectile points gave way to straight-stemmed types, and adzes became more common. In the Big Sandy phase, a few Adena projectile point types have been found. The Adena point, a long ovate-triangular form with a tapered stem, may indicate contacts with Burial Mound I period and Woodland tradition cultures to the north. Pottery still was not in wide use, but some Baumer fabric-marked sherds have been found, probably representing contact with peoples of the Woodland tradition rather than being of local manufacture.[15]

Lewis and Kneberg relate the Archaic cultures of the lower Tennessee to the cultures of the Green River region of Kentucky, where an Indian Knoll phase is equated chronologically as well as typologically with the lower Tennessee Three Mile phase. The Parrish and Ward sites of the Green River region then carry the Archaic tradition into the Burial Mound I Period and into acculturative contacts with the Woodland tradition.[16]

In northern Alabama, also along the Tennessee River, is another phase of the Archaic, the Lauderdale.[17] The stratigraphy of the northern Alabama deep shell mounds appears to span several thousand years, and sequent phases will probably be defined within what is considered as Lauderdale; for the present, it is safe to say that at least a part of the Lauderdale phase belongs to the Middle Archaic Period.[18] Among the artifacts recovered from the Lauderdale phase are atlatl weights, stone gorgets, bell-shaped pestles, mortars, bone and antler atlatl hooks, and sandstone and steatite bowls. In upper levels pottery has been found, not the fabric-marked pottery of the Woodland tradition which appeared in the Big Sandy phase in the lower Tennessee region, but forms of a general class called fiber-tempered.[19]

This fiber-tempered pottery, found throughout much of the Southeastern subarea, is here considered as the marker for the Late Archaic Period

Figure 5-7. Linear or "drag-jab" punctated sherds of fiber-tempered pottery from Stallings Island, Georgia. (Courtesy Peabody Museum, Harvard University.)

(2000–1000 B.C.). Its hearth appears to be in Georgia and Florida, where it has been dated by radiocarbon to the second millennium B.C.[20] It is possible, or even likely, that this fiber-tempered pottery did not reach northern Alabama until after 2000 B.C. and that it continued to be made and used there for some time after 1000 B.C., or into the Burial Mound I Period. This is a thick coarse ware, and, as the name implies, grass or rootlet fibers were mixed with the clay to strengthen the pottery. Firing was irregular and mottled the surfaces into shades of brown, gray-browns, and black. The vessels appear to have been molded, and the most common form was a round, medium-deep bowl with slightly flaring sides. Perhaps significantly, this form is very similar to the sandstone and steatite vessels of the preceding shell mound horizon. Most of the fiber-tempered pottery was undecorated, although some of it bore exterior dentate or linear-stamped impressions. Eventually, fiber-tempered pottery in the northern Alabama region was succeeded by Woodland tradition types.

The Lauderdale phase of northern Alabama relates closely with the Stallings Island phase. Stallings Island is a site in the Savannah River near Augusta, Georgia. A big tumulus of refuse shell and other debris, it is over 100 meters long and 100 meters wide and in some places reaches a depth of as much as 2.5 meters. The lower levels were pre-ceramic and contained stone mortars, atlatl weights, bar-gorgets, grooved axes, large-stemmed projectile points, bone atlatl hooks, bone pins, shell beads, and shell pendants. In the upper half-meter of refuse were fiber-tempered sherds, both plain and decorated with linear-punctations, fabric-impressions, or simple linear stamping. The vessel forms were all open bowls.[21]

Lewis and Kneberg have suggested two sub-traditional lines of development within the Archaic.[22] They call one of these the "Mid-Continent" and in it place the Eva continuum and the Green River phases of Kentucky. The other is referred to as the "Eastern" and includes Lauderdale and Georgia's Stallings Island. But it is interesting that a strictly geographical separation of the two does not always hold. For instance, a series of sites in the lower Tennessee region, all located near the Eva group of sites, are typologically closer to the "Eastern" subtradition than to the "Mid-Continent." These sites are the phases of the Kays-Weldon-Ledbetter continuity, and their presence on the lower Tennessee suggests an actual movement of Eastern groups into this region. Apparently, these Mid-Continent and Eastern phases lived peacefully side by side or at least co-existed. This idea of long-distance movements of peoples with generally related yet distinguishably Archaic cultures receives some support in this instance from the investigations of physical

anthropologists. As we mentioned, Archaic crania are generally long-headed, and this is true of the skulls of the Eva series. The skulls of the Kay phase, of the putatively intrusive Eastern peoples, on the other hand, are predominantly brachycranic. They, in turn, relate to the Stallings Island physical type, which also is broadheaded.

In Florida, fiber-tempered pottery specimens as abundant and more elaborately decorated than the Georgia examples have been found. The sites here are along the northward flowing St. Johns River, in northeastern Florida. This region was one of the richest in the entire Southeast in natural food resources. The shell middens are tremendously deep, some being as much as 10 meters. They attracted the attention of archaeologists as early as 1875 when it was realized that they were stratified in pre-ceramic and ceramic levels.[23] The pre-ceramic components are called the Mt. Taylor phase; the ceramic levels, the Orange phase. Fiber-tempered pottery types of the Orange phase are Orange Plain, Orange Incised, and Tick Island Incised. Orange Incised bore fine-line incisions, forming chevrons, nested squares, or diamonds, on the exterior walls of shallow bowls or bowls with slightly incurved rims. Tick Island Incised carried a curvilinear scroll design on a punctate or spot-filled, background.[24]

Origins of Fiber-Tempered Pottery. The origins of this Southeastern fiber-tempered pottery are still a mystery. Its context is definitely the Archaic cultural tradition. Its chronological position, as we mentioned, is the period defined as Late Archaic, with estimates of 2000–1000 B.C. There are indications, however, that it persisted somewhat later, especially in the north and west. Although distributed principally in the lower Southeast, centering in Georgia and northern Florida, examples also have been found in the Carolinas and Alabama and, in small amounts, as far to the west as the Mississippi Valley. It seems to have been the earliest pottery fashioned in eastern North America. At one time, archaeologists believed that it had been derived from the Woodland pottery tradition via stimulus diffusion.[25] This is still a possibility, but at present the earliest Woodland pottery of the north seems to date no earlier than about 1000 B.C.[26] Although occasional fiber-tempered sherds betray some Woodland influences (we have mentioned fabric or simple-stamped impressed surface treatments at Stallings Island and in northern Alabama), this is only a minor strain in a pottery tradition that is otherwise non-Woodland. Another possibility is that fiber-tempering was derived from Mesoamerica or South America, perhaps from the Caribbean Coast of Columbia where a very early fiber-tempered pottery has been found.[27] Another possibility is the completely local and independent development of fiber-tempered pottery in the Southeast. Certainly, Archaic stone vessels were logical prototypes. Some of these have been uncovered in the northern Alabama region, but they are most common in the country to the east of the Appalachians.

The Middle Atlantic. East of the Appalachians a Stallings Island or Savannah River Archaic winds through the Piedmont and Atlantic

Figure 5-8. Carolina piedmont country at the Gaston site, North Carolina. (Courtesy J. L. Coe; see also J. L. Coe, 1964.)

coastal plain for an undesignated distance to the north. J. L. Coe suggests that it, or something very similar, reaches southern Delaware.[28] Looking at the Archaic from the north, D. S. Byers refers to a related artifact complex that runs from southern New England southward at least to Virginia.[29] All the Archaic-type finds, from Georgia to New England, do not necessarily belong to a single culture phase, but it is evident that a significant general similarity exists all along the Piedmont and Atlantic coastal plain. This similarity is seen in tub-like steatite vessels, bannerstone and prismoidal atlatl weights, polished grooved axes, large-stemmed or notched projectile points, and, in the north, a semi-lunar flint knife. Fiber-tempered pottery has not been found beyond the southern piedmont, but the functional and chronological equivalent of it in the Middle Atlantic Late Archaic Period sites is the steatite ware. This is then followed by pottery of Woodland derivation which is similar to the type that developed at the close of the Archaic tradition in Kentucky. The chronology of these events in the Carolina piedmont and along the Atlantic coastal plain can be coordinated by trait comparisons with Middle and Late Archaic Period developments elsewhere in the Eastern Woodlands area; however, it is very likely that the Archaic tradition persisted in these regions beyond its chronological limits farther to the west and that Woodland pottery did not arrive in the country east of the Appalachians until after 1000 B.C.

In the North Carolina piedmont, the Archaic culture of the steatite vessels and the plentiful polished-stone implements is designated by J. L. Coe as the Savannah River phase. The Savannah River phase was preceded by a long Archaic development in that region. We have already touched on the earlier phases of this development in Chapter 2, but beginning at about 5000 B.C. the Stanly phase of the North Carolina sequence revealed the first characteristic polished-stone artifacts of the Middle Archaic Period. The succeeding Morrow Mountain and Guilford phases spanned the time from a little after 5000 to about

a

b

c

d

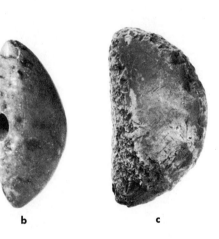

a

b

c

Figure 5-9. *Above:* Archaic stone-vessel fragments and axes from the Gaston site, North Carolina piedmont. *a:* Interior of Savannah River phase steatite rim sherd showing cross-hatching. *b:* Exterior of Savannah River phase rim sherd. *c:* Guilford phase rough-chipped axe. *d:* Savannah River phase grooved axe. Length of *c*, about 13 cm. (Courtesy J. L. Coe; see also J. L. Coe, 1964.)

Figure 5-10. *Center, left:* Archaic bannerstone type atlatl weights from the North Carolina piedmont, probably all Stanly phase. *a:* Fragment. *b:* Complete specimen. *c:* Unfinished specimen. Length of *b*, about 6 cm. (Courtesy J. L. Coe; see also J. L. Coe, 1964.)

Figure 5-11. *Bottom, left:* Archaic projectile points from the Doerschuk site, North Carolina piedmont. *a:* Stanly. *b:* Morrow Mountain I. *c:* Morrow Mountain II. *d:* Guilford. Length of *a*, 6.7 cm. (Courtesy J. L. Coe; see also J. L. Coe, 1964.)

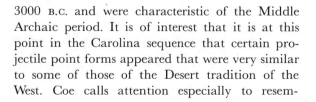

a

b

c

d

3000 B.C. and were characteristic of the Middle Archaic period. It is of interest that it is at this point in the Carolina sequence that certain projectile point forms appeared that were very similar to some of those of the Desert tradition of the West. Coe calls attention especially to resem-

259

blances between Morrow Mountain tapered-stemmed types and the western Gypsum Cave type. He also emphasizes that the occurrence of this type is on a time level two or three thousand years later than in the West. In the Carolina sequence the Guilford phase was overlain by levels containing artifacts of the Halifax phase, and these included point types that suggested influences from or a connection with Archaic cultures of the Northeast. The Halifax phase was then followed by the Savannah River phase which, as we have pointed out, was most characteristic of the Savannah River Basin and Georgia.[30]

The Northeast. In the Northeast, Byers distinguishes two main lines of Archaic development.[31] One of these divisions is the Coastal, which blends with and is similar to the Archaic of the piedmont and itself divides into periods, Early and Late, with the latter characterized by pollished-stone forms, including bannerstone atlatl weights and pestles. The other main line of development is the Boreal Archaic of the northern forests of New England, New York, and the Canadian Maritime Provinces. The discovery of bannerstones, plummets, and grooved axes reveals that Boreal Archaic was influenced from the south, but there were other more distinctive elements in the culture, such as woodworking tools, adzes and gouges, and a variety of slate knives and points.

Figure 5-12. *Top, right:* Archaic projectile points from the Doerschuk site, North Carolina piedmont, all of the Savannah River phase. Length of *a*, about 9 cm. (Courtesy J. L. Coe; see also J. L. Coe, 1964.)

Figure 5-13. *Bottom, right:* Chipped- and ground-stone artifacts of the Boreal Archaic, Maine. *a:* Gouge; length, 32 cm. *b:* Chipped point; length, 6.5 cm. *c:* Slate point; length, 9 cm. *d,e:* Plummets; lengths, about 7 and 5.5 cm. *f:* Gouge; length, 15 cm. *g:* Grooved bolas stone about 8 x 6 cm. *h:* Chipped-stone point; length, 13 cm. Specimens *c,d,g,h* are Early Boreal; others, Late Boreal. From Ellsworth Falls and other sites. (After Byers, 1959.)

One of the few definitive stratigraphies that has enabled archaeologists to order the development of the Boreal Archaic is at Ellsworth Falls on the Union River in Maine. The lowest levels of the Ellsworth Falls sequence have already been mentioned as evidence of a possible ancient percussion-flaked industry that might have served as a source of Archaic tradition development (Chap. 2). A fourth and final occupation level contained early Woodland pottery. It is in the second Ellsworth occupation that the first glimpse of a Boreal Archaic appeared. The diagnostic artifacts were adzes and gouges, roughly pecked from natural pebbles, polished-slate spear points, and curious "rods" of polished stone. Other objects, such as plummets and stemmed and unstemmed roughly chipped projectile points, were of a more generalized Archaic cast. The upper part of this second Ellsworth occupation is dated by radiocarbon to about 2000 B.C. Also Boreal is the third Ellsworth occupation (Fig. 5-13), from which many polished adzes and gouges, together with stemmed Archaic points, plummets, and bannerstones have been recovered. Radiocarbon dates this third occupation to 1400 B.C. It is this third occupation at Ellsworth that has been correlated with the burial complex, or cult, called the "Moorehead Complex." Graves of the complex have yielded additional polished-stone gouges and adzes and long, bayonet-like slate points. Many of these grave artifacts appear to have been non-utilitarian versions of the true tools, made in a softer and more easily worked stone.

In New York State the Boreal Archaic meets and blends with the Archaic cultures of the Ohio Valley. The earliest known Archaic culture of the region, the Lamoka, which is dated by radiocarbon to the fourth millennium B.C., has a bone artifact complement that is very similar to the Green River cultures of Kentucky. Its ground stone is more northern, however, with plano-convex adzes and the very diagnostic beveled adze. The latter, although not a specifically known Boreal form, certainly suggests that milieu rather than the Archaic cultures of the south. Lamoka was succeeded by the Laurentian or Boreal Frontenac and Brewerton phases which are associated with gouges, ground-slate weapons, and copper tools. Data gathered by physical anthropologists show that the Lamoka people were typical Archaic longheads, whereas the Frontenac-Brewerton people were round-headed.[32]

The Great Lakes and Upper Mississippi Valley. To the west, around the western Great Lakes and in the upper Mississippi Valley, the Old Copper Culture was affiliated with the Boreal Archaic; but the distinctiveness of this Archaic manifestation lies in its copper implements.[33] Two Wisconsin burial sites, Osceola and Oconto, have provided the best documented collections of these implements and the radiocarbon datings place the Old Copper Culture in the time span of the Middle Archaic Period. Copper was worked by cold- and hot-hammering techniques (never melted or cast) into spear points and knives which were then hafted by rat-tailed tangs or through semi-open sockets. Boreal-like copper forms included gouges, semi-lunar or ulu-type knives, and barbed harpoon points. Some southern Archaic items, such as bannerstone atlatl weights, were also imitated in copper. The stonework associated with the copper implements was definitely Archaic—long, narrow projectile points with side-notches, bannerstones, and rough grinding stones. The Old Copper Culture thus appears as a commingling of various lines of Archaic development in a copper technology that was almost certainly an independent invention of the Great Lakes region. In this connection, it is significant that large free copper nuggets are still imbedded in rock outcrops and in glacial deposits, especially around Lake Superior. Elsewhere in the Archaic occasional copper tools or ornaments have been identified. Presumably the copper, or the objects themselves, originated in the Great Lakes region of the Old Copper Culture; and the copper industry, as developed here in Archaic Period times, continued in various lesser ways in other traditions and in later periods in the East.

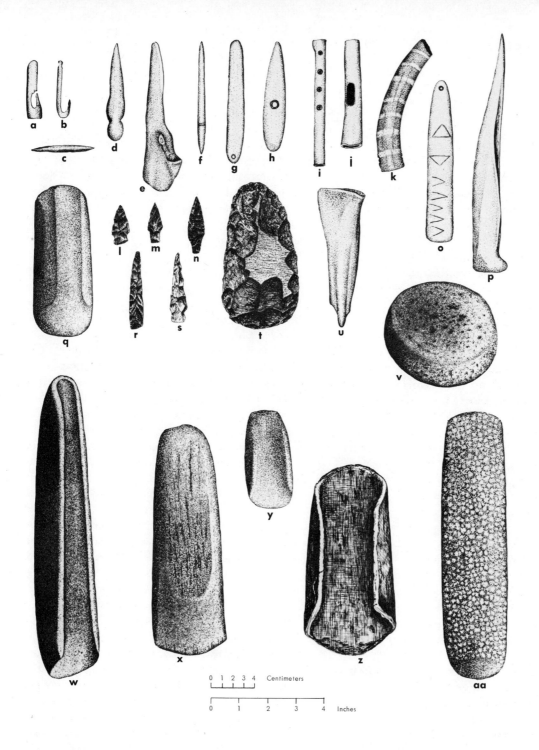

Figure 5-14. Representative stone, bone, and antler artifacts of the New York State Archaic cultures. Items a-v and aa pertain to the Lamoka phase; w-z are of the Laurentian phase. a: Bone fishhook in process. b: Completed fishhook. c: Bone gorge. d: Notched bone projectile (?) point. e: Deer ulna knife. f: Double-pointed, round, bone implement, scored near one end. g,h: Flat, perforated, bone netting tools (?). i,j: Bird-bone whistles. k,o: Split antler objects of unknown use, nicked along lower edges; first, striped with red paint; second, ornamented in intaglio. l: Side-notched flint point. m,n: Stemmed flint points. p: Bone dagger. q: Beveled adze. r,s: Flint drills (straight and side-notched, respectively). t: Sandstone chopper. u: Deer-scapula side-scraper. v: Stone muller. w,y: Stone gouges. x: Stone plano-convex adze. z: Native copper gouge. aa: Cylindrical stone pestle. (Courtesy of the New York State Museum and Science Service.)

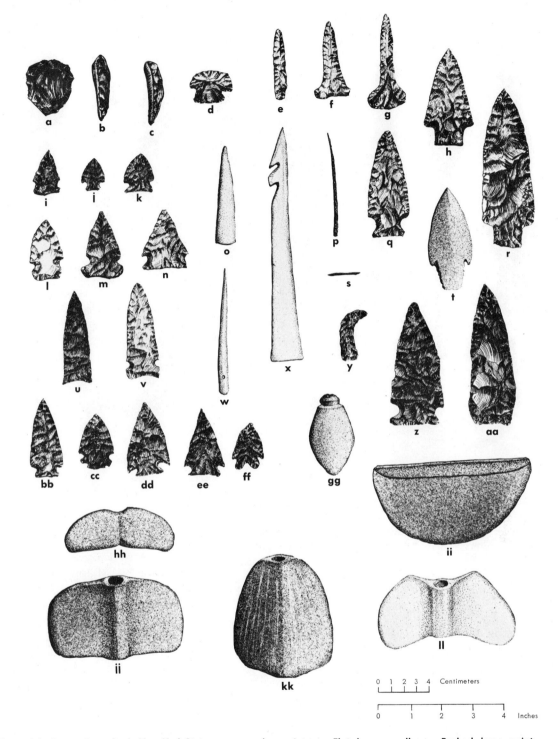

Figure 5-15. Artifacts of the Laurentian culture, New York State. *a-c:* Simple flint end-scrapers. *d:* Stemmed end-scraper. *e-g:* Straight and expanded base drills. *h,r:* Stemmed points, *i,q,l,m, v,z,bb:* Side-notched points. *j,k,n,dd,ee:* Corner-notched points. *o:* Hollowed antler tine projectile point. *p:* Native copper awl. *s:* Native copper gorge. *t:* Ground-slate knife. *u:* Eared trian-gular point. *w:* Flat bone needle. *x:* Barbed bone point. *y:* Curved flint knife. *aa:* Jasper knife. *cc:* Multiple side-notched point. *ff:* Corner-notched point with bifurcated base. *qq:* Stone plummet. *hh:* Notched bannerstone. *ii:* Ground-slate ulu. *jj-ll:* Perforated bannerstones. (Courtesy of the New York State Museum and Science Service.)

263

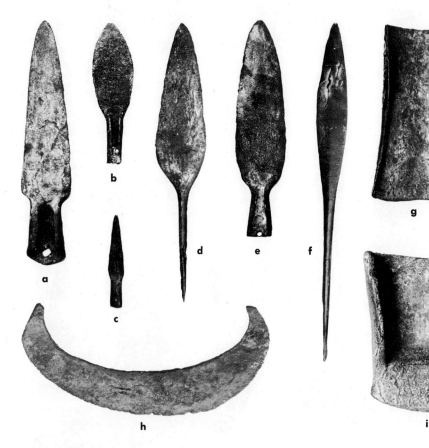

Figure 5-16. Old Copper culture artifacts from the Upper Great Lakes country. a-f: Socketed and rat-tailed spear and projectile points. g: Gouge. h: Crescent-shaped or ulu knife. i: Socketed axe. (Courtesy Chicago Natural History Museum; see also Quimby, 1960.)

South of the Great Lakes, in the Middle West, an Ohio Valley Archaic and a Plains Archaic meet in Illinois. The Faulkner site[34] and the middle and upper levels of the Modoc Rock Shelter[35] in southern Illinois, for example, shared most traits with either the Green River or lower Tennessee River regions; whereas the lanceolate points from the Archaic component at Starved Rock[36] in the northern part of Illinois and the absence there of polished-stone artifacts has a Plains cast. This merging of Eastern with Plains Archaic influences is even more evident in Missouri in the Dalton[37] and Nebo Hill[38] cultures and also at

Graham Cave.[39] The westernmost penetration of an Eastern Archaic complex is in the Late Archaic Period Fourche Maline phase of northeastern Oklahoma, with its bone atlatl hooks, boatstone weights, dog burials, and bone pins.[40]

The Ozarks. The culture of the sub-area of the Ozark hills in northwestern Arkansas and adjacent Oklahoma and Missouri, the Grove phase, was Archaic and was perhaps closer to the Archaic of northeast Texas than to any other variant. The only polished-stone form from either the Grove A or B subphases was the grooved axe; bone or shell artifacts were exceedingly rare. Projectile points were mainly stemmed, side-notched, or corner-notched although, as we saw in Chapter 2, some Plainview-like specimens also have been discovered.[41] The Grove phase is especially interesting, for the lower levels of the well-known

Ozark Bluff-Dweller sites presumably are related to it. The Bluff-Dweller sites are dry caves or shelters in which "perishables" such as basketry, wood, and plant remains have been preserved. Unfortunately, excavation data from the caves do not enable us to say if the cultivated plants found in them, including maize, were present in the Archaic strata.[42]

The Lower Mississippi Valley. In the lower Mississippi Valley, in Louisiana and Mississippi, Archaic cultures succeed those with fluted points and Dalton points. A Jones Creek phase, the type site of which is on an old prairie surface near Baton Rouge, Louisiana, has yielded large-stemmed projectile points similar to the Piedmont Kirk type and is believed to date somewhere around 5000 B.C. Jones Creek was succeeded by a number of later Archaic complexes—Amite River, Pearl River, Bayou Jasmine, Garcia, and Copell.[43] These complexes were regionally or locally differentiated, and some of them may also be chronologically differentiated, although at the present time the data available on them are very scanty. In general, they would appear to be bracketed between about 3500 and 300 B.C. From some of them have come such standard Middle to Late Archaic traits as plummets, boatstones, and bone atlatl hooks. In the upper part of their chronological range they almost certainly overlap with the famed Poverty Point phase, the principal sites of which are located in east-central and northeast Louisiana. Poverty Point, in addition to featuring projectile points of Archaic type, grooved stone axes, stone tubular pipes, two-holed bar-gorgets, and stone vessels, incorporated Woodland traits such as large and elaborate earthwork and mound construction. It is also believed to date largely in the first millennium B.C.[44] For these reasons, the Poverty Point phase sites seem more appropriately treated under the Woodland tradition and in the Burial Mound I Period.

Summary: Culture, Race, and Language. We have only sketched the archaeological record of the Archaic thus far, but we have said enough to afford us some idea of the Archaic tradition and its depth and its spread in the Eastern Woodlands area. In the societies concerned lived the forest, river, and coastal people. The artifacts we find are largely tools and weapons of the hunt or pertain to fishing or plant-collecting. Subsistence appears to have been uniformly better than it was for the approximately contemporary, and also non-agricultural, Desert people, and in some regions it was very favorable. As a result, small village groups became tied to favorable "food stations." Thus, life can be described as semi-sedentary and, perhaps, even fully sedentary, in some cases. Monumental constructions or fine arts were largely ignored by the Archaic peoples, but their craft skill was high and displayed an aesthetic dimension, best seen in some of the polished-stone objects. Bannerstone atlatl weights, for example, often were beautifully fashioned and highly polished; yet, obviously, they would have weighted the throwing-stick just as well if they had been only roughly shaped. Pride of craftsmanship certainly had developed. We should remember, too, that the archaeologist tends to reconstruct a picture of Archaic life that errs on the side of caution and, thereby, of primitiveness. In this connection the craft of woodworking comes first to mind. In several subareas of the East, it must have been a major field of technical and aesthetic expression during the Archaic Period. Almost all the products are lost to us now, but from ethnography or the occasional rare finds from prehistoric but post-Archaic contexts we have, at least, an intimation of its richness and excellence.[45]

Archaic culture varied regionally, and the pressures of natural environment are reflected in this variation; yet an examination of trait lists, from site component to site component and from phase to phase, shows a high degree of similarity. For the most part, there is a rather gradual blending of culture in space, from the Southeast to the Ohio Valley and Northeast, and from these eastern subareas westward to the Plains. This gradualness is also typical of change through time.

Two major technological innovations appeared during the Archaic tradition: the manufacture of polished-stone artifacts and the making of pottery. The first appearance of polished stone approximates the division point between the Early and Middle Archaic periods, at a time judged to be about 5000 B.C. The source from which it came into Archaic culture is unknown. One possibility is that it was introduced from the north and that its derivations may be traced back to northern Boreal culture of the Asiatic Mesolithic. Certain forms, such as adzes from the Northeastern Woodlands of North America and from Asia (Chap. 1), are quite similar. But no continuous, or even reasonably continuous, distribution has been traced between the Archaic of the North American Northeast and the Old World.[46] Furthermore, the evidence now at hand tends to indicate that the ground-stone forms of the Middle Archaic in the Southeast and the Ohio Valley—things like the bannerstone weights, for example—were appreciably earlier than the Mesolithic forms of the Boreal Archaic of the Northeast. In sum, although there is some likelihood of Asiatic diffusion or stimulus into the New World Archaic cultures, there are still considerable complications to be explained away. It is at least reasonable to suppose that some polished-stone forms and techniques of stone polishing were strictly independent New World inventions. The widespread presence of polished-stone artifacts in eastern South America in fairly early pre-Columbian times tends to enhance this possibility.

We have stated that fiber-tempered pottery appeared in the Southeastern subarea as early as 2000 B.C. and that this appearance, at the beginning of the Late Archaic Period, antedates Woodland grit-tempered pottery of the Northeast. Present radiocarbon datings support this stand. If the southern fiber-tempered pottery indeed appeared in the New World earlier than the Woodland tradition pottery, we must look to either local independent development or stimulus from Middle or South America. To support the latter explanation, no ready sources are at hand, although a very early fiber-tempered pottery was made in distant Caribbean Colombia.[47]

The populations associated with the Archaic tradition cultures were, for the most part, rather gracefully slender, with small though long heads, a type physical anthropologists call the Iswanid. The Iswanid prevailed in the Southeast, the Ohio Valley, and as far north and east as New York. A somewhat more rugged, larger-headed, and even longer-headed type, the Otamid, probably was also associated with Archaic cultures in the Northeast. This Otamid type was widely but randomly scattered in the New World, and may represent the most ancient sub-racial strain in the Americas. It was also the dominant physical type of the Woodland cultural tradition in the Eastern Woodlands. Both of these long-headed types seem to have been replaced by, or merged with, a round-headed type in the Middle and Late Archaic and in subsequent periods. This replacement or merger was not area-wide, occurring only in certain regions or subareas, especially in the Southeast. The round-headed type is sometimes referred to as the Walcolid. It may represent a new sub-racial strain which entered the New World from Asia; Neumann is inclined toward this interpretation. Or it may be a physical variety which developed in the Americas. In either case, the round-heads first were a minority element in Archaic tradition settings in the Middle and Late Archaic Periods.[48]

Archaeologists and other culture historians have been tempted to try to align cultural traditions, human physical types, and language families in the East. These reconstructions are highly speculative. One opinion expressed is that the Iswanid Archaic peoples were Proto-Siouan, and that the "remnant" Siouan tribes of the East, such as the Catawba and Tutelo, are their distant descendants, other Siouan groups having moved west to the Plains.[49] Another possibility is that the Archaic populations were of a Proto-Gulf-Algonquian language super-family and that the historic Algonquians (Northeast) and Muskogean-Gulf (Southeast) tribes were their very much later *in situ* descendants.[50]

The Woodland Tradition

Definitions and Origins. The Woodland cultural tradition may be defined, minimally, by the presence of Woodland pottery. W. H. Sears has argued for this definition, pointing out that in many regions of the East the essential difference between culture complexes or phases designated as Archaic and those designated as Woodland is the presence of cord-marked or fabric-marked pottery in the latter but not in the former.[51] A somewhat broader definition is often used, however, one which defines the Woodland tradition not only by its characteristic cord-marked and fabric-marked ceramics but by the construction of burial mounds and other earthworks and by at least the beginnings of agriculture. We shall follow this second definition in this discussion.

Such a Woodland tradition, expressed in many subareal and regional cultures and cultural phases, had its origins in the Burial Mound I Period (1000–300 B.C.), came to a climax in the earlier part of the Burial Mound II Period (300 B.C.–A.D. 700), and then waned but continued through the Temple Mound Periods (A.D. 700–1700). Its archaeological traces are found throughout nearly all of the Eastern Woodlands area and extend into the neighboring Plains area to the west. Whereas the Archaic tradition shared many traits with the Desert tradition of western North America, and the general outlines of Mesoamerican culture were reflected in the later Mississippian tradition, the Woodland configuration had no such related counterpart on the New World scene. In this sense it is the most unique of the three major traditions of the Eastern Woodlands.

If we are to assume that Woodland pottery, burial mounds, and agriculture were the three most significant traits in Woodland culture and were the traits which transformed the earlier Archaic pattern into Woodland, where are the origins of these traits or trait complexes and how do they enter or appear in the Eastern Woodlands?

First, let us look at Woodland pottery. It was as we have mentioned, usually cord-marked or fabric-marked. Such markings or impressions were made in the soft clay before the vessels were fired, and resulted from the paddling of the vessel surfaces with cord-wrapped or textile-wrapped wooden paddles, an operation carried out to smooth and anneal the construction coils. Woodland vessel forms were limited, the most common being a simple conoidal-based pot. Flat-bottomed jars and jars with little tetrapodal bases were also fashioned. The ware was tempered with grit, crushed rock, or clay. If the vessel surfaces were not cord-marked or fabric-marked, they were sometimes impressed with carved wooden paddles, which left designs of different sorts or they might be decorated by incision, punctation, rocker-stamping, surface-polishing, or, rarely, with red paint. Most finds of the simple cord-marked and fabric-marked wares have been made in the northern subareas, whereas the more elaborately decorated types tend to be associated with sites in the great river drainages and in the southern subareas. The most reasonable hypothesis for the appearance of Woodland pottery in Eastern North America is that it, or rather the ideas which produced it, were imported from cultures of the Siberian Mesolithic and Neolithic.[52] Even this hypothesis is not fully satisfactory, however, for some of the more specialized modes of treating or decorating the pottery surface, such as rocker-stamping or color-zoning, are as suggestive of Mesoamerica as they are of northern Asia. The problem of pottery origins in the Woodland tradition can be summarized only by saying that although the prevailing features of Woodland pottery were more reminiscent of northern Asia and Europe than they are of any other world areas, other features hint at Mesoamerican affiliations.

Burial mounds have been found throughout most of the Eastern Woodlands area, with the exception of parts of the Northeast. In simplest form, they are artificial tumuli of earth heaped over the remains of the dead. More elaborate variations included mounds built over specially prepared tombs, over the remains of burned ossuaries and crematoria. The most numerous, largest, and most structurally complicated mounds are in the Ohio Valley and Mississippi subareas. Here also are other forms of earthworks, such as enclosures and effigies, which may or may not have been places of burial but which are associated with Woodland tradition cultures. In general, the mounds are more difficult to attribute to Asiatic Boreal influences than the Woodland pottery. To be sure, mound burial, including the building of special tomb chambers, was an Asiatic and Old World trait complex; but as Chard has pointed out, no geographical continuity of the complex across Asia and into the New World can be established. A vast gap exists in eastern Asia and northern Canada.[53] Furthermore, mound burial was practiced in Mesoamerica and South America, and in Mesoamerica it had developed early enough to have influenced eastern North America.[54] It may be that more than one point of origin is involved, or it may be that the idea was a completely independent development of the Eastern Woodlands. In this last regard, it is important to mention that certain Archaic cultures placed great emphasis on elaborate grave offerings and on what has often been considered as the beginnings of a mortuary cult—the kind of phenomenon that might have led to a burial mound development.

With agriculture, the question is not so much one of origins, for the principal plants cultivated in native eastern North America were maize, beans, and squash, which must be attributed to Mesoamerican diffusion where the antiquity of such domesticates goes far back before 1000 B.C. The questions are, rather, at what time did the diffusion occur and how significant were these cultivated plants in the development of the Woodland cultural tradition? According to present excavation evidence, the earliest maize cobs do not appear in the Eastern Woodlands area until the Burial Mound II Period, when a number were recovered from Hopewell or Hopewellian sites. For Adena and other early Woodland sites of the Burial Mound I Period, the only cultigens appear to have been sunflower, marsh elder, squash, gourd, and perhaps chenopod.[55] In spite of this—and while admitting to the continued importance of Archaic tradition hunting patterns in Woodland cultures—I firmly believe that the growing of crops was more than a casual adjunct of Woodland economy and that economically significant maize farming was introduced into the Eastern Woodlands from Mesoamerica during the Burial Mound I Period or shortly after 1000 B.C. The huge earthwork constructions of some of the cultures of the Burial Mound I Period, together with their ceremonial and mortuary elaborations, are in my opinion insupportable on the kind of a subsistence base that one can envision for the environment with only hunting, fishing, food-collecting, and incipient agricultural techniques. Recent discoveries of maize in Burial Mound II Period sites reveal a development of the plant that suggests a long antecedent period of local domestication.[56] It should be made clear to the reader, however, that there is strong conflicting opinion on this question; and some authorities not only feel that agriculture was of no consequence in Burial Mound I times but that it played little part in the economy or the general development of Eastern Woodland cultures in the Burial Mound II Period.[57]

Adena. From what we have just said, it would seem highly unlikely that the three traits—Woodland pottery, burial mounds, and maize cultivation—had common origins or that they came into the Eastern Woodlands area together in a fully formed Woodland tradition. Rather, the tradition probably was synthesized somewhere in the area. If so, then where? Although there is no positive answer to this question, it would appear that one of the first flowerings of this synthesis was the Adena culture of the Ohio Valley.[58] As such, we are here considering Adena to mark the beginnings of the full Woodland tradition at the inception of the Burial Mound I Period (ca. 1000 B.C.). It is, however, possible, although not definite, that Woodland pottery had appeared in the Ohio Valley somewhat prior to the rise of Adena. In other words, the ceramic elements that were to go into the Woodland tradition may very well have arrived in the Ohio Valley subarea before the appearances of either burial mounds or agriculture.

Adena sites are found in southern Ohio, adjacent Indiana, northern Kentucky, southwestern Pennsylvania, and northwestern West Virginia. The culture takes its name from the Adena mound group in Ross County, Ohio, and the best known sites are marked by burial mounds, earthwork enclosures, or both. The burial mounds are conical tumuli of earth. They vary greatly in size, one of the largest being the famous Grave Creek Mound in West Virginia which is over 20 meters high. The earthwork enclosures appear to be ceremonial constructions rather than defense works. Many are almost perfectly circular. These "sacred circles" average 100 meters in diameter and are enclosed by low embankments, with the "moats," for these embankments within rather than outside the circle. Gateways open through the embankments. Burial mounds sometimes have been found inside the circles, and there are instances where several such circles were constructed together at a single site.

Excavation of the burial mounds has revealed the elaborate mortuary customs of the Adena people. Important individuals were buried in log tombs. These tombs were rectangular in outline and were made by placing timbers horizontally on the ground or in sub-surface pits. They were roofed over with poles and bark and then covered with a platform or mound of earth. After the first tomb was finished, other similar tombs might be built in or on the mound and still more earth added to cover these. Such tombs invariably collapsed because of the weight of the earth and the gradual rotting of the timbers, but careful excavation has revealed their original form and nature of construction. Usually the initial tomb burial within a mound was made within a wooden-post building. Such buildings may have been temples, ossuaries, or simply dwellings; but in any case,

the tomb was placed on the floor or in a sub-floor pit and the primary earth mound was raised over it within the house or building. Later the building was burned to the ground, apparently as part of the burial ceremony.

Bodies were placed on their backs in an extended position, apparently when the body was still in the flesh or, at least, in an articulated condition. Many bones have been recovered stained with red ocher. Either the skeleton was stripped of flesh before the red pigment was poured over it, or there was a period of exposure to decay after which the ocher was applied to the bones. The latter possibility would mean that some time elapsed between the time the body was placed in the tomb and the tomb was sealed. Meanwhile, the body may have lain in the tomb, which was sheltered only by the wooden-post building, or the mound may have been constructed and a tunnel cut to permit entry. Collapsed remains of these tunnel-like entrances, which had been walled and covered with timbers, have been found in some Adena mounds. Usually one to three persons were placed in a single log tomb. Single, separate skulls sometimes have been found in graves or in mounds. Perhaps these were trophy skulls or possibly skulls of revered ancestors. Flexed burials and

Figure 5-17. An Adena burial found in the sub-floor tomb of the Cowan Creek Mound (shown in Fig. 5-18, *left*). (Courtesy Ohio State Museum.)

secondary bundle burials, although occasionally discovered, were rare in Adena. Cremation actually was more common than burial. Bodies were burned in circular or elliptical clay basins, located either within buildings or in the village area. Sometimes the ash and burned bone were deposited with the extended burials; sometimes they were simply placed in the mounds; and at other times, they were left in the crematory basins and covered with clay or logs and the whole then was covered with the mound. Grave goods were interred with the bodies and with the remains of the cremated. Such goods had often been intentionally broken or been damaged by the crematory fires.

This brief exposition cannot do justice to the ranges of variation and combination that characterized Adena burials and mound construction. What is important to remember is that a cult of the dead was a central theme of Adena life and, in fact, a central theme of the entire Woodland tradition. Considerable labor was dedicated to the burial rites and constructions, fundamentaly for commemorative purposes—to set up permanent features on the landscape, such as mounds and ceremonial earthworks, to mark the spots sacred to the departed spirits. Such locations were in

a sense socio-political and religious "capitals" whether or not they were permanent habitation centers.

The habitation centers of the Adena people were very small village communities composed of two to five houses. These small hamlets, quite probably kin units of some sort, were a part of much larger aggregates of hamlets scattered over a considerable area. Perhaps these "greater villages," as Richard Morgan has termed the aggregates, were the sustaining populations for a burial mound or earthwork center.[59] Information on actual Adena architecture comes mainly from the mound sites where, as already mentioned, wooden-post buildings were frequently destroyed and covered over with the mounds. The post-mold patterns are of circular structures averaging about 11 meters in diameter, although some circles were much larger. Apparently the wall posts of the Adena buildings were always set in pairs in the line of the circle. Single post-molds, within the circle, served as central roof supports. Whether or not these sub-mound buildings were used only for ceremonial or funerary purposes or whether such ceremonial buildings duplicated ordinary dwellings in plan and form remain open as questions.

Large quantities of Adena artifacts have been taken from the burial mounds and some from village site debris. The Adena projectile point was a long, straight-stemmed form, not greatly different from Archaic prototypes. Ground- and polished-stone objects included the two-hole, expanded center bar-gorget, reel-shaped gorgets, and other

Figure 5-18. An Adena house. *Left:* Paired post-molds in a circular pattern. A sub-floor tomb had been dug within the circle. Cowan Creek Mound, Ohio. *Right:* Museum model of a house based on post-mold pattern at left. (Courtesy Ohio State Museum.)

Figure 5-19. A carved stone pipe from the Adena Mound, Ohio. The tobacco bowl is beneath the feet; the mouthpiece, on top of the head. Height, about 20 cm. (Courtesy Ohio State Museum.)

Figure 5-20. Adena tablets, both of a convenient size to hold in one hand. *Top:* The engraved stone Berlin tablet with an image of a raptorial bird with hooked beak and long talons. This tablet is unique in that it is the only one with a definite design on both sides, the one on the reverse being practically identical to the one shown. *Bottom:* The Gaitskill Clay tablet with bas-relief engraving. The design has been interpreted as a bird with human hands replacing wings. (Courtesy Ohio State Museum; see also Webb and Baby, 1957.)

gorget forms. Some of these were probably atlatl weights, as were the boatstones that have been found. Tubular pipes, which occur in some Archaic contexts of the late Archaic Period, were also a standard Adena feature. These were usually fashioned with either flattened or blocked-end mouthpieces. One unusually fine specimen is the effigy figure of a man. Adena decorative carving was expressed in small stone tablets. These were small, flat, a little over 1 centimeter thick, and measured about 10 by 8 centimeters on the other dimensions. On one or both flat sides were gracefully composed stylized zoomorphs or curvilinear geometric designs in deep relief. A. C. Spaulding has observed that these Adena tablets are often discovered with bundles of bone awls and that many of the tablets bore sharpening grooves on their backs. Because of these circumstances he believes they were stamps for imprinting or outlining tattooing designs.[60] Another possibility would be that they were used for textile stamps.

Among Adena ground-stone tools, the Archaic full-grooved axe had been replaced by the ungrooved axe, or celt. Somewhat rougher slab-like stones with chipped edges were probably used as hoes. Bone and antler were used in small tools but even more prominently in ornamental objects such as beads, combs, and worked animal-jaw gorgets or paraphernalia. Spoons, beads, and other implements were made from the marine conch, or *Busycon*. A few copper axes have been found, but

Figure 5-21. A gorget fashioned from a human skull cap from the Florence Mound, Ohio. The engraved design shows the raptorial bird theme common to both Adena and Hopewell art. (Courtesy Ohio State Museum.)

otherwise the metal was hammered into ornamental forms, such as bracelets, rings, beads, and reel-shaped pendants.

Adena pottery was not buried with the dead or the remains of the cremated, as were other artifacts. It is found in refuse. Tempered with grit or crushed limestone, it was largely plain, cord-marked, or fabric-marked, although one type bore a nested-diamond design executed in incision. The vessel forms were sub-conoidal or flat-bottomed jars, with some of the latter having small tetrapodal supports.

Adena textiles were woven in a variety of ways: plain plaiting, twilled plaiting, multiple-ply braid plaiting, plain twining, and twilled twining. The material was probably a local fiber, for there is no evidence for any cotton in the Eastern Woodlands at this time or even in later prehistoric times.

Human Physical Types. To this point, we have said nothing about human physical types in the Woodland tradition. In general, however, they were long-headed, resembling the dominant strain of the preceding Archaic populations of Eastern North America. However, the people of the Adena culture were round-headed and, because of this, some archaeologists have suggested that the brachycephalic Adenans represented a new and intrusive population element in the Ohio Valley who brought with them such traits as burial mounds and agriculture and whose arrival resulted in the synthesis of which we have already spoken. In this case the earlier resident culture was essentially Archaic with, perhaps, Woodland-type pottery which had diffused to the Ohio Valley from the north.[61] We favor this interpretation here, although we should mention that both long-headed and round-headed population groups lived in the Eastern Woodlands in Middle and Late Archaic Period times. This does not necessarily preclude a round-headed group from being the cultural innovators who moved into the Ohio Valley from the south, although it does lessen the possibility that the Adena brachycephals were new

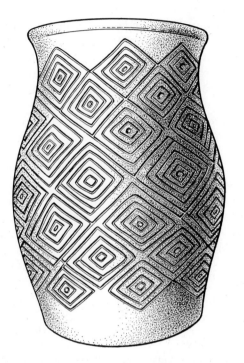

Figure 5-22. An Adena pottery vessel (Montgomery Incised). Height, 37 cm. (Drawn from Webb and Snow, 1945.)

immigrants from Mesoamerica. One distinctively different physico-cultural trait that does set the Adena people apart from earlier Eastern round-heads, however, is artificial occipital and bi-frontal head flattening,[62] a trait which could well have been derived from Mesoamerica.

Hopewell. The people who followed the Adena in the southern Ohio region, the Hope-wells, were, interestingly enough, long-headed, although they too practiced cranial deformation.[63] This seems to indicate another population change, at least within this region, and it may be that a more characteristically northern Woodland physical type had by this time assimilated to the Adena culture and developed a new brand of it, the Hopewell. For one of the most significant

things about Hopewell culture was that it repre-sented a continuation of the basic pattern of Adena life. The changes involved elaboration. This transition from Adena to Hopewell occurred in the latter part of the first millennium B.C. and may be said to mark the division between the Burial Mound I and II Periods.[64] The division, however, was by no means sharp. It appears, rather, that there was a basic continuity of village life in the Ohio Valley which was remarkably conservative. In a sense, separate Adena and Hope-well "cultures" are archaeological constructs based almost entirely upon funerary rites as these are found expressed in the burial mounds. In the main, the chronological changes we will record here serve to distinguish between an earlier Adena and a later Hopewell burial ceremonialism; how-ever, it must be understood that there was con-siderable overlap in time between Adena and Hopewell fashions. Present evidence from radio-carbon dates seems to indicate that although a maximum Hopewell florescence occurred in south-ern Ohio in the centuries 100 B.C. to A.D. 200, the Hopewell pattern—particularly as it was expressed in its unique pottery—first crystallized in central and southern Illinois and spread from there to southern Indiana and Ohio. It also spread from Illinois north and west to Michigan, Wisconsin, Iowa, and Missouri in the early centuries of the Christian era.

It is interesting to speculate on just what this spread of Hopewell influence signified in terms of cultural dynamics. If the elements which were spread or diffused were associated primarily with burial ritual—and to a great extent this seems to be the case—then it may well be that Hopewell "culture" was carried by a conquering or an elite group from Illinois to the many diverse regions of the Ohio, upper Mississippi, and Missouri drain-ages. In each instance, it was received into a less elaborate Woodland cultural context. The dif-ference in human physical type between Adenas and Hopewells in Ohio would seem to support this argument, at least insofar as the Ohio Valley is concerned. However, the cultural process involved in the Hopewell dissemination need not have been the same in every instance.[65]

The earthworks of the Ohio Hopewell phase were larger and more complex than their Adena counterparts. Some of them enclosed as much as a hundred acres, and the earth embankment walls rose to as high as 5 meters. Located in the valley flatlands, they were rectangular, circular, or octagonal. Sometimes two or more were connected by long, embankment-bordered passageways. Again, as with the Adena earthworks, it seems unlikely that they were erected for defense. Their curious forms, location on open ground, and the fact that the "borrow-trenches," or "moats," were inside rather than outside the enclosures all belie this interpretation. Burial mounds were associated with them, usually being within the enclosures.

Figure 5-23. The earthworks and mounds of the Edwin Harness Group, Ohio. (Redrawn from Mills, 1907.)

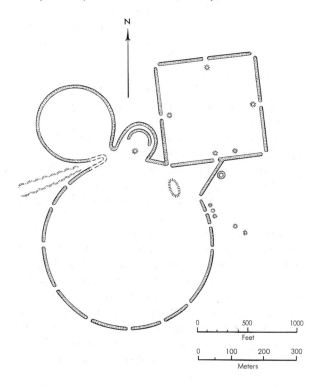

N

| 0 | 500 | 1000 |

Feet

| 0 | 100 | 200 | 300 |

Meters

Some of these were conoidal in form; others were elongate and very large. The Hopewell,[66] Seip,[67] Turner,[68] and Harness earthwork and mound groups are examples of burial and ceremonial centers of the Hopewell phase.[69] In addition to these strictly ceremonial earthwork sites there are others which, from their appearance, give the impression that they may have served as redoubts or fortified places of refuge. In these sites, walls, either of earth or stones, encircled hilltops, following the natural terrain in a way to suggest that they were intended as defensive constructions. Yet in these sites there also were burial mounds and other earthwork features which were similar to those found in non-fortified earthworks.[70]

As with Adena, Hopewell burials and cremations were held inside wooden-post buildings, which eventually were burned and their ruins covered over with the burial mounds. Some of the Hopewell buildings used for such mortuary purposes were small dwelling-type structures, but others were quite large and multi-roomed, built in the form of circles, ovals, and rectangles. The post-mold patterns by which they can be traced show that the walls were constructed of single rather than paired posts. It is doubtful if some of the largest buildings were completely roofed; more properly, they may be considered palisaded enclosures with smaller roofed apartments arranged around the inside of the main wall. In some multi-roomed buildings one chamber was set aside for the log-tomb burials, another for cremations, and a third apparently, as a storage place for ceremonial objects. The Hopewell log tombs, which were similar to the Adena, were the repositories for extended and in-the-flesh burials. The log cribbing of the rectangular tomb was built up on a low clay platform on the house floor; and the individual or individuals so honored were placed within the tomb accompanied, both inside and outside the immediate crypt, by quantities of ceremonially broken grave goods. The extensive store of implements and ornaments placed with the dead is one of the distinctive features of the Hopewell phase and contrasts with the fewer items

274

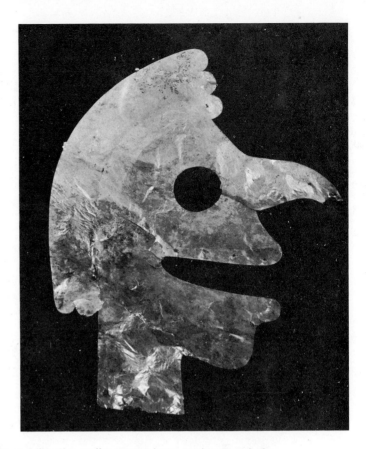

Figure 5-24. Hopewell copper and mica cut-out art. *Left:* Copper plaque from Mound City, Ohio, with hammered repousse design of raptorial birds, 28 cm. high. *Right:* Mica Sheet, 18 cm. high, fashioned into profile of a man, from Turner Mound Group, Ohio. (*Left,* courtesy Ohio State Museum; *right,* courtesy Peabody Museum, Harvard University.)

of grave furniture found in the Adena burials. It is impossible to list here all the items that the Hopewell buried with their dead; but the tombs, and the general area of the "houses of the dead" covered by the burial mounds, contained such things as huge sheet copper and mica cut-out figures of serpents, swastikas, heads, hands, animal claws, and geometric designs. Along with these esoteric objects were masses of freshwater pearls, heaped around the bones of the dead or around the cremated remains. Polished-stone ear spools, effigy monitor pipes, engraved human and animal bones, bird-stone type atlatl weights, and numerous other items of both copper and polished stone were all used as grave goods, as were caches of chipped flint and obsidian blades and points. Pottery occasionally was placed with the dead.

It has been estimated that over three-fourths of the Hopewell dead were cremated, tomb burial in the flesh apparently having been reserved for a distinguished minority of the population. Cremations were carried out in the mortuary houses.

Figure 5-25. Small carved-stone objects of the Hopewell culture. *a,b:* Engraved "marbles" or balls; diameter, 1.8 cm; from Seip Mound, Ohio. *c,d:* Two views of a "napkin-ring" ear spool; from the Hopewell Mound Group, Ohio. Diameter of *d,* 6.2 cm. (Courtesy Peabody Museum, Harvard University.)

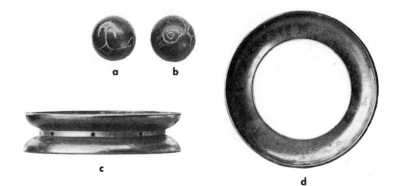

Figure 5-26. Clay-lined crematory basin and associated cache of obsidian flakes, Hopewell Mound Group, Ohio. (Courtesy Ohio State Museum.)

Bones were burned in rectangular clay-lined crematory pits, apparently after they had been denuded of flesh through either exposure and decay or by cleaning. Ashes and bone fragments were then placed in log crypt tombs on prepared platforms within the same houses or buildings.

Hopewell flint and obsidian work was of high quality, as the numerous finds of points, knives, and other implements indicate. In general, the large, broad-bladed, corner-notched or side-notched point, which with slight modification is a part of the Archaic and earlier Woodland heritage, was the common projectile form. These were used as atlatl dart tips. Both antler atlatl hooks and bar and birdstone weights attest to the use of the throwing-stick. Other typical Hopewell chipped-stone items were flake knives struck from cores and large, finely chipped blades or knives that do not appear to have been tools or weapons. The principal heavy cutting tools were ungrooved axes of polished stone, and axes and adzes of copper or meteoric iron. The metallurgy of the Hopewell people involved the same cold- and hot-hammering techniques that were practiced in the earlier Archaic cultures. We have already mentioned the sheet copper cut-out designs that were buried with the dead. Most of these were pierced with small holes and probably were fastened either to clothing or possibly to wooden backs or frames. Ear-spools, artificial noses or nose-masks placed on the faces of the dead, frames for headdresses, the Adena-style reel-shaped gorgets, and outer casings for reed Panpipes also were made of copper. Besides copper and meteoric iron, small amounts of silver and gold have been found in Hopewell mounds. These rare metals usually were hammered into very thin leaves, and some copper ear spools were covered with such silver sheeting.

It is through these metals found in the mounds that archaeologists have some knowledge of Hopewell textiles. The textiles have been found in fragments—some of them fortunately quite large —which were preserved by the oxidization of copper ornaments and other paraphernalia with which the cloth had been in contact. They were woven of plant fibers, presumably from wild plants and definitely not cotton, and they had been painted with bold curvilinear designs in two colors. From the appearance of the designs it would seem that the technique of painting may have been a batik-like or resist process, in which areas of the fabric had been covered with a paint or dye-resistant substance before the pigment was applied to the remainder of the cloth.

The Hopewell were sculptors. They worked in bone and stone and with both relief and full-round techniques. They carved stone tablets, in the same tradition as Adena tablets, and worked human and animal bones as ornaments or ritual objects, covering them with their distinctive stylized curvilinear designs. Full-round sculpture was best illustrated in the small effigy pipes, which were one of the most characteristic of Hopewell traits. Known as "monitor pipes," the bowl rested on the center of a flat, frequently curved-based element. One end of this basal element was a mouthpiece with a smoke-hole drilled into the bowl; the other end, of equal length, was identical in appearance except that it was undrilled. The sculptured portion of the pipe was the bowl. Sometimes these bowls were simply plain cylinders, but often they were fashioned as very life-like birds or animals which faced the smoker. The tobacco cavity was in the back of the zoomorph.

Like Adena pottery, most of the Hopewell vessels were either cord-marked or plain, and the

Figure 5-27. Carved horned serpent of slate or cannel coal. The horns were carved separately and inset. Length, about 24 cm. (Courtesy Peabody Museum, Harvard University.)

Figure 5-28. *Left:* A Hopewell carved-stone monitor effigy pipe. *Right:* A zoned rocker-stamped pottery vessel. These are characteristic or diagnostic features of classic Hopewell culture as revealed in Ohio. The mouthpiece of the pipe is at left; the tobacco bowl is in the bird's back. The vessel is a small tetrapodal jar, of a polished, brownish-black monochrome. The bird design is outlined in wide incised lines and left plain, but the background has been filled in with dentate rocker or roulette stamping. (Courtesy Ohio State Museum.)

Figure 5-29. Hopewellian pottery. *Top, left:* Zoned rocker-stamped rectanguloid jar of the type called Alligator Bayou Stamped, Santa Rose-Swift Creek phase, northwest Florida. Height, 23 cm. *Top, right:* Zoned-rocker-stamped jar from the Turner Mound, Ohio. Height, 19.5 cm. *Bottom, left:* Alligator Bayou Stamped bowl, northwest Florida. *Bottom, right:* Marksville Incised jar, Louisiana. Height, 10 cm. (*Top, right,* courtesy Peabody Museum, Harvard University; *others,* courtesy Museum of the American Indian, Heye Foundation.)

characteristic shape was a medium-to-small pot with a conoidal, rounded, or flattened base. Some pots had small tetrapodal supports. Another type, or series of types, were distinctly Hopewell, however; these were the incised and rocker-stamped pots or jars that presumably were of ceremonial rather than utilitarian significance. The upper rim of these jars bore a cross-hatched incised decoration which was set off from the body decoration by a row of deep hemiconical punctations. The body decoration was laid out by deep incised lines into zones of plain and rocker-stamped surfaces, with the positive element of the design usually being the part left plain. Designs were essentially curvilinear and often represented either bird or serpent figures or both. The art reflects

the same style as the Adena-Hopewell carved-stone tablets and the Hopewell carved-bone objects. Hopewell potters were more versatile than their Adena counterparts; besides the pot or jar, they turned out open bowls and plate shapes. Other Hopewell fired-clay items were platform pipes, similar to the stone ones, ear ornaments (frequently covered with copper sheeting), and figurines. These figurines are relatively rare but were well-rendered in a pleasing naturalistic style that was distinctive and quite unlike anything in Mesoamerica or the Southwest.[71]

Figure 5-30. A solid, hand-made Hopewell pottery figurine depicting a woman (front and side views); height, about 18 cm.; from the Turner Mound, Ohio; (Courtesy Peabody Museum, Harvard University.)

Our knowledge of the Hopewell settlement pattern is sketchy and incomplete. Some more or less permanent residents probably lived in and around the large ceremonial enclosures and burial mounds, although from the excavation records to date these sites could not be described as large permanent towns. Quite probably, many or most of the Hopewell lived in small semi-permanent villages, the majority of which were without burial mounds or other ceremonial earthworks. In this view, the mound and earthwork centers would have served as religious, and probably political and social, "capitals" for several villages.[72] The size of sites and the general elaboration of the culture, particularly in the wealth that was used as grave offerings in the mortuary cult, would indicate that agriculture was more firmly established in Hopewell than in the preceding Adena culture. Also, direct finds of charred maize have been found in the Ohio Hopewell sites as well as in other Hopewellian sites in regions outside the Ohio Valley.[73]

Viewed in broad geographical and long chronological perspective, the Hopewell development in the Eastern Woodlands was the first great cultural climax phenomenon of the area. This climax was best expressed in mounds and earthworks— truly monumental "public works"—and mortuary rituals which were commemorated with rich offerings. The power of the Hopewell idea of elaborate burial rites is further attested to by the expansive force of the complex—its remarkable radiations out of Illinois and Ohio in a relatively short period of time. Another testimony of this power was the far-flung network of trading relationships which were established by Hopewell cultures. Prufer has recently summarized this:

One of the hallmarks of most Hopewellian traits is the emphasis on exotic raw materials which were either manufactured into a variety of objects or remained deliberately unmodified. These exotic materials—copper from the Upper Great Lakes region, mica from the Appalachians, fancy flints from various sources, obsidian from the Rockies or from the Southwest, large conch shells from the Gulf Coast, various sea shells from the Atlantic and Gulf Coasts, Grizzly Bear canine teeth from the Rockies, silver, meteoric iron, fossil shark teeth, to mention only a few—seem to have been crucial components in the material maintenance of the Hopewellian idea system. In order to obtain these materials a vast, and undoubtedly complex, exchange network had to be maintained throughout large areas of the United States. Thus, each of these areas contributed vitally to the maintenance of the Hopewellian ceremonial system. The exchange network itself seems to have provided the mechanical basis upon which this system spread, leading to a vast dynamic interaction sphere, the aim of which appears to have been exclusively the production of ceremonial objects primarily intended for deposition with the dead.[74]

One of the most notable features of the decline and disappearance of Hopewell cultures was the breakdown of this system of trade in exotic raw materials.

The Hopewell culture of southern Ohio declined and disappeared during the latter half of the Burial Mound II Period. Following it, the record is perhaps semi-complete; or possibly this region ceased for a time to be an important cultural center. The succeeding local culture phase is known as the "Intrusive Mound Culture."[75] It was a continuation of the Woodland tradition, and it seems to have been a regional manifestation of a more widespread culture type. In Ohio this particular phase derives its name from the fact that the dead were buried in intrusive graves dug into the tops and sides of old Hopewell mounds. These bodies had been placed either in a primary flexed or extended position. Artifacts went into the graves—tools, weapons, and simple ornaments—but the rich and elaborate mortuary rites of Adena-Hopewell had been forsaken. Mound construction was not practiced, although elsewhere, as in Michigan, simple burial tumuli were thrown up by what appear to have been contemporaneous societies with a related culture.[76] Artifacts included large chipped points, suitable for the atlatl; ungrooved chipped-stone axes; unilaterally barbed harpoons of bone; hafted beaver-tooth chisels; and a variety of bone and antler tools. One Hopewell artifact that continued into the Intrusive Mound culture was the monitor pipe, now distinguished by a keeled ridge on the platform stem above the stemhole. However, the assemblage was, in general, Woodland, and the forest-hunting elements in it stand out clearly. The questions that arise are whether or not agriculture had regressed and if so, was this subsistence failure responsible for the Ohio Hopewell and general Hopewell decline in the northern subareas of the Eastern Woodlands.[77]

The Upper Mississippi and Great Lakes Subareas. This profile of Woodland tradition development—from Adena to the high peak of the Hopewell climax with, then, a recession or reduction of the tradition—was paralleled or reflected outside of Ohio. In central Illinois, for example, the Red Ocher (Roskamp) and Morton phases, believed to be approximately contemporaneous with Adena, exhibited a kind of minimal expression of the mortuary cult, with cord-marked pottery and flexed burials in small artificial burial mounds.[78] Other phases, such as Black Sand[79] in central Illinois, and Baumer[80] in the southern part of that state, are of Woodland affiliation but bear no trace of burial mounds or the elaborate mortuary cult. Perhaps these phases represented a pre-burial mound but pottery-using stage of the Woodland traditional development.[81]

Hopewell in Illinois differs from the earlier Woodland phases in that sites were larger and more numerous and the burial mound-mortuary complex is greatly enriched. A chronological seriation of three Hopewell subphases in the Illinois River Valley provides a detailed developmental picture. The early and middle subphases maintained the complex burial, mortuary, and mound-construction features, and the pottery of the middle subphase includes the so-called "classic Hopewell"—zoned, incised, and dentate-stamped decorated ware with bird figures. In fact, this seems to be the region in which this particular pottery style developed, and as we have said, it was in this region and at about this time that a crystallized Hopewell culture—or at least the elaborate mortuary aspects of a culture—were diffused or carried to southern Ohio. In the late Illinois Hopewell subphase bodies were buried in shallow pits which then were covered by relatively small, low mounds. The ceramics of this phase included little or none of the classic Hopewell ware; vessel surfaces were finished mostly with cord-marking or cord-wrapped stick impressions. This third subphase led into a Late Woodland culture, the Maples Mills phase, where burials—flexed, secondary bundle, or cremated remains—were made in cemetery areas. The pottery of this phase was in part derived from the preceding terminal Hopewell wares and in part from new northern influences which linked to the Lake Michigan Woodland cultures.[82]

To the north and west of the Ohio Valley, in the upper Mississippi subarea, the Burial Mound I Period cultures were reflected only in early Woodland tradition pottery, some of which was similar to the Baumer ware of southern Illinois. During Burial Mound II, there was a Hopewell blossoming manifested in an increase in the number of sites, burial mounds, mortuary customs, and distinctive Hopewell-style pottery. This flowering is best evidenced in the southern part of the subarea, in northwestern Illinois, northeastern Iowa, and adjacent portions of Wisconsin and Minnesota. Also in the upper Mississippi subarea is the Effigy Mound culture. Several phases are probably represented, and Wisconsin is the center of distribution, although there are other sites in neighboring states. The most distinguishing features of this culture were mounds shaped in animal effigies and other curious forms. These mounds usually were burial places of primary, secondary bundle, or cremated remains, although some that have been excavated contained no burials. The chronological position of the Effigy Mound culture is not fully clear. Associated pottery was of a general Woodland cast, with either conoidal or round-bottomed jars that bore cord-wrapped stick or cord-impressions, punctations, fingernail impressions, and dentate stamping. Most authorities believe that many of the sites were approximately contemporaneous with the upper Mississippi Hopewell phases and date, therefore, to the Burial Mound II Period. Other effigy mound sites may be somewhat later. The culture was obviously a part of the Woodland tradition, but a reduced, specialized, and geographically distinct version of it. Following the Hopewell horizon, the Woodland cultures of the upper Mississippi subarea, such as the Blackduck phase, began to abandon the mortuary cult and its associated ceramic and artifact styles. Mounds were still built and used for burial, but now were virtually empty of grave goods. Pottery was predominantly cord-marked, and the vessel form was a round-bottomed pot with a definite collar or neck. Still later Woodland cultures, persisting through the Temple Mound Periods, reveal a further diminution of the old mortuary customs. Some of these late phases, such as Keshena, in northeastern Wisconsin, can be linked to historic tribes like the Menominee.[83] Around the northern Great Lakes any Woodland-like cultures comparable to and contemporaneous with Adena are missing or only tentatively defined. The principal Hopewell phase in this subarea is the Goodall, and it was followed by later Woodland cultures, some of which bore close resemblances to the Intrusive Mound phase of Ohio.[84]

The Northeast and Middle Atlantic. Moving into the northeast, the Middlesex and Point Peninsula I phases of New York can be dated as Burial Mound I Period. Both these phases were characterized by a heavy, grit-tempered, cord-

Figure 5-31. Effigy mounds, Iowa. *Left:* Bird-effigy mound outlined in the snow. The mound measures 123 feet from wing-tip to wing-tip and is about 2½ feet in average elevation. *Right:* Bear-effigy mound outlined in white gravel. Measurements are 82 (length) by 44 (maximum width) feet. Both mounds are in Effigy Mounds National Monument, McGregor, Iowa, (Courtesy National Park Service and S. H. Maule.)

Figure 5-32. Vinette 1 Woodland cord-marked pottery. *a-c:* Vine Valley, New York. *d-f:* Long Island, New York. (Courtesy New York State Museum and Science Service.)

marked (interior and exterior surfaces) pottery which is termed the Vinette 1 type and is related to the other earliest occurrences of Woodland tradition pottery in Ohio (Fayette Thick type of Adena) and southern Illinois (Baumer type). Burials were flexed, secondary bundle, or cremated forms, accompanied by caches of grave goods (blades, blocked-end tubular stone pipes, and copper beads and tools), but burial mounds were not constructed. In other words, these phases represent the Woodland tradition without burial mounds and quite probably without agriculture. The New York Hopewell culture, which succeeded Middlesex and Point Peninsula, has revealed small burial mounds and reflects such Hopewell traits as copper ear ornaments and effigy platform pipes. The phase appears intrusive into the western New York region from Ohio and probably was established by a small group of immigrants. Farther east a non-burial mound Point Peninsula II phase was contemporaneous.[85] The Hopewell influences in New York were followed by a Woodland culture, the Owasco phase—which in its ceramics and many other traits was an integral part of the old Northeastern continuum of Middlesex-Point Peninsula-Owasco-Iroquois.[86]

In the Middle Atlantic states, east of the Appalachians, the Woodland tradition first appeared with the addition of cord-wrapped, stick-impressed, fabric-impressed, and cord-marked pottery. Later, artificial burial mounds with sub-floor pits appeared, along with other traits that were generally Hopewell. In both the Northeast and the Middle

Atlantic subareas the Woodland tradition continued beyond the Hopewell horizon.[87]

In the Carolina piedmont a Woodland sequence followed the Savannah River Archaic. The earliest phases were the Badin and Vincent, followed by Yadkin, Clements, and others. Here an essentially unmodified Woodland-type culture lasted not only throughout the Burial Mound Periods but through most of the Temple Mound Periods as well.[88]

Figure 5-33. *Top, left:* Vinette 2 pottery from New York State. *a-c:* Vinette Dentate-stamped. *d,e:* Point Peninsula rocker-stamped. *f-h:* Point Peninsula Corded. These sherds pertain to Early and Middle Point Peninsula cultures (early part of the Burial Mound II Period). (Courtesy New York State Museum and Science Service; see also Ritchie and MacNeish, 1949.)

Figure 5-34. *Below:* Northeastern pottery. *Left:* Guida style pottery from Massachusetts, showing Iroquoian influences, about 30 cm. high. *Right:* An Owasco vessel, Wickham Corded Punctate, from New York, 40 cm. high. (*Left,* courtesy R. S. Peabody Foundation, Andover; *right,* courtesy New York State Museum and Science Service.)

Figure 5-35. Woodland tradition pottery from the North Carolina piedmont. *a:* Badin Cord-Marked. *b:* Badin Fabric-Marked. *c:* Badin Net-Impressed. *d:* Vincent Cord-Marked. *e,f:* Vincent Fabric-Marked. All Burial Mound II Period, and perhaps earlier. (Courtesy J. L. Coe; see also J. L. Coe, 1964.)

Figure 5-36. Stone pipes from the Gaston site, North Carolina piedmont. *Top:* Pipe in the Hopewellian mode from the Woodland tradition Vincent phase (Burial Mound II Period). *Bottom:* Typical pipe of the historic period, associated with the Gaston phase. Length of *top*, 8 cm. (Courtesy J. L. Coe; see also J. L. Coe, 1964.)

Figure 5-37. (*Top,* p. 285) Woodland tradition fabric-marked vessels from the North Carolina piedmont. *Left:* Yadkin Fabric-Marked (Temple Mound I and II Periods); height, 25 cm. *Right:* Clements Fabric-Marked (Temple Mound II Period); height, 50.5 cm. (Courtesy J. L. Coe; see also J. L. Coe, 1964).

Figure 5-38. (*Bottom, left,* p.285) Post-Archaic Period projectile points from the North Carolina piedmont. *a-d:* Small triangular points of the historic period. *e,f:* Points of the late Woodland Clements phase, Temple Mound II Period. *g,h:* Points of the Woodland Yadkin phase, Temple Mound I and II Periods. *i,j:* Points of the Woodland Badin phase, Burial Mound II Period. Length of *g*, about 5.7 cm. *a-f,* from Gaston site; *g-j,* from Doerschuk site. (Courtesy J. L. Coe; see also J. L. Coe, 1964.)

Figure 5-39. (*Bottom, right,* p. 285) Late pottery from the North Carolina piedmont. *a:* Caraway Complicated Stamped. *b:* Caraway Simple Stamped. *c,d:* Pee Dee Complicated Stamped. *e:* Gaston Simple Stamped. The Caraway pottery dates ca. A.D. 1700; Pee Dee falls in the A.D. 1550–1650 range; Gaston dates ca. A.D. 1700 and later. All these types are essentially in the Woodland ceramic tradition although they reflect influences from such styles as Lamar of Georgia and South Carolina, which was a blend of Woodland and Mississippian elements. (Courtesy J. L. Coe; see also J. L. Coe, 1964.)

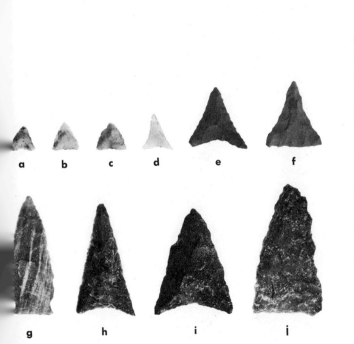

The Southeast. South of the Ohio Valley, in the upper Tennessee River drainage of eastern Tennessee, the Woodland cultures of the Burial Mound I Period, the Watts Bar and Candy Creek phases, reflected early Woodland ceramic traditions.[89] The Watts Bar pottery was a crude, heavy ware with plain-plaited fabric or cord-wrapped-stick impressions. The Candy Creek variety was somewhat better-made and revealed a greater variety of surface treatments, including cord-marking with a cord-wrapped paddle implement. Check-stamped and complicated-stamped types also appeared. These latter types related to and are undoubtedly derived from Georgia and northern Florida where vessel stamped decoration with carved wooden paddles developed during the Burial Mound I Period in such culture phases as Deptford and Swift Creek.[90] Burial mounds were not constructed during the Candy Creek and Watts Bar phases, although they appeared again in the succeeding Hamilton and Copena phases of the Middle Tennessee Valley, which are believed to date to the Burial Mound II Period.[91]

Still farther south, in Georgia and northern Florida, the early Woodland cultures were distinguished by a series of Southeastern pottery styles. These styles were variants of traditional Woodland

Figure 5-41. Reel-shaped copper gorgets from northern Alabama, characteristic of the Copena phase. Diameter of largest, about 15 cm. (Courtesy Museum of the American Indian, Heye Foundation.)

pottery with their grit or sand-tempering, the conoidal-bottom or tetrapodal-bottom pot forms, coiled or annular manufacture, and the obliteration of the coil lines by surface malleation and impression before firing; however, the more typically Woodland cord-wrapped paddle, fabric-wrapped paddle, cord-wrapped stick, or dentate impressions had been replaced by other kinds of stamping treatment; namely, check and linear-check stamping, simple stamping with a thong-wrapped or linear-grooved paddle, and stamping with a wooden paddle carved with complicated curvilinear or rectilinear designs. This last variant is known as "complicated stamped" ware, and one of the prime examples was the Swift Creek style, mentioned earlier as a trade ware or marginal influence north into Tennessee. The earliest

Figure 5-40. Steatite bird-effigy pipe from Tennessee, characteristic of the Copena phase. Length, 18 cm. (Courtesy Museum of the American Indian, Heye Foundation.)

286

Figure 5-42. Swift Creek Complicated Stamped pottery from northwest Florida. a: Early Swift Creek of the Santa Rosa-Swift Creek phase, about 20 cm. high. b,c: Late Swift Creek of the Weeden Island phase. Height of b, about 14 cm., of c, about 15 cm. (a,b, courtesy R. S. Peabody Foundation, Andover; c, courtesy Peabody Museum, Harvard University.)

of these Southeastern pottery styles were the Deptford of the Georgia and northwest Florida coasts, and the Mossy Oak of central and northwest Georgia. Deptford pottery was largely of check stamped or linear-check stamped surface finish, whereas Mossy Oak was simple stamped. The Deptford and Mossy Oak culture phases with which these styles are associated appear to have been on the Burial Mound I chronological horizon. Although evidence of small sand or earth burial mounds being built during these phases is not altogether convincing, the practice may have been followed. If so, it seems quite likely that it diffused into Florida and Georgia from along the Gulf Coast and the lower Mississippi Valley. However, another type of construction does seem to have been associated with the Mossy Oak phase—hilltop rock mound or rock effigy work. Two of these, near Eatonton, Georgia, are in the form of great bird figures with outstretched wings. These effigies may cover tombs, and there is reason to believe that small, dome-shaped rock mounds, sometimes found near the effigies, were burial covers.[92]

Mossy Oak and Deptford were succeeded by the complicated stamped styles, including Swift Creek. The Swift Creek culture is probably divisible into several phases, some of which can be arranged chronologically. Early Swift Creek featured the conoidal-bottom pot form, and the exterior surfaces of such vessels were virtually covered with concentric circles, scrolls, stars, and other forms integrated into complex unit patterns. In central Georgia, at the type site and elsewhere, there is no evidence of intentionally built burial tumuli;[93] in northwest Florida, however, the Santa Rosa-Swift Creek phase has yielded sand burial mounds and early and middle Swift Creek ceramics along with the Hopewellian types (Fig. 5-29).[94] The general chronological horizon seems to be that of the Burial Mound II Period. These Hope-

Figure 5-43. Negative-painted pottery from Crystal River, Florida, Hopewellian horizon or Burial Mound II Period. Diameter across rim, 9.5 cm. (Courtesy Museum of the American Indian, Heye Foundation.)

Figure 5-44. Hopewellian copper ear ornament from Crystal River, Florida Gulf Coast. Diameter, 8.5 cm. (Courtesy Museum of the American Indian, Heye Foundation.)

well pottery types in Santa Rosa-Swift Creek resemble forms from the lower Mississippi Valley, and it is likely that they diffused to northwest Florida from that direction. It is possible, however, that other Hopewell influences came into Florida by some more direct route from the Ohio Valley, as the exotic copper and other burial goods in the big burial mound at Crystal River on Florida's west coast suggest.[95] The Crystal River ceramic complex, while probably on the Burial Mound II horizon, was significantly different from Santa Rosa-Swift Creek.

The Southeast, however, deviated from the profile of Woodland tradition development that we have sketched for the North. Mortuary practices became more elaborate from Burial Mound I to Burial Mound II, undoubtedly conditioned by diffusion from the Ohio Valley centers. But these practices were not later abandoned, as they were in the North, nor did a northern Woodland culture appear. Instead, native cultures in regions like the Florida Gulf Coast and southwest Georgia bloomed. Population increased during the Weeden Island phases[96] of the coast, and their ceramics mark an aesthetic high point in Eastern prehistory. Outstanding were the incised and punctated designs that seem to have been highly stylized bird figures. A remote Hopewell inspiration, via Santa Rosa-Swift Creek, is thus suggested in the ancestry of the Weeden Island styles. Some Swift Creek Complicated Stamped types also persisted, but vessel forms grew more varied. Subglobular bowls and collared jars, the most common, mingled with trays, compartment vessels, and effigy vessels, often with rims decorated with bird, human, and animal effigies. Much of the Weeden Island pottery appears to have been made for burial purposes only. Such vessels were manufactured and fired with decorative holes in the sides and bottoms. Pottery and other artifacts were heaped in great mass offerings in burial mounds which today are found along the Gulf Coast, from Pensacola to Tampa and beyond, and on the streams flowing to the Gulf from the interior. There is also some evidence to indi-

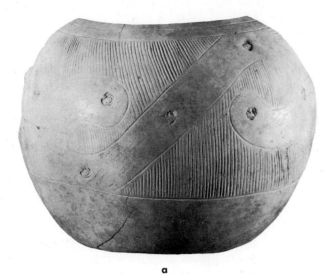

Figure 5-45. Weeden Island pottery, Florida Gulf Coast. a, Weeden Island Incised subglobular bowl about 18 cm. high. b: Weeden Island Punctated subglobular bowl about 20 cm. high. c: Human-effigy vessel about 32 cm. high. d: "Pre-fired killed" vessel about 22 cm. high. (a, courtesy Peabody Museum, Harvard University; b-d, courtesy Museum of the American Indian, Heye Foundation.)

cate that large, rectangular platform mounds, with ramp approaches, were constructed at some Weeden Island sites.[97] This kind of mound, and the implications of religious and social change which it carries, bespeaks another tradition, the Mississippian; so in a sense, the Weeden Island culture might be considered as one which bridged the transition from Woodland to Mississippian. Presumably, the latter phases of Weeden Island

Figure 5-46. A representative lot of polished-stone celt types, Santa Rose-Swift Creek, Weeden Island, and Ft. Walton cultures, northwest Florida. Celt at *top, left,* 16 cm. long. (Courtesy R. S. Peabody Foundation, Andover.)

lasted beyond the chronological limits of the Burial Mound II Period into Temple Mound I.

The Central and Lower Mississippi Valley. In our discussion of the Woodland tradition we have thus far ignored the alluvial lowlands of the central and lower Mississippi Valley. In turning to these subareas, let us go back to the Late Archaic Period. Archaic tradition sites are relatively rare in the alluvial bottoms of the river, probably because of recent stream and channel changes in the Mississippi drainage and the destruction and covering of early archaeological sites. You will recall, however, that some Archaic sites have been discovered in Louisiana and Mississippi and that some of these have contained typical Archaic artifacts found in association with mounds and earthworks. These sites appear to date from the close of the Late Archaic Period and from the beginnings of the succeeding Burial

Mound I Period. Poverty Point, in north Louisiana, is such a site.[98] It is located on an ancient alluvial fan or ridge left by an old channel of the Arkansas River. Although more recent stream action has destroyed part of the earthworks, those that remain are impressive. The principal mound is over 20 meters high and at its base measures about 200 meters. Tangent to this mound is a concentric octagonal figure over 1200 meters across composed of six rows of earth ridges. About a half-kilometer distant from the large mound and the octagon is a small conical mound, and over 2 kilometers away a second large mound. All these structures are believed to be contemporaneous, and there is little question but that they are all artificial. The purpose of the large mounds remains a mystery. They have not been excavated, although erosion gulleys in their sides disclose little else except basket-loaded clay fill. Owing to their somewhat irregular form, Ford and C. H. Webb have suggested that they may be huge bird-effigy figures, after the manner of the stone bird effigies of Georgia, except constructed of earth and much larger. It is, of course, quite possible that deep within their interiors, or under them, are tombs and burials. The small conical mound was excavated and contained a series of superimposed clay floors separated by lenses of fill. No building features could be detected on these floors, however. At mound base were traces of fires, ash beds, and some charred human bone fragments; thus it is possible that this mound was constructed to cover a crematory.

A number of test excavations were made in the ridges of the Poverty Point octagon, and Ford and Webb believe that the amount of refuse found on these ridges indicates a large planned town settlement. Although such an incipient urban development is not beyond the bounds of possibility (a minimum of 600 houses is estimated), the closest parallels to the Poverty Point octagon are the Ohio Adena and Hopewell ceremonial enclosures. Whether the concept of "town" or of "ceremonial enclosure" is more appropriate awaits further exploration of such works, although no house floors or post-mold patterns came to light during the Poverty Point excavations. As argued earlier, though, the Poverty Point mounds and enclosure are of such a size that it is difficult to imagine their construction in this environment by a people who were non-agriculturists.

Abundant artifacts and artifact fragments were found in mound fills and in the Poverty Point octagon enclosure ridges, including polished-stone and chipped-stone artifacts of Archaic types and thousands of tiny microlithic "perforators." The function of these implements is something of a mystery; the best explanation offered so far is that they are worn-out scrapers that were used in cutting antler and bone. The other characteristic and ubiquitous Poverty Point artifact was a fired clay object used in "stone-boiling," stones being scarce in the alluvial country of the lower Mississippi. These were fashioned in a great many different forms: balls or spheres, bicones, cylinders, and odd finger-squeezed shapes. Small, crude pottery figurines were also found. These represented human females but did not resemble the much more carefully modeled Hopewell figurines. Pottery at Poverty Point was represented by a very few sherds. Most imperishable containers were steatite or sandstone bowls. Of the pottery, most specimens were of fiber-tempered ware similar to specimens of the Late Archaic Period of the Tennessee River Valley.

The artifacts of Poverty Point were thus consistent with the Archaic tradition and with the Late Archaic Period; the mound and earthwork structures, on the other hand, were more like those of the Woodland tradition and the Burial Mound Period. The picture is the reverse of what we know about northern cultures such as Baumer. These northern cultures possessed Woodland pottery but built no mounds or earthworks. The mounds and earthworks existed at Poverty Point but not the ceramic component of Woodland. The actual date of Poverty Point is uncertain. A series of radiocarbon dates fall between 1200 and 100 B.C. The excavators, Ford and Webb, believe that site occupation and construction did not extend over such a long time span and settle on 800–600 B.C. as the best reasoned estimate. In so doing, however, they were conditioned in their thinking by the hypothesis that Poverty Point was a lower Mississippi Valley outpost of Adena-Hopewell mound-builders. This interpretation may be correct; but if the opposite view is taken—that the Poverty Point earthworks and an agricultural economy were introduced into the southern Mississippi River region from still farther south, or from Mesoamerica—a somewhat earlier date, perhaps in the vicinity of 1000 B.C., would be preferable.

If, indeed, the earthwork and mound-building pattern was first introduced, or first developed, in the lower Mississippi Valley, its subsequent developments were less spectacular in that subarea than in the Ohio Valley. Burial mounds are associated with the Tchefuncte[99] and Marksville[100] phases, which are believed to date from the Burial Mound I and II Periods. They reveal, respectively, some Adena and Hopewell similarities, although it is probable that they were somewhat later in time than the Ohio Valley climaxes of these latter cultures. The mounds of Tchefuncte and Marksville are burial tumuli, and enclosure-type earthworks are present at the Marksville site.[101] Ceramics of both Techefuncte and Marksville were more like the classic tradition of Hopewell pottery than like the cord-marked and cord-impressed wares of the north. Rocker-stamping, incision, punctation, and the usual red pigment were the decorative motifs (see Fig. 5-29). The stylized bird-form designs of classic Hopewell were utilized by Marksville potters, and their vessels were multi-shaped: small flat-bottomed and tetrapodal-support jars, hemispherical bowls, globular bowls, boat-shaped bowls or dippers, and deep jar-bowls of composite-silhouette outline. Clay temper, rather than grit or crushed rock, was standard to both Tchefuncte and Marksville. Unlike Adena and Hopewell, pottery was a common artifact placed in the burial mounds to accompany the dead of both Tchefuncte and Marksville. No data are available on the human physical type for the Poverty Point phase, but Tchefuncte and Marksville both included broad-headed elements in their populations.

As in Florida, no decline followed the Hopewell-influenced phases of the lower Mississippi Valley. In central Louisiana, Marksville was succeeded by a phase known as Issaquena, which appears to have been transitional into the local Mississippian tradition culture, the Coles Creek, of the Temple Mound I Period.[102] A similar development also unfolded up the Red River, in the Caddo region of northwest Louisiana and adjacent states, where the Woodland Fourche-Maline phase, or phases, was succeeded by the Caddoan Gibson culture.[103] Northward, in the central Mississippi Valley, information on the Woodland tradition cultures is scarcer, but the Tchula and Early Baytown phases of that subarea can be related to Tchefuncte and Marksville to the south and to Adena and Hopewell to the north and east. Significantly, the ceramic complexes of these central Mississippi-phase sites have yielded increasingly greater quantities of cord-marked and fabric-impressed pottery as one goes north. Early Baytown was succeeded by Late Baytown, in which the site pattern changes and in which burial mounds were replaced by flat-topped temple mounds of the Mississippian tradition.[104]

The Mississippian Tradition

Definitions and Origins. The Mississippian tradition stands in contrast to the Woodland tradition. There was some cultural continuity, but the differences are striking enough to justify regarding them as two separate traditions. For example, these differences are distinctly greater than those dividing the Basketmaker from the Pueblo phases in the Southwestern Anasazi culture or than those separating the subareal variants of the Southwestern tradition. To begin with, the pattern of the major Mississippian site was unlike that of the Woodland sites. It was marked by rectangular, flat-topped platform mounds which served as bases for temples, chiefs' houses, and other important buildings. Frequently these platform mounds were arranged around rectangular open plazas. Although burial mounds did not disappear entirely in Mississippian cultures, they were dwarfed by the platform mounds and were relatively minor features at the major sites. Generally, in both earthwork construction and extent of settlement, Mississippian sites were larger than Woodland sites. Although large Adena and Hopewell mound and embankment groups have been found and the Poverty Point site in Louisiana is unusually large, it is nevertheless true that the largest of the Mississippian centers, such as Cahokia (Illinois) or Moundville (Alabama), are even larger than these. Then, too, the density of living refuse and house remains in their large Mississippian villages give evidence of more stable occupation than do the Woodland sites. These facts, together with the now frequent finds of charred maize, beans, and squash, and the Mississippian appearance of new and improved strains of maize, point to an intensification of agriculture and its increased economic importance.

Associated with these changes in site patterns and subsistence were a host of other Mississippian traits, of which the most prominent were ceramic manufactures. New vessel forms, modes and manners of decoration, and aplastics appeared. Composite silhouette ollas, jars, and casuelas replaced the relatively simple pot forms of the Woodland. Handles and various appendages were added to the vessels. Incision, punctation, engraving, and painting tended to replace cord-marked, malleated, or stamped surfaces. In many Mississippian cultures, pulverized shell was the universal pottery temper. These ceramic innovations effected a near-complete break with the past, although in some regions they blended with and continued the older Woodland ways so that cord-marking or vessel-stamping, for instance, existed alongside the newer modes of surface treatment or decoration.

The Mississippian tradition was earliest and strongest in the central and lower Mississippi Valley subareas. According to the broad definition which is being used here, such cultures as the "Middle Mississippian" of the Central Valley and the Coles Creek and Caddo of the Lower Valley are all to be included in this tradition. The Mississippian tradition was also firmly established in the Southeast subarea, as represented by sites in the Tennessee River drainage and along other major river courses in Alabama and Georgia. It penetrated for short distances up the Ohio and Missouri valleys although here, and in the upper Mississippi subarea, its manifestations were somewhat more attenuated and fused considerably with the resident Woodland cultures. Around the Great Lakes, in the Northeast, in the Middle Atlantic states, and in the glades of southern Florida, no typically Mississippian sites have been found, although the local cultures, which were essentially Woodland or Woodland-Archaic, were exposed to Mississippian traits and influences. Similar circumstances also obtained in the Plains area to the west.

The Mississippian tradition began in the Temple Mound I Period, but the initial date of A.D. 700 for this period is most tentative and approximate. At about this time the earliest Mississippian cultures were in formation in the central Mississippi Valley subarea of northeastern Arkansas, southeastern Missouri, southern Illinois, and western Tennessee. More or less contemporaneously, the Coles Creek and related cultures of the lower Mississippi valley were making their appearance.

Owing to the nature of the essential Mississippian traits—the platform mound and plaza arrangement of sites, varieties of maize and maize cultivation, and certain ceramic features—there can be little doubt but that the ultimate inspiration of the tradition was in Mesoamerica. But just how these contacts were effected are not clear. A continuous geographical contact must be ruled out. In northeastern Mexico and much of Texas there are no sites which could be considered as either Mesoamerican or Mississippian. Nor is there in the Eastern Woodland area any evidence for Mesoamerican site-unit intrusion. That is, no archaeological sites have been found which in their total cultural complex reflect any known Mesoamerican culture. These facts strongly suggest that the Mesoamericanization of the Eastern Woodlands, a phenomenon of the Mississippian tradition and of the Temple Mound Periods, was accomplished by diffusion, intermittent contact, and occasional immigration rather than by mass movements of Mesoamerican tribes into the Mississippi Valley.

Within the Eastern Woodlands, in parts of the Southeast and in the upper Mississippi Valley, there is evidence of Mississippian site-unit intrusion. Here, in locations somewhat marginal to the main developments of the Mississippian tradition,

Figure 5-47. Mississippian temple mounds. *Left:* Mound B at Etowah, Georgia. *Right:* The great Monk's Mound at Cahokia, East St. Louis, Illinois. (Courtesy Peabody Museum, Harvard University.)

Mississippian sites are intruded into and in effect superimposed on the earlier resident Woodland sites and cultures. Thus although Mississippian culture could not have been brought from Meso-america to the Eastern Woodlands as a fully inte-grated, functioning entity, within the Eastern Woodlands area it appears to have been so propa-gated from its Mississippi Valley hearth.

Human Physical Types. In general, studies conclude that the Mississippian culture was associated with rugged, round-headed peoples—Neumann's Walcolid physical type.[105] However, the appearance of this type did not coincide with the advent of the Temple Mound I Period and the first Mississippian cultures. We have already men-tioned that round-headed elements were present in Archaic and Woodland populations. So it is possible, or even likely, that this minor brachy-cranic strain in the old local populations simply rose to later dominance and that there was no new immigration into the East from any other area. It is also quite likely, that this rise to domi-nance was related to the spread and propagation of the vigorous Mississippian cultural tradition with which brachycephalic peoples were associated. This is what seems to have occurred in the expan-sion of Mississippian culture out of the Mississippi Valley and into the marginal subareas. In the site-unit intrusions referred to in the preceding paragraph, the invading Mississippian populations tended to be more round-headed and heavy-boned than the earlier Woodland residents.

Languages. Linguistic data simi-larly suggest that Mississippian culture was devel-oped locally within the East by resident peoples. Muskogean, the language family of the Southeast which has been linked frequently with Mississip-pian culture, appears to have had an ancient history in the Eastern Woodlands area and to have been remotely related to Algonquian, the language family generally associated with Wood-land cultures.[106] The Siouan peoples, who may possibly have developed the Mississippian tradi-tion, form another major language family almost certainly long resident in the East. Neither the Muskogean nor Siouan have close linguistic rela-tives in Mesoamerica, and this holds for the Iro-quoian and Caddoan tribes of the East. In brief, the language families of the Eastern Woodlands appear to have been in that area for several mil-lennia and could not have been derived readily from language families in Mesoamerica, at least within a time span recent enough to throw light on the origins of Mississippian or Woodland cultures.[107]

The Temple Mound I Period: The Cen-tral and Upper Mississippi Valley and the Southeast.. The best known Temple Mound I community in the Mississippi Valley heartland is the great Cahokia mound and town site in East St. Louis, Illinois, in the northern part of the central Missis-sippi Valley subarea.[108] Cahokia has a long his-tory, but its earliest Temple Mound I Period com-ponent is a little-known phase which combined the new features of temple mounds with Woodland tradition pottery of the Jersey Bluff type.[109] This phase is believed to be contemporaneous with and related to the Late Baytown phase somewhat farther south.[110] At Cahokia it was succeeded by the better-known Old Village phase which was more fully and typically Mississippian.[111] Although excavation data for this phase have never been fully published, there is good reason to believe that Cahokia was a major political and religious center. The prominent features of this center were large flat-topped mound constructions. Such mounds, here and elsewhere in the Mississippian tradition, were constructed of clay or earth and were the bases on which stood temples, priests' quarters, or the houses of chiefs. Old Village phase ceramics were tempered either with finely crushed shell or pulverized limestone. Surfaces, charac-teristically, were well-polished. Chevron or scroll designs often were incised on vessel shoulders, and sometimes a red-slip was used. Angle-shouldered jars were most common, but beaker and bowl shapes also were made. Some specimens were equipped with loop handles; others bore small animal effigy heads on their rims. A mushroom-shaped pottery trowel was apparently used in fashioning the vessels.

This Old Village variety of early Mississippian culture spread northward up the Mississippi River Valley as far as Aztalan in southern Wisconsin. This great mound site, situated on a riverbank, was enclosed by a defensive earthwork and wooden palisade measuring about 500 by 200 meters. Within the enclosure are two pyramidal platform mounds as well as abundant village refuse. Additional village debris also lies outside the main enclosure. The Aztalan people were maize farmers who lived in rectangular wattle-daub houses. Their pottery was similar to that of the Old Village phase. Other artifacts included small triangular projectile points of flint; perforated shell hoes; numerous rough mortars, mullers, and grinders; stone hoes; ground-stone celts; copper-covered stone ear ornaments; and a variety of bone implements.[112]

Another phase of early Mississippian culture was the Obion in western Tennessee.[113] Obion was not so closely related to Old Village Cahokia as was Aztalan, but the Mississippian tradition affiliations are unmistakable in its platform mounds. Early Obion ceramics were clay-tempered, a variety that was succeeded by a later subphase of shell-tempered wares. Farther east, on the Tennessee River in eastern Tennessee, is still another early Mississippian phase known as Hiwassee Island.[114] The Hiwassee Island towns were stockaded. Within the fortified settlement zone are platform mounds and the remains of numerous dwellings. The mounds were surmounted by rectangular or circular buildings which had been constructed by digging wall trenches and setting saplings or small poles within these trenches. The poles were then bent over at the tops and lashed together, forming an arched roof. The walls were covered with wattle-daub sheathing and thatch was added to the roofs. Entrances were placed at the corners of rectangular buildings, and interior features, of clay, included fireplaces, small plat-

forms, and seats. Ramps or stairs led up the sides of the mounds to summit buildings. What appear to have been the ordinary dwelling houses, located on the flat ground surrounding the mounds, but within the palisaded enclosure, were similar in construction to the temples or public buildings. Hiwassee Island pottery was largely shell-tempered. Some of it was red-on-buff or red-slipped, although cord-marked and complicated-stamped types, heritages from the earlier local Woodland cultures, continued to be made. One characteristic Mississippian pottery type found at Hiwassee Island and at Obion and other phases was the textile-marked salt pan—huge, thick-walled vessels made in a broad, shallow pan shape. They were used for the production of salt presumably by evaporating water from salt springs or licks.

The fact that Mississippian sites of the Temple Mound I Period were frequently fortified suggests that they were often established in hostile territory. In addition to Aztalan and Hiwassee Island, the Macon Plateau is an example. The Macon site is farther away from the Mississippi Valley than either Aztalan or Hiwassee Island, being located in the heart of the Woodland Swift Creek country of central Georgia.[115] Two earthwork enclosures surround the site. Within are large platform mounds, community buildings, and dwellings. The dwellings are the wall-trench type and rectangular in outline. One of the community buildings is especially interesting. Circular, it was constructed on ground level, or slightly below ground level, rather than on a mound top. It is about 13 meters in diameter, and the floor plan reveals features that make it appropriate to designate the structure a council chamber. A large, circular, clay-lined fire pit is in the center and on the west side is a raised clay platform fashioned in the shape of an eagle, its head pointed toward the fire pit. There were 50 seats within the chamber, forty-seven of which were placed around the wall on a low clay bench, the individual seats being divided by clay ridges and marked by small depressions or receptacle-like basins at the front of each seat. Three similar depressions in the back

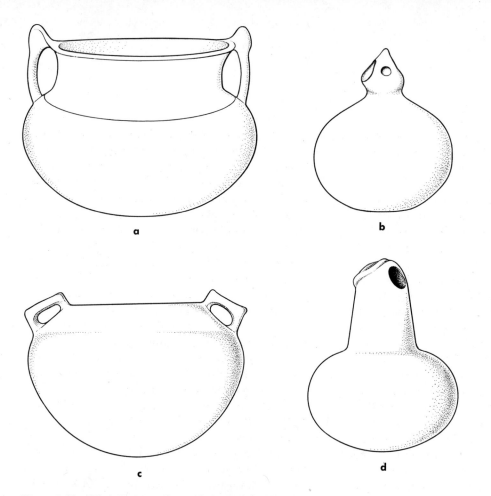

a

b

c

d

Figure 5-48. Mississippian pottery of the Temple Mound I Period. *a*: Loop-handled jar, Hiwassee Island phase, Tennessee; diameter, 44 cm. *b*: Blank-faced water bottle, Hiwassee Island phase, Tennessee; diameter, 26.5 cm. *c*: Loop-handled jar, Macon Plateau phase, Georgia; height, 14 cm. *d*: Blank-faced bottle, Macon Plateau phase, Georgia; height, 18 cm. (*a,b*, redrawn from Lewis and Kneberg, 1946; *c,d*, redrawn from Fairbanks, 1956.)

of the raised eagle-effigy altar mark the locations of the three other seats. On the east side, opposite the eagle platform is a long passage entrance. The walls of this building were made of clay. The roof was supported by four large floor posts, stringer-beams, and beams laid radially from the stringers to the clay wall. The whole was apparently covered with canes and earth, including the narrow passage entrance.[116] Macon pottery was either shell-or grit-tempered, but the forms were predominantly Mississippian, including the angle-shouldered jar, bottles, effigy ornamentations,

loop-handles, and fabric-marked salt pans. Although the principal burying ground was not located at Macon, a number of burials were found in log tombs beneath the lowest and earliest construction level of one of the platform or temple mounds.[117] This method of burial, like the earlier Woodland log-tomb interments of the Adena, Hopewell, and related cultures, suggests a marginal retention of an older local custom.

Early Mississippian penetrations into the Southeast subarea appear to have come mainly from the northwest, probably moving from the central Mississippi Valley up the Tennessee River and its tributaries and from this drainage southward into Alabama and Georgia. The Macon site is one of the southeasternmost outposts that can be confidently attributed to influences and peoples following such routes. There are, however, other indications of the early Mississippian tradition still farther south. We have already referred to the presence of platform mounds and exotic ceramic traits in the Weeden Island culture of the Florida Gulf Coast. These are in some way related to the general Mississippian tradition, although mound burial in Weeden Island followed the patterns of Hopewell-affiliated cultures. In this case, it seems most likely that the idea of temple mound construction spread eastward from the lower Mississippi Valley early in the Temple Mound I Period. The Kolomoki site in southwest Georgia, on a tributary of the Flint-Chattahoochee River system which empties into the Gulf of Mexico, boasts one of the largest rectangular flat-topped pyramidal mounds in the entire Southeast, yet the principal ceramic complex represented at the site is Weeden Island. Present also are small, dome-shaped burial mounds containing typical Weeden Island pottery and other offerings.[118]

The Temple Mound I Period: The Lower Mississippi Valley. The temple mound trait spread into southern Georgia and northwestern Florida probably from the Coles Creek continuum in Louisiana and adjacent Mississippi. This continuum succeeded the Woodland tradition-Marksville phase in this region. J. A. Ford has argued that the pyramidal platform mound is a feature of the earliest part of the continuum, dating from a phase designated as the Troyville.[119] Other authorities doubt Ford's contention, feeling that the ceramic complex associated with the Troyville phase belongs essentially to the latter part of Marksville and that the platform mound-plaza complex had not yet made its appearance. Great quantities of Troyville-Coles Creek pottery have been discovered in dwelling site refuse. It was clay-tempered, as was the preceding Marksville ware, and bore the Marksville deep incision, punctation, and rocker-stamping decorative techniques, although reflecting a shift from stylized bird figures to a greater emphasis on curvilinear meander or scroll designs or simple rectilinear patterns. New vessel forms also appeared—flat-bottomed beakers, subglobular bowls, and shallow bowls or trays with wide rim flanges.[120] These ceramic trends

paralleled the patterns in Florida pottery associated with the transition from Santa Rosa-Swift Creek into and through Weeden Island.

Coles Creek pottery is also similar to types found along the Red River in the Caddo region of northwest Louisiana and adjacent Texas, Arkansas, and Oklahoma. In this Caddo region the several phases of the Gibson culture established the Mississippian tradition. A. D. Krieger has argued that the early Gibson phase or subphase, the Alto 1, as represented at the Davis site in east Texas, was the earliest appearance of a Mississippian tradition culture in the Eastern Woodlands area and that the Gibson culture was, in effect, the link between Mesoamerica and the other Mississippian cultures of the East.[121] The propinquity of the Caddo region to Mexico tends to support this stand, as do Krieger's views about the "Gilmore Corridor" (see p. 336) as a route of migration or trait diffusion from Mesoamerica to the north;[122] however, much of the pottery of the Gibson culture can be related to the Coles Creek wares whose antecedents lie securely in the immediate environs of the lower Mississippi Valley rather than in the Caddo region. The interpretation favored here is that the Gibson culture spread up the Red River to the Caddo region from the Coles Creek region rather than the reverse.

The Temple Mound I Period: Conclusion. The first appearance of the Mississippian tradition in the East, remains clouded. Neither the place nor the exact time can be pinned down. Ultimate sources of origin are Mesoamerican, and the process of dissemination that crystallized in the Mississippian pattern appears to have been diffusion rather than massive migration of populations. The Mississippi Valley was the "forcing bed" of the tradition, but whether its earliest emergence was in the lower Mississippi Valley, the Caddo region, or in the central Mississippi Valley cannot yet be answered. Certainly the most vigorous and viable branch of the new tradition was located in the central Mississippi Valley, probably between St. Louis and Memphis; and it was

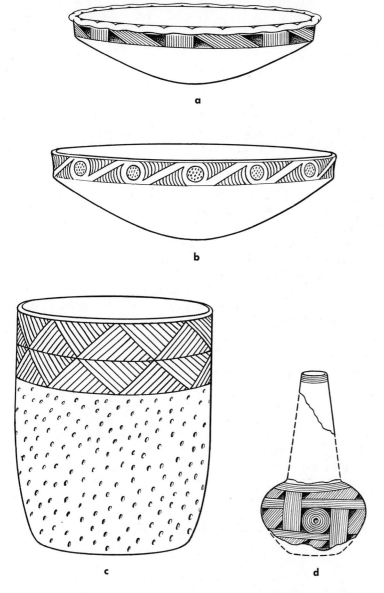

a

b

c   d

Figure 5-49. Temple Mound I Period pottery of Gibson Caddo affiliation. a: A carinated bowl with an engraved and incised decoration (Holly Fine Engraved). b: An incised and punctated carinated bowl (Crockett Curvilinear Incised). c: An incised and fingernail-punctated cylindrical vessel (Dunkin Incised). d: Bottle (Holly Fine Engraved). Diameter of a, about 36 cm. (Redrawn from Newell and Krieger, 1949.)

from here that emigrants set out to colonize places as distant as Aztalan, Wisconsin, and Macon, Georgia. Also at about the same time, influences spread and colonists perhaps moved from the lower Mississippi eastward into Florida and Georgia and probably northwestward up the Red River. These various events are estimated to have begun around A.D. 700, but it is likely the great Mississippian sites of the Temple Mound I Period did not reach their heyday until after A.D. 900.

The Temple Mound II Period: The Central Mississippi Valley. The Mississippian tradition attained its cultural climax during the earlier part of the Temple Mound II Period, presumably during those first two or three centuries following A.D. 1200, when population reached its maximum and the geographical extent of the tradition was greatest. All those regions formerly occupied by Mississippian peoples were included, as well as additional areas to the north, west, and east. As we have mentioned, the Temple Mound II period was also a time of regional culture differentiation and of modification of the Mississippian tradition by elements of antecedent Woodland cultures; yet in the majority of these blends the Mississippian patterns remained dominant.

The central Mississippi Valley subarea of the Eastern Woodlands continued as a major hearth of activity in Temple Mound II times. The great site of Cahokia was enlarged and its principal mound probably attained its final form in this period. This mammoth platform structure is over 30 meters high and measures about 300 by 200 meters at the base (see Fig. 5-47, *right*). In addition to the Cahokia group, over 80 smaller platform tumuli have been identified within a 3-to-4-mile radius, and it has been estimated that perhaps 200 smaller ones have been destroyed by plowing and cultivation in recent times. Abundant potsherds and other dwelling site debris have been found around these mounds, and there can be little doubt that these river bottom lands in the vicinity of what is now East St. Louis at one time sustained one of the largest population densities in pre-Columbian North America. Continual occupation from the earlier Old Village phase (Temple Mound I) into the later Trappist phase (Temple Mound II) is revealed in the Cahokia refuse stratigraphy. Shell-tempered ceramic vessels increased in variety, one new form revealing a dipper, or "beanpot," shape. Polished black-incised and painted types became the vogue.[123] South of Cahokia are other Temple Mound II sites, including Kincaid,[124] near the mouth of the Ohio, and the numerous mound groups and villages of the New Madrid (southeastern Missouri), Parkin (northeastern Arkansas), Walls (Memphis region), and Menard (lower Arkansas River) phases.[125] At all these site locations are pyramidal mounds,

Figure 5-50. Mississippian tradition pottery of the Temple Mound II Period, except f, which may be Temple Mound I. a: Walls phase (Arkansas or Tennessee) shell-tempered incised and punctate olla with arcaded handles; height, 21 cm. b: Effigy jar representing a hunchback figure (Arkansas); height, 21 cm. c: Frog-effigy jar of the Walls phase (Arkansas); height, 19 cm. d: Black ware jar with engraved hand-and-eye decorations (Moundville, Alabama); height, 11 cm. e: Effigy bowl in which human head on rim contains pellet rattle (Indiana); total height, 17 cm. f: Globular effigy jar representing an oppossum (Kentucky); height, 23 cm. (Courtesy Museum of the American Indian, Heye Foundation.)

a

b

c

d

e

f

although there is a regional variation in the nature of the mound groups and settlement pattern. At Kincaid and the sites of the New Madrid and Parkin phases, for example, the mound structures are much larger and more impressive than the Walls or Menard phase sites; and unlike the others, the New Madrid sites were fortified by encircling palisades. These sites and phases are linked by shell-tempered pottery and general ceramic features, including bowls with human and animal rim effigies, effigy vessels, bottles, handled bowls or ollas, and painted pottery. The pottery reflects both positive and negative (or resist-dye) techniques with color schemes in white and red, red on buff, and polychrome. There was a significant regional differentiation, however; for example, negative-painted pottery was characteristic of the New Madrid phase, but was rare or unknown in phases farther south. Burial customs also relate these and other late Mississippian phases and sites. In general, the dead were buried in cemetery areas (although sometimes in abandoned house sites or in small burial mounds) and the most frequent kind of interment was the single individual extended and placed on his back. Grave goods, including pottery vessels, were arranged around the body. Other means of disposing of the dead included primary flexed forms, secondary-bundle burial, mass inhumation, and cremation. Although regional and phase trends are apparent in these different funeral modes, all were employed in the same phases and even at the same sites.

The Temple Mound II Period: The Southeast. One of the most vigorous developments of the Mississippian tradition in Temple Mound II times occurred in the Tennessee and Cumberland River valleys in western and central Tennessee.[126] According to Kneberg, the Obion-phase peoples of the earlier Temple Mound I Period were never able to take full possession of the western Tennessee drainage where earlier Woodland groups continued to reside. But these Woodland groups were gradually acculturated to Mississippian ways. Although the ceramics of such a phase as Har-

mon's Creek continued to reflect Woodland patterns, house types followed the rectangular, open-cornered, wall-trench styles of Obion. Afterward, the Temple Mound II Mississippian cultures of the region—the Duck River and Gordon phases—emerged from this blending of traditions to reflect predominantly Mississippian themes. Rectangular, flat-topped, and ramped temple mounds were the salient features of the towns, which consisted of clusterings or arrangements of rectangular, wall-trench houses. Pottery was negative-painted or engraved, and the distinctly Mississippian bowl with human or bird-effigy heads on the rim made its appearance. Elaborately chipped ceremonial flints, including "monolithic axe" and "mace-like" forms, were produced. It was also in this Cumberland brand of Mississippian culture that the most ambitious stone sculpture of the eastern United States was fashioned. These sculptures, human figures from 40 to 50 centimeters tall, were usually quite realistically portrayed. Frequently, they depicted a kneeling (and perhaps speaking or singing) old man. Such images may have been revered in the temples as deities, perhaps as fire or sun gods in the manner of the elderly male fire gods of Mesoamerica. For burials, the Gordon and Duck River peoples used the "stone-box grave," a rectangular box-like tomb of rough stone slabs laid on edge to form the four upright walls which were covered with other slabs. The dead were placed full length and on their backs within the tombs.

In eastern Tennessee, the Dallas phase was the Mississippian culture contemporaneous with the Gordon and Duck River phases. Archaeologists believe that the Dallas phase represents a fusion of continuities from the earlier Hiwassee Island Mississippian phase of that region plus a strong increment of influences and peoples coming northward from the northwest Georgia center of Etowah.[127] Etowah shows the marks of the western and central Tennessee Cumberland variety of Mississippian culture. For example, stone idols and stone-box graves have been discovered at the Georgia site.[128]

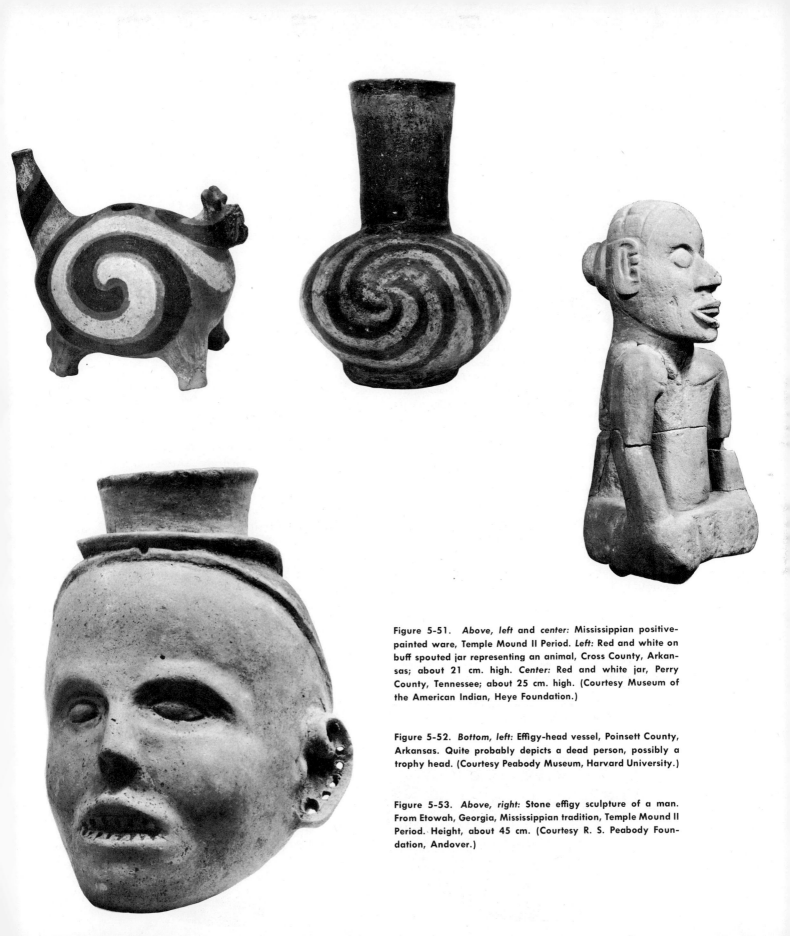

Figure 5-51. *Above, left and center:* Mississippian positive-painted ware, Temple Mound II Period. *Left:* Red and white on buff spouted jar representing an animal, Cross County, Arkansas; about 21 cm. high. *Center:* Red and white jar, Perry County, Tennessee; about 25 cm. high. (Courtesy Museum of the American Indian, Heye Foundation.)

Figure 5-52. *Bottom, left:* Effigy-head vessel, Poinsett County, Arkansas. Quite probably depicts a dead person, possibly a trophy head. (Courtesy Peabody Museum, Harvard University.)

Figure 5-53. *Above, right:* Stone effigy sculpture of a man. From Etowah, Georgia, Mississippian tradition, Temple Mound II Period. Height, about 45 cm. (Courtesy R. S. Peabody Foundation, Andover.)

Figure 5-54. Negative-painted pottery of the Mississippian tradition, Temple Mound II Period. *Left:* Black and white vessel with sun symbol design, Etowah, Georgia. *Right:* Black and white vessel with hand design, Moundville, Alabama. (*Left,* courtesy R. S. Peabody Foundation, Andover; *right,* courtesy Museum of the American Indian, Heye Foundation.)

old Southeastern complicated stamped ware tradition was modified by Mississippian contacts, so that typical Lamar pottery often bore complicated stamping and Mississippian-derived incised decoration on the same vessel. Other ceramic elements at the Etowah, Georgia, site include negative-painted wares (Fig. 5-54*a*). There are a great many other Lamar sites in addition to Etowah. Lamar proper, near Macon, the Nacoochee and Hollywood mound sites near Augusta, and the Irene mound near Savannah are among the best known. The pattern of settlement consisted of large and important towns with platform mounds and plazas and numerous smaller but residentially stable village sites scattered up and down the river bottoms. The Lamar site was enclosed by a pali-

The Georgia Etowah site is one of the largest temple mound groups (see Fig. 5-47, *left*) in the Southeast and this is a multiple-occupation site, although its heyday occurred in the Temple Mound II Period. Its basic ceramic pattern is that of the complicated stamped wares of the Georgian Lamar genre. In Lamar pottery, the

Figure 5-55. Temple Mound II Period complicated stamped pottery from Georgia, Nacoochee site. *Left:* Casuela bowl with complicated stamped decoration on lower portion and incision on upper zone. *Right:* Typical complicated stamped jar. (Courtesy Museum of the American Indian, Heye Foundation.)

Figure 5-56. Mississippian tradition (Temple Mound II Period) pipes. *Left:* A pottery pipe bowl with stylized bird-head effigies on rim from Montgomery County, Alabama. A reed stem was inserted in the tubular opening for smoking. Height, 7 cm. *Right:* Carved-stone pipe in the figure of an ocelot from Moundville, Alabama. The tobacco bowl is in the back of the animal, and a reed smoking stem was inserted at the rear. Length, about 15 cm. (Left, courtesy Museum of the American Indian, Heye Foundation; *right,* courtesy Peabody Museum, Harvard University.)

sade fortification. Burials were performed within the town and village areas. Lamar culture, with its characteristic pottery of deep jars and keel-like bowls, usually tempered with grit but sometimes with crushed shell, also spread to the north and east of its region of origin to sites in South and North Carolina. There now seems little doubt but that the Georgia Lamar culture was a creation of the Creek tribes, particularly the Lower Creeks and the Hitchiti, and that the large Lamar towns were in full vigor when De Soto made his famous entry into the Southeast in 1540–1542. However, in other regions, such as in the Carolinas and eastern Tennessee, Lamar pottery and culture were also associated with Cherokee and Siouan speaking groups of the proto-historic period.[129]

The huge ceremonial center and town site of Moundville, in northern Alabama, is representative of still another phase of Mississippian culture of the Temple Mound II Period. In sheer size the Moundville group of rectangular platform earthworks is second only to Cahokia. The cultural remains at Moundville present a much less adulterated version of the Mississippian tradition than Etowah or Lamar. Here, apparently, the resident Woodland cultures, such as the Copena, were less

tenacious or the Mississippian invasion was more obliterative of its predecessors than was the case farther to the east. The intensely Mississippian quality of Moundville is reflected in the pottery from that site, which includes large- and small-mouthed water bottles, beakers, and effigy forms which are shell-tempered and, when decorated, are incised, engraved, or negative-painted. Other characteristic Mississippian artifacts are greenstone celts of the flat cross-section, rectanguloid variety and equal-arm, elbow-form smoking pipes. The pipes were made of pottery and were used with an inserted reed stem. Another more unique Moundville pipe is a stone effigy of an ocelot (Fig. 5-56). Ornamental and ceremonial paraphernalia included such things as intricately carved shell gor-

Figure 5-57. *Above:* Two excellent examples of Mississippian (Temple Mound II Period) polished stonework from Moundville, Alabama. *Left:* A monolithic axe, 28.5 cm. long. *Right:* Bowl with a crested wood-duck effigy ornament, 29.5 cm. total height. (Courtesy Museum of the American Indian, Heye Foundation.)

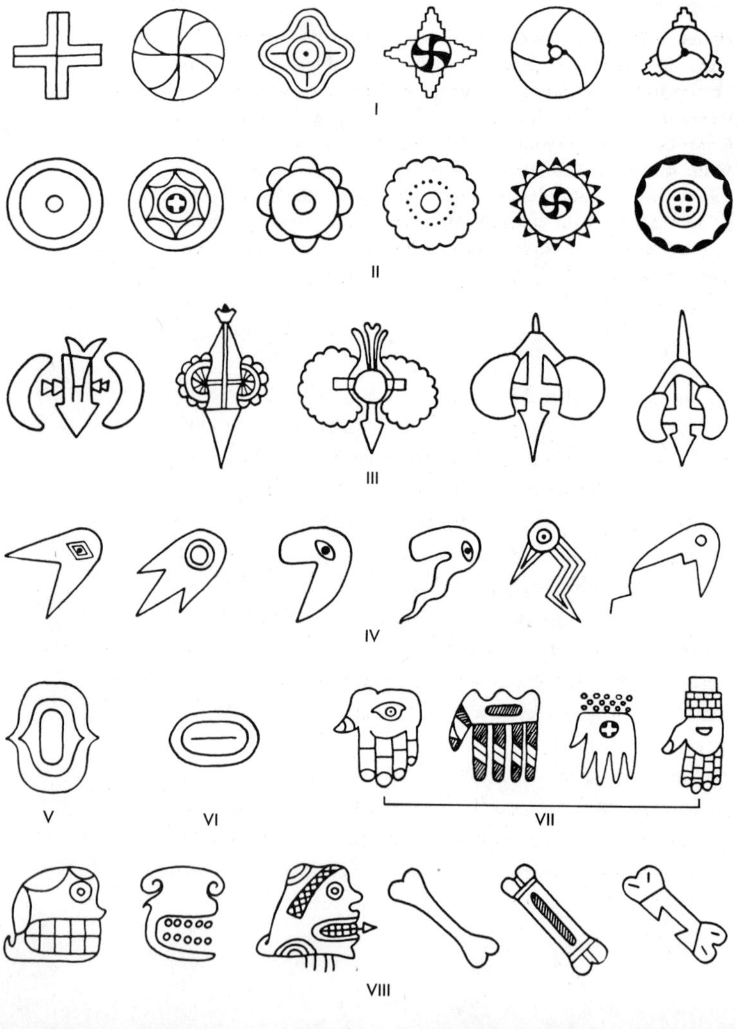

Figure 5-58. Design motifs of the Southern Cult. *I:* The cross. *II:* The sun circle. *III:* The bi-lobed arrow. *IV:* The forked eye. *V:* The open eye. *VI:* The barred oval. *VII:* The hand and eye. *VIII:* Death motifs. (After Waring and Holder, 1945. The designations or interpretations of motifs follow these authors.)

gets, embossed copper pendants, stone spatulate axes, monolithic axes (Fig. 5-57), stone "batons," stone vessels (Fig. 5-57), and engraved stone disks.[130]

The Southern Cult. Especially interesting in connection with the Mississippian tradition is the occurrence of a series of iconographic elements and objects which are associated as a complex and which apparently pertained to religious ritual. The complex existed throughout much of the southern part of the Eastern Woodlands during the Temple Mound II Period, and, reflecting its cult characteristics, it has been termed the Southeastern Ceremonial complex or the Southern Cult.[131] Significantly, the cult objects and design elements have appeared most often in the largest Mississippian temple and town sites such as Etowah and Moundville. These cult designs and objects also cross regional and subareal boundaries; in fact, one of the richest assemblages comes from Spiro in eastern Oklahoma, a site which is in the Caddo subtradition of the Mississippian tradition and which in its ceramic and other patterns differed considerably from Moundville, Etowah, or the Cumberland Valley sites of Tennessee. Cult designs were engraved on polished black shell-tempered pottery, carved on shell gorgets, or embossed on thin copper pendants. Among the designs were such things as a forked or "weeping" eye, a cross within a sunburst circle, a curious bi-lobed arrow form, human hands with eye or cross elements in the palm, human skull-and-bones motifs, and god-animal representations. Monolithic axes, mace-like batons, and ceremonial flint knives were a few of the objects associated with the Southern Cult. The god-animal themes and representations, including

eagles, serpents, winged-serpents, cats, and men masked as and impersonating animals, point to an affiliation with Mesoamerica.[132] This Mesoamerican derivation has been challenged, however, on the basis of the decidedly local style and rendering of the cult themes and of their possible prototypes in Hopewell and Burial Mound II Period art.[133] Rather than being the result of direct diffusion from Mexico, it has been argued that the Southern Cult manifestations were wholly Southeastern expressions of widely held native American mythological concepts. Although this latter explanation is a possibility, the total context favors somewhat more immediate Mesoamerican contact or stimuli. For it cannot be overlooked that, unlike the Archaic and Woodland traditions, the Mississippian has a strong Mesoamerican coloration.

Figure 5-59. Carved-shell gorgets with Southern Cult designs. *Left:* Sun symbol and pileated woodpecker designs, from Sumner County, Tennessee. Diameter, 8.5 cm. *Right:* Human figure, from Spiro, Oklahoma. Diameter, 12.5 cm. (Courtesy Museum of the American Indian, Heye Foundation.)

The concept of a cult to explain the widespread dissemination of these Southeastern design elements and ritual objects has also been questioned. At one time, students of the problem thought that such a cult may have been messianic and that it sprang up as a form of resistance and reassertion against the shock of the first Spanish invasions of the Southeast in 1540–1570.[134] Subsequent research has shown that Southern Cult art antedated by at least a couple of centuries the explorations of De Soto, and this dating has vitiated the messianic hypothesis. It is, however, still possible that a cult phenomenon was involved, although one wholly pre-Columbian. Such a cult, or widely shared religious ideology, could have been an expression of vitality rather than despair. A. J. Waring held this opinion and looking backward through time from the Creek "busk" or "green corn ceremony" of the historic horizon, he has suggested that the symbols of the Southern Cult were probably connected with harvest and renewal.[135]

The Ethnohistoric Horizon in the South. Insofar as we are able to tell, such great centers as Cahokia, Etowah, Moundville, Lamar, and many others were thriving when De Soto first came to southeastern North America. Native cultural decline did not set in until some little time later. This decline can be appraised in archaeological sequences in various regions. In central Georgia, as an example, a culture phase known as the Ocmulgee Fields succeeded Lamar some time during the seventeenth century. By this time, platform temple mounds were no longer being constructed. Populations had probably declined as a result of the introduction of European diseases. Ceramics were largely in the old native traditions, although the Ocmulgee Fields complex is debased

Figure 5-60. Ornamented copper of the Southern Cult, both from Etowah, Georgia. *Top:* Bi-lobed arrow element, possibly from a headdress. *Bottom:* God-animal representation or eagle-dancer. (Courtesy R. S. Peabody Foundation, Andover.)

and slovenly when compared to its ancestral Lamar standards. Ocmulgee Fields graves have yielded firearms and metal and glass utensils.[136] This kind of a blended Indian-European culture lasted for another century or so before the Creek Indians of the region, who can be identified with

Figure 5-61. God-animal representations of the Southern Cult. These objects, from Etowah, Georgia, and Spiro, Oklahoma, are either embossed copper sheets or sections of engraved conch shells. a,b,c,f: Representations of anthropomorphized eagle. The individual shown in g is holding a discoidal or chunkee stone as though to roll it. a,f, from Etowah; all others from Spiro. (After Waring and Holder, 1945.)

a

b

c

d

e

f

g

h

i

Figure 5-62. Mississippian discoidal stones from Tennessee. These objects are about 10 to 12 cm. in diameter and 4 to 5 cm. thick. (Courtesy Museum of the American Indian, Heye Foundation.)

Figure 5-63. Fort Walton phase pottery from northwest Florida. These specimens measure from 20 to 30 cm. in diameter. (a,b, courtesy Museum of the American Indian, Heye Foundation; c,d, courtesy Peabody Museum, Harvard University.)

the Ocmulgee Fields phase, were finally driven westward to settle in Oklahoma. Similar events were occurring elsewhere. On the Florida Gulf Coast and in northeast Florida, the Apalachee and Timucua tribes passed from the fully prehistoric Ft. Walton and related cultures to the Spanish Mission-Indian phases of the late seventeenth and early eighteenth centuries.[137] Farther west, in the lower Mississippi Valley, the Temple Mound II Period climax phase of Plaquemine[138] was succeeded by several historically identified phases, of which the best known is the Natchez.[139] As late as 1700, this tribe was still clinging to some remnants of an old hierarchical social and political system. A ceremonial center with temple and burial mounds was maintained, and the ruler of this petty state was supported by a class system which included nobles and commoners.[140] Up the

a

b

c

d

Figure 5-64. Pottery vessel of the historic Natchez culture; height, 11 cm. (Courtesy Museum of the American Indian, Heye Foundation.)

Red River from the Natchez were the various southern Caddo tribes represented by the later phases of the Fulton culture. These phases began to decline in the face of European contact by the late seventeenth and early eighteenth centuries.[141]

Temple Mound II Developments in the North. In the northern part of the Eastern Woodlands, the major cultures of the Temple Mound II Period were, in a very full sense, Mississippian-Woodland blends. Many of these cultures are referred to by the subarea geographical-cultural term of "Upper Mississippian." One such culture is the Fort Ancient,[142] of which several phases have been recognized in southern Ohio, southeastern Indiana, northern Kentucky, and adjacent West Virginia. This area is, in effect, the territory of the old Hopewell culture. Fort Ancient village sites were occupied throughout the Temple Mound II Period and, in some instances, until the late seventeenth century and the beginning of European contacts. Identifying the tribal members of the Fort Ancient culture is difficult, but the Shawnee (Algonquian-speaking) or Siouan groups are the most likely candidates. As with earlier peoples of the Ohio Valley subarea, both round and long-headed elements were represented in the Fort Ancient cranial series; and like many another Temple Mound II Period population of the East, skeletal materials have yielded considerable evi-

Figure 5-65. Caddoan pottery of the Fulton phase, both from northwest Louisiana. *Left:* Decorated with an engraved technique; height, 7 cm. *Right:* Incised; height, 12 cm. (Courtesy Museum of the American Indian, Heye Foundation.)

Figure 5-66. Caddoan pottery; polished black ware bottles with engraved decoration from southwest Arkansas. *Left:* Fulton phase. *Right:* Late Gibson or Gibson-to-Fulton transition. Height of bottle at *left*, 19 cm. (Courtesy Museum of the American Indian, Heye Foundation.)

dence of pathology, some of which may have resulted from syphilis.[143] The Fort Ancient villagers were successful farmers. Their communities were concentrated clusters or arrangements of large circular houses. Some villages may have been palisaded. There were no platform temple mounds. Burial patterns varied, but some interments were made in mounds, some in special cemetery areas, and some in and around the houses. Primary extended or flexed inhumation were the preferred modes. Ceramics bespeak the mixed Woodland-Mississippian heritage. Both grit and shell temper were employed and vessel surfaces were frequently cord-marked and then incised with guilloche designs or line-filled triangles. Abundant stone and bone tools were characteristic of Fort Ancient. Southern Cult designs were applied to tobacco pipes and other artifacts.

The historically well-known Iroquois tribes composed another northern Temple Mound II Period culture, but one which was considerably more oriented toward the Woodland tradition than was the Fort Ancient culture. Its local Northeastern prototype was the Woodland Owasco

phase. Iroquois culture flourished in central and northern New York State and extended westward to northern Ohio as well as southward into Pennsylvania and New Jersey.[144] J. B. Griffin has suggested that Iroquois ceramics may have had their origins in the west in Ohio Hopewell and that this derived ceramic complex was then carried east to New York.[145] The typical Iroquois vessel form was indeed reminiscent of Hopewell pottery, with its globular body and distinctly separate collar. A unique feature of the Iroquois vessel collar is that it was rectangulated or castellated. Long, obtuse-angle, elbow self-pipes and ornate bone combs are additional Iroquois culture diagnostics. Burial was in cemeteries or in ossuary deposits. Apparently, no burial or temple mounds were raised. The sites represent concentrated villages in which the big, extended-family, Iroquois long-houses, known from the historic horizon, were grouped together. Some villages were fortified.

West of the Fort Ancient culture, contemporaneous with it and related to it and to Iroquois as another manifestation of the Upper Mississippian branch of the Mississippian tradition, is the Oneota culture.[146] Oneota sites are scattered from Illinois to Nebraska and South Dakota and from central Wisconsin and southern Michigan as far south as Missouri. The culture was based on farming, but hunting was probably more important than it had been in Fort Ancient. Its ceramics were shell-tempered, typically globular olla-shapes with strap handles, and ornamented with simple geometric incised designs below the rim. One of the most characteristic traits was a small, short-stemmed disk-pipe of stone, sometimes called the "Siouan pipe." Cemetery burial was practiced, and there are no burial or platform mounds at the sites. Located on the western edge of the central and northern Woodlands area, Oneota was a transitional culture between Woodlands and Plains. House types, for example, were apparently pole structures in the east but earth lodges in the Nebraska Low Plains. Its late phases have been identified with several historic Siouan tribes of both the Woodlands and the eastern edge of the

Figure 5-67. Iroquois pottery from New York State. *Left:* about 34 cm. high. *Right:* 9 cm. high. (*Left,* courtesy New York State Museum and Science Service; *right,* courtesy Museum of the American Indian, Heye Foundation.)

Plains: the Winnebago, the Oto, the Ioway, the Missouri, and the Osage.

The Plains Area and Its Culture Sequence

The Area and Its Cultural Traditions. The culture history of the Plains area is closely bound up with the culture history of the Eastern Woodlands. As we mentioned at the beginning of this chapter, the same or only somewhat variant cultural traditions were shared by the two areas. Also, in our preceding discussion of the Mississippian tradition, we remarked that a culture such as the Oneota was to a degree transitional between the two areas. The same is true of the Caddo culture of the southern border of the Eastern Woodlands and the Plains. In general, then, as we move from the Eastern Woodlands area to the Plains area, we will be dealing with similar cultural forms and, in many instances, with adaptations of eastern-originated and developed elements to a new western environment.

The Plains area extends from southern Alberta, Saskatchewan, and Manitoba to central Texas.[147] Its eastern border follows the western edges of Minnesota, Iowa, and Missouri. As we said in the preceding section, this boundary is not sharp, either environmentally or culturally. The western border is the Rocky Mountains. In the Southwest, the Llanos Estacados of western Texas and eastern New Mexico also may be included in the Plains area, although here Plains cultures and those of the Southwestern tradition tended to merge. Terrain throughout the region is almost uniformly flat, with elevation generally rising gradually from east to west. Tall prairie grasses cover the eastern part of the Plains, and here the river valleys, which flow south and east into the Mississippi system, are wooded. To the west the prairie grasses give way to the shorter plains grasses, and rainfall becomes progressively less. Natural food resources were less varied on the Plains than in the Eastern Woodlands, but the lack of variety was compensated for by the quantity and quality of the big herd animals of the grasslands—in Pleistocene and early post-Pleistocene times the mammoth and now-extinct species of bison, later the modern bison (*Bison bison*).

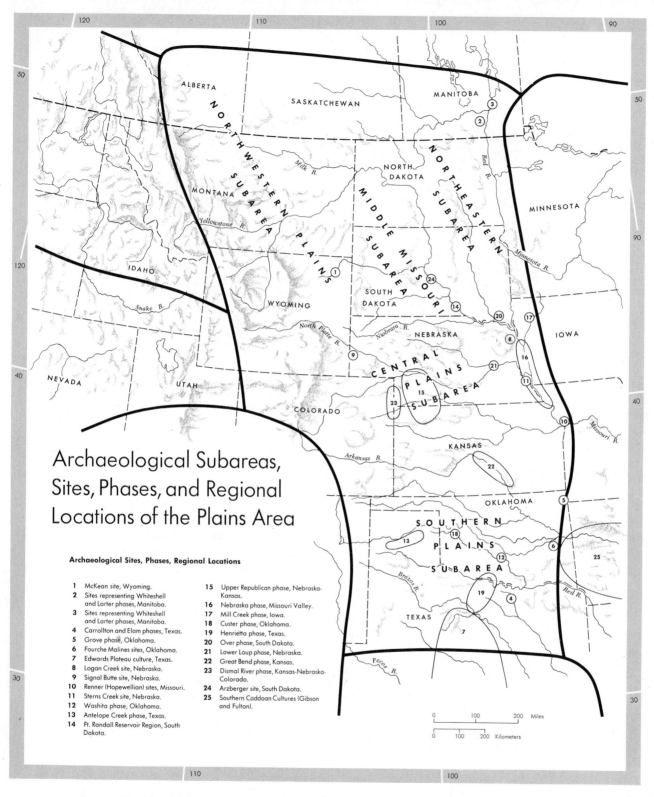

Archaeological Subareas, Sites, Phases, and Regional Locations of the Plains Area

Archaeological Sites, Phases, Regional Locations

1 McKean site, Wyoming.
2 Sites representing Whiteshell and Larter phases, Manitoba.
3 Sites representing Whiteshell and Larter phases, Manitoba.
4 Carrollton and Elam phases, Texas.
5 Grove phase, Oklahoma.
6 Fourche Malines sites, Oklahoma.
7 Edwards Plateau culture, Texas.
8 Logan Creek site, Nebraska.
9 Signal Butte site, Nebraska.
10 Renner (Hopewellian) sites, Missouri.
11 Sterns Creek site, Nebraska.
12 Washita phase, Oklahoma.
13 Antelope Creek phase, Texas.
14 Ft. Randall Reservoir Region, South Dakota.

15 Upper Republican phase, Nebraska-Kansas.
16 Nebraska phase, Missouri Valley.
17 Mill Creek phase, Iowa.
18 Custer phase, Oklahoma.
19 Henrietta phase, Texas.
20 Over phase, South Dakota.
21 Lower Loup phase, Nebraska.
22 Great Bend phase, Kansas.
23 Dismal River phase, Kansas-Nebraska-Colorado.
24 Arzberger site, South Dakota.
25 Southern Caddoan Cultures (Gibson and Fulton).

Figure 5-68. Subareal divisons follow Wedel (1961).

EASTERN NORTH AMERICA

There are four cultural traditions associated with the Plains area, and these succeeded one another, although in overlapping fashion. The earliest was the Big-Game Hunting tradition. In Chapter 2 we outlined how this long-dominant pattern of aboriginal life expired in the Plains during the Altithermal climatic stage at about 4000 B.C. It was replaced by a variant of the Archaic tradition called the Plains Archaic. This Plains Archaic tradition developed locally from the Big-Game Hunting tradition as the latter was modified by environmental pressures and was exposed to diffusion and interchange with the Archaic of the Eastern Woodlands area. Considerably later, the Woodland tradition penetrated the Plains from the East, bringing pottery and some agricultural techniques. The Plains Woodland was succeeded by the vigorous Plains Village tradition,[148] a synthesis of Archaic and Woodland elements plus influences from the expanding Mississippian tradition which occurred along the Missouri River and its tributaries in the eastern Plains. Sedentary village life based on river-valley farming and the more ancient tradition of buffalo-hunting characterized the Plains Village tradition. Some of its influences were felt farther west, but the far-western regions of the Plains remained non-agricultural and, at least in their subsistence pursuits, more akin to the older Plains Archaic mode of life. In the seventeenth and eighteenth centuries, the horse was introduced to the Plains tribes with significant modifying results on both the Plains Village and the more strictly buffalo-hunting cultures of the West. During the nineteenth century such tribes as Mandan (Siouan) and the Arikara and Pawnee (Caddoan) represented the Plains Village tradition in its fullest form, while to the west the Dakotas (Siouan) and the Blackfoot and Cheyenne (Algonquian) were marginal to that tradition. The map (Fig. 5-69) shows the locations of the many Plains area tribes in the nineteenth century. In many instances these ethnic groups can be identified with the late prehistoric or proto-historic archaeological cultures of their particular regions.

Chronology. The general archaeological chronology of the Plains area is given in Fig. 5-70. Keep in mind the distinctions between cultural traditions and culture periods. The Paleo-Indian Period, prior to 4000 B.C., was the time of the Big-Game Hunting tradition on the Plains. The Archaic Period, from 4000 B.C. to 0, was the time of the Plains Archaic tradition. The Woodland Period, from 0 to A.D. 1000, was characterized by the first appearances of the tradition of that same name and by the spread of this tradition in the Plains area. The final aboriginal period, the Plains Village Period, from A.D. 1000 to 1800, again bears the same name as the tradition that most characterized it, although some Woodland cultures persisted after A.D. 1000. The Early division of the Plains Village Period (A.D. 1000–1550) was prior to European contacts; the Middle Division (A.D. 1550–1800) was the proto-historic era of initial contacts and assimilation; the Late Division (after A.D. 1800) takes us into the fully historic period and into the still greater transformation of the native cultures.

The Plains Archaic Tradition. The origins of the Plains Archaic tradition are obscured by the millennium of extreme heat and aridity that marked the climax of the Altithermal climatic stage on the Plains between 4000 and 3000 B.C. During this time human occupation was at a minimum. At least, few archaeological sites from the Central or Northwestern Plains can be dated to this thousand-year span.[149] Not until around 3000 B.C. did a number of Plains Archaic site occupations appear. The evidence has been gathered from refuse and artifact complexes indicating a subsistence dependent on hunting and food-collecting. A good example would be the McKean phases or subphases of Wyoming in the Northwestern subarea of the Plains.[150] The principal projectile point of these complexes, the McKean point, was a lanceolate with an indented base which in its outline, although not in its indifferent chipping, resembled earlier Big-Game Hunting points of the same Wyoming region. Other points,

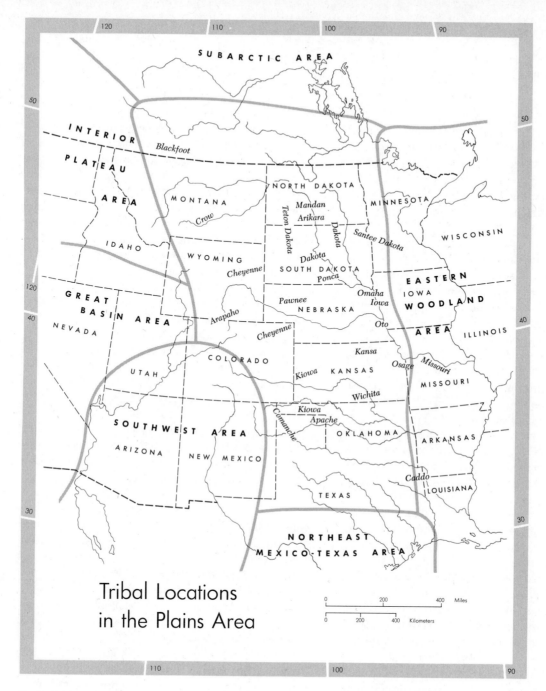

Figure 5-69.

Tribal Locations
in the Plains Area

stemmed and notched, were more reminiscent of the Desert or Eastern Archaic traditions. The same may be said for the milling and handstones that presumably were used to grind vegetable foods. It is impossible to say for certain whether influences were specifically Eastern Archaic or Desert owing

to the basic typological similarities between these two traditions; in view of the geographic location of the McKean culture, however, it seems most likely that borrowing or even migration, if there was any, came from the area of the Desert cultures. The McKean sites included camps, caves, and bison kills, and the deposits date from 3000 to 500 B.C. Some refuse locations show a depth that indicates fairly steady, if seasonally intermittent, occupation. McKean points and grinding stones were supplemented by an array of chipped-stone skin-dressing tools and bone implements. Collections of food debris have yielded the remains of bison, deer and antelope, birds, reptiles, and mussel-shells.[151]

Elsewhere in the Plains similar although not typologically identical assemblages have been found which can be dated to the Archaic Period. In the Northeastern subarea, the Whiteshell and Larter phases, covering about the same time span

as the McKean, have been identified from sites near Winnipeg, Canada. In these sites, McKean-like points were found mixed with more typically Archaic stemmed and notched forms, by which the McKean types later were replaced.[152] Influences here appear to have come mainly from the east. We know, of course, that at a much earlier date sites with Archaic projectile points were found all along the zone of contact between the Eastern Woodlands and the Plains, so that for a long time

Figure 5-70. Chronological chart for the Plains area. Only selected phases and cultures are shown in the subarea columns.

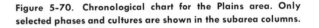

MAJOR PERIODS	DATES	NORTHWESTERN PLAINS	CENTRAL PLAINS	SOUTHERN PLAINS	MIDDLE MISSOURI	NORTHEASTERN SUBAREA
PLAINS VILLAGE	1700	Blackfoot Crow	Pawnee Omaha Dismal River	Comanche Kiowa	Mandan Arikara	Siouan Tribes
	1500		Lower Loup		Arzberger	
		(Plains Village-derived Pottery)		Henrietta Washita Custer	(Various Sites) Over Mill Creek	(Burial Mounds)
	1000		Upper Republican Nebraska	Antelope Creek		
WOODLAND		(First Appearance of Pottery?)			(Cord-roughened Pottery Sites)	
	500					Nutimik
			Loseke Creek			
	A.D.		Renner (Hopewellian)			? Anderson
	B.C.	(Various Later Sites)				
ARCHAIC						
	1000		Signal Butte I			
	2000				(Pre-ceramic Sites)	Larter Whiteshell
	3000	McKean		Edwards Plateau		
	4000		Logan Creek			
	5000			Portales	?	
PALEO-INDIAN	7000	Eden Scottsbluff Agate Basin	Simonsen Lime Creek	Plainview		
	9000	Folsom	Folsom Dent	Folsom Clovis		

Figure 5-71. The Red Smoke site, southwestern Nebraska. A representative Plains riverine early site location. The deeply buried occupation strata in this alluvial terrace were first exposed by stream-cutting. A great number of Plainview points were taken from a stratum of intermediate depth. Above this were later Plains Archaic artifacts; below were materials of earlier Big-Game Hunting cultures. (Courtesy Laboratory of Anthropology, University of Nebraska.)

inhabitants of the Plains were exposed to Eastern Archaic influences.

In the Southern Plains Eastern Archaic influences are quite definite. Phases such as the Grove and pre-ceramic Fourche Maline of Oklahoma and the Carrollton and Elam of north-central Texas occupy a border position between the Eastern Woodlands and the Plains.[153] The Edwards Plateau culture of central Texas is closely related to the Eastern Archaic, but also exhibits some Desert culture elements. It appears to have lasted a very long time and to have had its beginnings even prior to 4000 B.C. The Edwards Plateau culture is also called the "burned rock mound" culture, a designation taken from the typical midden heaps which contained ash and burned stone in addition to animal-bone refuse. Edwards Plateau was a part of an even larger entity designated as the Balcones culture, which extends from east to west across the entire state of Texas.[154] Sites which can be identified as Plains Archaic are also found from the Texas Panhandle, to the north of the Edwards Plateau group, and in the Oklahoma Panhandle and northeastern New Mexico. Some of the New Mexico sites have been found in dry caves, and as might be expected, their perishable artifacts and debris are similar to those of late Desert culture sites or the pre-ceramic levels of the Ozark Bluff Dwellers.[155]

There are fewer Archaic sites in the Central Plains, the geographic heart of the area. Some, like Logan Creek in eastern Nebraska, are earlier than 4000 B.C. and are in effect the westernmost representatives of the early Archaic culture of the Eastern Woodlands.[156] More typical of the Plains area, but considerably later, is the Signal Butte I phase of the North Platte Valley in western Nebraska. The Signal Butte site is a camp situated on the top of a high, eroded butte formation. The Signal Butte I phase has been identified from a basal level of midden at that site, fire hearths, and storage pits. Quantities of burned and split animal bones were found, and judging from these remains and from the chipped-stone weapons and tools, it seems probable that hunting was the most important economic activity of the inhabitants, but wild vegetal foods were also gathered. Signal Butte projectile points were both lanceolate and stemmed. Radiocarbon dates indicate an occupation of from about 1500–1000 B.C., and there is also evidence on the Butte of a later pre-ceramic occupation which may also be classed generally as Plains Archaic. Pottery appeared only in the uppermost level of the site.[157]

The Woodland Tradition. The hallmark of the Woodland tradition in the Plains area is of course pottery. This pottery first appeared at about the beginning of the Christian era and clearly derived from the Eastern Woodland area. It is reasonable to suppose that maize agriculture was associated with the first appearance of the Woodland tradition on the Plains, although the evidence is by no means uniform and conclusive. In the vicinity of Kansas City, on the Missouri River, Woodland sites of Hopewellian genre have yielded Indian corn, and these sites date from the early centuries A.D. A bit farther north and west, however, Woodland-type pottery has been found in sites that seem to be approximately contemporaneous with the Kansas City Hopewell examples but are devoid, or almost devoid, of direct evidences of maize. These distributions and circumstances may be only the result of fortuitous preservation of plant remains, or they may indicate that some Woodland tradition traits, such as pottery, preceded maize farming from the East onto the Plains.

The Hopewellian evidences in the Central Plains center around Kansas City and from there for 100 miles or more west into Kansas. The Hopewellian occupation was clearly riverine, with stable but small village sites. Dwellings may have been pole-and-mat structures, and the dead were buried in earth mounds containing rough-stone masonry chambers. This Kansas City Hopewell, or Renner, phase was obviously a western extension of the eastern Hopewell culture, presumably by a route from Illinois. Maize and

beans have been found in the village refuse along with deer and bison bones and a complement of large stemmed or corner-notched projectile points and skin-working tools. Hopewell-style platform pipes were a Renner item, and the pottery was clearly Hopewellian, with rouletted or rocker-stamped surface treatments.[158]

The non-Hopewellian Woodland tradition cultures of the Central Plains include such phases as Sterns Creek and Loseke Creek of the Missouri Valley in Nebraska, Iowa, and southern South Dakota, as well as other similar cultures in Kansas and eastern Colorado. The sites of these cultures are small. Dwellings must have been of pole-and-mat or some other perishable and flimsy type. The dead were either buried in the village or

Figure 5-72. The Signal Butte site, western Nebraska. (Courtesy Laboratory of Anthropology, University of Nebraska.)

Figure 5-73. Sterns Creek Woodland vessel. (Courtesy Nebraska State Historical Society.)

they are more easily related in content, as well as in chronological equivalence, to the Plains Village tradition. An exception is, of course, the Woodland horizon of the eastern fringe of the Southern Plains in Oklahoma, as represented in the later, pottery-bearing phases of Fourche Maline. Another is the presence of what appears to be early cord-roughened pottery at the far opposite edge of the Southern Plains in northeastern New Mexico and southeastern Colorado.[160] Other than these two marginal occurrences of the Woodland tradition or its influences, the Southern Plains cultures of the Woodland Period (0–A.D. 1000) appear to have remained in the Archaic tradition.

In the Missouri Valley of the Dakotas, a thick, cord-roughened Woodland pottery is stratigraphically the earliest ceramic of the subarea and frequently has been found beneath alluvial river

Figure 5-74. Woodland pottery vessel from the Valley site, Nebraska. (Courtesy Nebraska State Historical Society.)

placed in nearby ossuary pits or under small burial mounds. As we have mentioned, direct evidence of agriculture is absent or scanty. Artifact inventories were not radically different from those of the Plains Archaic tradition and included, besides chipped points, knives, and scrapers, food-grinding slabs and handstones. Pottery was not very plentiful and primarily took the form of jars which were rounded or pointed at the bottom and either undecorated or cord-roughened.[159]

In the Southern Plains little is known of the Woodland tradition, at least in an unadulterated and relatively early form. Later phases, such as the Washita or Antelope Creek, exhibit Woodland elements as, for example, cord-roughened pottery; but the total make-up of these phases is such that

deposits. Later pottery finds from the same localities were also cord-roughened and had rims that were frequently decorated with raised bosses or with the impressions of single cords in geometric patterns. There are burial mounds in the Middle Missouri subarea, and according to W. R. Wedel, they can be found all along the river valley through both Dakotas. It is assumed that they are associated with Woodland cultures and that some date from the Woodland Period of the Plains. Mound burials, both primary and secondary, have been discovered, and in the Fort Randall Reservoir region log-covered pit tombs have been found.[161]

Burial Mounds in the Plains. It is to the east and north of the middle Missouri Valley, however, that artificial mounds are most numerous.[162] These are found throughout eastern South and North Dakota and in southern Manitoba Province about as far north as Winnipeg. This territory composes the Northeastern subarea of the Plains. The mounds usually are situated on high ground, on bluffs above valleys, or on eminences overlooking lakes. We know nothing about their associations with villages or camp sites. Some are simple circular or oblong tumuli, of which the largest are 3 or 4 meters in height and 25 to 30 meters in diameter, although most are considerably smaller. Such mounds frequently occur in groups. Others are long, low, linear mounds or embankments which terminate in rounded ends or expansions. These linear mounds may be quite long and are often placed so that they are connected at right angles to one another. Both the circular-oblong and linear types were used for burials. These burials, both primary (usually flexed) and secondary, have been found in submound, timber-covered pits or in the mounds. Artifacts were buried in the graves, including rather specialized pottery vessels—small globular ollas with short, outflared, and quadrated collars. The body of the olla was often decorated with a continuous incised spiral line encircling the body or with vertically or horizontally placed incised lines. The type suggests the Mississippian rather than the Woodland tradition, and together with marine-shell gorgets bearing derivative Southern Cult designs, implies a relatively late date for the mounds in which the vessels were unearthed.

As Wedel has cautioned, however, very little is known of either the chronological position or the cultural affiliations of the Dakota and Manitoba mounds. Their exploration and excavation over the past 100 years has been casual and amateur, and we cannot say whether the mounds all pertain to the same cultural groups or the same time period. Apparently they antedate European contacts in this part of the Plains (A.D. 1650–1700). It is likely that they were constructed by peoples who were primarily hunters, fishers, and collectors rather than true farmers, for the Northeastern subarea lies largely north of the limits of aboriginal American agriculture. Their most probable cultural context is the Woodland tradition but the Woodland tradition in a marginal and essentially non-horticultural setting, and their most likely temporal position is in the later Woodland and Early Plains Village Periods of the Plains chronology.

Wedel has reviewed the hypothesis that the Dakota mound-builders were Siouan peoples who moved into the Plains from Minnesota, and he suggests the Blackduck phase of that state as a possible prototype.[163] Blackduck was a late Woodland culture and one which seems to have developed out of the Effigy-Mound culture of the upper Mississippi Valley. It in turn had eastern antecedents in the burial mound and mortuary practices of Adena and Hopewell. But in connection with the spread of the Woodland tradition into the Plains it should be kept in mind that village site materials, particularly pottery, show the presence of the tradition in the Northeastern Plains long before the time horizon of the Blackduck phase. Whether the burial mound idea was carried or diffused to the Dakotas and Manitoba as early as this, remains to be determined.

The Northwestern Margin of the Plains. Neither the Woodland nor the Plains Village traditions extended to the Northwestern subarea except in attenuated and modified forms. There are no burial mounds there, nor was agriculture practiced. The people hunted and collected food. In a sense a Plains Archaic tradition continued beyond the upper chronological limits (A.D. 1) of that period. However, significant changes appeared in the later cultures. Small side-notched or stemmed projectile points replaced the larger Archaic dart point, a shift undoubtedly indicative of the switch from the atlatl to the bow-and-arrow as the principal hunting weapon. Perhaps the bow was more successful against bison, for site remains attest to somewhat more bison- and other large-game hunting than during the immediately preceding millennia. The only Woodland tradition diagnostic was cord-marked pottery, only a few specimens of which have come to light. Along the eastern edge of the subarea, such pottery may antedate A.D. 1000; elsewhere, however, cord-marked pottery was later, as was the pottery which derived from the Plains Village tradition.[164]

The Plains Village Tradition: Prehistoric. The Plains Village tradition, which first appeared (ca. A.D. 1000) during the period of the same name, witnessed the establishment of a successful agricultural pattern in at least the eastern half of the Plains area. Subsistence still drew significantly on hunting, but maize, beans, and squash assumed equal if not greater importance in the economy. Gardens were tended in river bottoms. Nearby, on ridges or bluff tops, were small communities composed of substantial timber and earth-covered houses. Pottery was more plentiful than in Woodland sites, and there is in general every evidence of a more abundant life than formerly. The tradition was approximately contemporaneous with the Mississippian tradition of the Eastern Woodlands and, as might be expected, shows relationships to Mississippian cultures in ceramic work, including vessel forms, incised decoration, handles, and rim-effigy adornments; in smoking pipes; other artifacts; and in occasional design elements reminiscent of the Southern Cult. More generally, of course, the two traditions shared the same cultivated food plants and an increased dependence on such items as staples. Yet, agricultural subsistence on the Plains resulted in a different cultural adjustment from that of the Eastern Woodlands, and the Plains Village tradition should not be regarded as a direct and simple transferral of a Mississippian way of life to the Plains area. Rather, it involved a refashioning of certain Mississippian elements, including agriculture, to fit a new environmental setting and to be fused with the earlier heritages of the Plains Archaic and local Woodland traditions.

Early Plains Village tradition cultures are best documented in the Central Plains subarea. They include the Upper Republican (of western Nebraska and Kansas), the Nebraska (of eastern Nebraska and Kansas and adjacent Iowa), and the Smoky Hill (of eastern and north central Kansas). A highly characteristic feature of these cultures was the timber and earth-covered house type we mentioned previously. These earth-lodge houses were usually rectangular and the roofs were supported by four large central posts. Closely set smaller posts along the edge of the floor area supported the outer edges of the roof structure. A simple unlined fireplace was in the center of the floor, and the smoke from the fire ascended

Figure 5-75. Exposed post-mold and floor pattern of an Upper Republican house, Harlan County, south-central Nebraska. (Courtesy Laboratory of Anthropology, University of Nebraska.)

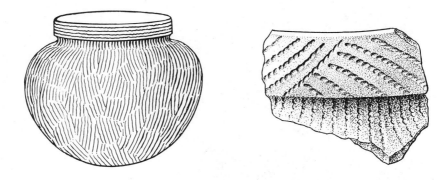

Figure 5-76. Upper Republican pottery from Nebraska. *Left:* Vessel from the Sweetwater site. The body is marked with a cord-wrapped paddle, the rim with cord-impressions. *Right:* Rim sherd. Again, body shows cord-wrapped paddle markings; the rim, diagonally placed cord-impressions. (*Left,* Redrawn from Champe, 1936; *right,* redrawn from Strong, 1935.)

through a central roof opening. Entry was through a long, narrow, covered passage. Storage pits were beneath the floor. In the eastern Plains, these houses were semi-subterranean; farther west they were constructed on the ground surface. This house was the prototype of similar, but modified, earth-lodge houses of the proto-historic and historic periods. The settlement pattern involved single houses, or small subclusters of from two to four houses, dotted at random and rather widely spaced over a small village or hamlet area. Wedel estimates that 50 to 100 persons lived in these earth-lodge villages.[165]

The ceramics of the early Plains Village tradition cultures exhibited a Woodland-Mississippian blend of features. In the Upper Republican complex, the Woodland elements were stronger. Jars were almost always cord-roughened. Rims were differentiated from the body wall by thickening and by incision, as in Hopewellian types, though the style and rendering was quite different from Hopewellian patterns. To the east in the Nebraska culture, Mississippian features were somewhat more pronounced. Vessels tended to be more globular, were more often smooth-bodied rather than cord-roughened, and bore rim lugs or handles. Through pottery we can most easily trace the routes and means by which Mississippian cultures influenced those of the Plains Village tradition. A major pathway was, of course, the Missouri River, and the definitely Mississippian pottery sites located near Kansas City on the east bank of this river must have been one source of contact. Farther north another zone of contact and acculturation lay in northwestern Iowa where the Mill

Creek culture, through its stratigraphic history, can be seen gradually moving from Mississippian-style pottery into something that was more like the early Plains Village wares.[166]

Although plant remains, including corn, are frequently found in early Plains Village tradition sites, corn-grinding implements were not well

Figure 5-77. Nebraska phase pottery vessel. (Courtesy Nebraska State Historical Society.)

Figure 5-78. Pottery effigy handle, Nebraska phase. (Courtesy Nebraska State Historical Society.)

Figure 5-79. Bone artifacts of the Nebraska phase, including pins, awls, tubes, beads, fishhooks, flaking tools, and what may be fragments of wrist-guard ornaments. (Courtesy Nebraska State Historical Society.)

developed. At some sites milling stones have been found, but none were specialized. It may be that wooden mortars and pestles, in the manner of the Eastern Woodlands, were used for maize-grinding. The principal agricultural digging tool was a hoe made of a bison shoulder blade. Bison, antelope, deer, and other animal bones have been identified in Nebraska and Upper Republican site refuse, and along the Missouri River fish were taken with bone hooks and with harpoons. Typical chipped-stone projectile points were small, triangular, side-notched arrowheads. This point was but another variety of the kind which came into use over much of North America in late pre-Columbian times. As might be expected, from the environmental setting and from the earlier cultural background of the Plains, the skin-dressing flint scraper (small snub-nosed end-type and side-scrapers) and the

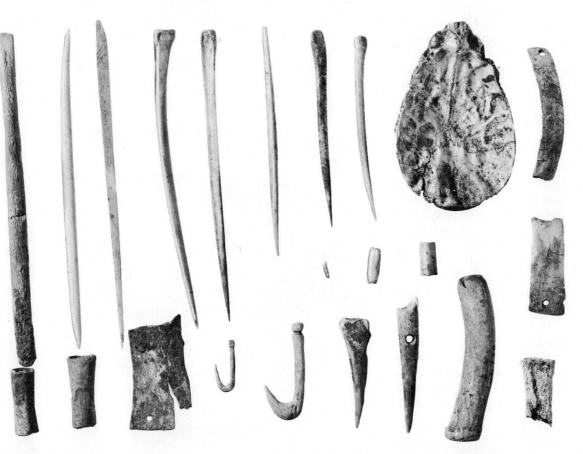

Figure 5-81. Shell ornaments and fragments of ornaments, Nebraska phase. (Courtesy Nebraska State Historical Society.)

Figure 5-82. A stone pipe, sculptured as a human head, Upper Republican phase. (Courtesy Nebraska State Historical Society.)

Figure 5-80. An engraved bow-guard or wrist-guard of bone, Upper Republican phase. Total length, about 14 cm. (Courtesy Nebraska State Historical Society.)

flint knife continued to be important items. Bone awls, bodkins, and needles were also used in preparing skin clothing. Ornaments such as gorgets, bow-guards or wrist-guards (Figs. 5-79, 5-80), bracelets, and pendants were made from bone and shell, but few have been recovered and these were relatively simple. The Upper Republican pipe was a stone, equal-armed elbow shape, whereas the Nebraska pipe, frequently of pottery, was curved and was sometimes effigy-modeled. In all these early Plains Village tradition cultures mass burial was practiced. Upper Republican pit ossuaries near villages have disclosed secondary burials.

Figure 5-83. Nebraska phase pottery pipes. (Courtesy Nebraska State Historical Society.)

Artifacts of all types have been found in these burials, although not in great numbers.[167]

Other early Plains Village tradition cultures developed on the Southern Plains. The Washita River phase peoples of central Oklahoma followed the same rectangular, four-center-post house pattern of construction that is associated with the Upper Republican culture. The economy here was also divided between hunting, fishing, and farming. The bison scapula hoe was utilized, as village site debris has indicated, and stone metates and manos were used to grind corn.[168] Other related phases are the Custer, also in Oklahoma, and the Henrietta, of the Brazos and Red River drainages of north central Texas.[169] On the east these Southern Plains village peoples were bordered by and had contacts with the somewhat more settled Caddo tribes of the late Gibson and early Fulton phases of southern Caddo culture. On the west along the Canadian River in the north Texas Panhandle we come to the Antelope Creek phase, to

which we have already referred in discussing the easternmost margins of Southwestern cultures (in Chapter 4). As we mentioned, Antelope Creek villages were made of stone and adobe, multi-roomed, Pueblo-like dwellings. Aside from the architectural style, however, the Antelope Creek phase was similar in its artifacts and economic basis to the Plains Village tradition cultures farther east.[170]

Early Plains Village cultures are well represented along the Middle Missouri in the Dakotas, and recent excavations by archaeologists of the Federal River Basins Surveys program have provided a rich inventory of materials on which to base cultural reconstructions. Middle Missouri houses, long and rectangular, were 30 to 65 feet long (about 9 to 20 meters). The superstructures were built in and over deep, straight-walled pits. Entry was through a long, descending passage. The fireplace was located on the midline of the long axis of the house but somewhat closer to the entrance than to the end wall. The roof was supported by both small wall posts and larger interior posts. Presumably it was of hip-form and was covered with grass thatch and possibly earth. The individual houses were built in ordered rows or more haphazardly arranged. Six to 20 houses composed a village, whose population probably totaled between 50 and 300 persons. Ditches and palisades usually surrounded these villages. The general pattern of life at this time in the Middle Missouri was very similar to life in the Central Plains, although the archaeological complexes differ in detail. A time trend has been worked out in ceramics in which earlier cord-roughened vessels were gradually replaced by vessels with smoothed or thong-wrapped paddle-marked surfaces.[171] East from the Middle Missouri, the sites of the Over phase in southeastern South Dakota also adopted the long-rectangular house type plus the bison shoulder-blade hoe and the underground storage pits of the Plains Village agricultural pattern. The ceramics, which included various cord-roughened, smoothed, and incised surface treatments, sometimes bore animal effigy handles and other traits which tend to link this phase to the Upper Mis-

sissippian cultures of the Eastern Woodlands.[172] Like Mill Creek, in Iowa, to which it is related, the Over phase of South Dakota also reveals affiliations with early Mississippian cultures (Temple Mound I Period) such as Old Village Cahokia and Aztalán.

The Plains Village Tradition: Proto-historic and Historic. The transition from the cultures of the Early Plains Village Period to those of the Middle (proto-historic) and Late (historic) periods has not yet been traced specifically and satisfactorily. To be sure, there are many Early Plains Village features which were obviously ances-

Figure 5-84. Excavated floor pattern of an Early Plains Village Period house in the Middle Missouri subarea. This rectangular structure is at the Langdeau site, South Dakota. Such structures, with a wide porch at front, were typical of the Grand Detour phase. This structure dates to about A.D. 1200. (Courtesy River Basin Surveys, Smithsonian Institution.)

Figure 5-85. Pottery vessels (restored) from the Middle Missouri subarea. *a:* A cord-impressed vessel (Foreman Cord Impressed) such as is typically associated with houses of the Early Plains Village Period in the Middle Missouri. *b:* An incised and handled vessel (Mitchell Broad Trailed) found in sites of the Early Plains Village Period in the Middle Missouri but apparently intrusive from Mississippian tradition cultures to the east. *c:* A vessel (Stanley Braced Rim) characteristic of the proto-historic to historic period Arikara sites of the Middle Missouri. (Courtesy River Basin Surveys, Smithsonian Institution.)

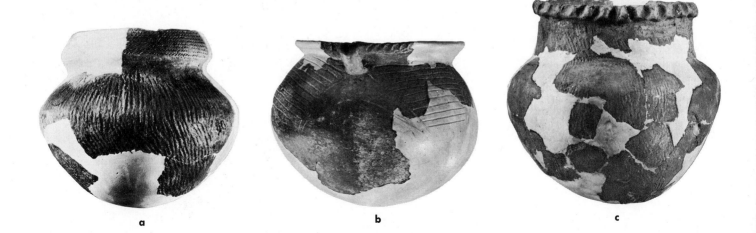

a   b   c

tral to later developments in the area, and it is evident that we are dealing with the same cultural tradition; yet cultural continuity is broken in the very heart of the area. At some time between A.D. 1400 and 1500 in the Central subarea the Upper Republican small villages were abandoned. Nomadic invaders from the west, such as the Plains Apache, may have been responsible. Or it may have been prolonged drought.[173] Whatever the circumstances, it seems most likely that the Upper Republican peoples were driven or attracted eastward toward the Missouri Valley, and it may be that they were the ones who here reconstituted a culture known as the Lower Loup phase.

Lower Loup sites are found on the banks of the Loup and Platte Rivers in east central Nebraska.[174] These sites were large villages ranging from 15 to 100 acres in extent, and this great change in village size from previous settlement patterns may reflect a banding together for defensive purposes against a raiding enemy. The sites are dotted with many earth-lodge rings from 25 to 50 feet (7.5 to 15 meters) in diameter, which are circular and slightly below ground level. They contained central fireplaces and bear evidence of four main post supports, a second series of smaller posts farther out toward the roof edge, and smaller wall posts at the perimeter. They also show traces of entrance passages and, in some instances, a small altar-like platform against the wall opposite the entrance. Some, but not all, of the Lower Loup sites were fortified. Individual primary burials accompanied by grave goods have been found in or near the villages. Pottery was not cord-roughened but usually was treated with a grooved paddle to produce a ridged surface. A distinctive ceramic feature was a series of small handles below the rim, which gave a cloistered or arcaded appearance to the upper part of the vessel. Incised triangles with hachure fillings around the shoulder of the jar were the usual decorative motif. Lower Loup villages were partly sustained by agriculture, the crops being cultivated with the Plains bison-bone hoe and stored in the traditional deep village cache pits. Hunting, of course, remained impor-

Figure 5-86. Lower Loup pottery vessel. (Courtesy Nebraska State Historical Society.)

tant. The dog was the only known domesticated animal, and it is likely that he was used to draw the pack travois. No archaeological finds attest to the presence of the horse; however, it is certain that at sometime in the Lower Loup cultural continuum horses were introduced, for they appear in the Pawnee villages in the same region during the

Figure 5-87. Historic Pawnee vessel from Nebraska. (Courtesy Nebraska State Historical Society.)

historic period. Very likely, the Lower Loup phase was the culture of the proto-historic Pawnee.[175]

In central Kansas a phase known as the Great Bend was related to and in contact with the Lower Loup, and this Great Bend phase is believed to have been the culture of the Indians of Quivira whom Coronado visited in 1541.[176] The Great Bend sites were agricultural villages and we know that they date to the sixteenth and seventeenth centuries by means of Pueblo glaze-paint trade wares and fragments of Spanish armour. It is likely that the people of Quivira were the Caddo-speaking relatives of the Pawnee, the Wichita.

The proto-historic and historic horizon of agricultural villagers is not well represented in the Southern Plains subarea, although certain sites on the Arkansas River in Oklahoma and on the Oklahoma-Texas border show some resemblances to the Great Bend phase.[177] For the most part, however, the marauding Apache and Comanche dominated this part of the Plains in late times.[178] Farther north along the western marches of the Central Plains in western Kansas and Nebraska and eastern Colorado, sites identified as Apache are known archaeologically as the Dismal River culture. The Dismal River sites reflect a culture that was only minimally horticultural, largely oriented toward hunting, and divided in its other material aspects between the Lower Loup and

Figure 5-89. Dismal River pottery vessel. (Courtesy Nebraska State Historical Society.)

Great Bend phases on the one hand and the Southwestern Pueblo cultures on the other.[179]

In the Middle Missouri subarea, circular-house villages replaced those of the earlier long-rectangular houses, a trend similar to what developed on the Central Plains. The proto-historic period here was also a time of convergence or coalescence of traditions with Mississippian Oneota influences from the east blending with resident Plains Village patterns. Also, there is some indication that the Upper Republican culture of the earlier Plains Village horizon may have contributed to the proto-historic cultures of the Middle Missouri. The large palisaded village known as the Arzberger site, east of Pierre, South Dakota, has been interpreted by A. C. Spaulding as representing a community of Upper Republican derivation influenced by both resident prehistoric Mandan culture and by Oneota.[180] In this connection Wedel has added that such an eastward and northward movement of an Upper Republican group could correspond to the time of the desertion of the Upper Republican sites of Nebraska at the end of the fifteenth century.[181] This movement may have marked the

Figure 5-88. Exposed post-mold and floor pattern of a Dismal River house, White Cat Village site, Nebraska. (Courtesy Laboratory of Anthropology, University of Nebraska.)

Figure 5-91. Oneota pottery vessel, Richardson County, Nebraska. (Courtesy Nebraska State Society.)

Figure 5-90. Plains Village house and fortification patterns of the proto-historic and historic period. *Top:* Two circular earth lodges excavated at the Fort George Village on the Missouri River near Pierre, South Dakota. The village was protected by a ditch and palisade and probably was occupied by the Arikara in the historic period. *Bottom:* Post-mold pattern of a defensive bastion at the palisaded Black Partisan site, a large village of the proto-historic period in central South Dakota. (Courtesy River Basin Surveys, Smithsonian Institution.)

separation of the Arikara from the parent Pawnee. Most of the circular-house villages of the Middle Missouri were not, however, fortified. The individual houses had shallowly excavated floors, central fire-basins, four centrally located large roof posts, and outer perimeter posts to support the edge of the roof and walls. The proto-historic Middle Missouri farmers, fishers, and hunters made cooking, storage, and water jars. Surfaces of this pottery were paddle-marked with a grooved or thong-wrapped paddle, and decoration, when applied, consisted of a diagonal line incision on the vessel shoulders.[182]

Although the exact lines of descent from these proto-historic Middle Missouri archaeological complexes cannot yet be traced in detail, we can be fairly certain that the later Mandan, Hidatsa, and Arikara tribes relate back to them. We know that in the eighteenth century there was a gathering together of Indian populations in large fortified village sites of as many as 200 houses. Horses were acquired from the south and west, guns and other European manufactures from the east, and for over 100 years these Middle Missouri villagers enjoyed a prosperity as traders, farmers, and buffalo hunters. Eventually, however, the Indians gave way to the encroachments and diseases of the whites, and the large settlements diminished or disappeared after the middle of the nineteenth century.[183]

The Far Western Plains. Only in the western Plains and particularly in the Northwestern subarea did native Indian culture continue vigorously in the nineteenth century. There the "classic" aborigine of the Plains pursued his way as a mounted bison hunter with little or no farming subsistence. Some of these tribes, such as the Assiniboine, Blackfoot, and Arapaho, were descendants of peoples who had never participated in the Plains Village tradition to any significant extent and who had always been nomadic or semi-nomadic hunters. Others like the Cheyenne and the Dakota Sioux had ancestral origins in the Plains Village tradition but their tribes had changed their mode of life as they moved farther westward onto the High Plains.[184]

Northeast Mexico-Texas

The Area—Its Peoples and Cultures. The Northeast Mexico-Texas culture area includes northern Tamaulipas, Nuevo León, Coahuila, eastern Chihuahua, and southern Texas (see map, Fig. 5-92).[185] It embraces that territory which lies surrounded by Mesoamerica, the Southwest, the Plains, and the Eastern Woodlands, so that its borders are drawn at the limits of spread of these neighboring areas. On the south the boundary is set at the Rio Soto la Marina, in Tamaulipas, about halfway between the Panuco River and the Rio Grande. This appears to be the northernmost frontier of firmly established Mesoamerican cultures of the Huasteca.[186] From the Soto la Marina,

Figure 5-92.

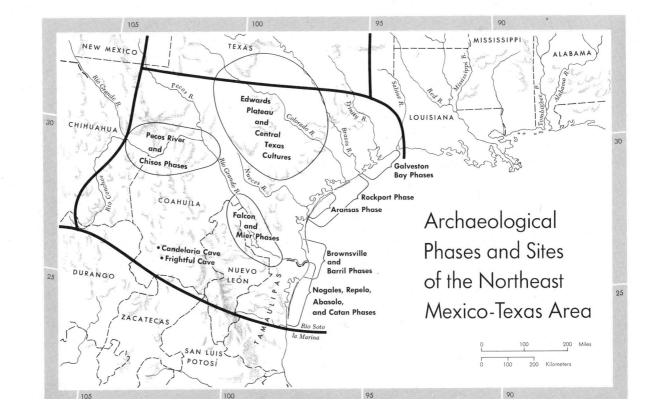

Archaeological Phases and Sites of the Northeast Mexico-Texas Area

the line runs northwestward, passing to the north of the Mesoamerican outposts of the Sierra de Tamaulipas, and then turns north to cross the Rio Grande so as to include the Big Bend subarea of Texas. Here the frontier is established by Pueblo sites which are found in the Rio Grande Valley as far south and east as the confluence of the Conchos.[187] The vast region that comprises the "horn" of southern Texas and all of the Texas coast are also a part of the Northeast Mexico-Texas area. Directly to the north, sharp limits are difficult to fix, since the Central Texas region can best be described as a transitional zone leading into the Southern Plains.[188]

The area is one ill-suited to or impossible for native agriculture. In Tamaulipas, the coastal plain is narrow and lined with dunes, ponds, and mud flats. Behind the plain a forbidding dissected peneplain of small mesas, hills, and arroyos rises to the Sierra Madre Oriental and the northern Mexican Desert Plateau. Climate is semi-arid or dry temperate. Precipitation is not unusually low on the coast, but it is spasmodic and not seasonally patterned and does not produce a suitable growing season. Occasional downpours alternate with droughts, so that conditions frequently vary from mud to dust. Vegetation is scrub thorn interspersed with some grasses.[189] Similar environments continue north into Texas. Here the coastal plain is wider, but the lagoons and sandy wastes of the shore are backed only by uninviting rolling plains and rocky outcrops. Mesquite and thorny bush cover still prevail, although there are grasses and stands of hardwood in the valleys of the rivers that flow into the Gulf.[190] In the absence of agriculture, native subsistence depended on a variety of natural resources. Along the immediate shore, fish and shellfish were caught; inland, the diet consisted primarily of seeds, nuts, cactus fruits, and roots. Hunting was pursued throughout the area. Most game was small, although there were bison and antelope in south Texas during the nineteenth century.

The Spanish explorer, Cabeza de Vaca, saw the hunting, food-collecting and fishing peoples of the Texas coast in 1534, and other Spanish explorers followed him into the Rio Grande Valley and to Tamaulipas during the next two centuries. For the most part the tribes of the area were broken up and the native cultures were dissolved by the close of the eighteenth century, although some groups continued until well into the nineteenth. The tribes of the proto-historic and historic periods include those grouped together under the names Tamaulipec, Coahuiltec, Karankawa, and Tonkawa. Generally all are lumped together into a Coahuiltec language family, although the linguistic evidence for such a classification is very limited. Only the Toboso and the Lipan to the west and north of the Coahuiltec belong to another major language group, the Athapascan. These two tribes are believed to be late proto-historic or historic arrivals to the area from the north.[191]

The Coahuiltec language family is sometimes classed together with the Hokan of Baja California and the Colorado River Valley into a Hokan Coahuiltec superstock.[192] W. W. Taylor, in commenting on the distribution of these tribes, has argued that the Hokan-Coahuiltec languages are among the oldest in the Americas and that a significant correlation appears between their locations and the marginal survivals of a Desert cultural tradition.[193] In this light, Northeast Mexico-Texas appears as a refuge where ancient Coahuiltec populations and non-agricultural Desert cultures maintained a long, continuous residence from ancient times almost down to the present day.

Scattered projectile point finds show that cultures of the Big-Game Hunting tradition of the North American Plains once were present in the area.[194] Later the dominant cultural pattern was one that relates closely to the Desert tradition. In fact some of the culture phases of Northeast Mexico-Texas are the same as those we already discussed in treating the Desert tradition and its incipient agricultural variants in the Mesoamerican area. The Northeast Mexico-Texas cultures also relate to the Archaic traditions of the Eastern Woodlands and the Plains. Without attempting to

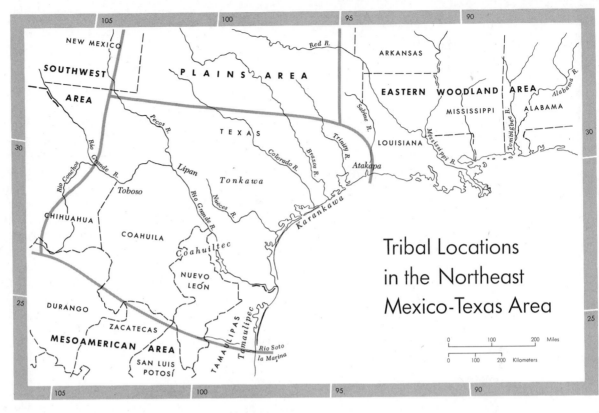

NEW MEXICO
SOUTHWEST AREA
PLAINS AREA
ARKANSAS
EASTERN WOODLAND AREA
Red R.
MISSISSIPPI
ALABAMA
Alabama R.
Tombigbee R.
Mississippi R.
Sabine R.
Trinity R.
Brazos R.
Colorado R.
LOUISIANA
TEXAS
Pecos R.
Rio Grande R.
Rio Conchos
Lipan
Toboso
Tonkawa
Atakapa
CHIHUAHUA
COAHUILA
Rio Grande R.
Nueces R.
Karankawa
Coahuiltec
NUEVO LEÓN
DURANGO
ZACATECAS
TAMAULIPAS
Tamaulipec
Rio Soto la Marina
MESOAMERICAN AREA
SAN LUIS POTOSÍ

Tribal Locations in the Northeast Mexico-Texas Area

0   100   200 Miles
0 100 200 Kilometers

Figure 5-93.

force a settlement of this taxonomic difficulty, we shall simply refer to Desert-Archaic cultures.

Chronology. For chronological reference we utilize three simply termed periods for the area—Early, Middle, and Late (see chart, Fig. 5-94). The Early Period antedated 5000 B.C. As we have just said, a Big-Game Hunting cultural tradition seems to have been represented in some regions, or possibly throughout the entire area at this time. There are, however, indications that Desert cultures also were in existence in Coahuila in the Early Period. The Middle Period extended from 5000 B.C. until A.D. 700. The period was completely dominated by Desert, Archaic, or Desert-Archaic cultures, which continued into the Late Period, the period which ran from A.D. 700–1850. The beginning date marked the advent of ceramics in some of the cultures concerned although not in all of them; the terminal date is an approximation of the final aboriginal occupations of parts of the area. The time from A.D. 1520 to 1850 refers to the proto-historic and historic periods.

The Tamaulipas and Texas Coasts: Pre-ceramic Cultures. Aside from those few indications of Big-Game Hunting projectile points which have come from the area, the beginnings of the Desert-Archaic tradition are most clearly seen in several culture phases or groups of phases. To turn first to Northern Tamaulipas, you will recall that a Nogales phase was a part of the Tamaulipas mountain sequence of the Huasteca subarea of Mesoamerica and that we classed it as a variant manifestation of the Desert tradition in which incipient plant cultivation was practiced (Chapter 3). According to MacNeish, this same Nogales phase extended throughout Northern Tamaulipas, where it has been identified in campsites by its flint projectile points and tools. Although traces of incipient cultivation have been found in the Nogales phase refuse levels of the Sierra de Tamaulipas caves, we do not know if the practice was followed at the open campsites farther to the north. Otherwise, insofar as the artifacts reveal it, the conditions of life were the same. Nogales is estimated as having lasted from about 5000 to

3000 B.C., and in Northern Tamaulipas it was succeeded by a complex known as Repelo. Repelo is differentiated from the earlier phase by the first appearance of stemmed dart points, although the unstemmed triangulars and round-based points of Nogales continued to be used. Side-notched and corner-notched types also appeared for the first time in this sequence, and mortars and rectangular metates were more widely used than in Nogales. There are artifact cross-ties with the La Perra and Almagre phases to the south and, to the north,

with the Falcon phase of the Southwest Texas region. Repelo is estimated to date from 3000–1800 B.C., and the succeeding Abasolo phase from 1800 B.C. to somewhere in the first millennium A.D. The Abasolo projectile points were smaller than the Nogales or Repelo varieties, but were still dart-type rather than arrow points, both stemmed and unstemmed. A significant cultural change is reflected in the first evidence of utilization of marine foods and seashore sites.[195]

In the Texas coastal region, the Aransas phase shell middens in the vicinity of Aransas and San Antonio Bays are judged to be approximately con-

Figure 5-94. Chronological chart for the Northeast Mexico-Texas area.

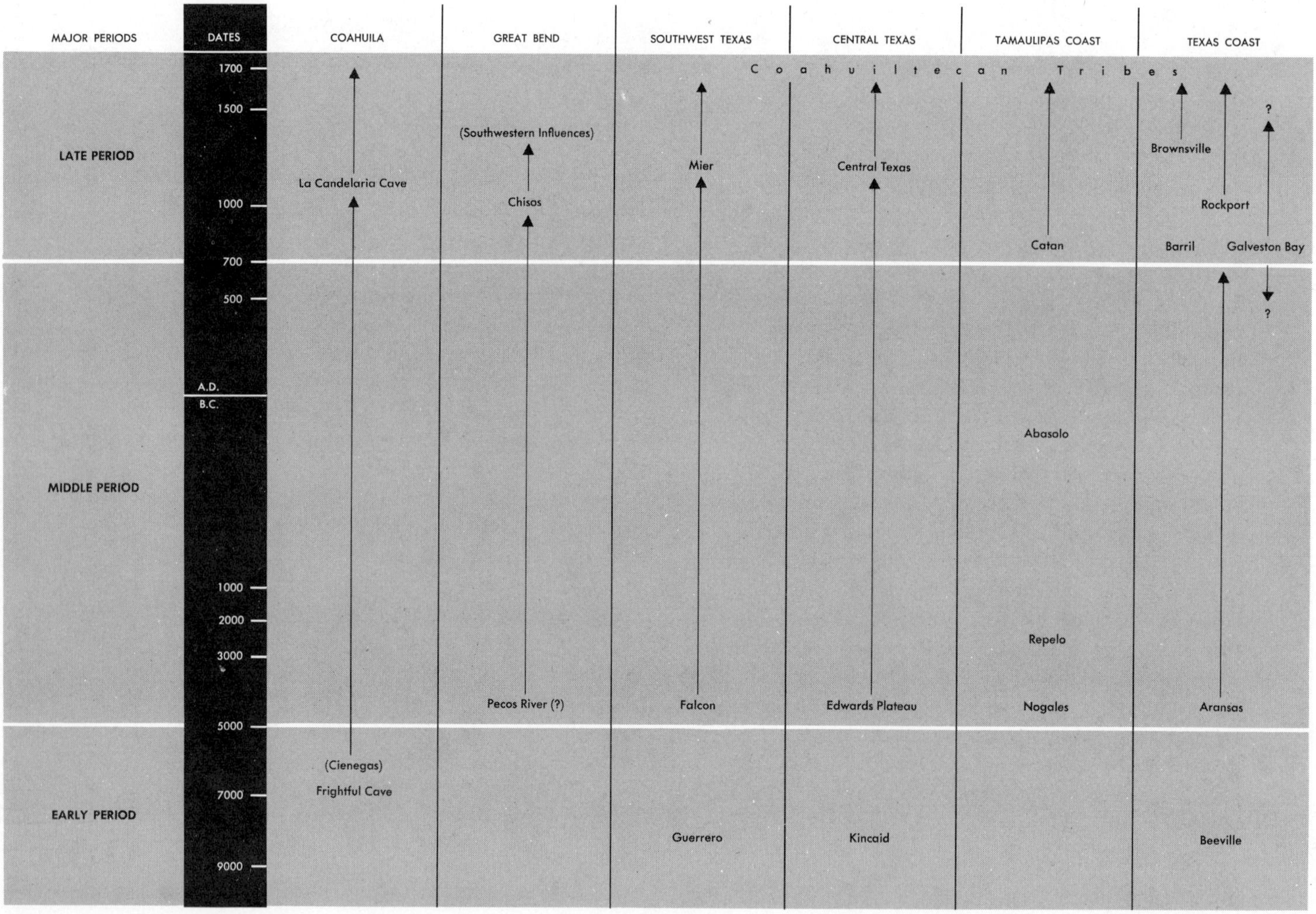

MAJOR PERIODS	DATES	COAHUILA	GREAT BEND	SOUTHWEST TEXAS	CENTRAL TEXAS	TAMAULIPAS COAST	TEXAS COAST
	1700				Coahuiltecan Tribes		
LATE PERIOD	1500			Mier	Central Texas		Brownsville
			(Southwestern Influences)				?
	1000	La Candelaria Cave	Chisos			Catan	Rockport
	700						Barril Galveston Bay
	500						?
	A.D.						
MIDDLE PERIOD	B.C.					Abasolo	
	1000						
	2000					Repelo	
	3000						
	5000		Pecos River (?)	Falcon	Edwards Plateau	Nogales	Aransas
EARLY PERIOD	7000	(Cienegas) Frightful Cave					
	9000			Guerrero	Kincaid		Beeville

temporaneous with the Nogales-Repelo-Abasolo cultures of Northern Tamaulipas. Aransas projectile point forms included the unstemmed rounded-base Abasolo type, although the more common varieties were stemmed, side-notched, or corner-notched. All are considered to be dart points. Drills, scrapers, gravers, knives, and milling stones and handstones also have been recovered. These artifacts link to the Edwards Plateau culture of central Texas as well as to Northern Tamaulipas. More distinctive of Aransas were shell implements, especially axes or adzes and gouges made from conch columellae. These were similar to some Eastern Archaic types and to specimens from later cultures of the Southeastern Gulf states, and also resemble such items from the West Indies and the Caribbean shore of Venezuela. As Suhm, Krieger, and Jelks observe, however, it is uncertain if an historical connection exists or if these shell implements were merely the result of adaptations to a common environmental condition.[196]

The Tamaulipas and Texas Coasts: Ceramic Cultures. What Suhm, Krieger, and Jelks refer to as "Neo-American" cultures followed these Northern Tamaulipas and Texas coast "Archaic" cultures.[197] The differentiation is based on the presence of pottery and of small arrow points in later levels. In our chronological organization, these pottery-bearing cultures fall into the Late Period (A.D. 700–1850); typologically, however, we continue to consider them a part of the Desert-Archaic traditions. In Tamaulipas, south of the Rio Grande delta country, the Catán phase is one of these cultures.[198] Catán was characterized by tiny arrowheads, including a type known as the Starr Concave point, which had a flared and fishtailed base. The associated pottery was almost certainly not a local product, but the result of trade from the Huasteca country of southern Tamaulipas. Catán is dated from somewhat before A.D. 1000 up to historic times. North of Catán on both sides of the Rio Grande delta are two phases which are designated as Barril and Brownsville.[199] Barril is presumed to be the earlier of the two,

and estimates indicate that the total time range of both parallel the Catán dates. Aransas influences are seen in the use of conch-shell implements and ornaments—projectile points, round-pointed at the tip and wedge-based, made of conch columellae; shell gouges; and engraved shell pendants. The pendants probably hark back to the Huasteca country. It is possible that the engraved shell pendant idea, so common to some eastern United States Mississippian cultures, was derived from Mesoamerica by this coastal route; however, the Barril and Brownsville forms were considerably less elaborate than either Huastecan or Mississippian pendants. Both Barril and Brownsville were shoreline fishing and hunting cultures. Barril sites occupied an area south of the Rio Grande delta; Brownsville sites lay mostly on the Texas side of that river. Guides to a chronological separation of the two complexes are Huasteca V (Las Flores) potsherds associated with Barril and Huasteca VI (Panuco) sherds associated with Brownsville. At Brownsville sites, glass arrow points have been discovered, an indication of European proto-historic and historic contact.[200] It seems most likely that these phases relate to the Coahuiltec Indians.

Farther north on the Texas coast the Rockport and Galveston Bay phases, located in the vicinities of these cities, followed the earlier Aransas phase and are probably the archaeological cultures to be associated with the Karankawa tribe. The sites are shell middens along the beaches or camps on the inland coastal plain, and the type of life implied was similar to that of the Barril or Brownsville phases. However, far fewer shell artifacts have been found here than at the Barril-Brownsville sites, and the ceramics associated with Rockport and Galveston Bay were quite different from those of the Rio Grande delta. Rockport pottery was decorated with a black asphaltum in rather carelessly made band, loop, dot, and wavy-line designs. Another characteristic was the deep interior scoring of bowls. Hemispherical and sub-globular bowls were two popular shapes, as was a narrow-necked bottle. No firm conclusions have been reached about the affiliations of Rockport pottery. It does

Figure 5-95. Rockport Black-on-gray sherds from various sites in Nueces and Aransas Counties, coastal Texas. (Courtesy Texas Archaeological Salvage Project, University of Texas.)

not seem to be related to the pottery complexes of the Eastern Woodlands, Plains, or Southwest, nor too obviously to the pottery of the Huasteca. It has all the appearances of a local development but certainly a local development stimulated by one of these neighboring pottery traditions. If one had to make a choice, stimuli from the south and the Huasteca seem the most likely possibility. The Rockport phase lasted until the nineteenth century, although its beginnings, fully prehistoric, go back perhaps to A.D. 1000.[201]

Although Galveston Bay culture was in many ways similar to Rockport, its ceramics were quite different. Incision rather than asphaltum paint was the common decorative technique. Deep cylindrical jars and deep wide-mouthed bowls with horizontal incised line patterns below the rim were prominent vessel types. Other design variations included pendant triangles filled with incised

lines or punctations, crossed diagonals or fields of diamonds, and lines ticked with punctations. The decorative technique and the designs were strongly reminiscent of the Coles Creek culture of the lower Mississippi Valley, and it is likely that inspiration for them came from that direction. Just what time span Galveston Bay pottery covered is uncertain, although the discovery of what might be a Tchefuncte trade sherd in one site suggests a date as early as A.D. 500, or even before. The dominant similarities to Coles Creek, on the other hand, imply a dating nearer A.D. 1000. There is no conclusive evidence whether or not the Galveston Bay phase survived into historic times.[202]

Before passing from the subject of these Texas coastal ceramics, we should mention that current research, as yet not fully published, indicates that there may be an early sand-tempered, pointed-bottom vessel, incised pottery complex, in the region underlying Galveston Bay and probably the Rockport phase wares. According to E. B. Jelks, who has propounded this idea, such a pottery horizon also reached farther north, in the Caddo region of northeastern Texas, where it underlies the Gibson phase pottery of the Caddo culture.[203] The affiliations of this earlier pottery horizon are no clearer than those of the Galveston Bay and Rockport ceramics; however, with reference to the eastern United States, connections with the Woodland rather than the Mississippian tradition seem more likely. It may well be that Galveston Bay pottery developed from such an early stratum and that Rockport pottery also had related origins but developed under influences from the Huasteca.

Southwest Texas and the Great Bend. Westward, away from the coast, the shell tools, pottery, and adaptations to the marine economy that marked the phases we have just been discussing were missing from the cultures of Southwest Texas. The Falcon phase, as we mentioned, may date back as early as 5000 B.C. The projectile points characteristic of the phase were the unstemmed, large, Tortugas (triangular), Abasolo (ovate-triangular), and Refugio (long-ovate or

Figure 5-96. Galveston Bay pottery from various sites in Chambers and Harris Counties, Coastal Texas. Item *j* is a pointed vessel base without decoration. (Courtesy Texas Archaeological Salvage Project, University of Texas.)

leaf-shaped) types. The economy reflected Desert tradition influences, although seeds probably were ground in wooden pestles, for ground-stone implements were not utilized. Falcon was succeeded by the Mier phase, in which a strong cultural continuity was maintained. The appearance of smaller dart points, stemmed points, and arrow points were the principal diagnostics of change. Mier occupies a chronological place between Falcon and the historic horizon.[204]

Farther west the Great Bend phases probably began as early as Falcon, although the earliest for which information is substantial is the Pecos River phase, which is believed to have lasted long enough to have spanned most of the first millennium A.D. The projectile points of the Pecos River phase were predominantly the large stemmed and barbed forms, but some unstemmed types similar to the Falcon variety have been found. Milling stones and handstones were widely used, and from dry caves have come a great many items such as wooden atlatls; atlatl darts; coiled, twined, and twilled basketry; and yucca-leaf sandals. The Chisos phase succeeded the Pecos River and continued the essentially Desert type culture up until about A.D. 1400; however, in later levels Southwestern trade pottery has been recovered along with corn, squash, and beans.[205]

Coahuila. South of the Big Bend subarea in southern Coahuila, a particularly dura-

ble variant of the Desert cultural tradition flourished. Taylor's discovery of the Cienegas phase at Frightful Cave indicates that it began as early, perhaps, as 6900 B.C., and there are signs that the same general pattern persisted up until Spanish colonial times. This pattern, according to some authorities, closely resembled the Big Bend cultures.[206] Another cave in the same region, La Candelaria, has produced an extremely rich inventory of burial artifacts dating to the twelfth to fourteenth centuries.[207] By this time, the atlatl had been largely replaced by the bow-and-arrow, and small stemmed and barbed projectile points were the common types. The economy of the Candelaria people is believed to have been divided between small-game hunting and fishing in nearby lakes. Oddly, the wild-plant food complex, generally so typical of the Desert tradition, was alien to the Candelarians, as the absence of milling stones and grinding stones indicate. Perhaps wooden pestles and mortars were used, yet their absence from the cave in which many other wood objects were found is curious.[208] Among the items from Candelaria are necklaces of fiber and of serpent vertebrae, ceremonial deer antler headdresses, shell beads and pendants, wooden bows-and-arrows, curved throwing sticks, and wooden "guardapúas" which may have been used for ritual blood-letting. This last may have been a custom diffused northward from the Mesoamerican civilizations.[209]

The Area As a Corridor for Mesoamerican Influences. Before turning from the Northeast Mexico-Texas area, we should say something about its role and position in the transmission of influences from Mesoamerica north to the Eastern Woodlands. As we know, both the Woodland and the Mississippian traditions of the East were significantly influenced by Mesoamerican cultures. The discovery of maize in Woodland sites is one definite testimony to this influence; mortuary mounds, rocker-stamped pottery, and figurines possibly are others. In the Mississippian tradition new species of maize were clearly Mesoamerican-developed, as were pyramid mounds, a variety of ceramic traits, and at least some of the iconography of the Southern Cult. The problem is not whether there are Mesoamerican elements in the Eastern Woodland area but rather the processes by which they arrived.[210]

Six possible routes have been proposed for Mesoamerican-Southeastern United States contacts. One of these involves northern South America, the West Indies, and a crossing to Florida, and refers more appropriately to South American than Mesoamerican diffusions. The case for such contacts is not convincing and can be dismissed as having played only a minor role, or no role, in the development of Eastern Woodland cultures.[211]

A second route is one wholly by water, across the Gulf from some point in Mesoamerica to the shores of the southeastern United States. Such a route is a possibility and cannot be ruled out; neither can it be directly verified or disproved.

The four routes which involve the Northeast Mexico-Texas area are: (1) a course from Coahuila to the Rio Grande and then eastward across the Texas Plains into the Woodlands; (2) along the islets and lagoons of the Tamaulipas and Texas coasts; (3) by an inland "Gilmore Corridor"; and (4) by an inland "Southern Overland Route." The first of these, the western route, may have

been used but probably not very intensively and only at a relatively late prehistoric to historic time. The remaining three routes are all possibilities, and it is likely that any or all of them were the ways by which the important Mesoamerican stimuli were passed to the Mississippi Valley.[212]

The north Tamaulipas-Texas coastal route would have had the advantage of offering canoe travel in and through a series of protected waterways. Unfortunately for the archaeologist, the off-shore islets of this coast are subjected to constant change and destruction from winds, tides, and hurricanes, and the mainland shore back of these islets and lagoons has been deeply covered in many places with thick mantles of clay and aeolian sand and clay. Hence the camp sites of Mesoamerican-Mississippi Valley travelers, if such there were, are likely to have been destroyed or buried. In this connection, however, it is worth mentioning that a small greenstone figurine, unmistakably Mesoamerican and probably of Guerrero origin, was found under a coastal dune near Corpus Christi, Texas, and a bird-effigy pottery vessel, reminiscent of both Mesoamerican and Mississippi Valley styles, was taken from a washout in the same locality.[213]

The Gilmore Corridor is a route which arches from northern Mexico through Texas to the pine forest country of eastern Texas and northern Louisiana. It lies well back from the coast, above the coastal plain but below the Edwards Plateau. The terrain is undulating prairie intersected by streams which flow southeastward to the Gulf. The Southern Overland Route parallels the Gilmore Corridor, but lies just south of it on the upper coastal plain. Both these routes were known to the Indians in historic times as a means of travel from Texas into Mexico. Both, however, cross terrain and environments inhospitable to native agriculture. The Coahuiltec tribes of the territories of the Gilmore Corridor and Southern Overland Route were non-agriculturalists who followed the hunting-collecting pattern of life described for the Desert-Archaic cultural tradition of the area. Thus any movements of Mesoamerican farming traits along these routes necessarily would have been rapid. Certainly they were transitory and had little effect on the local cultures.[214] Not until they reached the agricultural lands of Caddo country on the western margins of the Lower Mississippi valley did they find a receptive environment.

Such a set of circumstances favored the occasional and solitary movement of individuals, or small groups rather than mass migrations. The human mechanisms for this kind of diffusion through the Northeast Mexico-Texas area have been suggested by J. C. Kelley, who has used as a model the activities of the historical Coahuiltec tribes. These peoples followed a seasonally wandering food-search, ranging over considerable distances from coast to interior and from north to south. An individual Huasteca from the borders of Mesoamerica could have moved in a year's time to the fringes of the Mississippi Valley by attaching himself to one of these food-gathering bands after another. That such did happen is a reasonable supposition in view of the fact that in the seventeenth century Coahuiles Indians of southern Texas knew of and described to the Spaniards the Caddo Hasinai of eastern Texas. Members of their own tribe had obviously seen these village-and-town Indians, whose agricultural life was so different from their own.[215] It is also reasonable to suspect that they, or closely related peoples with whom they were in contact, were familiar with other villagers and townsmen of the Huasteca. In brief, these Coahuilteca and their relatives provided a kind of medium of survival and transit for the passage of the elements of village-and-town life which they in their environmental situation were unable to accept and assimilate. And such an hypothesis accords well with the appearance of Mesoamerican traits in the Eastern Woodlands, where we see them individually and thoroughly integrated into new patterns, as one would expect them to be if brought intermittently by few persons, and not implanted in full Mesoamerican complexes and contexts, as they would have been if introduced by large migrations of peoples.

Summary

In eastern North America, an Archaic cultural tradition became sufficiently distinctive by 5000 B.C. to characterize an Eastern Woodlands culture area. This tradition is believed to have had its earlier beginnings in the preceding two or three millennia and to have arisen from local adaptations of earlier Big-Game Hunting cultures to a woodland environment. Additional elements in its early formation appear to have been derived from the Desert tradition of the west. Still others, particularly the fashioning of utility and ornamental objects of polished stone, may have come from the north, ultimately from Asiatic boreal cultures; however, the extent to which these northern boreal zone cultures played a role in the development of the Eastern Woodlands Archaic tradition is uncertain, since many Archaic polished-stone artifacts are older in the southeastern United States than in the northern Woodlands.

A significant innovation in the Archaic tradition was the appearance of pottery around 2000 B.C. in the Southeastern subarea. This pottery was a thick, crude ware, tempered with plant fibers. The date of 2000 B.C. appears to be too early to explain the presence of fiber-tempered ware as the result of northern Asiatic and boreal influences; thus chances favor its appearance as a local invention or stimulation from Middle or South America.

A modified Archaic tradition existed in the Plains area, best explained as a diffusion from the east and a subsequent adaptation to Plains hunting conditions. South of the Plains, in the Northeast Mexico-Texas area, hunting and plant-collecting cultures were related to the Archaic tradition, although here that tradition seems best described as a blend between Archaic and Desert culture elements. This in brief was the situation in eastern North America at the climatic optimum of about 5000 B.C. and for the several millennia following.

At about 1000 B.C. a new pattern formed in the Eastern Woodlands area, the Woodland tradition. Woodland societies followed a mixed hunting and farming economy. Maize, derived from Mexico, probably was an important element in this new formation. Ceramics, cord-marked or fabric-impressed, most likely of boreal inspiration, was another. A third was a ceremonial complex involving burial in artificial mounds and maintained with other earthworks as special ceremonial sites. The Woodland tradition spread from the Ohio, Mississippi, and lower Missouri valleys westward into the Plains, becoming successfully established in the eastern river valleys of that area, although thinning out and disappearing in the drier, less favorable climates of the western and southern Plains. Except for some possible ceramic influences, it never penetrated to the Northeast Mexico-Texas area.

In the latter half of the first millennium A.D. another new and highly viable tradition, the Mississippian, began spreading from a center or centers in the Mississippi Valley. This tradition was firmly agricultural. Its settlements were permanent villages or towns, many of ceremonial importance, as is attested by the presence of rectangular, flat-topped mounds which were topped with temples, chiefs' houses, or other special buildings. The Mississippian tradition also introduced new ceramic techniques, including vessels with handles, bottle forms, a proliferation of effigy adornments, and frequent resort to engraving and painting to decorate the vessels. The new tradition blended with as well as replaced the older resident Woodland cultures. Thus while it became firmly established in the lower and central Mississippi valleys and in the Southeast, its imprint elsewhere was less; and cultures in the upper Mississippi Valley, Ohio Valley, Great Lakes, Northeastern, and Middle Atlantic subareas, although significantly modified, retained many Woodland elements.

Westward in the Plains, Mississippian influence appears to have been the crucial factor in the development of what has been called the Plains Village tradition, a blend of the earlier Woodland cultures of the Plains with those of Mississippian background. As might be anticipated, this Plains Village tradition, with its strong dependence on farming, became rooted only in the river valleys of the eastern Plains and did not, at least in its full form, move to the High Plains of the west or southward beyond the northern regions of Texas.

Mississippian culture did not spread into the Northeast Mexico-Texas area. The cultures here remained relatively static and conservative. Living sites were seasonal camps. Hunting, collecting, and fishing continued as the modes of subsistence. Pottery was introduced to the area a few centuries before A.D. 1000. At least one source of inspiration for some of this pottery was Mesoamerica, and this suggests the routes and means by which other, and earlier, influences passed northward from Mesoamerica through northeastern Mexico and Texas and on to the Eastern Woodlands, where they sparked the development of the Woodland and Mississippian traditions.

Footnotes

[1]Kroeber (1939, pp. 60–95, 101–108 and map 6) discusses the East as a culture area, or aggregate of culture areas, with reference to natural environment. He summarizes the views of earlier writers, particularly Thomas (1894), Holmes (1903), and Wissler (1922), with respect to both archaeological and ethnographic data. Kroeber's East is, in effect, the two areas described here as the Eastern Woodlands and the Plains. Kroeber does not include the Northeast Mexico-Texas area in his East.

[2]The Eastern Woodlands definition of this book approximates, but does not exactly fit, the culture areas of the ethnologists. It would correspond, more or less, to what Wissler (1922) designates as the Southeastern and Eastern Woodlands areas, the principal difference being that Wissler's Eastern Woodlands is extended farther north to include much of eastern Canada. The present definition would embrace all of Driver's (1961, map 2) "East" plus the eastern half of what he calls the "Prairie" area. These differences are largely the result

of fashioning the areas of this survey in accordance with archaeological rather than ethnographic data.

[3]The Woodland and Mississippian traditions have long been recognized as major cultural entities of the East. They are sometimes referred to as "Basic Patterns," "Basic Cultures," or "Patterns" in the Midwestern Taxonomic Classification. See, for example, Deuel (1935) or McKern (1939).

[4]Paleo-Indian is here used as a *period* name for the Eastern Woodlands *area*. It is not used as a *stage* or a *tradition* designation.

[5]The Ford-Willey (1941) chronological scheme for the East employs the terminology: Archaic, Burial Mound, Temple Mound. The Griffin (1952 a) scheme uses the names Archaic, Woodland, and Mississippian for similar divisions. I have used the former terminology for the periods of the area chronology in this chapter, especially to distinguish between cultural traditions (Woodland and Mississippian) and culture periods (Burial Mound and Temple Mound). For the Archaic tradition and the Archaic Period the term is, unfortunately, the same, and the particular usage will be specified in any given context in the text.

[6]For instance, in the Griffin (1952 a) chronology, a "Late Woodland Period" is indicated as being contemporaneous with the Mississippian Period. It is to avoid this particular kind of terminological inconsistency that I have used a separate set of terms for the cultural traditions and the periods (with the above-noted exception of Archaic).

[7]Lewis and Kneberg (1959).

[8]These subareas are conveniences and compromises. To be more accurate their boundaries would have to be redrawn for each time period.

[9]Sources for tribal and linguistic distributions include such works as Wissler (1922, 1938), Eggan (1952), and Driver (1961).

[10]Lewis and Kneberg (1959).

[11]See Goslin (1957); Struever (1962); Yarnell (1963, 1964).

[12]Lewis and Kneberg (1959, 1961).

[13]Neumann (1952). See also Chap. 1, p. 14.

[14]Lewis and Kneberg (1959).

[15]Lewis and Kneberg (1959).

[16]Lewis and Kneberg (1959).

[17]W. S. Webb and De Jarnette (1942, 1948).

[18]A four-period Archaic sequence is described by Webb and De Jarnette (1948) for the Flint River site and for the northern Alabama region in general. "Archaic 1" pertains to the lowest levels of shell mound sites and is defined by the presence of bone tools alone. "Archaic 2" is the period from the advent of chipped stone until the advent of polished stone, "Archaic 3" is defined by polished stone, and it terminates with the "Pottery 1" period which is characterized by fiber-tempered wares. (The subsequent "Pottery 2" and "Pottery 3" periods takes us beyond a concern with the Archaic.) Presumably, "Pottery 1" corresponds to what we have called here the Late Archaic; "Archaic 3" is the equivalent of the Middle Archaic Period; and "Archaic 2" is probably our Early Archaic Period. The curious "pre-flint" or "pre-chipped stone" horizon of "Archaic 1," in which only bone implements have been found, is unknown elsewhere in the Eastern Woodlands and suspect as a cultural isolate.

[19]W. S. Webb and De Jarnette (1942).

[20]Bullen, (1961).

[21]Claflin (1931); Fairbanks (1942).

[22]Lewis and Kneberg (1959).

[23]Wyman (1875).

[24]Goggin (1949); J. B. Griffin (1945); J. W. Griffin (1952).

[25]See, for instance, J. B. Griffin (1952 a).

[26]Ritchie (1962 b).

[27]Reichel-Dolmatoff (1961).

[28]J. L. Coe (1952, 1964).

[29]Byers (1959).

[30]J. L. Coe (1952, 1964).

[31]Byers (1959).

[32]Ritchie (1932, 1938, 1940, 1944, 1946); MacNeish (1952).

[33]Ritzenthaler (1946); Ritzenthaler and Wittry (1952); Miles (1951); Libby (1955).

[34]MacNeish (1948).

[35]Fowler (1959 a, b). See also Chap. 2, pp. 62–63.

[36]Mayer-Oakes (1951).

[37]Logan (1952).

[38]Wormington (1957, pp. 146–147).

[39]Logan (1952).

[40]Baerreis (1951, 1959); Bell and Baerreis (1951).

[41]Baerreis (1959).

[42]Harrington (1924).

[43]Gagliano (1963); Ford and Quimby (1945).

[44]C. H. Webb (1948); Ford, Phillips, and Haag (1955); Ford and C. H. Webb (1956).

[45]Various summaries of Archaic culture may be consulted: Haag (1942); Fairbanks (1949); Ford and Willey (1941); Griffin (1946, 1952 a, 1964); Phillips (1958, pp. 111–118); Byers (1959); Sears (1964).

[46]Byers (1959) summarizes this problem.

[47]Reichel-Dolmatoff (1961).

[48]See Neumann (1952) for a description and discussion of these physical types.

[49]Neuman (1952).

[50]Willey (1958).

[51]Sears (1948).

[52]See McKern (1937); Spaulding (1947). An opposing view would derive Woodland pottery from Old World boreal cultures but by way of the north Atlantic rather than across the Bering Strait (A. B. Kehoe, 1962).

[53]Chard (1961).

[54]See the stone chambers, covered with earth mounds, at La Venta, Tabasco (Drucker, Heizer and Squier, 1959).

[55]Yarnell (1964).

[56]Prufer and others (1965).

[57]Caldwell (1958).

[58]Webb and Snow (1945); Webb and Baby (1957); Morgan (1952).

[59]Morgan (1952).

[60]Spaulding (personal communication, 1965).

[61]Spaulding (1952).

[62]Morgan (1952).

[63]Morgan (1952).

[64]Griffin (1958).

[65]See Prufer and others (1965) for a discussion of this.

[66]Moorehead (1922); Shetrone (1926).

[67]Mills (1909); Shetrone and Greenman (1931).

[68]Willoughby and Hooton (1922).

[69]For general summaries of Hopewell culture see Shetrone (1930, pp. 185–222) and Morgan (1952).

[70]Prufer and others (1965) believe that these fortified Hopewell sites date from near the end of the period of Hopewell florescence (ca. A.D. 500) and reflect a period of disruption or troubles.

[71]For figurines see, especially, Willoughby and Hooton (1922) and McKern, Titterington, and Griffin (1945).

[72]Morgan (1952); Griffin (1956). Prufer and others (1965) have recently found evidence for this kind of a Hopewell settlement pattern in Ohio.

[73]Morgan (1952); Griffin (1960).

[74]Prufer and others (1965, p. 132).

[75]Morgan (1952).

[76]Quimby (1941).

[77]Griffin (1960).

[78]Cole and Deuel (1937); Wray (1952).

[79]Cole and Deuel (1937); Wray (1952).

[80]Maxwell (1952).

[81]See Maxwell (1952) for a discussion of this and a summary of opinion of various authorities.

[82]Wray (1952).

[83]J. W. Bennett (1952).

[84]Quimby (1952).

[85]Ritchie (1944); MacNeish (1952).

[86]Ritchie (1944).

[87]Schmitt (1952).

[88]J. L. Coe (1964).

[89]Kneberg (1952); C. W. Rowe (1952); Lewis and Kneberg (1946).

[90]A. R. Kelly (1938); Willey (1949 a).

[91]Lewis and Kneberg (1946).

[92]A. R. Kelly (1938); Willey (1949 a); Fairbanks (1952).

[93]A. R. Kelly (1938).

[94]Willey (1949 a).

[95]Moore (1903, 1907 a).

[96]Willey (1949 a).

[97]Willey (1949 a); also see Sears (1953, 1956).

[98]Ford and Webb (1956).

[99]Ford and Quimby (1945).

[100]Ford and Willey (1940).

[101]Setzler (1933).

[102]Greengo (1964); Ford (1951).

[103]K. G. Orr (1952).

[104]Phillips, Ford, and Griffin (1951); Griffin (1952 b).

[105]Neumann (1952).

[106]Haas (1958).

[107]Notwithstanding my own (Willey, 1958) earlier surmises on the possibilities of Iroquoian-Caddoan and Siouan migrations from Mesoamerica as being the agencies by which Adena-Hopewell and Mississippian culture elements were carried into the Eastern Woodlands. This hypothesis appears to be seriously weakened by linguists' caution in accepting the validity of the Hokan-Siouan superstock in which the Coahuiltec languages of northeast Mexico were included (Haas, 1958).

[108]Moorehead (1928); A. R. Kelly (1933).

[109]Wray (1952).

[110]Phillips, Ford, and Griffin (1951).

[111]Wray (1952).

[112]Barrett (1933); McKern (1946); McKern and Ritzenthaler (1946); J. W. Bennett (1952).

[113]Kneberg (1952).

[114]Lewis and Kneberg (1946).

[115]A. R. Kelly (1938).

[116]Fairbanks (1946).

[117]Fairbanks (1956).

[118]Sears (1953, 1956), for the Kolomoki site. Sears interprets the dominant burial mound complex, which he terms the Kolomoki complex, as being essentially post-Weeden Island. Willey's (1949 a) chronology and interpretations would place it as early Weeden Island or Weeden Island I phase.

[119]Ford (1951).

[120]Ford (1951).

[121]Newell and Krieger (1949).

[122]Krieger (1949).

[123]Wray (1952).

[124]Cole and others (1951); Maxwell (1952).

[125]J. B. Griffin (1952 b).

[126]Kneberg (1952).

[127]Kneberg (1952).

[128]Moorehead (1932); Fairbanks (1952).

[129]A. R. Kelly (1938); Fairbanks (1952); Caldwell and McCann (1941); Heye, Hodge and Pepper (1918).

[130]Moore (1905, 1907 b); De Jarnette and Wimberly (1941); De Jarnette (1952).

[131]Waring and Holder (1945); Ford and Willey (1941).

[132]Waring and Holder (1945).

[133]Krieger (1945); however, Krieger, in a later paper (Krieger, 1953) is convinced of Mesoamerican contact as a force in the development of the Southern Cult and cites several parallels between iconography in the Codex Nuttal and the Dresden Codex, on the one hand, and engraved shell gorgets from Spiro, Oklahoma, on the other.

[134]Ford and Willey (1941); J. B. Griffin (1944 a).

[135]Personal communication (1945–46).

[136]A. R. Kelly (1939).

[137]Willey (1949 a); H. G. Smith (1948).

[138]Quimby (1951); personal communication from Philip Phillips and Stephen Williams (1960–64).

[139]Quimby (1942).

[140]Swanton (1911).

[141]K. G. Orr (1952).

[142]J. B. Griffin (1943) is the principal source. The great earthworks at the Fort Ancient site proper, from which the culture takes its name, are of earlier date and of Hopewell affiliation.

[143]The skeletal material in question is definitely pre-Columbian.

[144]Ritchie (1938, 1961); MacNeish (1952).

[145]J. B. Griffin (1944 b).

[146]J. W. Bennett (1952).

[147]As defined by Wedel (1961). Wedel (1961) has been used as the principal reference in this section. See also a later summary by Wedel (1964).

[148]A term proposed by D. J. Lehmer (1954 a).

[149]See chronological chart in Wedel (1961, fig. 25).

[150]The Plains subareas (Central, Southern, Middle Missouri, Northwestern, and Northeastern Periphery) follow Wedel's definitions (1961).

[151]Mulloy (1954); Wedel (1961, pp. 250–251).

[152]Wedel (1961, pp. 235–236).

[153]See Chap. 2, section on "The Archaic Tradition" and Suhm, Krieger,

and Jelks (1954, pp. 76–80).

[154]See Chap. 2, section on "The Archaic Tradition"; see also Wedel (1961, pp. 135–136) and Suhm, Krieger, and Jelks (1954, pp. 102–112).

[155]Wedel (1961, pp. 133–135).

[156]Wedel (1961, p. 87).

[157]Strong (1935, pp. 224–239). Strong's classic volume marks the beginnings of modern archaeology in the Plains area. For additional comments on Signal Butte see Wedel (1961, pp. 85–86).

[158]Wedel (1943, pp. 15–62, 106–137, 193–208); see also 1961, pp. 88–89).

[159]Kivett (1952); Wedel (1961, pp. 89–92).

[160]Wedel (1961, p. 152).

[161]Wedel (1961, pp. 165–168).

[162]Wedel (1961, pp. 215–228); see also Hewes (1949) and MacNeish (1958).

[163]Wedel (1961, pp. 224–225).

[164]Wedel (1961, pp. 244–246, 255–259).

[165]Wedel (1961, pp. 92–100); Strong (1935, pp. 69–144, 124–175, 245–267); Wedel (1959, pp. 557–571).

[166]Wedel (1961, pp. 96–99).

[167]Wedel (1961, pp. 92–100).

[168]Bell and Baerreis (1951, pp. 75–81); Wedel (1961, pp. 139–140).

[169]Krieger (1946, pp. 87–159).

[170]Krieger (1946, pp. 17–74); Wedel (1961, pp. 142–144).

[171]Lehmer (1954 a, b); Wedel (1961, pp. 168–182).

[172]Meleen (1938); Over and Meleen (1941); Hurt (1951); Wedel (1961, pp. 212–213).

[173]Wedel (1941, 1953, 1961, pp. 100–101).

[174]Dunlevy (1936, pp. 147–247); Wedel (1961, pp. 109–111).

[175]Wedel (1938, 1961, pp. 108–111).

[176]Wedel (1942, 1959, pp. 211–377, 571–589, 1961, pp. 104–107).

[177]Bell and Baerreis (1951, p. 91); Steen (1953, pp. 177–188); Krieger (1946, pp. 161–164); Suhm, Jelks, and Krieger (1954, pp. 92–98); Wedel (1961, pp. 146–147).

[178]Wedel (1961, p. 146).

[179]Champe (1949); Gunnerson (1960); Wedel (1961, pp. 111–117).

[180]Spaulding (1956).

[181]Wedel (1961, p. 182).

[182]Wedel (1961, pp. 184–190).

[183]Wedel (1961, pp. 190–208).

[184]Wedel (1961, pp. 241–243).

[185]This is somewhat less than the size of the territory indicated by Driver (1961, map 2) as his northeastern Mexico area. He extends it considerably farther south and west into Mexico, but his data are essentially ethnographic.

[186]R. S. MacNeish (1958 a, p. 186) notes a few Huasteca sites for another 50 miles north of this, going as far as the San Fernando River; however, these sites at best are but small and quite late encroachments beyond the Soto la Marina frontier.

[187]Suhm, Krieger, and Jelks (1954, pp. 41, 45).

[188]The northeastern Mexico area can be divided into the following subareas, at least tentatively and for present organization and working purposes: (1) Northern Tamaulipas; (2) Nuevo León-Coahuila (those Mexican states up to just below the Rio Grande Valley); (3) Trans-Pecos or Big Bend (the Rio Grande Valley between the confluences of the Conchos and the Pecos, including portions of northern Coahuila and adjacent Texas); (4) Southwest Texas (The Texas Horn back away from the Gulf Coast); and (5) the Texas coast. Central Texas may be included in the area or in the Plains area. See Suhm, Krieger, and Jelks (1954, fig. 1).

[189]MacNeish (1958 a, pp. 10–14).

[190]Suhm, Krieger, and Jelks (1954, p. 118).

[191]See MacNeish (1958 a, pp. 14–21); Mason (1940); Driver (1961, maps 37, 38).

[192]Driver (1961, p. 576).

[193]Taylor (1961).

[194]See various observations on "Paleo-American Stage" in Suhm, Krieger, and Jelks (1954); see also Gonzalez Rul (1959).

[195]MacNeish (1958 a, pp. 178–183).

[196]Suhm, Krieger, and Jelks (1954, pp. 121–125); Campbell (1947).

[197]Suhm, Krieger, and Jelks (1954, pp. 20, 125–133).

[198]MacNeish (1958 a, p. 183).

[199]MacNeish (1958 a, pp. 184–192); Suhm, Krieger, and Jelks (1954, pp. 130–133); Sayles (1935); Campbell and Frizzell (1949).

[200]See MacNeish's chart (1958 a, p. 192).

[201]Suhm, Krieger, and Jelks (1954, pp. 125–128).

[202]Suhm, Krieger, and Jelks (1954, pp. 128–130); Wheat (1953).

[203]E. B. Jelks (personal communication, 1964).

[204]Suhm, Krieger, and Jelks (1954, pp. 136–143).

[205]Little known complexes (Maravillas, Santiago, and Red Bluff) appear to be the earliest representatives of a Desert-Archaic tradition in this subarea. These are succeeded by Pecos River and Chisos. A late, Livermore phase shows contact with Southwestern farmers. Suhm, Krieger, and Jelks (1954, pp. 51–62); Kelley, Campbell, and Lehmer (1940); Kelley (1952).

[206]Taylor (1956).

[207]Radiocarbon dates cited by Aveleyra Arroyo de Anda (1964).

[208]However, La Candelaria is a burial cave, not a living site, and it may be that the absence of grinding implements of either stone or wood is to be explained by this.

[209]Aveleyra Arroyo de Anda, Maldonado-Koerdell, and Martinez del Rio (1956).

[210]A sampling of papers on the question of Mesoamerican influences in Southeastern United States cultures includes: Phillips (1940); Griffin (1949); Krieger (1953).

[211]See my own summary of the question in Willey (1949 a, pp. 570–574 and 1949 b). See also Sturtevant (1960).

[212]See Krieger (1949); Kelley (1952).

[213]Krieger (1953).

[214]See Krieger (1953) for notes on occasional finds of Mesoamerican provenience reported from these regions of Texas.

[215]Kelley (1952).

In this chapter we deal with the culture history of those areas of North America which lie essentially outside and to the west of the principal pre-Columbian agricultural establishments. The exceptions, as we shall see, are marginal and relatively minor, brief, or late occurrences of native farming. Aside from this circumstance—that either hunting, fishing, or some manner of food-collecting were the dominant subsistence modes rather than agriculture—the native societies and cultures of the vast territory of western North America cannot be viewed in a unitary fashion, at least from the standpoint of culture history. This does not mean that there were no significant cultural interrelationships among the several areas which are included here. Such relationships did exist; the point to be made is rather that the historical tracing of the major cultural traditions with which we shall be here concerned is more readily accomplished within the framework of culture area divisions. The culture areas employed are conventional archaeological and ethnographical ones. (see Fig. 1-1).[1]

The first area is the Great Basin, embracing most of Nevada and Utah with adjacent portions of California, southern Oregon, southern Idaho, and southwestern Wyoming. This area is the ancient hearth of the Desert cultural tradition (see Chap. 2, pp. 55–60), the place where the tradition persisted in purest form down to historic and even modern times. Although for a relatively brief

Western North America

period the Southwestern cultural tradition (see Chap. 4) did spread into the Great Basin area, its influences there soon waned and by the time of European contact the way of life of the peoples of the Basin had returned once more to the earlier tradition which had been modified but never completely disrupted. Thus, for a time, it might be said that the northern boundary of the Southwest culture area could be extended to include a Northern Periphery which encompassed much of the physiographic Great Basin.

A second area is Baja California, comprising most of that peninsula. This was a non-farming area down to historic times, and although the archaeological evidence is still thin, the cultural pattern would appear to be that of the Desert tradition. Superficially at least, the Baja California tribes were similar to those of the Northeast Mexico-Texas culture area in that they followed a Desert hunting and collecting subsistence supplemented in coastal localities by marine foods.

A third culture area is California proper, including the interior valleys, mountains, and coast of most of that state. In early times (Chap. 2, pp. 53–55) this area was dominated by an Old Cordilleran hunting-collecting tradition which gave rise after about 5000 B.C. to a California Coast and Valley tradition. This too was a food-collecting, fishing, and hunting subsistence pattern which continued until late historic times.

The Northwest Coast area is a fourth. It is well-known to ethnographers for its spectacular salmon-fishing culture of the historic period. This culture had deep roots in the past and is designated here as the Northwest Coast tradition. Some of its remote antecedents may be found in the Old Cordilleran tradition. The area comprises a bit of northern California, coastal Oregon, Washington, British Columbia, and southern Alaska.

The fifth area is the Plateau, consisting mostly of interior portions of Oregon, Washington, and British Columbia, and of most of Idaho. The parent tradition here also was the Old Cordilleran, which gave rise, sometime after 5000 B.C. (Chap. 2, pp. 51–55), to the Northwest Riverine, another hunting, fishing, and food-collecting tradition.

The Persistence of the Desert Tradition in the Great Basin

The Geographic Scope of the Desert Tradition. In Chapter 2 we postulated that the Desert cultural tradition, that ancient way of life built around seed-collecting and seed-grinding and small-game hunting, had its beginnings as early as 8000–7000 B.C. and that its form and distinctiveness probably were attained in the next two or three thousand years in the Great Basin. We emphasized the long persistence of the tradition, but directed most of our interest toward the earlier manifestations; and although we commented about subareal and regional differences among the desert cultures, we were concerned mainly with cultural similarities. In this chapter we shall turn our gaze on the later continuities of the North American Desert way of life and summarize the subareal and regional variations.

There are several cultural subarea divisions included within the limits of the Great Basin area itself: southeastern Oregon, western Utah, northwestern Nevada, and southeastern California. Going beyond the physiographic province of the Basin proper,[2] but still remaining within somewhat similar arid environmental conditions, another territorial unit with a distinctive variety of the Desert culture is eastern Utah. This is the subarea that was for a time within the compass of the Southwestern tradition but then reverted to the Desert pattern. Still farther away, in Arizona and New Mexico, we recognize another variant of the Desert tradition in the Cochise cultural continuum, which underlies the Southwestern tradition cultures. Even more remotely and with the broadest application of the Desert tradition concept, other examples of the old Desert way of life are suggested by the Coahuila Lake cultures in northeastern Mexico (Chap. 5, p. 335) and by the pre-village farming levels revealed in the Mexican highlands prior to the rise of the Mesoamerican tradition (Chap. 3, pp. 78–83).

In sum, according to this view, a Desert tradition culture area might be said to have once covered most of arid western North America. In some places, such as Mesoamerica and the Southwest, and even for a time in a part of the Great Basin, it was replaced by other traditions. In most of the Great Basin physiographic province, however, the Desert cultural tradition continued into historic times, and it is there that we return to see it in its later manifestations.

Danger Cave, Utah. The stratigraphy at Danger Cave, in northwestern Utah, was our starting point for reviewing Desert culture evidences as these bore on the problem of early man in the Americas. We return to the cave and its stratigraphy to examine the continuity of this Desert culture into later times. The cave is situated a few miles from the Utah-Nevada border, near Wendover, Utah,[3] in a setting that is typical of the Great Basin desert. The cavern itself is in the rocky slope of an embayment of hills or low mountains that once formed the shore of an old glacial lake. Below the cave entrance, at the foot of the hills, are the saline flats of the Great Salt Lake Desert. Elevation is about 4250 feet above sea level. Summers are extremely hot, winters cold; rainfall is less than an annual 10 inches. Grasses and scrub bushes grow on the desert floor, and there are brackish seep springs along the edge of the desert which sustain thickets of bulrushes. Higher up in the surrounding mountains the precipitation is, of course, heavier. Here there are forests, and a somewhat different fauna from what is found on the desert floor. Such circumstances afforded primitive peoples two separate environmental niches within the radius of a few miles. The nature of plant foods in such a setting has already been described (Chap. 2, pp. 55–56). In addition, antelope, bison, mountain sheep, deer, rabbits, squirrels, various rodents, and waterfowl were available for the hunt.

You will recall that a Desert culture pattern, indicated by milling stones, baskets, stemmed and notched projectile points, and evidences of a seed-collecting and hunting existence, was represented in Zone II of the Danger Cave refuse as early as 7000 B.C. This pattern continued with enrichments into Zone III, believed to date somewhere in the range of 5000–3000 B.C.,[3a] and even into Zones IV and V of the dry cave refuse. The terminal date for Zone V is around the beginning of the Christian era.[4] Even later the cave was used occasionally by Indians so that more recent items, continuing up to the historic period, have been found superficially at the site. In this present resumé, we will pay most attention to Zones III through V (see chronological chart, Fig. 6-2).

The Danger Cave III culture phase carried over as the most common types from phase II the me-

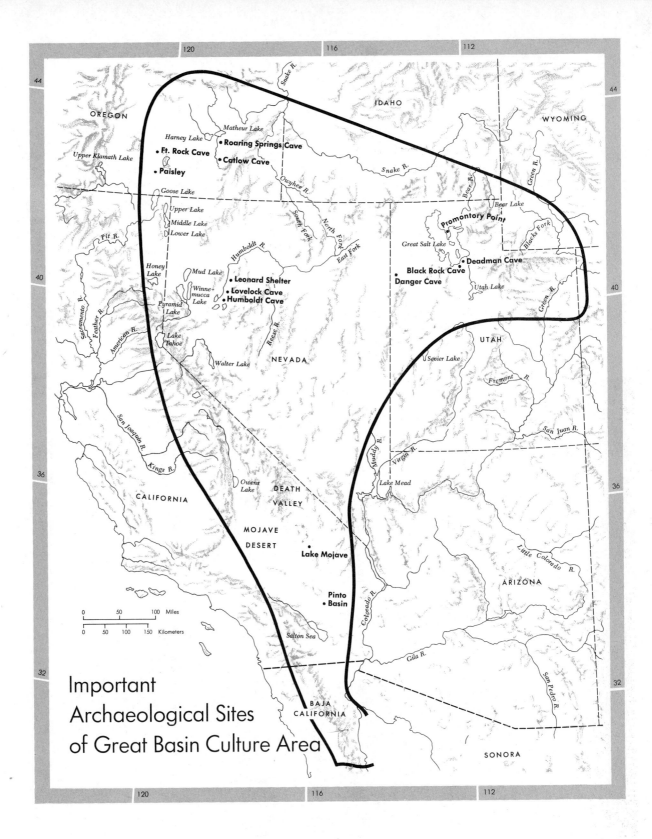

Important
Archaeological Sites
of Great Basin Culture Area

Figure 6-1.

dium-to-small stemmed, side-notched, and basal-notched projectile points. In Zone III one such point, broken, was found still attached to a wooden dart foreshaft about 25 centimeters long and about 1 centimeter thick. The flint point had been fitted into an end slot, or nock, and firmly lashed with sinew. Apparently such a foreshaft was inserted into the hollow end of a longer reed spear shaft.

Milling stones and handstones were other carry-overs from phase II. The first were slabs or blocks of fine-grained abrasive stone, generally of an elongated-oval shape, and ranging from 20 to 50 centimeters in length. One or both faces had worked concave surfaces formed by a rotary grinding motion. Otherwise they were unshaped. The manos, or handstones, resembling flattened, oval buns, fitted the milling slabs, but otherwise most were unshaped except by use. The technique of

Figure 6-2. Chronological chart for the Great Basin culture area. The Colorado River (Patayan) column has been carried over from the Southwestern area chronological chart (see Chap. 4, Fig. 4-6).

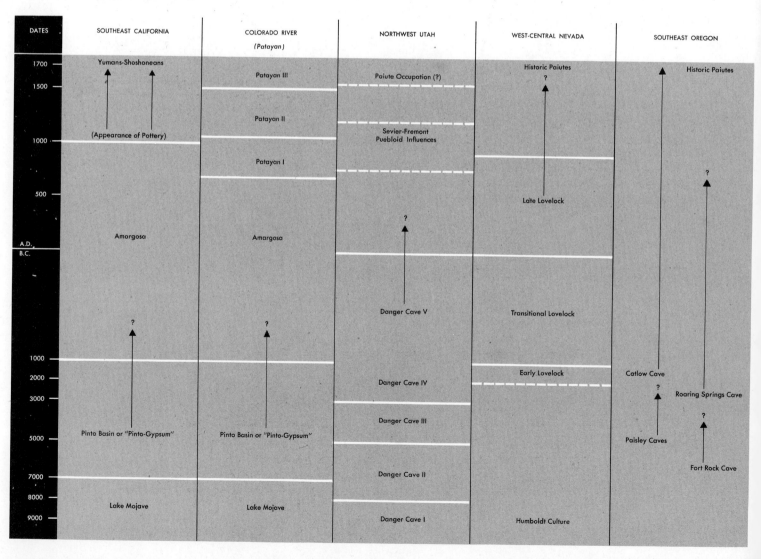

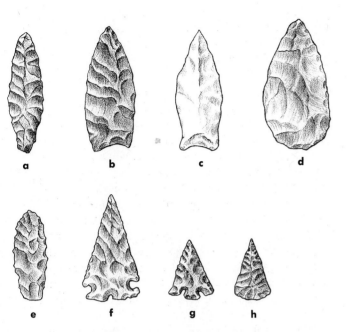

a b c d

e f g h

Figure 6-3. Projectile points from Danger Cave, Utah. *a,d,e*: Types well represented in Level II. *c,f*: Types well represented in Levels II-III. *b*: A common Level III type. *g,h*: Level V types. Length of *a*, 5.2 cm. (After Jennings, 1957.)

nants of the desert saline water bulrushes (*Scirpus Americanus*). Most authorities believe that the Danger Cave peoples chewed them as a food, not as a narcotic. It is also possible that they were chewed to obtain the fibers which then were used for net-making. Nets were a common item, and were made of hemp (*Apocynum*), cedar (*Juniperus*), and flax (*Linum*), as well as the bulrush fibers. Such netting was used in making drawstring traps and, probably, carrying bags. A great many basketry pieces come from phase III deposits, most made from sandbar willow splints. These baskets were constructed by simple and diagonal twining, techniques also used in phase II, and by coiling, which appeared for the first time in III.

In phase IV of Danger Cave, unstemmed trianguloid or lanceolate points were more common than stemmed and notched types. Most of them were rather roughly chipped. A number of wooden pegs or skewers have been recovered. The most common material for cordage was sagebrush bark. Otherwise, there were no significant changes from phase III.

Phase V saw the first appearance of the small, notched, barbed, and expanded-stem arrow points. Older dart forms also were used. Milling stones and handstones remained much the same, except that more of the handstones were deliberately shaped. A few beads and pendants were made from ground and polished stone. The L-shaped awls had disappeared, most such tools being splinter-shaped; however, more bone and horn items have been recovered than in lower levels. Among these are large bone tubes, some of which contain caked car-

deliberate shaping did not become common until later, particularly in phase V. The only other ground-stone artifacts found in phase III were abraders.

From phase III also have come a number of bone awls, including an L-shaped type made from an antelope scapula. An eyed bone needle and bone tubes (shamanistic?) also form part of the phase III inventory, along with an *Olivella* shell ornament and a few mussel shells. There was a quantity of food bones in the refuse zone, including antelope, mountain sheep, bison (rare), rodent, rabbit, and bird. All these species were associated with the preceding Zone II. Deer bones were notably absent, and the only remains of this animal in the cave were antlers found in Zone V. A number of leather scraps indicate that hides were tanned.

Chewed quids turned up throughout the cave refuse, including that of Zone III, most being rem-

Figure 6-4. L-shaped bone awl, Level IV, Danger Cave. Length, about 9 cm. (After Jennings, 1957.)

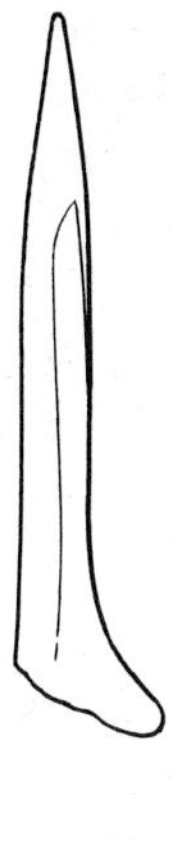

bon and presumably were smoking devices. Spoons were made of sheep horn, and small bone disks and slabs perhaps served as game counters. Wooden objects were also more numerous in phase V. These included dart mainshafts and foreshafts; arrows, some of which still have split-feather fletchings bound with sinew and one of which is a compound form with reed shaft and hardwood nock-end; fire drills and hearths; bows, which are small and either toys or perhaps drill-bows; a forked-stick snare; and six "gaming" sticks, all 25 centimeters long and 1 centimeter in diameter, and all painted in varying patterns of red stripes. The netting reveals a greater variety of knot styles than earlier specimens and cordage now was made of milkweed, bulrush fibers, and sagebrush bark. Coiling was the preferred basketry technique, and Jennings makes the observation that basket-making methods were quite distinct from those practiced in the Anasazi country to the south. In his opinion, Southwestern Basketmaker influences were not important, although an approximate contemporaneity is indicated. No pottery has been found in level V proper, although a few crude small animal effigies of fired clay have turned up.

A post-Zone V horizon of Danger Cave has been indicated by the superficial discovery of a few potsherds. These, indeed, may span a considerable period of time. Some are identified with the Sevier-Fremont peripheral Pueblo culture and probably date to the A.D. 750–1250 range; others are Shoshoni ware fragments and may have been left from historic period Paiute camps.

Humboldt Basin, Nevada. Besides Danger Cave, another important locus in which to examine the continuity of the Desert tradition is the Humboldt Basin region of west-central Nevada. You will remember (see Chap. 2, p. 57) that there in the Leonard Rock Shelter, traces of human occupation, termed the Humboldt Culture, were found to date as early as 9000 B.C., although these earliest remains were not clearly of Desert culture type.[5] Overlying these traces were Desert tradition culture levels which intermittently carry

the story of the cave's occupancy up to late prehistoric times. In this particular case, it is quite probable that the last dwellers in the shelter were northern Paiute.

It is with the late prehistoric culture of the Leonard shelter that we are here most concerned. Actually, this culture, named the Lovelock by R. F. Heizer, is seen to better advantage in the excavations and collections from two other nearby caves, Lovelock proper and Humboldt.[6] Radiocarbon and other dating estimates from the three caves place the Lovelock culture between 2000 B.C. and about A.D. 900. Subdivisions are Early Lovelock, 2000–1000 B.C.; Transitional Lovelock, 1000 B.C.–0; and Late Lovelock 0–A.D. 900.[7] The full time span essentially paralleled the Medithermal climatic stage and correlates, at least in part, with the estimated dates for Zones IV and V of Danger Cave.

The Humboldt Basin setting of the Lovelock culture is a remnant of ancient Lake Lahontan. A so-called Humboldt Lake, or sink, is the terminus of the Humboldt River as this stream runs itself out into the desert sands. Until very recently in historic times, the sink contained a small body of shallow water surrounded by tule marshes.[8] Fish and shellfish were found in this brackish pond, as well as tule and rush used in basketry and mats, and edible tubers, shoots, and seeds. In prehistoric times it had obviously been a desirable oasis for the Desert culture peoples, particularly during the climatic amelioration at the beginning of the Medithermal. The Leonard-Lovelock and Humboldt sites are all within a few miles of the former shoreline of the sink.

The Lovelock Cave site was first excavated by L. L. Loud in 1912 and again by M. R. Harrington and Loud in 1924.[9] Minor operations, including the collection of radiocarbon samples, have been carried out since by University of California field parties.[10] The cave, on a mountain slope overlooking the old lake basin, is in a limestone formation and was carved out by wave action of Lake Lahontan sometime during the Pleistocene. Actually a rockshelter rather than a deep cave, it is about 12 meters deep, 50 meters wide, and up to 6 meters in height. At around 9000 B.C., with the last major recession of Lake Lahontan, the shelter became available for occupancy. It does not, however, seem to have been occupied by man at this time, for the earliest radiocarbon dates, in the vicinity of 4000 B.C., come from culturally sterile bat guano deposits overlying the rock floor of the cave. The earliest human occupation above the basal bat guano was during the Early phase of the Lovelock culture.

The artifacts of the Early Lovelock phase included medium-sized stemmed and basally notched projectile points which were used on atlatl darts. These darts were equipped with wooden foreshafts generally similar to the type recovered from Danger Cave. Fiber netting was used for snares, shredded fiber for clothing, and blankets were made of birdskins and furs. Both twined and coiled baskets have been found, the latter variety including bowls, trays, jugs, and large carrying baskets. L-shaped bone awls made up part of the inventory, along with shells from the Pacific Coast, which were drilled and strung as beads and pendants.

Following a period when the cave was unoccupied, the Transitional phase set in, its accompanying changes written in the Lovelock intermediate levels. Among these innovations were the introduction of the bow-and-arrow, accompanied by the small-stemmed and barbed arrow points; slate knives used to cut bulrushes, replacing the horn sickles that had been used earlier; a wickerwork technique used in making large carrying baskets; and twined tule bags. The only grinding tools found in the cave, rough stone "hullers," were associated with the Transitional phase deposits. Generally, milling stones and mano stones seem to have been very scarce items in all phases of the Lovelock culture; not only the Lovelock Cave proper, but other sites as well are quite barren of them.[11] The archaeologists who have worked with the Lovelock culture, however, believe that such items probably were a part of the technical equipment of these people, although for some reason they were rarely brought into the cave quarters. But to continue

with the Transitional phase, moccasins, sandals, and tubular stone pipes also were new additions. Horn and wooden pendants were fashioned during the Early Lovelock phase, although the wooden ones died out during the Transitional phase. Hoof rattles and pendants were common to both phases. Decoys to lure water fowl were used only during the Transitional phase.

In the Late Lovelock phase, the bow-and-arrow became the principal weapon; coiled and wicker basketry continued, to be made, along with tule mats, although the mats now were made with cordage wefts. Wooden pins, a wooden fishhook-shaped object, and carved stone art in the form of a ring with two protruding heads were other additions to the Late level inventories. As in the Leonard shelter, the Late Lovelock phase probably represents the culture of the immediate ancestors of the northern Paiute. Certain traits in the Late phase levels can be matched with historic northern Paiute material culture: the bow-and-arrow with wooden foreshaft and side-notched barbed points, matting and twined tule bags, shredded fiber aprons, fur and birdskin blankets, and hoof rattles. On the other hand, northern Paiute basketry was twined, not coiled or wicker.[12] The Lovelock Cave deposits do not, however, continue up to the historic horizon. The site was abandoned some time earlier, for from 3 to 6 feet of sterile bat guano overlie the cultural refuse.

Southeastern Oregon. The Fort Rock Cave, in the southeastern Oregon subarea of the Great Basin, has already been mentioned in connection with both the Old Cordilleran tradition and the earliest manifestations of the Desert tradition (Chap. 2, pp. 56–57). Radiocarbon dates have been obtained from twined sandals found in the cave, and these indicate that the lower layer of the rockshelter dates to about 7000 B.C., approximately equivalent to the Danger Cave II stratum. The sandals in question, of which almost 100 charred fragments were recovered, were woven of sagebrush bark shreds with five warp strands forming the foundation for an elongate-oval sole. Tie-cords

Figure 6-5. Desert country of Southeast Oregon. *Left:* The entrance to Catlow Cave No. 1. *Right:* The Alkali flats of Catlow Valley. (Courtesy Luther S. Cressman.)

and loops and toe-flaps were then added to the sole piece. A single piece of twined basketry was also taken from this level. The leaf-shaped and notched projectile points from this layer have already been mentioned. They were accompanied by numerous flint scrapers and some drills, as well as by a few manos, a metate-like stone, bone awls, and a bone atlatl hook.[13]

This early Desert culture was succeeded by other related manifestations in the same subarea. These sequences have been revealed through discoveries made at Paisley Nos. 1 and 2 Caves, from Roaring Springs Cave, and from Catlow Cave.[14] The later Oregon Desert complexes date from about 5000

B.C. to the historic horizon, essentially paralleling the Utah and Nevada cave sequences. The richest inventories date from after 2000 B.C. and include numerous samples of basketry, sandals, wooden and bone tools and other objects, flint projectile points and scrapers, and grinding stones. The basketry from these caves included the type called Catlow Twined (see examples in Figs. 6-6, *left;* 6-7, *bottom*); which utilized tule reeds for both the two-ply warp strands and the wefts. The Catlow basketmakers preferred deep receptacles and trays, which they often decorated by alternating dark- and light-colored strand elements to effect bands of diamonds, triangles, or stepped figures. They also used "overlays," in which weft strands were wrapped with other fibers dyed in various shades. Catlow Twined basketry was the same or similar to types found in the Lovelock culture in Nevada and in the Utah Danger Cave levels II and III. It was also essentially similar to the twined basketry of the Anasazi Basketmaker phases of the Southwest. Coiled baskets (Fig. 6-7, *top*) were found

Figure 6-6. Oregon cave textiles from Roaring Springs Cave. *Left:* Section of Catlow Twined basket with woven design. *Right:* Basketry section of twilled twining. (After Cressman, 1942.)

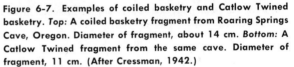

Figure 6-7. Examples of coiled basketry and Catlow Twined basketry. *Top:* A coiled basketry fragment from Roaring Springs Cave, Oregon. Diameter of fragment, about 14 cm. *Bottom:* A Catlow Twined fragment from the same cave. Diameter of fragment, 11 cm. (After Cressman, 1942.)

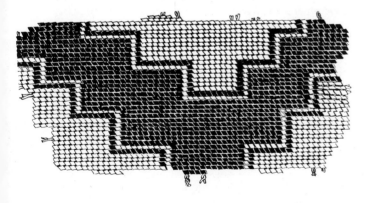

Figure 6-9. Section of twilled twining weave, partly covered with false embroidery, from Roaring Springs Cave. (After Cressman, 1942.)

Figure 6-8. A stepped decoration motif in twilled twining. (After Cressman, 1942.)

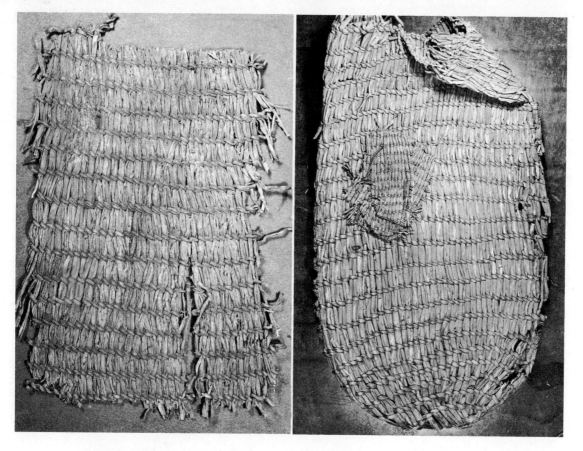

Figure 6-10. Mat (*left*) and coarse bag or container (*right*), Oregon caves. (After Cressman, 1942.)

Figure 6-11. Bone awls from Roaring Springs Cave and Catlow Cave No. 1, Oregon. *a,b:* L-shaped type. *e:* Retains textile wrapping around handgrip. Length of *a,* 8 cm. (After Cressman, 1942.)

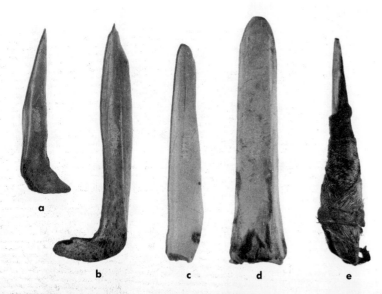

in Catlow and Roaring Springs Caves, but the specimens probably were somewhat later than the twined variety. You will recall that coiling succeeded twining in the Danger Cave stratigraphy.

The sandals of the later Oregon caves included the presumably earlier Fort Rock type (which is found in Catlow Cave) as well as multiple warp and spiral weft examples. The multiple warp form had from 8 to 14 strands; a heel pocket feature; toe-flaps, which were extensions of these warp strands; and tie-loops, which were extensions of the weft strands. There is a vague suggestion in the Catlow Cave stratigraphy that the multiple warp type was earlier than the Fort Rock type; but the evidence is inconclusive and the radiocarbon dates for the Fort Rock finds, as well as the technological simplicity of the Fort Rock sandal, would seem to indicate the reverse chronological order.

L-shaped bone awls, like the ones taken from Lovelock Cave, were found in Roaring Springs Cave, as were various bone beads and pendants. Wooden specimens included atlatl handle fragments, dart shafts, bow fragments, and arrow shafts. The stratigraphy of these items, as well as of the projectile points, again shows that the bow-and-arrow gradually replaced the throwing-stick and dart. Many projectile points have been found, mostly with stemmed, barbed, or notched haft features. L. S. Cressman, who excavated the Oregon caves, states that many of the same forms were both large and heavy (dart varieties) and small and light (arrow-tip). The abundant flint scrapers speak of the economic importance of hunting and hides, and articles of leather were among the cave finds. The handstones, or manos, associated with these other materials did not adhere to any set shape or size, and the same is true for the basins or metate stones, which were very irregular. Their presence, however, is indicative of seed-collecting and grinding.

Southeastern California. At the southern end of the Great Basin, the interior deserts of southeastern California have yielded archaeological finds that may be classed in the Desert tradition or at least discussed in the same general frame of reference. In our survey of early remains in Chapter 2, we referred to the Lake Mojave phase finds of the late pluvial. These were, putatively, a part of or possible local protopyes of the Desert tradition.[15]

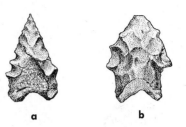

Figure 6-13. Pinto Basin projectile points, California desert. Length of a, 3.5 cm. (After M. J. Rogers, 1939.)

The succeeding Pinto Basin culture or phase was more "Desert-like" in its artifact inventories. Authorities differ on the time span to be assigned to Pinto Basin, or "Pinto-Gypsum" as it is sometimes called.[16] Bennyhoff suggests a range of from 7000 to 1000 B.C., although his chart allows for a later continuation of another millennium or so.[17] Meighan concurs essentially with Bennyhoff, placing it from 6000 B.C. to A.D. 0.[18] W. J. Wallace, on the other hand, is doubtful if the Mojave and Colorado desert lake basins were occupied during the height of the Altithermal and would prefer restricting Pinto Basin to a period of from 3000 B.C. to A.D. 0.[19] No clear answer to the dating problem is yet available, but it is sufficient to say that in the time span of the early-to-middle ranges of the Desert cultural tradition the old southeastern California lake basins were occupied by numerous bands of food-collectors and hunters. According to Wallace, the population of the California desert subarea was much greater at this time than during the period of the Lake Mojave culture, and he attributes this increase to the cycle of increased rainfall that followed the close of the Altithermal. He refers to large campsites in the Pinto Basin proper, a locality in northeastern Riverside County, to others on old beach lines around Owens Lake and near Little Lake, to locations in Death Valley, and to a rockshelter site in southeastern San Diego County in the far south.[20] The unifying feature of the Pinto Basin culture or complex—the various regional manifestations of it are much too diverse to refer to a Pinto Basin culture phase—is the Pinto Basin point form, a projectile almost certainly used to tip a dart rather than an arrow. We have already

Figure 6-12. Lake Mojave or Playa projectile points, California desert. Length of a, 5.8 cm. (After M. J. Rogers, 1939.)

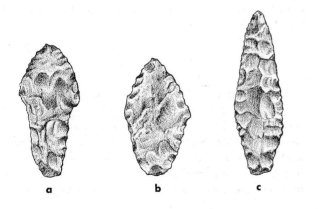

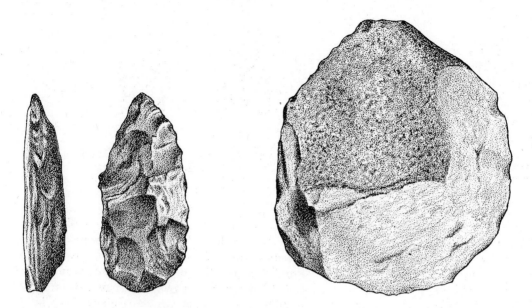

Figure 6-14. *Above:* Side and top views of a Pinto Basin or "Pinto-Gypsum" plano-convex knife, California desert. Length, 6.3 cm. (After M. J. Rogers, 1939.)

Figure 6-15. *Above, right:* A Pinto Basin or "Pinto-Gypsum" bifacial hand-chopper, California desert. Length, 8.7 cm. (After M. J. Rogers, 1939.)

referred to these points (Chap. 2, Fig. 2-24*b*); Wallace describes them as being "marked by weak, narrow shoulders and concave bases."[21] Some leaf-shaped points also were associated with the Pinto points, along with knives, drills, scrapers, scraper-planes, rough choppers, handstones, and milling stones.

Following the Pinto Basin complex, the evidences of human habitation in the California desert basins are rather slim. The period we are now concerned with would appear to begin somewhere between 1000 B.C. and A.D. 0 and to last up until about A.D. 1000. M. J. Rogers has designated the culture of this horizon as the Amargosa, and Wallace follows this terminology.[22] What may be an earlier phase (Fig. 6-16, *left*) featured a broad, triangular-bladed, notched, square-based dart point which Wallace describes as being similar to Southwestern Basketmaker forms. Blades, drills,

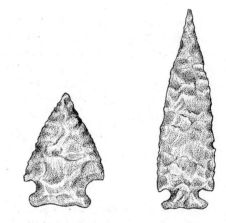

Figure 6-16. Amargosa dart points, California desert. *Left:* Phase I. *Right:* Phase II. *Left* is 4.4 cm. long. (After M. J. Rogers, 1939.)

flake-scrapers, and slate pendants also made up the artifact complex. A later phase of the Amargosa (see Figs. 6-16, *right*, and 6-17) saw a longer, more slender notched dart type and small, light-weight arrow points appear. Handstones and milling stones were used during the Amargosa, and in the late phase occasional Anasazi sherds have turned

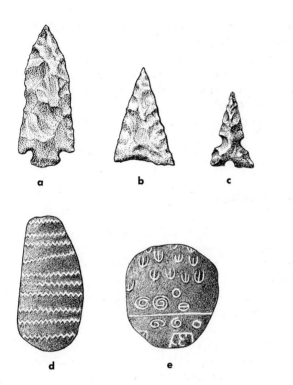

Figure 6-17. Amargosa II artifacts, California desert. a,b,c: Projectile points. d,e: Incised slate pendants. Length of a, 4.2 cm. (After M. J. Rogers, 1939.)

up.[23] Reports of Amargosa camp site discoveries have come from the Mojave Desert north to Owens Valley and Death Valley. They have been found along intermittent water courses or near water holes, and are believed to have been occupied during climatic conditions much like those that exist today.

After A.D. 1000, archaeologists believe, the ancestors of the present Shoshone and Yuma Indians entered the southeastern California subarea of the Great Basin, although it is not beyond the bounds of possibility that some of these people—perhaps the Yuma—were already there during Amargosa times.[24] In any event, there were significant culture changes after that date. For one thing, sites grew much more numerous. They appear to have been the camping stations of peoples who were constantly shifting to follow the seasonal maturation of plant foods. Judging from artifact inventories, heavy with handstones, milling stones, pestles, and bedrock mortars, seed-collecting became more important than formerly and hunting declined. The standard projectile point was the tiny triangular arrow-tip, which varied in terms of side and basal notching. Sea shells were used for beads. The dead were cremated. Pottery was manufactured locally and was influenced by two ceramic traditions. In the north, the coiled and scraped vessels relate to Great Basin wares; farther south, the coiled but paddle-anvil thinned pots can be more easily linked with Patayan pottery-making of the lower Colorado region.[25]

In Chapter 4 we discussed the westward extension of the Patayan culture during the Patayan II Period. M. J. Rogers believed that this expansion carried agriculture as well as pottery into the Mojave Desert region.[26] Wallace, on the other hand, does not mention farming as a part of the native economy of the Mojave in the post-A.D. 1000 period but stresses, instead, plant-collecting.[27] Thus the westward spread of Southwestern horticultural traditions is somewhat tenuous and doubtful. The expansion of the Patayan pattern is, rather, documented by its pottery. The significant observation is that the southeastern California deserts mark the essential western barriers of the Southwest culture area into which the Southwestern tradition penetrated only weakly and relatively late.

Summary. These samplings of the Desert cultural tradition, although varying in space and in time, betray an over-all similarity that reflects, if not a single common point of origin, a long interrelated history in comparable environments. To summarize, the Desert tradition had its hearth in the Great Basin region, that interior drainage of western North America centering on the state of Nevada and including adjacent portions of surrounding states. In this area it persisted until historic times. The tradition extended beyond the physiographic limits of the

Basin proper to other similar areas, such as Arizona and New Mexico, where it was replaced by the Southwestern tradition of native farming, and to northwestern and central Mexico, where it was succeeded by the Mesoamerican tradition. In the areas of Northeast Mexico-Texas and Baja California the Desert tradition was modified by other environmental-cultural factors and persisted in modified forms to the historic horizon.

The native peoples living in the Great Basin and surrounding areas in historic times were of Uto-Aztecan (Utes, Paiutes, Shoshone) and Hokan (Yuma and others) speech. In many instances, their material culture closely resembled that of the late prehistoric Desert tradition complexes. Just how far back in time these ethnic identities may be pushed remains uncertain.

The life of the Desert tradition peoples was always semi-nomadic and based on hunting and the collecting of desert plants. Camps were established along lake shores, near streams, and by water holes. Today the environment is semi-arid to arid. It probably was somewhat more favorable under the Anathermal conditions at the end of the pluvial, the era that marked the beginnings of the Desert pattern. Under succeeding Alithermal conditions, the climate grew more severe and water more limited than before or after, but there are evidences of habitation in some parts of the Basin even during this period.

The standard artifacts of the Desert tradition included stemmed and notched dart points, forms which were reduced in size and weight during the later prehistoric periods as the bow-and-arrow replaced the atlatl. Milling stone and handstones have been found in most Desert culture complexes, along with simple bone tools, ornaments, and gaming objects. A typical Desert culture feature was an L-shaped bone awl, although it was restricted chronologically and has not been found in all regions of the Great Basin. Nets, mats, sandals, and baskets were made of available fibers and reeds; twined basketry preceded the coiled variety. In addition to these various textiles, objects of wood and leather have been found, usually where climatic and other conditions of preservation were favorable. Admittedly the archaeological image of the Desert cultures has been strongly enhanced by fortunate conditions of preservation guaranteed by the dry climate. In characterizing a Desert tradition these wood, fiber, and hide "perishables" have probably been stressed too much by archaeologists; but they cannot be ignored, and the student can only be cognizant of the circumstances.

Baja California

The Area and Its Ethnography. In Baja California there are archaeological indications that the Desert cultural tradition was carried into the isolated peninsula from the Great Basin and the southeastern California deserts relatively early. In its local evolution here, however, it underwent modifications, mainly in response to seashore adaptations, so that it is best to consider this areal variant of Desert culture separately and within the geographic frame of reference of a Baja California culture area.

Baja California is a peninsula separated from mainland Mexico by the Gulf of California and extending all the way from the mouth of the Colorado River south to the peninsular tip at Cabo Falso. It is almost 800 miles long and averages less than 100 miles in width. It has a mountainous backbone, numerous small valleys and interior basins, and both coastlines are indented by many bays. It is a semi-arid desert land, especially in the central and northern portions. In the south below La Paz Bay on the Gulf of California side, rainfall is more plentiful, with summer showers feeding intermittent streams that flow from the mountains to the coast through alluvial valleys. Here wild plant and animal foods were more abundant in aboriginal times. Throughout the peninsula pre-Columbian peoples sustained themselves by hunting, fishing, and plant-collecting. Fish and shellfish were available on both coasts, although somewhat more plentiful on the Gulf side than on the Pacific.

The native languages and tribes of Baja California may be divided into three groups.[28] In the north were the California Yuman tribes—the Diegueño, who were also found north of the international border in California, the Kamia, the Paipai, the Ñakipa and the Kiliwa—all speaking Yuman languages. These tribes and their immediate kinsmen and neighbors were found southward on the peninsula to a point about 150 miles south of the international border or to 31 degrees north latitude. South of the California Yuma were the Peninsular Yuma, also of the Yuman tongue but linguistically forming a sub-family apart from the California Yuma and displaying a significant number of cultural differences. The Borjeño and Ignacieño were two of these Peninsular Yuman tribes, and there were also others. Their southern border is just south of the town of Loreto on the Gulf Coast, or at about 26 degrees north latitude. From here southward to the end of the peninsula were the tribes of the Guaicuran language family, including the Guaicura, Huchiti, and Pericú, the last named occupying the very southern tip of Baja California. The Guaicuran language family is not Yuman although it may possibly be related to Yuman in the larger Hokan linguistic grouping. In culture traits, as exhibited on the ethnographic horizon, the Guaicuran tribes differed noticeably from their Peninsular Yuman neighbors and even more from the more distant California Yuma in the north.

The ethnographic horizon for the Indians of Baja California is essentially the eighteenth century. Prior to that time, there had been contacts, with Spaniards from the Mexican mainland from 1535 until 1685, but none of these resulted in successful European settlements. In 1697, however, Loreto was founded on the Gulf of California, and from this date until 1767 Jesuit missions were established in the peninsula. Although missionization of the tribes proceeded peacefully, the aboriginal populations were decimated by disease, so that toward the end of the eighteenth century in the period of the Franciscan and Dominican missions the old native life had become

drastically altered. In the nineteenth and twentieth centuries only a few reduced groups remained, all in the far north.

Many anthropologists have commented about the "layering" of native tribes, languages, and cultures from north to south in the long Baja California peninsula.[29] Almost certainly, various peoples have made their way into the cul-de-sac of the peninsula and have gradually drifted or have

Figure 6-18. The heavy line delimits the culture area, following Massey (1949, 1961 a). Tribal groupings, principal tribal names, and archaeological and geographical locations are shown.

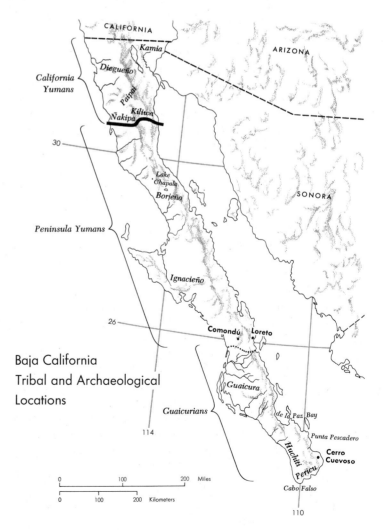

Baja California Tribal and Archaeological Locations

been forced by the pressure of newcomers to locations farther south. Thus tribes such as the Pericú, at the extremity of the peninsula, and other Guaicurans are believed to represent descendants of the oldest migrants into Baja California; they were followed by Peninsular Yumans; and these, in turn, were succeeded by Californian Yumans of the north. In general the archaeology of the area substantiates this hypothesis. So, too, do the few findings made by physical anthropologists, for the crania found in Pericú territory, the Pericú, or Cerro Cuevoso, type,[30] are markedly dolichocephalic and physical anthropologists consider them related to similar marginal populations on the Texas coast and in the eastern Brazilian highlands.[31]

These age-area considerations, the archaeological data, and comparisons of both ethnographic and archaeological data from Baja California with data from areas to the north and northeast have led W. C. Massey to define a Baja California culture area as being composed of the territory of the Peninsular Yuman and the Guaicuran tribes alone[32] (see Fig. 6-18). In other words, the northern boundary of the area falls at about the 31st parallel.

Problems of Culture Sequence and the Early Horizons. The territory of the California Yumans in Baja California to the north of the 31st parallel is best divided between the Great Basin area on the northeast[33] and the California area to the northwest. The culture sequences which pertain to these far northern parts of Baja California are thus those of Southeastern California and South Coastal California. The first began with a Lake Mojave horizon and extended upward through a Pinto Basin (or Pinto-Gypsum) culture, continued into Amargosa, and terminated with the Patayan (or Yuma) levels. The second sequence ran from an early San Dieguito culture through the La Jolla phases into the California Late Period and historic cultures of the southern California coast.

These archaeological sequences, which actually lie outside Baja California proper at what Massey has termed the "gateway" to Baja California, arc our best guides to chronological ordering farther south.[34] Neither sequence can be imposed *in toto*, but each is pertinent to the interpretations of findings from the middle and southern peninsula, especially the southeastern California sequence. Pinto Basin-type remains have been found in both the Peninsular Yuman and Guaicuran subareas of Baja California. These specimens include Pinto Basin projectile points and other points reminiscent of the Gypsum type but with long, exaggerated tangs, the so-called La Paz point. Milling stones and mano stones were associated in the same camp sites.[35] These widespread Pinto Basin, or Pinto-Gypsum, culture remains in Baja California argue for the extension of the Desert tradition into the peninsula several thousands of years before the beginning of the Christian era. Perhaps these remains hark back to the first human habitation of the area. Or possibly man entered the peninsula still earlier, on a Lake Mojave or early San Dieguito cultural level. As yet the evidence is uncertain. Massey is of the opinion that San Dieguito artifacts can be found but little farther south than the California-Mexico international border.[36] Perhaps one of the artifact complexes associated with the lower lake-line levels in the Lake Chapala Basin in central Baja California may be this early, although the frequency of grinding stones associated with both complexes suggests a Pinto Basin rather than a Lake Mojave horizon.[37]

It is also possible, as we mentioned in Chapter 2, that a very early, pre-projectile point occupation of Baja California is represented by the artifact assemblage found on the highest of the Lake Chapala beach lines. This is the complex which its discoverer, Arnold, has referred to as the Elongated-Biface Assemblage and which featured crude, ovoid, or elliptical bifacially chipped implements.[38]

If a Pinto Basin variety of the Desert tradition provides the basis for later developments in Baja California, the story of these developments remains largely unknown. Local adaptations and evolutions are certainly a part of it. Similarly, continued contacts with the north are sure to be another. According to Massey, all phases of Amargosa culture are found in the peninsula, and presumably this would include the late pre-Patayan brand of Amargosa seen in the South-eastern California deserts. Just when peoples of Yuman speech entered Baja California is specu-lative, and may even remain so; but as Massey has argued, the Peninsular Yumans were ignorant of pottery and other Patayan traits, so it is likely that they descended to their present geographical location before the rise of the Patayan culture on the lower Colorado River and in the adjacent deserts.[39] This probably puts the date of their arrival back prior to the beginning of the Christian era and on an Amargosa or Pinto Basin cultural level. Following this reasoning, Guaicurans at the southern end of Baja California preceded Peninsular Yumans and thus entered the area during Pinto Basin times or before.

Figure 6-19. Chronological chart for Baja California based on comparisons with South Coastal and Southeastern (desert) California.

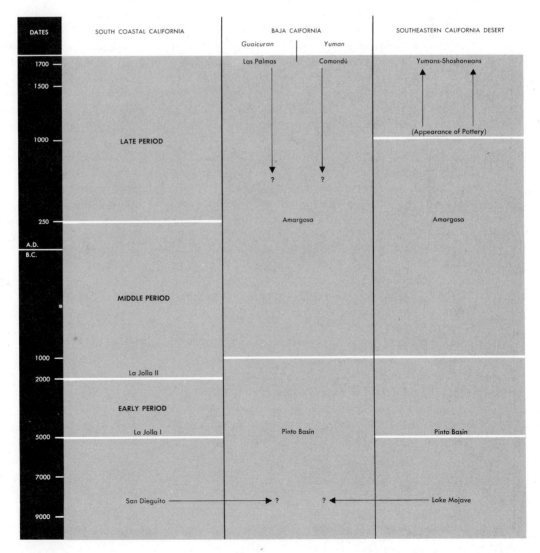

Late Cultures. The late prehistoric-to-proto-historic cultures of Baja California clearly led into the ethnohistoric cultures. Massey has tentatively defined two such cultures. One for the far south, the Las Palmas was beyond much doubt of Guaicuran affiliation; the other, the Comondu, located farther north, was related to the Peninsular Yumans.[40] Quite possibly Las Palmas culture extended over the whole Guaicuran subarea, although this is merely a supposition. Nor has the duration of the Las Palmas culture been established, but presumably it extended from the historic horizon of the eighteenth century downward for a good many centuries or even millennia. Subsequent phases remain to be defined; as has been indicated, these may carry back into a Pinto Basin-like horizon. Sites include extensive shell middens along the coasts and inland stations, some of them caves. Some of the best known from the southern Cape region of the Peninsula are Cerro Cuevoso, Piedra Gorda, and Punta Pescadero.

Both the bow-and-arrow and the spear-thrower or dart-thrower were elements of the Las Palmas material culture. The bow probably was not introduced until the later phases. The dart-thrower, although earlier, continued in use, however, until historic times. Four of these throwing-sticks were found in the Cerro Cuevoso cave accompanying a primary burial. They measure about 80 centimeters in length and have a projecting hook or prong, carved from the same stick, near the end to engage the concave butt of the dart.[41] The large projectile points, which must have tipped the darts, were long, slender, tanged-stem and broad convex-stem types. Other Las Palmas stone implements included manos and milling stones and chipped heavy hand-axes and scrapers made from flint cores. Coiled basketry was rare. The most common and typical "basket" was, instead, nothing more than a container made of palm bark sewn together. A little flat bipointed wooden object, with a shark-tooth set at one end, was another typical item. Perhaps it was used for carving or engraving or perhaps for ceremonial blood-letting. Bone spatulas and carved oyster shell ornaments also were characteristic. According to Massey, secondary bundle burial was the usual form of interment, but he also mentions extended and flexed primary burials and possible cremations.[42] The historic Pericú, at the tip of the peninsula, cremated their dead. Shellfish clearly were important in the Las Palmas diet, to judge from the size and extent of coastal middens. It is less certain, however, if fish were of equal economic consequence. No fishhooks or remains of nets have been discovered, and the historic Guaicura used only spears for fishing.

The Comondú culture of the Peninsular Yumans flourished during the period 1697 to 1767. In the Peninsular Yuma subarea are numerous coastal shell middens, especially on the Gulf side, and also cave sites and inland open-camp sites. Along the coasts nets and hooks-and-lines were used for taking fish. Coiled baskets were common, as were tubular-stone smoking or shamanistic pipes. Foreshafted arrows have been found in cave sites. These arrows were tipped with small delicately chipped points, including some made from obsidian. Manos and milling stones were, of course, used.[43] Relationships between the Comondú culture and earlier horizons, such as the later complexes of Lake Chapala,[44] are blurred; but a sharing of some traits, such as the milling and mano stones, certainly suggests a continuity in food habits. In the Comondú culture proper, as defined by Massey, ceramics have been discovered only at historic sites of the Mission period.[45] This pottery appears to be linked to the Southwestern Patayan or Hohokam traditions; and in this connection, at the very north of the Peninsular Yuman subarea, a few red and brown ware sherds indicate contacts with the Southwest on a prehistoric level.[46] An unusually spectacular feature of the archaeology of the Peninsular Yuma subarea are cave pictographs and petroglyphs. These representations have been reported from several localities, but one of the most notable is in the San Borjita Cave in Ignacieño territory. The entire roof of this large cavern is covered with multicolored renderings of humans and animals.[47] Quite probably these paintings pertain to the Comondú archaeological culture of late prehistoric times.

Summary. In retrospect we see the peninsula of Baja California as an area which, following possible earlier immigrants, peoples of the hunting and collecting Desert cultural tradition entered in early post-glacial times. It seems likely that these people were of Guaicuran and Peninsular Yuman speech, in that chronological order. Specifically their culture was closely allied to that of their immediate northern neighbors, the Pinto Basin people, who probably spoke Yuman. By late prehistoric times, perhaps near the beginning of the Christian era, the Guaicurans and the Peninsular Yumans had developed a variant brand of the Desert tradition, which was reflected in the Las Palmas and Comondú cultures which persisted until the historic horizon of the eighteenth century. These cultures defined a Baja California culture area for the southern three-quarters of the peninsula. In the northern quarter of the peninsula, the old Desert tradition was modified in different ways—in the east, by the Patayan development, a branch of the Southwestern farming tradition; to the west, on the Pacific Coast, by what we are calling a California Coast and Valley tradition.

California

The Area. The California archaeological area includes most of that state. It embraces the western slopes of the high Sierra Nevadas, the interior great north-south valleys of the Sacramento and the San Joaquin, the coastal ranges, and the Pacific littoral. As we pointed out in the foregoing section, its southern boundary is set between California and Baja California at 31 degrees north latitude. Also in the south is an essentially level passage from the coast eastward, south of the high mountain ranges, into the California deserts of the Great Basin. At this point, the line between a California area and a Great Basin archaeological area is most approximate

and arbitrary. On the north, Cape Mendocino can serve as a dividing point between the Californian and Northwest Coast areas. In both of these instances, ethnohistoric cultural and tribal distributions tend to coincide with archaeological distributions to help us set the outer borders of the area.

The California area is characterized by marked subareal and regional variability in natural environment. Elevations range from sea level to over 14,000 feet; annual precipitation may be less than 10 inches or as much as 100. In some places, the vegetation cover is oak or redwood forest; in others it is of meager scrub Mediterranean type or the land is virtually treeless. Wild game and plant resources are, or were, accordingly variable, but generally ample. Along the shore, shellfish, fish, and sea mammals abound. In overview, the south is drier and more barren; the north has more rainfall and tree cover.

Ethnography and Language. Ethnically, the California area was a notorious patchwork of tribes and languages, a condition sometimes explained by a "fish-trap" theory of human migrations.[48] That is, numerous separate groups entered the area at various times in the past. Many of them probably came in through the mountain passes to the east, leaving the less favorable hunting and food-gathering environments of the Great Basin or the Interior Plateau. Finding the California valleys and coastal locations far preferable to the lands they had left, they remained, with each newcoming group squeezing into yet another small ecological niche. Whether or not this explanation is correct, we know that at the historic period, beginning in the sixteenth century, California was certainly one of the most densely populated of North American aboriginal areas and that these populations presented a diverse ethnic pattern.

California was dominated by two major linguistic families: the California Penutian and Hokan. The Penutians held the larger share of the territory. Among them were such tribal clusters as

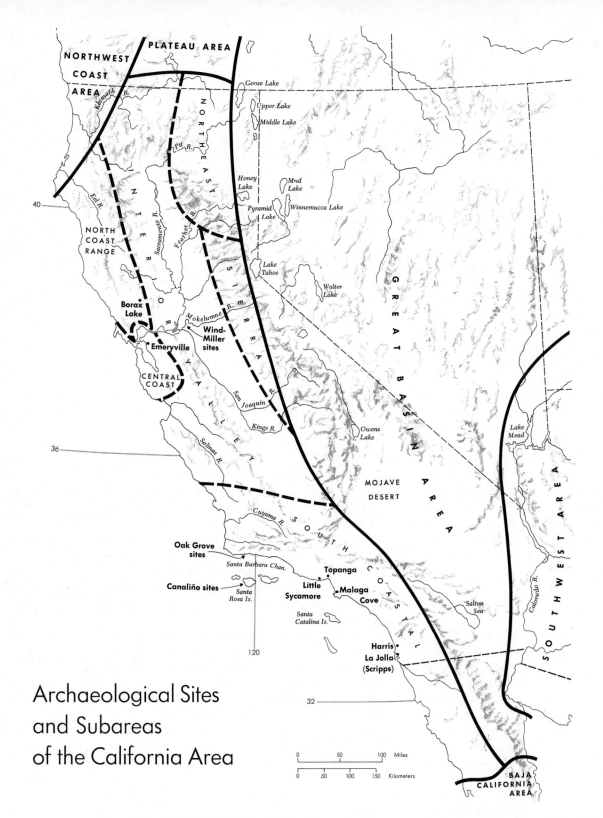

The following labels appear on the map:

PLATEAU AREA

NORTHWEST COAST AREA

Klamath R.

Goose Lake

Upper Lake

Middle Lake

NORTHEAST

Pit R.

Honey Lake

Mud Lake

Winnemucca Lake

Pyramid Lake

40

Eel R.

NORTH COAST RANGE

Sacramento R.

Feather R.

INTERIOR

SIERRA

Lake Tahoe

Walter Lake

GREAT BASIN AREA

Borax Lake

Mokelumne R.

Wind-Miller sites

Emeryville

VALLEY

San Joaquin R.

CENTRAL COAST

Kings R.

Owens Lake

Lake Mead

36

Salinas R.

MOJAVE DESERT

Cuyama R.

SOUTH

Oak Grove sites

Santa Barbara Chan.

Topanga

Little Sycamore

Malaga Cove

COASTAL

Salton Sea

Colorado R.

SOUTHWEST AREA

Canaliño sites

Santa Rosa Is.

Santa Catalina Is.

Harris

La Jolla (Scripps)

120

32

BAJA CALIFORNIA AREA

0   50   100 Miles

0   50   100 150 Kilometers

Archaeological Sites
and Subareas
of the California Area

Figure 6-20. The California Northwest subarea (or region) has
been placed in the Northwest Coast major culture area, and
the Desert subarea (or region) has been placed in the Great
Basin major culture area. Compare with Fig. 6-21.

Archaeological Regions
of California

After Meighan, 1959 a.

- - - - County Boundaries

Figure 6-21.

count only the larger and inclusive tribal units, we still are dealing with some 25 to 30, and within each of these, the actual independent political units, were the smaller tribelets.

The native cultures of the historic horizon were largely non-agricultural, minor exceptions being some groups in the south who had acquired farming practices from the Southwest area in late pre-Columbian or early historic times. Hunting, fishing, and plant-collecting provided subsistence.

Figure 6-22.

the Wintun and Yokuts of the interior valleys, the Miwok and Maidu adjoining them on the east, and the Costanoan of the central coast. The Hokan tribes occupied what might be interpreted as somewhat more marginal positions, being split among peoples like the Pomo of the north coast and mountains, and the Salinan, Chumash, and various California Yuman tribes of southern California and northern Baja California. In addition, there were also a few small enclaves of completely unrelated tongues—the Uto-Aztecan affiliated Luiseño of the southern California coast, and the Athapascan tribes of the far north coast. But these general statements, couched in the broadest categories of linguistic classification, do not reflect the tribal heterogeneity of the area. Even if we

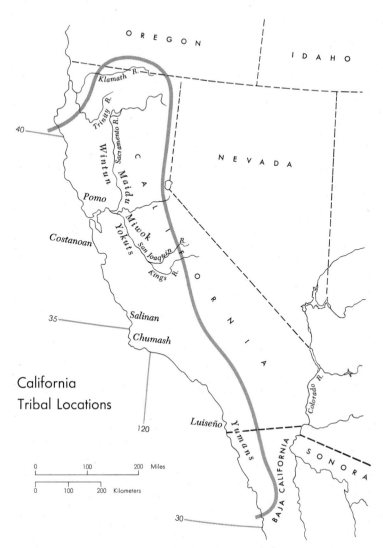

California
Tribal Locations

Since these subsistence patterns can be projected well back into the prehistoric past with strong regional and local continuities traced in archaeological sequences, the material culture of the California Indians has been described as exhibiting an extreme conservatism over several millennia. The old native ways of life remained in force following the first European contacts throughout the sixteenth, seventeenth, and early eighteenth centuries; but Spanish missionary activities in the latter part of the eighteenth century began the attrition of Indian peoples and cultures which was brought to a destructive climax with the heavy European-American settlement of the mid-nineteenth century.

Early Sites (Pre-5000 B.C.). Chronologically, the archaeological story of settlement in the California area may begin with the putative pre-projectile point horizon of 20,000 or more years ago. Some of these finds have been mentioned in Chapter 2. They include the hearths on Santa Rosa Island and near La Jolla and the deeply buried possible artifacts from Texas Street, San Diego. Others include the finds of human skeletons, such as the "Los Angeles Man," which came from a probable geological association with the extinct Imperial elephant.[49]

Coming up in time to the late Wisconsin ice age, and to the horizon of the fluted projectile points, there are some scattered signs of what might have been the presence or the marginal influence of the Big-Game Hunting tradition in California. These are best seen at the Borax Lake site in the northern California coastal range country, where several fluted flint projectile points have been found which resemble very closely those of the general Clovis-Folsom category.[50] The artifact context in which they were found, however, would not appear to be of an age equivalent to either the Clovis or Folsom complexes of the Plains, and it is possible that they represent some kind of a marginal and late retention of the fluting technique. In any event, however the Borax Lake discoveries are interpreted, we cannot now claim that the Big-Game Hunting tradition was truly represented in the California area.

It would seem, rather, that the earliest cultures of the California archaeological area about which we can be certain follow in a tradition, or traditions, which can best be analyzed as a blend between the Old Cordilleran pattern of northwestern North America and the Desert, or proto-Desert, pattern of the Great Basin. We have already referred to such cultural complexes in Chapter 2 and in the preceding sections of this chapter. Specifically these complexes are the Lake Mojave of the southeastern California deserts, and

Figure 6-23. Synoptic diagram of Topanga culture traits, Southern California. (After Meighan, 1959 a.)

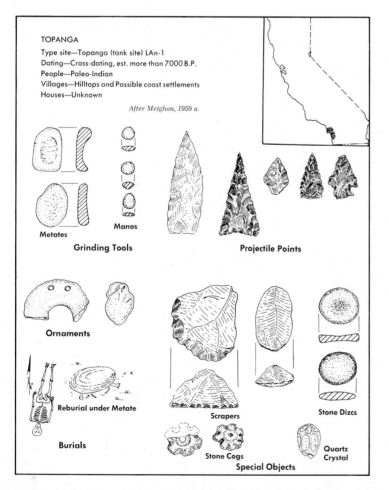

TOPANGA

Type site—Topanga (tank site) LAn-1
Dating—Cross-dating, est. more than 7000 B.P.
People—Paleo-Indian
Villages—Hilltops and Possible coast settlements
Houses—Unknown

After Meighan, 1959 a.

Metates

Manos

Grinding Tools

Projectile Points

Ornaments

Reburial under Metate

Scrapers

Stone Dizcs

Burials

Stone Cogs

Quartz Crystal

Special Objects

the related San Dieguito, Malaga Cove I, and early Topanga cultures of the Southern California subarea. Just how ancient these various cultures are we cannot say. Perhaps they began as early as 8000 B.C., perhaps around 6000 B.C. All authorities, however, place them before 5000 B.C.[51] One of the best stratified sites in which a San Dieguito complex has been isolated in its lowermost levels is the Harris site in San Diego County.[52] The technology, like that of Lake Mojave, was all chipped stone. The projectile points were leaf-shaped bifaces—Old Cordilleran point forms—associated with a good many heavy bipointed blades or knives, scraper-planes, a variety of scrapers, curious eared-crescent forms, heavy choppers, pebble hammerstones, and hammerstones made from cores. Grinding stones, as at Lake Mojave, were missing.[53] Their absence throws some doubt on the Desert classification of the complex, but as we said in our brief survey of Great Basin cultures, milling stones are sometimes rare or absent in sites which otherwise seem to adhere to Desert tradition patterns. The caution to be interjected here is that not all site inventories may be fully representative of the manufactures and activities of a former society, and that such a thing as seasonal occupancy during a period of the year devoted to hunting might explain the absence of seed-grinders from a camp location. Yet viewed in the full perspective of the California area archaeological sequences, it seems most likely that grinding implements were, if not unknown, at least uncommon in such cultures as Lake Mojave and the neighboring San Dieguito complex. For immediately following this horizon they became more common, and it is with the succeeding chronological horizon, dated after 5000 B.C., that what we are here generalizing as a California Coast and Valley tradition came into being.

The California Coast and Valley Tradition. The California Coast and Valley cultural tradition appears to have been shaped from Old Cordilleran and Desert hunting and collecting antecedents. The most likely explanation is that Old Cordilleran and Desert hunters and food collectors from the interior pushed southward and westward into California during the last millennia of the Pleistocene (prior to 5000 B.C.). In their new environment, these people adapted to marine ecological niches and to such wild crops as the acorn in the interior and coastal valleys. The California pattern emerged in response to these adjustments. Quite possibly or even probably, more newcomers entered California in the millennia after 5000 B.C., bringing with them new traits and techniques.

The California Coast and Valley tradition may be described as one of favorable or near-optimum subsistence adjustments under hunting-fishing-collecting conditions. In the development of the tradition there is a very definite chronological trend toward increasingly efficient ecological adaptations. Sites tended to grow larger in the later periods, reflecting both an increase in the local populations and a more sedentary existence. One of the features of the time trend is an increasingly effective exploitation of sea foods in all the coastal regions. C. W. Meighan, who has carefully analyzed site refuse from a number of California locations, describes three broad categories of prehistoric economic adjustment:[54]

1. Primary dependence upon plant seeds and small game. The perishable nature of foods utilized makes this one of the most difficult of environmental adaptations to define archaeologically. However, living desert Indians of California, in particular the Cahuilla, provide a good picture of such environmental use. . . . The Oak Grove and Topanga archaeological cultures are Californian representatives of this group. . . .

2. An economy based upon acorns, fish, birds, and larger game animals such as deer and elk. This is typical of the central valleys and most of the mountainous areas of the state.

3. A marine economy based upon resources of the Pacific Ocean. There is a wide divergence within this category. Some groups depended primarily upon shellfish, others upon hunting sea mammals, still others upon fish.

Meighan was not addressing himself to the problem of an historical line of development but was, rather, considering California archaeological cultures from a developmental standpoint as manifestations of an American-wide Archaic level.[55] Nevertheless, his designation of these cultures as a California Archaic, and his treatment of them in an area chronology frame of reference, implies their interrelatedness and presages the tradition concept applied here. He goes on from his observations on subsistence and ecology to lay out certain technological or artifactual characteristics of the California Archaic, or what is here synthesized from the point of view of history as the Coast and Valley tradition. Ground stone was employed in a diversity of forms which we can group here under two headings: grinding implements and ornamental devices. Grinding implements included the ubiquitous metates and manos or mortars and pestles, the ornamental devices, such items as charmstones or plummet-like pendants and pipes. The atlatl and dart (earlier periods) and the bow-and-arrow (later periods) were used, and among the chipped-stone projectile points were large bi-pointed, straight-based, and fish-tailed lanceolates and stemmed and notched forms, as well as smaller points for arrow tips. Vessels were made of steatite and other stone in some regions and periods, but baskets were apparently the principal containers. Pottery-making was not practiced until very late, and then only in regions influenced by the neighboring Southwest area. Widely distributed bone objects included fish gorges, awls, whistles, fish-spears, and wedges. Marine shells, especially the abalone (*Haliotis*), were usually made into ornaments. Meighan concludes his survey of California technology by observing that while few devices could be called complex, and most of them were tools or objects similar to those known in other areas of the world, the majority exhibited excellent workmanship and were efficient or aesthetically pleasing, or both. Furthermore, in his words: ". . . there is an increased elaboration of artifacts (through time), with more attention being paid to artistic embellishment and the production of ornaments and other non-functional objects."[56]

From archaeological remains and from projecting ethnohistorical sources backward in time, Meighan has inferred that the largest political units were probably villages, usually numbering no more than a few hundred persons. Society was stratified, but according to a person's individual qualities rather than by class. Warfare was carried out on a small-scale raiding basis. Trade was often conducted over long distances, some by hand-to-hand passage of objects but often by trips undertaken by certain groups. Standardized mortuary practices give some indications of a cult of the dead. Burial offerings were sometimes elaborate. Archaeological charmstones and pipes or sucking tubes had ethnographic counterparts in types used by shamans in curing, sorcery, and controlling nature.

In brief the California Coast and Valley tradition, which persisted from at least 5000 B.C. up until the historic period, was a pattern which had been elaborated within the limits of a hunting-collecting and chipped- and polished-stone technology. Although comparable patterns in other parts of the New World have been transformed by the introduction of agriculture, this development did not unfold in the California area. But in some regions, as has been pointed out by Meighan,[57] Heizer,[58] and others, the California development did, in the sizable increase in its population groups during the late periods (some numbering over 1,000 persons) and in its allowance of leisure time for aesthetic and ceremonial pursuits, match strides with agricultural areas such as the Southwest.

Subareas and Chronology. The archaeological record of the California tradition can best be examined in a frame of reference which is described in several subareas (see Fig. 6-20) and in three major periods. Authorities agree on a South Coastal subarea which extends for 100 miles or so in from the coast and runs from northern Baja California north to a point somewhere above Santa

Barbara.[59] Central California is divided variously, but Central Coast, Interior Valley (Sacramento-San Joaquin drainages), and Sierra (western slopes of the Sierra Nevada) are the subareas usually indicated. A North Coast Range subarea, of the coast and coastal mountains north of San Francisco Bay, is sometimes set apart from the Central Coast. And a northeast subarea, consisting mainly of Modoc and Lassen counties in the far northeast corner of the state, also is sometimes treated separately, although the archaeological cultures here, from what little is known of them, tend to shade

off into Great Basin patterns. A Northwest subarea, above Cape Mendocino, can also be discussed in connection with California archaeology, but here we assign it to the major Northwest Coast area (see pp. 380–382). For the most part we will be concerned in our survey with the South Coastal and Central subareas, which are best known and which

Figure 6-24. **Chronological chart for the California South Coastal subarea, with selected regional phases. Culture phases from other subareas referred to in text may be correlated by major period reference.**

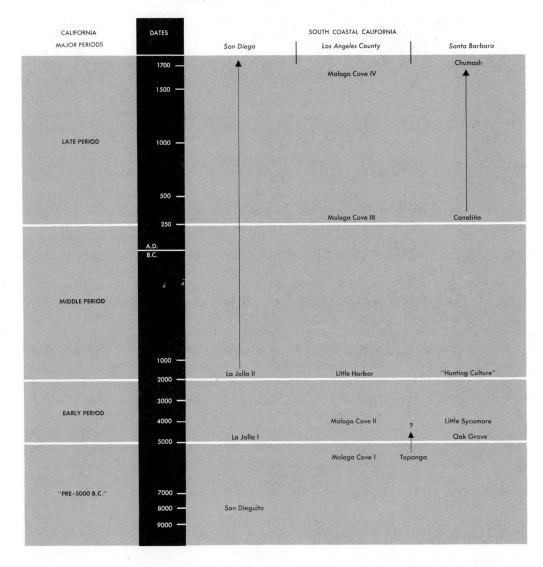

seem to typify best the California Coast and Valley tradition.

The three major periods, as designated by scholars of the tradition, are the Early, Middle, and Late. The dating of the beginning of the Early Period has been obscured by differences of opinion over the ages of such South Coastal cultures as Topanga and Oak Grove. Meighan has been inclined to date them as early as 6000 B.C. and to group them, in spite of the discovery of grinding stones at Topanga and Oak Grove sites, along with San Dieguito I.[60] Heizer, on the other hand, places all the grinding-stone cultures in his Early, but post-San Dieguito I, bracket, and traces their beginnings to 5000 B.C.[61] In this period presentation we follow Heizer and set the approximate dates of the California Early Period at 5000 to 2000 B.C., the Middle or Intermediate Period from 2000 B.C. to a date of A.D. 250,[62] and the Late Period from A.D. 250 to the historic horizon.

The California Early Period (Post-5000 B.C.). In the South Coastal subarea (which also includes the Channel Islands) the Early Period cultures have been grouped under the rubrics of the Milling Stone horizon or the La Jolla I culture.[63] Topanga,[64] Malaga Cove II,[65] Little Sycamore,[66] the Scripps Estate site,[67] and Oak Grove[68] are among the best known stations of this culture and horizon. A wealth of metate and muller, or mano, stones have been recovered from these sites. At the Little Sycamore site, for instance, 116 metates were recovered. Seventy-five of these were basined, some quite deeply, but the rest had no marked concavities. All were large and cumbersome and, except for the effects of grinding on the surface, were unshaped. One hundred twenty-three mullers were found. These specimens were natural pebbles, and again their surfaces were worn from grinding, but only on one side. Flake scrapers, scraper-planes, pebble hammerstones, and pitted hammerstones were other common artifacts. Projectile points taken from Little Sycamore were mostly leaf-shapes or large triangular forms, for the most part unstemmed. Also excavated were "cogstones,"

stone disks with deeply notched edges, but just how these were used remains a mystery.[69] Other ground-stone objects such as small stone discoidals, perforated flat pendants or ornaments, charmstones, and steatite pipes completed this particular inventory. A few bone and shell artifacts have been recovered. At Little Sycamore, these included bone awls; spatulate bone pins; bipoints, or gorges; tubes; and a possible atlatl hook of antler, as well as a few *Olivella* shell beads; abalone and cowry pendants; and shell trumpets.

Burials were flexed, prone extended, or secondary. The graves were frequently covered with metates or with cairns made up of metates. At the Little Sycamore site a huge cairn of metates, many with their bottoms knocked out, has been partially uncovered. Fragments of human bones were found beneath the stones and scattered among them, perhaps indicating a mass burial place.

Little Sycamore, on the shore in Ventura County, is on a promontory overlooking the sea at the mouth of a small creek.[70] Sycamores, willows, and oaks grow along the creek bottom. The area of site refuse on the promontory is about 125 by 160 meters and a meter-and-a-half in depth. Mollusks and abalone shells were found throughout the midden. Some bones of the mule deer, the sea otter, and various water fowl have been preserved, but generally mammal and bird remains were rare. No vegetable remains were found in the debris, but the milling stones attest to the importance of nut and seed foods. Fish appear to have been rarely caught and eaten. Tapping of ocean resources by these Early Period populations had not yet attained the proportions it reached in later periods.

In central California in the Interior Valley subarea the Early Period is represented by the Windmiller phase.[71] Windmiller sites are located on clay knolls which protrude through the silts of the flats of the lower Sacramento Valley. Near the river shores are grasslands and oak groves which not only provided plant harvests but once teemed with animal life. Slab metates and bowl mortars have been found in the sites, but the preponderance of large, stemmed, chipped projectile points;

been suggested by finds of baked clay balls which were apparently used in basket "stone-boiling" in place of stones (Fig. 6-27*k–m*). Many burials have been exposed at the Windmiller sites. These burials were primary interments, the bodies having been placed in an extended, prone position. A majority of them were accompanied by artifacts, including *Olivella* and abalone beads, chipped-

Figure 6-25. Milling stones of the California Early Period, Central Valley. *Top:* Mortar with long, narrow trough. Diameter, 21.5 cm. *Bottom:* A cobble mortar. Diameter, 18 cm. (After Heizer, 1949.)

Figure 6-26. Projectile points of the California Early Period, Central Valley. Point at *top, left,* 4.2 cm. long. (Courtesy R. F. Heizer.)

bone fishhooks and gorges; and bone trident fish spears imply that game and fish from the river were more important in the diet than seeds and nuts. Other bone implements were rather scarce, but specimens recovered included bone splinter awls, daggers, pins (see examples in Fig. 6-27*a–c*), needles, bird-bone tubes, and flat spatulate bone objects. No slim-pointed awls of the type characteristically associated with the manufacture of coiled baskets have been discovered, nor have any coiled basketry impressions, although impressions of twined weaving indicate that the technique was practiced. That baskets were important as containers, and perhaps as cooking vessels, has

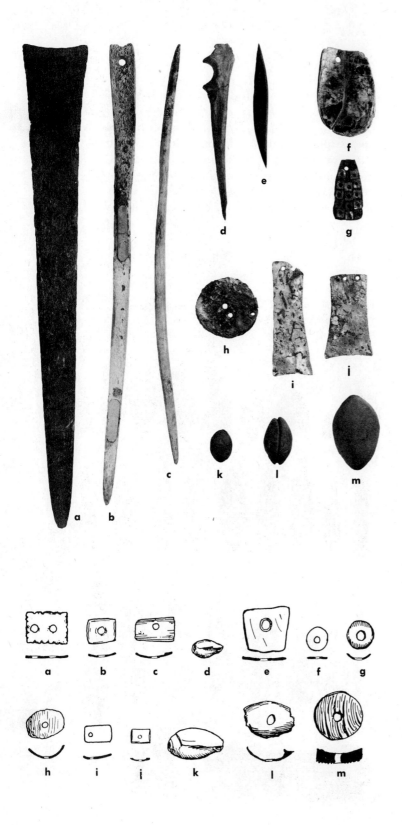

stone projectile points, quartz crystals, and charm-stones. The charmstones were ground and polished out of alabaster, granite, and blue schist and were fashioned in flattened or cylindrical forms tapering to either end from a central bulge (see Fig. 6-29a–h).

According to Heizer, remains from the southern San Joaquin Valley also may be attributed to the Early Period. But comparable evidence of the Early Period has not yet come from the Central Coast subarea around San Francisco Bay, although the horizon probably is represented there at the bases of some of the large shell middens. North of San Francisco Bay, in the North Coast Range subarea, the Mendocino and Borax Lake complexes may fall into the Early bracket, although this association is as yet uncertain. Similarly, in the east on the Sierra Nevada slopes, certain artifact forms suggest the Early Period, but more definite confirmation is needed.[72]

The Middle Period. Middle, or Intermediate, Period sites appear to be more widespread throughout the California area than those of the Early Period. The sites themselves are also larger. On the South Coast Heizer includes the La Jolla II phase of the San Diego region and the "Hunting Culture" phase of the Santa Barbara region in this Middle Period.[73] Meighan, for the same subarea, remarks that this was the time when the distinctive maritime adaptation that was later to characterize the Chumash and Gabri-

Figure 6-27. *Top, left:* Early Period artifacts, Central California. *a–c:* Long antler or bone daggers or pins. *d:* Bone awl. *e:* Double-pointed bone object (gorge ?). *f:* Biotite pendant. *g:* Turtle carapace pendant set with *Haliotis* beads. *h–j:* Haliotis ornaments. *k–m:* Baked-clay objects. Length of *a*, 32 cm. (Courtesy R. F. Heizer.)

Figure 6-28. *Bottom, left:* Shell beads, Central California. *a–d:* Early Period. *e–i:* Middle Period. *j–m:* Late Period. Length of *a*, 1.5 cm. (After Heizer and Fenenga, 1939.)

eliño of historic times developed.[74] In this connection he describes the site of Little Harbor which he considers ". . . provides some understanding of the shift from a land-oriented economy to one dependent almost entirely on the sea."[75]

Little Harbor is located on the seaward side of Santa Catalina Island. The island, one of the larger of the southern California offshore group, lies some 20 miles from the mainland. The site is a shell midden, averaging over a meter in depth, which caps a headland or promontory overlooking the ocean. A radiocarbon date of about 1900 B.C. was obtained from charcoal taken from a basal level. The artifacts from Little Harbor also reflect close continuities with the Early Period which, given the dating, is not surprising. Thus for example, the Little Harbor projectile points were of Early Period leaf-shaped or side-notched forms rather than the more typically Middle Period long-stemmed forms. No milling or metate stones have turned up; the principal grinding implements were the mortar and pestle. A variety of charmstones, small perforated stones, crude steatite effigies, pitted hammerstones, bone pries (for detaching abalone shells from the rocks?), awls, fish gorges, and shell beads were among the other Little Harbor artifacts. An analysis of the natural environment and the midden contents, however, throws more light on subsistence than inferences from tool and weapon forms. Catalina has a steep, hilly terrain, a relatively sparse vegetation cover, and a limited land fauna; and there is every reason to believe that these conditions have prevailed there for several thousand years. Seed and nut foods, therefore, would not have been abundant in this setting and land game would have been scarce. The refuse deposits at the site support these environmental observations. The Little Harbor debris was almost a solid mass of mussel (*Mytilus*) shells, abalone (*Haliotis*) shells, and marine mammal bones. Among the latter were dolphins and porpoises (*Cetacea*) and seals (*Pinnipedia*). Together, these composed 97 per cent of the animal bones found in the refuse. The remaining 3 per cent of the bones were of land mammals, principally deer.

Such a finding does not necessarily carry the same implications for all mainland sites of the Middle Period, but it does demonstrate that at least some groups were becoming highly adapted to marine living.

Such a marine adaptation implies great skill in handling small boats or canoes, for there is no way to catch porpoises and dolphins in any numbers except by going after them in such craft. Pre-

Figure 6-29. Ground- and polished-stone artifacts of the California Early Period, Central Valley. *a–h*: Charmstones. *i*: Hammerstone. *j*: Tubular or funnel-shaped pipe. *k*: Pendant. *l*: ring. *m*: Quartz crystal. *n*: Long slate, pencil-like object. Item *a*, 22 cm. long. (Courtesy R. F. Heizer.)

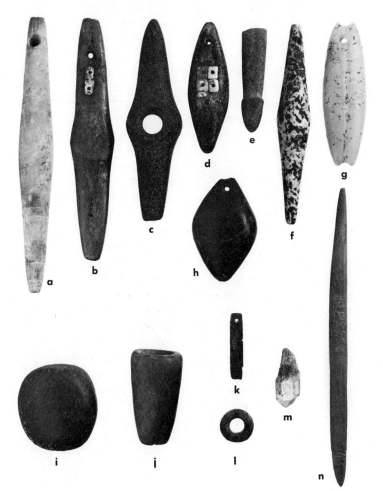

sumably the animals were hunted with the atlatl and dart or spear, tipped with the chipped-stone projectile points found in the site refuse. At least, no other suitable weapons were revealed by the excavations.

In the Interior Valley subarea of Central California during the Middle Period, populations had increased. The Middle Period, too, marked the beginning of the accumulation of the great shell refuse deposits of the Central Coast subarea, such as the Emeryville Shell Mound on San Francisco Bay.[76] Beardsley has outlined several culture phases, or subphases, of the Middle Period in each of these subareas.[77] The two subareas are linked by shared traits, but they are also distinguished by cultural differences. Many of these differences relate to differing subsistence patterns: the communities of the coast were rapidly moving toward a maritime and shellfish economy; those of the interior continued to rely more on hunting, river fishing, and plant-collecting. In the Interior subarea, where Early Period levels exist, the Middle Period occupations show some continuity with the earlier horizon but also exhibit a number of differences. Among these was a change in burial practices. Middle Period interments were usually tightly flexed, whereas formerly the bodies of the dead frequently were extended. Also, cremation was practiced in the Middle Period in the interior. We should mention, furthermore, that fewer grave goods accompanied the flexed burials than had been the case with the Early Period extended burials. A few Middle Period flexed burials, however, were replete with burial furniture, and all cremations had associated artifacts. Insofar as the skeletons themselves are concerned, it is interesting to observe that although all the Early Period crania relate to long- and high-headed individuals, the Middle Period peoples tended more toward meso- or brachycephaly. This trend continued into the California Late Period. It is another example of the general, almost American-wide shift from dolicho- to brachycephaly. Whether in this specific instance the change can be attributed to the appearance of new peoples who interbred with the

Early Period residents or whether it was caused by "genetic drift" is a moot question.

In Central California, the use of mortars and pestles was much more widespread in the Middle Period than in the Early Period, although they were rare commodities in the Interior Valley subarea, where suitable natural stone was scarce. In these alluvial valley regions, wooden mortars may have been used instead. For projectile points, obsidian was used more frequently in the Middle Period than it had been earlier, but otherwise the point types were similar—large and suited to the lance or dart but not to the arrow.[78]

Figure 6-30. Projectile and lance points of the California Middle Period, Central Valley. Point at *top*, *left*, 20 cm. long. (Courtesy R. F. Heizer.)

Fishing gear was used by both Interior and Coastal peoples. In the Interior, however, the bipointed bone fish-gorge and the unilaterally barbed bone fish-spear were preferred, implying line and spear fishing (Fig. 6-31*b–d*). Along the Coastal subarea, notched stone weights, presumably used for anchoring nets, suggest a seining technique.

In both subareas, bone tools were much more widely used during the Middle Period than ever before, particularly the slender, sharp awl, (Fig. 6-31*h*) which was used to make coiled baskets. Bone, along with antler, also was carved into ornaments. Typical Coastal specimens were long spatulate objects, which may have been head-scratchers or hair pins. In graves, they are usually found near the head of the individual. In the Interior, long pendants, beads, tubes, and perforated or grooved animal teeth were more fashionable.

In shell, circular or rounded rectangular beads of abalone were a diagnostic of the Middle Period. These were strung or attached like sequins and scattered over the burial. Larger circular and perforated abalone shell ornaments were also characteristic. In general, both in numbers and variety, shell ornaments were plentiful (see Figs. 6-28*e–i*; 6-31*m–n*).

In ground-stone ornaments, the Interior Valley featured ring-shaped and elongated perforated slate ornaments (Figs. 6-31*j,k;* 6-32, *right*), beads, and spool earplugs. Along the Central Coast, prismatic obsidian splinters known as tinklers and pentagonal ornaments of perforated mica were popular. Charmstones have been found in both subareas,

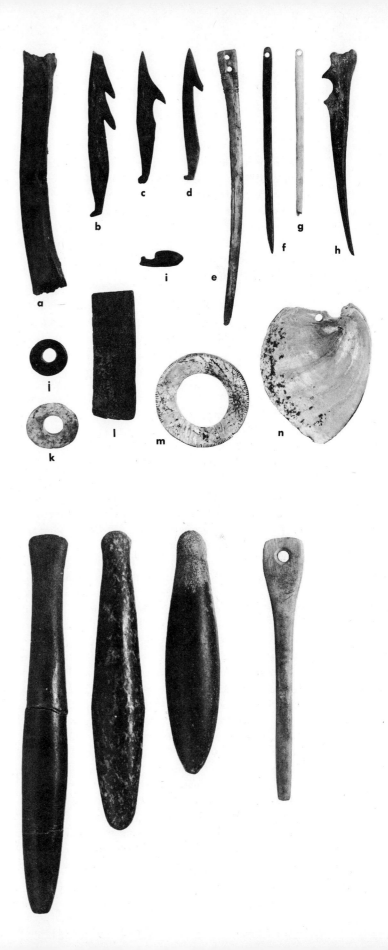

Figure 6-31. *Top, right:* Middle Period artifacts, Central California. *a:* Bone whistle. *b–d:* Bone fish-spears, each one-half of a pair. *e:* Bone pin or hair ornament. *f–g:* Matting needles. *h:* Bone awl. *i:* Atlatl hook. *j,k:* Stone rings. *l:* Flat bone net gauge (?). *m,n:* Abalone-shell ornaments. Length of *a*, 16 cm. (Courtesy R. F. Heizer.)

Figure 6-32. *Bottom, right:* Charmstones and perforated stone of the California Middle Period, Central Valley. Object at left, 20 cm. long. (Courtesy R. F. Heizer.)

the common Interior form featuring a flattened or "fish-tail" end (see Fig. 6-32), the Coastal variety, a pyriform stone with a short stem.

Baked clay balls used for basket-boiling have been taken in great quantities from Interior Valley sites, but are missing from the Coast, where the only fired clay artifacts so far discovered are crude human figurines.

Elsewhere in the state, as in the North Coastal subarea, the Sierra Nevadas, and in the far south of the San Joaquin Valley, there is substantial evidence of Middle Period habitation. Via these antecedents, we move to examine the cultures of the Late Period, which lead us directly to the historic tribes of the area.

The Late Period. Both Heizer and Beardsley, in summarizing the Late California Period, speak of regional and local differentiation of cultures, especially with reference to the South Coastal, Central Coastal, and Interior Valley subareas.[79] Apparently by the beginning of the period (during the first half-millennium of the Christian era) population growth was at or near a maximum and was divided into the politically independent and culturally differentiated tribes or tribelets that characterized the California area in the sixteenth century. Both men, however, make clear that the cultural differences among regional and local groups were essentially matters of elaboration or of emphases deriving out of microenvironmental subsistence adjustments. Overriding similarities were also apparent. Thus the bow-and-arrow was the dominant weapon throughout the area, replacing the spear-thrower; projectile points were small triangular, stemmed or side-notched forms, frequently with serrated edges and usually made from obsidian. Steatite became a common substance for long tubular pipes and for cooking vessels except in the south and east, where pottery cookware had been introduced from the Patayan culture of the Southwest. In the Central subareas, larger mortars and pestles came into much wider use. Throughout the period, stone and shell beads and ornaments become more numerous, more

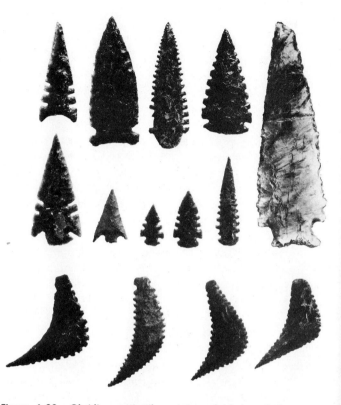

Figure 6-33. Obsidian projectile points and blades of the California Late Period, Central Valley. Point at *top, left,* 5.2 cm. long. The four objects at bottom are "Stockton curves" and, from ethnographic evidence, reputedly were tied to the fingers of a dancer to imitate bear claws. (Courtesy R. F. Heizer.)

elaborate, and more diversified (see Fig. 6-28 and also Fig. 6-35), and they serve, in their peculiarities, as some of the most distinguishing markers of the period. As an example, in the Central Interior Valley, a diagnostic bead type for the earlier part of the Late Period is a small *Olivella* form, rectangularly shaped, drilled at the center or at one end, and frequently found laid in shingled rows on the skull of a burial or on carbonized textiles associated with burials. On the South Coast, Heizer describes a circular shell fishhook which, although probably appearing slightly earlier, is a Late Period diagnostic.

The Late Period culture of the South Coastal subarea has been designated the Canaliño in the

Santa Barbara coastal and Channel Island region. Drawing upon both archaeology and ethnohistory, D. B. Rogers has reconstructed the life of these people.[80] Presumably they were the Chumash and their immediate ancestors.

Canaliño villages were located in the bottoms of small canyons through which intermittent streams flowed into the ocean. Nearby were brackish lagoons surrounded by thickets of scrub bush and reeds, excellent localities for wild fowl and small game; and at hand, of course, was the sea with its fish, shellfish, and sea mammals. House pat-

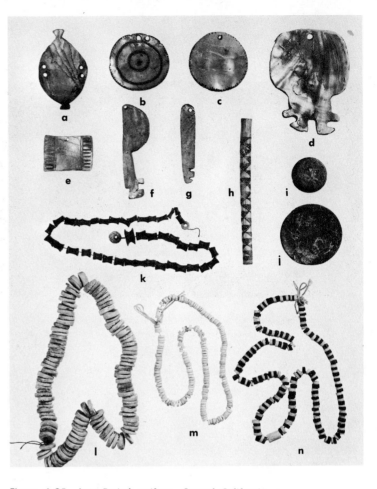

Figure 6-35. Late Period artifacts, Central California. *a–g: Haliotis*-shell ornaments. *h:* Incised-bone tube. *i,j:* Ground-stone lip or ear plugs. *k:* Beads of imitation (stone) fish vertebrae. *l:* Clam-shell disk beads. *m:* Disk beads of white magnesite. *n:* String of alternating white magnesite and black steatite beads. Length of *a*, 6.5 cm. (Courtesy R. F. Heizer.)

Figure 6-34. Late Period artifacts, Central California. *a:* Antler wedge. *b–d:* Mammal-bone awls. *e:* Bone whistle. *f:* Long, ceremonial, serrated spear point of flint. *g–i:* Stone tobacco pipes. *j,k:* Cylindrical stone (magnesite) beads. Length of *a*, 14 cm. (Courtesy R. F. Heizer.)

terns have been traced from debris. In the center was a fireplace, a dense bed of ashes usually filled with broken vessels and other artifacts and food debris. In a circle around the fireplace were other artifacts, frequently unbroken, and whole stone vessels and items of jewelry. From the distribution of these materials, it would seem that the dwellings were circular in plan and measured from about 4 to 7 meters in diameter. These inferences accord with ethnographic descriptions of Spanish priests in the latter half of the eighteenth century who described the huts as circular and dome-shaped, with a central fire area and roof smoke-hole. The dome shape was effected by driving

375

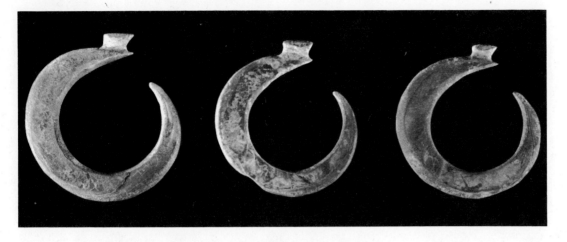

Figure 6-36. *Haliotis*-shell fishhooks, San Nicolas Island, California. Outer diameters of hooks, about 3 cm. (Courtesy Clement Meighan.)

poles into the ground and bending them inward. The pole frameworks were then covered with dried grass or reeds which was woven between the poles.

In addition to these "jacales," as they were called by the Spanish, the villagers also constructed sweat-houses, usually one to a village. These semi-subterranean structures had heavy pole frameworks which could sustain the weight of earth coverings. Entrances were in the roofs. Rogers mentions that these sweat-houses, or "temescales," were built on the order of the ordinary dwellings of the Oak Grove people, who occupied the same general region many centuries before in the Early Period, and suggests that they indicate a veneration for ancient forms in "public" or ceremonial structures comparable to the Pueblo subterranean kivas of the Southwest.

Two other types of constructions also found in some of the Canaliño villages are what Rogers calls "dance floors" and "sacred council chambers." The dance floors, if indeed this is what they were,[81] were slight oval depressions in the ground measuring about 20 meters or more across their maximum diameter. They contained hard-packed earth, usually free of stones and other debris, and were surrounded by low embankments of boulders and earth. Usually, they were located near the

temescal. Close at hand, also apparently of some ceremonial significance, were the so-called council chambers.[82] Rogers quotes Cabrillo,[83] the sixteenth-century explorer, to the effect that the Indians of the region built circular stone enclosures within which they placed wooden posts bearing pictures or insignia. Archaeologists have uncovered such stone circles, and these may relate to Cabrillo's descriptions. They are 6 to 7 meters in diameter, and the outer ring is of massive boulders. Within the outer circle is a smaller ring composed of small stones set on end. In one of these structures caches or arrangements of special paraphernalia were found, including charmstones, small stone effigies of whales, phallic-like "snakeheads," and what appears to be a gaming die. Whether or not such enclosures were roofed in full or in part is unknown.

The Canaliño buried their dead in cemetery areas within the village precincts. The typical interment was primary, tightly flexed, and in a small pit into which grave goods had been placed. A stone bowl was frequently inverted over the head or hips of the corpse. In some instances grave furniture, including steatite vessels and projectile points, had been broken, or "killed," before being placed with the dead. Some grave pits had been prepared by firing the sides of the excavation. Other pits had been lined with stone slabs, smeared with clay, and then fired. These practices do not, however, indicate *in situ* cremation, for the

376

Figure 6-37. Steatite sculptures of the Late Period or Canaliño culture of the Southern California coast. *Top:* A killer-whale effigy inlaid with shell beads, reportedly from a grave on Catalina Island. Length, about 10 cm. *Bottom:* So-called "pelican stone," unknown use. Height, 15 cm. (*Top,* courtesy Catalina Island Museum; *bottom,* courtesy Clement Meighan.)

bones of the dead show no effects of fire and were obviously placed in the graves after the burning.

The Canaliño were exceptional stone-carvers. They worked with sandstone and steatite and turned out hemispherical, flat-bottomed inverted conical, subglobular, and shallow elongate bowls. The stone was carefully pecked, ground, and smoothed. Large vessels were used for storing water or for "stone-boiling." Smaller specimens probably served as dishes. The shallow elongate types frequently found with traces of carbon around their rims may have been oil lamps. Yet another Canaliño stone vessel was an acorn mortar with a bottomless basket glued to the rim with asphaltum. This basket-mortar, or hopper-mortar, was used in hulling, grinding, and winnowing nuts, the meat of which was then leached with warm water. Although not perfected until the Late Period Canaliño phase, the basket-mortar was in use during the preceding Middle Period. Acorns were also ground in mortar holes which had been hollowed out of large boulders or other live-rock exposures near the villages. The stone pestles used with all of these mortars were long, cylindrical, and carefully formed, and frequently had carved ornamental handles (Fig. 6-39, *bottom*).

The full material culture inventory of the Canaliño is extensive and cannot be detailed in a summary survey. Many items, such as charm-stones, perforated stone disks, pitted stones probably used as small anvils or hammers, grooved stones used as net-weights or bolas, bone tools and hair ornaments, shell fishhooks and shell beads, and chipped-stone spear and arrow points were carry-overs from the preceding period, although in many cases these were modified in form and distinctive to the late horizon. Typical Canaliño small projectile points, apparently arrow-tips, were either triangular and fish-tailed or leaf-shaped.

The Late Period in the Interior Valley subarea of Central California must almost certainly be identified with the California Penutian-speaking tribes of that territory. The archaeological complexes reveal the general culture changes which we have already referred to: an elaboration and

Figure 6-38. *Above:* Late Period or Canaliño stone bowls, Southern California. *Left:* Steatite globular. Diameter, 28 cm. *Right:* Sandstone open. Diameter, 50 cm. (After D. B. Rogers, 1929.)

Figure 6-39. *Center, left:* Canaliño ground-stone implements. *Top:* A basket-mortar, showing asphaltum on rim where top was attached, and pestle. Diameter, 24 cm. *Bottom:* Typical carved pestle. Length, 36 cm. (After D. B. Rogers, 1929.)

Figure 6-40. *Bottom, left:* Late Period projectile points from Southern California. Length range, 2 to 3 cm. (Courtesy Clement Meighan.)

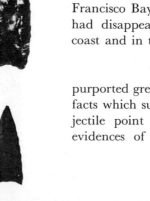

profusion of shell ornaments, the large stone mortar, and the long steatite smoking pipes. Cremation, practiced here in the Middle Period, increasingly became the accepted means of disposing of the dead.[84] Toward the end of the Late Period, European metal items and Chinese porcelains (brought by Spanish ships) were introduced in the vicinity of San Francisco Bay. Some of the sites in which these objects have been found date from the end of the sixteenth century; but for the most part, European articles, and in particular glass trade beads, belong to the latter part of the eighteenth century. It is from this later date that the truly Historic Period may be said to date. Native cultures vanished soon after in the San Francisco Bay region, and within 50 to 100 years had disappeared elsewhere along the California coast and in the interior.[85]

Summary. Leaving aside finds of purported great antiquity, as well as scattered artifacts which suggest affiliation with the fluted projectile point complexes, the earliest substantial evidences of habitation in the California area

378

Figure 6-41. Model canoes carved from steatite, from Catalina Island and, presumably, Canaliño graves. *Top:* Specimen is decorated with *Olivella* shell beads set in asphaltum. Length, 18 cm. *Bottom:* Length, 15 cm. (Courtesy Catalina Island Museum.)

pertain to people who were following in the technological traditions of the Old Cordilleran and Desert patterns. Perhaps the term "proto-Desert" would be more appropriate than "Desert," for these earliest California horizons lacked the diagnostic Desert tradition seed-grinding tools. At any event these artifact assemblages of Old Cordilleran and Desert-like flint implements were found in southern California on a time horizon preceding 5000 B.C. Subsequently, and apparently growing out of these earlier hunting and food-collecting complexes, the dominant area tradition arose. We have designated it by the name of California Coast and Valley, after its prime ecological settings.

The villages of the California Coast and Valley tradition were found along the Pacific shores or back in the great interior valleys of the Sacramento and San Joaquin Rivers. Archaeologists divide the tradition by several subareas and by three major periods: the Early, from 5000 to 2000 B.C.; the Middle, from 2000 B.C. to A.D. 250; and the Late, from A.D. 250 until the gradual extinction of native cultures in the eighteenth century. The basic economy throughout the history of the tradition was, of course, hunting and collecting, with those communities located along the seashore exploiting marine resources. For the most part subsistence was ample, owing particularly to the abundant acorn harvests of the interior valleys and to the plentiful fish, shellfish, and sea mammals along the coast. In addition to developing a chipped-stone technology, the peoples of the California Coast and Valley tradition were adept at grinding and polishing stone. From stone they fashioned implements for grinding seeds and nuts and a variety of ornamental or ceremonial forms. Ground- and polished-stone implements became more plentiful and elaborate throughout the archaeological sequences, but they also were in use during the Early as well as the Late and Middle Periods. Thus insofar as we are able to determine, these grinding and polishing techniques were as early in the California area as they were along the Northwest Coast or Interior Plateau areas to the north, and no fully convincing case can be made for deriving them from elsewhere. They may very well have been completely local developments.

Other chronological trends and changes that marked the California Coast and Valley tradition were an increasing maritime adaptation of the shore villages, over-all population growth for the area, and a population increase in individual village or town concentrations. During the Late Period, the bow-and-arrow replaced the dart or spear as the principal weapon, a change more or less concurrent with this event in other parts of native North America. Pottery was introduced from the Southwestern area into southern California toward the end of this period, and steatite vessels for cooking were developed locally and widely used.

The history of the California area and its Coast and Valley cultural tradition is a success story of diversified hunters and collectors who took advantage of a rich natural environment and fashioned a conservative and slow-changing adjustment to it. Perhaps because of their success and their conservatism, they resisted taking up agriculture, which they could have borrowed from their not-too-distant Southwestern area neighbors. In seeking for cause here, however, it is well to remember that the California coasts and valleys, with their Mediterranean type climate of winter rains and dry summers, were not ideally suited to maize cultivation.

The Northwest Coast

The Area and Its Subareas. The Northwest Coast area stretches along the north Pacific Coast from Cape Mendocino in northern California to Yakutat Bay in southern Alaska. It is essentially a maritime province. Toward the interior lie the Plateau and Subarctic areas, which are divided from the Northwest Coast by the Coastal Mountains of British Columbia and, farther south, by the Cascade Mountains of Oregon and Washington.

The terrain of the Northwest Coast varies from the islands, "drowned" fiord-type valleys, and mountains of the north to the gentler rounded hills and coastal estuaries of Washington and Oregon. Throughout, the area has a heavy forest cover of firs, spruce, cedar, redwood, and some deciduous trees. These wood resources were extremely important in the native material culture. Innumerable streams descend from the Pacific mountains to the coast, and great continental rivers, like the Columbia and the Fraser, also have their outlets in the area. Rainfall is high, but in spite of the wet, the climate is not disagreeably cold, because the Japanese Current exerts a moderating effect at this latitude. The sea and the rivers abound in fish, and these were a dietary staple from ancient to modern times. They include salmon, halibut, cod, herring, smelt, and olachen (candle-fish). Mollusks were once very plentiful, as is attested by the numerous prehistoric shell midden piles. For the sea hunter, seals, otter, porpoises, and whales thrived in the offshore waters. Along the shores were water fowl, and inland roamed deer, elk, mountain goats, bears, and smaller animals. In fact, there are few places in

Figure 6-42. (P. 381) Northwest Coast subareas follow Drucker (1955 b.) Certain archaeological sites and regions and neighboring culture areas are indicated.

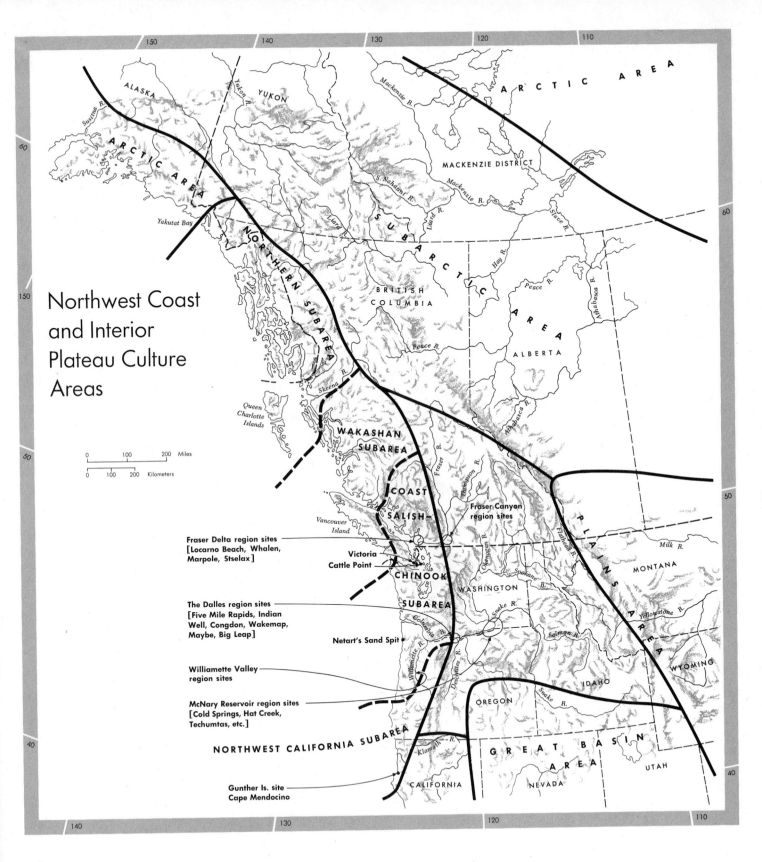

Northwest Coast and Interior Plateau Culture Areas

ARCTIC AREA

ALASKA

Suitna R.

Yukon R.

YUKON

A R C T I C   A R E A

Mackenzie R.

MACKENZIE DISTRICT

ARCTIC AREA

Yakutat Bay

S. Nahanni R.

Mackenzie R.

Liard R.

Liard R.

Slave R.

S U B A R C T I C

BRITISH
COLUMBIA

Peace R.

Athabasca R.

NORTHERN SUBAREA

Skeena R.

A R E A

Peace R.

ALBERTA

Queen
Charlotte
Islands

WAKASHAN
SUBAREA

Fraser R.

Thompson R.

Fraser Canyon
region sites

P L A I N S

Flathead R.

Milk R.

COAST
SALISH

Fraser Delta region sites
[Locarno Beach, Whalen,
Marpole, Stselax]

Vancouver
Island

Victoria
Cattle Point

CHINOOK

Okanogan R.

Spokane

MONTANA

A R E A

The Dalles region sites
[Five Mile Rapids, Indian
Well, Congdon, Wakemap,
Maybe, Big Leap]

SUBAREA

WASHINGTON

Snake R.

Columbia R.

Salmon R.

Yellowstone R.

Netart's Sand Spit

Williamette Valley
region sites

Williamette R.

Deschutes R.

IDAHO

WYOMING

McNary Reservoir region sites
[Cold Springs, Hat Creek,
Techumtas, etc.]

OREGON

Snake R.

NORTHWEST CALIFORNIA SUBAREA

Klamath R.

G R E A T   B A S I N

A R E A

UTAH

Gunther Is. site
Cape Mendocino

CALIFORNIA

NEVADA

0   100   200   Miles

0   100   200   Kilometers

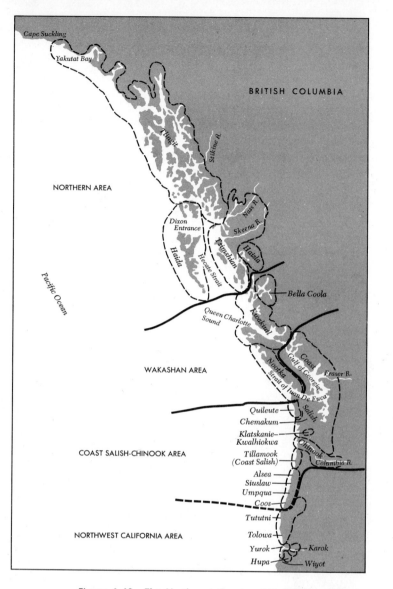

Figure 6-43. The Northwest Coast and its historic tribes. In this chapter Drucker's four areas are subareas: Northern, Wakashan, Coast Salish-Chinook, and Northwest California. (After Drucker, 1955 b.)

subareas may be meaningful in distinguishing archaeological culture differences has not yet been fully determined; however, it is likely that they will have some significance in this regard. The Northern subarea extended from Yakutat Bay to Queen Charlotte Island. Its major tribal groupings were the Tlingit, Haida, and Tsimshian. These peoples are generally considered of independent linguistic status, although some authorities group the Tlingit and Haida, together with the Athapascans, as Na-Dene, and classify the Tsimshian with the major Penutian stock. The second subarea, traveling southward, was the Wakashan. This territory embraced Queen Charlotte Sound and most of Vancover Island and its main inhabitants were the Kwakiutl, Nootka, and Bella Coola tribes. As the subarea name implies, the principal language family was the Wakashan, although the Bella Coola were Salishan. South and to the east of the Wakashan was the Coast Salish-Chinook subarea, which included the Gulf of Georgia, the southeastern shores of Vancouver Island, the Strait of Juan de Fuca, the Washington coast, and the upper Oregon coast. The Coast Salish, Chinook, Siuslaw, and other groups held this subarea, their principal language affiliations being Salishan and Chinook. This is the subarea, incidentally, in which archaeological knowledge and time depth is most developed. The fourth and southernmost subarea, the Northwest Californian, extends from the Coquille River in southern Oregon to Cape Mendocino, California. The tribes here included the Yurok (Ritwan-speaking), Karok (Hokan-speaking), and Hupa (Athapascan-speaking).

History. The tribes of the North- west Coast area were not touched by European influences until considerably later than their California neighbors to the south. Russians and Danes reached their shores during the early half of the eighteenth century, and Captain Cook arrived there in 1778. During the latter part of the eighteenth century, English, American, and Russian fur traders were competing in the area from sail-

the world where land and sea combine to offer such a rich and regular bounty for human consumption, and the Indians of the Northwest Coast, at least in later times, exploited it to the full.[86]

Philip Drucker has subdivided the Northwest Coast into four subareas (Figs. 6-42; 6-43).[87] These subareas show a close coincidence between cultures, as seen on the ethnographic level, tribal groupings, major language groupings, and physical type of inhabitants. The extent to which these

ing vessels. In 1821, a land-based fur trade began. In general, the Indians were materially enriched during the period. Metal tools were introduced, and these were important influences in the subsequent flowering of an already established wood-carving tradition. The Indians were largely successful, however, in keeping the actual fur-trading posts out of their immediate territories; and this undoubtedly preserved the native peoples from the erosive effects of Indian-White contacts. Thus many of them remained independent and culturally more or less intact. Such a continuity of vigorous Indian life persists in parts of British Columbia and southern Alaska down to the present day.

The Ethnographic Pattern.   The Northwest Coast has long been one of the classic culture areas of the ethnographer. Although displaying subareal differentiation, it has a general, area-wide ethnographic pattern which is in effect the historical end-product of what we have chosen here to call the Northwest Coast cultural tradition.[88] This general ethnographic pattern was based during the late nineteenth and twentieth centuries on a fishing and sea-mammal-hunting economy. Traps, angling devices, harpoons, and dugout canoes were the technical appurtenances. The canoes also were particularly important, for water transport along the rugged embayed coasts of the northern part of the area. Woodworking was emphasized, not merely in making the dugout canoes but also in constructing rectangular plank houses and carving household articles, masks, and totem poles. Woodworking tools of polished stone, bone, and antler later gave way to metal implements. Garments were untailored and aboriginally, were woven of plant fibers or in some cases of mountain-goat hair. The natives usually went barefoot. The basic socio-political unit was the lineage-local group. These usually autonomous units composed the larger tribes that we have just discussed. Social differences were rigid and were based on heredity and the accumulation of wealth. Slavery was practiced. Common ceremonial fea-

tures linked the various regions and subareas. One of the most conspicuous was the "potlatch," or the ceremonial display and dispersal of wealth. Another was the "first salmon rites," a propitiation to insure the continuity of the annual salmon "harvests" which were as secure and as bountiful as the agricultural harvests of successful farming peoples. In brief, although the Northwest Coast Indians were hunters, fishers, and gatherers, their level of subsistence and their material and non-material attainments were equal to or better than those of many agricultural societies.[89]

The Cultural Tradition as Seen Archaeologically.   A current problem for archaeologists is determining the antiquity and origins of this ethnographic pattern of the Northwest Coast. How is the pattern recognizable in the archaeological record? To answer this question involves trying to translate the ethnographically observed institutions and activities into their material exponents. We have already given some general indications along this line in regard to fishing and hunting equipment and to woodworking implements. Let us now take a more detailed look at an archaeological trait list for a Northwest Coast tradition. First are some of the hunting items—bone harpoons and points. Harpoons were of two types. The toggling type had a basal socket which fitted onto the blunt tip of a shaft or foreshaft the way a thimble fits onto a finger. The second type had a barbed head with a conical butt which was simply inserted into a socket at the end of the harpoon shaft. The term "fixed barbed points," which is often used by archaeologists, refers to a barbed bone point which was not normally intended to be detachable, but as the term implies, was firmly and permanently fastened to the shaft as a dart, arrow, or spear head is so attached.[90] Unbarbed bone and antler points were also widely used, as were large or medium-size chipped-stone projectile tips, leaf-shaped, stemmed, or barbed forms. Slate points and knives were also used fairly widely. Various notched and perforated stones were used for anchoring fishing nets. For woodworking, the diagnostic implements are heavy antler wedges and pestle-shaped stone hammers, as well as polished-stone adzes and celts. Sculpture and carving runs strongly throughout the Northwest Coast tradition, and the work in wood is only one aspect of it, perhaps a relatively late one. Bone, antler, and stone were also carved—as ornaments, figurines, vessels, effigies, pipes, and ornamented stone clubs (the so-called "slave-killers") —in the archaeological past. This early stone carving—in its peculiar renderings of animals and people—was clearly parent to the great historic woodcarving style of the area. All these elements, then, varying regionally and chronologically in terms of details of form, quantity, and quality, provide us with a sort of core which can be recognized and set apart on the American native scene as a Northwest Coast cultural tradition.

Hypotheses About Northwest Coast Culture Development. As to the origins and ages of these various traits and weaving them into a pattern, archaeological research in the Northwest Coast area is still too limited to offer any definite answers. But both ethnography and archaeology supply clues which bear on the problem, and various hypotheses have been constructed which deal with external influences, internal growth, and the rise of Northwest Coast culture. We will review some of these briefly before citing the specific archaeological finds.

In general, there have been two themes which run through the theories concerning Northwest Coast culture development. One of these sees the essential elements as being northern imports, from the Arctic Eskimo or from Asia. The other is more locally oriented. It conceives of peoples, culture traits, or both, moving to the coast from the Interior Plateau. Afterward, Northwest Coast culture flowered as a result of a maritime adaptation to the original land-oriented elements. Actually, these two points of view are not mutually exclusive, and it is almost certain that each contains some truth. The questions are rather in what combinations and how, when, and where did events occur. The late

Franz Boas, viewing the situation without benefit of archaeological research,[90a] leaned toward the Asiatic diffusion thesis. He pointed out that such things as slat-and-plate armor, the compound bow, and the tambourine drum were obviously of Asiatic origin and postulated a continuous distribution of such elements around the north Pacific rim from Siberia down the Northwest Coast of North America. This Asiatic to Northwest Coast continuity, in his hypothesis, had been broken and disrupted by the appearance of the Eskimo in Alaska.[91] Drucker, although accepting the Asiatic derivation of the traits Boas lists, plus a good many others, sees an important difference in the interpretation. Since archaeologists have now traced the origins of the Eskimo culture pattern to western Alaska, and carried them back at least to the first millennium B.C. if not earlier, he feels that the Eskimo must have been important participants in any Asia-to-Northwest Coast diffusion rather than its disrupters. In other words, he would see Northwest Coast culture arising from an early Eskimo base in southern Alaska and the Aleutians.[92]

A. L. Kroeber, drawing upon both ethnographic information and some of the early archaeological work of Harlan I. Smith, was one of the first to propound the Interior Plateau-to-Northwest Coast migration and diffusion hypothesis, whereby inland hunters worked their way down the various rivers to the coast and adjusted to maritime conditions.[93] A serious objection to this interpretation is that Northwest Coast culture is so much more elaborate in its ceremonial aspects than Plateau culture that it is difficult to see the latter as the source or, at least, the sole source of the former.

More recently, archaeologist C. E. Borden refurbished Kroeber's concept.[94] According to Borden's first opinions, the initial population and cultural pattern of the coast was derived from northern or "Eskimoid" sources. Then followed an important diffusion to the coast from the Plateau, bringing in such new traits and patterns as heavy stone adzes, antler wedges, and the woodworking complex. The blending of these two streams, the "Eskimoid," or maritime, with the Interior Plateau land-oriented pattern then gave rise to the classic Northwest Coast developments. Osborne and his associates challenged this reconstruction on two grounds: lack of evidence in the Interior Plateau of sufficient antiquity or even the presence of the traits and patterns which Borden would derive from that area, and the strong possibility that the "Eskimoid" elements of Borden's early coastal period are more likely to be a part of an ancient pre-Eskimo circum-polar diffusion from Asia to northern North America.[95]

In yet other and more recent statements, Borden has modified his views.[96] He now believes that the first occupants of the coast were Plateau hunters, perhaps as long ago as 6000 B.C. or earlier. Much later, but perhaps beginning as early as the second millennium before Christ, other groups found their way down the rivers from the Plateau to the coast. These peoples brought with them many traits which they had acquired indirectly from north Asiatic sources, especially polished-stone implements and a tradition of woodworking. Such traits and traditions were a part of a general circum-polar or circum-boreal distribution, related also to the comparable features of the Archaic tradition of the Eastern Woodlands of North America, which had also drawn on the same Asiatic inspiration. And these were the elements or the raw materials with which the peoples of the Northwest Coast built their unique culture. In this modification of his earlier ideas, Borden jettisons the Eskimo, or "Eskimoid," derivation of the Northwest Coast tradition. Instead, he sees many of its most important traits as appearing earlier on the Northwest Coast than in either the Aleutians or western Alaska and the Eskimo as the receivers rather than the donors of a Siberian Mesolithic-Neolithic technology which had passed down into northern North America by interior routes and then been taken westward to the Northwest Coast.

Such, in very brief form, are some of the highlights of the arguments about Northwest Coast culture origins. As of the present writing, they remain unresolved. What does stand out most clearly and certainly, however, is that the Northwest Coast tradition, in addition to the marvelous native food resources of the area, owed much of its material richness and probably some of its color and flamboyance to an Asiatic ancestry. This ancestry, while traceable back a considerable distance in time, was not of the very remote Paleo-Indian past but of the middle chronological ranges, possibly from 4000 to 1000 B.C. It is an ancestry which can be identified beyond much doubt with Siberian Mesolithic and Neolithic complexes. It also seems to be an ancestry to which certain elements of the Eastern Archaic tradition can be traced. Just how these distantly derived but important Asiatic influences became implanted upon the Northwest Coast and how they became combined with the earlier local traditions to form the Northwest Coast culture is the story which still remains for archaeologists to reveal.

Old Cordilleran Antecedents. You will recall that in Chapter 2 we discussed the Old Cordilleran tradition of northwestern North America as a probable local parent tradition of both the Northwest Coast and the Northwest Riverine (Plateau) traditions. By "local parent" we mean, in this instance, an ancient resident culture of the late Pleistocene which gave rise to certain hunting and fishing practices that carried down through the millennia into late prehistoric and historic cultures. It does not mean, as should be clear from the foregoing discussion of the extra-areal influences which impinged on both the Northwest Coast and the Plateau developments, that the full pattern and "set" of the later traditions can be derived *in toto* from the Old Cordilleran stock. It implies, rather, that the Old Cordilleran culture provided the matrix for later developments. To date the best evidences of the Old Cordilleran tradition come from the lower Columbia River Valley in the vicinity of The Dalles.[97] This area is some 180 to 190 miles upstream from the coast and within the Plateau area rather than the Northwest Coast proper. Farther north, in the Fraser Canyon, the Old Cordilleran culture is again revealed in deep stratigraphic levels on the western edge of the Plateau area.[98] It is generally believed that these Old Cordilleran occurrences date at the latest from about 7000 to 5000 B.C.[99] Quite probably, as we stated previously, the tradition goes back much earlier. Although these Old Cordilleran finds lie largely within the province of what is now the Plateau area, there have been land-sea changes there since the termi-

nal Pleistocene and the early post-Pleistocene. At that time, geologists feel both the Fraser Canyon and Dalles regions were much nearer the sea than they are today, and deep embayments extended up the present river mouths. Certainly sea mammals were hunted and killed by the early Dalles inhabitants, who used barbed-bone harpoon points as well as the Old Cordilleran marker type, the leaf-shaped point of chipped stone. These early Dalles hunters were also great salmon fishermen; thus in

Figure 6-44. Chronological chart showing Northwest Coast sequences from the Coast Salish-Chinook subarea and Interior Plateau area sequences from The Dalles and elsewhere.

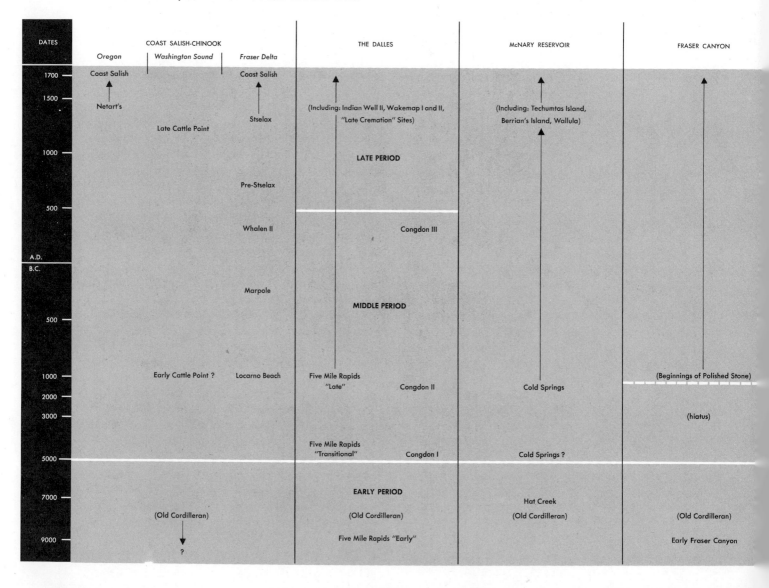

DATES	COAST SALISH-CHINOOK			THE DALLES		McNARY RESERVOIR	FRASER CANYON
	Oregon	Washington Sound	Fraser Delta				
1700	Coast Salish		Coast Salish				
1500	Netart's			(Including: Indian Well II, Wakemap I and II, "Late Cremation" Sites)		(Including: Techumtas Island, Berrian's Island, Wallula)	
		Late Cattle Point	Stselax				
1000				LATE PERIOD			
			Pre-Stselax				
500							
			Whalen II		Congdon III		
A.D.							
B.C.							
			Marpole				
				MIDDLE PERIOD			
500							
1000	Early Cattle Point ?	Locarno Beach	Five Mile Rapids "Late"	Congdon II			(Beginnings of Polished Stone)
2000						Cold Springs	
3000							(hiatus)
5000				Five Mile Rapids "Transitional"	Congdon I	Cold Springs ?	
7000				EARLY PERIOD		Hat Creek	
	(Old Cordilleran)			(Old Cordilleran)		(Old Cordilleran)	(Old Cordilleran)
9000	?			Five Mile Rapids "Early"			Early Fraser Canyon

an Old Cordilleran context the basic economic adaptations of the later Northwest Coast tradition were beginning to emerge.

In the Northwest Coast area proper, there are also hints of the early presence of the Old Cordilleran pattern. On the east coast of Vancouver Island, for example, Old Cordilleran, or Lerma-like, leaf-shaped points dating to about 6300 B.C. have been found.[100] Elsewhere it is undoubtedly significant that the lower levels of later prehistoric sites were always characterized by abundant leaf-shaped points, which then tend to be replaced at least partially by stemmed and notched types. Present research, however, indicates that a gap of some several millennia exists in the coastal archaeological record, between about 6000 B.C and the later prehistoric cultures which take up the sequence at around 1000 B.C. or perhaps slightly before. One possible candidate for this hiatus is the undated Island phase which A. R. King has reported from the lowest levels of Cattle Point on San Juan Island in Washington Sound.[101] King has described this complex as reflecting a preoccupation with land hunting. Deer and other land-mammal bones were most conspicuous in the midden refuse, along with some fish bones and seal remains. King believes that the site was a seasonal fishing camp for a people who were primarily land hunters. Leaf-shaped points were the most common chipped-stone projectile form found in the area, plus some bone awls and points, including fixed barbed types, and some ground-slate weapons. No trace of toggle harpoons has appeared. As we shall see, this assemblage has a transitional cast to it—transitional, that is, between the more strictly Old Cordilleran adjustment and the later maritime adaptations. Perhaps it is significant that the east coast of Vancouver Island and San Juan Island are in the Coast Salish-Chinook subarea of the Northwest Coast, and it is into this subarea that both the Columbia and Fraser Rivers flow.

The Fraser Delta Sequence. It is in the Coast Salish-Chinook subarea that we have our first view of the fully emerging Northwest Coast tradition. At the delta of the Fraser River, Borden has defined several culture phases which would appear to span the period from about 1000 B.C. to the historic horizon. The chronology of these phases is, as yet, uncertain. Originally, Borden grouped his Locarno Beach I and II phases, together with a Whalen I phase, into an Early Period. These were followed by an Intermediate Period composed of the Marpole, Point Grey, and Whalen II phases; and this in turn was succeeded by a Late Period Stselax phase.[102] Although some recent radiocarbon dates have cast doubt on the order of succession of the Early and Intermediate phases, it is likely that Borden's sequence is substantially correct.[103] The Early Period phases of Locarno Beach and Whalen I, now jointly called the Locarno Beach phase, probably spanned the centuries from 1000 B.C. to the beginning of the Christian era. The Intermediate Period phases of Marpole, Point Grey, and the more recently excavated Beach Grove component, now grouped together under the name Marpole phase, have been dated to 300 B.C. to A.D. 400. The other Intermediate Period phase, Whalen II, which is typologically quite distinct from the Marpole phase sites, lasted from A.D. 300–700. That the Stselax phase is late prehistoric-to-historic Coast Salish has been well documented, and the occupation is dated as A.D. 1250 to, in effect, the modern Musqueam community which today lives on a part of the site. Borden has also hypothesized another phase, which he tentatively calls "Pre-Stselax," and for which he has some surface collection indications from other sites. He places this Pre-Stselax phase at A.D. 700–1250, or between Whalen II and Stselax.[104] (See Fig. 6-44.)

In the Locarno Beach phase, Borden found conclusive evidence of the hunting of sea mammals. Besides the animal bone refuse, he discovered toggling harpoons of antler, including plain one-piece toggle heads, some slotted for cutting blades, and composite, or two-piece, toggles. No harpoons were barbed, but some fixed barbed points and unbarbed bone points also were taken from the refuse. Heavy mussel shells, as well

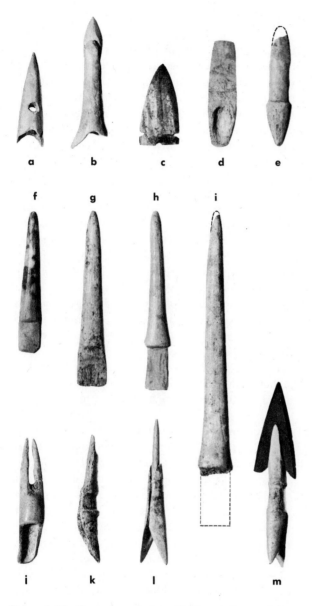

as bone and antler, were used for making points, scrapers, and knives. Chipped-stone was not very common, but the standard projectile point was the stemless leaf-shape. The ground-slate industry, on the other hand, was highly developed, and a variety of points and knives were made of this

Figure 6-46. Fixed barbed points from Northwest Coast cultures. a–c: Locarno Beach phase. d–l: Marpole phase. a,b: Bone. c–l: Wapiti antler. Length of a, 26 cm. (Courtesy Charles Borden.)

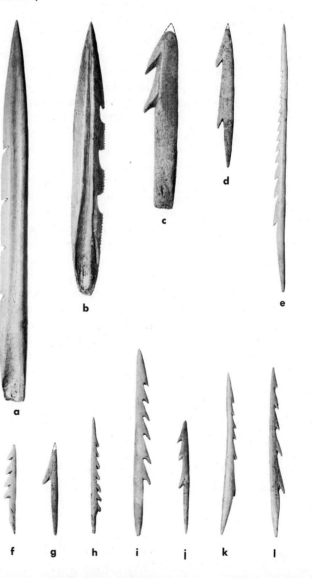

Figure 6-45. Harpoon parts from Northwest Coast cultures. a: Unarmed toggle harpoon head. b: Toggle head, slotted and armed with bone point. c: Side and basally notched point of ground mussel shell. d,e: Valves for composite toggle heads: d a ventral view, and e a dorsal view. f–i: Fore-shafts for toggle heads. j: Toggle head, slotted for point. k: Valve for composite toggle, side view. l: Composite toggle armed with slender bone point. m: Composite toggle armed with ground-slate point. All made from wapiti antler except where speci-fied otherwise. a–i: Locarno Beach phase. j: Marpole phase. k: Whalen II phase. l,m: Stselax phase. Length of a, 6 cm. (Courtesy Charles Borden.)

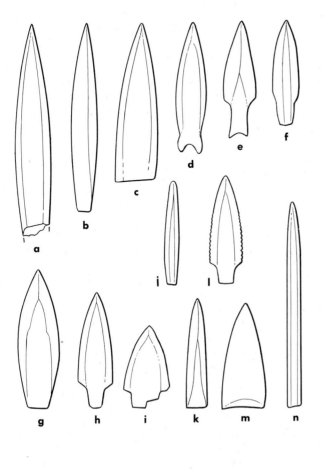

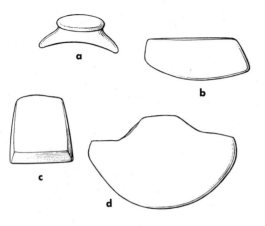

material (Figs. 6-47a–h; 6-48b). The outstanding ground- or polished-stone implements were small adzes and chisels of nephrite, suitable for small-scale or light woodworking, but not for constructing such things as dugout canoes. Since his searches revealed no heavy adzes nor wedges, Borden infers that skin boats must have been used rather than dugouts. Besides the nephrite tools, other finely polished items of stone from the site were ear spools and labrets. That a tradition of carving and sculpturing already existed, if on a very small-scale, has been attested by the discovery of a bone throwing-stick hook carved as a human head.

The Marpole[105] phase is similar to Locarno Beach in its maritime adjustment except that this culture was even more specialized to its environmental niche. The barbed-antler harpoon, rather than the toggle type, was the common Marpole form, and in many varieties. Fixed points of antler (Fig. 6-46d–l) were also used for fish spears, darts, and, perhaps, arrow tips. Perforated net-weights were another frequent item in Marpole sites. Chipped-stone items were more carefully fashioned than those from Locarno Beach. Leaf-shaped points, some with incipient stems, stemmed and barbed points, and a variety of knives, scrapers, and other tools were also found. Ground-slate (Fig. 6-47i–n) implements continued to be made but differed from Locarno specimens in that such things as ulu knives (Fig. 6-48d) were thinner and more carefully polished. Small sculptured stone bowls fashioned in anthropomorphic or zoomorphic forms (Figs. 6-50; 6-51, right) were another distinctive item. Beads of stone and shell

Figure 6-47. *Top, left:* Ground-slate blades, Northwest Coast. a–h: Locarno Beach phase. i–n: Marpole phase. Length of a, 16 cm. (After Borden, 1962.)

Figure 6-48. *Bottom, left:* Marpole and Locarno Beach polished-stone artifacts. a: Labret, Marpole phase. b: Slate ulu, Locarno Beach phase. c: Jadeite adze, Marpole phase. d: Slate ulu, Marpole phase. (After Borden, 1962.)

were especially popular. A major departure from Locarno Beach was heavy woodworking, reflected in the large stone adze blades, (Fig. 6-52*a–e*) stone hand mauls (see Fig. 6-53), and antler wedges (Fig. 6-54*a–c*), which have been recovered. These implements were undoubtedly used in constructing dugout canoes and plank houses. In general, the Marpole phase represents a first full blooming of the Northwest Coast tradition which was anticipated but not fully achieved at Locarno Beach. The villages were large, extending over several acres. Although the archaeological evidence is still quite sparse, it is highly likely that the big wooden houses, known from later prehistoric and historic times, were present in Marpole. Furthermore, from caches of beads and rare native copper ornaments, and from the occasional lav-

Figure 6-49. *Below, left:* Wapiti antler barbed harpoons, Marpole phase. Length of *a*, 8.7 cm. (Courtesy Charles Borden.)

Figure 6-50. *Below, right:* Stone-head mortar, Marpole phase. Height, 20.5 cm. (Courtesy Charles Borden.)

Figure 6-51. (*Top,* p. 391) Seated human-figure bowls of carved stone. *Left:* From North Saanich; height, 35 cm. *Right:* From Marpole site, Marpole phase; height, 10 cm. (*Left,* courtesy Wilson Duff; *right,* courtesy Charles Borden.)

Figure 6-52. (*Bottom, left,* p. 391) Adze blades of nephrite from the Northwest Coast. *a–e:* Marpole phase. *f:* Stselax phase. Length of *a*, 5.5 cm. (Courtesy Charles Borden.)

Figure 6-53. (*Bottom, right,* p. 391) Stone hand mauls, Marpole phase, Northwest Coast. Height of *a*, 20.7 cm. (Courtesy Charles Borden.)

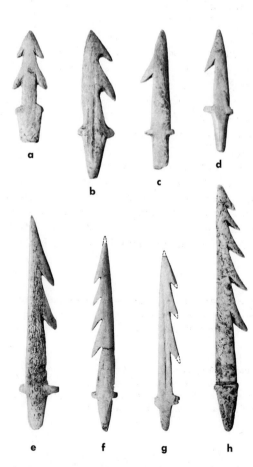

a

b

c

d

e

f

a

b

391

Figure 6-54. Wapiti antler wedges. *a–c:* Marpole phase. *d,e:* Stselax phase. Length of *a,* 14 cm. (Courtesy Charles Borden.)

Figure 6-55. Northwest Coast bone carvings. *Top:* Great blue heron, Marpole phase. Height, 11 cm. *Bottom:* Whale or fish effigy. Length, 12 cm. (After Borden, 1962.)

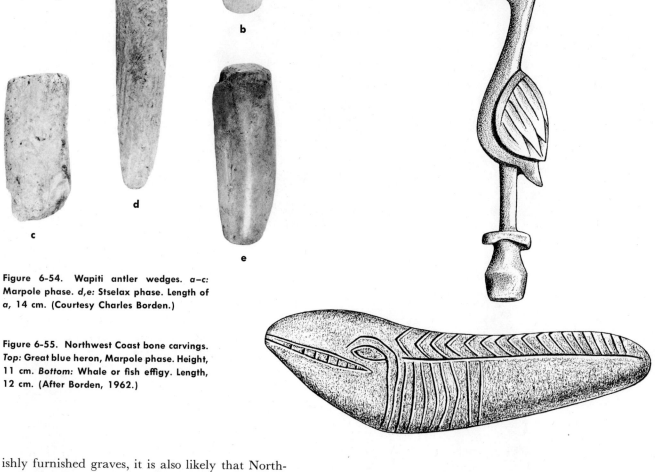

ishly furnished graves, it is also likely that Northwest Coast concepts of wealth and social stratification were emerging at this time.

The Whalen II phase witnessed a synthesis of some Locarno Beach and Marpole elements, such as toggling harpoons and heavy woodworking tools; however, slate work and stone sculpture had been abandoned. Some sculptural tradition was retained locally, however, as witnessed by carved-bone objects. (For harpoons, see Fig. 6-45*k.*)

This Fraser delta sequence, as it is now known, does not necessarily apply universally to the Northwest Coast or even to the Coast Salish-Chinook subarea. Almost certainly, the Locarno Beach-Marpole-Whalen II sequence was not a closed, unilinear development or cultural evolution. Quite likely each of these culture phases, as seen in the rich coastal environment of the delta, represented a society whose history was somewhat sepa-

392

Figure 6-56. Three views of seated human-figure bowl of carved stone, from Lytton, British Columbia. Height, 12 cm. (Courtesy Wilson Duff.)

rate from that of the others. Thus Borden speculates that the Locarno Beach phase may have been formed on the coast somewhat farther north, although to the south of Alaska, while Marpole probably originated inland on the Fraser River and the Plateau. Whalen II may have been a local synthesis, although there is a distinct possibility that it represented the movement of still another group to the Fraser delta.[106] In this last connection, the absence of Whalen II ground-slate and stone sculpture almost certainly was not typical of the entire Coast Salish-Chinook subarea; and other cultures, contemporaneous but as yet undiscovered, must have carried on these two traditional technologies. In any event, we can definitely say that in the millennium before the beginning of the Christian era, a Northwest Coast tradition was being assembled and synthesized in that area and that by the close of that millennium it was fully formed.

Fraser River Stone Sculpture. Two aspects of the Northwest Coast development deserve special mention. One of these is the stone carving of the Fraser River. This carving included small objects such as labrets, pipes, ornaments, figurines, and what may be throwing-stick weights; but it is

best known for its larger stone bowl and effigy forms of seated humans (Fig. 6-51, *left;* Fig. 6-56; holding bowls in their lap or between their legs. Some were over 30 centimeters high, and many of them were sophisticated works of art. The carvings seem to center on the lower Fraser River although they are also found farther up that stream in Plateau country and on the islands in

Figure 6-57. Zoomorphic stone bowl, Northwest Coast, from the Upper Skagit River, British Columbia. Length, 14 cm. (After Duff, 1956.)

the Gulf of Georgia. Most were made of steatite, although some were of sandstone. We have already mentioned that such sculpture was practiced in the Marpole phase, but its origins may go back even farther. Significantly, in the Fraser River Canyon on the edge of the Plateau, Borden found small steatite animal effigies—apparently prototypical of later Fraser River sculptural developments—which date to as early as 800 B.C.[107] Thus these carvings had early roots, although Wilson Duff, who has written a definitive monograph on the subject, feels that the finest specimens probably fall in the first millennium A.D.[108] The Fraser stone-carving is especially interesting, of course, since it appears to be the prototype of the Northwest Coast wood sculpturing of the ethnographic horizon. Duff compares it most closely with the Wakashan subarea wood sculpture style, an interpretation which fits in with Drucker's designation of the Wakashan subarea as a refuge for earlier Northwest Coast customs and patterns.[109] Presumably the seated-stone-figure-vessels depict guardian spirits. There is evidence that they were used by Salish shamen or ritualists in even recent times; however, to quote Duff: "Their use seems to have been on the decline, and the decline may have been well under way in pre-contact times."[110]

Burial Mounds or Cairns. The other Northwest Coast feature of unusual interest is the burial mound or cairn. The existence of these mounds has been known and reported for many years, but unfortunately most of the excavations conducted in such mounds were carried out before archaeological recording techniques were refined. Near Victoria, B.C. small dome-shaped mounds of earth and stone apparently covered single, partially cremated burials. The skeletal remains were placed in a shallow subsurface pit which then was covered with earth and rock. An outer ring of large stones was set up about the central cairn, and then the whole was mounded again to a height of a meter or more.[111] Similar mounds have also been found elsewhere on Vancouver Island and on the Puget Sound mainland. It is

not clear if the burials, in all these instances, showed signs of cremation or not. A noteworthy, if negative, feature is that grave artifacts were virtually never associated with the mounds; hence it is difficult to date them. Since such mounds are frequently found in close proximity to midden sites, however, and since these middens contain materials of a developed Northwest Coast pattern, it is possible that they may have been constructed at any time in the prehistoric past back to 1000 B.C.

Late Prehistoric-to-Historic Developments. Outside of the Coast Salish-Chinook subarea, Northwest Coast archaeology seems to pertain to what can be called a late prehistoric-to-historic period. Presumably earlier levels of occupation will be found in these subareas, but whether these will reveal a Northwest Coast cultural tradition or something else remains to be seen. In the Northwest California subarea, the Gunther Island site on Humboldt Bay carries a radiocarbon date of A.D. 900 for its earliest level, and other sites in the subarea carry the story on from A.D. 1200 to 1600.[112] The Gunther Island artifact complex included the heavy antler and bone wedges and stone mauls used in large-scale woodworking. Carved zoomorphic clubs, tubular steatite pipes, and stone bowls represented the stone-carver's art. The site also has yielded barbed harpoons and toggle harpoons; chipped-stone points, both stemmed and notched; and an unusual Northwest Coast feature, a fired clay figurine. In the early subphase at Gunther Island, ceremonies for the dead included burning grave goods in the grave pit prior to placing the corpse on the burning embers. In the later subphase, burials were simple primary, extended interments without offerings. The Gunther Island site probably was occupied by the historic Wiyot tribe.[113]

On the Oregon coast, the late prehistoric and historic remains of the Tillamook (Coast Salish) have been discovered at the Netarts sand spit site, which lies within the Coast Salish-Chinook subarea.[114] This site was occupied from about

A.D. 1400 to 1800, and of particular interest are the seventeenth-century remains of a rectangular wooden house. The building measured 16 by 4.5 meters and was constructed with four large corner posts. Smaller supporting wall posts had been placed between the corner posts, and the side walls were made of horizontal cedar planks. Mats covered the end openings of the building, which had a single-pitch roof. Inland in Oregon in the Willamette Valley are refuse mounds which served as both camp sites and burial places for the Calapuya. These sites show some Plateau affinities but are essentially within the Northwest Coast orbit.[115]

Much farther to the north, in the Wakashan and Northern subareas, the late prehistoric, protohistoric, and historic periods are represented by the numerous midden sites along the coasts, which Drucker has explored.[116] Drucker characterized the Wakashan subarea as lacking, or only weakly reflecting, those elements which might be traceable to interior influences. His position seems consistent with the ethnographic picture here, for tribes like the Kwakiutl had very little contact with interior groups. But he does point out some archaeological signs of interior contacts in the Northern subarea—heavy splitting adzes and hafted stone mauls. Composite harpoons, fixed bone points, and serpentine celts were widely used; very few ground-slate weapons and stone splitting adzes have been recovered. Mound, or cairn, burial was not practiced in either the Wakashan or the Northern subareas. Here the dead were placed directly in the middens or in wooden boxes and left in rock shelters or caves. Cremation was practiced in the Northern subarea only on the ethnographic horizon.

Now to return to the Coast Salish-Chinook subarea. During the late prehistoric-to-historic continuum of the postulated Pre-Stselax and well-documented Stselax phases, hunters and fishermen plied their trades with composite and toggle harpoons and slate weapons. Intact, a variety of slate artifacts have been found. Woodworker's wedges, mauls, and adzes, attest to the vigor at

Figure 6-58. Stone hand mauls, Stselax phase, Northwest Coast. Height of maul at *left*, 18.5 cm. (Courtesy Charles Borden.)

his craft, whereas the paucity of chipped-stone finds bespeaks the decline of this industry. In certain localities shellfish may have become scarce, perhaps because the beaches were drying up, as King argues with reference to the Late phase at Cattle Point.[117] As a result, population pockets may have grown smaller, although in general the subarea and the entire Northwest Coast area can hardly be said to have been suffering from any very serious cultural decline. The evidence for house types is now secure. At the Stselax village, huge rectangular wooden buildings were constructed by suspending hand-split cedar planks between paired upright posts. The planks were clapboarded. Roofs were of the single-pitch type. Stone-carving was no longer practiced but wood-carving was. Personal ornaments were rather scarce. Antler combs carved with zoomorphic and anthropomorphic elements were most popular. This seems to have been the time when the idea of spinning and weaving was introduced, using mountain goat and dog wool. Carved spindle whorls of whalebone have been found in the middens. Burial practices changed at some time in this late prehistoric period. Corpses were wrapped in mats or blankets and stored in a mortuary house. In brief, the stage on which the colorful and rich native life of ethnographic record was to be enacted was fully set.

Summary. In retrospect, the interpretation of the development of the Northwest Coast tradition which we prefer, given our present state of knowledge, is one which saw an Old Cordilleran hunting pattern of the Interior Plateau become specialized toward a river fishing, hunting, and shellfishing existence. Probably sometime prior to 5000 B.C. this pattern was shared both by Plateau river societies, at the gateways to the coastlands on the Columbia and Fraser, and by groups that had recently descended to the coast proper. Out of this resident base the Northwest Coast tradition was developed through adaptation to a maritime environment and through the acquisition, modification, and specialization of new traits which in the broadest sense may be attributed to a circum-polar diffusion from Asiatic Mesolithic and Neolithic sources. This process probably began sometime after 5000 B.C. By the first millennium B.C., a Northwest Coast tradition was a functioning, viable entity. It seems most likely that the main courses of this diffusion were from the Arctic, down through the Subarctic, into the Interior Plateau area and from there westward by the river valleys to the Northwest Coast. This point, however, remains moot; and it may be that diffusion from Alaska southward along the coast was equally or more important. Borden has argued that many of the characteristic Northwest Coast features were earlier within that tradition than they were in Eskimo culture and that probabilities favor a northward Pacific coastal diffusion from the Northwest Coast into Alaska rather than the reverse.[118] To support his case he cites such things as ground-slate implements, nephrite and serpentine celts, carved labrets and ear spools, and stone-effigy sculpture as being more ancient on the Northwest Coast than in Eskimo contexts.

Diffusion from Asia, by way either of the interior or the coast, had not run its course before 1000 B.C. Other elements later were added to the Northwest Coast pattern, some of which may have been passed southward by the Eskimo, others probably coming from Athapascan peoples of the northern interior. In fact, peoples such as the Haida and Tlingit were probably relatively latecomers to the Northwest Coast from the interior.

By the end of the first millennium A.D., a Northwest Coast tradition had reached its near-final form. At this time it was spread throughout the area from southern Alaska to northern California. How early this spread occurred is unknown; it is only in the centrally located Coast Salish-Chinook subarea that the earlier levels of the tradition have been found. Throughout the area the tradition seems to lead directly into ethnographically recorded Northwest Coast cultures which enjoyed a material post-European flowering as a result of the fur trade during the eighteenth and nineteenth centuries.

The Interior Plateau

The Area and Its Peoples. The Interior Plateau like the Northwest Coast is mainly an ethnographer's area (see Figs. 6-42; 6-59). Its cultural distinctiveness is, however, less sharp; and it has been debated whether the Plateau should stand apart as a culture area or simply be considered as a sort of transitional zone between the Plains, the Great Basin, and the Northwest Coast.[119] Our position follows Shiner and Osborne in that we examine the question from historical and archaeological as well as ethnographic perspective and hold that the Plateau was the hearth of a separate major cultural tradition.[120] This tradition was fully evident in late prehistoric times. Its Plains area coloration is easily ascribed to quite late, even historic and post-European, contacts. Its Great Basin affiliations are ancient ones that for the most part appear to antedate the rise of the distinctive Plateau culture. Its Northwest Coast affinities cannot be dispensed with so easily. They are prehistoric although relatively late, and the relationship between the two areas was intimate. The problems surrounding this relationship are far from settled, as we have seen from the preceding section; nevertheless, the late prehistoric Plateau pattern seems now sufficiently different from that of the Northwest Coast to justify its separate areal and traditional treatment here.

The Interior Plateau area is bounded on the west by the slopes of the Cascades and the Coastal Mountains of British Columbia. On the east it extends to the Flathead River in western Montana and, farther south, to the continental divide. Its southern boundary abuts on the Great Basin in central Oregon and southern Idaho. The northern boundary is less clearly fixed but falls somewhere along the divide separating the upper Fraser and the upper Mackenzie tributaries, perhaps a little south of the 55th parallel. In terms of modern political divisions, central and northeastern Oregon, eastern Washington, most of Idaho and a western edge of Montana, and interior southern British Columbia are included. The major drainages are the Klamath, Columbia-Snake, and Fraser-Thompson river systems, all of which eventually cut through the western mountains and fall to the Pacific.

Structurally the southern part of the Plateau is a vast basin surrounded on the west, north, and east by mountains. Its geological under-structure is volcanic lava. General elevation is about 5000 feet, although there are deep canyons and high mountain slopes which range from almost sea level to as high as 10,000 feet. Annual rainfall is slightly less than 20 inches. Summers are warm; winters go below freezing but are not severely cold. The southern, volcanic part of the Plateau, which grades imperceptibly into the Great Basin to the south, has a somewhat similar vegetation to that of the Basin—dry, treeless, and covered only with cactus and sagebrush. The exceptions to this pattern, and these were important on the primitive economic level, are the major river valleys. These carried a great volume of water from the east through the semi-arid Plateau and provided a constant supply of fish. Forests and timber were available to the inhabitants of the Plateau in certain regions, especially on the western slopes of the Rockies, where pines, Douglas fir, and even maple grew. In general, the northern part of the Interior Plateau which is composed of the northern Rockies of Canada is more heavily forested and better watered than the southern part.

The two principal language families of the Plateau were the Salishan peoples of the north, extending from well into British Columbia down to about the Columbia River, and the Klamath-Sahaptin peoples, who occupied the territory to the south of the Columbia. Among the Salishan-speakers were such tribal groups as the Shuswap, Okanogan, Wenatchi, Sanpoil, Kalispel, Flathead, and Coeur d'Alene. Those who spoke Sahaptin included, among others, the Nez Percé, Cayuse, Umatilla, Yakima, and Tenino. The linguistically independent Kutenai occupied the northeastern edge of the area. On the Columbia River, the Chinook-speaking Wishram and Wasco once lived as far east as The Dalles rapids. To the far south, some northern Shoshone groups held the marches of the area on the Great Basin periphery. The Sahaptin tribes, in their southern position, were exposed to Plains influence earlier than the Salishans and were more receptive to it. Such things as horses, guns, concepts of war honors, and tribal organization spread from Plains tribes such as the Blackfoot to the Nez Percé and from them to groups still farther west. The Salishan tribes remained more conservative. European influences came to them at first indirectly, via the Northwest Coast and took the form of items of trade such as copper and glass beads, which date to the latter part of the eighteenth century. Lewis and Clark made their famous expedition through the Plateau and the northwest country early in the nineteenth century. At that time they found the native cultures quite untouched by the white man's ways, but shortly afterward this condition changed quite rapidly. Traders were established in the area in the 1820's and missionaries by the 1830's.[121]

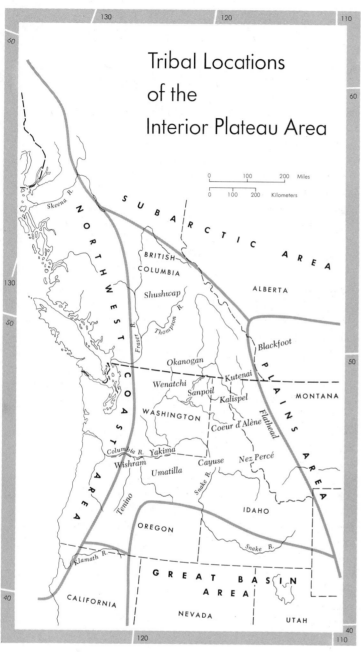

Tribal Locations
of the
Interior Plateau Area

100 200 Miles

100 200 Kilometers

SUBARCTIC AREA

NORTHWEST COAST AREA

BRITISH COLUMBIA

ALBERTA

Skeena R.

Shushwap

Fraser R.

Thompson R.

Okanogan

Blackfoot

Wenatchi

Kutenai

Sanpoil

Kalispel

MONTANA

WASHINGTON

Coeur d'Alène

Flathead

PLAINS AREA

Columbia R.

Yakima

Wishram

Cayuse

Nez Percé

Umatilla

Snake R.

Tenino

IDAHO

OREGON

Snake R.

Klamath R.

GREAT BASIN AREA

CALIFORNIA

NEVADA

UTAH

Figure 6-59.

Culture Sequences at The Dalles and the Early and Middle Periods. A consideration of the earliest occupations of the Plateau area take us back again to the Dalles-Deschutes region of the Columbia River Valley and to the lower levels of

archaeological sites in that region. These levels contained, you will recall, the remains of river hunting and salmon-fishing peoples who had settled there near the close of the Pleistocene. The culture of these ancient hunters and fishers has been designated as the Old Cordilleran. Insofar as we are now able to determine, this Old Cordilleran tradition was the matrix culture for the subsequent Northwest Coast tradition and for the later cultural tradition of the Interior Plateau, which R. D. Daugherty has named the Northwest Riverine tradition.[122]

The Dalles-Deschutes region of the Columbia Valley is one of the most important in the archaeology of northwestern North America, a direct reflection of its earlier significance as a living zone for aboriginal populations. The natural setting of The Dalles is at that point where the Columbia River begins its passage through the Cascade Mountains to descend to the lowlands. The immediate environment is the dry shrub and bush country of the Plateau, but only a few miles farther west the landscape changes to the wet, forested world of the Pacific zone. The river valley is extremely deep, and along the banks of the great stream are willows and cottonwoods and a microenvironment considerably more lush than the Plateau uplands which lie on both sides. The Dalles proper are a series of rapids located 5 miles east of the present city of The Dalles, Oregon. They are one of the great salmon-fishing grounds on the river, just as they were in the time of Lewis and Clark, who observed Indians living and fishing here, and for many millennia prior to the arrival of the white man. Archaeological remains including dwelling sites, burial grounds, and petroglyphs occur along both shores of the river. L. S. Cressman has excavated in two habitation mounds on the Oregon side.[123] It is from one of these, known as the Five Mile Rapids site, that Old Cordilleran artifacts and huge amounts of fish-bone debris have been dated to well before 7000 B.C., perhaps as early as or earlier than 9000 B.C.

The complex which can be identified as a manifestation of the Old Cordilleran tradition corre-

Figure 6-60. Projectile points from the Early Period, The Dalles. a–e: Cascade or Old Cordilleran. f–i: Lanceolate, slightly modified toward stem process (suggestive of Lake Mohave). j–m: Stemmed types (probably the latest of the Early Period series.) Length of a, 6 cm. (Courtesy Luther S. Cressman; see also Cressman and others, 1960.)

Figure 6-61. Flint blades of the Early Period, The Dalles. a–e: Bifacially flaked. f,g: Unifacially flaked. Length of a, 6 cm. (Courtesy Luther S. Cressman; see also Cressman and others, 1960.)

sponds to what Cressman and his associates have designated as their Early Period. Too few radiocarbon datings have been made to define this period exactly, but as we mentioned, it began around 9000 to 7000 B.C. and lasted until perhaps 5000 B.C.[124] Its characteristic projectile was the leaf-shaped flint point, which was accompanied by similar leaf-shaped and stemless triangular blades and large ovate-triangular forms with broad ta-

Figure 6-62. Bone and antler artifacts of the Early Period. a: Harpoon prong. b: Carved-bone fragment. c: Harpoon section. d–f: Unidentified worked fragments. g: Flaker. (After Cressman and others, 1960.)

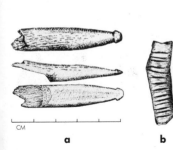
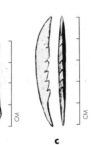
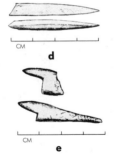

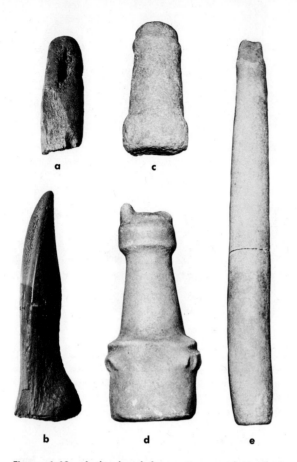

Figure 6-63. Antler bevel faces, stone mauls, and stone pestle, from The Dalles. a,b: Antler bevel faces or wedges; a, about 8 cm. long; b, 20 cm. long. c,d: Mauls; c, about 17 cm. long; d, about 27 cm. e: Pestle; about 48 cm. long. Antler tools, Early Period; mauls and pestle, Late Period. (Courtesy Luther S. Cressman; see also Cressman and others, 1960.)

enough to permit an adequate characterization of the period. The site stratigraphy takes up after this, however, and apparently runs from about 4100 B.C. to historic contact times. The artifacts from this long period (designated by Cressman as his Late Period) present a rich inventory. The projectile points were, at first, long triangular stemmed and barbed forms and, later, small triangles. Ground- and carved-stone items included mauls, carved pestles, carved mortars, pipes, charmstones, notched-stone sinkers, and stone sculptures. In Cressman's opinion, most of these specimens fall after 1000 B.C.[125]

B. R. Butler, also writing of The Dalles region, has proposed a sequence somewhat similar to Cressman's. Butler's synthesis is based on his excavations at the Indian Well and Congdon sites on the north bank of the river in the same locality of the rapids, as well as on a review of other excavations and artifact collections in the region.[126] His Early Period, which corresponds approximately to Cressman's, he sets from 8000 to 5500 B.C. It is represented by the bottom levels of the Indian Well site in which he found the leaf-shaped Old Cordilleran or Cascade points, various flake and bifacially chipped blades, and various scrapers, cobble choppers, and flaked pebbles. Butler's Middle

pered stems. The antler and bone tools and weapons taken from the site all belonged to this earliest complex. These items included harpoon prongs, atlatl spurs or hooks, and beveled-antler implements perhaps used for dressing skins. Grooved or girdled bolas stones (or net-weights?) and flint burins completed the picture. These specimens were all found in a context of salmon- and animal-bone refuse.

During Cressman's succeeding Transitional Period (ca. 5000 to 4100 B.C.) the bone and antler artifacts and the more distinctive stone forms all declined and eventually disappeared. Then perhaps for several centuries, the site was used only as an occasional camp. Refuse is thin and the tool types insufficient in quantity or not distinctive

Figure 6-64. Projectile points from the Late Period, The Dalles. Length of point at top, left, 3.6 cm. (Courtesy Luther S. Cressman; see also Cressman and others, 1960.)

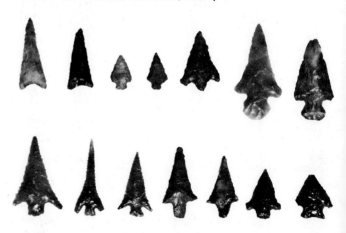

Period lasted from 5500 B.C. to A.D. 500. In it he grouped a number of site components, including the three sequent phases of the Congdon site (Congdon I, II, and III). The earliest of these phases, Congdon I, probably corresponded, at least in part, to the weak Transitional Period at Five Mile Rapids. Its characteristics were flat basalt grinding slabs, crude shallow-basin mortars, cobble choppers and hammerstones, scrapers, and flint and basalt projectile points, including large triangular side-notched and smaller stemmed points. Butler believes that Congdon I could probably be correlated with the onset of Altithermal climatic conditions, and regards its artifact complex as similar to that of contemporaneous Great Basin Desert tradition cultures. Congdon II saw substantial and important additions to the trait list,[126a] among them ground- and polished-stone forms such as paddle-shaped stone mauls, tubular pipes, atlatl weights, two-holed stone gorgets, perforated circular stones (probably net-weights), nicely shaped

stone pestles and deep mortars, slate fish-gorges, and zoomorphic stone sculptures. In brief, many of the traits of the Northwest Riverine tradition appeared at this time, and they continued into the Congdon III phase with minor changes and some new increments. Butler feels that this "enormous influx" of new elements in Congdon II, "indicating Boreal Archaic or Eastern Woodland influences," dates at around 1500 to 1000 B.C., or at a time not significantly different from Cressman's estimate of the appearances of the same or similar traits in the Five Mile Rapids site sequence.

Figure 6-65. *Below, left:* Bone sculpture from the Columbia River. Human head with bird-head crest, similar in motif to later Northwest Coast wood sculpture. Height, about 4 cm. (Courtesy Emory Strong.)

Figure 6-66. *Below, right:* Stone sculptures from The Dalles. *Left:* Owl-effigy vessel. *Right:* "Slave-killer" club with animal-effigy projection. (*Left,* courtesy John Krussow; *right,* courtesy Emory Strong.)

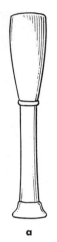

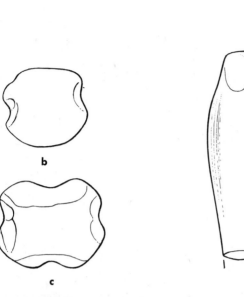

Figure 6-67. *Above, left:* Stone pipe (*a*) and chipped-stone sinkers (*b,c*) from The Dalles. Length of *a*, 12 cm. (After Strong, Schenck, and Steward, 1930.)

Figure 6-68. *Above, right:* Stone wedge and stone chisel from The Dalles. *Left:* Wedge; length, 18 cm. *Right:* Chisel. (After Strong, Schenck, and Steward, 1930.)

The Significance of the "Boreal" Traits. These approximate dates and the various ground-, polished-, and carved-stone objects are extremely important landmarks in our attempt to follow the courses of culture history in the Interior Plateau and on the Northwest Coast. Consider again similar elements as they pertain to the adjacent Pacific Coast. Here, too, they entered the archaeological record around 1000 B.C. As we have mentioned before, they may have been of ultimate north Asiatic origin and a part of a circum-polar Mesolithic tradition. In the interpretation we prefer, they appeared earlier in the Plateau than on the Northwest Coast, though chronological control in neither area is secure enough now to decide this question. If one had to pick focal points, however, at which such traits found a receptive setting for their eventual development as a part of the Northwest Riverine and Northwest Coast traditions, they would be the great and rich fishing rapids on the Plateau edge descents of the Columbia and Fraser Rivers. For these were the regions in which human societies in this part of the New World would have found the most optimum conditions given their state of technological advancement.

The Fraser River Canyon. The Fraser River canyon, several hundred miles to the north of The Dalles and about 100 miles inland from the Fraser delta, offers another series of salmon rapids comparable to those on the Columbia. Here on the east bank of the canyon interposed between deep stratified sands and gravels, Borden has uncovered a series of early artifact complexes which are dated by radiocarbon as falling between about 7000 and 5400 B.C.[127] The lowest level contained leaf-shaped points and blades. Another level dating to approximately 6200 B.C. has yielded leaf-shaped points clearly in the Old Cordilleran tradition, cobble choppers, and other flint tools. These occupations were certainly related to the Cressman-Butler Early Period. They were followed, after a long interval represented by river gravels and sediments, by a horizon which bore smaller stemmed and notched projectile points, mortars and pestles, stone mauls, pipes, pendants, labrets, adze blades, carved-stone animal and human figurines, and ground-slate knives. Borden, as we mentioned in the preceding

402

section, states that the effigy figurines of steatite may be dated as early as 800 B.C. and that the ground-slate knives, which resemble those from the Marpole phase of the Fraser delta, date from 400 B.C. Thus the Fraser Canyon sequence has parallels to The Dalles sequence, although it lacks the Desert-like complex of Congdon I. Such a complex, presumably reflecting the arid-lands environmental adjustment found farther south in the interior of the continent, would hardly be expected in the Fraser River setting of the northern part of the Plateau. Unfortunately a very crucial part of the story for the Plateau, as well as for the Northwest Coast, is in the still poorly documented span of millennia from around 5000 to 1000 B.C.

Early and Middle Period Evidences Elsewhere on the Plateau. Evidences of the Old Cordilleran tradition are found up the Columbia River from The Dalles in the McNary Reservoir. In the pre-volcanic ash layer at Hat Creek site in that region were found leaf-shaped Cascade points, cobble hammers and choppers, and bone awls and beads. These items were gathered from refuse, mixed with salmon, deer, and rabbit bones.[128] Butler also has referred to a similar complex found in a deep deposit in a cave on the lower Snake River.[129] Other early Plateau remains include the Lind Coulee finds in eastern Washington. Here, however, both the projectile points and the faunal debris seem more reminiscent of the later phases of the Big-Game Hunting tradition of the Plains than of the Old Cordilleran tradition.[130] Farther east, in the Idaho Rockies, Swanson's Bitterroot culture, with its projectile point forms resembling those of the Desert tradition, may antedate 5000 B.C.[131]

Other signs of the Butler Middle Period, in addition to The Dalles and the Fraser River Canyon, are not evident as yet in other parts of the Plateau. Possibly some of the sites in the McNary Reservoir may belong to this bracket, although this is uncertain. At one of them, Cold Springs, there is an apparent carry-over of the Old Cordilleran Hat Creek artifact types, although these are associated with new forms. In the stratigraphy of this site,

side-notched points replaced the unnotched leaf-shaped forms and many long basalt knives were recovered along with various net-weights and tubular pipes and pendants. Thus in its lower and middle components, Cold Springs presents something of a Middle Period aspect. In connection with Cold Springs, it is important to mention the semi-subterranean pithouse remains found in the middle levels. All that remains of them today are circular depressions in the ground, a meter or less in depth. Probably they were once surrounded by low earth embankments. Fires had been made in the centers. No post remains or post-molds reveal structural foundations, and it is likely that coverings were of light poles and mats. One such house measured 12 to 13 meters in diameter. Such dwellings apparently were cleaned out, refurbished, and re-used over long periods of time. Another feature at Cold Springs, and one which, like the semi-subterranean house, had a long history on the Plateau, was the earth oven. Archaeologists have linked these ovens to pits in the ground filled with layers of fire-

Figure 6-69. A generalized projectile point form sequence for the McNary region of the Plateau. Chronology runs from bottom to top row, with row c earliest, b intermediate, and a latest. (After Shiner, 1961.)

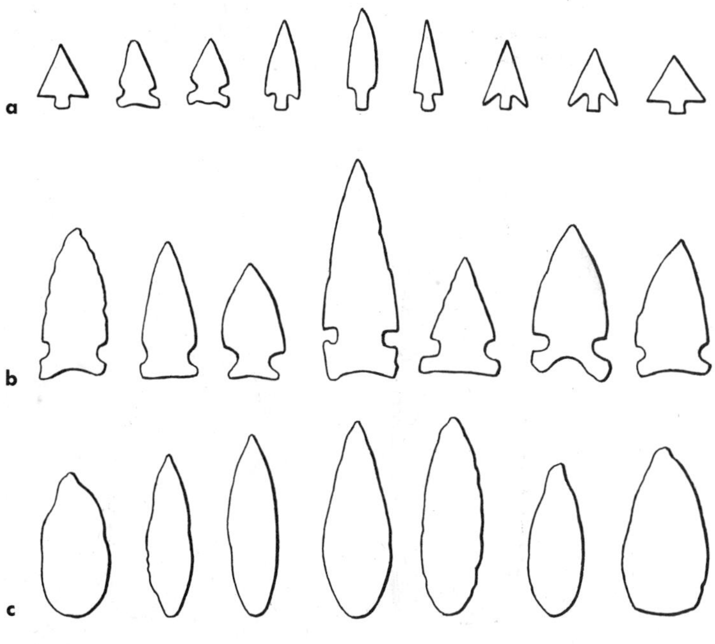

blackened stones and earth. They were used for heated-stone baking or for roasting the camas root, a dietary staple on the Plateau.

The Late Period and the Northwest Riverine Tradition. Butler dates his Late Period at The Dalles from A.D. 500 to the historic horizon, around 1800.[132] In it he places the upper level of the Indian Well site (Indian Well II), both the Wakemap I and II phases, and what he designates as the "Late Cremation" sites. In the McNary Reservoir, upstream from The Dalles, Shiner and Osborne excavated other sites which apparently fall into this period: Techumtas Island, Berrian's Island, Wallula, the burial site near Umatilla designated as 45-BN-3, and the upper levels at the Cold Springs site.[133] Continuing upriver, in northeastern Washington, Collier, Hudson, and Ford surveyed and tested a great many habitation and burial sites above and below the Spokane River confluence. All these belonged to a late prehistoric-to-historic time level.[134] Regional and undoubtedly chronological differences are distinguishable in all these Plateau sites; but a common heritage is obvious, a heritage which was brought up from the preceding Middle Period phases of both the

Columbia and Fraser Rivers. To put it in other words, a Northwest Riverine tradition had its roots in the Middle Period; by the Late Period the pattern could be recognized throughout the area.

These interpretations of change, continuity, and the emergence of a Northwest Riverine or a Plateau tradition are not viewed in exactly the same way by all archaeologists working in the area. E. T. Swanson, Jr., in an analysis of cultural and natural environmental changes based on his field work in the Vantage region of the Columbia River Valley in central Washington, sees matters somewhat differently.[134a] He, too, emphasizes the importance of an ancient Plateau culture—a tradition which seems essentially the same as the Old Cordilleran; and in his opinion there is also a significant change which became established on the Plateau around 1500 B.C. This last he refers to as the "Northern Forest Culture." It has some Old Cordilleran antecedents, but whether he would consider it still within the same cultural tradition is not clear. Apparently, however, this Northern Forest Culture is related to the polished-stone "boreal traits," to which other Northwest prehistorians have referred. In Swanson's view, this Northern Forest Culture, with its increments of the Old Cordilleran heritage, persisted on the Plateau until about A.D. 1200–1300. At this time a number of rapid and significant changes occurred: larger riverine villages appeared; new items emerged in site inventories; and trade—particularly with the Pacific Coast—became very important. In brief, it was at this time that the Interior Plateau ethnographic culture pattern—or what others have called, and what we are calling, the Northwest Riverine tradition—came into being. The difference between this interpretation and the one we have been inclined to follow in this chapter is that in the latter the crystallizing elements of the Northwest Riverine tradition have been taken to be the "forest" or "boreal" traits which appear ca. 1500 to 1000 B.C. Swanson, on the other hand, sees the late prehistoric and ethnographic Plateau pattern as not really coalescing until some two millennia later.

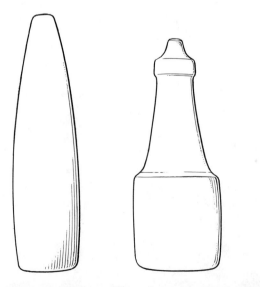

Figure 6-70. **Stone pestle and maul from the McNary region.** *Left:* Pestle; length 26 cm. *Right:* Maul; length, 23 cm. (After Osborne, 1957.)

404

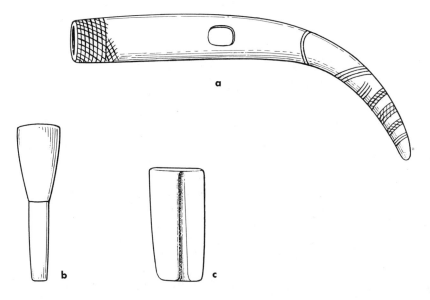

Figure 6-71. Artifacts from the Upper Columbia Valley. *a:* Antler digging-stick handle; length, 28 cm. *b:* Stone pipe; length, 13.5 cm. *c:* Stone shaft-straightener; length, 10 cm. (After Collier, Hudson, and Ford, 1942.)

Shiner has synthesized a Plateau or Northwest Riverine cultural tradition, using largely late prehistoric and early historic data.[135] Among the most universal traits were cobble hammers and choppers and leaf-shaped blades, all carried over from the chronologically remote Old Cordilleran tradition. To these items we can add smaller side-notched, corner-notched, and stemmed flint points; lozenge-shaped flint blades; stone mallets, or mauls; polished-stone pestles and celts; tubular pipes; stone bowls; notched net-weights; antler digging-stick handles; and antler and horn wedges. Stone sculptures, thin-walled stone bowls, stone clubs, and in general a greater virtuosity in stone-grinding and polishing differentiated The Dalles and the Fraser Canyon sites from the regions farther inland. The same was also true of fancy, non-utilitarian work in bone. Bone points and harpoons, on the other hand, although they have been found at The Dalles,[136] were more typical of the upper Columbia drainage in northeastern Washington.[137]

House types varied, and a clear chronological-distributional picture of plateau dwellings has not yet emerged. On the lower Spokane River and around its confluence with the Columbia, there were no pithouses, and it is likely that here the

above-ground, perishable mat-covered structures prevailed.[138] We have mentioned the evidences of pithouses in the McNary region at the Cold Springs site, and similar depressions were also uncovered at Techumtas Island and at 45-BN-53.[139] Pithouse remains were also found in the upper levels of the Wakemap Mound (Wakemap II) and at Miller's Island, sites in The Dalles region explored by Strong, Schenck, and Steward.[140] These dwellings also appear to have been circular and were probably earthcovered. Strong and his collaborators suggest a dwelling-type sequence for The Dalles region which began with surface mat-and-pole houses (Wakemap I), continued with earth-covered semi-subterranean structures (Wakemap II), and finally ended with the semi-subterranean rectangular plank houses which Lewis and Clark reported on their trip down the Columbia River. Strong and his associates believe that this third type of house had been brought into the region only shortly before the beginning of the nineteenth century by the Upper Chinook Wishram tribe, which came from the coast and did not have a long Plateau history. The earlier earth-covered, flimsily-built pithouses, they speculate, were the dwellings of the Salishan tribes, who formerly had occupied The Dalles and the river to the east. At the time of the Lewis and Clark journey, the above-ground, pole-and-mat lodging was the only dwelling in the region of the McNary Reservoir, and it is the belief of Strong and his collaborators that this house type was being brought downriver from the east to supplant the old semi-subterranean pithouse in late prehistoric-to-historic times.

To sum up, Interior Plateau area houses appear to have been mainly of two types: semi-subterranean pit-dwellings, circular in form and covered with light superstructures and probably earth; and above-ground pole-and-mat dwellings. The antiquity of the latter form is difficult to trace through archaeology, but it may well be very ancient. The semi-subterranean pithouse is definitely prehistoric, and may date back to earlier than A.D. 500. Certainly the widespread presence in the northern Plateau of the pithouse, although of a heavier timbered style than the early ones on the Columbia River, argues for its extreme age in the area. Plank houses were clearly a late Northwest Coast innovation.

The manner of burial and disposal of the dead also varied within the Plateau area and within what we are conceiving of as a Northwest Riverine tradition. Osborne has discussed the subject at length and for the area as a whole.[141] Unfortunately archaeological data on either burials or cremations are missing for many of the regions. Using the McNary Reservoir information and other findings from the Columbia Valley, he summarizes a sequence which begins with simple pit burial of a flexed or semi-flexed body. This stage was then succeeded by cremation which, in his opinion, was a trait diffused downriver from the northern part of the Plateau. Cremation was followed by a third fashion—enclosing the dead in cists, usually made of wooden planks. In this method, the grave was dug, the flexed body was placed within the grave, and the boards were placed within the grave to surround and shelter the corpse. The grave was then covered with earth or stones until only the tops of the wooden planks protruded above the surface. These were sometimes burned off or sometimes left in place as grave markers. Osborne believes this burial practice was also of northern origin. It met with another mortuary mode, however, which was spreading upriver from the Northwest Coast, probably with the Chinook tribes. This was the semi-subterranean wooden burial vault, house, or shed. Both the plank cist and the wooden burial vault customs were replaced in the early 1800's by a simpler practice: that of marking a plain pit grave with a little tent or cone of small poles or sticks or of merely placing a single pole marker over the grave.

The full chronological depth of this sequence is difficult to estimate. It seems likely that both pit burial and cremation were extremely old in the Plateau. Butler describes cremated human remains, apparently covered with small stone cairns, at both the Maybe and Big Leap sites, which he equates chronologically with the Congdon II phase and with his Middle Period (or before A.D. 500).[142] However, the particular cremations which Osborne was describing were comparable to those which Butler assigned to his "Late Cremation I" (very late prehistoric) and "Late Cremation II" (post-European contact) phases at The Dalles. Judging from grave goods, the plank cist burials of the McNary at the 45-BN-3 site, were both late prehistoric and post-European contact. The Chinook wooden vault was also this late, or even later, while the terminal traits of stick-tents or pole-markers for graves are considered to be early nineteenth century. In all types of burial and at all periods for which we have record, including the Middle Period Maybe site cremations, grave goods were the rule in the Plateau, and frequently artifacts were broken or otherwise "killed" before being placed with the dead.

The ethnographic picture of the Plateau Indians in the period between 1800 to 1840 corresponds very well with this archaeologically-derived description of the Northwest Riverine tradition of the late prehistoric era. The Indians at this time followed a seasonal migratory pattern of life. During the winter they occupied the river villages from which they ventured out to hunt for deer and other animals. Such villages also served as fishing stations at other times of the year. Other groups migrated to the fishing grounds periodically. Temporary camps were set up at root-gathering or berry-picking locations. Eye-witness accounts of early European explorers described the Indians netting and spearing fish and gathering tuberous roots such as the camas (*Camassia*) and kouse (*Lomatium caus*). "First fruits" and "first salmon" rites were the rituals associated with these economic activities. The material culture described by early travelers included such archaeological items as the ubiquitous stone mauls and antler wedges, stone pestles, antler-handled digging sticks, and fishing tackle and hunting weapons. The houses and the burial practices were the ethnohistoric counterparts of at least some of those uncovered in archaeological sites. In brief, the Northwest Riverine tradition was fully alive during the early nineteenth century, and even if adulterated, traces of it still remain.

Summary.   The Plateau appears to be the hearth of the Old Cordilleran hunters and fishers, one of the earliest American traditions. They occupied the area perhaps as early as 9000 B.C. Insofar as their way of life can be appraised, it changed very little for the next 4 or 5 millennia. Between about 5000 B.C. and 1000 B.C., the Plateau archaeological record is rather obscure. Presumably during this time these early hunters and fishermen were adapting slowly to a river existence and were probably assimilating "boreal" traits which were being diffused to them from a general northerly, and ultimately Asiatic, direction. They were also influenced during this period by the Great Basin Desert tradition. At about 1500 to 1000 B.C., where adequate archaeological sampling breaks into the story again, we see a drastically changed culture. Ground- and polished-stone implements—for food preparation, heavy woodworking, ornament, and ritual—were now characteristic. A distinctive art style, also revealed in stone carving, was beginning to develop. Some of these new developments were also shared with the new, emergent tradition of the Northwest Coast. Whichever way the lines of influence were running, the histories of the two areas were significantly related at this point. They were to continue to be related, but also to differ significantly. The Northwest Coast tradition appeared in the first millennium B.C.; the story for the Plateau is less clear. Perhaps it was not for another two thousand years or so that a fully formed Northwest Riverine tradition came into existence.

Footnotes

[1] These areas approximate, although do not duplicate, the ethnographic areas of Driver (1961, map 2).

[2] See Bennyhoff (1958, map 1). The physiographic area of the Great Basin is somewhat smaller than the culture area which is generally designated by the same name.

[3] Jennings (1957).

[3a] Baumhoff and Heizer (1965) question the estimated dating of Danger Cave III and wonder if it might not date from Post-Altithermal (after 3000 B.C.) times.

[4] See also Bennyhoff (1958).

[5] Heizer (1951).

[6] Heizer and Krieger (1956).

[7] Grosscup (1960). Bennyhoff (1958) gives slightly different estimates.

[8] Heizer (1951); Heizer and Krieger (1956).

[9] Loud and Harrington (1929).

[10] Grosscup (1960).

[11] For example, only a single milling slab and a few small handstones are reported from Humboldt Cave (Heizer and Krieger, 1951).

[12] Grosscup (1960); Heizer and Krieger (1956).

[13] Cressman (1942, 1951); Wormington (1957, p. 184).

[14] Cressman (1942).

[15] W. J. Wallace (1962).

[16]The joint term "Pinto-Gypsum" is a dubious one. It is likely that the Gypsum-type projectile points, named after Gypsum Cave, Nevada, were considerably earlier than the Pinto Basin-type points.

[17]Bennyhoff (1958).

[18]Meighan (1959 a).

[19]Wallace (1962).

[20]Wallace (1962); Campbell and Campbell (1935).

[21]Wallace (1962) questions the inclusion of Lake Mojave, and of the succeeding southeastern California desert cultures, in a Desert tradition.

[22]W. J. Wallace (1962). This follows the terminology of the earlier Rogers (1939) scheme. In Rogers' new terminology (Rogers, 1959; Haury and others, 1950) the name Amargosa III would correspond to the old Amargosa phase or period with Amargosa I and II replacing the former designation Pinto-Gypsum.

[23]Wallace's (1962) later Amargosa phase, as described here, would seem to correspond to the very late pre-ceramic and pre-Patayan I culture that is described by Rogers (1945) (Chapter 4, pp. 228–231). Also, it is probable, following the estimated dating, that the later Amargosa phase of the California desert is, in part, contemporaneous with the Patayan I Period of the Colorado River Valley to the east.

[24]Wallace (1962). This apparently corresponds to the Patayan II Period expansion, from the Colorado River Valley westward into the California deserts (M. J. Rogers, 1945) (see also Chapter 4, pp. 228–231).

[25]Wallace (1962).

[26]M. J. Rogers (1945).

[27]Wallace (1962).

[28]Massey (1949, 1961 a).

[29]Kroeber (1939); Kirchhoff (1942); Massey (1947, 1949, 1961 a).

[30]Massey (1947).

[31]This is Neumann's "Otamid" type (see Chapter 1, p. 14).

[32]Massey (1961 a).

[33]This is qualified, of course, by how one defines the western extension of the Southwestern Patayan subarea. In this survey we are considering the southeastern California desert and adjacent portions of northern Baja California as a part of the Great Basin area rather than the Southwest.

[34]Massey (1961 a). Treganza (1942) is also considering this far northern part of Baja California in his survey article.

[35]Massey (1961 a). In a letter of 8 February 1965, Massey confirms the presence of Pinto and Gypsum-points and artifacts throughout the peninsula, noting that in the central regions the Pinto Basin forms are more common on the Pacific side, the Gypsum Cave types on the Gulf side.

[36]Massey (1961 a).

[37]Arnold (1957).

[38]Arnold (1957).

[39]Massey (1949).

[40]Massey (1961 a).

[41]Massey (1961 b).

[42]Massey (1961 a). It is not always clear what archaeological elements of the region, as described in an earlier paper (Massey, 1947), are to be included in this presumably late prehistoric-to-historic Las Palmas complex.

[43]Massey (1961 a).

[44]Arnold (1957).

[45]Massey (1961 a).

[46]Massey (1947).

[47]Dahlgren and Romero (1951).

[48]Heizer (1964).

[49]Heizer (1952).

[50]Harrington (1948), and Meighan (1959 a).

[51]Bennyhoff (1958); also Meighan (1959 a); Wallace (1962); Heizer (1964).

[52]Warren and True 1961); Heizer (1964).

[53]Grinding stones are also missing from the Malaga Cove I level (Walker, 1951).

[54]Meighan (1959 a).

[55]See also Willey and Phillips (1958).

[56]Meighan (1959 a).

[57]Meighan (1959 a).

[58]Heizer (1964).

[59]Compare Heizer's (1964) subareas or regions with those of Meighan (see fig. 6-21). A southern California Interior Desert subarea is sometimes defined as part of the California archaeological area, but in this survey it is included as a part of the Great Basin area.

[60]Meighan (1959 a).

[61]Heizer (1964); see also W. J. Wallace (1955) for dating estimates.

[62]This is a mean of Heizer's estimate of "0 to A.D. 500."

[63]W. J. Wallace (1954, 1955); Heizer (1964).

[64]Treganza and Bierman (1958).

[65]Walker (1951).

[66]W. J. Wallace (1954).

[67]Shumway, Hubbs, and Moriarty (1961).

[68]D. B. Rogers (1929).

[69]Eberhart (1961).

[70]W. J. Wallace (1954).

[71]See Beardsley (1948) for summary and bibliography; see also Heizer (1964).

[72]Heizer (1964).

[73]Heizer (1964); D. B. Rogers (1929).

[74]Meighan (1959 b).

[75]Meighan (1959 b).

[76]Schenck (1926).

[77]Beardsley (1948).

[78]Heizer (1964) appears to disagree with Beardsley (1948) on this matter, seeing the introduction of the bow as early as the Middle Period.

[79]Heizer (1964); Beardsley (1948).

[80]The following account of the Canaliño culture is based on D. B. Rogers (1929, pp. 367–419). Rogers sees new immigrants with a maritime culture as being responsible for many of the Late Period Canaliño developments. In his opinion the incoming Canaliño merged with and assimilated the earlier Middle Period residents (his "Hunting Culture").

[81]D. B. Rogers (1929) quotes Spanish missionary sources to this effect.

[82]Perhaps an archaeological example of the widespread California "men's houses" of the ethnographic horizon.

[83]Rogers (1929).

[84]Heizer (1964).

[85]Beardsley (1948).

[86]Drucker (1955 a) is the best summary source for the area.

[87]Drucker (1955 a, b).

[88]Daugherty (1962) suggests the idea of a "Northwest Coast tradition" although does not actually name or define it.

[89]Drucker (1955 b).

[90]These descriptions of harpoon types and "fixed" point types have been clarified for me by C. E. Borden (personal communication, 1964).

[90a]At least without stratigraphic or chronologically oriented archaeological research.

[91]Boas (1905, 1933).

[92]See Drucker (1955 b) for a review of some of these hypotheses.

[93]Kroeber (1923); H. I. Smith (1907, 1909).

[94]Borden (1953–1954).

[95]Osborne, Caldwell, and Crabtree (1956). For further reading in archaeologic-ethnographic reconstructions of Northwest Coast culture history see M. W. Smith (1950, 1956).

[96]Borden (1962). Borden has also made a manuscript (1964) available to me which amplifies, and to some extent modifies, his 1962 conclusions.

[97]Cressman and others (1960).

[98]Borden (1960, 1962) and also Borden's manuscript of 1964 referred to in footnote 96.

[99]See Borden (1962) for radiocarbon dates; see also dating estimates by Butler (1959) and by Cressman and others (1960).

[100]Capes (1964).

[101]King (1950).

[102]Borden (1951).

[103]Borden (1962) revealed dates of 943 B.C. to A.D. 179 for Marpole and others of ca. 500–400 B.C. for Locarno Beach. He now (1964 ms. and personal communication, 1964) has a revised date on the 943 B.C. Marpole sample which is 390 B.C. He prefers the latter.

[104]Borden (1964 ms.) is the principal source for this sequence outline and for the following phase descriptions.

[105]Marpole is a famous site in Northwest Coast archaeology, formerly called Eburne (see H. I. Smith, 1903; Hill-Tout, 1895, 1928; Borden, 1950, 1951).

[106]Borden (personal communication, 1964, and 1964 ms.).

[107]Borden (personal communication, 1964).

[108]Duff (1956).

[109]Drucker (1955 a, b).

[110]Duff (1956, p. 95).

[111]Capes (1964) summarizes earlier literature on the mounds and cairns.

[112]Heizer (1964).

[113]Heizer and Elsasser (1964); Heizer (1964); Loud (1918).

[114]T. M. Newman (1959).

[115]Laughlin (1941, 1943).

[116]Drucker (1943).

[117]King (1950).

[118]Borden (1962). Wilson Duff (personal communication, 1964) differs from Borden on this and prefers an Eskimo-to-Northwest Coast diffusion.

[119]See Kroeber (1931); Ray (1939); Shiner (1961).

[120]Osborne (1957); Shiner (1961). The reader is also referred to Swanson (1962 b) who sees the Interior Plateau and the Northwest Coast as culturally very similar in earlier times but with a trend toward divergences in the later prehistoric periods.

[121]Osborne (1957); Shiner (1961).

[122]Daugherty (1962).

[123]Cressman and others (1960).

[124]Cressman and others (1960).

[125]Cressman and others (1960).

[126]Butler (1958 c, 1959). Butler (1965) would place The Dalles region and the lower Columbia Valley in the Northwest Coast area rather than the Plateau area.

[126a]Stone and bone sculptures and stone pipes, wedges, chisels, and other ground stone items (such as those shown in Figs. 6-65, 6-66, 6-67, and 6-68, and attributed to The Dalles region) are representative of the kinds of things that begin to appear in Butler's Congdon II phase; however, such artifacts persist at The Dalles until much later times.

[127]Borden (1960, 1961, personal communication, 1964).

[128]Shiner (1961).

[129]Butler (1959).

[130]Daugherty (1956).

[131]Swanson (1962 a).

[132]Butler (1959). This would span only the terminal centuries of what Cressman has called the "Late Period."

[133]Shiner (1961); Osborne (1957).

[134]Collier, Hudson, and Ford (1942).

[134a]Swanson (1962 b).

[135]Shiner (1961).

[136]See Strong, Schenck, and Steward (1930).

[137]Collier, Hudson, and Ford (1942).

[138]Collier, Hudson, and Ford (1942).

[139]Shiner (1961).

[140]Strong, Schenck, and Steward (1930). See also a well-illustrated semipopular account of the Wakemap Mound (Oregon Archaeological Society, 1959).

[141]Osborne (1957, pp. 143–159).

[142]Butler (1959).

The Areas, Their Peoples, and Cultures

The Arctic area includes the Alaskan coast, from Yakutat Bay in the northern Pacific northward through the Bering Strait and then eastward along the Arctic coast. Also included are the islands of the Aleutian chain and those in the Bering Sea, as well as the adjacent mainland on the Asiatic side of Bering Strait. Eastward from Alaska the coasts and tundras of the Yukon and Canadian Northwest Territories, together with the Canadian islands to the north, fall within the area; as does the great island of Greenland, or at least those coastal portions of it that were occupied by the aborigines. Eastern Canada, northern Quebec, coastal Labrador, and Newfoundland also can be included in the Arctic area, although Newfoundland is a transitional zone between Arctic and Subarctic (see Fig. 7-1).

The Subarctic area lies to the south, or inland from the Arctic area. In the east it borders on the North American Eastern Woodlands area and consists of Canada north of the St. Lawrence River and the Great Lakes, except southern Ontario and southern Quebec. Farther west it lies north of the Plains and includes northern Manitoba, Saskatchewan, Alberta, and those portions of the Canadian Northwest Territories, the Yukon, and Alaska

The Arctic and Subarctic

7

which lie well inland from the sea. On the west and southwest, the Subarctic abuts on the Northwest Coast and Interior Plateau areas (see Fig. 7-1).

From an environmental point of view, the essential line between Arctic and Subarctic is the tree line that separates the barren tundras of the north from the coniferous forests to the south; from a cultural and ethnographic point of view, it is the division between Eskimo and Indian. Environment and culture correspond rather closely. The Arctic area is the Eskimo area, and the Subarctic is the home of the Indian tribes.[1]

These distributions are, of course, modern, historic, and late prehistoric ones. In early times, after the last glacial advance, Arctic tundras extended farther south into what is now the Subarctic. Afterward, during Altithermal times and later, the boreal forests advanced over the Subarctic, creating the environmental conditions that exist today.

We do not know who the early inhabitants of the Arctic and Subarctic were from the ethnic and physical standpoints. Presumably the very earliest of them were of the proto-Mongoloid or pre-Mongoloid stock that, according to the physical anthropologists, first peopled the New World. These early immigrants from Asia may have been associated with such archaeological complexes as the British Mountain, if MacNeish is correct in his dating of that complex (Chap. 2). In any event, no such early human remains have yet been found in the Arctic or Subarctic, nor have any skeletal remains been discovered from cultures dating prior to about 2000 B.C.

Skeletons and crania thus far found date from relatively late prehistoric times, and they display the dichotomy recognized from historic and modern times between Subarctic Indians (the Deneid type of Neumann) and Arctic Eskimo-Aleuts (the Inuid type of Neumann) (Chap. 2). According to W. S. Laughlin, the Eskimo-Aleut is racially closer to the Asiatic Chukchi—in physical structure and in blood grouping—than to his New World Indian neighbors. That is, the Eskimo-Aleut is the most Mongoloid of all the American aborigines. Laughlin also believes that the crucial period marking the beginning of the dichotomy between Eskimo and Indian was somewhere between 4000 and 2000 B.C.[2] He is not explicit about just how this division came about, whether from migrations of a new physical stock from Asia or from genetic changes in the resident populations of northern North America; since, however, Eskimo culture received substantial increments of northeastern Asiatic cultural elements, the Eskimo-Aleut physical type probably derived from Asiatic Mongoloid progenitors no earlier than three or four millennia B.C. Perhaps significantly, the Indians of the western Subarctic, the Deneid physical type, are, although standing apart from the Eskimo-Aleut or Inuid, more Mongoloid in appearance than any

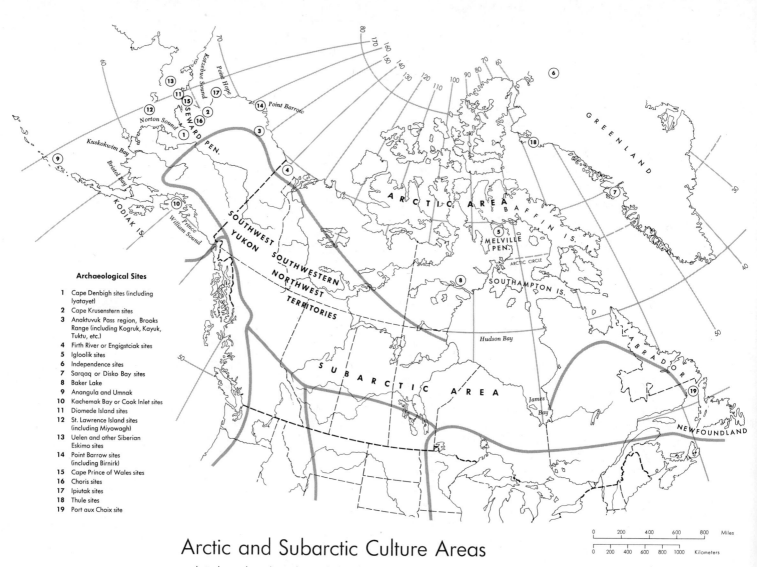

Arctic and Subarctic Culture Areas

with Selected Archaeological Regions and Site Locations

Figure 7-1.

Archaeological Sites

1 Cape Denbigh sites (including
   Iyatayet)
2 Cape Krusenstern sites
3 Anaktuvuk Pass region, Brooks
   Range (including Kogruk, Kayuk,
   Tuktu, etc.)
4 Firth River or Engigstciak sites
5 Igloolik sites
6 Independence sites
7 Sarqaq or Disko Bay sites
8 Baker Lake
9 Anangula and Umnak
10 Kachemak Bay or Cook Inlet sites
11 Diomede Island sites
12 St. Lawrence Island sites
   (including Miyowagh)
13 Uelen and other Siberian
   Eskimo sites
14 Point Barrow sites
   (including Birnirk)
15 Cape Prince of Wales sites
16 Choris sites
17 Ipiutak sites
18 Thule sites
19 Port aux Choix site

other American Indians. Their racial history may be that of earlier resident Indians who have become more Mongolized through contact and mixture with the Eskimo or proto-Eskimo; or, and perhaps more likely, they too may represent another wave of late immigrants from Asia. If so, it seems probable that they preceded the Eskimo-Aleut and diverged from a common Asiatic parent stock at a time somewhat prior to the pronounced Mongoloid specialization of the Eskimo-Aleut.

As we mentioned, the Arctic area was the Eskimo or Eskimo-Aleut area. On the historic horizon, and as late as the twentieth century, tribes speaking an Eskimo-Aleut language were in possession of the entire territory from the Aleutian chain to Greenland. In language, the Aleut are most distinctive, and are believed, on the basis of glottochronological reckonings, to have separated from the Eskimo proper at around 2600 B.C.[3] As their name implies, the Aleut occupied the Aleutian chain of islands. A great many different Eskimo tribes lived along the Alaskan Pacific and Bering Sea coasts and adjacent islands, as well as on the

Asiatic side of the Bering Sea. Farther north, on the Alaskan Arctic coast, were the Point Barrow Eskimo, and continuing east and naming only some of the better known groups, were the Mackenzie, Copper, Polar, and Greenland Eskimos. All these people were linked by language, general physical type, and culture.

The Subarctic area was held by Indian tribes of two major linguistic stocks: Athapascan and Al-

gonquian, the former in the west, the latter in the east. All of interior Alaska was in the solid possession of Athapascan tribes such as the Kutchin, Tanana, Ahtena, and Ingalik; and in the interior of western Canada, extending down to the northern Plains, were the Kaska, Dog Rib, Slave, Yellow Knife, Beaver, and Chipewyan tribes. On the

Figure 7-2.

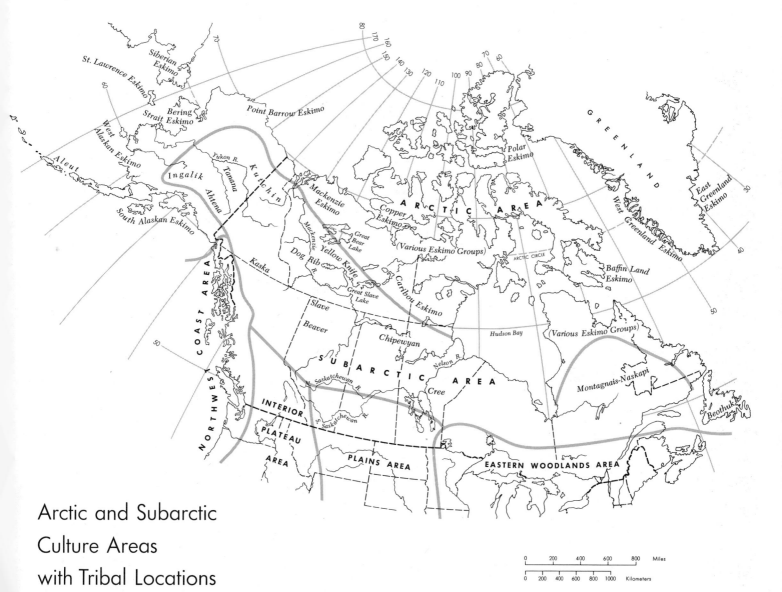

Arctic and Subarctic
Culture Areas
with Tribal Locations

southwest side of Hudson Bay these groups were fronted by the Algonquian Cree; and east of Hudson Bay, in interior Quebec, were the Algonquian Montagnais-Naskapi. These Subarctic Algonquian peoples were a part of a larger linguistic grouping of tribes, including those found to the south in the Eastern Woodlands and Plains country of the United States. Physically and culturally, as well as linguistically, their heritage differs from that of the Athapascans. Although the archaeological record of the Subarctic is still quite fragmentary, it is highly probable that the cultural background of the northern Algonquian area derives from the Archaic tradition of eastern North America.

In discussing the archaeology of the Arctic and Subarctic, we shall not proceed by formal chronological or subareal organization. Data are too scarce, except for the later chronological ranges of the Eskimo cultures, and the archaeologists working in the areas have not formalized any such schemes as yet. We will, rather, deal with several

Figure 7-3. Chronological chart for the Arctic area and the Western Subarctic.

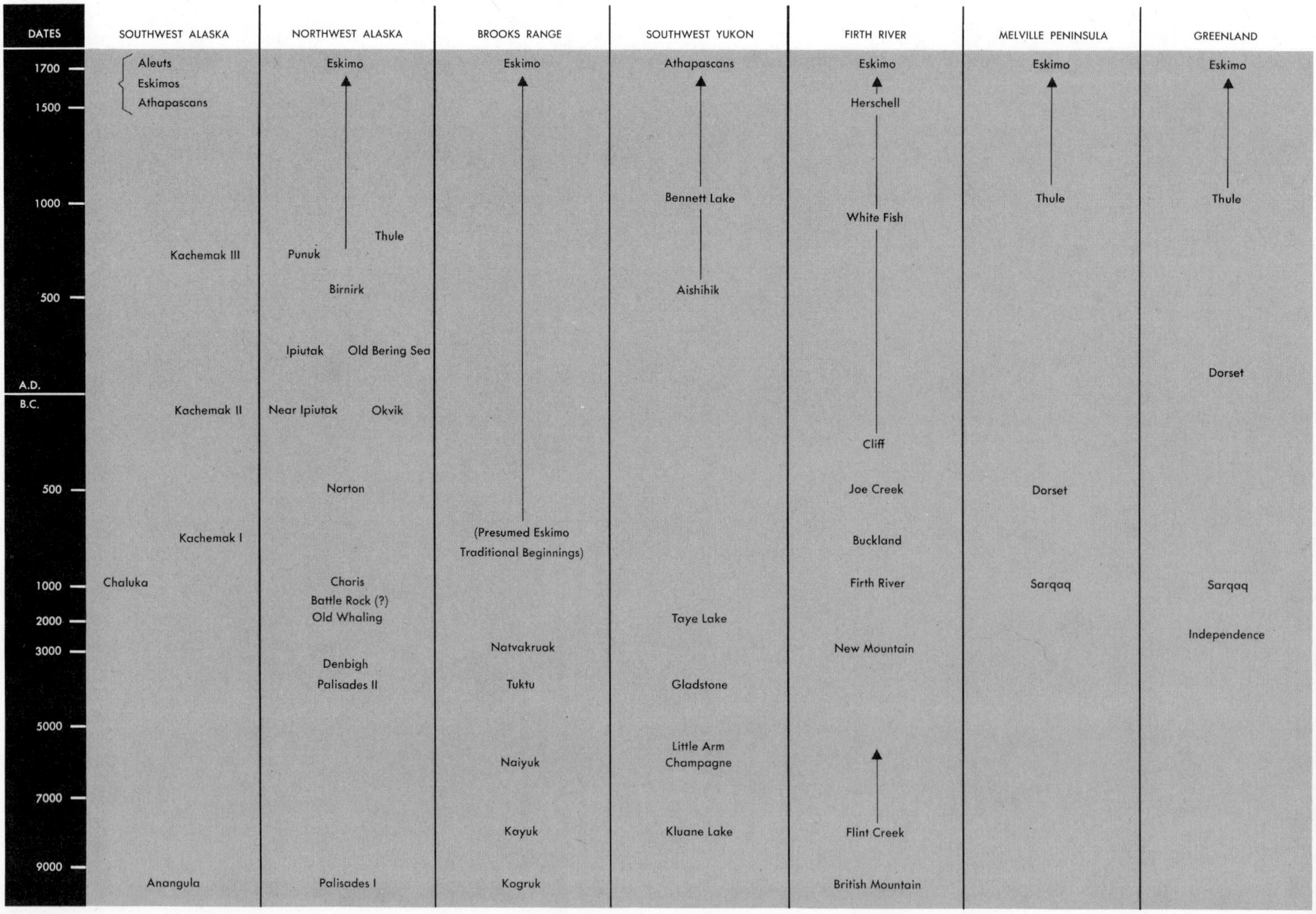

DATES	SOUTHWEST ALASKA	NORTHWEST ALASKA	BROOKS RANGE	SOUTHWEST YUKON	FIRTH RIVER	MELVILLE PENINSULA	GREENLAND
1700	Aleuts / Eskimos / Athapascans	Eskimo	Eskimo	Athapascans	Eskimo	Eskimo	Eskimo
1500					Herschell		
1000				Bennett Lake	White Fish	Thule	Thule
	Kachemak III	Punuk / Thule					
500		Birnirk		Aishihik			
		Ipiutak / Old Bering Sea					
A.D.							Dorset
B.C.	Kachemak II	Near Ipiutak / Okvik					
					Cliff		
500	Kachemak I	Norton	(Presumed Eskimo Traditional Beginnings)		Joe Creek	Dorset	
					Buckland		
1000	Chaluka	Choris / Battle Rock (?) / Old Whaling			Firth River	Sarqaq	Sarqaq
2000				Taye Lake			Independence
3000		Denbigh / Palisades II	Natvakruak / Tuktu	Gladstone	New Mountain		
5000			Naiyuk	Little Arm Champagne			
7000			Kayuk	Kluane Lake	Flint Creek		
9000	Anangula	Palisades I	Kogruk		British Mountain		

major cultural or technological traditions, as these have been defined by various scholars, placing these in space and in time and in their relationships to one another insofar as possible.

In Chapter 2 we surveyed the earliest of these traditions: the little-known British Mountain; the Old Cordilleran, in which several Arctic and Subarctic finds hint at a connection with that tradition as it has been defined from the northwestern United States; and the Plano projectile point tradition, which seems certainly linked with the later stages of the Big-Game Hunting tradition of the North American Plains and Woodlands. This brought our story up to around 5000–6000 B.C., or to the beginnings of the amelioration of early postglacial climates. At this point we resume with the later traditions of these areas, those in which we see the foreshadowings of traits and complexes that can be traced into late prehistoric and early historic times. These traditions include the earlier Northwest Microblade and Arctic Small-Tool technological traditions and the later and more amply documented Eskimo cultural tradition. We shall also refer to the much less well known Denetasiro cultural tradition of the Subarctic Athapascans and to a northern or Boreal extension of the Archaic tradition that is associated with the Subarctic Algonquian tribes.

Some Early Traditions and Industries

The Northwest Microblade Tradition. The Northwest Microblade tradition has been defined and discussed by both MacNeish and W. N. Irving.[4] According to the latter, it is not a complete or full cultural tradition, at least insofar as it can now be described, but rather an aggregate of tool-type complexes that persisted over a relatively long period of time. It shared distinctive artifact types which have a more or less continuous geographic distribution, implying a derivation from common sources. As the name suggests, the tradition was distributed northwesterly. Representative sites have been found in several places in Alaska, in the

Yukon Territory, and in the southwestern part of the Canadian Northwest Territories. MacNeish estimates that its time depth was greatest in Alaska, where it may have begun as early as 6500 B.C. It lasted until around 4000 or 3500 B.C. in Alaska and the western Arctic. In the southwestern Yukon and the Canadian Northwest Territories it probably persisted until 1000 B.C.[5] Characteristic of the tradition were numerous microblades struck from either conical or tongue-shaped cores, burins which were never retouched for hafting, rather carelessly chipped large bifacial knives, large and small endscrapers, and a variety of projectile points, including large stemmed and notched forms and lanceolate types reminiscent of the Plano tradition.[6]

One of the best sequences of the Northwest Microblade tradition is in the Subarctic forest country of the southwest Yukon.[7] The earliest of three phases, Little Arm (5500–4000 B.C.), was a hunting culture, based probably on large animals such as buffalo, elk, and caribou, and on small game and fishing. Included in the tool complex were microblades, the diagnostic tongue-shaped cores, burins, lanceolate projectile points, and stone net-sinkers. Little Arm was succeeded by the Gladstone phase (4000–2000 B.C.), which witnessed a shift from large lanceolate points to smaller types and also to stemmed and side-notched forms. Also in the artifact complex was a beaver-tooth gouge for woodworking, an implement destined to have a long history in Subarctic cultures. Gladstone gave way in turn to the third member of the continuum, Taye Lake (2000–1000 B.C. or later). Taye Lake sites are larger and more numerous than those of the preceding phases. Notched points and half-moon side-blades for harpoons were common weapon types, and probably associated with the complex was a polished stone three-quarter-grooved adze. By now the microblade, core, and burin industry was definitely on the wane.

It seems most likely that the Northwest Microblade tradition was an interior forest development which provided an ancient ancestral base for the later Denetasiro tradition of the Athapascan

Figure 7-4. Chipped-flint artifacts of the Northwest Microblade tradition from Pointed Mountain site, Northwest Territories, Canada. a–d: Lamellar flakes. e: Large-stemmed projectile point. f: Side and front views of tongue-shaped core. g: Conoidal core. h: Side and top views of small end-scraper. i,j: Side and top views of larger end-scrapers. k–n: Burins. o: Large bifacial knife. Length of e, 6.8 cm. (Courtesy National Museum of Canada; see also MacNeish, 1954 b.)

Subarctic hunters. Perhaps the first Athapascans entered the New World at this time, although the complex could have been developed by peoples who occupied the western Subarctic and who were subject only to Asiatic influences rather than invasions. In any event, the Northwest Microblade tradition seems to have had its beginnings toward the close of the early post-glacial period and at a time when the coniferous forests were spreading.[8] Over time it adapted to a boreal environment. Its derivations seem mixed. Obviously it drew upon specialized core, microblade, and burin-making techniques from Asiatic Mesolithic cultures; but its associated projectile points probably had other origins. The lanceolates suggest the dying Plano tradition of the north, the stemmed and notched types of Boreal Archaic cultures of the Great Lakes. The presence of the stemmed and notched points raises problems of dating. If these particular specimen types can be derived from Late Archaic complexes of the Great Lakes, as J. B. Griffin surmises, then they are probably no older than 2000 B.C.[9] Yet in the northernmost complexes of the Northwest Microblade tradition, Palisades II and Tuktu in Alaska, such side-notched points are thought to date to the fourth millennium B.C.[10]

The Arctic Small-Tool Tradition. At some time between 4000 and 3000 B.C. another industrial tradition in flint-working appeared in the western Arctic. Irving has named it the Arctic Small-Tool tradition.[11] Much more clearly defined than the Northwest Microblade tradition in typology, distribution, and chronology, the Arctic Small-Tool tradition might with some justification be called a cultural tradition. It persisted from the above date until about 1000 B.C. Thus, in general, it was later than the Northwest Microblade tradition, although paralleling in time some of the later manifestations of that tradition. The Arctic Small-Tool tradition stretched from southwestern and western Alaska across the Arctic to Greenland, with clear indications of a movement from the west to east. Some of its elements, al-

416

though by no means the full complex of tools, were retained in almost all later Eskimo cultures.

Irving's formulation of the concept of the Arctic Small-Tool tradition followed some years after the discovery of Giddings' remarkable type site for the tradition—Iyatayet, at Cape Denbigh, on the south side of the Seward Peninsula.[12] Giddings found his Denbigh complex or culture phase stratigraphically below a layer in which artifacts of the much later Eskimo tradition occurred, the two cultural zones being separated by a sterile soil layer. The Denbigh complex, and the Arctic Small-Tool tradition as a whole, are characterized by a unique style of fine pressure-flaked flint, by the generally small size of these artifacts, and by the fact that it was a blade or bladelet industry. The numerous microblades found at Denbigh and at other sites were struck from prepared polyhedral cores. Among the diagnostic types were small, bifacial points and knives without stems or notches, bifacially retouched crescent-shaped side-blades which were probably set in the grooved sides of antler and bone points or handles, burins prepared for hafting and retouched on one or both faces, and minute burin spalls which had also been retouched as engraver's tools. One of the features of the flint-flaking was its oblique, parallel arrangement on the blade face (see Fig. 7-6a–f).

In his detailed and careful reconstruction of the old life of the Denbigh flint-knappers, Giddings sees them as sea-mammal hunters who used an end-bladed thrusting harpoon for walrus, and as caribou hunters who employed the small finely chipped points as arrow tips. He comments on the

Figure 7-5. Chipped-stone artifacts of the Arctic Small-Tool tradition from Iyatayet, Cape Denbigh. a: Obsidian core. b: Chert microblade. c: Obsidian microblade. d,e: Retouched obsidian microblades. f,g: Channeled knife blades of chert. h: Lunate knife blade of obsidian. i: Unifaced knife of chert. j–l: End-scrapers of chert or jasper. m: Bifaced 3-edged knife or scraper of jasper. Height of b, 4 cm; and a–e are to this scale. Height of f, 7.5 cm; and f–m are to this scale. (Courtesy Haffenreffer Museum and Brown University Press; see also Giddings, 1964.)

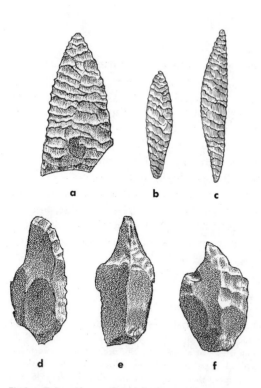

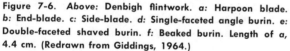

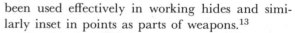

Figure 7-6. *Above:* Denbigh flintwork. *a:* Harpoon blade. *b:* End-blade. *c:* Side-blade. *d:* Single-faceted angle burin. *e:* Double-faceted shaved burin. *f:* Beaked burin. Length of *a*, 4.4 cm. (Redrawn from Giddings, 1964.)

Figure 7-7. *Above, right:* Denbigh burin spall artifact of flint or chert. Length, 10.6 cm. (Redrawn from Giddings, 1964.)

absence of house pits, which suggests that either the Denbigh people did not spend the winter on the Bering Sea coast or, if they did, built their winter quarters on ground surface. Unlike the later Eskimos who occupied the same site, the Denbigh people had no stone or pottery lamps for burning seal oil nor pottery for cooking. The presence of fire-cracked stone around the hearths implies, instead, that food was stone-boiled in bark baskets. Burins and burin chip artifacts indicate an extensive antler and ivory carving craft, both for utilitarian and aesthetic purposes, although no specimens have been found. The numerous micro-blades set in bone or antler handles could have

been used effectively in working hides and similarly inset in points as parts of weapons.[13]

The Arctic Small-Tool tradition was confined to the Arctic culture area. There is a Denbigh-like station on the Cape Krusenstern beaches on the north side of the Seward Peninsula,[14] and Campbell's Natvakruak complex in the Brooks Range is clearly affiliated with it.[15] MacNeish's New Mountain phase, in the Firth River sequence of the Yukon Arctic coast, also may be included within the tradition,[16] along with sites farther east at Baker Lake in the Keewatin District of the Northwest Territories,[17] at Igloolik on the Melville Peninsula,[18] and in Greenland.[19] As we mentioned, the tradition seemed to describe a sloping horizon as it moved from west to east, and such later complexes in Greenland as Independence II and Sarqaq, which date to around 1000 B.C., also may be considered a part of it.[20]

As to its origins, Irving has discovered similarities between some Arctic Small-Tool types and specimens from the Lena River Basin in

Siberia, although the Lena River types seem too recent to have provided the first impulses for the Arctic Small-Tool tradition.[21] Irving probably is correct in feeling that as a complex or a tradition, it was essentially formed in the Bering Strait region. Nevertheless the technological aspects of flint work are, as Giddings has emphasized, distinctly Old World with similarities spanning the Upper Paleolithic, Mesolithic, and Siberian "Neolithic."[22] And Griffin seems correct in surmising that both the Arctic Small-Tool tradition and the Northwest Microblade tradition exhibit Asiatic technologies following, respectively, Arctic coastal tundra and Subarctic forest adaptations and developments.[23]

The Aleutian Core and Blade Industry. It seems appropriate to refer again to the Aleutian Core and Blade Industry which we mentioned in Chapter 2 as a possible very early Arctic complex from Anangula, dating back to 6000 B.C. or before.[24] Characteristic blades of the industry, which Irving describes as being much thicker than the Arctic Small-Tool and Northwest Microblade types, have been found in the lower levels of the Chaluka midden site on the nearby Aleutian island of Umnak. In this context, which dates to 1000 B.C.,[25] they were associated with bifaced stemmed points, knives, and other artifacts which Laughlin and Marsh have identified with an early Aleut or proto-Aleut-Eskimo culture.[26] From these finds, we might speculate that the so-called Aleutian Core and Blade Industry long persisted in the Aleutians, running contemporaneously with the Northwest Microblade and Arctic Small-Tool traditions, and that it provided the matrix culture for the later Eskimo cultures of the Aleutians or all of the Pacific-Aleut regions.

The Eskimo Tradition

General Statement. From what we now know, the Eskimo cultural tradition had its inception some time between 2000 and 1000 B.C.

in the region of the Bering Strait in northeastern Siberia and western Alaska. The process of this development involved the assimilation and adaptation of new culture traits and perhaps new peoples into earlier, resident cultural traditions. The most important of these resident traditions was the Arctic Small-Tool, and the Aleutian Core and Blade Industry apparently was equally important in the Aleutians. The source of the new elements which were to transform the resident traditions lay in Siberian Mesolithic and Neolithic traditions. The argument, thus, is not that Eskimo culture was imported or brought fully formed from Siberia to America but that it was fashioned by peoples living around the Bering Strait and in western Alaska who drew upon old, local knowledge and upon new inspiration from their more advanced neighbors of northern Asia.

Eskimo culture spread from the Bering Strait region south along the Alaskan shores of the Bering Sea, into the Aleutians, and down the Alaskan Pacific coast. It also spread north from the Bering Strait and east across Arctic Canada to Greenland, Labrador, and Newfoundland. The southern spread may have been the earlier of the two, for old Eskimo archaeological levels in Pacific Alaska are as early (1000 B.C. or before) as those of the Bering Sea and Bering Strait. However, the history of the early Eskimo settlements in Pacific Alaska and the Aleutians is complicated by what may be additional diffusion from Japan and Kamchatka by way of the Aleutian chain. The northern spread, as might be anticipated, describes a horizon which slopes upward in time from west to east, as did the horizon of the Arctic Small-Tool tradition, so that Eskimo culture does not appear in eastern Canada and in Greenland until after 1000 B.C.

Because of the close historical association of the Eskimo cultural tradition, the Eskimo language, and the Mongoloid Eskimo physical type, scholars assume that the tradition was indeed created and carried by peoples of this language and racial stock. And this assumption seems well supported by both glottochronological reckonings and archaeological-physical anthropological reconstructions. We cannot be certain, however, that the dissemination of the Eskimo cultural tradition throughout the Arctic was also accompanied by a spread of Eskimo as a new language and by Eskimos as a new physical type. In fact it is quite likely that the carriers of the earlier Arctic Small-Tool tradition, which was similarly widely distributed in the Arctic, also spoke an Eskimo language and were of the same general physical type as the later Eskimo. Hence, the Eskimo cultural tradition could have spread from its western Arctic base largely by diffusion, being taken up by the various resident tribes who had been following in the Arctic Small-Tool tradition. Only closely coordinated archaeological and physical anthropological research in the many regions of the Arctic can give us the exact story. The only thing we can be fully certain of is that the Eskimo hunters were preceded by either direct ancestors or by others who had already made considerable strides in adjusting to a life on the frozen treeless tundras of the far north.

The Eskimo cultural tradition has been conditioned by the severe environment of the Arctic and is well known for its efficient adaptation to this environment. This conditioning and adaptive response are seen most clearly in those northern regions where the climate is dramatically harsh, where ice and snow, sub-zero weather, and long, dark nights persist for most of each year. Conversely, the distinctiveness of the culture is less pronounced in regions such as the Aleutians and the Alaskan Pacific coast where the climate is milder.

In general the Eskimo tradition was based on hunting—hunting of sea mammals, including seals, walruses, and whales; and of land animals, principally the caribou. Fish and birds provided dietary supplements. Within the history of the tradition there seems to be a chronological drift toward a greater maritime dependence and away from land-hunting. This drift or trend should not be over-emphasized, however, for, as we already have mentioned, even the earlier Arctic Small-Tool cultures were equipped for sea- as well as land-hunting, and many late prehistoric and historic Eskimo cultures were as dependent on land game as on the walrus and the seal.

Eskimo winter houses were frequently semi-subterranean and constructed of driftwood or whale-bone frames covered with turf and stones; in some regions, such as the Canadian Arctic, however, the winter house was the classic igloo made of ice and snow. Skin tents were generally used during summer months. Clothing was made of skins and fur, and skins were stretched over wooden frames to make the mens' covered hunting canoe, or kayak, and the larger umiak, or "woman's boat."

This utilization of skins and furs, for clothing, shelters, and boats is only another aspect of the Eskimos heavy dependence on game animals. Besides furnishing meat and skins, animals supplied the Eskimo with many other essentials. The whale lent his bone for construction and his oil for cooking and illumination. The bones of smaller animals were converted into artifacts. Ivory from the tusks of the walrus became tools and ornaments. The principal weapon for sea-mammal hunting was the ivory harpoon, usually equipped with a slate end-blade. Land animals were taken with spears or arrows tipped with barbed bone or with chipped-stone points.

A very characteristic Eskimo implement was the slate ulu, or crescent-shaped knife, the "woman's knife." The lamps for burning whale oil were made of both stone and pottery, and pottery vessels are characteristic of many although not all regions and phases of the Eskimo tradition. Some of the most distinctive Eskimo gear pertains to land travel over the snow and ice fields. Among the items are sleds (for either human or dog traction), ice-creepers for walking, and the narrow-slitted ivory snow-goggles to protect the eyes of the traveller from the fierce glare of the sun on ice and snow.

The Eskimo cultural tradition is usually divided into major sub-traditions by archaeologists. MacNeish, for example, follows a two-fold split between what he calls the North Pacific tradition and the Inuk.[27] The first embraces the cultures of Pacific Alaska; the second refers to all the Eskimo cultures of the Bering Strait region and the northern Arctic. H. B. Collins treats of four traditional or sub-traditional divisions.[28] His Pacific-Aleut approximates MacNeish's North Pacific, although he includes the Aleutian Islands as well as the Alaskan Pacific coast within his category. He then divides the remaining Eskimo archaeological cultures into three branches: Northern Maritime; Choris-Norton-Near Ipiutak; and Dorset. We will utilize Collins' four-fold division in our survey presentation, after a few prefatory comments.

Other Arctic scholars as well as MacNeish and Collins separate the Pacific-Aleut subtradition from the remainder of prehistoric and historic Eskimo cultures.[29] This cultural split coincides with the natural environmental differences between Pacific Alaska and the northern Arctic regions that we already have pointed out.

The second and third subtraditions, the Northern Maritime and the Choris-Norton-Near Ipiutak, were closely intertwined, and Collins' conception of them as two semi-separate lines of development, although useful as an hypothesis, is not always easy to follow. The Northern Maritime subtradition is well represented on the Asiatic side of the Bering Strait, on the St. Lawrence and Diomede Islands, at Cape Prince of Wales at the end of the Seward Peninsula, at Point Barrow in Arctic Alaska, and in its later stages, from Barrow eastward across the Arctic to Greenland. The Choris-Norton-Near Ipiutak sub-tradition was distributed, in Alaska, from Point Hope on the Arctic Sea southward to Kotzebue Sound, the Seward Peninsula, Norton Sound, and on to Bristol Bay. Thus although archaeological sites and complexes which represent it tend to lie to the south of those of the Northern Maritime subtradition, there is a partial territorial correspondence of the two between Point Hope and Norton Sound. Furthermore, there was also considerable trait-sharing between the cultures of the two subtraditions.

The fourth, or Dorset, subtradition stands apart from the Pacific-Aleut, the Northern Maritime, and the Choris-Norton-Ipiutak. Restricted to the eastern Arctic it was essentially a simpler expression of Eskimo material culture than was found in the west. In parts of the eastern Arctic, Dorset occurs consistently on an earlier chronological horizon than the late manifestations of the Northern Maritime subtradition which appear to have replaced it.

The Pacific-Aleut Subtradition. The Pacific-Aleut cultural subtradition can be traced in the Aleutian Islands and southern Alaska from about 1000 B.C. to historic and even modern times. Its history seems to have been one of gradually increasing divergence from the other Eskimo subtraditions, apparently because of geographic separation and local developments, especially local development under natural environmental conditions that are, as we have said, much less severe than in the Arctic subareas to the north. In general, the findings of linguists and physical anthropologists support what archaeologists have learned about this separatist drift of the Pacific-Aleutian peoples. Glottochronological reckoning indicates that the Aleut language once was the same as Eskimo or proto-Eskimo, and the two are thought to have split apart some time during the third millennium B.C. Moreover even within the Eskimo language, the dialects of the Pacific Alaskan mainland are the most divergent. In physical type, although the old Aleut were long and high-headed as were the prehistoric and historic Eskimo of the Northern Maritime subtradition, the later Aleut showed a tendency toward broader, lower-vaulted heads.

Although all this Pacific-Aleut branching—cultural, linguistic, and physical—may have resulted from a semi-isolated local development, this probably is much too simple an explanation. To begin with, you will recall that the Aleutian chain leads westward toward the Kamchatka Peninsula and Asia, and that this chain of islands, as well as the Bering Strait crossing, could have served as a path of migration and diffusion from Old World to New. New Mongoloid varieties could have reached America by this route in relatively late prehistoric times and new culture traits could have been carried this way.[30] In this connection, too, it is worth remembering that the Aleutian path from Asia to the New World was an old one and that the ancient cultural heritage here, which antedated the rise of the Eskimo tradition, was somewhat different from that of the rest of the Arctic. As we have just observed, the Arctic Small-Tool tradition, so widespread in all other parts of the Arctic, does not seem to have existed in the Aleutians. Instead, the analogous complex there—the Aleutian Core and Blade Industry— seems related only in the sense of having the same general and remote Asiatic Mesolithic parentage.

Another important factor that must have been at least partly responsible for the distinctiveness of the Pacific-Aleut subtradition is the Northwest Coast, the culture area to the south that we surveyed in the preceding chapter. We know that there was cultural interchange along the Northwest Coast-Arctic frontier between Eskimo and Northwest Coast tribes during late prehistoric and historic times. And Borden and others (see pp. 385, 396) have argued that in the first millennium B.C. or earlier, a number of important traits, such as ground-slate weapons and tools, effigy stone-carving, and the use of labrets were diffused from the Northwest Coast to the Eskimo.

Aside from the Chaluka midden in the Aleutians which, with its radiocarbon date of 1000 B.C. may lie near the transition point from pre-Eskimoid into more typically Eskimoid levels, the earliest phase of the Pacific-Aleut Eskimo subtradition is probably Kachemak Bay I on the mainland.[31] The Kachemak Bay sequence, worked out by Frederica de Laguna in Cook Inlet, offers a continuity from phases I through IV, or from about 750 B.C. to historic times.[32] It is the basic sequence of the subtradition, and it relates to discoveries in Prince William Sound, on Kodiak Island, and in the Aleutians.

The Kachemak Bay villages were located along the shore, and the houses were semi-subterranean affairs, built up of stone and whalebone or wood. They had central fireplaces, and in the late phases at least, were rectangular in plan and had passage entrances. The cultures were clearly oriented toward sea-hunting and fishing, as well as toward land game and food-collecting. Hunting gear included leaf-shaped chipped-stone projectile points and knives. In general chipped implements, including end-blades, were more common during the earlier phases. Later the same types and forms were made of ground slate. Bone toggle harpoons were used, although not so liberally as a type of barbed-bone dart with a tang-hole for attaching the line and a slate end-blade. Fishing remnants included bone and wood composite hooks and perforated-stone sinkers. Many woodworking tools characterized the sequence—splitting and planing adzes of ground stone, stone saws and hammers, and bone wedges. These implements, of course, differ markedly from a typical northern Eskimo artifact inventory. More Eskimo-like were oval and circular stone lamps for burning oil. Completing the inventory were a great many small bone tools, including such Eskimo-like items as needles, pins, punches, and needle-cases.

Kachemak art initially was rather crude, but realistic stone and ivory effigy carvings had begun to appear in Kachemak Bay II along with the strongly characteristic Eskimo bone and ivory engraving in which fine spurred lines were combined with dot and circle motifs in the manner of Northern Maritime styles such as Okvik and Old Bering Sea. Presumably this engraving was done with copper tools. Not until Kachemak Bay III did copper ornaments appear, along with numerous bone, stone, and ivory items. Beads and bracelets were made of the metal and pendants and labrets of the other materials. Phase III also marked the emergence of a very crude Eskimo pottery. One of the most interesting features of the Kachemak culture, associated with phase II, were human burials dressed out with carved ivory eyeballs. This mortuary trait also was practiced in the Ipiutak culture of the Arctic.[33]

422

In contrasting Kachemak and Pacific-Aleut culture with the other Eskimo subtraditions, Collins has summed the matter up by listing those traits in which the former stand apart. These traits included specialized forms of slate blades, wider use of the barbed bone dart than of the toggle-headed harpoon, composite fishhooks and line weights, oval and round stone lamps, and finally the greater emphasis on woodworking and, from historic times, on weaving.[34]

In summary, we can see that the Pacific-Aleut subtradition and cultural subarea differ from most other chapters in the Eskimo story. The evidence at hand indicates that this situation became more pronounced in later prehistoric times than it had been earlier, although there are hints at ancient differences as well. Certainly one factor in this cultural differentiation was the natural environmental setting of the Pacific-Aleut subarea—its milder climate and stands of forest, so unlike the northern Arctic tundra. But diffusion from and contact with other surrounding peoples also must be taken into account. Asia, by way of the Kamchatka Peninsula and the Aleutian chain of islands, was one probable source of such outside influences. The cultures of the Northwest Coast were another. With respect to the latter, however, it is as yet uncertain whether Northwest Coast tribes or Pacific-Aleut Eskimos were in primary possession of ground-slate weapons and polished-stone woodworking tools in the first millennium B.C.

The Northern Maritime Subtradition. In examining the Eskimo tradition, we have begun with a division of it—the Pacific-Aleut subtradition—which is least typical of its most characteristic line of development. Let us move now to that most characteristic line, the Northern Maritime subtradition. As a culture continuum, it begins with the Okvik phase and runs successively through Old Bering Sea, Birnirk, Punuk, and Thule cultures. Thule then provided the immediately antecedent base for the historic and modern Eskimo cultures of northern Alaska, Arctic Canada, and Greenland. In Greenland, it was the Thule culture which blended with the culture of the medieval Norsemen who colonized parts of this vast northern island during the thirteenth to the fifteenth centuries. The resultant cultural fusion, which was dominated by the Eskimo, is called the Inugsuk phase.[35]

Information about the pre-Thule stages of the continuum have come down to us only from discoveries in the west, around the Bering Strait and in northern Alaska, indicating that the movement of this subtradition originally was from west to east; during Thule times, however, there was a backdrift of both peoples and cultures from the central Arctic all the way to the Bering Strait, resulting in the cultural and linguistic uniformity seen all across the Arctic on the historic horizon. The southern boundary of this westernmost spread of Thule Eskimo culture was Norton Sound, and Eskimo dialects spoken just to the north of Norton Sound were more closely related to those of far-off Greenland than to the dialects of tribes immediately to the south. Similarly, in physical type the Eskimos to the north and east of Norton Sound were long-headed and high-headed, whereas those to the south were broad-headed, with lower cranial vaults, similar to the late Pacific-Aleuts.[36]

The known chronology for the Northern Maritime subtradition begins with the date for Okvik, determined by radiocarbon to be about 300 B.C.[37] Old Bering Sea then followed Okvik in the first half of the first millennium A.D., to be succeeded by Birnirk after A.D. 500. Thule and Punuk, which are largely contemporaneous, began some time prior to A.D. 1000 and led eventually into modern Eskimo culture. The Okvik date, which is substantially later than the earliest date for the Pacific-Aleut subtradition, or to the earliest radiocarbon dates now available for the Choris-Norton-Near Ipiutak subtradition, is viewed by Collins as marking a point well along in the Northern Maritime development; and he warns against assuming that the Northern Maritime line is necessarily more recent than, or derivative of, the other two.[38] He apparently leans instead toward the interpretation that both the Northern Maritime and Choris-Norton-Near Ipiutak Eskimo cultures arose from a common Denbigh-like, or Arctic Small-Tool tradition base and that their development was more or less co-ordinate in time although accomplished in different geographical locations.[39] Presumably a third contemporaneous development, but one in which the process of increasing "Eskimo-ization" was occurring on the somewhat different Aleutian Core and Blade technological base, was that of the Pacific-Aleut locus that we have just discussed. In all three instances, these acculturation processes must have begun around 1000 B.C. or a bit before.

The Okvik and Old Bering Sea phases are known best from sites on St. Lawrence Island, the Diomede Islands, and from Uelen and other sites on the Siberian side of the Bering Strait. Artifacts in Okvik and Old Bering Sea styles were more widely distributed than this, however, occurring as far north as Point Hope and Point Barrow and south as far as Bristol Bay. On St. Lawrence Island in the vicinity of Gambell, Collins seriated a number of village occupations by stratigraphy, old beach line locations, and artifact stylistic

changes.[40] The oldest of the village locations was on the lower slope of a hill overlooking a geologically recent gravel spit on which the younger villages were found. The houses and refuse of this oldest site yielded many artifacts with incised designs in Okvik and early Old Bering Sea art styles. These Old Bering Sea objects related in turn to incised ivory from the second oldest of the Gambell sites which lay at the base of the hill on the oldest of the gravel spit beach lines. In the upper levels of this second site, overlying the Old Bering Sea artifacts, were items in the Punuk style. This second site, Miyowagh, is worth a closer look as a representative station of the Northern Maritime subtradition during its Old Bering Sea and Punuk phases.

The Miyowagh midden is about 100 meters in diameter, and Collins' excavations proved that it was as much as 2 meters deep in some places. As a living site it had been on or nearer the sea; today it is over a half-mile distant as a result of the successive building out of the strand lines of the gravel spit. A small lake, fed by a little stream from the adjacent hills, was nearby and probably offered a freshwater source. The earliest houses at Miyowagh were built directly on the gravel plain, and the debris which had accumulated around them was made up almost entirely of decomposed animal remains and other organic materials. The rich black matrix of the midden contained great quantities of animal bones and baleen (a horny substance from the mouths of whales) and artifacts and rejectage of stone, bone, wood, and ivory. As at many Arctic sites, the frozen soil kept the remains in an excellent state of preservation. Several houses were uncovered in the Miyowagh excavations. The most complete specimen dates to the early part of the Punuk phase; another, also reasonably intact, was found stratigraphically beneath the Punuk house and probably dates to late Old Bering Sea. The houses were rectangular, had been floored with stone slabs, and the walls were constructed of driftwood logs and whalebone laid up horizontally and held in place by upright posts, large bones, and stones.

Figure 7-8. Three-sided view of a decorated ivory object in the Okvik style from Little Diomede Island. (After Collins, 1937.)

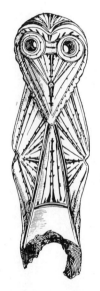
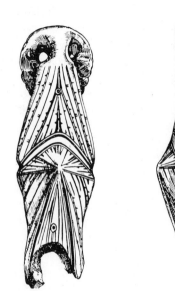

Presumably they were roofed with horizontal timbers. Both houses had long entrance passages. In the Punuk house there was an entrance antechamber (Fig. 7-9) roughly oval in outline and measuring about 3.5 by 2 meters. The floor was of stone, and the random utilization of building materials in the superstructure of this antechamber is evident from the following description:

> The roof was formed of timbers placed transversely across two (extended) whale jaws. The inner wall consisted principally of a small whale skull which had been placed base downward on cross timbers beneath which the occupants had to crawl to enter the passageway leading to the house.[41]

The stone-floored entrance passage proper was about 1.5 meters wide and about 5 meters long. The walls of stone, whalebones, and walrus skulls were capped by transverse wooden logs and overlying poles laid parallel to the long axis of the passage. There was a step-up of about 32 centimeters from the passage to the floor of the house proper. The house proper was about 6 by 6.75 meters. The earlier house was smaller, but otherwise similar, and had a long but curved entrance passage.

The abundant whale, walrus, and seal bones in the Miyowagh midden, and the use of bone in house construction, leaves little doubt but that sea-mammal hunting was a primary economic activity of the Northern Maritime Eskimo at this site. Apparently this pursuit of sea game grew in importance from Okvik and Old Bering Sea times through the Punuk, proto-historic, and historic periods. This trend is indicated by the increase in the number of harpoon parts found in the later midden at Miyowagh and other Gambell sites. The harpoon was, of course, the weapon used in sea-mammal hunting. Its basic principle was that the barbed point, on becoming detached from the shaft of the spear, remained in the swimming animal. The point or head was attached to a line, the other end of which was held by the hunter so that the wounded quarry could not escape in the

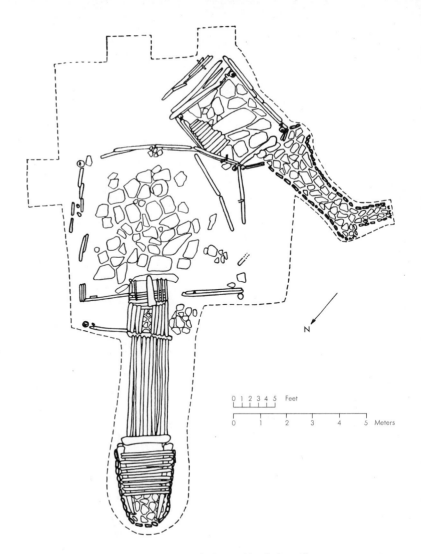

Figure 7-9. House plans at Miyowagh. House No. 3, from the early Punuk phase, is larger and was partially superimposed over House No. 4, which probably dates from late Old Bering Sea times. (After Collins, 1937.)

water. As a composite artifact, the Eskimo harpoon consisted of a wooden mainshaft, a slender bone or ivory foreshaft, and a detachable toggle-head of bone or ivory. The wooden mainshaft also was equipped with an ivory icepick set in the butt-end, an ivory or bone finger rest at mid-section, and a bone socket-piece attached to the fore-end into which the foreshaft was set. These various parts were among the most numerous small items in the village refuse and are extremely important in Arctic archaeology, for their minor technical and stylistic changes serve to mark off the culture

425

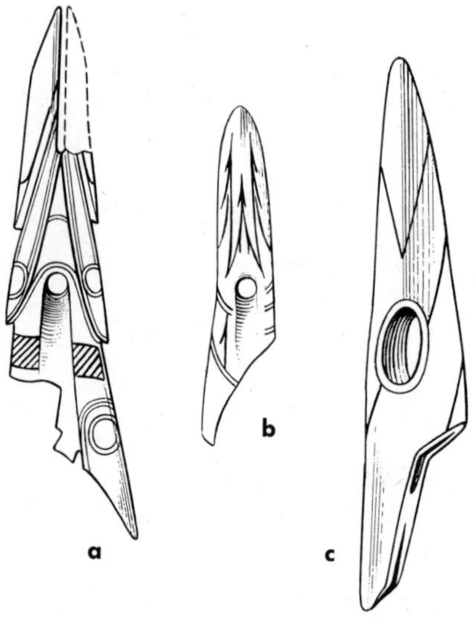

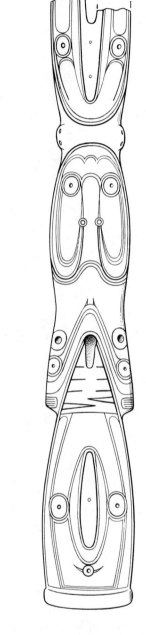

sequence. This is particularly true of the bone or ivory points for, in Collins' words:

The toggle harpoon head is the most dependable criterion of cultural change at our disposal, and as such it is destined to bear the main weight of the chronology that must be established if we are to have a clear understanding of the stages of development in Eskimo culture. As a "time indicator," the harpoon head occupies a position in Eskimo culture analogous to that of pottery in the Southwest.[42]

A number of variable features distinguished types and varieties among these toggle harpoon heads—the nature of the socket for engaging the end of the foreshaft; the lashing slots for further securing the head to the foreshaft; the pointed lower end or spur; the perforation or line hole by which the head was attached to the line; the lateral barbs or inset stone blades; and the tip which may or may not have been slit for an end-blade.[43] A detailed examination of Eskimo harpoon head types would go beyond our survey purpose, but in general those of the Okvik and Old Bering Sea phases are complicated and highly variable in form and are further distinguished by engraved designs in the Old Bering Sea art style. In the Punuk phase, as they become more numerous, they become simpler both in form and decoration, and more standardized; and these trends culminated in the simple, utilitarian, but highly effective harpoon head used by the modern Eskimo.[44] It may also be significant that the larger whaling harpoon heads found in the St. Lawrence Island sites date no earlier than the Punuk phase and then become more frequent. Perhaps only seal and walrus were hunted during the Okvik and Old Bering Sea periods; however, whale bone and whale baleen were put to a variety of uses in these earlier cultures. The whaling harpoon heads averaged perhaps 20 centimeters in length, whereas those used for seal and walrus were about one-half that size.[45]

Another item of hunting gear which underwent similar changes was a winged or butterfly-like object of ivory (Fig. 7-12, *top*) that was probably attached to the butt-end of a harpoon of a dart

Figure 7-10. *Above, left:* Ivory harpoon points. *a:* Old Bering Sea. *b:* Punuk. *c:* Punuk whaling. Length of *a,* 13.4 cm.; *b,* 8.1 cm.; *c,* 20.2 cm. (After Collins, 1937.)

Figure 7-11. *Above, right:* Socket-piece for harpoon, Old Bering Sea style. Length, 11.5 cm. (After Collins, 1937.)

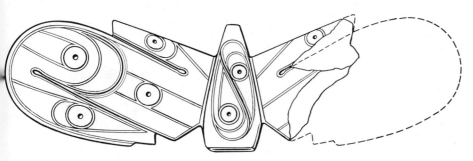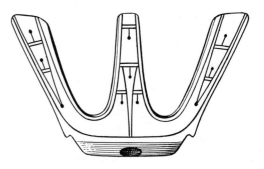

Figure 7-12. Eskimo winged ivory objects of Old Bering Sea (*left*) and Punuk phases. Diameter of *left*, about 21 cm. (After Collins, 1937.)

shaft to serve as a "wing" and counterweight to guide and balance the flight of the missile. A full cycle of elaborative and aesthetic development unfolds in these little objects. On the Okvik level they were small and plain; in the Old Bering Sea phases they became large, butterfly-shaped, and ornamented with engraved geometric designs; in early Punuk they were large and trident-formed; and, finally, in late Punuk they were reduced in size and left undecorated.[46]

Additional artifacts from the debris of the St. Lawrence Island sites were stone points and knives, barbed points of ivory or bone, and prongs for bird darts and fish spears, also of ivory and bone. The stonework included both chipped chert and slate and rubbed-slate points and knives, with the chipped types tending to be replaced by the rubbed forms in Punuk times and later. Some of the points were small triangular blades which were fixed in the slotted ends of the ivory harpoon heads. Other points or knives were larger, broad-bladed, and stemmed types that could have served to arm harpoons, although they may have been hafted as knives. One wooden knife handle from Miyowagh still held a chipped chert blade in its socket, and a number of other wooden handles were recovered from which the blades had been lost. Some slate ulus were found as well, including specimens still hafted in handles of wood or ivory. Besides the points and knives, many drills, scrapers, and adzes have been taken from the midden refuse. The adzes had been hafted into handles of either wood or ivory.

A great many utensils besides those already mentioned had been fashioned of ivory, bone, and baleen. For example, whole or nearly whole walrus tusks had been notched for hafting to wooden han-

dles for use as picks to dig in the ice or frozen ground. Wedges for splitting wood were also made of walrus ivory, and walrus scapulae were turned into snow shovels. Smaller items included ivory drills and drill-rests and implements such as fat-scrapers, awls, needles, buttons, pendants, brow-bands, and combs. Ice creepers, which were attached to the soles of boots to keep them from slipping on ice, were made of flat pieces of bone or baleen inset with ivory spikes. Among the most common household utensils were ivory spoons or ladles and pails of stitched baleen fitted with wooden bottoms and bone or ivory handles.

One interesting and important Eskimo trait was the manufacture of models or toys. Toy specimens have been found throughout the St. Lawrence sequence, and they offer testimony of various activities otherwise not definitely documented. Thus small toy bows furnish sound evidence of the use of the sinew-backed bow in the Punuk, but not in the earlier Old Bering Sea phase. Toy umiaks and kayaks from both Old Bering Sea and Punuk contexts imply the use of those familiar Eskimo boats during these times.

Potsherds were abundant at the Gambell sites, and the pottery tradition remained remarkably unchanged throughout the sequence. Both lamps and cooking vessels were made of a coarse, thick, poorly fired ware which had been tempered with either grass fibers or gravel. The cooking pots were of an undistinguished round-bottomed form, and the surfaces of some had been impressed before firing with a parallel-grooved or a checked wooden

427

paddle. The pottery lamps were deep, saucer-like dishes. These two utensils, in spite of their crudity, were of utmost importance to the Eskimo in cooking his food and in lighting and heating his dwellings.

The most distinctive thing about the Northern Maritime subtradition, however, is its art style, seen to good advantage in the materials recovered from the St. Lawrence Island sites. The most distinguished style of the subtradition, associated with the Okvik and Old Bering Sea phases, generally is called Old Bering Sea art. It is coherent, sophisticated, and easily recognizable. Collins recognizes three sequent substyles or subphases: 1

(Okvik), 2 and 3 (early and late Old Bering Sea). The Old Bering Sea 1, or Okvik, substyle was simpler than the subsequent Old Bering Sea 2 and 3 phases. It was essentially linear, characterized by radiating lines, long spurs, broken lines, and some concentric circles. Phase 2 was the apogee. Although employing some of the same elements as phase 1, it was distinctly curvilinear. Circles, lobed forms, forked-tailed lobes, rhomboidal, and triangulate elements all were incorporated in graceful, rhythmic conceptions. Small dots and broken lines served as fillers. Biomorphic themes—whales, seals, human faces—were incorporated in some of the designs, but in a highly stylized method. Phase 3 art emphasized concentric circles, often suggesting animal eyes. The phase was further defined by a reduction in the use of filler elements. The Punuk

Figure 7-13. Principal decorative motifs of Old Bering Sea Style 1. (After Collins, 1937.)

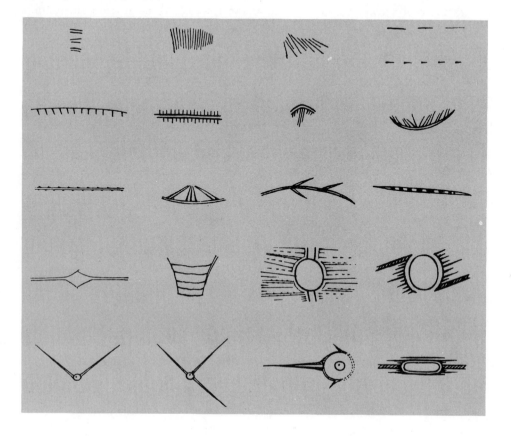

style, which followed, was clearly in the same line of development, although the full story of the transition was not revealed in the Miyowagh or other Gambell middens. Punuk art also featured the circles and circle-and-dot motifs, but these were perfectly round, compass-made elements. Old Bering Sea and Punuk art, like all Eskimo art, was confined to relatively small objects, utility items such as harpoon heads, the winged objects, adze handles, pail handles, and needle cases. It was also a sculptural art or an engraver's art, and the prime material for its expression was walrus ivory. In Okvik and Old Bering Sea times, the sculpturing was done with stone gravers, probably of chipped chert. One of the important changes in the Punuk phase was the introduction of iron-pointed engraving tools.[47]

Before leaving the St. Lawrence Island sequence, let us take a summary glance at the changes which are recorded there in the Northern Maritime subtradition. The art style moved from moderately complex linear arrangement of design to arrangements which were increasingly complicated and curvilinear. After the close of the Old Bering Sea phase, they again became simplified in Punuk and still more so in the historic and modern periods. The hunting economy and technology was marked by increased adaptation to large marine game, especially the whale. Although a great many artifact types were present in Old Bering Sea times and remained the same or underwent only slight modifications, others were more significantly changed. Chipped stone gave way to rubbed slate. New forms and implements also appeared. In the transition from Old Bering Sea to Punuk, such innovations as the larger whaling harpoon head, blunt bird arrows, bolas for hunting birds, ivory and bone wrist guards for archers, the sinew-backed bow, slat armor, and iron-pointed engraving tools appeared. Collins also enumerates other changes which characterize modern Eskimo life on St. Lawrence Island and which were probably brought in during late prehistoric or early historic times. He mentions modifications in pottery types and in the semi-subterranean houses, to include

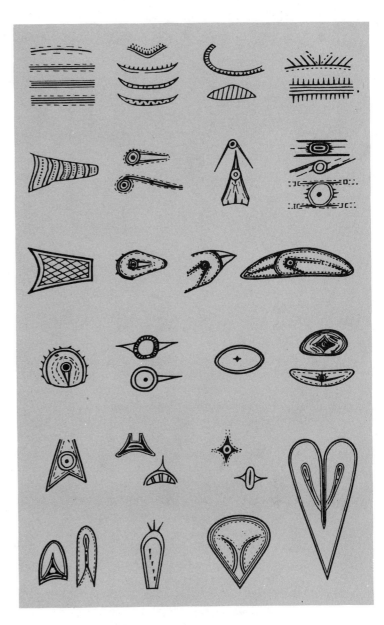

Figure 7-14. Principal decorative motifs of Old Bering Sea Style 2. (After Collins, 1937.)

such features as sleeping benches, and the use of iron lance blades. One extremely important new complex, distinguished by several artifactual features, was the dog-traction sled. Ivory sled runners date back to the Old Bering Sea middens, but these sleds were apparently pushed or drawn by humans.

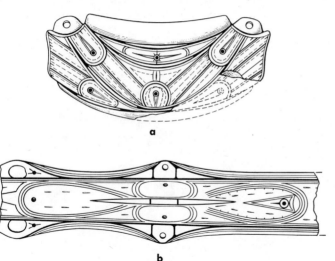

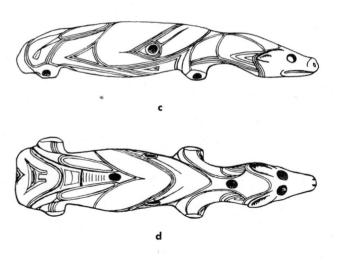

Figure 7-15. Ivory carving in Old Bering Sea style. *a*: Ornament, 11.2 cm. in diameter. *b*: Needle case, 8.5 cm. long. *c,d*: Two views of a polar bear in Old Bering Sea style. Length, 9 cm. (After Collins, 1937.)

The dog-traction complex included such material items as swivels and trace buckles for harnesses and ferrules for the ends of whip handles.[48] Some of these traits, such as the use of iron and the dog sled, appear to have been of Asiatic derivation. Others were either of New World origin or were Arctic area reformulations of an ancient Asiatic heritage which had spread back to western Alaska and St. Lawrence Island from the northern and eastern ranges of the Northern Maritime subtradition.

The northern and eastern extensions of the Northern Maritime subtradition probably diverged from the parent stock toward the close of the Old Bering Sea phase, around A.D. 500, simultaneous with the beginning of the Birnirk-Thule line of development. The Birnirk phase is best revealed at Point Barrow on the Arctic coast of Alaska,[49] but excavations at Kurigitavik on Cape Prince of Wales have revealed it in stratigraphic relationship to an early subphase of the Thule culture which immediately overlies it and which appears to have developed out of it. Birnirk crossdates with terminal Old Bering Sea and with the earlier part of Punuk, whereas Thule at Kurigitavik is coeval with, and in many ways parallel in development to, late Punuk.[50] The Birnirk-Thule branch of Northern Maritime culture spread east-

ward from Alaska to Greenland in prehistoric times and became, as we pointed out, the immediate forerunner of historic and modern Eskimo culture all across the Arctic.[51]

The Choris-Norton-Near Ipiutak Subtradition. The Choris-Norton-Near Ipiutak line of development has been studied most closely in the regions of Norton Sound, Kotzebue Sound, and Point Hope. As we pointed out before, this distribution overlaps with the Northern Maritime subtradition, and the two are interrelated in their earlier histories. According to Collins, the later inheritors of the Choris-Norton-Near Ipiutak subtradition were the historic and modern Eskimo of the Bering Sea coast from Norton Sound to Bristol Bay, who held a geographically intermediate position between Pacific-Aleut and Northern Maritime tribes.[52] Collins further contends that the Choris-Norton-Near Ipiutak and Northern Maritime cultures shared a common base in the Denbigh culture of the Arctic Small-Tool tradition. To support this contention, he cites an archaeological complex known as Battle Rock, located a few miles north of Cape Krusenstern in Kotzebue Sound, which contains elements common to both Choris-Norton-Ipiutak and early Northern Maritime phases and which may be intermediate in time between them and Denbigh. Battle Rock, thus, would be a transitional link between the earlier Arctic Small-Tool tradition and the Eskimo tradition, possessing, significantly, items of engraved Eskimo art in a sort of

430

proto-Okvik style. It would also represent that point in time when what were to be the Choris-Norton-Near Ipiutak and Northern Maritime branches of the Eskimo tradition were still undifferentiated.[53] Collins' hypothesis is reasonable, but nothing more. For one thing, the Battle Rock complex has not been satisfactorily dated and may be as late or later than Choris, the earliest member of the Choris-Norton-Near Ipiutak line.[54] Also, the picture of events in the interval between 2000 to 1000 B.C., or from about the end of the Denbigh phase until the beginning of Choris, is still very clouded.

This period from 2000 to 1000 B.C. was undoubtedly a crucial one in the development of Eskimo culture, with new elements being introduced from Asia and perhaps also from the boreal lands of interior Alaska and Canada. Except for Battle Rock, the interval appears largely unfilled, although Giddings has defined another complex at Krusenstern which he calls the Old Whaling culture and which is seriated between Denbigh and Choris and dates to 1800 B.C.[55] Old Whaling, however, in no way provides a transition from Denbigh to Choris-Norton. Old Whaling debris is characterized not by finely chipped microliths and caribou bones but by large flint bifaces that seem to be whaling harpoon blades, by whale bones, and by lanceolate side-notched points. It is, at least up to the present, the earliest Arctic complex which betrays signs of accomplished whale-hunting, although its odd mixture of whaling harpoon blades and large side-notched points, the latter suggesting not the Arctic nor northeastern Siberia but the Boreal Archaic of the North American Subarctic, is difficult to explain. From what we know now, it would not appear to have been involved directly in the evolution of either the Choris-Norton-Near Ipiutak or Northern Maritime subtraditions but suggests instead another line of development. Such a line may have been aborted or it may have been assimilated in some as yet untraced way to find a much later expression in the late prehistoric and historic whaling activities of the Eskimo. We allude to it here not because it elucidates the early history

of the Choris-Norton-Near Ipiutak continuum, which it does not, but because it points up the historical complexity of events in the western Arctic during the second millennium B.C.

Both the Choris and Norton phases are related to the Arctic Small-Tool tradition, which suggests that they are descendants in this ancestral line. These ancestral connections are glimpsed in flint-chipping techniques.[56] Norton, which dates to about 500 B.C., has yielded a few microblade elements, including small side-blades, but has otherwise ceased to follow in the old patterns of stone-flaking. The earlier Choris phase, estimated to about 1000 B.C., lacked the microblade, burin, side-blade assemblage, although it retained the trait of fine diagonal flaking on some larger blades. From this evidence there can be little doubt but that there was a break in the Denbigh-to-Choris continuity and that Denbigh culture ceased to exist some time prior to 1000 B.C. Perhaps it was broken or disrupted by the Old Whaling culture to which we have just referred, or perhaps its demise was earlier, around 2500 B.C., as Giddings suggests.[57] Most likely, the elements shared by Denbigh and Choris and Norton resulted from contacts with other groups not too distant from the Norton Sound and Kotzebue regions who persisted in the old Arctic Small-Tool modes of flint-working. We have in this connection already seen how the Arctic Small-Tool tradition was retained as a more or less integrated pattern into the second millennium B.C. in eastern sections of the Arctic.

The Norton culture has been examined in detail in the component of that phase excavated at Iyatayet by Giddings.[58] It was at this site that Giddings found it overlying the earlier Denbigh remains, the two being separated by a sterile soil zone. This was a coastal site of substantial winter houses. One such house plan was rectangular, measuring a little over 5 by 5 meters, and with a long entrance passage. The wall structure was of vertical driftwood poles, and there were signs of a fireplace on the floor. Apparently such dwellings were heated both by open fires as well as by oil lamps. Seal, beluga, and walrus bones were liber-

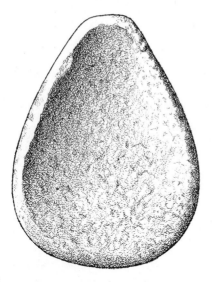

Figure 7-16. Lamp made of igneous rock, Norton phase. Long diameter, 26 cm. (Redrawn from Giddings, 1964.)

ally scattered throughout the village refuse. No direct archaeological remains prove that the kayak was used to hunt such animals. Due to broken ice conditions now present near the site, Giddings feels that the breathing-hole technique of seal-hunting would have been impractical for the Iyatayet inhabitants then as now, and that the kayak was probably an important item in the arsenal of the Norton hunters. Numerous notched stone sinkers attest to the importance of fishing. Although caribou bones were rather scarce at Iyatayet, many small points, side-blades (arrows), and large (lance) points found at the site indicate that this game, and other land animals, probably were hunted seasonally, perhaps at some distance from the winter seaside camp. Heavy adze blades for woodworking were alien to the Norton culture, but small polished blades of silicified slate were apparently used for cutting antler and bone. Polished-stone labrets were also found, and lamps and dishes made of ground stone. Ulus and skinning knives were made of slate, but in general rubbed-slate tools were not carefully made, and this industry was poorly developed. Stone-chipped cherts and other flints were relatively rare, basalt being the material most commonly used for points, blades, and scrapers. Unlike the early cultures of the

Northern Maritime subtradition, toggle-harpoons were few and rather crude, and ivory engraving was negligible.

For the most part, the earlier Choris phase, as revealed at Kotzebue Sound, exhibits a less ample tool and artifact inventory than Norton, lacking polished adzes, net-weights, and side-blades. The Norton economy seems to have been more oriented toward the caribou than toward sea mammals.[59]

Before leaving Cape Denbigh, it should be noted that the Iyatayet site is also the location of deep and extensive refuse of the later Nukleet phase.[59a] The Nukleet phase is representative of proto-historic and historic Eskimo culture. The lines of its development would be continuities out of the earlier Choris-Norton-Near Ipiutak subtradition plus a strong infusion of traits from the expanding late prehistoric Northern Maritime subtradition. Harpoons, spears, bows-and-arrows, snow goggles, plate armor, and numerous other items of Nukleet gear are, in general, characteristic of late Eskimo material culture of northern Alaska and the northern Arctic (Figs. 7-17, 7-18, 7-19, 7-20, 7-21).

Figure 7-17. (*Bottom, left,* p. 433) Harpoon points of antler and ivory, Nukleet culture. Late Eskimo tradition, Cape Denbigh region, Iyatayet site. Length of *a,* 10.8 cm. (Courtesy Haffenreffer Museum and Brown University Press; see also Giddings, 1964.)

Figure 7-18. (*Top,* p. 433) Arrowheads and fish spears of the Nukleet culture from the Iyatayet site. Late Eskimo tradition, Cape Denbigh region. *a–e:* Antler arrowheads. Length of *a,* 22 cm. *f:* Fish arrow barb, antler. *g:* Fish spear center prong, ivory. *h:* Fish arrow shaft, wood. *i:* Fish spear center prong, antler. *j:* Leister prong, antler. Length of *f,* 9.5 cm. (Courtesy Haffenreffer Museum and Brown University Press; see also Giddings, 1964.)

Figure 7-19. (*Bottom, right,* p. 433) Wooden bow fragments, Nukleet culture. Late Eskimo tradition, Cape Denbigh region, Iyatayet site. *a–c:* Fragments of regular bows. *d,e:* Fragments of drills or toys. Length of *a,* 19.5 cm. (Courtesy Haffenreffer Museum and Brown University Press; see also Giddings, 1964.)

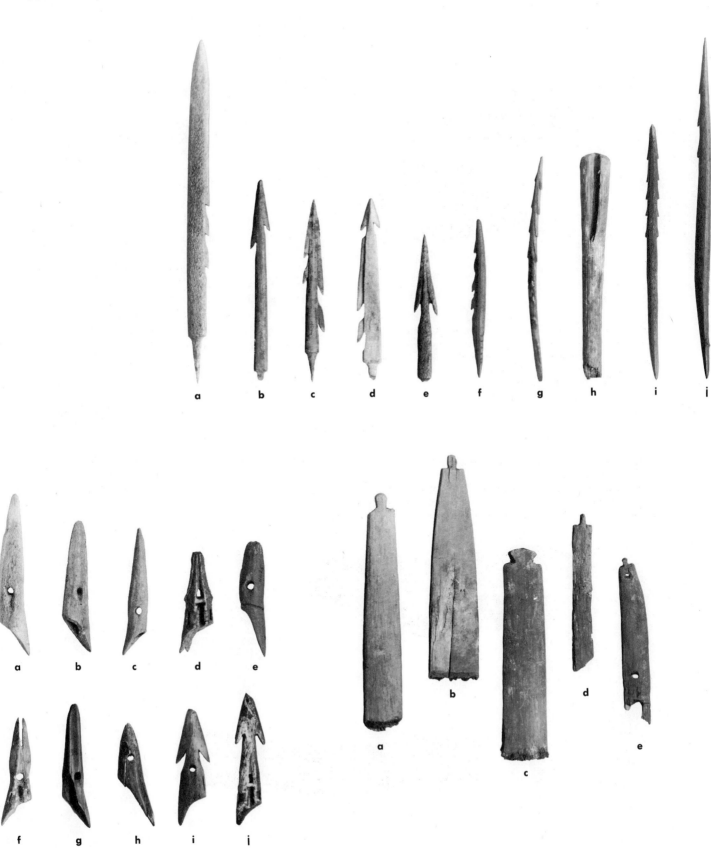

a   b   c   d   e   f   g   h   i   j

a   b   c   d   e

a   b   c   d   e

f   g   h   i   j

Figure 7-20. Slate blades, Nukleet culture. Late Eskimo tradition, Cape Denbigh region, Iyatayet site. a: Single-edged blade. b: Double-edged blade. c,d: Stemmed ulu blades. Length of a, 8 cm. (Courtesy Haffenreffer Museum and Brown University Press; see also Giddings, 1964.)

Figure 7-21. Antler and wooden items, Nukleet culture. Late Eskimo tradition, Cape Denbigh region, Iyatayet site. a: Wooden snow goggles. b: Antler comb. c,d: Antler spoons. e: An antler armor plate. Length of a, 17 cm. (Courtesy Haffenreffer Museum and Brown University Press; see also Giddings, 1964.)

Pottery in the Arctic. One important trait that links both Choris and Norton is the presence of a pottery complex which appears to be the earliest in the Arctic. Known as the Norton Complex, or as Norton Ware, the pottery included three types: Norton Check Stamped (see Fig. 7-22*a–c*), Norton Linear Stamped (see Fig. 7-22*f*), and Norton Plain.[60] It was a relatively coarse, thick pottery, tempered with plant fibers or sand. The standard vessel shape was a deep, flat-bottomed pot. Exterior surfaces, in the checked and linear stamped types, were impressed with carved wooden paddles before firing. All three of the types have been identified from the Norton phase at Iyatayet, but only the Norton Linear Stamped was recovered from the earlier Choris phase component. Griffin and Wilmeth suggest a time span for the Norton Pottery Complex of from 500 to 100 B.C. or essentially the span of the Norton phase. This estimate would appear to be conservative, however, if the preceding Choris phase can be dated back as early as 1000 B.C. The general distribution of the Norton pottery types in the Arctic was from Kuskokwim Bay on the south then northward and eastward around the Alaskan Arctic coast to the Firth River region in the northern Yukon Terri-

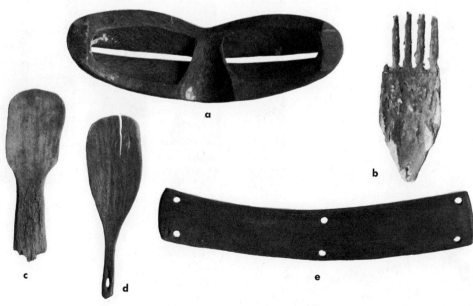

Figure 7-22. Pottery from Iyatayet, Alaska. *a–c*: Norton Check Stamped. *d,e*: Barrow Curvilinear Paddled or Stamped. *f*: Norton Linear Stamped. *g–h*: Yukon Line-Dot. Diameter of *a*, about 8 cm. (Courtesy J. B. Griffin; see also Griffin and Wilmeth, 1964.)

tory. Specimens also have been discovered at Eskimo sites in the Chukchi Peninsula of Siberia.

Griffin is inclined to derive this earliest Arctic pottery of the Norton Complex from the Lena Valley in Siberia where similar types were in use between 1500 and 1000 B.C. With Wilmeth, he states:

The logical area in Alaska for this complex to have been first established is the region immediately adjacent to Bering Strait, where a group of sites yielding Norton ware have been reported (Iyatayet, Choris, Near Ipiutak). The spread along the north coast of Alaska would be subsequent to its initial appearance, so that the Norton ware of the Firth River area must be later, rather than earlier, as would be indicated by MacNeish's estimates.[61]

MacNeish's reference is to the appearance of pottery in the Firth River, Buckland, Joe Creek, and Cliff phases of the Engigstciak site.[62] The first two of these phases MacNeish placed in the Arctic Small-Tool tradition, the latter two in his Inuk tradition (Northern Maritime subtradition).[63] In our story, we follow Griffin's interpretation that these four phases occupied a relatively brief span of time and came later than MacNeish's estimate of from 2000 to 500 B.C.[64] A post-1000 B.C. date for their inception seems preferable. Whether the arrival of Norton pottery at the Firth River delta could be said to mark the appearance in that region of a Choris-Norton-Near Ipiutak or Northern Maritime brand of Eskimo culture would depend on a much closer analysis of the data than

we are able to make here. Speaking generally, what was undoubtedly occurring in the Engigstciak sequence at this particular point was a switch from a culture which embodied a delayed version of the Arctic Small-Tool tradition to a culture of the Eskimo tradition.

In looking at this early pottery in the Arctic from a hemispheric perspective, we should mention that the Norton Complex does not answer the description of the kind of ceramic ware that we would anticipate as the forerunner of early Woodland pottery as found in the northeastern United States (Chap. 5). Typologically it cannot be compared with the cord-marked Vinette wares or other early Woodland types of the northern part of the Eastern Woodlands area. Although linear- and check-stamping were practiced in the eastern United States, these traits developed earlier in the Southeast than in the north and appear to have been independent and local developments. Norton pottery is also too recent to have served as the inspiration for the earliest of the Eastern Woodland area wares. It is of course possible, as Griffin has suggested, that there is an earlier, pre-Norton cord-marked pottery horizon in the Arctic which is responsible for similar early northeastern United States types like Vinette 1; but if so, it has not yet been disclosed.[65]

Later Eskimo pottery of the Arctic appears to have derived from the Norton complex. The later wares had thicker walls, their paste was coarser, and they were tempered with more and larger peb-

Figure 7-23. Potsherds from the Firth River region. a: Norton Check Stamped. b,c: Barrow Curvilinear Paddled. (Courtesy National Museum of Canada; see also MacNeish, 1959 a.)

a   b   c

Figure 7-24. Coarse Eskimo pottery. Thule Fiber-Tempered ware, Herschel Island phase, Firth River region, Canada. Height, about 40 cm. (Courtesy National Museum of Canada; see also MacNeish, 1959 a.)

bles and sand. Vessel rims and lip forms were more or less stable, and the principal changes that occurred chronologically involved shifts in surface treatment, from linear and check stamping to curvilinear stamped motifs, and then from the latter to incised and punctate decoration. The first of these shifts occurred during the latter half of the first millennium A.D., a shift clearly revealed in pottery associated with the Northern Maritime subtradition phases. For example, the Okvik and Old Bering Sea phases of St. Lawrence Island featured check-stamped and linear-stamped types, but later Birnirk was a curvilinear paddle-stamped pottery of the general category of Barrow ware. This Barrow ware has been found over about the same geographical range in Alaska as the preceding Norton ware, and its chronological range is estimated from about A.D. 800 to 1400. Barrow ware was in turn succeeded by Yukon ware. The most characteristic type Yukon ware bore incised and punctate decoration, and its geographical distribution was more limited than that of either Norton or Barrow ware. It is found on the Seward Peninsula, around Norton Sound, and from there south to Kuskokwim Bay; but it has not been found to the north and east of the Seward Peninsula. Yukon ware dates from after A.D. 1400 and continued much later into the historic period[66] (for Barrow ware, see Fig. 7-22d,e; for Yukon ware, Fig. 7-22g,h).

Our digression into Arctic pottery at this point in the narrative is occasioned by the fact that its earliest manifestations were found in the initial phases of the Choris-Norton-Near Ipiutak subtradition. As should be clear from what we have said, however, all this Arctic pottery may be regarded as a single ceramic tradition; and its principal wares and types were associated with both the Choris-Norton-Near Ipiutak and Northern Maritime Eskimo cultural subtraditions. Whether early Norton ware will be found in the hypothetical beginning stages of the Northern Maritime subtradition, as has been proposed by Collins, remains to be seen, when and if these stages are discovered and excavated. Of the other Eskimo subtraditions, we have mentioned that pottery appeared in the

Kachemak III phase of the Pacific-Aleut development. This pottery seems to have derived from Alaskan Eskimo sources and, considering its late date and general crudity, was probably most closely related to the later Barrow or Yukon wares rather than to the earlier Norton ware. The Dorset subtradition remained barren of ceramics.

The Ipiutak Site. Point Hope lies several hundred miles to the north of the Seward Peninsula and the Bering Strait, on the Chukchi Sea. In 1939 the remarkable Ipiutak site was discovered there.[67] In many ways Ipiutak stands apart from all other Eskimo sites. The Ipiutak phase, named for the site, reflects new infusions of Siberian traits, particularly in its exotic carved ivory. But it also shows connections with both the Northern Maritime and Choris-Norton-Near Ipiutak subtraditions. In fact it would appear to be something of a blend of the two plus the new elements of Scytho-Siberian art.

The peninsular tip of Point Hope is formed by two converging gravel bars which enclose a shallow inlet. Several old Eskimo occupations, including the Ipiutak site, are situated on these bars between the open sea and the inlet. Considering these several occupations in chronological order, the earliest is not the Ipiutak site proper but another location called Near Ipiutak. The name derives from its

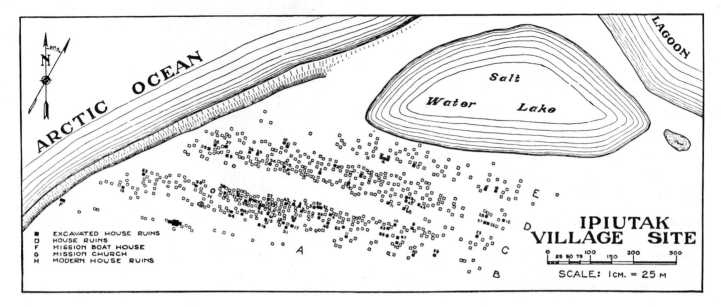

Figure 7-25. The Ipiutak site. (After Larsen and Rainey, 1948.)

proximity to the main Ipiutak site. Near Ipiutak is culturally affiliated with the Ipiutak phase proper, and also is related to the Choris and Norton phases of the Norton, Seward, and Kotzebue regions. In fact the relationships in this latter direction are so strong that Near Ipiutak is considered the terminal member of Collins' Choris-Norton-Near Ipiutak continuum, or Eskimo subtradition. The chronological ordering of Choris, Norton, and Near Ipiutak, in that sequence, is best substantiated by the seriation of old beach line villages at Cape Krusenstern. It is also in this same seriation that Ipiutak immediately follows Near Ipiutak.[68] Thus at Point Hope it would appear that following Near Ipiutak, the gravel bars next were occupied by the people who built the large Ipiutak village proper. Radiocarbon findings date the Ipiutak site probably to the first few centuries of the Christian era. This time span is contemporaneous with the Okvik-Old Bering Sea phases of St. Lawrence Island, and evidences of early Old Bering Sea art and other traits in Ipiutak strengthen this correlation. They also indicate a cultural fusion between Northern Maritime and Choris-Norton-Near Ipiutak subtraditions in the Ipiutak phase. After the abandonment

of the Ipiutak village, the next occupation of the Point Hope bars was by Northern Maritime peoples of the Birnirk phase, presumably during the latter half of the first millenium A.D. Subsequently this Birnirk culture evolved or was transformed into a variety of Thule culture, Western Thule. Western Thule in turn became the proto-historic local Tigara culture. Finally the Tigara culture evolved into the culture of the modern Eskimo village of New Tigara, which is also located on the Point Hope peninsular bars.[69] But here our main interest is the Ipiutak site and phase; let us look at them.

The Ipiutak site consists of an amazing concentration of buried house floors and foundations which extend for over a kilometer along a series of five low beach ridges. Helge Larsen and Froelich Rainey counted over 500 slight pit-like depressions, the surface indications of these houses, and excavated over 60 of them. They estimate that there must have been in the neighborhood of 600 to 700 of these dwellings. The thin layer of refuse on the floors and the relative homogeneity of house styles and artifacts found in them suggest a relatively brief period of occupation. The Ipiutak house was semi-subterranean, with the floor level about 50 centimeters below ground surface. The ground plan was square or squarish with rounded corners.

438

In diameter, the houses were between 3 and 6 meters. Fireplaces were built near the center of the houses. The floors were either of packed gravel or had been covered with logs or poles. Sleeping benches of gravel and earth had been built up along the north, east, and south walls. The walls probably were constructed of perpendicular logs or poles which were leaned against horizontal stringers that capped the four main upright corner posts of the superstructure. Smaller poles and sticks were then placed between the interstices of the larger timbers and the whole was covered with moss turf. The roofs, also of timbers, probably were more or less flat and had centrally located smoke-holes. The entrance to a house was from the side, probably the west side in most cases, and the floor of the entrance passage was higher rather than lower than the house floor. Presumably, such entrances also were covered.[70]

The cemetery was discovered to the southeast of the village site on a long strip of land along the inlet or lagoon side of the Point Hope spit. Graves were found for a distance of over 4 kilometers. These were all located by test digging, not by surface indications. One burial type was distinguished by a log coffin which had been constructed in a half-meter-deep pit. Some of the logs were placed on the pit floor and others were stacked horizontally to form the sides. These sides were held in position by stakes driven into the ground. More logs had then been laid over the rectangular box thus formed to serve as a lid. Individual coffins usually contained a single skeleton in an articulated, extended position. Some of the coffins contained grave goods, for the most part artifacts similar to those recovered in and around the houses, but never in great numbers. The other principal type of Ipiutak burial was found quite superficially, none being over a few centimeters below present ground level. The dead must have been placed on the surface and then probably were covered with some sort of wooden frames or with piles of logs. As viewed archaeologically, they were usually partially disarticulated skeletons mixed with wood debris, black midden soil, and numerous artifacts. The elaborate Ipiutak ivory carvings were invariably associated with burials of this kind, suggesting that the individuals involved were persons of special status in the society, perhaps shamans.[71]

The most flamboyant aspect of Ipiutak material culture were these ivory carvings found with the superficial burials, and it is in them that Larsen and Rainey saw Scytho-Siberian "animal style" influences. The most elaborate items were small sculptures of bears, walruses, and other natural and fantastic animals, curious delicate spiral or swivel-like objects, linked chains of ivory, and composite mask-like ornaments that were probably fastened to wooden grave coverings (see Figs. 7-26c; 7-27a, b,c,d). In addition to these carvings, Ipiutak art was applied by the sculptor and engraver to every-day utensils and weapons. Harpoon sockets were fashioned as animal heads, and similar decorations were placed on the ends of dagger and knife handles. Ivory harpoon heads were engraved, as in the Okvik or Old Bering Sea phases of the Northern Maritime subtradition. In general, although Ipiutak art was related to the carvings and engravings of these phases, it was much richer and more elaborate.[72]

Larsen and Rainey inferred complex burial customs and religious beliefs from the association of the remarkable non-utilitarian ivory objects with burials. In their reconstruction:

A ghost cult and shamanism were the two most conspicuous elements of the spiritual culture of the Ipiutak people. We have already suggested the possibility that the animal figures with the skeleton design represent spirits, possibly a shaman's guardian spirits. The adornment of the deceased with artificial eyes (of ivory), a mouth cover, and noseplugs is probably also evidence of the existence of a ghost cult. . . . Some of the animal carvings, a few carved human heads and skulls, and the fantastic openwork carvings have been interpreted as shamans' regalia. This interpretation is based on their resemblance to the carvings attached to the Tlingit (Northwest Coast) shaman's costume and to a comparison with the Siberian shaman's costume. An analysis of the design composition of the openwork carvings reveals

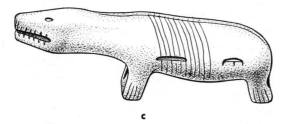

Figure 7-26. *Above:* Ipiutak ivory art. *a:* Snow-goggles; *b:* Ornamental band. *c:* Polar bear with skeleton design on body. *d:* Human skull. (After Larsen and Rainey, 1948.)

Figure 7-27. *Left:* Ipiutak ivory art. *a:* Animal or human figure. *b:* Curious pretzel-like ivory piece. *c:* Swivel. *d:* Chain links. Length of *b,* 10 cm.; length of *c,* 25 cm.; length of *d,* with extended links, about 15 cm. (After Larsen and Rainey, 1948.)

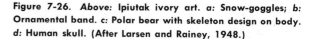

that the majority are composed of one or more of the following three elements: animal figure, chain, and swivel, all of which have been found in metal on Siberian shamans' costumes. They are considered as symbolic objects, but so far their meaning is obscure.[73]

The subsistence pattern of the Ipiutak people was similar to that of other prehistoric and historic Eskimo groups but closest to the Choris-Norton-Near Ipiutak subtradition. The Ipiutaks were both sea and land hunters and must have followed a seasonal round of coastal and interior living. To date, no interior sites of the culture have been located, but a number of features suggest this aspect of their lives. For example, the open fire-places in the houses and the absence of stone or pottery lamps indicate that wood was used as fuel. Judging from the number and variety of arrow-heads recovered, caribou hunting must have been of considerable importance. These heads were usu-ally made of antler and were set with end-blade points or small inset blades along the sides. The points and blades were finely chipped from flint, frequently were parallel-flaked, and in general hark back to the excellent flint-working technologies of Norton, Choris, and the earlier Arctic Small-Tool tradition. The use of birchbark vessels also implied

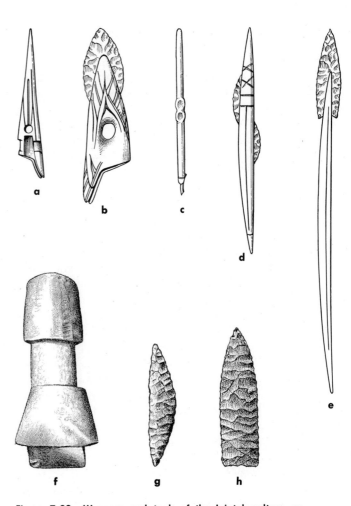

Figure 7-28. A set of Ipiutak ivory carvings which form a mask-like element. These must have adhered to a wooden backing. (After Larsen and Rainey, 1948.)

Figure 7-29. Weapons and tools of the Ipiutak culture. a: Ivory harpoon point. b: Ivory harpoon point armed with flint end-blade. c: Engraving tool with squirrel-tooth point. d: Antler or ivory arrowhead with flint side-blades. e: Antler or ivory arrowhead with flint end-blade. Length of a, 8 cm.; all of above to this scale. f: Antler adze head with ground-stone adze blade. Length, about 10–11 cm. g: Side-blade. Length 5 cm. h: End-blade. Length 5.8 cm. (After Larsen and Rainey, 1948.)

some knowledge of the interior. But of course at the coastal location on Point Hope there is plentiful evidence of seal- and walrus-hunting, of a full knowledge of the complex toggle harpoon gear, and of the walrus ivory-carving—all of which testify to an Eskimo type of maritime existence.[74]

The Ipiutak people were adept at making ground-stone items, as their adze blades and chisels of silicified slate, stone labrets, and jet ornaments and inlays on ivory indicate. They fashioned no pottery. Wood, bone, antler, and ivory were of course skillfully converted into various knife, adze, and other tool handles and into bows, shafts, dart pieces, shovels, wedges, needle cases, and many other items. Particularly interesting is one small ivory engraving tool equipped with a tiny iron point, probably the earliest instance of the use of iron in the native Arctic.[75]

In centering our attention on Ipiutak, we have ignored the related Near Ipiutak phase. The latter, as we mentioned, was earlier and would appear to provide a link between the more spectacular Ipiutak phase and its Choris-Norton antecedents. At Point Hope, the Near Ipiutak finds came from burials, a house foundation, and midden refuse, all situated within a few hundred meters of the big Ipiutak village and the Ipiutak cemetery zone. Arrowheads of the Near Ipiutak phase were similar to the Ipiutak variety, although Near Ipiutak harpoon heads were more primitive. Unlike the Ipiutaks, the Near Ipiutaks used stone lamps, a Norton-type pottery, and more slate.[76] As we stated at the outset, Near Ipiutak furnished one source of Ipiutak development, and the elements from this source, presumably coming to Point Hope from the south, appear to have converged with streams of influence from both the early aspects of the Northern Maritime subtradition and from Siberia to the west.

The Dorset Subtradition. The Dorset subtradition of the eastern Arctic is known from various locations in the eastern part of the Canadian Northwest Territories, including Southampton Island, the Melville Peninsula, Baffin Island, the eastern Hudson Bay region, Labrador, Newfoundland, and Greenland.[77] Its earliest appearances, from radiocarbon dating of materials from Southampton Island and the Melville Penin-

sula, are in the neighborhood of 800–600 B.C. Dorset persisted until it was replaced by the Northern Maritime Thule culture around A.D. 1000–1200.[78] As we already have mentioned, the spread of Thule culture probably was accompanied by a movement of the immediate ancestors of the modern eastern Eskimo across the Arctic from the west. According to Collins, small groups of the Dorset Eskimo continued to occupy pockets of their old territory for some centuries after the invading Thule Eskimo had taken possession of most of the area; however, they and their culture either died out or were absorbed by the Thule prior to the historic horizon.[79]

The Dorset subtradition, like the other Eskimo branches, had its origins in the cultures of the earlier Arctic Small-Tool tradition. As you will recall, this Small-Tool tradition was diffused or carried across the Arctic between 3000 and 1000 B.C., with a marked chronologic lag in this spread. Presumably the transition from Arctic Small-Tool cultures to Dorset was in part a story of local evolution. It was also in part a process of the acceptance and assimilation of what are considered to be more characteristically Eskimo traits. Whether the latter were carried by new peoples from the west who overran the earlier populations of the Arctic Small-Tool cultures in much the same manner as the Thule peoples superseded the Dorset is uncertain. It is possible that a gradual diffusion of ideas and elements would have been sufficient to have effected the changes that occurred between pre-Dorset and Dorset levels in the east. You will remember that the Eskimo tradition first appeared in the Aleutians and on Norton Sound around 1000 B.C., or perhaps a bit before. Here, especially in the Choris-Norton-Near Ipiutak subtradition, it transformed the resident Arctic Small-Tool tradition cultures, such as the Denbigh. Significantly, the earliest Dorset dates are only a few centuries later, and undoubtedly the changes from pre-Dorset to Dorset in the east were a part of the same wave of early "Eskimoization" that was going on in the Arctic at about the beginning of the first millennium B.C.

442

Just where the Dorset culture developed as a distinct entity is unknown. Jorgën Meldgaard leans toward the hypothesis that it first crystallized somewhere in the east, perhaps as far east and south as the region within the triangle of the Great Lakes, James Bay, and Newfoundland.[80] However, Meldgaard's clearest evidence for a pre-Dorset to Dorset transition, while eastern, is somewhat north, on Melville Peninsula. Elmer Harp, who is most familiar with Dorset in its Labrador and Newfoundland manifestations, is unconvinced of its eastern origins and speculates that it probably first developed somewhere in Alaska and was carried east along the northern fringes of the continent and then passed northward to Greenland and southward to Labrador-Newfoundland.[81] Both authorities, as well as Collins, agree, however, that wherever the point of origin, the matrix culture was some aspect of the Arctic Small-Tool tradition.

At Meldgaard's Igloolik sites on the Melville Peninsula a sequence of Sarqaq (pre-Dorset), Dorset, and Thule houses and debris has been revealed. The Sarqaq houses were round or oval with central fireplaces. The Dorset houses were rectangular, fairly large, semi-subterranean, and equipped with side-benches. The Arctic Small-Tool chipped assemblage of the Sarqaq phase included tiny burins of flint, small curved microblades, tanged or faintly side-notched points and blades of flint, flint arrowpoints of pointed oval form, bone lances, and open-socketed bone harpoon heads. A continuity with succeeding Dorset levels is evident in the general smallness of the flintwork and in the presence of numerous microblades in the later culture. These blades were, however, larger and straighter than the Sarqaq specimens. A burin-like implement continued into the Dorset, but by then usually was made of ground slate rather than flint. Slate also tended to replace flint in points and blades which became sharply side-notched, sometimes with paired notches. The pointed oval arrowpoint of Sarqaq disappeared, and the common chipped-stone Dorset form was the triangular harpoon end-blade which was fre-

quently fluted at the tip. The Dorset bone lance points differed only slightly from the Sarqaq types; the open-socket bone harpoon heads were converted to a closed-socket type. Stone lamps became much more common in Dorset and were square rather than round. Completely new Dorset innovations included multi-barbed bone fish spears, ulu-like knives of bone, snow knives, and bone sledge-shoes.[82] In brief, the change from Sarqaq to Dorset at Igloolik was an *in situ* evolution accompanied by some new traits.

What might be considered as a typical Dorset community dating from the later period of the culture (ca. A.D. 100–650) is the Port aux Choix-2 site in western Newfoundland.[83] The location is on Cape Riche, overlooking the Gulf of St. Lawrence near Belle Isle Strait. It was surveyed and excavated by Harp, who describes it as an area 3 acres in extent containing some 35 to 40 house pits along old strand lines. Several of these house depressions were excavated. Apparently the original dwellings were rectangular and had been constructed with floor levels dug down several centimeters below the surrounding ground level. Fire-pits and storage-pits had been lined with rocks, but apparently walls and roofs were relatively flimsy wood and pole, skin-covered structures. There were no definite signs of interior benches. An analysis of the ample bone remains around one house yielded a count and percentages showing overwhelming dependence on seal meat. Whales, fish, birds, caribou, and other land mammals made up the remainder of the debris. In Harp's opinion the Port aux Choix-2 location was a seasonal (spring-summer) camp where the Eskimo:

. . . erected their skin-covered semi-subterranean tents, and exploited the whelping St. Lawrence seal herd as it followed the retreating ice northward through the Strait of Belle Isle. As spring turned to summer this rich food resource was supplemented from bird rookeries on various offshore islands, from salmon runs in the nearby streams, and the trapping of minor game. . . . With the coming of the fall, the settlement probably dispersed into the interior Long Range barrens for a major caribou hunt, or possibly some family

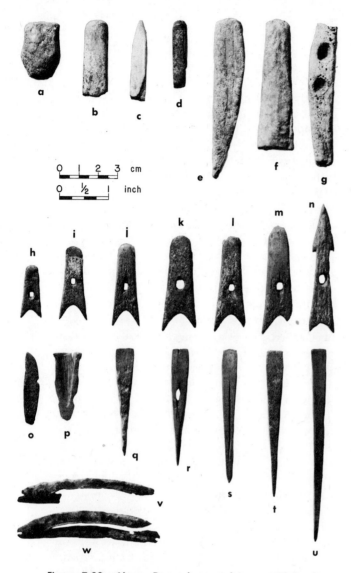

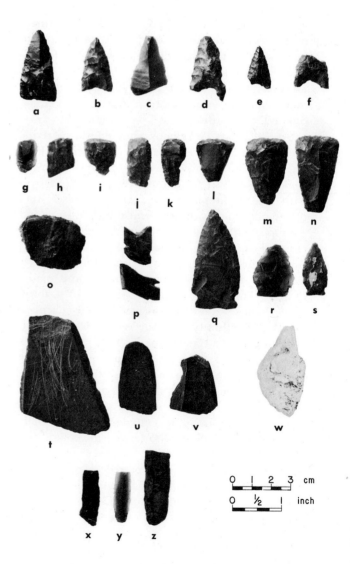

groups made their way back to Labrador for the same purpose. But this phase of their lives must remain indefinite until we know more about the inland archaeology of the region.[84]

The relatively late Dorset culture of Port aux Choix-2 still retained vestiges of the old Arctic Small-Tool heritage. Prismatic blades, including some microblades, were found in and around the house locations. The most common stone points

Figure 7-30. *Above:* Dorset bone and ivory artifacts, from a cave burial at Cape Riche, Newfoundland. *a–g:* Bone and ivory flaking hammers and flaker tips. *h–n:* Bone harpoon heads with rectangular shaft sockets, all slotted for end-blades except *n. o,p:* Two bone support pieces for knife blade hafting. *q–u:* Harpoon foreshafts with "screwdriver" end to fit rectangular sockets in heads above. *v,w:* Two unidentified slotted bone plates, probably garment decorations. (Courtesy Elmer Harp, Jr.)

Figure 7-31. *Right:* Dorset artifacts, same associations as Fig. 7-30. *a–f:* Harpoon points. *g–n:* End-scrapers. *o:* Side-scraper *p:* Two fragments of side-notched polished "groovers." *q–s:* Side-notched knives. *t–v:* Bevelled slate knives and scrapers. *w:* Quartz crystal micro-core. *x–z:* Unworked prismatic blades. (Courtesy Elmer Harp, Jr.)

were double side-notched forms, and these were probably hafted as harpoon head end-blades. However, Hårp believes that a number of quite small side-notched forms, of both chert and slate, were arrowheads. Snub-nosed end-scrapers, knives, and what may be large spear points also were part of the Port aux Choix-2 flint inventory. The knife handles and harpoon heads into which flint and slate blades or points were set were made of bone and antler and were frequently found in the midden. Bilaterally barbed fish spears, leisters (pronged spears), adze handles, and sledge runners were also made of these materials. Ivory was used for bag-handles and was carved into ornaments, small amulets, and little walrus effigies (despite the scarcity of this animal's remains). Adze blades were small and usually made of polished slate, and a few large, bevelled, slate points were found in addition to the slate end-blades we have already mentioned. One ancient trait—or modified ancient trait—were burin-like gravers made of slate rather than chipped stone. Lamps and cooking pots of steatite were a part of the village refuse.

Such, in selected sample, is the archaeological picture of the Dorset culture in a late and southerly manifestation. It is interesting that, in Newfoundland and in Labrador, Dorset sites are found in the same vicinity with those of the Boreal Archaic tradition, but there is little evidence of contact or inter-influencing. At least in its beginnings, and for much of its life span, the Archaic cultures of this northeasternmost periphery of the Eastern Woodlands environment were too early to have influenced Dorset Eskimo.[85] Later, after the arrival of the Dorset peoples, it seems quite likely that the two—Eskimo newcomers and earlier resident Indians—were in contact in these marginal regions of Labrador and Newfoundland which lie on the transitional zone between Arctic barrens

Figure 7-32. Dorset bone and ivory amulets (actual size), same associations as Fig. 7-30. *a,b*: Conventionalized seals (?). *c–f*: Conventionalized bears (?). (Courtesy Elmer Harp, Jr.)

and Subarctic coniferous forests. As yet, however, little archaeological evidence of this contact has been found.

Indian Cultures

The Denetasiro Tradition. In the western Subarctic are prehistoric remains which appear to be considerably later than those of the Northwest Microblade tradition but which probably are representative of a culture which developed from a Northwest Microblade base. MacNeish has grouped these findings under the general synthetic term of the Denetasiro tradition.[86] There is every reason to believe that this Denetasiro tradition was immediately ancestral to historic Athapascan Indian culture in this part of northwestern North America. In fact, historic Athapascan culture in some regions, such as the Southwest Yukon, is regarded as a late phase of the tradition.

According to MacNeish, the Denetasiro tradition existed in the Southwest Yukon and in the interior forested parts of the Canadian Northwest Territories.[87] Quite probably it also extended into interior Alaska, and may have spread eastward into northern Alberta, northern Saskatchewan, and northern Manitoba; its over-all distribution, however, is really unknown. Perhaps it may have corresponded more or less to the Athapascan linguistic distribution in western Canada as opposed to Algonquian-held land to the east and south, but this thesis remains to be demonstrated. The Denetasiro time span can be estimated only most approximately. In the Southwest Yukon its earliest manifestations date to after A.D. 300 and its latest to A.D. 1900. It is of course possible that in some places the tradition dates back earlier, perhaps to 1000 B.C., although it is unlikely that it can be pushed back much beyond this time.

MacNeish's definition of Denetasiro is based on the Southwest Yukon sequence. Here the terminal phase of the Northwest Microblade tradition is the Taye Lake in which microblades and burins were definitely on the wane and in which polished-

Figure 7-33. Views of Southwest Yukon country. *Left:* Wooded valley east of Kluane Lake. *Right:* Grasslands with sparse and stunted trees east of Kluane Lake. (Courtesy R. S. Peabody Foundation, Andover.)

Figure 7-34. Denetasiro tradition artifacts from various sites in the Mackenzie River drainage, Canada. *a:* Bone netting needle. *b:* Bone beamer. *c:* Bone fish spear. *d:* Bone bird-stunning point with pointed base. *e:* Same, with bifurcated base. *f:* Same, with hollow base. *g–i:* Bone pins. *j:* Ground deer or caribou phalanx for cup-and-pin game. *k:* Brass arrowhead with bone shaft. *l,m:* Multibarbed unilateral bone harpoon heads. Length of *a,* about 28 cm. (Courtesy National Museum of Canada; see also MacNeish, 1953.)

stone wood-cutting tools were first becoming important. Taye Lake was dated after 2000 B.C., and it or related phases may have lasted late enough to effect a gradual transition into the Aishihik phase of the Denetasiro tradition. Aishihik was subsequent to A.D. 300. In it the microblade tradition has completely disappeared; projectile points were corner- or side-notched forms; and some of these points were quite small and suitable for arrows. Polished-stone adzes were a common tool. Aishihik was immediately ancestral to the Bennett Lake phase. Bennett Lake sites were seasonal trapping, hunting, and fishing camps, and the artifacts in them were preponderantly bone and antler tools and weapons, as opposed to chipped stone. These items included antler arrow points, leisters and gorges for fishing, bone-fleshers, beamers, and awls. The chipped-stone points taken from these sites were almost all uniformly of the small triangular, notched or unnotched, variety. Copper was also used to make points as well as tinkler ornaments and pins, awls, and gorges. From the ethnographic horizon, the material culture of Bennett Lake can be filled out with wooden implements, such as bark containers and other household utensils. Bennett Lake appears to date to the late prehistoric and historic centuries leading up to A.D. 1900; and, as found in the Southwest Yukon, it is indeed the archaeological or material culture inventory of the northern Athapascans.[88]

To summarize, the Denetasiro tradition was the culture of the hunters, trappers, and fishermen of interior Alaska and northwestern Canada. The environment was one of lakes, ponds, creeks, marshes, wooded ridges, and flat areas. Forests were of spruce and dwarf birch. Available game included moose, caribou, and other mammals, fish, and birds. The local antecedents of the tradition can be discerned in the technology of the Northwest Microblade tradition, to which were added new culture traits brought into the area, perhaps by way of the early Eskimo cultures and the Eskimos or perhaps by Asiatic immigrants who became the northern Athapascan tribes. The Denetasiro pattern appears to have crystallized some time after 2000 B.C. Formed in and adapted to a Subarctic forest environment, it stands in marked contrast to the coastal and tundra cultures of the Eskimo tradition. Although not yet adequately documented from an archaeological point of view, its details and nature are undoubtedly contained in the modern Athapascan ethnographic accounts of the area.[89]

The Archaic Tradition. A consideration of the Eastern Subarctic brings us back again to the Archaic tradition of the North American Eastern Woodlands. In Chapter 5 we related how a Boreal branch or subtradition of the Archaic was the dominant and long-persistent pattern in northern New England, northern New York, and the Canadian Maritime Provinces. Archaeological sites are also found still farther to the north in Ontario, Quebec, Labrador, and Newfoundland. Characteristic Boreal Archaic artifacts found by Harp in his surveys in southern Labrador and Newfoundland, along the Belle Isle Strait, included large stemmed, side-notched, and corner-notched projectile points of chipped stone, chipped adzes, stemmed ground-slate points, and ground- and polished-stone adzes and gouges.[90] Related implement types have been discovered by Strong and Bird as far north as northeastern Labrador in the Nain-Hopedale region[91] and to the west in Quebec, near Tadoussac, and in eastern Ontario.[92] Going still farther west and northwest into Canada, it would appear that the Archaic tradition left its traces in early hunting cultures such as those found in the Thelon River region of the District of Keewatin, Northwest Territories.[93] Here, however, these probable influences manifest themselves as stemmed and side-notched points; the more complete complex of both chipped- and ground-stone points and woodworking tools is missing. Even more distantly, there were, of course, the Archaic-like side-notched points that appeared in the Northwest Microblade tradition contexts of the southwest Yukon (Taye Lake phase) and in Alaska (Tuktu phase or complex); but whether these were really the results of Archaic diffusion from the south is less certain.

The dating of the Boreal Archaic in the Subarctic has not definitely been established. As Harp and others have pointed out, the tool types from Newfoundland and Labrador are strikingly similar to those from New England, and Byers' radiocarbon date of 2000 B.C. for Boreal Archaic levels at Ellsworth Falls, Maine, in the Northeastern subarea of the Eastern Woodlands, would seem to be applicable to at least some of the Subarctic materials.[94] Most authorities now agree that the Boreal Archaic pattern was fully formed long before similar ground-slate artifacts appeared in the eastern Eskimo Dorset culture.[95] Both Archaic and Dorset must have received the polished-slate technical tradition from a source as yet unidentified.[96] Certainly, the heavy stone woodworking tools—adzes, gouges, and chisels—are not Eskimo. Nor are they at home in the Arctic or Subarctic, except in those two places where their origins can be attributed to contacts with the south. One of these places was the eastern Subarctic instance we are now discussing. There such implements may have derived from the Woodlands of the northeastern United States, where they had a long history. The other place was the North Pacific Coast. Here Eskimo cultures bordered those of the Northwest Coast and Plateau traditions, where heavy polished-stone tools had appeared early. Whether or not a link exists between Boreal Archaic and these polished-stone implements of the west is unknown.[97]

In the eastern Subarctic, the Boreal Archaic subtradition persisted to historic times. It is quite likely that the vanished Beothuk of Newfoundland represented one of the last phases of this line of development. Most likely the Beothuk were Algonquian-speaking Indians, maintaining to the last their distinctive culture which was probably the first to gain a foothold in the region, which withstood the Eskimo incursions of Dorset times, and which remained little changed by its Eskimo contacts.[98]

Summary

During historic times the Arctic barrens and tundras of the far north were occupied by the Eskimo, a people who were physically and linguistically distinct from the American Indian. The Eskimo also had a distinctive culture, one well adapted to a hunting life amid conditions of severe cold, ice, and snow. The Subarctic was occupied by Indian groups. Tribes in the west spoke Athapascan languages; in the east, Algonquian. The culture of the Indian tribes differed significantly from that of the Eskimo, although some traits were shared. These Subarctic peoples also were hunters, but their technologies and skills were adapted to the interior forests rather than to the coastal tundras.

Eskimo origins—racially, linguistically, and culturally—are Asiatic and probably derived out of the northeast Siberian-Kamchatka regions at a relatively late period. By relatively late, we mean the Siberian Mesolithic and early Neolithic periods. It is likely that contacts across the Bering Strait, as well as along the chain of the Aleutian Islands, were maintained between Asia and America, more or less steadily, from the Mesolithic until the historic period. These contacts continued to modify and add to Eskimo culture until only a few centuries ago; however, an Eskimo cultural tradition, associated with peoples of a recognizable Eskimo physical type, had come into being in the Aleutians and along the shores of the Bering and Chukchi Seas by at least the onset of the first millennium B.C. Shortly afterward Eskimo culture spread eastward across the Arctic, reaching as far as Greenland. The general early picture is one of greater cultural elaboration in the west, (in Alaska) with a somewhat simpler version of Eskimo culture in the east. In later prehistoric times, however, an important secondary center of Eskimo culture arose in the northern and central Arctic and spread back toward the west. This movement is believed to account for a great deal of the uniformity that has marked Eskimo culture from about A.D. 1000 until the historic and modern horizons.

Whether the earlier archaeological horizons of the Arctic—those antedating 1000 B.C.—are to be identified as Eskimo is debatable. The cultural remains show some affinities and proto-typical relationships to the later Eskimo levels, but they are, nevertheless, quite different. Unfortunately, no human skeletal material has been recovered from these earlier cultures, so that from a racial or subracial point of view we cannot say if the peoples associated with them were Eskimo or not. Speaking only of the archaeological evidences, the earlier culture history of the Arctic, and Subarctic, may be recapitulated as follows.

What may be the earliest Arctic archaeological complex is called British Mountain. It is represented by collections of rather crudely chipped choppers, scrapers, and unifacial points discovered in northwestern Alaska and on the Arctic coast of the Yukon Territory. The complex has not been firmly dated although it may be very old. A few fluted points have also been found in the Arctic along with many Cordilleran leaf-shaped points. These points possibly antedate similar forms found much farther south on the North American High Plains and in the Pacific mountain regions. If so, they could well mark the southward migrations of some of the first hunters to enter the New World by way of a Bering Strait land bridge in Pleistocene times and, as such, could be the first technical traces of the North American Big-Game Hunting and Old Cordilleran traditions. On the other hand, these fluted and leaf-shaped points of the Arctic and Subarctic may represent only a backwash of influence from the centers of these traditions as they developed much farther south.

Perhaps the earliest technological horizon of the Arctic and Subarctic which can be defined with any typological clarity and with reasonable chronological certainty is that of the Plano projectile points. These points were lanceolate, frequently parallel-flaked, forms which derived from the areas of the northern United States Plains and the Great Lakes between about 8000 and 4000 B.C., apparently later than the British Mountain complex and the scattered fluted points and Cordilleran points. Authorities generally believe that their presence represents a northern movement of buffalo hunters in post-glacial times.

Subsequent to the Plano point horizon, and perhaps overlapping it chronologically, was a technological tradition known as the Northwest Microblade. Its distribution was western, and it seems to be best represented in Subarctic interior environments, although it also invaded some Arctic coastal localities. Its most characteristic features were microblades and certain burin forms, traits which almost certainly came from the Siberian Mesolithic. Possibly it was associated with migrations from Asia to northern North America, and it may be that the ancestors of the later Athapascan Indians of the western Subarctic entered the New World at this time. We should mention, however, that both Plano-like projectile points and large stemmed and notched points, similar to specimens of the eastern North American Archaic tradition, were associated in Northwest Microblade assemblages, so the tradition represented a mixture or fusion of both American and Asiatic elements. It probably began as early as 6000 B.C. By 4000–3000 B.C., the Northwest Microblade tradition had disappeared in some regions, although in others, especially the interior forested country of the western Subarctic, it persisted down to 2000–1000 B.C.

At some time between 4000 and 3000 B.C., a new technological tradition appeared in the western Arctic, the Arctic Small-Tool tradition. Along the Bering Sea it replaced the Northwest Microblade tradition and is best known from this region as the Denbigh culture. The Denbigh was a core and bladelet industry of fine craftsmanship, with definite antecedents in Siberia. The implements were smaller and finer than Northwest Microblade types. Tiny points and side-blades exhibited oblique parallel-flaking. Burins were retouched for hafting. The milieu of the Arctic Small-Tool tradition cultures, which developed in all parts of the Arctic and as far east as Greenland, was definitely the coastal tundras, and these people were both sea-mammal hunters as well as land hunters. Its geographical distribution, its apparent ecological adaptation, and its chipped-stone technology all suggest that the Arctic Small-Tool tradition was the American Arctic base culture for the subsequent development of the Eskimo cultural tradition. It may be that its bearers, who in many places were the first peoples ever to explore the far northern Canadian Arctic and Greenland, were of Eskimo physical type, although this thesis cannot yet be proved.

As we have observed, the Eskimo cultural tradition seems to have come into being around 1000

B.C. It may be that new immigrant waves from interior Asia were responsible, or perhaps the resident Arctic populations who participated in the Arctic Small-Tool tradition were its originators. I prefer the latter interpretation, one which sees the Arctic Small-Tool cultures as being associated with an Eskimo physical type and these societies and cultures responding to new cultural stimuli from northern Siberia and Kamchatka. Four subtraditional lines have been proposed for the Eskimo tradition: Pacific-Aleut; Northern Maritime; Choris-Norton-Near Ipiutak; and Dorset. Of these, the Northern Maritime subtradition, which appears to have originated on both the Asiatic and Alaskan sides of the Bering Strait and on St. Lawrence Island, was the most viable. After its Okvik and Old Bering Sea phases, it spread northward and eastward across the Arctic in its Birnirk-Thule development, and it is this particular branch of Eskimo culture that became the classic whale- and sea-mammal hunting culture of the Arctic from Alaska to Greenland in historic and modern times.

The Pacific-Aleut subtradition stands most apart from the others. It centered on the Aleutian Islands and in Pacific coastal Alaska, where the climate was milder, and its technological adaptations reflect this circumstance. Then, too, cultural factors may account for some of the Pacific-Aleut divergences from the main Eskimo pattern. The underlying culture of the Aleutians was probably not that of the Arctic Small-Tool tradition but of a related, yet different, complex known as the Aleutian Core and Blade Industry. This difference in earlier, proto-typical traditions was probably also further augmented by a somewhat different line of diffusion from Asia, from Kamchatka along the Aleutian chain of islands as opposed to a Bering Strait route.

The Choris-Norton-Near Ipiutak subtradition was both geographically and typologically intermediate between Northern Maritime and Pacific-Aleut Eskimo. It seems to have centered at Norton Sound and from there southward, although sites representing the subtradition are also known to the north of the sound. Its earlier phases or begin-

nings, dating to the first millennium B.C., quite clearly emerged from the Arctic Small-Tool tradition, and in general it seemed less well adapted to maritime hunting than the Northern Maritime subtradition. Some of its influences merged with the earlier phases of the Northern Maritime in northwestern Alaska, but the historic and modern Eskimo cultures that can be most directly traced back to the Choris-Norton-Near Ipiutak line are those found to the south between Norton Sound and Bristol Bay.

The Dorset subtradition was the eastern branch of Eskimo culture, best known from the north and east of Hudson Bay as well as from Greenland and Newfoundland. Dorset, too, resembled the underlying cultures of the Arctic Small-Tool tradition in many respects and represented a blend of this base tradition with Eskimo elements from the west. After A.D. 1000, it was superseded by the Thule cultures of the Northern Maritime subtradition.

In the Western Subarctic the Denetasiro tradition appears to have developed from the earlier Northwest Microblade tradition. It was a hunting culture of the forests, imperfectly known from archaeology but more fully perceived in Athapascan ethnography.

In the Eastern Subarctic the Boreal branch, or subtradition, of the Archaic cultural tradition of eastern North America persisted from several millennia before the Christian era down to the Algonquian Indian societies of historic times. Camp sites were found in the Canadian Maritime Provinces, Newfoundland, Labrador, Quebec, and Ontario. Insofar as can be told, the Boreal existed in these regions prior to the arrival of either the Arctic Small-Tool or the later Dorset cultures. While there seems to have been some interchange between Archaic and Arctic Small-Tool and Northwest Microblade traditions, as witnessed, for instance, by the presence of large stemmed and side-notched points of Archaic character well north and west in the Subarctic, there is little evidence for significant borrowing or contact between Boreal Archaic and Dorset Eskimo cultures. The former's hearth was well to the south in the northeastern

United States and Ohio Valley subareas of the Eastern Woodlands, with traces of distinctive patterns beginning as early as 5000 B.C. The latter came from the Arctic, and ultimately from the western Arctic, and developed its distinctive origins no earlier than 1000 B.C. Their common traits, such as ground-slate work, seem more likely to have descended from an ancient mutual heritage, the lines of which remain untraced, or which developed separately and independently.

Footnotes

[1] These area definitions are essentially the same as Driver's (1961).

[2] Laughlin (1962 a, b).

[3] Laughlin (1962 a).

[4] MacNeish (1964 a); Irving (1962).

[5] MacNeish (1964 a).

[6] Irving (1962); MacNeish (1964 a).

[7] MacNeish (1964 a).

[8] For a detailed consideration of natural environmental history of the region, see Johnson and Raup (1964).

[9] Griffin (1962).

[10] MacNeish (1964 a); Giddings (1964, pp. 252–253); Campbell (1962), however, would date the Tuktu complex at about 2000 B.C.

[11] Irving (1957, 1962).

[12] Giddings (1951, 1961, 1964).

[13] Giddings (1964).

[14] Giddings (1961).

[15] Campbell (1962).

[16] MacNeish (1964 a). In this work MacNeish also includes the subsequent, pottery-bearing Firth River and Buckland phases in the Arctic Small-Tool tradition. This interpretation would place the Engigstciak pottery of these phases as the earliest yet discovered in the Arctic. This interpretation is open to serious question (see Griffin, 1962), as is the inclusion of these phases in the Arctic Small-Tool tradition.

[17] Harp (1962).

[18] Meldgaard (1960).

[19] Giddings (1961).

[20] Meldgaard (1952); Mathiassen (1958); Tauber (1960).

[21] Irving (1962).

[22] Giddings (1964).

[23] Griffin (1962).

[24] Irving (1962); Black and Laughlin (1964).

[25] Collins (1964).

[26] Laughlin and Marsh (1954, 1956).

[27] MacNeish (1964 a).

[28] Collins (1964).

[29] For example, see the summary of Martin, Quimby, and Collier (1947, pp. 490–502, the "Southwestern Eskimo area").

[30] An argument against such late movements from west to east, along the Aleutian chain is offered by Spaulding's (1962) findings on Agattu, one of the westernmost islands. Here, a culture (Krugloi Point) comparable to that dated at 1000 B.C. at the Chaluka midden yields a radiocarbon reading of 615 B.C., implying an east-to-west drift of Eskimo culture in the islands. This does not, however, negate the idea of earlier, pre-Eskimo movements along the Aleutians from Asia to America.

[31] The lower levels at Krugloi Point on Agattu Island in the western Aleutians have yielded radiocarbon dates as early as 615 B.C.

[32] De Laguna (1934); Collins, 1964.

[33] De Laguna (1934); see also Martin, Quimby, and Collier (1947, pp. 490–502) for summarization.

[34] Collins (1964).

[35] See Martin, Quimby, and Collier (1947, pp. 508–509) for a summary of the Inugsuk culture.

[36] Collins (1964).

[37] Ackerman (1962).

[38] Compare Giddings (1964, pp. 252–253) and Collins (1964).

[39] Collins (1964).

[40] Collins (1937); Giddings (1960).

[41] Collins (1937, p. 70).

[42] Collins (1937, p. 97).

[43] Collins (1937, p. 98).

[44] Collins (1964).

[45] Collins (1937, pp. 215–217).

[46] Collins (1964); see also Collins (1937).

[47] Collins (1937, pp. 76–97).

[48] Collins (1937, pp. 251–256).

[49] Ford (1959).

[50] Collins (1964). For data on interrelationships of Birnirk and Punuk see Ackerman (1962).

[51] Mathiassen (1927); Collins (1940). For an ethnographic summary of Eskimo life at Thule (northwestern Greenland) see Murdock (1938, pp. 192–220).

[52] Collins (1964).

[53] Collins (1964).

[54] Compare Giddings (1961) and Collins (1964).

[55] Giddings (1961, 1962, 1964).

[56] Giddings (1960).

[57] Giddings (1964, p. 270).

[58] Giddings (1960, 1961, 1964, pp. 119–190).

[59] Giddings (1960).

[59a] Giddings (1964).

[60] Griffin and Wilmeth (1964).

[61] Griffin and Wilmeth (1964, p. 283).

[62] MacNeish (1962).

[63] MacNeish (1964 a).

[64] Griffin (1962).

[65] Griffin (1962).

[66] Griffin and Wilmeth (1964).

[67]The monographic reference on Ipiutak and Near Ipiutak is Larsen and Rainey (1948).

[68]Giddings (1960, 1961).

[69]Larsen and Rainey (1948).

[70]Larsen and Rainey (1948, pp. 40–57).

[71]Larsen and Rainey (1948).

[72]Larsen and Rainey (1948).

[73]Larsen and Rainey (1948, p. 149).

[74]Larsen and Rainey (1948).

[75]Larsen and Rainey (1948).

[76]Larsen and Rainey (1948, pp. 162–168); see also Collins (1964).

[77]In addition to specific citations here, some general references on Dorset include Mathiassen (1927); Rowley (1940); Leechman (1943); Meldgaard (1960).

[78]Meldgaard (1962); Collins (1964).

[79]Collins (1964).

[80]Meldgaard (1962).

[81]Harp (1964, ms. 1964). W. E. Taylor, Jr. (1964) has recently reported Dorset sites from Bernard Harbor, more than 400 miles west of their previously known western limit of distribution.

[82]Meldgaard (1962).

[83]Harp (1964, ms. 1964).

[84]Harp (ms. 1964).

[85]Ritchie (1951, 1962 a); Byers (1962); Harp (1963).

[86]MacNeish (1964 a).

[87]MacNeish (1964 a).

[88]MacNeish (1962 b, 1964 a).

[89]See, for example, Osgood (1937 or 1940).

[90]Harp (1963).

[91]Strong (1930); Bird (1945).

[92]Harp (1963 and various references cited therein).

[93]Harp (1961).

[94]Harp (1963); Byers (1959).

[95]Ritchie (1962 a); Byers (1962); Harp (1964).

[96]Byers (1962).

[97]Collins (1962); Griffin (1962).

[98]Harp (1963, 1964).

Cultural Traditions: The Lines of History

Throughout this book we have been following the growth, development, modification, or dissolution of the major cultural traditions of pre-Columbian North and Middle America. These traditions, as they can be traced in the archaeological record through space and time, are, indeed, the main lines of history of the native New World. By way of summary, let us review their salient configurations, their principal events, and their probable relationships.

Early Man in America: Problems and Considerations. Before reviewing the earliest of the New World cultural traditions, certain preliminary observations seem necessary. To begin with, we do not know just when man first entered America from northeastern Asia. He may have crossed in the Bering Strait region, by land-bridge connection, as far back as the middle or the early Wisconsin ice age, or the Sangamon interglacial, 20,000 to 40,000 or more years ago. At the upper chronological limit, his entrance to the New World may have been as recent as the Two Creeks interstadial, separating the Mankato and Valders ice advances, no longer ago than about 10,000 B.C.

If the first immigrants from Asia came over during the early or middle Wisconsin stage, it is likely

Summary and Perspective

that their technological equipment and skills were modest and primitive. Most probably, they would have been derived from such flint-chipping industries as the Asiatic or Southeast Asiatic Chopper-Chopping Tool complex. Although no New World artifact assemblage found under conditions of antiquity, or presumed antiquity, closely matches such Asiatic industries, there are a number of discoveries and artifact assemblages which are so unspecialized that it is entirely possible that they could have been derived from distant Asiatic Lower or Middle Paleolithic traditions. These American artifacts in question usually consist of rather amorphous, thick flint scrapers, chopper-like implements, and worked flakes. Characteristically, like their presumed Asiatic forerunners, they lack well-formed, bifacially flaked blades, and projectile points. Unfortunately, as we have seen in our survey of the problem, none of these artifacts have as yet been found under conditions that indicate undisputed extreme age. Most of them are, in fact, surface discoveries which have been assigned to a "pre-projectile point horizon" (Fig. 8-1) because of their typology and their isolation from other, and presumably later, complexes of artifacts. Thus, the case for man in America in early or middle Wisconsin times, while a possibility and a definite problem in archaeological research, remains unproven.

The earliest secure evidences of man in the New World date from the millennium between about 10,000 and 9000 B.C. This was apparently the time of the Two Creeks interstadial just prior to the last major Wisconsin glacial advance known as the Valders. These evidences are included in this book under the rubric and concept of the Big-Game Hunting tradition. More specifically, they refer to the earliest known manifestations of that tradition, the Llano complex and its marker-type artifact, the Clovis fluted projectile point. Although it is true that the earliest and most firmly associated radiocarbon dates place the Big-Game Hunting tradition as no earlier than the tenth millennium B.C., it is probable that the tradition is older than this and that man was established in the Americas before this time. In fact, various inferences and extrapolations from North American discoveries and excavations suggest otherwise, as well as do finds in far southern South America, which are almost as old as the earliest well-dated artifacts from North America. Just how early is a matter of speculation which is guided largely by distant and somewhat tenuous comparisons with the Old World.

These comparisons with the Old World, particularly with Siberia, concern the origins of the Big-Game Hunting and the other early American tradition, the Old Cordilleran. The comparisons involve bifacially flaked lanceolate or leaf-shaped projectile points or blades which were found in western Siberia in Mousterian-like Paleolithic contexts dated to about 20,000 B.C. Such would seem to be the earliest possible Asiatic sources for the early American projectile point traditions. Admittedly, the link is tenuous. The distributional data are few, the distances involved enormous, and the level of typological comparison quite general. Still, it is a suggestive lead which permits the hypothesis that man, carrying the kinds of skills and adaptations which characterized the American Big-Game Hunting tradition, could have arrived in the New World at any time after 20,000 B.C. (Fig. 8-1).

An alternative view of the origins of the Big-Game Hunting and Old Cordilleran technologies

Figure 8-1. Schematic diagram of the major cultural traditions of North and Middle America viewed diachronically. Compare with Fig. 2-31, Chap. 2.

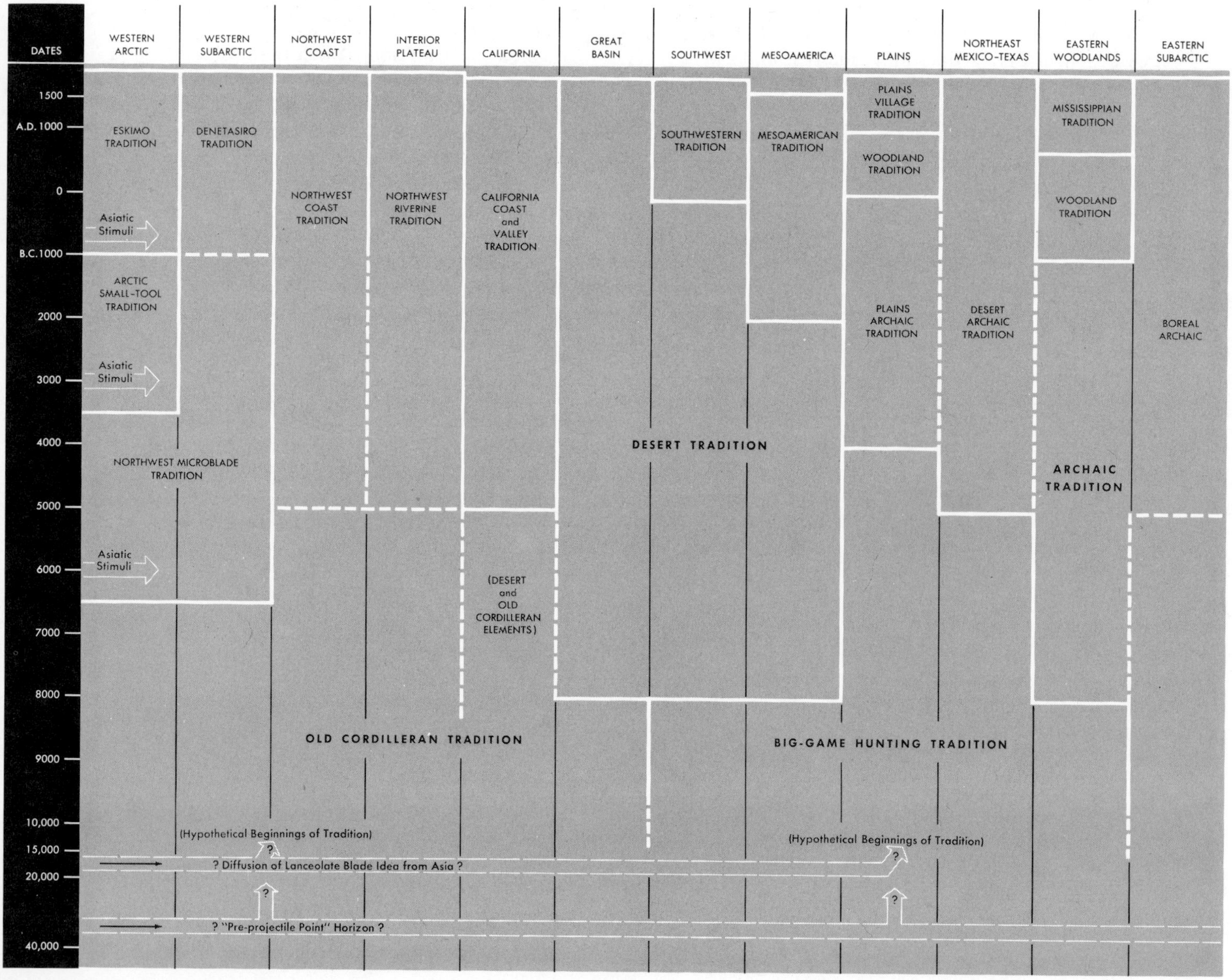

| DATES | WESTERN ARCTIC | WESTERN SUBARCTIC | NORTHWEST COAST | INTERIOR PLATEAU | CALIFORNIA | GREAT BASIN | SOUTHWEST | MESOAMERICA | PLAINS | NORTHEAST MEXICO-TEXAS | EASTERN WOODLANDS | EASTERN SUBARCTIC |

(Diagram labels, from the chart:)

1500 / A.D.1000 — ESKIMO TRADITION, DENETASIRO TRADITION, SOUTHWESTERN TRADITION, MESOAMERICAN TRADITION, PLAINS VILLAGE TRADITION, MISSISSIPPIAN TRADITION, WOODLAND TRADITION

0 / B.C.1000 — Asiatic Stimuli, NORTHWEST COAST TRADITION, NORTHWEST RIVERINE TRADITION, CALIFORNIA COAST and VALLEY TRADITION, WOODLAND TRADITION

2000 — ARCTIC SMALL-TOOL TRADITION, Asiatic Stimuli, PLAINS ARCHAIC TRADITION, DESERT ARCHAIC TRADITION, BOREAL ARCHAIC

3000 — Asiatic Stimuli

4000 — NORTHWEST MICROBLADE TRADITION, DESERT TRADITION, ARCHAIC TRADITION

5000 —

6000 — Asiatic Stimuli, (DESERT and OLD CORDILLERAN ELEMENTS)

7000 —

8000 —

9000 — OLD CORDILLERAN TRADITION, BIG-GAME HUNTING TRADITION

10,000 / 15,000 — (Hypothetical Beginnings of Tradition), ? , ? Diffusion of Lanceolate Blade Idea from Asia ?, (Hypothetical Beginnings of Tradition), ?

20,000 — ? , ?

40,000 — ? "Pre-projectile Point" Horizon ?

would hold that they developed independently in the New World out of the ancient pre-projectile point horizon technology and that their only relationships with Asia lie on this ancient level of connection.

The Big-Game Hunting Tradition. This term has been used to describe a pattern of life that was organized around the hunting of herd animals on the North American Plains (see Fig. 8-1). The camp and "kill" sites were distinguished by bifacially flaked, lanceolate projectile points and by other artifacts of chipped stone that are related to the tool kit of the hunter and skin-dresser. The most notable of the projectile points are the Clovis, Sandia, Folsom, and the various Plano types. Sites of the Big-Game Hunting tradition have been found throughout the North American Plains, in parts of the Southwest, and in eastern North America. Occasional discoveries of the diagnostic projectile point types of the tradition also have been reported from far western North America and the Arctic. In Middle America there are some "kill" sites and some scattered finds which appear to pertain to the tradition. In South America projectile points which are related in form also have been discovered under conditions implying substantial age.

As we have seen, the time of origin of the Big-Game Hunting tradition is unknown. It could date anywhere from 20,000 to 10,000 B.C., but an estimate of 14,000 or 13,000 B.C. seems reasonable. The best documented sites and finds of the tradition fall, however, between 10,000 and 8000 B.C. After 8000 B.C., with the gradual disappearance of Pleistocene environments, the tradition began to wane or to undergo marked modifications. In the eastern United States it was replaced by the Archaic tradition. On the Plains the Big-Game Hunting complexes which date after 8000 B.C. frequently have yielded new artifact types such as seed-grinding stones, although old projectile point types and the emphasis on the hunting of herd animals continued. This was the time of the Plano points.

The geographical locus of the origin of the Big-Game Hunting tradition was probably the North American High Plains where the Clovis Fluted point could have been developed from the technological seed idea of the bifacially flaked lanceolate point that had been brought to the New World by migrant hunters from Asia. From here the pattern spread rapidly to eastern North America and, as seen, certain elements of it diffused even more widely. Alternative views hold, however, that the tradition may have developed originally in eastern North America or in the Arctic.

The Big-Game Hunting tradition was apparently contemporaneous with the Old Cordilleran tradition. There are interrelationships between the two, and the two traditions probably also had a common Asiatic technological ancestry. In both the eastern United States and in the Plains, the Big-Game Hunting tradition was ancestral to the Archaic tradition. In the west—in the Great Basin, California, and the Pacific Northwest—the Old Cordilleran tradition seems to have been the matrix culture for the Desert tradition and for other later traditions.

The Old Cordilleran Tradition. This tradition relates to a series of early culture complexes in the Pacific Northwest (Fig. 8-1). The pattern of life, insofar as it can be inferred from the archaeological evidence, was one of rather unspecialized and diversified hunting, including some marine hunting. Fishing was also important, as was plant-collecting. The most characteristic artifact type was a willow-leaf or bipointed projectile of chipped stone. These points were associated with oval knives of flint and with edge-ground cobble pounders. The pattern is best seen in early sites along the Pacific edge of the Interior Plateau, but other sites have been uncovered through much of Washington and Oregon. Elements of the pattern, particularly the leaf-shaped bipoint, also appeared early in California and the Great Basin and, farther afield, in the Arctic and in Middle and South America.

The Old Cordilleran tradition appears to have extended back as far as 10,000 to 9000 B.C. in the Pacific Northwest, and may well be earlier. In the Interior Plateau and in the Northwest Coast areas, which appear to have been its homeland, the Old Cordilleran tradition persisted until at least 5000 B.C. After this time the record is obscure; but at some time between this date and 1000 B.C. it appears to have evolved—with the help of diffused traits—into the later Northwest Riverine and Northwest Coast traditions. In the Great Basin, it was much shorter-lived, being replaced by the Desert tradition by 8000 B.C. In California, Old Cordilleran elements which are found in the cultures of that area were replaced by the California Coast and Valley tradition. In both Middle and South America the Old Cordilleran willow-leaf projectile points have long histories, are very widespread, and may be the earliest point types in these areas. These findings are not sufficient, however, to define an Old Cordilleran cultural tradition for Middle America or for the southern continent.

The Desert Tradition. This tradition was an adaptation to life in arid western North America. It was based on a subsistence pattern of wild seed and plant foods supplemented by hunting. In some local situations around inland lakes, fish and waterfowl were also important factors in the diet. Characteristic artifacts included relatively crude milling stones and handstones, baskets, nets, sandals, a few simple bone tools and ornaments, and stemmed or notched chipped-stone projectile points. Social groups were small and seem to have followed a practice of cyclic wandering for wild foods. (See Fig. 8-1 for Desert tradition.)

Archaeological and ethnographic evidences of the tradition have come from the Great Basin (which includes eastern California, Nevada, western Utah, southeastern Oregon, and southern Idaho), the Southwest (Arizona and New Mexico), the western edges of the High Plains and the eastern Rockies, the Northeast Mexico-Texas area, the northern and central highlands of Mexico, and

Baja California. The Great Basin area, however, appears to have been the heartland of the tradition and probably its place of origin. The tradition seems to have first arisen between 8000 and 7000 B.C., to have derived out of the Old Cordilleran tradition, and to be, in fact, a specialization of that tradition in response to environmental pressures. Within the Great Basin, the Desert tradition has persisted from that early period until historic times.

Along the western edge of the High Plains and in the eastern Rockies, the Desert tradition also lasted up to the historic horizon, although here it was blended with and modified by the Archaic and later traditions of the Plains. In both the Northeast Mexico-Texas and the Baja California areas, the Desert tradition lasted to the historic period, although substantially modified. In the former area it blended with the Archaic tradition, especially in the east along the coast of the Gulf of Mexico. In the latter area, it was modified by its adaptation to the coastal living conditions of Baja California. In California proper, Desert tradition influences, merging with those of the Old Cordilleran tradition, provided the matrix culture for the California Coast and Valley tradition.

In upland Mesoamerica, the Desert tradition began to be modified by 5000 B.C., or earlier, by incipient plant cultivation practices. By 2000 B.C., it gave way to the newly crystallizing Mesoamerican tradition. A similar process also occurred in the Southwest, some time later, where the Desert tradition provided the base for the rise of the southwestern farming tradition.

The Archaic Tradition. The subsistence core of the Archaic tradition (Fig. 8-1) of the Eastern Woodlands was the adaptation of hunting, fishing, and collecting to a temperate forest and river environment. While the food quest here was similar to that of the contemporaneous Desert tradition of the arid west, the natural environment was quite different. It is likely that in the Archaic tradition the pursuit of game was more important than in the Desert tradition. There was considerable regional variation in food resources, with river and coastal shellfish, seeds and nuts, and animal game all being exploited. Archaic sites varied from small camp locations to fairly large, apparently semi-permanent or seasonal villages. Characteristic artifact types were large, proportionately broad, stemmed and notched chipped-stone dart points, polished-stone "bannerstones" and other throwing-stick weights, polished-stone axes and adzes for woodworking, stone vessels, and a large complement of bone artifacts and ornaments.

Archaic tradition cultures existed from the Gulf of Mexico well into southeastern Canada and from the Atlantic Coast westward into the Plains. Within the Eastern Woodlands of the United States the cultures date from as far back as 8000 B.C. and lasted until 1000 B.C. In the Plains, a Plains Archaic variant of the tradition arose somewhat later and lasted up until the beginning of the Christian era. In Subarctic eastern Canada, the Boreal Archaic tradition complex lasted until historic times, as did a blended Desert-Archaic tradition in the Northeast Mexico-Texas area.

The most likely origins for the Archaic tradition lie in the Big-Game Hunting tradition as it developed in the Eastern Woodlands area. An alternative proposal sees it originating in an unspecialized lithic industry and hunting-gathering pattern which derived from an ancient pre-projectile point horizon. Almost certainly the pattern was assembled and formed in the Eastern Woodlands, and its growth paralleled the development of the Desert tradition from Old Cordilleran prototypes in the west.

Old World boreal zone Mesolithic cultures possibly influenced the development of the Archaic. Certain polished-stone artifact forms such as adzes and axes have been cited in this connection; however, the forms in question appeared earlier in the middle and southern latitudes of the Eastern Woodland area than they did in northern regions closer to the presumed boreal sources.

The profile of development of the Archaic tradition in the East seems to include a less specialized period of from 8000 to 5000 B.C. during which the transition from the Big-Game Hunting pattern was occurring. After 5000 B.C., the polished-stone forms, so typical of the Archaic, appeared, and the tradition moved toward its climax. Beginning at about 2000 B.C., certain significant new features, such as fiber-tempered pottery, appeared in parts of the Eastern Woodlands. Finally, after 1000 B.C., Archaic cultures were transformed into those of the Woodland tradition.

We have indicated already relationships between the Big-Game Hunting and Archaic traditions, suggesting that the former was the forerunner of the latter. There were also other and later relationships between the two traditions along the western edge of the Woodland area and the eastern edge of the Plains. Close contacts also existed between the Desert and Archaic traditions, especially in the South; and in the Northeast Mexico-Texas area, the two patterns blended. Farther afield, certain Archaic-like elements, such as projectile points, appeared in the Subarctic and Arctic pre-Eskimo cultures of the Northwest Microblade and Arctic Small-Tool traditions.

In the Far West, there were similarities between the polished-stone woodworking implements of the Northwest Riverine, Northwest Coast, and California Coast and Valley traditions and those of the Archaic. It has been surmised that all these traditions were linked by a common source of diffusion or inspiration derived from Asiatic Mesolithic cultures. But this hypothesis is not conclusive, and it is possible that the Eastern Woodland and Pacific polished-stone industries were quite separate developments and that both were independent of Old World boreal sources.

The Mesoamerican Tradition. The Mesoamerican cultural tradition (Fig. 8-1) had its subsistence basis in the successful cultivation of maize, beans, squashes, chili peppers, cacao, maguey, and a host of other lesser crops. Slash-and-burn or milpa farming methods were generally practiced, although in certain upland regions intensive techniques, such as irrigation, terracing, and the creation of artificial island garden plots were followed. Maize and other plant foods were carefully stored. Maize was ground in stone metate instruments and the meal made into tortilla cakes, tamales, or gruel. The importance of agriculture was reflected in the native religions of the area.

The Mesoamerican tradition was characterized further by sedentary village communities, by the organization of these villages around ceremonial centers or principal towns, and by the development of these towns, at least in the later phases of the tradition, into true cities. The ceremonial centers and cities were marked by earthen, stone, or adobe platforms, and these platforms were surmounted by temples and palaces ornamented with sculptures and paintings. These centers and cities were the seats of power maintained by hereditary rulers and priests who often held sway over large territorial states or empires. Throughout, stone-carving, ceramics, textiles, and other industries, reached a high level of development. Religion was intimately interwoven with learning. Among the intellectual achievements were astronomy, mathematics, and hieroglyphic writing.

The geographical distribution of the tradition was the Mesoamerican area that extended from central Honduras and northwest Costa Rica on the south, to central Tamaulipas and northern Sinaloa on the north. This is a territory of varied topography and vegetation. It lies largely in tropical latitudes, but these latitudes are moderated by altitude, so that regional climates may vary from temperate to tropical.

Insofar as we are able to trace them at present, the roots of the Mesoamerican tradition lie in the Desert tradition cultures of upland Mexico. These cultures began early to diverge from the main line of Desert tradition development as the result of plant cultivation. By 2000 B.C., this "incipient cultivation" can be said to have passed over to a condition of "established agriculture" capable of sustaining sedentary village life. With the attainment of this threshold, the Mesoamerican cultural tradition was under way. Within the next thousand years, the sedentary village agricultural pattern spread to most of the rest of the Mesoamerican area.

It is, of course, possible that the Mesoamerican tradition had other roots, but so far we have uncovered no sound evidence of early cultures from the lowland or coastal regions of Mesoamerica that might have contributed to the formation of the Mesoamerican pattern. However, pre-agricultural or early agricultural cultures existed to the south in Panama, Colombia, and Venezuela; and it is possible that similar ones may be discovered in lowland and coastal Mesoamerica.

One of the features of Mesoamerican cultural development was the multiplicity of its subareal centers. There were at least ten of these, all drawing on the common heritage of the Early Preclassic Period (2000–1000 B.C.) of the tradition. These subareas began to follow distinct subtraditional lines of development during the succeeding Middle Preclassic (1000–300 B.C.) and Late Preclassic (300 B.C.–0) Periods. This subtraditional diversification continued into the Proto-Classic and Classic Periods (A.D. 0–900) and was marked by the rise of some of the most brilliant Mesoamerican civilizations, such as the Maya, the Zapotec, the Totonac, and Teotihuacán. During the latter part of the Classic Period and into the Postclassic Period (A.D. 900–1520) Mesoamerican society was disrupted from time to time by wars, invasions, and migrations of peoples. These disruptions are frequently associated with Toltec and other Nahua-speaking nations whose ancient homeland was in northwest Mexico. In the last century before the arrival of the Spanish, the Aztecs, a Nahua tribe, held imperial domain over a large part of Mesoamerica.

The relationships of the Mesoamerican tradition were, as we have seen, with the antecedent Desert tradition or a southern variant of that tradition and, perhaps, with early local or northern South American pre-agricultural cultures which were adapted to coastal or lowland environments. Later, during the Preclassic Period, and also continuing up through the Classic and Postclassic Mesoamerican cultural elements were carried southward to the Intermediate and Peruvian areas, especially to Ecuador and to Peru. Some contact may have been by sea, with the exchange passing in both directions. Metallurgy, which was incorporated into the Mesoamerican tradition in relatively late pre-Columbian times, was acquired from the Andean cultures. To the north, the Mesoamerican influence was felt in the Southwest and the Eastern Woodlands areas as early as the first millennium B.C. and became progressively more important. The agricultural traditions of these areas in large part were derivatives of Mesoamerica.

The Southwestern Tradition. The subsistence basis of the Southwestern tradition (Fig. 8-1) was the maize-beans-squash complex inherited from Mesoamerica, but the hunting and plant-collecting continued to be of some economic importance. The sedentary village was the early and fundamental settlement unit of the Southwestern tradition. Later, large towns appeared. Social, political, and religious organization seems to have been structured upon the local community or the small region; and it is unlikely that ancient Southwestern society was ever highly stratified or that royal lineages developed as in Mesoamerica.

Southwestern architecture included the individual pithouse; the small above-ground jacal, adobe, or stone house; and the larger, above-ground, multi-storied apartment-like building of adobe or stone masonry. Specialized or ceremonial architecture included the subterranean kiva chamber and, in some regions, the ball court and the small platform mound. Typical Southwestern tradition artifacts were the stone metate and mano for corn-grinding, pottery painted in black-on-white or red-on-buff modes, small chipped-stone arrow points, ornamental objects in Pacific sea shells and in turquoise, and basketry and textiles, including cotton cloth.

The distribution of the Southwestern cultural tradition defines the Southwest area—Arizona, New Mexico, southern Utah, southeastern Nevada, western and southwestern Colorado, west Texas, and Sonora and Chihuahua in Mexico.

The Southwestern tradition appears to have been synthesized between 100 B.C. and A.D. 400, and its antecedents are seen in the resident Desert culture (the Cochise), with important infusions of Mesoamerican cultural elements. The centuries between about A.D. 400 and 1000 saw the change from pithouses to above-ground architecture and the steady development of the four subtraditional lines of the Southwestern culture: the Mogollon, Anasazi, Hohokam, and Patayan. Climaxing this period and immediately following it, the great pueblos or towns of the Anasazi were constructed, and the Hohokam subarea flourished. During the thirteenth century many of the Anasazi towns were abandoned, and some groups appear to have moved south to join with Hohokam communities in the Arizona desert while others settled in New Mexico along the Rio Grande drainage. Drought and incursions by semi-nomadic Athapascan peoples have been suggested as causes for these changes. After A.D. 1400 the southern Arizona groups dwindled.

Diffusion to the Southwest from Mesoamerica did not cease with the beginning of the Christian era but continued almost to the historic horizon. The strongest influences are seen in the Hohokam subarea. In the west, California Desert cultures were in contact with the Southwest through the Patayan subarea. In the north, Anasazi influence penetrated into and blended with the later Desert cultures of Utah; but from the north came the invading Athapascans. The exact date of this Athapascan invasion is uncertain, but it probably began about A.D. 1300. Athapascan influences seem to have contributed little to the Southwestern tradition; their effects were, rather, the reverse. On the other hand, the Athapascan peoples appear to have borrowed massively from the resident Southwesterners. What their culture was when they entered the area is rather obscure. Quite probably it derived from the Denetasiro tradition of the western Subarctic, but other elements may have been assimilated from Desert tradition Utes and Paiutes and from cultures of the Plains. Finally, there are signs of Southwestern contacts with the Plains and the eastern United States along the eastern borders of the Southwest. They do not seem to have had important formative influences on the Southwestern tradition; they seem mostly to date from late prehistoric times.

The Woodland Tradition. The economy of the Woodland tradition of eastern North America was a mixture of hunting-collecting and farming. The hunting-collecting pattern seems to have been stronger during the earlier phases of the tradition, with agriculture increasing in importance as time went on. There was also a geographic differential, with regions farther to the north and east and more remote from the major river valleys being less oriented toward farming than regions nearer the Mississippi Valley. The tradition was characterized by cord-marked or fabric-marked pottery fashioned in simple, pointed-bottom pot-shapes. Other ceramic styles sometimes associated with Woodland tradition cultures are more elaborate surface finishings or decoration, including incised and rocker-stamped designs and painted incised zone elements. Pottery figurines were sometimes fashioned. Non-ceramic artifacts carried over from the antecedent Archaic tradition; chipped-stone projectile points tended to be large stemmed or notched types, and polished-stone utility and ornamental objects continued to be popular. Among the latter were tubular smoking pipes, a trait known from the Archaic tradition but more common in the Woodland cultures. (For Woodland tradition, see Fig. 8-1.)

Woodland living sites were either small villages or camp locations. The degree of permanent residency is difficult to establish, but it would appear that in certain regions and periods village communities were relatively stable. A frequent feature of Woodland cultures was a burial or mortuary mound. Some of these were quite simple; others were very elaborate, with specially constructed tombs containing large amounts of grave furniture. The large mound and earthwork sites would appear to have been ceremonial or, possibly, politico-religious centers for surrounding villages.

The geographical distribution of Woodland cultures included the entire Eastern Woodlands area from southern Canada to the Gulf of Mexico and from the Atlantic to the Plains. A variant of the Woodland culture was also found in the Plains area (Fig. 8-1).

The chronological range of the Woodland cultural tradition in the Eastern Woodlands area was from 1000 B.C. until A.D. 1700, or even later. In many parts of the East it was replaced by the Mississippian cultural tradition, which began to expand at the expense of the Woodland around A.D. 700; however, in the northern and eastern parts of the area it continued as a viable way of life until historic times. The dawn of Plains Woodland culture has been traced to about the beginning of the Christian era and its eclipse to A.D. 1000, although here, too, it persisted until later in some regions.

The origins of the Woodland tradition lie primarily in the antecedent and resident Archaic tradition of the Eastern Woodlands. At about 1000 B.C., this Archaic tradition began to be transformed by the appearance of several new traits: maize-farming, Woodland-type pottery, and burial mounds and specialized mortuary customs. Maize was certainly derived from the Mesoamerican tradition. The pottery, on the other hand, especially the earliest Woodland pottery, suggests an Asiatic inspiration; but the course and history of such a diffusion, if it did occur, has not been traced. The pottery relationships of the Woodland tradition are also complicated by the fact that some ceramic traits, especially those of the middle and later chronological ranges of the tradition, may have been of Mesoamerican origin. The mortuary mounds and mortuary customs cannot readily be traced to Mesoamerica, nor to Asia, nor to elsewhere in North America; they may have been local developments.

The particular region or regions where the Woodland tradition was first synthesized in the Eastern Woodlands area remain undetermined. During the Burial Mound I Period (1000–300 B.C.), the Ohio Valley witnessed the richest elaboration of mounds and earthworks in the Adena culture. At the beginning of the subsequent Burial Mound II Period (300 B.C.–A.D. 700), the Hopewell cultures of the Ohio Valley again represented a developmental peak for the tradition, and it was about this time that Hopewell influence spread widely through the East and westward to the Plains. During the latter part of the Burial Mound II Period, the cultures of the Ohio Valley seem to have declined somewhat, and cultural leadership within the Woodland tradition passed to the south, especially to the Lower Mississippi Valley and the Gulf Coast. Also at this time influences from Mesoamerica probably became more pronounced in the southern part of the Eastern Woodlands. After the rise and spread of the Mississippian tradition in the Temple Mound I Period (A.D. 700–1200), Woodland cultures were overrun, superseded, or rolled back from the Mississippi and Ohio Valley regions. Some of them continued in the old ways, as we have mentioned, up to the historic period; others tended to fuse with the Mississippian tradition to produce many of the regional cultures of the Temple Mound II Period (A.D. 1200–1700).

The Mississippian Tradition. The Mississippian tradition of the Eastern Woodlands area was a development of the resident and antecedent Woodland tradition plus important diffused influences from Mesoamerica and the Mesoamerican tradition. Maize agriculture was of greater economic significance in Mississippian than in Woodland cultures; hunting-collecting assumed a definitely secondary subsistence role. Mississippian sites tended to be larger, and they give more of an appearance of sedentary permanence than those of the Woodland tradition. Major Mississippian sites were marked by flat-topped platform mounds, arranged around open plazas, which served as bases for temples and chief's houses. The similarity to Mesoamerica is apparent. Some such sites were large towns, often fortified. Mississippian pottery assumed a variety of new modes. Many were in vessel form, including collared and spouted jars,

casuelas, effigy shapes, plates, and handled vessels. Decoration, too, differed from Woodland norms in that most of it was incised, punctated, engraved, or painted. Usual Mississippian artifacts included small triangular arrow points of chipped stone and elbow-form pottery pipes. (For Mississippian tradition, see Fig. 8-1.)

The geographic distribution of the Mississippian tradition clearly radiated from the main axis of the central and lower Mississippi Valley, covering most of the Southeast but extending for only short distances up the Ohio and Missouri drainages. In both of these latter valleys the tradition became attenuated and noticeably blended with Woodland elements. It underwent the same changes as it extended into the upper Mississippi Valley.

A date of A.D. 700 has been selected as the approximate time of the inception of the Mississippian tradition. The tradition appeared originally in the central and lower Mississippi valleys and southward along the Gulf Coast. These appear to be the subareas of its synthesis; these were also the subareas of its peak development. Between A.D. 700 and 1200, during the Temple Mound I Period, it spread to other parts of the East. In many cases the nature of this spread was by actual movement of peoples. Later, in the Temple Mound II Period, it was best represented in these outlying subareas and regions in blended Mississippian-Woodland cultures. By the historic period, the tradition either had dominated or influenced in some way all of the Eastern Woodlands area and much of the Plains area.

The Plains Village Tradition. We have pointed out that the Archaic tradition spread into the Plains from the East, merging with elements of the old Big-Game Hunting tradition and with others derived from the Desert tradition. This Archaic way of life dominated the Plains area from 4000 B.C. up until the first centuries of the Christian era; and in some places, such as the far western Plains and the south, it persisted until historic times. In the east the Archaic pattern was succeeded by the Woodland tradition, which brought with it pottery and cultivation of plants. The importance of farming in these Plains Woodland cultures is difficult to appraise. Apparently it was of greater significance in the river valleys of the eastern Plains than elsewhere, but even here it probably was a minor or partial element in the economy. Around A.D. 1000 the more vigorous agricultural practices of the Mississippian tradition spread into the river valleys of the Plains and served as the dynamic force in the synthesis of what has been called the Plains Village tradition (Fig. 8-1).

Plains Village people grew corn, beans, and squash in the river bottoms of the Missouri and its tributaries. They supplemented their agricultural stocks with buffalo, river fish, and wild plants. Their villages consisted of groups of semi-subterranean or surface timber-and-earth lodges. At first these were small, open communities; later they were enlarged and fortified. Common tools of the tradition were bison shoulder-blade hoes and an ample chipped-stone selection of points, knives, and skin-dressing tools. Pottery was more abundant than in the Plains Woodland cultures and was a development of the earlier Woodland styles modified by Mississippian influences. In brief, the tradition might be thought of as a re-integration and new adaptation of Mississippian traits to a Plains environment. Certain distinctive features of the Mississippian tradition, such as the platform temple mounds, had been abandoned.

The Plains Village tradition developed in the central and middle Missouri subareas, in Nebraska, Kansas, western Iowa, and parts of the Dakotas. Its influences, of course, spread beyond, but as an integrated culture pattern it was essentially confined to the suitable river valley locations of the eastern part of the Plains. In the fifteenth century the tradition was disrupted by drought, nomadic incursions (Apache ?), or both. After this, changes set in, such as the increase in the size of villages and their frequent fortification. The introduction of horses and guns to peoples of the Plains Village tradition in the seventeenth and eighteenth centuries further modified the tradition, and the tendency toward large village concentration increased. Such villages continued to depend to a considerable degree on river-bottom crops, but the greater mobility which the horse gave to the huntsmen also boosted the importance of buffalo-hunting. The historic Mandan, Arikara, and Pawnee tribes of the eastern Plains were the terminal representatives of the Plains Village tradition in its fullest sense; farther west, the Dakotas, Blackfoot, and Cheyenne were contemporaneous hunters who had been influenced by the tradition as well as by the European innovations of the gun and horse.

The California Coast and Valley Tradition. The California Coast and Valley tradition (Fig. 8-1) was a subsistence economy that was based on hunting, fishing, and collecting along the sea-shore, on offshore islands, in small coastal valleys, and in the larger interior valleys of the area. Along the shore the marine adaptation was effective and the resources—fish, shellfish, and sea mammals—abundant. The peoples in such seaside communities also collected nuts and seeds for food. Inland, wild plant foods, especially the acorn, were the main staples, and these harvests were much more substantial than the arid or semiarid desert country farther to the east yielded. The sites were camp, semi-sedentary village, and permanent village locations. Milling stones and handstones, mortars and pestles, fishing gear of stone and shell and bone, and various polished-stone objects of both a utilitarian and ceremonial nature were found in site refuse and as burial furniture. Among the latter were pendant-like "charmstones," tubular pipes, net weights, cogged stones, effigies, and vessels. A profusion of projectile points and other chipped-stone implements and bone implements and shell ornaments also have been recovered. Basketry was an important craft.

The tradition characterized almost the entire area of the present state of California, excepting portions of the far north and the eastern interior deserts.

The California Coast and Valley tradition probably had its origins in the earlier Old Cordilleran tradition and in the early manifestations of the Desert tradition around 5000 B.C. Its ground- and polished-stone work may have been the result of local invention; however, the possibilities of early contacts between the California Coast and Valley tradition and the Northwest Coast tradition should not be ruled out.

The California Coast and Valley tradition can be observed through a sequence of three major periods: Early (5000–2000 B.C.); Middle (2000 B.C.–A.D. 250); and Late (A.D. 250 to historic times). The principal trends during this time were an increasing utilization of marine resources by communities situated near the sea, over-all growth in the population and in the size and stability of individual villages, an increase in the manufacture of polished-stone artifacts and shell ornaments, and the replacement of the throwing-stick and dart by the bow-and-arrow. Pottery and agriculture were relatively unimportant in the tradition, both being introduced from the Southwestern area via the Patayan and Southern California Desert cultures during very late prehistoric or proto-historic times.

The Northwest Coast Tradition. The life pattern of the Northwest Coast tradition can be described from late nineteenth- and twentieth-century accounts of these Indians, some of whom continue in their native ways today (Fig. 8-1). The Northwest Coast Indians were salmon fishermen and sea-mammal hunters. They made dugout canoes and plank houses and were otherwise adept at woodworking and wood sculpture. They lived in settled or semi-sedentary villages along the shores, some of which were fairly large. The basic social and political unit was the local lineage group. Material goods were plentiful, and social differences were based on wealth and inheritance. This pattern was conditioned and modified to some extent by contacts with European traders. Iron tools, for example, were used in woodworking; woolen blankets acquired from the white man replaced local products woven of plant fibers and mountain-goat hair; and, in general, much of the material affluence of the Northwest Coast Indian societies de-

rived from the fur trade, which was organized and operated by Europeans. Nevertheless, the underlying aboriginal pattern of the culture shone through clearly, and this pattern has since been traced back in time by archaeologists.

Archaeological evidence of the fishing and sea-mammal hunting economy of the Northwest Coast tradition is supplied by bone harpoons, fixed barbed-bone points, and other projectile tips of chipped stone and ground slate. The woodworking industry can be traced through the antler wedge, pestle-shaped stone hammer, adze, and celt. The Northwest Coast art style, illustrated by carved totem poles, canoes, or plank houses, is preserved in stone prototypes such as ceremonial clubs, vessels, and animal and human-effigy sculptures.

Both ethnographic and archaeological testimony of the presence of the Northwest Coast cultural tradition are found throughout the Northwest Coast area, from Cape Mendocino in northern California, to Yakutat Bay in southern Alaska.

The origins of the tradition lie, at least in part, in the earlier Old Cordilleran tradition of the Interior Plateau country to the east. Sometime prior to 5000 B.C., Old Cordilleran groups, already specializing in river salmon fishing, descended to the coastal country and added maritime hunting to their riverine subsistence. Between 5000 B.C. and 1000 B.C., they acquired a series of characteristic Northwest Coast traits: the polished-stone and antler woodworking tools, the use of ground-slate weapons, and the tradition of stone effigy sculpture. The nature of this acquisition, as well as the more exact time at which it occurred, remains obscure. Such traits may have been derived from Asiatic Mesolithic and Neolithic boreal zone complexes, and their appearance along the Northwest Coast may be but a part of a general diffusion which embraced the North American Archaic cultures of the East as well as the cultures of the Pacific Northwest and California. If so, such traits may have been brought to the Northwest Coast via the Interior Plateau area, which is the interpretation I favor. Or they may have passed south to the Northwest Coast by way of early, unrevealed Eskimo or Eskimoan cultures of the Arctic. It is also possible that these artifact types, associated with woodworking, and this stone sculptural development arose locally somewhere in Pacific North America—along the Northwest Coast, in the Interior Plateau, or, possibly, in California. Whatever the source of the new elements, they were established by the opening of the first millennium B.C., and it can be said that the Northwest Coast tradition had its beginnings at least as early as this. The tradition developed and spread in the next 2000 years. Its early hearth was probably in the Coast Salish-Chinook subarea around the Fraser delta, Puget Sound, and the Columbia delta. By A.D. 1000, if not before, the Northwest Coast cultural pattern had spread throughout the area.

The Northwest Coast tradition, whatever its origins, maintained definite contacts with the Northwest Riverine and Eskimo traditions in later prehistoric times, so its history cannot be understood except in conjunction with Interior Plateau and Arctic culture history. There also appear to have been direct late contacts between the Northwest Coast and both the Denetasiro tradition of the Athapascan Indians of interior Canada and the California Coast and Valley tradition.

The Northwest Riverine Tradition. This tradition was based on river-fishing, forest-hunting, and wild-plant collecting. Villages along the rivers were the most permanent loci of population, but even these were abandoned for parts of the year while the inhabitants hunted or gathered roots and berries. House types varied, regionally and chronologically, but the most common forms were circular, earth-covered pithouses and above-ground pole-and-mat lodges. The dead were buried in pits or were cremated. Grave goods were common. Characteristic artifacts of the tradition included cobble hammers, leaf-shaped and side-notched or stemmed flint points, bone points and harpoons, polished-stone mauls, mallets, adzes, celts, vessels, net weights, antler wedges, zoomorphic stone sculptures, and effigy sculptures in bone. These materials reflected the hunting, fishing, and woodworking

traits of the culture and its common artistic themes. (See Fig. 8-1 for Northwest Riverine tradition.)

The Northwest Riverine tradition, traced either archaeologically or ethnographically, has been found throughout all those parts of the Interior Plateau area which have been explored to date. The area is best defined as lying between the Pacific mountain ranges and the continental divide and between the Great Basin on the south and the upper drainages of the Fraser River on the north. The southern part of the area has been studied and excavated more thoroughly than the northern part.

The Northwest Riverine Culture grew out of the earlier resident Old Cordilleran culture, and focal points of this development may have sprung up along The Dalles rapids of the Columbia River and in the Fraser River canyon. Old Cordilleran sites did exist in these localities prior to 5000 B.C., but the period between 5000 B.C. and about 1000 B.C. is shrouded in mystery. Archaeological cultures that arose after 1500 to 1000 B.C., exhibited certain Old Cordilleran-like traits, such as leaf-shaped projectile points and cobble hammers, so some local continuity probably was maintained. Beginning around 1500 to 1000 B.C., some new traits made their appearance, particularly polished-stone forms, including woodworking tools. Some authorities have considered this new infusion of traits to be of Asiatic boreal zone inspiration, part of a more general diffusion to the New World which also included similar traits in the Archaic tradition of the Eastern Woodlands area of North America. These are, of course, the same traits which made their appearance on the Pacific Northwest Coast at about the same time. The interpretation we have favored is that they moved from Plateau to Coast.

It might be argued that the Northwest Riverine culture pattern came into being with the appearance and integration of the various polished-stone traits around 1500 to 1000 B.C., more or less coordinate with the beginnings of the Northwest Coast tradition. But some authorities argue that a Northwest Riverine tradition—if such is to be considered the same as the culture of the Plateau ethnohistoric

466

horizon—did not come into being until considerably later, at around A.D. 1200–1300. Following this interpretation the Plateau area culture of the 1500 B.C. to A.D. 1800 period is one designated as a "Northern Forest Culture." This "Northern Forest Culture," presumably deriving out of the earlier Old Cordilleran tradition, plus increments of the so-called "boreal" influence, was ancestral to later Plateau or Northwest Riverine culture but differed in that its orientations were more toward forest hunting than toward riverine village life.

Relations between the Northwest Riverine and Northwest Coast traditions were always close. The Desert tradition of the Great Basin and probably the Subarctic cultures of the Denetasiro tradition which lay to the east and north also contributed to the development of the Northwest Riverine tradition. In historic times contacts also were established with the western tribes of the Plains area.

The Pre-Eskimo Traditions of the North. The earliest evidences of man in the Arctic and Subarctic areas consist of projectile points which appear to belong to the Old Cordilleran and Big-Game Hunting traditions and which have been found isolated or as parts of otherwise undistinctive lithic complexes. To these indications may be added the scantily represented and poorly defined British Mountain complex, which may have been the earliest of all.

It was not until about 6000 B.C., however, that a technological tradition both characteristically northern and reasonably well known appeared in the Arctic and Subarctic. This tradition was the Northwest Microblade flint industry (Fig. 8-1). Artifacts were found in interior forest camp sites and the people who made them and occupied the sites lived by hunting caribou, elk, and buffalo. The most diagnostic features of the tool complex were microblades which were struck from tongue-shaped cores. These blades were accompanied by large bifacial knives, large stemmed and notched projectile points, and lanceolate points. Such assemblages have been found in the northwestern Arctic and Subarctic, as the name for the tradition implies, and in Alaska, the Yukon Territory, and the southwestern portions of the Canadian Northwest Territories. The earliest have come from Alaska and the west, where they date from about 6500 to 3500 B.C. Elsewhere, they endured to 1000 B.C.

The origins of the Northwest Microblade technological tradition are mixed, but the diagnostic elements, such as the microblades and cores, appear to have derived from Asiatic Mesolithic sources. The large stemmed points suggest the Archaic tradition of eastern North America and the Great Lakes region, and the lanceolate points are similar to those of the Plano style of the North American Plains.

The Northwest Microblade tradition probably provided the local matrix culture for the development of the Denetasiro tradition of the western Subarctic.

The Arctic Small-Tool technological tradition was undoubtedly the product of coastal and tundra-hunting peoples rather than interior forest hunters. Sites have been discovered all along the Arctic coasts from Alaska to Greenland. Its diagnostics are finely flaked, small artifacts of flint, including numerous blades and bladelets, polyhedral cores, small bifacial points or knives, crescent-shaped side-blades, and retouched and hafted burins. The small points and side-blades were set in harpoons and spear points of bone and antler, and these were used for hunting seal, walrus, and caribou. The delicate burins indicate that antler and ivory carving was widely practiced.

The Arctic Small-Tool tradition first appeared in the western Arctic between 4000 and 3000 B.C. (Fig. 8-1), where it persisted until about 2000 B.C. The course of its diffusion in the Arctic was clearly from west to east, and in the east Arctic Small-Tool cultures may have existed until 1000 B.C. The tradition seems to have derived from Asiatic sources. In the New World it was probably in contact with the later manifestations of the Northwest Microblade tradition in the west and with the Archaic tradition in the east. Throughout most of the Arctic it appears to have served as the matrix culture for the later Eskimo tradition.

The Aleutian Core and Blade Industry appears to have originated early from Asiatic roots. It may have been the local base technology from which Eskimo culture in the Aleutians emerged.

The Eskimo Tradition. The Eskimo cultural tradition was based on a sea-mammal and land-hunting subsistence pattern adapted to the Arctic tundra and coasts. This culture was shared by peoples of an Eskimo-Aleut physical type and language affiliation. It was, and to a degree still is, found throughout the Arctic area. Its maximum geographic extension reaches from eastern Siberia across the Arctic to Greenland (Fig. 8-1).

The Eskimo adapted spectacularly well to the ice and snow of the far north. With bone and ivory harpoons set with slate end-blades, they hunted seal, walrus, and sometimes whale from their frame-and-skin kayaks and larger umiak boats. On land they pursued the caribou with darts and spears. Sleds and ice-creepers (cleats worn on boots) facilitated their travel across the ice and frozen snow. Their winter houses were usually semi-subterranean, roofed with driftwood or whale-bone, and covered with earth and rocks. In some regions, however, the classic igloos made of ice and snow were used. Summer dwellings were skin tents. These various domiciles were heated and lighted with stone or pottery lamps in which animal oils were burned. Clothes were tailored and made of skins. A great many household utensils were made of bone, ivory, or antler. The finest representations of Eskimo art are engravings on ivory.

The Eskimo tradition, which first appeared in the western American Arctic at about 1000 B.C., may owe its origins to new immigrants from Siberia; but it is more likely that the basic Eskimo population was already in the New World and that peoples who were following in the tradition of the Arctic Small-Tool industry gradually became assimilated to a new cultural pattern. Such a pattern would have been the result of new diffused traits from Siberia being blended into the resident Arctic Small-Tool cultures.

There are four subtraditional lines of development in Eskimo culture history: the Pacific-Aleut, the Northern Maritime, the Choris-Norton-Near Ipiutak, and the Dorset. Of these, the Pacific-Aleut is most divergent, probably as the result of its milder natural environmental setting and its somewhat different Asiatic heritage. The Northern Maritime tradition proved to be the most viable; and the classic Eskimo whale-hunting culture of historic times, which is found all across the northern Arctic, descended from this line. The Choris-Norton-Near Ipiutak subtradition, which in its early phases centered around Norton Sound, was somewhat less adapted to maritime hunting. The Dorset branch, the most limited of the four in its material inventories, was the earliest Eskimo culture to spread to the eastern Arctic. Here it was superseded by the Northern Maritime subtradition in late prehistoric times.

In general, the main developmental trends in Eskimo culture, particularly in the dominant Northern Maritime branch, reflect an increasing adaptation to polar climates, especially in an increased efficiency in sea-mammal hunting. Through time, the pattern was enriched by the addition of new elements, either invented locally or received from Asia. The prevailing drift of diffusion was from west to east. Although some kind of contact was maintained with Asian cultures throughout the history of the tradition, there was an observable trend away from Asiatic modes, particularly in art forms. For example, some of the most Siberian-appearing art features occurred quite early in the Northern Maritime and Choris-Norton-Near Ipiutak sequences, and then were steadily transformed into local styles. This transformation tended toward simplification and loss of iconographic content; and one wonders if elements of Old World myth, religion, and ritual, were not lost or diluted at the same time.

The Denetasiro Tradition. In the western Subarctic the term Denetasiro tradition refers to forest-hunting, trapping, and fishing cultures that arose sometime after 2000 B.C. (Fig. 8-1). The people involved were probably the Athapascans; at least the later prehistoric and historic phases of the tradition can be so identified. The seasonal camp sites representing the tradition are known best from the Southwest Yukon country, but they have also been found in the interior forest lands of the Canadian Northwest Territories. Future excavations and study may reveal that the tradition extended into interior Alaska and possibly along the northern margins of the provinces of Alberta, Saskatchewan, and Manitoba.

The Athapascans subsisted on moose, caribou, small game, fish, and wild berries; chipped-stone work included small triangular arrow points and other tools. Most weapons and tools, however, were made of bone and antler, although the polished-stone woodworking adze was widely used. The old microblade industry of the Northwest Microblade tradition had vanished. Cold-hammered copper was used for a few implements and utensils, and from the ethnographic horizon comes proof of the manufacture and use of bark containers.

The origins of the Denetasiro tradition probably lie in the older resident cultures of the Northwest Microblade tradition and in diffusions from Eskimo cultures and possibly from Asiatic sources in pre-Eskimo times. The earliest documented evidences of Denetasiro cultures are late, after A.D. 300; but probably the tradition will be traced back earlier than this. Relationships also were established with the Northwest Riverine and Northwest Coast traditions.

Correlation of Cultural Traditions and Area Chronologies

The main lines of our story have dealt with the cultural traditions. Except for the foregoing summary, where we extracted them from their contexts to treat them individually, we have examined the traditions in their geographical area settings and with the aid of the archaeological constructs of area chronologies. In so doing we have been at pains to make clear the conceptual differences between cultural traditions and culture periods; but since these are frequently coterminous and sometimes bear the same names, it seems advisable to review the two in this summary chapter, which we shall do with the aid of the two charts, Figs. 8-1 and 8-2. Figure 8-1, to which we constantly referred in the preceding section, is a diachronic presentation of the major cultural traditions of North and Middle America set in the framework of the major culture areas with which we have been dealing. Figure 8-2, drawn to the same scale and with the same geographical arrangement, presents the area chronologies or culture sequences from which the cultural traditions have been derived. These are, for the most part, simplified versions of area chronology charts that appear in the several chapters.

Figure 8-2 is arranged on a more or less east-west axis through North America, no perfect arrangement of this kind being possible on a single chart. The eastern, or right-hand, column represents the Eastern Subarctic; the most westerly, or left-hand, column is the Arctic. However, in discussing each column and its chronology we can begin at any point, so we shall follow the order of area presentation of the book.

The Mesoamerican Area. The Mesoamerican area chronology embraces five major periods. The earliest of these, the *Paleo-Indian Period,* arose at an unknown time and ended at 7000 B.C. The cultural remains of the period include some which relate to the Big-Game Hunting tradition, such as the mammoth "kill" site at Santa Isabel Iztapán, in the Valley of Mexico; however, the chart plotting the cultural traditions (Fig. 8-1) oversimplifies the situation. As brought out in the text discussions (Chap. 2), early finds of Middle America relate to both the Old Cordilleran and Big-Game Hunting traditions. The *Food-Collecting and Incipient Cultivation Period* extended from 7000 B.C. to 2000 B.C. The cultures of the period were those of the southern extension of the Desert tradition into Mesoamerica. The period was terminated by the appearance of settled agricultural village life and pottery in the southern part of the Mesoamerican area and, in effect, by the beginnings of the Mesoamerican cultural tradition. The third, fourth, and fifth periods of the Mesoamerican area chronology all pertain to this Mesoamerican cultural tradition. They are designated as the *Preclassic, Classic,* and *Postclassic Periods.* They fall between 2000 B.C. and A.D. 1520, and, as indicated on the time chart (Fig. 8-2), they are further subdivided.

The Southwest Area. In the Southwest area, the earliest period is also designated the

Figure 8-2. A correlation of major area chronologies for North and Middle America.

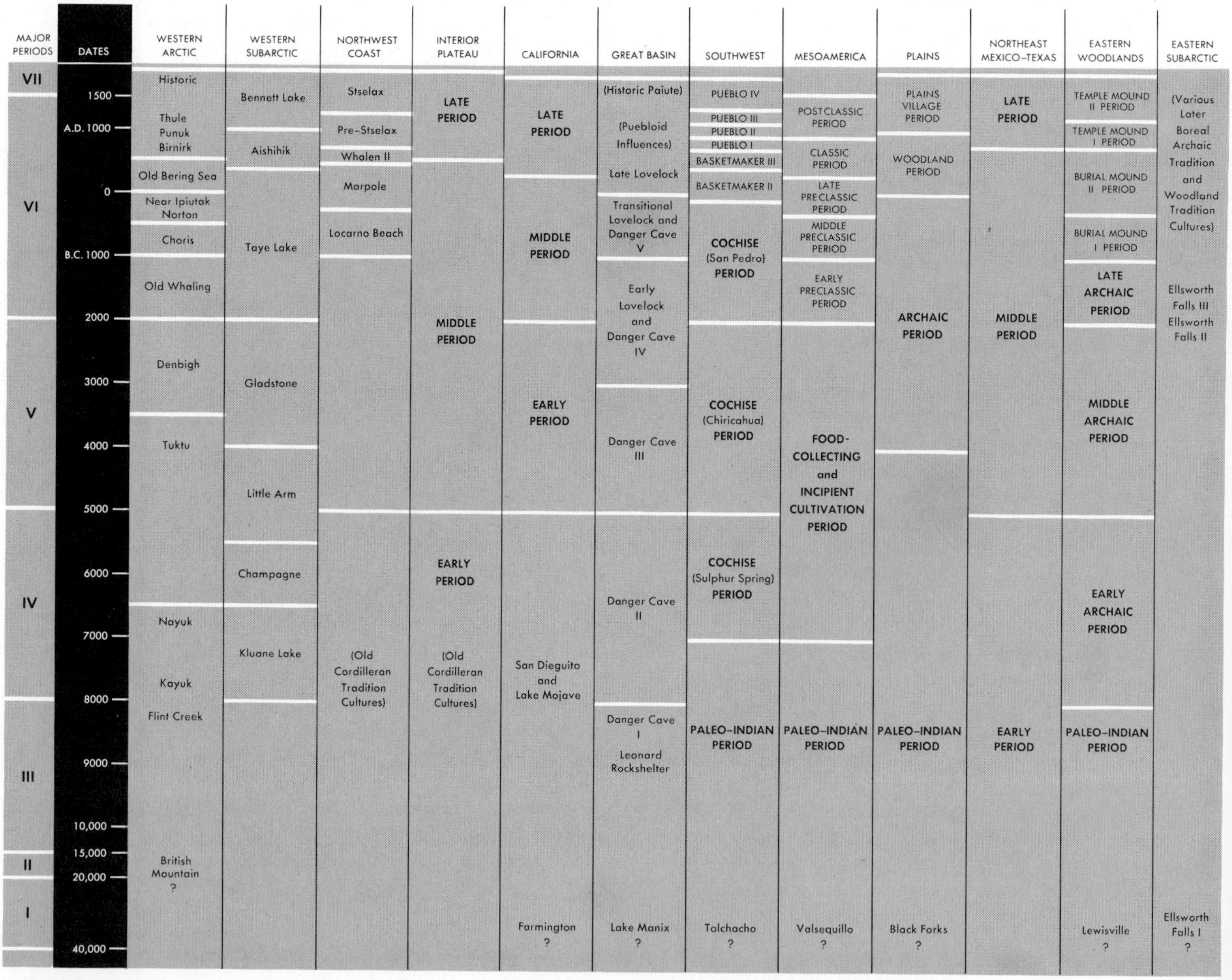

MAJOR PERIODS	DATES	WESTERN ARCTIC	WESTERN SUBARCTIC	NORTHWEST COAST	INTERIOR PLATEAU	CALIFORNIA	GREAT BASIN	SOUTHWEST	MESOAMERICA	PLAINS	NORTHEAST MEXICO–TEXAS	EASTERN WOODLANDS	EASTERN SUBARCTIC
VII	1500	Historic	Bennett Lake	Stselax	LATE PERIOD	LATE PERIOD	(Historic Paiute)	PUEBLO IV	POSTCLASSIC PERIOD	PLAINS VILLAGE PERIOD	LATE PERIOD	TEMPLE MOUND II PERIOD	(Various Later Boreal Archaic Tradition and Woodland Tradition Cultures)
	A.D. 1000	Thule Punuk Birnirk	Aishihik	Pre-Stselax			(Puebloid Influences)	PUEBLO III / PUEBLO II / PUEBLO I	CLASSIC PERIOD	WOODLAND PERIOD		TEMPLE MOUND I PERIOD	
				Whalen II			Late Lovelock	BASKETMAKER III					
	0	Old Bering Sea		Marpole				BASKETMAKER II	LATE PRECLASSIC PERIOD			BURIAL MOUND II PERIOD	
VI		Near Ipiutak Norton				MIDDLE PERIOD	Transitional Lovelock and Danger Cave V		MIDDLE PRECLASSIC PERIOD				
	B.C. 1000	Choris	Taye Lake	Locarno Beach				COCHISE (San Pedro) PERIOD				BURIAL MOUND I PERIOD	
		Old Whaling					Early Lovelock and Danger Cave IV		EARLY PRECLASSIC PERIOD			LATE ARCHAIC PERIOD	Ellsworth Falls III / Ellsworth Falls II
	2000				MIDDLE PERIOD					ARCHAIC PERIOD	MIDDLE PERIOD		
	3000	Denbigh	Gladstone			EARLY PERIOD		COCHISE (Chiricahua) PERIOD				MIDDLE ARCHAIC PERIOD	
V							Danger Cave III		FOOD-COLLECTING and INCIPIENT CULTIVATION PERIOD				
	4000	Tuktu											
	5000		Little Arm										
	6000		Champagne	(Old Cordilleran Tradition Cultures)	EARLY PERIOD		Danger Cave II	COCHISE (Sulphur Spring) PERIOD				EARLY ARCHAIC PERIOD	
IV		Nayuk											
	7000		Kluane Lake		(Old Cordilleran Tradition Cultures)	San Dieguito and Lake Mojave							
	8000	Kayuk Flint Creek					Danger Cave I						
	9000						Leonard Rockshelter	PALEO-INDIAN PERIOD	PALEO-INDIAN PERIOD	PALEO-INDIAN PERIOD	EARLY PERIOD	PALEO-INDIAN PERIOD	
III													
	10,000												
II	15,000 / 20,000	British Mountain ?											
I	40,000					Farmington ?	Lake Manix ?	Tolchacho ?	Valsequillo ?	Black Forks ?		Lewisville ?	Ellsworth Falls I ?

Paleo-Indian. Terminating at 7000 B.C., it was largely the period of the Big-Game Hunting tradition. The subsequent *Cochise Period,* which ran from 7000 B.C. to 100 B.C., took its name from a subtraditional line of development within the Desert tradition. It is divided into three subperiods. Sites of Cochise affiliation and dating have been found in the Mogollon and Hohokam subareas of the Southwest.[1] From 100 B.C. to the historic horizon, the cultures of the Southwest may be considered a part of the Southwestern tradition. They can be traced through time in the archaeological chronologies of each subarea. The best known of these chronologies is the one for the Anasazi subarea with its periods: *Basketmaker II, Basketmaker III, Pueblo I, Pueblo II, Pueblo III,* and *Pueblo IV.* (See Chap. 4 for details of dates for this and Southwest subarea chronologies.)

The Eastern Woodlands Area. In the Eastern Woodlands area, a *Paleo-Indian Period* terminated at 8000 B.C. The cultures of the period were of the Big-Game Hunting tradition. An *Archaic Period,* divided into three subperiods, ran from 8000 to 1000 B.C. It has the same name as the Archaic cultural tradition which characterized it. From 1000 B.C. to A.D. 700 was the time of the *Burial Mound Period,* the time when the Woodland tradition dominated the area. The period is divided into two subperiods. The *Temple Mound Period,* lasting from A.D. 700 to A.D. 1700, is also divided into two subperiods. It was the time of the Mississippian cultural tradition in the East.

The Plains Area. In the Plains area the *Paleo-Indian Period* is plotted as lasting until 4000 B.C. The Big-Game Hunting tradition lasted throughout the period. Following the Paleo-Indian Period, between 4000 B.C. and 0, was the *Archaic Period,* which took its name from the dominant cultural tradition in the area at that time. The *Woodland Period* lasted from 0 to A.D. 1000, and it too was named for the prevalent cultural tradition of the period, the Woodland. The *Plains Village Period* is named for the Plains Village cultural tradition which lasted from A.D. 1000 to 1800, or later, in the Plains.

The Northeast Mexico-Texas Area. The *Early Period* in the area seems primarily related to the Big-Game Hunting Tradition, although certain Desert tradition elements and Archaic tradition elements may also have influenced it. It was followed, from 5000 B.C. to A.D. 700, by a *Middle Period,* A.D. 700 being an approximate date for the appearance of pottery in some parts of the area. The cultural tradition of the period revealed a blend of Desert tradition and Archaic tradition elements and has been named the Desert-Archaic tradition. A *Late Period,* from A.D. 700 to the historic horizon, remains dominated by this Desert-Archaic tradition.

The Great Basin Area. No general area chronology has been devised for the Great Basin. On the chart (Fig. 8-2) we have used culture phase names from the western Utah and Nevada subareas. Phases like *Leonard Rock Shelter* (lower levels) and *Danger Cave I* comprise a pre-8000 B.C. period, and have here been interpreted as being within the Old Cordilleran tradition rather than the Desert tradition. From 8000 B.C. until A.D. 1800, the column is marked off in a series of Periods: *Danger Cave II; Danger Cave III; Early Lovelock and Danger Cave IV;* and *Late Lovelock.* All these periods were represented by cultures which were a part of the Desert tradition.

The Baja California Area. No Baja California column is shown on the chart. Most authorities believe, however, that a period recognized by its Pinto Basin-like complexes can be set at 7000 to 1000 B.C. This *Pinto Basin Period* was succeeded by an *Amargosa Period,* which lasted from 1000 B.C. to 0. From 0 to A.D. 1800, a period can be named after the two dominant late cultures, which are geographically distinct but coeval, the *Las Palmas* and the *Comondú.* Throughout the sequence the cultures were all of the Desert tradition or a later modification of that tradition.

The California Area. One period, tentatively named for two cultures, the *Lake Mojave* and the *San Dieguito*, began at an undetermined time and ran until 5000 B.C. In Fig. 8-1 these cultures are indicated as being essentially of Old Cordilleran affiliation, though with Desert or "proto-Desert" elements. From 5000 B.C. on to the historic period, the California area was the setting of the California Coast and Valley tradition. This time span has been divided into *Early, Middle,* and *Late Periods,* as shown on the chart (Fig. 8-2).

The Northwest Coast Area. No general area chronology has been formulated. Prior to 5000 B.C., culture complexes of the Old Cordilleran tradition existed or are surmised to have existed. From about 5000 B.C. to 1000 B.C., there is no definite archaeological record. After 1000 B.C., five culture phase names from the Fraser River region sequence have been used as period names: *Locarno Beach; Marpole; Whalen II; Pre-Stselax;* and *Stselax*. The last of these terminated with the historic Northwest Coast cultures. All these phases, and all other archaeological remains of the area which seem to fall into the span of centuries between 1000 B.C. and A.D. 1800, are considered a part of the Northwest Coast cultural tradition.

The Interior Plateau Area. The area chronology used for the Interior Plateau area is based on one generalized for The Dalles region of the Columbia River. Prior to 5000 B.C. there was an *Early Period,* a time of cultural complexes relating to the Old Cordilleran tradition. A *Middle Period* spanned the time from 5000 B.C. to A.D. 500. The earlier ranges of this period are not well documented, but after about 1000 B.C. its culture phases were affiliated with the Northwest Riverine tradition. This tradition persisted through a *Late Period,* set at A.D. 500 to the historic horizon.

The Western Subarctic. There is no general area chronology for the western part of the Subarctic area. The period names in the column are taken from a regional sequence in the south-west Yukon. *Kluane Lake* is dated from 8000 B.C. to 6500 B.C., and its cultural affiliations are thought to be Old Cordilleran. The succeeding *Champagne* phase, from 6500 B.C. to 500 B.C., betrays signs of both Old Cordilleran and Big-Game Hunting elements, the latter being in the form of Plano-type projectile points. *Little Arm,* from 5500 B.C. to 4000 B.C., was a Northwest Microblade tradition phase and so were the succeeding *Gladstone* (4000 B.C.–2000 B.C.) and *Taye Lake* (2000 B.C. to before A.D. 300) phases. The *Aishihik* and *Bennett Lake* phases date from A.D. 300 to A.D. 1000, and from A.D. 1000 to the historic, respectively. Both these phases belong in the Denetasiro tradition.

The Arctic Area. Leaving aside a *British Mountain* phase, which is hesitantly placed in the vicinity of 20,000 to 14,000 B.C., the next Arctic area phases in order of time were the *Flint Creek, Kayuk,* and *Nayuk,* which date prior to 6500 B.C. The first two generally are linked to the Old Cordilleran tradition; the last was characterized by Plano points. The *Tuktu* phase, beginning at 4000 B.C., was affiliated with the Northwest Microblade tradition. The fifteen-hundred years from 3500 to 2000 B.C. was the period of the *Denbigh* phase, the best known Arctic Small-Tool tradition phase of the western Arctic. The *Old Whaling Culture,* dating to around 1800 B.C., is bracketed after Denbigh but it is unplaced as to tradition affiliation. Beginning at 1000 B.C., several phases from the western Arctic are representative of a sequence of periods: *Choris; Norton; Near Ipiutak; Old Bering Sea; Birnirk; Punuk;* and *Thule.* The last leads into historic and modern Eskimo culture. All these phases, from 1000 B.C. forward, are within the Eskimo cultural tradition.

As is obvious from this summary, there is no general area chronology for the Arctic. The sequence described and shown on the chart (Fig. 8-2) pertains to the western Arctic. The Eskimo tradition phases that make up the upper part of the column are a pastiche of phases from the Choris-Norton-Near Ipiutak and Northern Maritime subtraditional lines. Keep in mind, although the charts (Figs. 8-1, 8-2) do not indicate it, that significant chronological differences obtain in the persistence of culture traditions between the western and the eastern Arctic.

The Eastern Subarctic. We have omitted any discussion of culture sequences for the eastern Subarctic. Leaving aside Dorset Eskimo sites, which are found in a transitional Arctic-to-Subarctic zone, all the archaeological cultures of the eastern Subarctic fall within the Archaic or the Boreal Archaic tradition.[2] Apparently this tradition persisted until historic times. It may have arisen anywhere between 2000 and 5000 B.C.

Some Synchronic Perspectives of Major American Periods

To this point we have reviewed and summarized the several cultural traditions and have placed these in diachronic perspective with reference to the various archaeological area chronologies of North and Middle America. With this background we turn now to a consideration of a series of synchronic perspectives or time horizons as these may be drawn, in continental-wide fashion, across the time chart (Fig. 8-2). In so doing we are attempting for the first time in this book to construct major American culture periods and to ask the question how meaningful these may be as aids to the study of New World prehistory. Remember that we are talking about *periods* and *not* about *stages*. Periods are defined as segments of past time marked off in absolute years. The way in which they may be described by the culture content which they demarcate is secondary to their definition.

Period I: 40,000–20,000 B.C. Man may or may not have been in the New World this early. If he was, presumably he had arrived recently from Asia. He must have lived in small, widely scattered groups, but he may very well have distributed himself over most of North, Middle,

and South America. The crude percussion choppers and scrapers from places such as Lake Chapala in Baja California, Black Forks in Wyoming, Lake Maracaibo in Venezuela, and the Patagonian marine terraces in Argentina—to name only a few—may represent the technology of these early Americans. All we can say or infer about such implements is that their makers were probably hunters and food-collectors.

Period II: 20,000–15,000 B.C. It has been surmised (see chart, Fig. 8-2) that the idea of a bifacially flaked lanceolate point or knife was brought or diffused to the New World during this period. If so, such a technological innovation would have been added to existing resident industries if such were already present. If they were not, this period would mark man's first entry into the New World from Asia. It also has been speculated that a complex like the British Mountain of the Arctic is representative of such a technological spread from Asia to America and is also representative of the period. This is still mere speculation, however.

Period III: 15,000–8000 B.C. We can only guess about the initial date of this period, which marks the hypothetical beginnings of the Old Cordilleran and Big-Game Hunting traditions (Figs. 8-1, 8-2), which may have stemmed from the heritages of Period I, Period II, or both, or may have derived immediately out of migrations or diffusions from Asia. The first secure datings of these traditions fall between 10,000 and 9000 B.C.

By 9000 B.C. we know that the Big-Game Hunting tradition had spread throughout the North American Plains, to the Eastern Woodlands, and to the Southwest. Elements of it also appeared in Mesoamerica and South America. At this date the mammoth and other Pleistocene animals were on the wane in the Plains area, and the Big-Game Hunting tradition was being adapted to the buffalo.

The Old Cordilleran tradition is less clearly dated, but it is reasonably certain that it was established by this time in the Pacific Northwest and in much of western North America. Elements of it, too, can be traced into Mesoamerica and South America.

The Big-Game Hunting tradition was a sophisticated subsistence pattern based on the hunting of large herd animals and on the utilization of their meat, hides, and bones. The contemporaneous Old Cordilleran tradition was less distinctive, but in the Pacific Northwest it was a successful, if less specialized, hunting way of life supplemented by river-fishing.

During Period III, North and Middle America were dominated by these two traditions. If, however, either or both of the antecedent periods truly pertain to man in the New World, then it is quite possible that in some areas and regions unspecialized hunting cultures, making crude rough-flaked tools, still persisted. If one should attempt to project the period to South America as well, then this possibility seems even more likely. The period ended at 8000 B.C., the approximate point of the first appearances of cultures of two new major traditions, the Archaic and the Desert.

Period IV: 8000–5000 B.C. During this period, the cold, wet Pleistocene climate was steadily moderated. In some places, such as the Great Basin of western North America, extreme dryness set in. Of the two new major traditions, the Archaic appears to have arisen out of the Big-Game Hunting tradition in the Eastern Woodlands, and during the period gradually adapted to this environment. The Desert tradition, arising from Old Cordilleran antecedents, prevailed in the Great Basin, the Southwest, parts of California, Baja California, and in upland Mesoamerica (Figs. 8-1, 8-2).

On the Plains, the late cultures of the Big-Game Hunting tradition continued to exist, and in the Pacific Northwest and parts of California the Old Cordilleran tradition persisted.

In the Arctic and Subarctic some cultures related most closely to the Old Cordilleran tradition appeared; others were influenced by a new tradi-

tion, the Northwest Microblade, which seems to have derived from Siberia.

In general, the cultures of this period were in transition from predominantly hunting toward regionally adapted mixed economies of hunting, fishing, and plant-collecting. Ground-stone implements, used especially for food-grinding, made their first appearance.

Period V: 5000–2000 B.C. This period saw the disappearance of the Old Cordilleran and Big-Game Hunting traditions (see Figs. 8-1, 8-2).

In the Eastern Woodlands, the Archaic tradition reached its maturity with large semi-sedentary village sites and a diverse exploitation of natural resources, including shellfish, fish, game, and wild plants.

In the west, the Desert tradition, with its emphasis on wild seed foods, was firmly established in the Great Basin, the Southwest, upland Mexico, and Baja California. In upland Mexico, plant cultivation was underway as an adjunct to the collection of wild vegetable foods.

New traditions were also appearing. Among these was the California Coast and Valley tradition, with its emphasis on wild plant foods and sea foods. It is believed to have developed from Old Cordilleran and Desert tradition prototypes. Farther north, the Old Cordilleran tradition of the Interior Plateau and the Northwest Coast probably was developing along the lines of the new Northwest Coast and Northwest Riverine traditions.

Still farther north, the Arctic Small-Tool tradition had made its appearance, probably largely in response to the Mesolithic influences from Siberia.

In general, the traditions that had arisen in the preceding period were maturing; hunting, fishing, and collecting techniques were being refined; the populations were adapting to a number of different environments; and polished-stone and bone implements and ornaments were being manufactured.

Period VI: 2000 B.C.–A.D. *1500.* The beginning date for this period marks the first appearance of successful village agriculture in Mesoamerica and the beginnings of the Mesoamerican cultural tradition. Somewhat later, agriculture spread from Mesoamerica to some but not all North American areas, although not simultaneously.

Pottery also appeared at about 2000 B.C. in Mesoamerica and spread to various North American areas during this period, but again, not simultaneously.

Period VI saw the origin and rise of the Mesoamerican, Southwestern, Woodland, and Mississippian cultural traditions (Figs. 8-1, 8-2), all or partly agricultural, and the first appearances of Northwest Coast, Northwest Riverine, Denetasiro, and Eskimo traditions, all non-agricultural. In some areas, the non-agricultural Archaic, Desert, and California Coast and Valley traditions still persisted.

The soundest generalizations we can make for the period are that some of the cultures were agricultural but many were not and that pottery was fashioned and used in some areas but not in all. Insofar as they can be appraised archaeologically, cultures which knew neither pottery nor agriculture continued along their accustomed ways. In the northern part of the continent, Asiatic contacts continued to play an important role in the development of cultures in those areas.

It is obvious that within the time span of this period many important events were occurring in the New World, but to best appreciate these it is necessary to view them in terms of particular area chronologies. Thus, for example, in Mesoamerica the rise of true cities and development of large territorial states and warring empires are extremely important to an understanding of the cultures of that area, but they and the particular periods in which they occurred have little relevance outside of that area and culture sphere.

Period VII: A.D. *1500–Present.* This is the Historic Period of the New World, the time after Columbus' first arrival. During the first two hundred years of the period, the advanced civilizations of Mesoamerica and of South America and native cultures elsewhere were radically transformed by European acculturation. Since then, these processes have continued there and elsewhere, so that now only a few Indian or Eskimo societies approximate their old patterns of life.

Observations. This organization of New World cultural history by strict time periods provides some interesting and informative synchronous perspectives, but as a device for generalizing or recapitulating cultural history it leaves much to be desired. In general, the clearest coincidences of cultural content and cultural events with time horizons relate to the early periods. Forgetting the first two periods, which are hypothetical constructs, there is a definite correspondence between Period III and the Big-Game Hunting and Old Cordilleran traditions. Leaving aside the differences between these two traditions, the period could be described succinctly as one pertaining to hunters who made lanceolate projectile points and other chipped-stone weapons and tools. Complications might arise, of course, if we presumed that a number of non-projectile point complexes also fell in the same period. These could be accommodated to a general period definition only if we eliminated the lanceolate points as a diagnostic feature of the period. Period IV, too, might be generalized, although somewhat less succinctly, by stating that it was a time of Big-Game Hunting and of Old Cordilleran and Desert and Archaic tradition hunters and food-collectors. With Period V the picture grows more complicated, and with Period VI the difficulties of generalization become formidable.

Even if we cut our seven periods to three, cogent description is still difficult. In the tri-fold scheme favored by some American archaeologists a Paleo-Indian Period would correspond to our Period III (or, perhaps, to Periods I, II, and III). A Meso-Indian Period would bracket our Periods IV and V, and a Neo-Indian Period would be essentially the same as Period VI. As is obvious, however, the problems remain. Perhaps the most important thing to be learned by looking at New World prehistory in this fashion is that many important events did not occur simultaneously. Only if we shift our point of view from synchronized periods to culture stages can we offer more satisfactory generalizations.[3]

Major American Culture Stages

Culture stages are defined by a general similarity of culture content—i.e., "hunting-gathering cultures," "agricultural cultures," or "urban cultures." Such cultures so grouped in a stage may or may not be generically related to one another. In North and Middle America, and, in fact, within the New World as a whole, such generic relationships often do exist. But these relationships are not the basis for stage classification. To repeat, the criteria for such classification are those of similarity of general culture type.

Culture stages also have an important reference in time, but they are not defined by time in the way that periods are. Thus, we may set a stage defined by agricultural cultures. In a certain area, this agricultural stage may follow a stage defined by hunting cultures, and the change from the one stage to the other in that area may have occurred in A.D. 100. However, in a neighboring area this changeover from a hunting to an agricultural stage may have been delayed until A.D. 1000. The succession of stages in the two areas is the same, but the events which the device of stages would describe for the two areas would not be described by the same time period.

In an earlier work with Phillips, we outlined a series of New World culture stages, projecting these for all of the Americas.[4] These previous formulations, modified somewhat, are the basis for our present observations on the subject. Although this volume deals largely with Middle and North America, the stages set down here could also be applied to the prehistory of South America. Running in a general time order from earliest to latest, these stages are as follows: Lower Lithic, Upper Lithic, Proto-Archaic, Full Archaic, and Agricultural. We will discuss each, briefly, in turn.[5]

Lower Lithic Stage. The name Lower Lithic follows terminology used in the Willey-Phillips presentation.[6] A. D. Krieger has applied the term "Pre-Projectile Point Stage" to the same data.[7]

The artifacts that characterize the stage are rough, percussion-flaked stone scrapers, choppers, and knives that we have discussed under our Period I and, in greater detail, in Chapter 2, pp. 29–33.[8] The inference is that these artifact assemblages were left by hunters and food-gatherers who were relatively unspecialized or left few traces of specialization in their manufactures or camp sites.

This stage, if it is accepted as such, is thought to have begun as early as our Period I (40,000–20,000 B.C.), and it may have lasted as late as Period III (15,000–8000 B.C.).

Upper Lithic Stage. This stage name, again, follows the terminology of the Willey-Phillips 1958 presentation.[9] Krieger called this same stage the "Paleo-Indian Stage."[10]

The primary archaeological criteria here were bifaced lanceolate projectile points, including the fluted forms of the Big-Game Hunting tradition and the leaf-shaped forms of the Old Cordilleran tradition, along with a variety of other chipped-stone artifacts such as the knives and skin-dressing tools of the hunter. Some bone tools and artifacts also were fashioned.

The definition of the stage we present here follows Krieger's modifications of the Willey-Phillips application of the Upper Lithic concept.[11] That is, the stage now pertains to cultures of our Period III (15,000–8000 B.C.), cultures of the Big-Game Hunting and Old Cordilleran cultural traditions. The Period IV (8000–5000 B.C.) continuities of the Big-Game Hunting tradition in the Plains, which in the 1958 formulation were included as Upper Lithic, now fall within the succeeding Proto-Archaic stage.

I agree with Krieger's arguments for making such a change; the late Big-Game Hunting tradition cultures of the Plains were characterized quite frequently by food-grinding implements as well as hunting gear.

The Upper Lithic stage also subsumes Middle and South American complexes which relate to the Big-Game Hunting or Old Cordilleran traditions. Probably it should also pertain to those hypothetical complexes of Period II (20,000–15,000 B.C.) which may contain lanceolate points.

Proto-Archaic Stage. The criteria of this stage were food-grinding implements: milling stones, handstones, and mortars and pestles. These have been found in contexts which indicate that seed-collecting activities were an important part of the subsistence economy. Hunting was carried over from the preceding stage, varying according to natural environmental circumstances.

The Proto-Archaic stage as so conceived began during our Period IV (8000–5000 B.C.) and pertains especially to cultural complexes of the Desert and Archaic traditions during this period. As we mentioned, and following Krieger's reasoning, the later complexes of the Big-Game Hunting tradition of the North American Plains also are included in this stage.[12]

Although most cultures attributed to the stage fall into the 8000–5000 B.C. time period, some persisted later. Examples would be Desert tradition cultures of the Great Basin and Baja California areas which date later than 5000 B.C. or post-5000 B.C. cultures of the Desert-Archaic tradition of the Northeast Mexico-Texas area.

Full Archaic Stage. Polished-stone artifacts—axes, celts, adzes, vessels, pipes, various weights, and ceremonial objects—and general indications of a more successfully adapted subsistence economy than had developed during the Proto-Archaic stage are criteria of the Full Archaic. Sites were larger and contained deeper concentrations of refuse than in prior stages, indicating a more sedentary life, larger groups, or both.

As defined, the stage first appears in what we have designated as Period V (5000–2000 B.C.). It was particularly well expressed in the Archaic tradition cultures of the Eastern Woodlands and in the California Coast and Valley tradition.

The Full Archaic stage lasts, in some places, through Period VI (2000 B.C.–A.D. 1500) and into Period VII (A.D. 1500–Present). Notable examples would be the Archaic or Boreal Archaic tradition cultures of the Eastern Subarctic, the California Coast and Valley tradition cultures, those of the Northwest Coast and Northwest Riverine traditions, and the Eskimo and Denetasiro cultures of the Arctic and western Subarctic.

The use of the Full Archaic stage concept here is taken from Willey and Phillips, with Krieger's suggested revisions.[13]

Agricultural Stage. This stage embraces cultures sustained primarily by growing cultivated food plants.[14]

The appearance of cultigens under conditions where these were not the primary basis of subsistence is not sufficient to define the stage. Thus the incipient cultivation practices of the Desert tradition cultures of the Mesoamerican or Southwest areas remain within contexts classified on the Proto-Archaic or Full Archaic stages.

Sedentary village life appeared as a concomitant of the Agricultural stage condition in many places, although some non-agricultural Full Archaic stage cultures also were characterized by sedentary village communities.

Pottery accompanied all the Agricultural stage cultures of North and Middle America, as well as those of South America; but pottery also occurred in some Full Archaic contexts.

In North and Middle America the Mesoamerican, Southwestern, Mississippian, and Plains Village traditions belong in the Agricultural stage. The Woodland tradition is more difficult to appraise, but in some of its phases is on this level.

In absolute time, the Agricultural stage is a phenomenon of Periods VI (2000 B.C.–A.D. 1500) and VII (A.D. 1500–Present).

In the Willey-Phillips presentation of New World culture stages, what is here designated as the Agricultural stage was divided into three sequent parts: a *Formative* stage, a *Classic* stage, and a *Postclassic* stage. This subdivision derived from considerations of Mesoamerican and Peruvian cultures. As far as the present volume is concerned, the two later stages pertain only to the Mesoamerican area. They are based on criteria of urban population concentrations, other aspects of city life, and the rise of large-scale territorial states and militarism.[15]

Concluding Remarks

In this summary chapter I have tried to bring together not only the highlights of substantive data on New World prehistory but a recapitulation of the methodology involved throughout the book. This methodology was referred to briefly in the first chapter. We mentioned then that our principal vehicle of presentation was to be the major cultural traditions of native America. These are the historic continuities, the unique patterns or ways of life which have persisted through long periods of time in the New World. They are, in a sense, generic units in that the various cultures and phases of culture which may be grouped together in a tradition are related one to another. We have defined sixteen such major traditions for North and Middle America.[16] The histories of these sixteen cultural traditions make up the body of this work. They are reviewed in this chapter.

We have followed out the histories of the major cultural traditions by plotting them in geographic space. To do this we used the basic concept of the culture area. Twelve such culture areas were defined for North and Middle America.[17] Each of these were, on occasion, subdivided into subareas, regions, and localities. This was done on a selective rather than on a comprehensive basis. In examining the major cultural traditions in the settings of culture areas, some pains were taken to point out cultural-environmental relationships.

Within each culture area the histories of the cultural traditions were plotted out through time by means of chronologies. These chronologies or sequences of periods were examined for individual archaeological sites, for localities, regions, subareas, and entire areas. This, again, could not be done systematically and comprehensively but was, instead, selective. We attempted, however, to give both a general area picture of culture development through time as well as to substantiate this with localized, specific examples. In this summary we have carried this chronological examination of the cultural traditions farther by projecting the major traditions of North and Middle America on continental-wide time charts (Figs. 8-1, 8-2). In so doing, we reviewed the correlation of cultural traditional histories in the frameworks of individual area chronologies. We then devised seven major time periods, each established with reference to absolute dates, in which to describe cultural events throughout North and Middle America.

Lastly, and for the first time in the book, we set forth five major cultural stages by which New World culture history could be recapitulated. These major culture stages, which may also be applied to South America, cross-cut the cultural traditions, culture areas, and chronological periods. They are defined not by the lines of historical relationships nor strictly by the horizon lines of chronology but by general cultural type. The dynamics of their development are, to be sure, sometimes found in diffusion and historical interrelationships. They are also to be found in the interactions of technology and environment, in the relationships of these two factors to demographic changes, and in the momentum of cultural development.[18]

Throughout this book the basic, life-giving circumstances of technology, environment, and subsistence have been emphasized. These strands of human history may have been over-emphasized. As we mentioned in the beginning, this is a one-sidedness peculiar to archaeology and deriving out of the very nature of its data. But until archaeologists can follow more surely, other equally important and more humanly appealing strands of man's endeavor from the distant past, it remains our limitation. Ethnohistory and ethnology are the disciplines that will enable the American archaeologist to transcend this limitation; however, the archaeologist must also develop methods and theories of his own—particularly methods and theories in the realm of general comparative analogy.[19] American archaeology of the future undoubtedly will march forward swiftly with inquiry into areas as yet little known, with greater chronological control, and with more precise comparative methods; yet its greatest victories remain to be achieved through sound interpretation of the life that is past by analogy with the life of the living.

Footnotes

[1]In the Anasazi subarea Cochise-related cultures, such as the San Jose, precede the Basketmaker II phase of the Southwestern tradition. In the Patayan sequence column a *Lake Mojave phase* would correspond in time with the Paleo-Indian Period for the rest of the Southwest. The closest affiliations of the Lake Mojave culture are with the Old Cordilleran and Desert traditions. In this sequence Lake Mojave would be succeeded by a *Pinto Basin phase,* definitely a part of the Desert tradition. The Pinto Basin phase would parallel, in time, the Cochise culture of the Mogollon and Hohokam subareas (7000–1000 B.C.). It would be succeeded by an *Amargosa phase,* still within the Desert tradition, which lasted from 1000 B.C. until A.D. 650. At A.D. 650 the sequence takes up with the three periods: *Patayan I, Patayan II, Patayan III.* The last of these runs to the historic horizon, and all fall within the Southwestern cultural tradition.

[2]Depending on where the line is drawn between the Northeastern subarea of the Eastern Woodlands and the eastern Subarctic, Woodland tradition pottery may be found on late prehistoric sites. (Byers, 1959). Most of the eastern Subarctic, however, lies north of the distribution of pottery.

[3]The Paleo-Indian, Meso-Indian, Neo-Indian scheme may be applied either in a *period* or a *stage* sense. Sometimes there is ambiguity on this distinction. A. G. Smith (1957), who propounds it, refers to these concepts as ". . . major time periods, or culture stages."

[4]Willey and Phillips (1955, 1958).

[5]The reader should also consult Beardsley and his associates (1956), Hester (1962), and Krieger (1964) for further considerations of New World culture stages.

[6]Willey and Phillips (1958, pp. 79–86).

[7]Krieger (1964).

[8]See also Krieger (1964).

[9]Willey and Phillips (1958, pp. 86–103).

[10]Krieger (1964).

[11]Krieger (1964); Willey and Phillips (1958, pp. 86–103).

[12]Krieger (1964).

[13]Willey and Phillips (1958, pp. 104–143); Krieger (1964).

[14]In our earlier consideration of New World stages (Willey and Phillips, 1955), the criterion of agriculture or a successful agricultural economy sustaining sedentary village life was taken as diagnostic for the formative stage. Later (Willey and Phillips, 1958, pp. 144–147), we revised this, making agriculture or any other form of subsistence capable of sustaining settled village life the criterion. Or in other words, the degree of sedentism, as expressed in permanent villages, was the stage diagnostic. Here I have returned to the original formulation and have, in fact, referred to the stage as "Agricultural." This is not to deny that settled village life was possible with a Full Archaic stage subsistence. This, indeed, occurred in the Americas (see Willey and Phillips, 1958). It is rather that agriculture was the dynamic of the new stage that had great potential—a potential over and beyond that of the richest Full Archaic stage economy. The later substages (Classic and Postclassic) of the Agricultural stage in Mesoamerica, substages which did not occur elsewhere in North America, are testimony to this potential. In considering this problem, refer to Hester (1962).

[15]Willey and Phillips (1958, pp. 182–199). See also Steward (1948, 1955).

[16]These are: (1) the Big-Game Hunting; (2) the Old Cordilleran; (3) the Desert; (4) the Archaic; (5) the Mesoamerican; (6) the Southwestern; (7) the Woodland; (8) the Mississippian; (9) the Plains Village; (10) the California Coast and Valley; (11) the Northwest Coast; (12) the Northwest Riverine; (13) the Northwest Microblade; (14) the Arctic Small-Tool; (15) the Eskimo; and (16) the Denetasiro. Significant variants of some of these traditions might also be counted as separate traditions: the Desert-Archaic blend of the Northeast Mexico-Texas area; the Boreal Archaic of the eastern Subarctic; the Mexican Highland Desert tradition variant; and the Baja California Desert tradition variant.

[17]These are: (1) Mesoamerica; (2) the Southwest; (3) the Eastern Woodlands; (4) the Plains; (5) Northeast Mexico-Texas; (6) the Great Basin; (7) Baja California; (8) California; (9) the Northwest Coast; (10) the Interior Plateau; (11) the Subarctic; and (12) the Arctic. Of these, the Subarctic could be split into eastern and western divisions.

[18]The reader's attention is also called to various other summary works of New World prehistory. For example, see Willey (1960 a, 1960 b); Griffin (1953); Armillas (1956); Meggers (1963, 1964); and Bernal (1964 b).

[19]See, for example, Binford (1962).

Glossary

Bannerstone: A stone atlatl, or throwing-stick weight, placed on the stick shaft to give greater propulsive force to a thrown dart. The stone is perforated for hafting and often has a bi-pennate, "butterfly," or banner-like appearance.

Bar-gorget: Bar-like ornament(?), usually of polished stone and perforated; worn suspended around the neck(?).

Blow-outs: Concavities or depressions in the earth caused by the wind-removal or erosion of sandy or soft soils.

Boatstone: A boat-shaped stone used as an atlatl, or throwing-stick weight. (See *bannerstone.*) Unlike the bannerstone, it was apparently lashed to the stick shaft.

Bolas: Grooved stones attached to the opposite ends of a section of cord or thong, which, when thrown, entangled the legs or wings of animals or birds.

Brachycephalic, brachycranic: Physical anthropological terms meaning broad-headed (i.e., the maximum width of the cranium being 80% or more of the maximum length).

Breccia: A geological term referring to rock composed of angular fragments cemented together.

Bundle burial: A form of secondary burial in which the bones of the deceased are gathered together and interred in a non-articulated pile or bundle. (See *Secondary burial.*)

Burin: A flint implement used for engraving bone, characterized by a small beak or point which was fashioned by chipping.

Caliche: A calcareous conglomeritic gravel typical of the desert basins of southern Arizona.

Caryatid: A supporting base (as in architecture) of columns fashioned as human figures.

Celt: An ungrooved axe blade.

Chert: A dark, impure, flintlike rock.

Couvade: A custom, practiced by many primitive tribes of the world, in which the father of a new-born child takes to "confinement" or seclusion for a specified period at the time of birth.

Dendrochronology: The science of the comparative study of tree-rings to determine the age of trees, beams, or other timbers.

Diatomaceous: Referring to soils containing diatomaceae, or minute fossil plants. Such soils are freshwater or marine sediments.

Disconformity: A geological term referring to a weathered surface of a soil or rock stratum covered by an overlying stratum. The disconformity of the two strata, occasioned by the weathered surface of the older stratum, indicates a lapse of time before the deposition of the younger stratum.

Dolichocephalic, dolichocranic: Physical anthropological terms meaning long-headed (i.e., the maximum width of the cranium being 75% or less of the maximum length).

Epicanthic fold: The skin and flesh immediately above the upper eyelid.

Ethno-historic: Pertaining to ethnographic or ethnological data at the historic period.

Glottochronology: Science of the comparative study of language vocabularies for measuring linguistic change through absolute time.

Gorge: Usually a bipointed object of bone (although other materials may be used) which was tied to a fishline and which caught in the fish's mouth.

Guardapúa: Pointed wooden implement, possibly used in ritual blood-letting.

Guilloche: A pattern made by interlacing curved lines.

Hematite: An iron-ore mineral.

Interstadial: A term used in glacial geology to refer to periods or eras between stages of glaciation or glacial advance.

Jacal: A type of house construction in which walls are made of poles coated with mud plaster.

Labret: A lip-plug or ornament inserted in an incision in the lower lip.

Lacustrine: Of or pertaining to lakes.

Lanceolate: Lance-shaped, referring to projectile points.

Laterite: Soils rich in alumina and iron oxides, as in tropical areas. Such soils are usually reddish in color.

"Lost-wax" (or *cire perdue*): A method of casting metals in which the desired form was carved in wax, coated with charcoal and clay, and then the wax replaced by pouring molten metal into the casing of clay.

Mano: A handstone used in a metate for grinding seeds, usually maize. (See *Metate*.)

Mesocephalic: A physical anthropological term meaning "medium-headed" (i.e., the maximum width of the cranium being between 75% and 80% of the length). (See *Brachycephalic* and *Dolichocephalic*.)

Metate: A stone trough-like basin used for grinding seeds, usually maize. (See *Mano*.)

Midden: A refuse heap marking a former human habitation area. Midden debris usually contains decayed organic material, bone-scrap, artifacts (broken and whole), and miscellaneous detritus.

Milpa: Usually refers to an agricultural technique whereby forest vegetation is cut down annually and burned in place to prepare fields for crops. A term used particularly in Latin America. (See *Swidden*.) However, its actual derivation is Nahuatl, and in this language it means any field where maize is cultivated regardless of the system of farming.

Negative painting: A technique of painting (usually pottery surfaces) in which a design area is covered with a paint resistant substance (probably a gum or wax), after which the vessel surface is dipped in paint or dye, dried, and fired. After firing, the design area that had been covered with the resistant substance stands out, in the lighter ground color of the vessel, in contrast to the areas covered with the paint or pigment. The technique is also known as "resist-dye."

Olivella: A marine univalve genus; a small spiral shell.

Ossuary: A charnel house or a place where bones of the dead are kept or deposited.

Paramos: Wet grasslands or forests at high elevations.

Peneplain: A geological term referring to a region that is almost a plain (e.g., a low, fan-like deposition or outwash at the mouth of a ravine).

Phenotype: A biological type determined by the visible characters common to a group as distinguished from their hereditary characters.

Plinth: An architectural term referring to the lowest member of a base.

Podzols: Leached, acid soils formed under conditions of boreal or northern forest vegetation cover.

Positive painting: The direct application of a design by use of pigments (as in painting pottery). (See *Negative painting*.)

Pre-ceramic: Before ceramics, referring to a period antedating the use of ceramics or pottery.

Primary burial: Direct inhumation of the fully articulated corpse. (See *Secondary burial*.)

Prognathic: A physical anthropological term referring to the forward projection, beyond the vertical plane, of the alveolar process and mandible (mouth area).

Rebus writing: A mode of expressing words and phrases by pictures of objects whose names resemble those words or the syllables of which they are composed.

Secondary burial: Burial of a dismembered corpse. In American archaeology it frequently refers to human remains which have been exposed to decay, after which the bones are cleaned and buried. (See *Primary burial; Bundle burial*.)

Self pipe: Smoking pipe in which a stem, which is a part of the stone or clay of the pipe, is inserted into the mouth of the smoker. This is in contradistinction to stone or clay pipe bowls which were made for the insertion of a reed or wooden stem.

Sipapu: The hole in a kiva floor which symbolized the mythical entrance to the underground chamber of origin of a people (Southwestern United States native mythology and archaeology).

Stela, stelae: Singular and plural of a stone column monument.

Stone-boiling: Cooking that is done by heating stones and placing them in the liquid or substance to be cooked. This is often done in baskets or containers that cannot be placed directly in or over a fire.

Sweat-house: A special building for taking sweat-baths. It usually features a fire-area for heating stones. Water is then poured over the stones to produce steam.

Swidden: An agricultural technique whereby forest vegetation is cut down annually and burned in place to prepare fields for crops. The system is called *milpa* in Latin America.

Tablero-talud: A special architectural term referring to a sloped basal apron surmounted by a recessed vertical tablet.

Tang: Projectile, spear, or knife stem or handle.

Travertine: A limestone deposition that has been formed by limestone in solution (e.g., the stalactites and stalagmites in limestone caves).

Travois: A carrying device dragged along the ground on two poles behind a dog or a horse. The opposite ends of the poles are attached to the body of the animal.

Ulu: A crescent-shaped knife, usually of slate, in which the blade of the knife is the lower element of an inverted T and the handle the vertical upright element.

Yuguito: A carved stone, presumably a replication of a wooden yoke-section, used in the ceremonial ballgames.

Ackerman, R. E. (1962), "Culture Contact in the Bering Sea: Birnirk-Punuk Period," in *Prehistoric Cultural Relations Between the Arctic and Temperate Zones of North America,* J. M. Campbell, ed., Technical Paper No. 11, pp. 27–34, Arctic Institute of North America, Montreal.

Acosta, J. R. (1956), "Resumen de las Exploraciónes Arqueológicas en Tula, Hidalgo, durante los VI, VII y VIII Temporadas, 1946–1950," *Anales,* Vol. 8, pp. 37–116, Memorias del Instituto Nacional de Antropología e Historia, Mexico, D.F.

Adams, R. M. (1961), "Changing Patterns of Territorial Organization in the Central Highlands of Chiapas, Mexico," *American Antiquity,* Vol. 26, No. 3, pp. 341–360, Salt Lake City.

Agogino, G. A. (1960), "The San Jose Sites: A Cochise-like Manifestation in the Middle Rio Grande," *Southwestern Lore,* Vol. 26, No. 2, pp. 43–48.

Agogino, G. A. (1961), "A New Point Type from Hell Gap Valley, Eastern Wyoming," *American Antiquity,* Vol. 26, No. 4, pp. 558–560, Salt Lake City.

Agogino, G. A. (1963), "The Paleo Indian in North America," *Genus,* Vol. 19, Nos. 1–4, pp. 3–17, Rome.

Alexander, H. L., Jr. (1963), "The Levi Site: A Paleo-Indian Campsite in Central Texas," *American Antiquity,* Vol. 28, No. 4, pp. 510–528, Salt Lake City.

Amsden, C. A. (1937), "The Lake Mohave Artifacts," in *The Archaeology of Pleistocene Lake Mohave: A Symposium,* Southwest Museum Papers, No. 11, pp. 51–98, Los Angeles.

Andrews, E. W. (1960), "Excavations at Dzibilchaltún, Northwestern Yucatán, Mexico," *Proceedings, American Philosophical Society,* Vol. 104, No. 3, pp. 254–265, Philadelphia.

Andrews, E. W. (1961), *Preliminary Report on the 1959–60 Field Season, National Geographic Society—Tulane University, Dzibilchaltún Program,* Miscellaneous Series, No. 11, Middle American Research Institute, Tulane University, New Orleans.

Antevs, Ernst (1962), "Late Quarternary Climates in Arizona," *American Antiquity,* Vol. 28, No. 2, pp. 193–198, Salt Lake City.

Armillas, Pedro (1944), "Exploraciónes recientes en Teotihuacán, Mexico," *Cuadernos Americanos,* July-August, pp. 121–136, Mexico, D.F.

Bibliography

Armillas, Pedro (1948 a), "A Sequence of Cultural Development in Meso-America," in *A Reappraisal of Peruvian Archaeology,* W. C. Bennett, ed., pp. 105–112, Memoir No. 4, Society for American Archaeology, Menasha, Wisconsin.

Armillas, Pedro (1948 b), "Arqueológia del occidente de Guerrero," in *El Occidente de Mexico,* pp. 74–76, Mesa Redonda, Sociedad Mexicana de Antropología, Mexico, D.F.

Armillas, Pedro (1950), "Teotihuacán, Tula, y los Toltecas: Las Culturas Post-Arcaicas y Pre-Aztecas del Centro de Mexico—excavaciónes y estudios, 1922–50," *Runa,* Vol. 3, pp. 37–70, Buenos Aires.

Armillas, Pedro (1956), "Cronología y periodificación de la historia de la America precolombina," *Journal of World History,* Vol. 3, No. 2, pp. 463–503, Paris.

Armillas, Pedro (1964), "Northern Mesoamerica," in *Prehistoric Man in the New World,* J. D. Jennings and E. Norbeck, eds., pp. 291–330, University of Chicago Press, Chicago.

Ascher, Robert (1961), "Analogy in Archaeological Interpretation," *Southwestern Journal of Anthropology,* Vol. 17, pp. 317–325, Albuquerque.

Aschmann, Homer (1952), "A Fluted Point from Baja California," *American Antiquity,* Vol. 17, pp. 262, Salt Lake City.

Arnold, B. A. (1957), *Late Pleistocene and Recent Changes in Land Forms, Climate, and Archaeology in Central Baja California,* University of California Publications in Geography, Vol. 10, No. 4, Berkeley and Los Angeles.

Aveleyra Arroyo de Anda, Luis (1956), "The Second Mammoth and Associated Artifacts at Santa Isabel Iztapán, Mexico," *American Antiquity,* Vol. 22, No. 1, pp. 12–28, Salt Lake City.

Aveleyra Arroyo de Anda, Luis (1961), "El Primer hallazgo Folsom en territorio Mexicano y su relación con el complejo de puntas acanaladas en Norteamerica," *Homenaje a Pablo Martinez del Rio,* pp. 31–48, Instituto Nacional de Antropología e Historia, Mexico, D.F.

Aveleyra Arroyo de Anda, Luis (1962), *Antigüedad del Hombre en Mexico y Centroamerica: Catálogo Razonado de Localidades y Bibliografía Selecta (1867–1961),* Cuadernos del Instituto de Historia, Serie Antropológica No. 14, Universidad Nacional Autonoma de Mexico, Mexico, D.F.

Aveleyra Arroyo de Anda, Luis (1963), "An Extraordinary Composite Stela from Teotihuacán," *American Antiquity,* Vol. 29, No. 2, pp. 235–237, Salt Lake City.

Aveleyra Arroyo de Anda, Luis (1964), "Sobre dos fechas de radiocarbono 14 para la Cueva de la Candelaria, Coahuila," *Anales de Antropología,* Vol. 1, pp. 125–130, Instituto de Investigaciónes Historicas, Universidad Nacional Autonoma de Mexico.

Aveleyra Arroyo de Anda, Luis and Manuel Maldonado-Koerdell (1953), "Association of Artifacts with Mammoth in the Valley of Mexico," *American Antiquity,* Vol. 18, No. 4, pp. 332–340, Salt Lake City.

Aveleyra Arroyo de Anda, Luis, Manuel Maldonado-Koerdell, and Pablo Martinez del Rio (1956), "Cueva de la Candelaria," Vol. 1, *Anales,* Vol. 5, Memorias del Instituto Nacional de Antropología e Historia, Mexico, D.F.

Baerreis, D. A. (1951), *Preceramic Horizons in Northeastern Oklahoma,* Anthropological Paper, No. 6, Museum of Anthropology, University of Michigan, Ann Arbor.

Baerreis, D. A. (1959), "The Archaic as Seen from the Ozark Region," *American Antiquity,* Vol. 24, No. 3, pp. 270–275, Salt Lake City.

Bandelier, A. F. (1878), *On the Distribution and Tenure of Lands, and the Customs with Respect to Inheritance, Among the Ancient Mexicans,* 11th Annual Report, Vol. 2, pp. 385–448, Peabody Museum, Cambridge.

Bandelier, A. F. (1880), *On the Social Organization and Mode of Government of the Ancient Mexicans,* 12th Annual Report, Vol. 2, pp. 557–699, Peabody Museum, Cambridge.

Barbour, E. H. and C. B. Schultz (1932), *The Scottsbluff Bison Quarry and Its Artifacts,* Bulletin 34, Vol. 1, Nebraska State Museum, Lincoln.

Barrett, S. A. (1933), *Ancient Aztalan,* Bulletin 13, Milwaukee Public Museum, Milwaukee.

Bartlett, Katherine (1943), "A Primitive Stone Industry of the Little Colorado Valley, Arizona," *American Antiquity,* Vol. 8, No. 3, pp. 266–268, Menasha, Wisconsin.

Batres, Leopoldo (1903), *Visita a los Monumentos Arqueológicos de "La Quemada," Zacatecas,* Inspección y Conservación de Monumentos Arqueológicas de la Republica Mexicana, Mexico, D.F.

Baudez, C. F. (1962), "Rapport Préliminaire sur les Recherches Archéologiques Entreprises dans la Vallée du Tempisque, Guanacaste, Costa Rica," *Proceedings, 34th International Congress of Americanists,* pp. 348–357, Vienna.

Baudez, C. F. (1963), "Cultural Development in Lower Central America," in *Aboriginal Cultural Development in Latin America: An Interpretative Review,* B. J. Meggers and C. Evans eds., Smithsonian Miscellaneous Collections, Vol. 146, No. 1, pp. 45–54, Smithsonian Institution, Washington, D.C.

486

Baudez, C. F. and M. D. Coe (1962), "Archaeological Sequences in Northwestern Costa Rica," *Proceedings,* 34th International Congress of Americanists, pp. 366–373, Vienna.

Baumhoff, M. A. and R. F. Heizer (1965), "Postglacial Climates and Archaeology in the Desert West," *The Quaternary of the United States,* H. E. Wright and D. G. Frey, eds., pp. 697–708, 7th Congress of the International Association for Quaternary Research, Princeton University Press, Princeton.

Beals, R. L. (1934), *Material Culture of the Pima, Papago, and Western Apache,* United States Department of Interior, National Park Service, Field Division of Education, Berkeley, California.

Beardsley, R. K. (1948), "Culture Sequences in Central California," *American Antiquity,* Vol. 14, No. 1, pp. 1–28, Menasha, Wisconsin.

Beardsley, R. K., *et al.* (1956), "Functional and Evolutionary Implications of Community Patterning," in *Seminars in Archaeology: 1955,* R. Wauchope, ed., Memoir No. 11, Society for American Archaeology, Salt Lake City.

Bell, R. E. (1960), "Evidences of a Fluted Point Tradition in Ecuador," *American Antiquity,* Vol. 26, pp. 102–106, Salt Lake City.

Bell, R. E. (1963), *Archaeological Investigations at the Site of El Inga, Ecuador,* Mimeographed MS., Department of Anthropology, University of Oklahoma, Norman.

Bell, R. E. and D. A. Baerreis, (1951), *A Survey of Oklahoma Archaeology,* Bulletin, Vol. 22, pp. 7–100, Texas Archaeological and Paleontological Society, Lubbock.

Bennett, J. W. (1952), "The Prehistory of the Northern Mississippi Valley," in *Archaeology of Eastern United States,* J. B. Griffin, ed., pp. 108–123, University of Chicago Press, Chicago.

Bennyhoff, J. A. (1958), "The Desert West: A Trial Correlation of Culture and Chronology," in *Current Views on Great Basin Archaeology,* University of California Archaeological Survey Report, No. 42, pp. 98–113, Berkeley.

Berlin, Heinrich (1952), "Excavaciones en Kaminaljuyú; Monticulo D-III-13," *Ideah,* Vol. 4, No. 1, Instituto de Antropología e Historia de Guatemala, Guatemala City.

Bernal, Ignacio (1949 a), *La Ceramica de Monte Albán IIIA,* Ph.D. thesis, University of Mexico, Mexico, D.F.

Bernal, Ignacio (1949 b), "Distribución geográfica de las culturas de Monte Albán," *El Mexico Antiguo,* Vol. 7, pp. 209–216, Mexico, D.F.

Bernal, Ignacio (1958 a), *Monte Alban and the Zapotecs,* Boletín de Estudios Oaxaqueños, No. 1, Mexico City College, Mexico, D.F.

Bernal, Ignacio (1958 b), *Archaeology of the Mixteca,* Boletín de Estudios Oaxaqueños, No. 7, Oaxaca, Mexico.

Bernal, Ignacio (1959), *Tenochtitlán en Una Isla,* Serie Historia II, Instituto Nacional de Antropología e Historia, Mexico, D.F.

Bernal, Ignacio (1964 a), "Arqueología Mixteca del Valle de Oaxaca," *Proceedings, 35th International Congress of Americanists,* Vol. 1, pp. 453–461, Mexico, D.F.

Bernal, Ignacio (1964 b), "Concluding Remarks," in *Prehistoric Man in the New World,* J. D. Jennings and E. Norbeck, eds., pp. 559–566, University of Chicago Press, Chicago.

Bernal, Ignacio and Eusebio Davalos Hurtado (1953), "Huastecos, Totonacos y Sus Vecinos," *Revista Mexicana de Estudios Antropológicos,* Vol. 13, Nos. 2–3, Mexico, D.F.

Beyer, Hermann (1933), *Shell Ornament Sets from the Huaxteca, Mexico,* Middle American Research Series, No. 5, Tulane University, New Orleans.

Binford, L. R. (1962), "Archaeology as Anthropology," *American Antiquity,* Vol. 28, No. 2, pp. 217–225, Salt Lake City.

Bird, J. B. (1938), "Antiquity and Migrations of the Early Inhabitants of Patagonia," *Geographical Review,* Vol. 28, No. 2, pp. 250–275, New York.

Bird, J. B. (1945), *Archaeology of the Hopedale Area, Labrador,* Anthropological Papers, Vol. 39, Pt. 2, American Museum of Natural History, New York.

Bird, J. B. (1946), "The Archaeology of Patagonia," in *Handbook of South American Indians,* J. H. Steward, ed., Vol. 1, pp. 17–24, Bureau of American Ethnology, Bulletin 143, Smithsonian Institution, Washington, D.C.

Bird, J. B. (1948), "Preceramic Cultures in Chicama and Viru," in *A Reappraisal of Peruvian Archaeology,* W. C. Bennett, ed., Memoir No. 4, pp. 21–28, Society for American Archaeology, Menasha, Wisconsin.

Birdsell, J. B. (1951), "The Problem of the Early Peopling of the Americas as Viewed from Asia," in *Papers on the Physical Anthropology of the American Indian,* W. S. Laughlin, ed., pp. 1–68, Viking Fund., New York.

Black, F. and W. S. Laughlin (1964), "Anangula: A Geologic Interpretation of the Oldest Archeologic Site in the Aleutians," *Science,* Vol. 143, pp. 1321–1322, Washington, D.C.

Blom, Frans (1932), *The Maya Ball-Game Pok-ta-pok, Called Tlachtli by the Aztec,* Middle American Research Series, No. 4, pp. 485–

530, Tulane University, New Orleans.

Boas, Franz (1905), "The Jesup North Pacific Expedition," *Proceedings, 13th International Congress of Americanists,* pp. 91–100, New York.

Boas, Franz (1933), "Relations Between Northwest America and Northeast Asia," in *The American Aborigines,* pp. 357–370, Toronto.

Boos, F. H. (1964), "An Analysis and Classification of the Oaxacan Urns in the Collection of the Museum für Völkerkunde Leipzig," *Jahrbuch des Museums für Volkerkunde zu Leipzig,* Band 20, pp. 360–373, Akademie-Verlag, Berlin.

Bopp-Oeste, G. (1961), "El análisis de polen con referencia especial a dos perfiles polinicos de la Cuenca de Mexico," *Homenaje a Pablo Martinez del Rio,* pp. 49–57, Instituto Nacional de Antropología e Historia, Mexico, D.F.

Borden, C. E. (1950), "Preliminary Report on Archaeological Investigations in the Fraser Delta Region," *Anthropology in British Columbia,* No. 1, pp. 13–27, British Columbia Provincial Museum, Victoria, B.C.

Borden, C. E. (1951), "Facts and Problems of Northwest Coast Prehistory," *Anthropology in British Columbia,* No. 2, pp. 35–52, British Columbia Provincial Museum, Victoria, B.C.

Borden, C. E. (1953–54), "Some Aspects of Prehistoric Coastal-Interior Relations in the Pacific Northwest," *Anthropology in British Columbia,* No. 4, pp. 26–32, British Columbia Provincial Museum, Victoria, B.C.

Borden, C. E. (1960), *DjRi 3, an Early Site in the Fraser Canyon, British Columbia,* Bulletin 162, pp. 101–118, National Museum of Canada, Ottawa.

Borden, C. E. (1961), *Fraser River Archaeological Project, Progress Report, April 20, 1961,* Anthropology Papers, No. 1, pp. 1–6, National Museum of Canada, Ottawa.

Borden, C. E. (1962), "West Coast Crossties with Alaska," in *Prehistoric Cultural Relations Between the Arctic and Temperate Zones of North America,* J. M. Campbell, ed., Technical Paper No. 11, pp. 9–19, Arctic Institute of North America, Montreal.

Borden, C. E. (1964), "Archaeology in British Columbia," MS., to be published as chapter in a general book, *Archaeology in Canada,* Canadian National Museum, Ottawa.

Bradfield, Wesley (1931), *Cameron Creek Village: A Site in the Mimbres Area in Grant County, New Mexico,* Monograph No. 1, School of American Research, Santa Fe.

Brainerd, G. W. (1951), "Early Ceramic Horizons in Yucatán," *Selected Papers, 29th International Congress of Americanists, Vol. 1, The Civilizations of Ancient America,* S. Tax, ed., pp. 72–78, University of Chicago Press, Chicago.

Brainerd, G. W. (1954), *The Maya Civilization,* Southwest Museum, Los Angeles.

Brainerd, G. W. (1958), *The Archaeological Ceramics of Yucatán,* Anthropological Records, No. 19, University of California Press, Berkeley and Los Angeles.

Brew, J. O. (1946), *Archaeology of Alkali Ridge, Southeastern Utah.* Peabody Museum Papers, Vol. 21, Harvard University, Cambridge.

Brush, C. F. (1965), "Pox Pottery: Earliest Identified Mexican Ceramic," *Science,* Vol. 149, pp. 194–195, Lancaster.

Bryan, A. L. (1962), "Paleo-American Culture History—A New Interpretation," MS., thesis submitted for Ph.D. degree, Harvard University, Cambridge.

Bryan, Alan L. (1964), "New Evidence Concerning Early Man in North America," *Man,* September-October 1964, No. 186, pp. 152–153, London.

Bryan, Alan L. and Ruth Gruhn (1964), "Problems Relating to the Neothermal Climatic Sequence," *American Antiquity,* Vol. 29, No. 3, Salt Lake City.

Bryan, Kirk (1941), "Pre-Columbian Agriculture in the Southwest as Conditioned by Periods of Alluviation," *Annals,* Vol. 31, No. 4, pp. 219–242, Association of American Geographers, New York.

Bryan, Kirk and J. H. Toulouse, Jr. (1943), "San José Non-Ceramic Culture and Its Relation to a Puebloan Culture in New Mexico," *American Antiquity,* Vol. 8, No. 3, pp. 269–280, Menasha, Wisconsin.

Bullard, W. R., Jr. (1960), "The Maya Settlement Pattern in Northeastern Peten, Guatemala," *American Antiquity,* Vol. 25, pp. 355–372, Salt Lake City.

Bullard, W. R., Jr. (1962), *The Cerro Colorado Site and Pithouse Architecture in the Southwestern United States Prior to A.D. 900,* Peabody Museum Papers, Vol. 44, No. 2, Harvard University, Cambridge.

Bullen, R. P. (1961), "Radiocarbon Dates for Southeastern Fiber-Tempered Pottery," *American Antiquity,* Vol. 27, No. 1, pp. 104–106, Salt Lake City.

Bullen, R. P. and W. W. Plowden, Jr. (1963), "Preceramic Archaic Sites in the Highlands of Honduras," *American Antiquity,* Vol. 28, No. 3, pp. 382–386, Salt Lake City.

Bushnell, G. H. S. and Charles McBurney (1959), "New World Origins Seen from the Old World," *Antiquity,* Vol. 33, pp. 93–101, London.

Butler, B. R. (1959), "Lower Columbia Valley Archaeology: A Survey and Appraisal of Some Major Archaeological Resources," *Tebiwa,* Vol. 2, No. 2, pp. 6–24, Idaho State University Museum, Pocatello.

Butler, B. R. (1961), *The Old Cordilleran Culture in the Pacific Northwest*, Occasional Papers, No. 5. Idaho State University Museum, Pocatello.

Butler, B. R. (1965), "Perspectives on the Prehistory of the Lower Columbia Valleys," *Tebiwa*, Vol. 8, No. 1, pp. 1–16, Idaho State University Museum, Pocatello.

Byers, D. S. (1954), "Bull Brook—A Fluted Point Site in Ipswich, Massachusetts," *American Antiquity*, Vol. 19, No. 4, pp. 343–351, Salt Lake City.

Byers, D. S. (1955), "Additional Information on the Bull Brook Site, Massachusetts," *American Antiquity*, Vol. 20, No. 3, pp. 274–276, Salt Lake City.

Byers, D. S. (1959), "The Eastern Archaic: Some Problems and Hypotheses," *American Antiquity*, Vol. 24, pp. 233–256, Salt Lake City.

Byers, D. S. (1962), "New England and the Arctic," in *Prehistoric Cultural Relations Between the Arctic and Temperate Zones of North America*, J. M. Campbell, ed., Technical Paper No. 11, pp. 143–153, Arctic Institute of North America, Montreal.

Caldwell, J. R. (1954), "The Old Quartz Industry of Piedmont Georgia and South Carolina," *Southern Indian Studies*, Vol. 6, pp. 27–39, Chapel Hill, North Carolina.

Caldwell, J. R. (1958), *Trend and Tradition in the Prehistory of the Eastern United States*, Scientific Papers, Vol. 10, Illinois State Museum, Springfield, and Memoir 88, American Anthropological Association, Menasha, Wisconsin.

Caldwell, J. R. and Catherine McCann (1941), *Irene Mound Site, Chatham County, Georgia*, University of Georgia Press, Athens.

Cambron, J. W. and D. C. Hulse (1960), "An Excavation on the Quad Site," *Tennessee Archaeologist*, Vol. 16, pp. 14–26, Knoxville.

Cambron, J. W. and S. A. Waters (1959), "Flint Creek Rock Shelter, Pt. 1," *Tennessee Archaeologist*, Vol. 15, pp. 73–87, Knoxville.

Campbell, E. W. C. (1949), "Two Ancient Archaeological Sites in the Great Basin," *Science*, Vol. 109, p. 340, Washington, D.C.

Campbell, E. W. C. and W. H. (1935), *The Pinto Basin Site*, Southwest Museum Papers, No. 9, Los Angeles.

Campbell, E. W. C. and W. H. (1937), "The Lake Mohave Site," in *The Archaeology of Pleistocene Lake Mohave: A Symposium*, Southwest Museum Papers, No. 11, pp. 9–43, Los Angeles.

Campbell, J. M. (1961), "The Kogruk Complex of Anaktuvuk Pass, Alaska," *Anthropologia*, Vol. 3, No. 1, pp. 1–18, Ottawa.

Campbell, J. M. (1962), "Cultural Succession at Anaktuvuk Pass, Arctic Alaska," in *Prehistoric Cultural Relations Between Arctic and Temperate Zones of North America*, J. M. Campbell, ed., Technical Paper No. 11, pp. 39–54, Arctic Institute of North America, Montreal.

Campbell, T. N. (1947), *The Johnson Site: Type Site of the Aransas Focus of the Texas Coast*, Bulletin, Vol. 18, pp. 40–76. Texas Archaeological and Paleontological Society, Abilene.

Campbell, T. N. and J. Q. Frizzell (1949), *Notes on the Ayala Site, Lower Rio Grande Valley, Texas*, Bulletin, Vol. 20, pp. 63–72, Texas Archaeological and Paleontological Society, Abilene.

Canby, J. S. (1951), "Possible Chronological Implications of the Long Ceramic Sequence Recovered at Yarumela, Spanish Honduras," *Selected Papers, Vol. 1, 29th International Congress of Americanists, The Civilizations of Ancient America*, S. Tax, ed., pp. 79–85, University of Chicago Press, Chicago.

Capes, Katherine H. (1964), *Contributions to the Prehistory of Vancouver Island*, Occasional Papers, No. 15, Idaho State University Museum, Pocatello.

Cardich, Augusto (1958), *Los Yacimientos de Lauricocha: Nuevas Interpretaciónes de la Prehistória Peruana*, Studia Praehistorica I, Centro Argentino de Estudios Prehistóricos, Buenos Aires.

Cardich, Augusto (1960), "Investigaciónes Prehistóricas en los Andes Peruanos," in *Antiguo Peru: Tiempo y Espacio*, pp. 89–118, Libería-Editorial Juan Baca, Lima.

Carter, G. F. (1957), *Pleistocene Man at San Diego*, Johns Hopkins Press, Baltimore.

Caso, Alfonso (1938), *Exploraciónes en Oaxaca, Quinta y Sexta Temporadas, 1936–37*, Publicación 34, Instituto Pan-americano de Geografiá e Historia, Mexico, D.F.

Caso, Alfonso (1941), *Culturas Mixtecas y Zapotecas*, Biblioteca del Maestro, El Nacional, Mexico, D.F.

Caso, Alfonso (1947), *Calendario y Escritura de las Antiguas Culturas de Monte Albán*, Capítulo, como homenaje, en Obras Completas de Miguel Othon de Mendizábal, Mexico, D.F.

Caso, Alfonso (1953 a), "New World Culture History: Middle America," in *Anthropology Today*, A. L. Kroeber, *et al.*, eds., pp. 226–237, University of Chicago Press, Chicago.

Caso, Alfonso (1953 b), *El Pueblo del Sol*, Fondo Cultura Economica, Mexico, D.F.

Caso, Alfonso and Ignacio Bernal (1952), *Urnas de Oaxaca*, Vol. 2, Memorias del Instituto Nacional de Antropología e Historia, Mexico, D.F.

Champe, J. L. (1936), "The Sweetwater Culture Complex," in *Chapters in Nebraska Archaeology*, E. H. Bell, ed., Vol. I, Nos. 1–6, pp. 249–300, University of Nebraska, Lincoln.

Champe, J. L. (1949), "White Cat Village," *American Antiquity,* Vol. 14, No. 4, pp. 285–292, Menasha, Wisconsin.

Chard, C. S. (1959 a), "New World Origins: A Reappraisal," *Antiquity,* Vol. 33, No. 129, pp. 44–49, London and Tonbridge, Great Britain.

Chard, C. S. (1959 b), "Old World Sources for Early Lithic Cultures," *Actas del 33ra Congreso Internacional de Americanistas,* pp. 314–320, San Jose, Costa Rica.

Chard, C. S. (1963), *The Old World Roots: Review and Speculations,* Anthropological Papers, Vol. 10, No. 2, University of Alaska, Fairbanks.

Chard, C. S. (1961), "Invention Versus Diffusion: The Burial Mound Complex of the Eastern United States," *Southwestern Journal of Anthropology,* Vol. 17, pp. 21–25, Albuquerque.

Cigliano, E. M. (1961), "Noticia sobre una nueva industria precerámica en el Valle de Santa María (Catamarca): el Ampajanguense," *Anales de Arqueología y Etnología,* Vol. 16, pp. 169–179, Universidad Nacional de Cuyo, Mendoza, Argentina.

Claflin, W. H., Jr. (1931), *The Stalling's Island Mound, Columbia County, Georgia,* Papers, Vol. 14, No. 1, Peabody Museum, Harvard University, Cambridge.

Coe, J. L. (1952), "The Cultural Sequence of the Carolina Piedmont," in *Archaeology of Eastern United States,* J. B. Griffin, ed., pp. 301–311, University of Chicago Press, Chicago.

Coe, J. L. (1964), *The Formative Cultures of the Carolina Piedmont,* Transactions, Vol. 54, Pt. 5, American Philosophical Society, Philadelphia.

Coe, M. D. (1957), "Cycle 7 Monuments in Middle America: A Reconsideration," *American Anthropologist,* Vol. 59, pp. 597–611, Menasha, Wisconsin.

Coe, M. D. (1960 a), "Archaeological Linkages with North and South America at La Victoria, Guatemala," *American Anthropologist,* Vol. 62, No. 3, pp. 363–393, Menasha, Wisconsin.

Coe, M. D. (1960 b), "A Fluted Point from Highland Guatemala," *American Antiquity,* Vol. 25, pp. 412–413, Salt Lake City.

Coe, M. D. (1961), *La Victoria, an Early Site on the Pacific Coast of Guatemala,* Papers, Vol. 53, Peabody Museum, Harvard University, Cambridge.

Coe, M. D. (1962 a), *Mexico,* Ancient Peoples and Places, No. 29, G. Daniel, ed., Hazell Watson and Viney, Ltd., Aylesbury and Slough, Great Britain.

Coe, M. D. (1962 b), "Preliminary Report on Archaeological Investigations in Coastal Guanacaste, Costa Rica," *Proceedings, 34th International Congress of Americanists,* pp. 358–365, Vienna.

Coe, M. D. (1963), "Cultural Development in Southeastern Mesoamerica," in *Aboriginal Cultural Development in Latin America: An Interpretative Review,* B. J. Meggers and C. Evans, eds., Smithsonian Miscellaneous Collections, Vol. 146, No. 1, pp. 27–44, Smithsonian Institution, Washington, D.C.

Coe, M. D. (1964), "The Chinampas of Mexico," *Scientific American,* Vol. 211, No. 1, pp. 90–98, New York.

Coe, M. D. and C. F. Baudez (1961), "The Zoned Bichrome Period in Northwestern Costa Rica," *American Antiquity,* Vol. 26, pp. 505–515, Salt Lake City.

Coe, W. R. (1955), *Excavations in El Salvador,* University Museum Bulletin, Vol. 19, No. 2, Philadelphia.

Coe, W. R. (1962), "A Summary of Excavation and Research at Tikal, Guatemala: 1956–1961," *American Antiquity,* Vol. 27, No. 4, pp. 479–507, Salt Lake City.

Coe, W. R. (1963), "A Summary of Excavation and Research at Tikal, Guatemala, 1962," *Estudios Cultura Maya,* Vol. 3, pp. 41–64, Universidad Nacional de Mexico, Mexico, D.F.

Cole, F. C. and Thorne Deuel (1937), *Rediscovering Illinois: Archaeological Explorations in and around Fulton County,* University of Chicago Press, Chicago.

Cole, F. C., *et al.* (1951), *Kincaid, A Prehistoric Illinois Metropolis,* University of Chicago Press, Chicago.

Collier, Donald, A. E. Hudson, and Arlo Ford (1942), *Archaeology of the Upper Columbia Region,* University of Washington Publications in Anthropology, Vol. 9, No. 1, Seattle.

Collins, H. B. (1937), *The Archaeology of St. Lawrence Island, Alaska,* Smithsonian Miscellaneous Collections, Vol. 96, No. 1, Smithsonian Institution, Washington, D.C.

Collins, H. B. (1940), *Outline of Eskimo Prehistory,* Smithsonian Miscellaneous Collections, Vol. 100, pp. 533–592, Smithsonian Institution, Washington, D.C.

Collins, H. B. (1962), "Bering Strait to Greenland," *Prehistoric Cultural Relations Between the Arctic and Temperate Zones of North America,* J. M. Campbell, ed., Technical Paper No. 11, pp. 126–139, Arctic Institute of North America, Montreal.

Collins, H. B. (1964), "The Arctic and Subarctic," in *Prehistoric Man in the New World,* J. D. Jennings and E. Norbeck, eds., pp. 85–116, University of Chicago Press, Chicago.

Colton, H. S. (1945), "The Patayan Problem in the Colorado River Valley," *Southwestern Journal of Anthropology,* Vol. 1, No. 1, pp. 114–121, Albuquerque.

Colton, H. S. (1946), *The Sinagua: A Summary of the Archaeology of the Region of Flagstaff, Arizona,* Bulletin 22, Museum of Northern Arizona, Flagstaff.

Cortes, Hernando (1908), *Letters of Cortes,* 2 Vols., translated by F. A. MacNutt, New York and London.

Cosgrove, H. S. and C. B. (1932), *The Swarts Ruin,* Peabody Museum Papers, Vol. 15, No. 1, Harvard University, Cambridge.

Cotter, J. L. (1937), "The Occurrence of Flints and Extinct Animals in Pluvial Deposits near Clovis, New Mexico: Report on the Excavations of the Gravel Pit in 1936," *Proceedings, Philadelphia Academy of Natural Sciences,* Vol. 89, pp. 2–16, Philadelphia.

Cotter, J. L. (1938), "The Occurrence of Flints and Extinct Animals in Pluvial Deposits near Clovis, New Mexico, Pt. VI: Report on Field Season of 1937," *Proceedings, Philadelphia Academy of Natural Sciences,* Vol. 90, pp. 113–117, Philadelphia.

Covarrubias, Miguel (1957), *Indian Art of Mexico and Central America,* Alfred A. Knopf, Inc., New York.

Cowgill, G. L. (1964), "The End of Classic Maya Culture: A Review of Recent Evidence," *Southwestern Journal of Anthropology,* Vol. 20, No. 2, pp. 145–159, Albuquerque.

Cowgill, U. M. (1961), *Soil Fertility and the Ancient Maya,* Transactions, Vol. 42, pp. 1–56, Connecticut Academy of Arts and Sciences, New Haven.

Cowgill, U. M. and G. E. Hutchinson (1963), "Ecological and Geochemical Archaeology in the Southern Maya Lowlands," *Southwestern Journal of Anthropology,* Vol. 19, No. 3, pp. 267–286, Albuquerque.

Crane, H. R. and J. B. Griffin (1958 a), "University of Michigan Radiocarbon Dates III," *Science,* Vol. 128, pp. 1117–1123, Lancaster.

Crane, H. R. and J. B. Griffin (1958 b), "University of Michigan Radiocarbon Dates II," *Science,* Vol. 127, No. 3306, pp. 1098–1105, Lancaster.

Cressman, L. S. (1942), *Archaeological Researches in the Northern Great Basin,* Publication 538, Carnegie Institution of Washington, Washington, D.C.

Cressman, L. S. (1951), "Western Prehistory in the Light of Carbon 14 Dating," *Southwestern Journal of Anthropology,* Vol. 7, No. 3, pp. 289–313, Albuquerque, New Mexico.

Cressman, L. S. and A. D. Krieger (1940), *Early Man in Oregon,* University of Oregon Studies in Anthropology, No. 3, Eugene.

Cressman, L. S., *et al.* (1960), *Cultural Sequences at The Dalles, Oregon,* Transactions, Vol. 50, Pt. 10. American Philosophical Society, Philadelphia.

Crook, W. W. and R. K. Harris (1952), *Trinity Aspect of the Archaic Horizon: The Carrollton and Elam Foci,"* Bulletin, No. 23, pp. 7–38, Texas Archaeological and Paleontological Society, Abilene.

Crook, W. W. and R. K. Harris (1957), *Hearths and Artifacts of Early Man near Lewisville, Texas, and Associated Faunal Material,* Bulletin, Vol. 28, pp. 7–97, Texas Archaeological and Paleontological Society, Abilene.

Crook, W. W. and R. K. Harris (1958), "A Pleistocene Campsite near Lewisville, Texas," *American Antiquity,* Vol. 23, No. 3, pp. 233–246, Salt Lake City.

Cruxent, J. M. (1962), "Artifacts of Paleo-Indian Type, Maracaibo, Zulia, Venezuela," *American Antiquity,* Vol. 27, No. 4, pp. 576–579, Salt Lake City.

Cruxent, J. M. and Irving Rouse (1956), "A Lithic Industry of Paleo-Indian Types in Venezuela," *American Antiquity,* Vol. 22, No. 2, pp. 172–179, Salt Lake City.

Cummings, Byron (1933), *Cuicuilco and the Archaic Culture of Mexico,* University of Arizona Bulletin, Vol. 4, No. 8, Social Science Bulletin No. 4, Tucson.

Cushing, F. H. (1920), *Zuñi Breadstuffs,* Indian Notes and Monographs, Vol. 8, Museum of the American Indian, Heye Foundation, New York.

Dahlgren, Barbro (1954), *La Mixteca, Su Cultura e Historia Prehispanicas,* Imprenta Universitaria, Mexico, D.F.

Dahlgren, Barbro and Javier Romero (1951), "La Prehistoria Bajacaliforniana," *Cuadernos Americanos,* Vol. 10, No. 4, Mexico, D.F.

Daifuku, Hiroshi (1952), "A New Conceptual Scheme for Prehistoric Cultures in the Southwestern United States," *American Anthropologist,* Vol. 54, pp. 191–200, Menasha, Wisconsin.

Daugherty, R. D. (1956), "Archaeology of the Lind Coulee Site, Washington," *Proceedings, American Philosophical Society,* Vol. 100, No. 3, Philadelphia.

Daugherty, R. D. (1962), "The Intermontane Western Tradition," *American Antiquity,* Vol. 28, No. 2, pp. 144–150, Salt Lake City.

Davis, E. M. (1953), "Recent Data from Two Paleo-Indian Sites on Medicine Creek, Nebraska," *American Antiquity,* Vol. 18, No. 4, pp. 380–386, Salt Lake City.

Davis, W. A. and E. M. (1960), *The Jake Martin Site,* Archaeological Series, No. 3, Department of Anthropology, University of Texas, Austin.

De Jarnette, D. L. (1952), "Alabama Archaeology: A Summary," in *Archaeology of Eastern United States,* J. B. Griffin, ed., pp. 272–284, University of Chicago Press, Chicago.

De Jarnette, D. L., E. B. Kurjack, and J. W. Cambron (1962), "Stanfield-Worley Bluff Shelter Excavations," *Journal of Alabama Archaeology,* Vol. 8, Nos. 1–2, University.

De Jarnette, D. L. and S. B. Wimberly (1941), *The Bessemer Site: Excavation of Three Mounds and Surrounding Village Areas Near Bessemer, Alabama,* Geological Survey, Museum Paper 17, University of Alabama.

De Terra, H., J. Romero, and T. D. Stewart (1949), *Tepexpán Man,* Viking Fund Publications in Anthropology, No. 11, New York.

Deuel, Thorne (1935), "Basic Cultures of the Mississippi Valley," *American Anthropologist,* Vol. 37, pp. 429–445, Menasha, Wisconsin.

Diaz del Castillo, Bernal (1908–1916), *The True History of the Conquest of New Spain,* 5 Vols., translated by A. P. Maudslay, Hakluyt Society, London.

Di Peso, C. C. (1955), "Two Cerro Guamas Fluted Points from Sonora," *Kiva,* Vol. 21, pp. 13–15, Arizona Historical Society, Tucson.

Di Peso, C. C. (1963), "Cultural Development in Northern Mexico," in *Aboriginal Cultural Development in Latin America: An Interpretative Review,* B. J. Meggers and C. Evans, eds., Smithsonian Miscellaneous Collections, Vol. 146, No. 1, pp. 1–16, Smithsonian Institution, Washington, D.C.

Di Peso, C. C., *et al.* (1956), *The Upper Pima of San Cayetano del Tumacacori: An Archaeological Reconstruction of the Ootam of the Pimeria Alta,* Publication No. 7, Amerind Foundation, Dragoon, Arizona.

Dixon, K. A. (1959), *Ceramics from Two Pre-Classic Periods at Chiapa de Corzo, Southern Mexico,* Papers, No. 5, Publication No. 4, New World Archaeological Foundation, Orinda, California.

Dixon, R. B. (1923), *The Racial History of Man,* Scribner's, New York.

Dixon, R. B. (1928), *The Building of Cultures,* Scribner's, New York.

Driver, H. E. (1961), *Indians of North America,* University of Chicago Press, Chicago.

Driver, H. E. and W. C. Massey (1957), *Comparative Studies of North American Indians,* Transactions, Vol. 47, Pt. 2, American Philosophical Society, Philadelphia.

Drucker, Phillip (1943 a), *Ceramic Sequences at Tres Zapotes, Veracruz, Mexico,* Bureau of American Ethnology, Bulletin 140, Smithsonian Institution, Washington, D.C.

Drucker, Phillip (1943 b), *Ceramic Stratigraphy at Cerro de las Mesas, Veracruz, Mexico,* Bureau of American Ethnology, Bulletin 141, Smithsonian Institution, Washington, D.C.

Drucker, Phillip (1943 c), *Archaeological Survey on the Northern Northwest Coast,* Anthropological Paper, No. 20, Bureau of American Ethnology, Bulletin 133, Smithsonian Institution, Washington, D.C.

Drucker, Phillip (1948), *Preliminary Notes on an Archaeological Survey of the Chiapas Coast,* Middle American Research Records, Vol. 1, No. 1, Tulane University, New Orleans.

Drucker, Phillip (1952), *La Venta, Tabasco: A Study of Olmec Ceramics and Art,* Bureau of American Ethnology, Bulletin 153, Smithsonian Institution, Washington, D.C.

Drucker, Phillip (1955 a), *Indians of the Northwest Coast,* Anthropological Handbook No. 10, American Museum of Natural History, New York.

Drucker, Phillip (1955 b), "Sources of Northwest Coast Culture," in *New Interpretations of Aboriginal American Culture History: 75th Anniversary Volume of the Anthropological Society of Washington,* pp. 59–81, Washington, D.C.

Drucker, Phillip and R. F. Heizer (1960), "A Study of the Milpa System of La Venta Island and Its Archaeological Implications," *Southwestern Journal of Anthropology,* Vol. 16, No. 1, pp. 36–45, Albuquerque.

Drucker, Phillip, R. F. Heizer, and R. J. Squier (1959), *Excavations at La Venta, Tabasco, 1955,* Bureau of American Ethnology, Bulletin 170, Smithsonian Institution, Washington, D.C.

Duff, Wilson (1956), "Prehistoric Stone Sculpture of the Fraser River and Gulf of Georgia," *Anthropology in British Columbia,* No. 5, pp. 15–151, British Columbia Provincial Museum, Department of Education, Victoria, B.C.

Dunlevy, M. L. (1936), "Comparison of Cultural Manifestations of the Burkett and the Gray-Wolfe Sites," in *Chapters in Nebraska Archaeology,* Vol. 1, No. 2, pp. 147–247, University of Nebraska, Lincoln.

Du Solier, Wilfrido (1945), "La Cerámica Arqueológica de El Tajín," *Anales,* Vol. 3, Epoca 5, pp. 147–192, Museo Nacional de Arqueológia, Historia y Etnografía, Mexico, D.F.

Dutton, Bertha P. (1955), "Tula of the Toltecs," *El Palacio,* Vol. 62, Nos. 7–8, pp. 195–251, Santa Fe.

Dutton, B. P. and H. R. Hobbs (1943), "Excavations at Tajumulco, Guatemala," Monographs, No. 9, School of American Research, Santa Fe.

Eberhart, Hal (1961), "The Cogged Stones of Southern California," *American Antiquity,* Vol. 26, No. 3, pp. 361–370, Salt Lake City.

Eggan, F. R. (1952), "The Ethnological Cultures and Their Archaeological Background," in *Archaeology of Eastern United States,* J. B. Griffin, ed., pp. 35–45, University of Chicago Press, Chicago.

Ekholm, G. F. (1942), *Excavations at Guasave, Sinaloa, Mexico,* Anthropological Papers, Vol. 38, Pt. 2. American Museum of Natural History, New York.

Ekholm, G. F. (1944), *Excavations at Tampico and Panuco in the Huasteca, Mexico.* Anthropological Papers, Vol. 38, Pt. 5. American Museum of Natural History, New York.

Ekholm, G. F. (1946), "The Probable Use of Mexican Stone

Yokes," *American Anthropologist*, Vol. 48, pp. 593–606, Menasha, Wisconsin.

Ekholm, G. F. (1948), "Ceramic Stratigraphy at Acapulco, Guerrero," in *El Occidente de Mexico*, pp. 95–104, Mesa Redonda, Sociedad Mexicana de Antropología, Mexico, D.F.

Ekholm, G. F. (1949), "Palmate Stones and Thin Stone Heads: Suggestions on their Possible Use," *American Antiquity*, Vol. 15, pp. 1–9, Menasha, Wisconsin.

Ekholm, G. F. (1958), "Regional Sequences in Mesoamerica and their Relationships," in *Middle American Anthropology*, G. R. Willey, E. Z. Vogt, A. Palerm, eds., Social Science Monograph 5, pp. 15–24. Pan American Union, Washington, D.C.

Ekholm, G. F. (1964), "Transpacific Contacts," in *Prehistoric Man in the New World*, J. D. Jennings and E. Norbeck, eds., pp. 489–510, Rice University Semi-centennial Publications, University of Chicago Press, Chicago.

Emperaire, Jose and Annette Laming (1961), "Les Gisements des Iles Englefield et Vivian dans la Mer D'Otway, Patagonia, Australie," *Journal, Société des Américanistes*, Vol. 50, pp. 7–75, Paris.

Engel, Frederic (1957), "Early Sites on the Peruvian Coast," *Southwestern Journal of Anthropology*, Vol. 13, pp. 54–68, Albuquerque.

Epstein, J. F. (1959), "Dating the Ulua Polychrome Complex," *American Antiquity*, Vol. 25, pp. 125–129, Salt Lake City.

Epstein, J. F. (1963), "The Burin-faceted Projectile Point," *American Antiquity*, Vol. 29, No. 2, pp. 187–201, Salt Lake City.

Estrada, Emilio, B. J. Meggers, and Clifford Evans (1962), "Possible Transpacific Contact on the Coast of Ecuador," *Science*, Vol. 135, No. 3501, pp. 371–372, Lancaster.

Estrada, Emilio and Clifford Evans (1963), "Cultural Development in Ecuador," in *Aboriginal Cultural Development in Latin America: An Interpretative Review*, B. J. Meggers and C. Evans, eds., Smithsonian Miscellaneous Collections, Vol. 146, No. 1, pp. 77–88, Washington, D.C.

Ezell, P. H. (1961), *The Hispanic Acculturation of the Gila River Pimas*, Memoir 90, American Anthropological Association, Menasha, Wisconsin.

Fairbanks, C. H. (1942), "The Taxonomic Position of Stallings Island, Georgia," *American Antiquity*, Vol. 7, pp. 223–231, Menasha, Wisconsin.

Fairbanks, C. H. (1946), "The Macon Earth Lodge," *American Antiquity*, Vol. 12, No. 2, pp. 94–108, Menasha, Wisconsin.

Fairbanks, C. H. (1949), "A General Survey of Southeastern Prehistory," in *The Florida Indian and His Neighbors*, J. W. Griffin, ed., pp. 55–76, Rollins College, Winter Park, Florida.

Fairbanks, C. H. (1952), "Creek and Pre-Creek," in *Archaeology of Eastern United States*, J. B. Griffin, ed., pp. 285–300, The University of Chicago Press, Chicago, Illinois.

Fairbanks, C. H. (1956), *Archaeology of the Funeral Mound, Ocmulgee National Monument, Georgia*. Archaeological Research Series, No. 3, National Park Service, U.S. Department of Interior, Washington, D.C.

Fenneman, N. M. (1928), *Physiographic Divisions of the United States*, Annals, Vol. 18, No. 4, pp. 264–353, Association American Geographers, Albany.

Ferdon, E. N. (1955), *A Trial Survey of Mexican-Southwestern Architectural Parallels*, Monographs, No. 27, School of American Research, Santa Fe.

Figgins, J. D. (1927), "The Antiquity of Man in America," *Natural History*, Vol. 27, No. 3, pp. 229–239, American Museum of Natural History, New York.

Finch, V. C., G. T. Trewartha, A. H. Robinson, and E. H. Hammond (1957), *Elements of Geography, Physical and Cultural*, McGraw-Hill, New York.

Flint, R. F. (1957), *Glacial and Pleistocene Geology*, John Wiley & Sons, New York.

Forbis, R. C. and J. D. Sperry (1952), "An Early Man Site in Montana," *American Antiquity*, Vol. 18, No. 2, pp. 127–132, Salt Lake City.

Ford, J. A. (1951), *Greenhouse: A Troyville-Coles Creek Period Site in Avoyelles Parish, Louisiana*, Anthropological Papers, Vol. 44, Pt. 1, American Museum of Natural History, New York.

Ford, J. A. (1959), *Eskimo Prehistory in the Vicinity of Point Barrow, Alaska*, Anthropological Papers, Vol. 47, Pt. 1, American Museum of Natural History, New York.

Ford, J. A., Philip Phillips, and W. G. Haag (1955), *The Jaketown Site in West-Central Mississippi*, Anthropological Papers, Vol. 45, Pt. 1, American Museum of Natural History, New York.

Ford, J. A. and G. I. Quimby (1945), *The Tchefuncte Culture, an Early Occupation of the Lower Mississippi Valley*, Memoir No. 2, Society for American Archaeology, Menasha, Wisconsin.

Ford, J. A. and C. H. Webb (1956), *Poverty Point: A Late Archaic Site in Louisiana*, Anthropological Papers, Vol. 46, Pt. 1, American Museum of Natural History, New York.

Ford, J. A. and G. R. Willey (1940), *Crooks Site: A Marksville Period Burial Mound in LaSalle Parish, Louisiana*, Anthropological Study 3, Department of Conservation, Louisiana Geological Survey, New Orleans.

Ford, J. A. and G. R. Willey (1941), "An Interpretation of the Prehistory of the Eastern United States," *American Anthropologist*,

Vol. 43, pp. 325–363, Menasha, Wisconsin.

Forde, C. D. (1931), *Ethnography of the Yuma Indians,* University of California Publications in American Archaeology and Ethnology, Vol. 28, pp. 83–278, Berkeley.

Fowler, M. L. (1959 a), "Modoc Rock Shelter: An Early Archaic Site in Southern Illinois," *American Antiquity,* Vol. 24, pp. 257–270, Salt Lake City.

Fowler, M. L. (1959 b), *Summary Report of Modoc Rock Shelter,* Illinois State Museum Report of Investigations 8, Springfield.

Frye, J. C. and H. B. Willman (1960), *Classification of the Wisconsin Stage in the Lake Michigan Glacial Lobe,* Circular 285, Illinois State Geological Survey, Springfield.

Furst, P. T. (1965), "Radiocarbon Dates from a Tomb in Mexico," *Science,* Vol. 147, No. 3658, pp. 612–613, Lancaster.

Gagliano, S. M. (1963), "A Survey of Preceramic Occupations in Portions of South Louisiana and South Mississippi," *The Florida Anthropologist,* Vol. 16, No. 4, pp. 105–132, Gainesville.

García Payón, José (1943), *Interpretación Cultural de la Zona Arqueológica de El Tajín,* Universidad Nacional Autónoma de Mexico.

García Payón, José (1949 a), *Arqueologia del Tajín,* Universidad Nacional Autónoma de Mexico, Mexico, D.F.

García Payón, José (1949 b), *Zempoala: Compendio de su Estudio Arqueológica,* Uni-Ver., Vol. 1, No. 8, Universidad Veracruzana, Jalapa.

García Payón, José (1949 c), *Arqueología de Zempoala,* III. Univ-Ver., Vol. 1, No. 10, Universidad Veracruzana, Jalapa.

García Payón, José (1950), *Restos de una Cultura Prehispanica Encontrados en la Región de Zempoala, Veracruz,* Uni-Ver., Vol. 2, No. 15, Uni-

versidad Veracruzana, Jalapa.

García Payón, José (1954), *El Tajín: Descripción y Comentarios,* Univ-Ver., Vol. 4, pp. 18–43, Universidad Veracruzana, Jalapa.

Gates, William (1932), *The Dresden Codex,* Maya Society Publication, No. 2, Johns Hopkins University, Baltimore.

Giddings, J. L. (1951), "The Denbigh Flint Complex," *American Antiquity,* Vol. 16, No. 3, pp. 193–203, Salt Lake City.

Giddings, J. L. (1960), "The Archaeology of Bering Strait," *Current Anthropology,* Vol. 1, No. 2, pp. 121–138, Wenner-Gren Foundation, Chicago.

Giddings, J. L. (1961), "Cultural Continuities of Eskimos," *American Antiquity,* Vol. 27, No. 2, pp. 155–173, Salt Lake City.

Giddings, J. L. (1962), "Side-Notched Points Near Bering Strait," in *Prehistoric Cultural Relations Between the Arctic and Temperate Zones of North America,* J. M. Campbell, ed., Technical Paper No. 11, pp. 35–38, Arctic Institute of North America, Montreal.

Giddings, J. L. (1964), *The Archaeology of Cape Denbigh,* Brown University Press, Providence.

Gifford, E. W. (1950), *Surface Archaeology of Ixtlán del Rio, Nayarit,* University of California Publications in American Archaeology and Ethnology, Vol. 43, No. 2, Berkeley.

Girard, Rafael (1962), *Los Mayas Eternos,* Antigua Librería Robredo, Mexico, D.F.

Gladwin, H. S. (1928), *Excavations at Casa Grande, Arizona,* Papers, No. 2, Southwest Museum, Los Angeles.

Gladwin, H. S. (1943), *A Review and Analysis of the Flagstaff Culture,* Gila Pueblo Medallion Papers, No. 31, Globe, Arizona.

Gladwin, H. S. (1948), *Excavations at Snaketown IV: Reviews and Conclusions,* Gila Pueblo Medallion

Papers, No. 38, Globe, Arizona.

Gladwin, H. S. (1957), *A History of the Ancient Southwest,* Bond Wheelwright Company, Portland, Maine.

Gladwin, H. S., *et al.* (1937), *Excavations at Snaketown—Material Culture,* Gila Pueblo Medallion Papers, No. 25, Globe, Arizona.

Gladwin, Winifred and H. S. (1930), *Some Southwestern Pottery Types, Series I,* Gila Pueblo Medallion Papers, No. 8, Globe, Arizona.

Goggin, J. M. (1949), "Cultural Traditions in Florida Prehistory," in *The Florida Indian and His Neighbors,* J. W. Griffin, ed., pp. 13–44, Rollins College, Winter Park.

Goggin, J. M. (1950), "An Early Lithic Complex from Central Florida," *American Antiquity,* Vol. 16, No. 1, pp. 46–49, Menasha.

Gonzalez, A. R. (1960), "La Estratigrafía de la Gruta de Intihuasi, Prov. de San Luís y Sus Relaciónes con Otros Sitios Precerámicos de Sudamerica," *Revista del Instituto de Antropologiá,* Vol. 1, pp. 9–296, Universidad Nacional de Cordoba.

Gonzalez Rul, Francisco (1959), "Una Punta Acanalada del Rancho" La Chuparrosa, *Publicaciónes, Dirección de Prehistoria,* No. 8, Instituto Nacional de Antropologiá e Historia, Mexico.

Goslin, R. M. (1957), "Food of the Adena People," in *The Adena People, No. 2,* W. S. Webb and R. S. Baby, eds., pp. 41–46, Ohio Historical Society, Ohio State University Press, Columbus.

Green, F. E. (1963), "The Clovis Blades: An Important Addition to the Llano Complex," *American Antiquity,* Vol. 29, No. 2, pp. 145–165, Salt Lake City.

Greenberg, J. H. (1960), "The General Classification of Central and South American Languages," in *Men and Cultures,* A. F. C. Wallace, ed., *Selected Papers, 5th International Congress of Anthropological and Ethnological Sciences,* pp. 791–

794, University of Pennsylvania Press, Philadelphia.

Greengo, R. C. (1964), *Prehistory in the Lower Mississippi Valley: The Issaquena Phase,* Memoir 18, Society for American Archaeology, Salt Lake City.

Griffin, James B. (1943), *The Fort Ancient Aspect; Its Cultural and Chronological Position in Mississippi Valley Archaeology,* University of Michigan Press, Ann Arbor.

Griffin, J. B. (1944 a), "The De Luna Expedition and the 'Buzzard Cult' in the Southwest," *Journal of Washington Academy of Science,* Vol. 34, No. 9, pp. 299–303, Washington, D.C.

Griffin, J. B. (1944 b), *The Iroquois in American Prehistory,* Papers, Vol. 29, pp. 357–374, Michigan Academy of Science, Arts, Letters, Ann Arbor.

Griffin, J. B. (1945), "The Significance of the Fiber-Tempered Pottery of the St. Johns" *Journal of Washington Academy of Science,* Vol. 35, pp. 218–223, Washington, D.C.

Griffin, J. B. (1946), "Cultural Change and Continuity in Eastern United States Archaeology," in *Man in Northeastern North America,* F. Johnson, ed., Papers of R. S. Peabody Foundation for Archaeology, Vol. 33, pp. 37–95, Andover, Massachusetts.

Griffin, J. B. (1949), "Meso-America and the Southeast: A Commentary," in *The Florida Indian and His Neighbors,* J. W. Griffin, ed., pp. 77–100, Rollins College, Winter Park, Florida.

Griffin, J. B. (1952), "Prehistoric Florida: A Review," *Archaeology of Eastern United States,* J. B. Griffin, ed., pp. 352–364, University of Chicago Press.

Griffin, J. B. (1952 a), "Culture Periods in Eastern United States Archaeology," in *Archaeology of Eastern United States,* J. B. Griffin, ed., pp. 352–364, University of Chicago Press, Chicago.

Griffin, J. B. (1952 b), "Prehistoric Culture of the Central Mississippi Valley," in *Archaeology of Eastern United States,* J. B. Griffin, ed., pp. 226–238, University of Chicago Press, Chicago.

Griffin, J. B. (1953), "United States and Canada: Indigenous Period," *Program of the History of America,* Vol. I, No. 3, Instituto Panamericano de Geografía e Historia, Mexico, D.F.

Griffin, J. B. (1956), "Prehistoric Settlement Patterns in the Northern Mississippi Valley and the Upper Great Lakes," in *Prehistoric Settlement Patterns in the New World,* G. R. Willey, ed., pp. 63–71, Viking Fund Publications in Anthropology, No. 23, New York.

Griffin, J. B. (1958), *The Chronological Position of the Hopewellian Culture in the Eastern United States.* Anthropological Papers, No. 12, Museum of Anthropology, University of Michigan, Ann Arbor.

Griffin, J. B. (1960), "Climatic Change: A Contributory Cause of the Growth and Decline of Northern Hopewellian Culture," *The Wisconsin Archaeologist,* Vol. 41, pp. 21–33, Milwaukee.

Griffin, J. B. (1962), "A Discussion of Prehistoric Similarities and Connections Between the Arctic and Temperate Zones of North America," in *Prehistoric Cultural Relations Between the Arctic and Temperate Zones of North America,* J. M. Campbell, ed., Technical Paper No. 11, pp. 154–163, Arctic Institute of North America, Montreal.

Griffin, J. B. (1964), "The Northeast Woodlands Area," in *Prehistoric Man in the New World,* J. D. Jennings and E. Norbeck, eds., pp. 223–258, University of Chicago Press, Chicago.

Griffin, J. B. and Antonieta Espejo (1950), "La Alfarería Correspondiente al Ultimo Periode de Ocupación Nahua de Valle de Mexico," in *Tlatelolco a Través de los Tiempos,* Vol. 9, pp. 10–26; Vol. 11, pp. 15–90, Memorias de la Academia Mexicana de la Historia, Mexico, D.F.

Griffin, J. B. and R. H. Wilmeth, Jr. (1964), "The Ceramic Complexes at Iyatayet," in *The Archaeology of Cape Denbigh,* by J. L. Giddings, pp. 271–310, Brown University Press, Providence.

Grosscup, Gordon L. (1960), *The Culture History of Lovelock Cave, Nevada,* University of California Archaeological Survey, No. 52, Department of Anthropology, University of California, Berkeley.

Guernsey, S. J. (1931), *Explorations in Northeastern Arizona,* Papers, Vol. 12, No. 1, Peabody Museum, Harvard University, Cambridge.

Guernsey, S. J. and A. V. Kidder (1921), *Basket-Maker Caves of Northeastern Arizona,* Papers, Vol. 8, No. 2, Peabody Museum.

Gunnerson, J. H. (1960), *An Introduction to Plains Apache Archaeology—The Dismal River Aspect,* Bureau of American Ethnology, Bulletin 173, No. 58, Smithsonian Institution.

Haag, W. G. (1942), "Early Horizons in the Southeast," *American Antiquity,* Vol. 7, pp. 209–222, Menasha, Wisconsin.

Haas, Mary R. (1958), "A New Linguistic Relationship in North America: Algonkian-Gulf Relationships," *Southwestern Journal of Anthropology,* Vol. 14, No. 3, pp. 231–264, Albuquerque.

Haberland, Wolfgang (1958), "A Preclassic Complex of Western El Salvador," *Anales,* Vol. 8, pp. 11–16, Museo Nacional, San Salvador.

Haberland, Wolfgang (1959, "Zentral Amerika: Begriff, Grenzen, und Probleme," *Amerikanistische Miszellen,* pp. 53–59, Hamburg.

Haberland, Wolfgang (1960), "Ceramic Sequence in El Salvador," *American Antiquity,* Vol. 26, pp. 21–29, Salt Lake City.

Haberland, Wolfgang (1963 a),

"Conferencia y Exposición Arqueológica," *Nicaragua Indígena,* Segunda Epoca, No. 36, pp. 25–39, Managua.

Haberland, Wolfgang (1963 b), "Ometepe," *Nicaragua Indígena,* Segunda Epoca, No. 37, pp. 7–10, Managua.

Hack, J. T. (1941), *The Changing Physical Environment of the Hopi Indians of Arizona,* Papers, Vol. 35, No. 1, Peabody Museum, Harvard University, Cambridge.

Hall, E. T., Jr. (1944 a), *Early Stockaded Settlements in the Governador, New Mexico: A Marginal Anasazi Development from Basket Maker III to Pueblo I Times,* Columbia Studies in Archaeology and Ethnology, Vol, 2, Pt. 1, Columbia University Press, New York.

Hall, E. T., Jr. (1944 b), "Recent Clues to Athapaskan Prehistory in the Southwest," *American Anthropologist,* Vol. 46, pp. 98–105, Menasha, Wisconsin.

Harp, Elmer, Jr. (1961), *The Archaeology of the Lower and Middle Thelon, Northwest Territories,* Technical Paper No. 8, Arctic Institute of North America, Montreal.

Harp, Elmer, Jr. (1962), "The Culture History of the Central Barren Grounds," in *Prehistoric Cultural Relations Between the Arctic and Temperate Zones of North America,* J. M. Campbell, ed., Technical Paper No. 11, pp. 69–75, Arctic Institute of North America, Montreal.

Harp, Elmer, Jr. (1963), *Evidence of Boreal Archaic Culture in Southern Labrador and Newfoundland,* Bulletin No. 193, Contributions to Anthropology, 1961–1962, Pt. 1, National Museum of Canada, Ottawa.

Harp, Elmer, Jr. (1964), *The Cultural Affinities of the Newfoundland Dorset Eskimo,* Bulletin 200, Anthropological Series, No. 67, National Museum of Canada, Ottawa.

Harp, Elmer, Jr. (1964), "The Prehistoric Indian and Eskimo Cultures of Labrador and Newfoundland," MS.

Harrington, M. R. (1924), "The Ozark Bluff-Dwellers," *American Anthropologist,* Vol. 26, No. 1, pp. 1–21, Menasha, Wisconsin.

Harrington, M. R. (1933), *Gypsum Cave, Nevada,* Southwest Museum Papers, No. 8, Los Angeles.

Harrington, M. R. (1948), *An Ancient Site at Borax Lake, California,* Southwest Museum Papers, No. 16, Los Angeles.

Harrington, M. R. and R. D. Simpson (1961), *Tule Springs, Nevada, with Other Evidences of Pleistocene Man in North America,* Southwest Museum Papers, No. 18, Los Angeles.

Haury, E. W. (1936 a), *The Mogollon Culture of Southwestern New Mexico,* Gila Pueblo Medallion Paper, No. 20, Globe, Arizona.

Haury, E. W. (1936 b), *Some Southwestern Pottery Types, Series IV,* Gila Pueblo Medallion Paper, No. 20, Globe, Arizona.

Haury, E. W. (1945), *The Excavation of Los Muertos and Neighboring Sites in the Salt River Valley, Southern Arizona,* Papers, Vol. 24, No. 1, Peabody Museum, Harvard University, Cambridge.

Haury, E. W. (1953), "Artifacts with Mammoth Remains, Naco, Arizona, I: Discovery of the Naco Mammoth and the Associated Projectile Points," *American Antiquity,* Vol. 19, No. 1, pp. 1–14, Salt Lake City.

Haury, E. W. (1957), "An Alluvial Site on the San Carlos Indian Reservation, Arizona," *American Antiquity,* Vol. 23, pp. 2–27, Salt Lake City.

Haury, E. W. (1958), "Evidence at Point of Pines for a Prehistoric Migration from northern Arizona," in *Migrations in New World Culture History,* R. H. Thompson, ed., University of Arizona Social Science Bulletin No. 27, pp. 1–8, Tucson.

Haury, E. W. (1962), "The Greater American Southwest," in *Courses Toward Urban Life,* R. J. Braidwood and G. R. Willey, eds., Viking Fund Publication in Anthropology, No. 32, pp. 106–131, New York.

Haury, E. W., *et al.* (1950), *The Stratigraphy and Archaeology of Ventana Cave, Arizona,* University of Arizona, Tucson, and University of New Mexico, Albuquerque.

Haury, E. W. and E. B. Sayles, (1947), *An Early Pit House Village of the Mogollon Culture, Forestdale Valley, Arizona,* Bulletin, Vol. 18, No. 4, University of Arizona, Tucson.

Haury, E. W., E. B. Sayles, and W. W. Wasley (1959), "The Lehner Mammoth Site, Southeastern Arizona," *American Antiquity,* Vol. 25, pp. 2–30, Salt Lake City.

Hay, C. L., *et al.* (1940), *The Maya and their Neighbors,* Appleton-Century, New York.

Haynes, C. V., Jr. (1964), "Fluted Projectile Points: Their Age and Dispersion," *Science,* Vol. 45, pp. 1408–1413, Washington, D.C.

Haynes, Vance and George Agogino (1960), "Geological Significance of a New Radiocarbon Date from the Lindenmeier Site," *Proceedings,* No. 9, Denver Museum of Natural History, Denver.

Heine-Geldern, Robert von (1953), "Die Asiatische Herkunft der Südamerikanischen Metalltechnik," *Paideuma,* Band 5, pp. 347–423, Frobenius-Institute—J. Wolfgang Goethe-Universität, Frankfurt am Main.

Heine-Geldern, Robert von (1959 a), "Representations of the Asiatic Tiger in the Art of the Chavín Culture: A Proof of Early Contacts Between China and Peru," *Actas del 33rd Congreso Internacional de Americanistas,* pp.

321–326, San Jose, Costa Rica.

Heine-Geldern, Robert von (1959 b), "Chinese Influences in Mexico and Central America: The Tajín Style of Mexico and the Marble Vases from Honduras," *Actas del 33rd Congreso Internacional de Americanistas*, pp. 195–206, San Jose, Costa Rica.

Heine-Geldern, Robert von (1959 c), "Chinese Influence in the Pottery of Mexico, Central America, and Colombia," *Actas del 33rd Congreso Internacional de Americanistas*, pp. 207–210, San José, Costa Rica.

Heizer, R. F. (1949), *The Archaeology of Central California, 1: The Early Horizon*, University of California Anthropological Records, Vol. 12, pp. 1–84, Berkeley.

Heizer, R. F. (1951 a), "Preliminary Report on Leonard Rock Shelter, Pershing County, Nevada," *American Antiquity*, Vol. 17, pp. 89–98, Menasha, Wisconsin.

Heizer, R. F. (1951 b), "An Assessment of Certain Radiocarbon Dates from Oregon, California, and Nevada," in *Radiocarbon Dating*, F. Johnson, ed., pp. 23–25, Memoir No. 8, Society for American Archaeology, Salt Lake City.

Heizer, R. F. (1952), "A Review of Problems in the Antiquity of Man in California," in *Symposium on the Antiquity of Man in California*, pp. 3–17, University of California Archaeological Survey, Report No. 16, Berkeley.

Heizer, R. F. (1959), "Specific and Generic Characteristics of Olmec Culture," *Actas del 33rd Congreso Internacional de Americanistas*, Vol. 2, pp. 178–182, San Jose, Costa Rica.

Heizer, R. F. (1964), "The Western Coast of North America," in *Prehistoric Man in the New World*, J. D. Jennings and E. Norbeck, eds., pp. 117–148, University of Chicago Press, Chicago.

Heizer, R. F. and J. A. Bennyhoff (1958), "Archaeological Investigation of Cuicuilco, Valley of Mexico, 1957," *Science*, Vol. 127, No. 3292, pp. 232–33, Lancaster.

Heizer, R. F. and R. A. Brooks (1965), "Lewisville—Ancient Campsite or Wood Rat Houses?" MS., courtesy of R. F. Heizer.

Heizer, R. F. and A. B. Elsasser (1964), *Archaeology of Hum-67, the Gunther Island Site in Humboldt Bay, California*, Reports of the University of California Archaeological Survey, No. 62, Berkeley.

Heizer, R. F. and F. Fenenga (1939), "Archaeological Horizons in Central California," *American Anthropologist*, Vol. 41, pp. 378–399, Menasha, Wisconsin.

Heizer, R. F. and A. D. Krieger (1956), *The Archaeology of Humboldt Cave, Churchill County, Nevada*, University of California Publications in American Archaeology and Ethnology, Vol. 47, No. 1, pp. 1–190, Berkeley and Los Angeles.

Hester, J. J. (1962 a), "A Comparative Typology of New World Cultures," *American Anthropologist*, Vol. 64, No. 5, pp. 1001–1015, Menasha, Wisconsin.

Hester, J. J. (1962 b), *Early Navajo Migrations and Acculturation in the Southwest*, Papers in Anthropology, No. 6, Museum of New Mexico, Santa Fe.

Hewes, Gordon W. (1949), "Burial Mounds in the Baldhill Area, North Dakota," *American Antiquity*, Vol. 14, No. 4, pp. 322–327, Menasha, Wisconsin.

Heye, G. G., F. W. Hodge, and G. H. Pepper (1918), *The Nacooche Mound in Georgia*, Contributions from Museum of American Indian, Vol. 4, No. 3, Heye Foundation, New York.

Heyerdahl, Thor (1952), "Aboriginal Navigation in Peru; Objects and Results of the Kon-tiki Expedition; Some Basic Problems

in Polynesian Anthropology," *Proceedings, 30th International Congress of Americanists*, pp. 72–85, Royal Anthropological Institute, London.

Hibben, F. C. (1938), "The Gallina Phase," *American Antiquity*, Vol. 4, pp. 131–136, Menasha, Wisconsin.

Hibben, F. C. (1941), *Evidences of Early Occupation of Sandia Cave, New Mexico, and Other Sites in the Sandia-Manzano Region*, Smithsonian Miscellaneous Collections, Vol. 99, No. 23, Smithsonian Institution, Washington, D.C.

Hill-Tout, Charles (1895), "Later Prehistoric Man in British Columbia," *Proceedings, Royal Society of Canada*, Vol. 1, Sect. 2, pp. 103–122.

Hoijer, Harry (1946), "Introduction," in *Linguistic Structures of Native America*, H. Hoijer, ed., pp. 9–29, Viking Fund Publications in Anthropology, No. 6, New York.

Holmes, W. H. (1903), *Aboriginal Pottery of the Eastern United States*, Annual Report, Bureau of American Ethnology, Vol. 20, Smithsonian Institution, Washington, D.C.

Hooton, E. A. (1947), *Up From the Ape*, rev. ed., The MacMillan Company, New York.

Hough, Walter (1915), *The Hopi Indians*, Torch Press, Cedar Rapids.

Howard, E. B. (1935 a), "Evidence of Early Man in North America," *The Museum Journal*, Vol. 24, Nos. 2–3, University of Pennsylvania Museum, Philadelphia.

Howard, E. B. (1935 b), "Occurrence of Flints and Extinct Animals in Pluvial Deposits near Clovis, New Mexico, Pt. 1, Introduction," *Proceedings, Philadelphia Academy of National Sciences*, Vol. 87, pp. 299–303.

Howard, E. B., Linton Satterthwaite, Jr., and Charles Bache

(1941), "Preliminary Report on a Buried Yuma Site in Wyoming," *American Antiquity,* Vol. 7, No. 1, pp. 70–74, Menasha, Wisconsin.

Howells, W. W. (1946), *Mankind So Far,* The American Museum of Natural History Science Series, Doubleday, New York.

Hughes, J. T. (1949), "Investigations in Western South Dakota and Northeastern Wyoming," *American Antiquity,* Vol. 14, No. 4, Menasha, Wisconsin.

Hurt, W. R. (1951), *Report of the Investigations of the Swanson Site, 39 Br 16, Brule County, South Dakota,* Archaeological Studies, No. 3, South Dakota State Archaeological Commission.

Hurt, W. R. (1956), "The Lagoa Santa Project," *Museum News,* Vol. 18, Nos. 9–10. W. H. Over Museum, University of South Dakota, Vermillion.

Hurt, W. R. (1960), "The Cultural Complexes from the Lagoa Santa Region, Brazil," *American Archaeologist,* Vol. 62, pp. 569–585, Menasha, Wisconsin.

Hurt, W. R. (1964), "Recent Radiocarbon Dates for Central and Southern Brazil," *American Antiquity,* Vol. 30, No. 1, pp. 25–33, Salt Lake City.

Huscher, B. H. and H. A. (1942), "Athapascan Migration via the Intermontane Region," *American Antiquity,* Vol. 8, No. 1, pp. 80–88, Menasha, Wisconsin.

Huscher, B. H. and H. A. (1943), *The Hogan Builders of Colorado,* Colorado Archaeological Society, Gunnison.

Hutchinson, Joseph (1959), *The Application of Genetics to Cotton Improvement,* Cambridge University Press, Cambridge, England.

Hutchinson, Joseph (1962), "The History and Relationships of the World's Cottons," *Endeavour,* Vol. 21, No. 81, pp. 5–15, London.

Hutchinson, J. B., R. A. Silow, and S. G. Stephens, (1947), *Evolution of Gossypium,* Oxford University Press, London.

Hymes, D. H. (1957), "A Note on Athapaskan Glottochronology," *International Journal of American Linguistics,* Vol. 23, pp. 291–297, Baltimore.

Ibarra Grasso, D. E. (1955), "Hallazgo de Puntas Paleolitcas en Bolivia," *Proceedings, 31st International Congress of Americanists,* Vol. 2, pp. 561–568, Sao Paulo.

Imbelloni, Jose (1958), "Nouveaux Apports à la Classification de l'Homme Américain," *Miscellanea Paul Rivet, Octogenaria Dictata,* Vol. 1, pp. 107–136, Universidad Nacional Autónoma de Mexico, Mexico, D.F.

Irving, W. N. (1957), *An Archaeological Survey of the Susitna Valley,* Anthropological Papers, Vol. 6, No. 1, pp. 37–52, University of Alaska, Fairbanks.

Irving, W. N. (1962), "A Provisional Comparison of Some Alaskan and Asian Stone Industries," in *Prehistoric Cultural Relations Between the Arctic and Temperate Zones of North America,* J. M. Campbell, ed., Technical Paper No. 11, pp. 55–68, Arctic Institute of North America, Montreal.

Ishida, Eiichiro, *et al.* (1960), Andes, Report of the University of Tokyo Scientific Expedition to the Andes in 1958, University of Tokyo.

James, P. E. (1959). *Latin America,* 3rd ed., Cassel's, London.

Jenness, Diamond (1940), "Prehistoric Culture Waves from Asia," *Journal of Washington Academy of Sciences,* Vol. 30, No. 1, pp. 1–15, Washington, D.C.

Jennings, J. D. (1957), *Danger Cave,* Memoir 14, Society for American Archaeology, Salt Lake City.

Jennings, J. D. (1964), "The Desert West," in *Prehistoric Man in the New World,* J. D. Jennings and E. Norbeck, eds., pp. 149–174, University of Chicago Press, Chicago.

Jennings, J. D. and Edward Norbeck (1955), "Great Basin Prehistory: A Review," *American Antiquity,* Vol. 21, pp. 1–11, Salt Lake City.

Jennings, J. D. and E. K. Reed (1956), "The American Southwest: A Problem in Cultural Isolation," in *Seminar in Archaeology: 1955,* R. Wauchope, ed., Memoir No. 11, Society for American Archaeology, Salt Lake City.

Jimenez Moreno, Wigberto (1942), "El Enigma de los Olmecas," *Cuadernos Americanos,* Vol. 1, No. 5, pp. 113–145, Mexico, D.F.

Jimenez Moreno, Wigberto (1954–1955), "Síntesis de la Historia Precolonial del Valle de Mexico," *Revista Mexicana de Estudios Antropológicos,* Vol. 14, Pt. 1, pp. 219–236, Mexico, D.F.

Jimenez Moreno, Wigberto (1959), "Síntesis de la Historia Pretolteca de Mesoamerica," in *Esplendor del Mexico Antiguo,* C. Cook de Leonard, Coordinador, Vol. 2, pp. 1019–1108, Centro de Investigaciónes Antropológicas de Mexico, Mexico, D.F.

Johnson, A. E. (1963), "The Trincheras Culture of Northern Sonora," *American Antiquity,* Vol. 29, No. 2, pp. 174–186, Salt Lake City.

Johnson, A. S. (1958), "Similarities in Hohokam and Chalchihuites Artifacts," *American Antiquity,* Vol. 24, pp. 126–130, Salt Lake City.

Johnson, Frederick (1940), "The Linguistic Map of Mexico and Central America," in *The Maya and Their Neighbors,* C. L. Hay, *et al.,* pp. 88–116, Appleton-Century, New York.

Johnson, Frederick and H. M. Raup (1964), *Investigations in the Southwest Yukon: Part I: Geobotanical and Archaeological Reconnaissance,* Papers of the R. S. Peabody Foundation for Archaeology, Vol. 6, No. 1, Phillips Academy, Andover, Massachusetts.

Jones, V. H. and R. L. Fonner (1954), "Plant Materials from Sites in the Durango and La Plata Areas, Colorado," in *Basket Maker II Sites near Durango, Colorado,* E. H. Morris and R. F. Burgh, eds., Publication No. 604, Carnegie Institution of Washington, Washington, D.C.

Judd, N. M. (1954), *The Material Culture of Pueblo Bonito,* Smithsonian Miscellaneous Collections, Vol. 124, Smithsonian Institution, Washington, D.C.

Judd, N. M. (1964), *The Architecture of Pueblo Bonito,* Smithsonian Miscellaneous Collections, Vol. 147, No. 1, Smithsonian Institution, Washington, D.C.

Kehoe, A. B. (1962), "A Hypothesis on the Origin of Northeastern American Pottery," *Southwestern Journal of Anthropology,* Vol. 18, pp. 20–29, Albuquerque.

Kelley, J. C. (1952), "Some Geographic and Cultural Factors Involved in Mexican-Southeastern Contacts," in *Indian Tribes of Aboriginal America,* S. Tax, ed., *Selected Papers, 29th International Congress of Americanists,* Vol. 3, pp. 139–144, University of Chicago Press, Chicago.

Kelley, J. C. (1953), "Reconnaissance and Excavation in Durango and southern Chihuahua, Mexico," *Year Book of the American Philosophical Society,* pp. 172–176, Philadelphia.

Kelley, J. C. (1956), "Settlement Patterns in North-Central Mexico," in *Prehistoric Settlement Patterns in the New World,* G. R. Willey, ed., Viking Fund Publications in Anthropology, No. 23, pp. 128–139, New York.

Kelley, J. C. (1959), "The Desert Culture and the Balcones Phase: Archaic Manifestations in the Southwest and Texas," *American Antiquity,* Vol. 24, pp. 276–288, Salt Lake City.

Kelley, J. C. (1960), "North Mexico and the Correlation of Mesoamerican and Southwestern Cultural Sequences," *Selected Papers, 5th International Congress of Anthropological Sciences,* A. F. C. Wallace, ed., pp. 566–573, Philadelphia.

Kelley, J. C., T. N. Campbell, and D. J. Lehmer (1940), *The Association of Archaeological Materials with Geological Deposits in the Big Bend Region of Texas,* No. 10, West Texas Historical and Scientific Society.

Kelley, J. C. and W. J. Shackelford (1954), "Preliminary Notes on the Weicker Site, Durango, Mexico," *El Palacio,* Vol. 61, No. 5, pp. 145–160, Santa Fe.

Kelley, J. C. and H. D. Winters (1960), "A Revision of the Archaeological Sequence in Sinaloa, Mexico," *American Antiquity,* Vol. 25, No. 4, pp. 547–561, Salt Lake City.

Kelly, A. R. (1933), *Some Problems of Recent Cahokia Archaeology,* Transactions, Vol. 25, No. 4, pp. 101–103, Illinois State Academy of Science, Springfield.

Kelly, A. R. (1938), *A Preliminary Report on Archaeological Exploration at Macon, Georgia,* Anthropological Papers, No. 1, Bureau American Ethnology, Bulletin 119, pp. 1–69, Smithsonian Institution, Washington, D.C.

Kelly, A. R. (1939), "The Macon Trading Post—An Historical Foundling," *American Antiquity,* Vol. 4, pp. 328–333, Menasha, Wisconsin.

Kelly, Isabel T. (1938), "Excavations at Chametla, Sinaloa," *Ibero-Americana,* No. 14, University of California, Berkeley.

Kelly, Isabel T. (1945–1949), "The Archaeology of the Autlán-Tuxcacuesco Area of Jalisco: I: The Autlan Zone; II: The Tuxcacuesco Zapotitlan Zone," *Ibero-Americana,* Nos. 26–27, University of California, Berkeley.

Kelly, Isabel T. (1947), *Excavations at Apatzingan, Michoacan,* Publications in Anthropology, No. 7, Viking Fund, New York.

Keur, D. L. (1941), *Big Bead Mesa,* Memoir No. 1, Society for American Archaeology, Menasha, Wisconsin.

King, A. R. (1950), *Cattle Point: A Stratified Site in the Southern Northwest Coast Region,* Memoir No. 7, Society for American Archaeology, Salt Lake City.

Kirchhoff, Paul (1942), "Las Tribus de La Baja California y el Libro del P. Baegert," in *Noticias de la Peninsula Americana de California* by J. J. Baegert, translated by P. R. Hendricks, Mexico, D.F. (Cited from Massey, 1961 b.)

Kirchhoff, Paul (1943), "Mesoamerica," *Acta Americana,* Vol. 1, pp. 92–107, Mexico, D.F.

Kirchhoff, Paul (1954), "Gatherers and Farmers in the Greater Southwest: A Problem in Classification," *American Anthropologist,* Vol. 56, No. 4, Pt. 1, pp. 529–550, Menasha, Wisconsin.

Kidder, A. V. (1924), *An Introduction to the Study of Southwestern Archaeology, with a Preliminary Account of the Excavations at Pecos,* Papers, Southwestern Expedition, Phillips Academy, No. 1, Yale University Press, New Haven.

Kidder, A. V. (1931), *The Pottery of Pecos,* Vol. I, Papers, Southwestern Expedition, Phillips Academy, Yale University Press, New Haven.

Kidder, A. V. and Guernsey, S. Y. (1919), *Archaeological Exploration in Northeastern Arizona,* Bureau of American Ethnology, Bulletin 65, Smithsonian Institution, Washington, D.C.

Kidder, A. V., J. D. Jennings, and E. M. Shook (1946), *Excavations at Kaminaljuyú, Guatemala,* Publication No. 561, Carnegie Institution of Washington, Washington, D.C.

Kidder, A. V. and A. O. Shepard (1936), *The Pottery of Pecos,*

Vol. II, Papers, Southwestern Expedition, Phillips Academy, Yale University Press, New Haven.

Kivett, M. F. (1952), *Woodland Sites in Nebraska,* Publications in Anthropology, No. 1, Nebraska State Historical Society, Lincoln.

Kneberg, Madeline (1952), "The Tennessee Area," in *Archaeology of Eastern United States,* J. B. Griffin, ed., pp. 190–198, University of Chicago Press, Chicago.

Krickeberg, Walter (1956), *Altmexikanische Kulturen,* Safari-Verlag, Berlin.

Krieger, A. D. (1945), "An Inquiry Into Supposed Mexican Influence on a Prehistoric Cult in the Southern United States," *American Anthropologist,* Vol. 47, No. 4, pp. 483–515, Menasha, Wisconsin.

Krieger, A. D. (1946), *Culture Complexes and Chronology in Northern Texas,* Publication, No. 4640, University of Texas, Austin.

Krieger, A. D. (1947), "The Eastward Extension of Puebloan Datings Toward Cultures of the Mississippi Valley," *American Antiquity,* Vol. 12, No. 3, Pt. 1, Menasha, Wisconsin.

Krieger, A. D. (1949), *Importance of the "Gilmore Corridor" in Culture Contacts between Middle America and the Eastern United States,* Bulletin 19, Texas Archaeological and Paleontological Society, Abilene.

Krieger, A. D. (1953), "Recent Developments in the Problem of Relationships between the Mexican Gulf Coast and Eastern United States," in *Los Huastecas, Los Totonacos, y sus Vecinos,* I. Bernal and E. Davalos Hurtado, eds., pp. 497–518, Sociedad Mexicana de Antropología, Mexico, D.F.

Krieger, A. D. (1962), "The Earliest Cultures in the Western United States," *American Antiquity,* Vol. 28, No. 2, pp. 138–143, Salt Lake City.

Krieger, A. D. (1964), "Early Man in the New World," in *Prehistoric Man in the New World,* J. D. Jennings and E. Norbeck, eds., pp. 23–84, University of Chicago Press, Chicago.

Kroeber, A. L. (1923), "American Culture History and the Northwest Coast," *American Anthropologist,* Vol. 25, pp. 1–20, Menasha, Wisconsin.

Kroeber, A. L. (1939), *Cultural and Natural Areas of Native North America,* University of California Publications in American Archaeology and Ethnology, Vol. 38, Berkeley.

Kroeber, A. L. (1948), *Anthropology,* Harcourt, Brace & World, New York.

Kubler, George (1961), "Chichén Itzá y Tula," *Estudios de Cultura Maya,* Vol. 1, pp. 47–80, Seminario de Cultura Maya, Universidad Nacional Autonoma de Mexico, Mexico, D.F.

Kubler, George (1962), *The Art and Architecture of Ancient America: The Mexican, Maya, and Andean Peoples,* Penguin Books, Baltimore.

Lacerda, A. (1882), *Documents pour Servir a L'Histoire de L'Homme Fossile du Brésil,* Memoires de la Societé d'Anthropologie de Paris, 2nd Série, Tome 2, Fasc. 4, Paris.

de Laguna, Frederica (1934), *The Archaeology of Cook Inlet, Alaska,* University of Pennsylvania Press, Philadelphia.

Lanning, E. P. (1963), "A Pre-Agricultural Occupation on the Central Coast of Peru," *American Antiquity,* Vol. 28, No. 3, pp. 360–371, Salt Lake City.

Lanning, E. P. and E. A. Hammel (1961), "Early Lithic Industries of Western South America," *American Antiquity,* Vol. 27, No. 2, pp. 139–154, Salt Lake City.

Larsen, Helge and F. G. Rainey (1948), *Ipiutak and the Arctic Whale Hunting Culture,* Anthropological Papers, Vol. 42, American Museum of Natural History, New York.

Lathrap, D. W. (1957), *The Classic Stage in Mesoamerica,* Kroeber Anthropological Society Papers, No. 17, pp. 38–74, Department of Anthropology, University of California, Berkeley.

Laughlin, W. S. (1941), "Excavations in the Calapuya Mounds of the Willamette Valley, Oregon," *American Antiquity,* Vol. 7, No. 2, pp. 147–155, Menasha, Wisconsin.

Laughlin, W. S. (1943), "Notes on the Archaeology of the Yamhill River, Willamette Valley, Oregon," *American Antiquity,* Vol. 9, No. 2, pp. 220–229, Menasha, Wisconsin.

Laughlin, W. S. (1962 a), "Generic Problems and New Evidence in the Anthropology of the Eskimo-Aleut Stock," in *Prehistoric Cultural Relations Between the Arctic and Temperate Zones of North America,* J. M. Campbell, ed., Technical Paper No. 11, pp. 100–112, Arctic Institute of North America, Montreal.

Laughlin, W. S. (1962 b), Bering Strait to Puget Sound: Dichotomy and Affinity Between Eskimo-Aleut and American Indians," in *Prehistoric Cultural Relations Between the Arctic and Temperate Zones of North America,* J. M. Campbell, ed., Technical Paper No. 11, pp. 113–125, Arctic Institute of North America, Montreal.

Laughlin, W. S. and G. H. Marsh (1954), "The Llamellar Flake Manufacturing Site on Anangula Island in the Aleutians," *American Antiquity,* Vol. 20, No. 1, pp. 27–39, Salt Lake City.

Laughlin, W. S. and G. H. Marsh (1956), *Trends in Aleutian Chipped*

Stone Artifacts, Anthropological Papers, Vol. 5, No. 1, pp. 5–21, University of Alaska, Fairbanks.

Leechman, Douglas (1943), "Two New Cape Dorset Sites," *American Antiquity,* Vol. 8, pp. 363–375, Menasha, Wisconsin.

Lehmer, D. J. (1954 a), *Archaeological Investigations in the Oahe Dam Area, South Dakota, 1950–51,* River Basin Survey Papers, No. 7, Bureau American Ethnology, Bulletin 158, Smithsonian Institution, Washington, D.C.

Lehmer, D. J. (1954 b), "The Sedentary Horizon of the Northern Plains," *Southwestern Journal of Anthropology,* Vol. 10, pp. 139–159, Albuquerque.

Leighton, M. M. (1960), "The Classification of the Wisconsin Glacial Stage of North Central United States," *The Journal of Geology,* Vol. 68, pp. 529–552, University of Chicago Press, Chicago.

Le Paige, Gustavo R. P. (1958), "Antiguas culturas atacamenas en la cordillera chilena," *Revista Universitaria Catolica de Chile,* Vol. 43, pp. 139–165, Santiago.

Le Paige, Gustavo R. P. (1960), "Antiguas culturas atacamenas en la cordillera chilena," *Revista Universitaria Catolica de Chile,* Vols. 44–45, pp. 191–206, Santiago.

Lewis, T. M. N. and Madeline Kneberg (1946), *Hiwassee Island,* University of Tennessee Press, Knoxville.

Lewis, T. M. N. and Madeline Kneberg (1958), "The Nuckolls Site," *Tennessee Archaeologist,* Vol. 14, pp. 60–79, Knoxville.

Lewis, T. M. N. and Madeline Kneberg (1959), "The Archaic Culture in the Middle South," *American Antiquity,* Vol. 25, No. 2, pp. 161–183, Salt Lake City.

Lewis, T. M. N. and Madeline Kneberg Lewis (1961), *Eva, an Archaic Site,* University of Tennessee Study in Anthropology, University of Tennessee Press, Knoxville.

Libby, W. F. (1955), *Radiocarbon Dating,* 2nd ed., University of Chicago Press, Chicago.

Linne, Sigvald (1934), *Archaeological Researches at Teotihuacán, Mexico,* Publication No. 1, Ethnographical Museum of Sweden, Stockholm.

Linne, Sigvald (1938), *Zapotecan Antiquities,* Publication No. 4, Ethnographical Museum of Sweden, Stockholm.

Linne, Sigvald (1942), *Mexican Highland Cultures, Archaeological Researches at Teotihuacán, Calpulalpán and Chalchicomula in 1934–35,* Publication No. 7, Ethnographical Museum of Sweden, Stockholm.

Linton, Ralph (1944), "Nomad Raids and Fortified Pueblos," *American Antiquity,* Vol. 10, No. 1, pp. 28–32, Menasha, Wisconsin.

Lister, R. H. (1955), *The Present Status of the Archaeology of Western Mexico: A Distributional Study,* University of Colorado Studies, Series in Anthropology No. 5. Boulder, Colorado.

Lister, R. H. and A. M. Howard (1955), "The Chalchihuites Culture of Northwestern Mexico," *American Antiquity,* Vol. 21, pp. 123–129, Salt Lake City.

Logan, W. D. (1952), *Graham Cave, an Archaic Site in Montgomery County, Missouri,* Memoir No. 2, Missouri Archaeological Society, Columbia.

Longacre, R. E. and R. F. Millon (1961), "Proto-Mixtecan and Proto-Amuzgo-Mixtecan Vocabularies: A Preliminary Cultural Analysis," Anthropological Linguistics, Vol. 3, No. 4, pp. 1–44, Bloomington.

Longyear, J. M., III (1944), *Archaeological Investigations in El Salvador,* Memoirs, Vol. 9, No. 2, Peabody Museum, Harvard University, Cambridge.

University of Tennessee Press, Knoxville.

Lorenzo, J. L. (1953), "A Fluted Point from Durango, Mexico," *American Antiquity,* Vol. 18, pp. 394–395, Salt Lake City.

Lorenzo, J. L. (1955), "Los Concheros de la Costa de Chiapas," *Anales,* Vol. 7, pp. 41–50, Instituto Nacional de Antropología e Historia, Mexico, D.F.

Lorenzo, J. L. (1964), *Dos puntas acanaladas en la región de Chapala, Mexico,* Boletín, No. 18, pp. 1–6, Instituto Nacional de Antropología e Historia, Mexico, D.F.

Lothrop, S. K. (1924), *Tulum,* Publication No. 335, Carnegie Institution of Washington, Washington, D.C.

Lothrop, S. K. (1927), *Pottery Types and Their Sequence in El Salvador,* Indian Notes and Monographs, Vol. 1, No. 4, pp. 165–220, Museum of the American Indian, Heye Foundation, New York.

Lothrop, S. K. (1939), "The Southeastern Frontier of the Maya," *American Anthropologist,* Vol. 41, pp. 42–54, Menasha, Wisconsin.

Lothrop, S. K. (1952), *Metals from the Cenote of Sacrifice Chichén Itzá, Yucatan.* Memoirs, Vol. 10, No. 2, Peabody Museum, Harvard University, Cambridge.

Loud, L. L. and M. R. Harrington, (1929), *Lovelock Cave,* University of California Publications in American Archaeology and Ethnology, Vol. 25, No. 1, Berkeley.

Lowe, G. W. (1959 a), *The Chiapas Project, 1955–58,* Papers, No. 1, Publication No. 3, New World Archaeological Foundation, Orinda, California.

Lowe, G. W. (1959 b), "The Long Sequence of Preclassic Architectural Development at Chiapa de Corzo, Chiapas," *Abstracts of Papers, 24th Annual Meeting, Society for American Archaeology,* p. 38, University of Utah, Salt Lake City.

Lowe, G. W. (1962 a), "Algunos Resultados de la Temporada 1961 en Chiapa de Corzo, Chiapas," *Estudios de Cultura Maya,* Vol. 2, pp. 185–196, Mexico, D.F.

Lowe, G. W. (1962 b), *Mound 5 and Minor Excavations, Chiapas, Mexico,* Papers, No. 12, New World Archaeological Foundation, Provo, Utah.

Lowie, R. H. (1946 a), "Eastern Brazil: An Introduction," in *Handbook of South American Indians,* J. H. Steward, ed., Vol. 1, pp. 381–398, Bureau American Ethnology, Bulletin 143, Smithsonian Institution, Washington, D.C.

Lowie, R. H. (1946 b). "The Bororo," in *Handbook of South American Indians,* J. H. Steward, ed., Vol. 1, pp. 419–434, Bureau American Ethnology, Bulletin 143, Smithsonian Institution, Washington, D.C.

Lumholtz, C. (1902), *Unknown Mexico,* Charles Scribner's Sons, New York.

MacGowan, Kenneth and J. A. Hester, Jr. (1962), *Early Man in the New World,* rev. ed., Doubleday, New York.

MacNeish, R. S. (1948), "The Pre-Pottery Faulkner Site in Southern Illinois," *American Antiquity,* Vol. 13, No. 3, pp. 232–243, Menasha, Wisconsin.

MacNeish, R. S. (1952), "The Archaeology of the Northeastern United States," in *Archaeology of Eastern United States,* J. B. Griffin, ed., pp. 46–57, University of Chicago Press, Chicago.

MacNeish, R. S. (1953), *Archaeological Reconnaissance in the Mackenzie River Drainage,* Bulletin No. 128, Annual Report of the National Museum of Canada, Ottawa.

MacNeish, R. S. (1954), *An Early Archaeological Site near Panuco, Veracruz,* Transactions, Vol. 44, Pt. 5, American Philosophical Society, Philadelphia.

MacNeish, R. S. (1956), *The Engigstciak Site on the Yukon Arctic Coast,* Anthropological Papers, Vol. 4, No. 2, University of Alaska, Fairbanks.

MacNeish, R. S. (1958 a), *Preliminary Archaeological Investigations in the Sierra de Tamaulipas, Mexico,* Transactions, Vol. 48, Pt. 6, American Philosophical Society, Philadelphia.

MacNeish, R. S. (1958 b), *An Introduction to the Archaeology of Southeast Manitoba,* Bulletin 157, National Museum of Canada, Ottawa.

MacNeish, R. S. (1959 a), *Men Out of Asia; As Seen from the Northwest Yukon,* Anthropological Papers, Vol. 7, No. 2, University of Alaska, Fairbanks.

MacNeish, R. S. (1959 b), "A Speculative Framework of Northern American Prehistory as of April 1959," *Anthropologia,* Vol. 1, pp. 7–23, Canadian Research Center for Anthropology, University of Ottawa.

MacNeish, R. S. (1961), *First Annual Report of the Tehuacán Archaeological-Botanical Project,* Project Reports No. 1, R. S. Peabody Foundation, Andover.

MacNeish, R. S. (1962 a), *Second Annual Report of the Tehuacán Archaeological-Botanical Project,* Project Reports, No. 2, R. S. Peabody Foundation for Archaeology, Andover.

MacNeish, R. S. (1962 b), "Recent Finds in the Yukon Territory of Canada," in *Prehistoric Cultural Relations Between the Arctic and Temperate Zones of North America,* J. M. Campbell, ed., Technical Paper No. 11, pp. 20–26, Arctic Institute of North America, Montreal.

MacNeish, R. S. (1964 a), *Investigations in the Southwest Yukon: Part II: Archaeological Excavation, Comparisons and Speculations,* Papers, Vol. 6, No. 1, R. S. Peabody Foundation for Archaeology, Phillips Academy, Andover.

MacNeish, R. S. (1964 b), "Ancient Mesoamerican Civilization," *Science,* Vol. 143, pp. 531–537, Lancaster.

Maldonado-Koerdell, Manuel and Luis Aveleyra Arroya de Anda (1948), "Nota Preliminar sobre dos Artefactos del Pleistoceno Superior Hallados en la Región de Tequixquiac, Mexico," in *Tomo Especial de Homenaje al Dr. Eduard Seler,* Mexico, D.F.

Mangelsdorf, P. C. and R. H. Lister (1956), "Archaeological Evidence on the Evolution of Maize in Northwestern Mexico," *Botanical Museum Leaflets,* Vol. 17, No. 6, Harvard University, Cambridge.

Mangelsdorf, P. C., R. S. MacNeish, and W. C. Galinat (1964), "Domestication of Corn," *Science,* Vol. 143, No. 3606, Lancaster.

Mangelsdorf, P. C., R. S. MacNeish, and G. R. Willey (1964), "Origins of Agriculture in Mesoamerica," *Handbook of Middle American Indians,* R. Wauchope, ed., Vol. 1, pp. 427–445, University of Texas Press, Austin.

Mangelsdorf, P. C. and R. G. Reeves (1959), "The Origin of Corn—Five Papers Commemorating the Darwin Centennial," *Botanical Museum Leaflets,* Vol. 18, Nos. 7–10, pp. 329–440, Harvard University, Cambridge.

Mangelsdorf, P. C. and C. E. Smith, Jr. (1949), "New Archaeological Evidence on Evolution in Maize," *Botanical Museum Leaflets,* Vol. 13, No. 8, Harvard University, Cambridge.

Marquina, Ignacio (1951), *Arquitectura Prehispanica,* Memorias del Instituto Nacional de Antropología e Historia, No. 1, Mexico, D.F.

Marshack, Alexander (1964), "Lunar Notation on Upper Paleolithic Remains," *Science,* Vol. 146, pp. 743–745, Lancaster.

Martin, P. S. (1940), *The SU Site Excavations at a Mogollon Village, Western New Mexico, 1939,* Anthropological Series, Vol. 32, No. 1, Field Museum of Natural History, Chicago.

Martin, P. S. (1943), *The SU Site Excavations at a Mogollon Village, Western New Mexico, Second Season, 1941,* Anthropological Series, Vol. 32, No. 2, Field Museum of Natural History, Chicago.

Martin, P. S. and others (1952), *Mogollon Cultural Continuity and Change: The Stratigraphic Analysis of Tularosa and Cordova Caves,* Fieldiana: Anthropology, Vol. 40, Chicago Natural History Museum, Chicago.

Martin, P. S., G. I. Quimby, and D. Collier (1947), *Indians Before Columbus,* University of Chicago Press, Chicago.

Martin, P. S. and J. B. Rinaldo (1940), *The SU Site, Excavations at a Mogollon Village, Western New Mexico 1939,* Anthropological Series, Vol. 32, No. 1, Field Museum of Natural History, Chicago.

Martin, P. S. and J. B. Rinaldo (1947), *The SU Site Excavations at a Mogollon Village, Western New Mexico, Third Season, 1946,* Anthropological Series, Vol. 32, No. 3, Field Museum of Natural History, Chicago.

Martin, P. S. and J. B. Rinaldo (1950 a), *Turkey Foot Ridge Site, a Mogollon Village, Pine Lawn Valley, Western New Mexico,* Fieldiana: Anthropology, Vol. 38, No. 2, Chicago Natural History Museum, Chicago, Illinois.

Martin, P. S. and J. B. Rinaldo (1950 b), *Sites of the Reserve Phase, Pine Lawn Valley, Western New Mexico,* Fieldiana: Anthropology, Vol. 38, No. 3, Chicago

Natural History Museum, Chicago.

Martin, P. S. and J. B. Rinaldo (1951), "The Southwestern Co-Tradition," *Southwestern Journal of Anthropology,* Vol. 7, pp. 215–229, Albuquerque.

Martin, P. S., J. B. Rinaldo, and Ernst Antevs (1949), *Cochise and Mogollon Sites, Pine Lawn Valley, Western New Mexico,* Fieldiana: Anthropology, Vol. 38, No. 1, Chicago Natural History Museum, Chicago.

Martin, P. S., James Schoenwetter, and B. C. Arms (1961), *Southwestern Palynology and Prehistory: The Last 10,000 Years,* Geochronology Laboratories, University of Arizona, Tucson.

Mason, J. A. (1937), *Further Remarks on the Pre-Columbian Relationships between the United States and Mexico,* Bulletin, Vol. 9, pp. 120–129, Texas Archaeological and Paleontological Society, Abilene.

Mason, J. A. (1940), "The Native Languages of Middle America," in *The Maya and Their Neighbors,* C. L. Hay, *et al.,* eds., pp. 52–87, Appleton-Century, New York.

Mason, R. J. (1958), *Late Pleistocene Geochronology and the Paleo-Indian Penetration into the Lower Michigan Peninsula,* Anthropological Papers, No. 11, Museum of Anthropology, University of Michigan, Ann Arbor. (Cited from Wilmsen, 1964.)

Mason, R. J. (1962), "The Paleo-Indian Tradition in Eastern North America," *Current Anthropology,* Vol. 3, No. 3, pp. 227–246, Wenner-Gren Foundation, Chicago.

Massey, W. C. (1947), "Brief Report on Archaeological Investigations in Baja California," *Southwestern Journal of Anthropology,* Vol. 3, No. 4, pp. 344–359, Albuquerque.

Massey, W. C. (1949), "Tribes and

Languages of Baja California," *Southwestern Journal of Anthropology,* Vol. 5, No. 3, pp. 272–307, Albuquerque.

Massey, W. C. (1961 a), "The cultural distinction of aboriginal Baja California," in *Homenaje a Pablo Martinez del Rio,* pp. 411–423, Instituto Nacional de Antropología e Historia, Mexico, D.F.

Massey, W. C. (1961 b), "The Survival of the Dart-thrower on the Peninsula of Baja California," *Southwestern Journal of Anthropology,* Vol. 17, No. 1, pp. 81–93, Albuquerque.

Mathiassen, Therkel (1927), *Archaeology of the Central Eskimos,* Report of the Fifth Thule Expedition, 1921–24, Vol. 4, Copenhagen.

Matthiassen, Therkel (1958), *The Sermermiut Excavations, 1955,* Meddelelser om Grønland, Vol. 161, No. 3, Copenhagen.

Mattos, Anibal (1946), "Lagoa Santa Man, in *Handbook of South American Indians,* Julian H. Steward, ed., Vol. 1, pp. 399–400, Bureau of American Ethnology, Bulletin 143, Smithsonian Institution, Washington, D.C.

Maudslay, A. P. (1889–1902), *Archaeology, Biologia Centrali Americana,* 4 Vols., R. H. Porter and Dulau and Company, London.

Maxwell, M. S. (1952), "The Archaeology of the Lower Ohio Valley," in *Archaeology of Eastern United States,* J. B. Griffin, ed., pp. 176–189, University of Chicago Press, Chicago.

Mayer-Oakes, W. J. (1951), "Starved Rock Archaic, A Pre-Pottery Horizon from Northern Illinois," *American Antiquity,* Vol. 16, pp. 313–323, Salt Lake City.

Mayer-Oakes, W. J. (1959), "A Stratigraphic Excavation at El Risco, Mexico, D.F.," *Proceedings,* Vol. 103, No. 3, American Philosophical Society, Philadelphia.

Mayer-Oakes, W. J. and R. E. Bell (1960), "Early Man Site Found in Highland Ecuador," *Science,* Vol. 131, No. 3416, pp. 1805–1806, Lancaster.

McCary, B. C. (1951), "A Workshop Site of Early Man in Dinwiddie County, Virginia," *American Antiquity,* Vol. 17, No. 1, pp. 9–17, Salt Lake City.

McGregor, J. C. (1941), *Southwestern Archaeology,* John Wiley and Sons, Inc., New York.

McKern, W. C. (1937), "An Hypothesis for the Asiatic Origin of the Woodland Culture Pattern," *American Antiquity,* Vol. 3, pp. 138–143, Menasha.

McKern, W. C. (1939), "The Midwestern Taxonomic Method as an Aid to Archaeological Study," *American Antiquity,* Vol. 4, pp. 301–313, Menasha, Wisconsin.

McKern, W. C. (1946), "Aztalan," *The Wisconsin Archaeologist,* Vol. 27, No. 2, pp. 41–52, Milwaukee.

McKern, W. C., P. F. Titterington, and J. B. Griffin (1945), "Painted Pottery Figurines from Illinois," *American Antiquity,* Vol. 10, No. 3, pp. 295–302, Menasha, Wisconsin.

McQuown, Norman (1964), "Los Origenes y la diferenciación de Los Mayas segun se infiere de estudio comparativo de las lenguas Mayanas," in *Desarollo Cultural de Los Mayas,* E. Z. Vogt, and A. Ruz, eds., Publicación Especial del Seminario de Cultura Maya, pp. 49–81, Universidad Nacional Autónoma de Mexico, Mexico, D.F.

Medellin Zenil, Alfonso (1960), *Cerámicas del Totonacapan,* Universidad Veracruzana, Instituto de Antropología, Veracruz.

Meggers, B. J. (1954), "Environmental Limitation on the Development of Culture," *American Anthropologist,* Vol. 56, pp. 801–824, Menasha, Wisconsin.

Meggers, B. J. (1963), "Cultural Development in Latin America: An Interpretative Overview," in *Aboriginal Cultural Development in Latin America: An Interpretative Review,* B. J. Meggers and C. Evans, eds., Smithsonian Miscellaneous Collections, Vol. 146, pp. 131–145, Smithsonian Institution, Washington, D.C.

Meggers, B. J. (1964), "North and South American Cultural Connection and Convergences," in *Prehistoric Man in the New World,* J. D. Jennings and E. Norbeck, eds., pp. 511–526, University of Chicago Press, Chicago.

Meighan, C. W. (1959 a), "Californian Cultures and the Concept of an Archaic Stage," *American Antiquity,* Vol. 24, pp. 289–305, Salt Lake City.

Meighan, C. W. (1959 b), "New Findings in West Mexican Archaeology," *The Kiva,* Vol. 25, No. 1, pp. 1–7, Journal of the Arizona Archaeological and Historical Society, University of Arizona, Tucson.

Meighan, C. W. (1959 c), "The Little Harbor Site, Catalina Island: An Example of Ecological Interpretation in Archaeology," *American Antiquity,* Vol. 24, pp. 383–405, Salt Lake City.

Meldgaard, J. A. (1952), "Paleo-Eskimo Culture in West Greenland," *American Antiquity,* Vol. 17, No. 3, pp. 222–230.

Meldgaard, J. A. (1960), "Prehistoric Culture Sequences in the Eastern Arctic as Elucidated by Stratified Sites at Igloolik," *Selected Papers, 5th International Congress of Anthropological and Ethnological Sciences,* A. Wallace, ed., pp. 588–595, Philadelphia.

Meldgaard, J. A. (1962), "On the Formative Period of the Dorset Culture," in *Prehistoric Cultural Relations Between the Arctic and Temperate Zones of North America,* J. M. Campbell, ed., Technical Paper No. 11, pp. 92–95, Arctic Institute of North America, Montreal.

Meleen, E. E. (1938), *A Preliminary Report of the Mitchell Indian Village Site and Burial Mounds, on Finesteel Creek, Mitchell, Davison County, South Dakota,* Archaeological Studies, Circular No. 2, South Dakota Archaeological Commission, Vermillion.

Mendizabal, Othon de and W. Jimenez Moreno (1939), *Lenguas Indígenas de Mexico,* a linguistic map, Instituto Panamericano de Geografiá e Historia, Mexico, D.F.

Menghin, O. F. A. (1952), "Fundamentos Cronológicos de la Prehistoria de Patagonia," *Runa,* Vol. 5, pp. 23–43, Buenos Aires.

Menghin, O. F. A. (1953–1954), "Culturas Precerámicas en Bolivia," *Runa,* Vol. 6, Pts. 1–2, pp. 125–132, Buenos Aires.

Menghin, O. F. A. and Marcelo Bormida (1950), "Investigaciónes prehistoricas en cuevas de Tandilia, Provincia de Buenos Aires," *Runa,* Vol. 3, Pts. la and 2, Buenos Aires.

Mera, H. P. (1938), "Some Aspects of the Largo Cultural Phase, Northern New Mexico," *American Antiquity,* Vol. 3, No. 3, Menasha, Wisconsin.

Metraux, Alfred (1946), "Ethnography of the Chaco," in *Handbook of South American Indians,* J. H. Steward, ed., Vol. 1, pp. 197–370, Bureau of American Ethnology, Bulletin 143, Smithsonian Institution, Washington, D.C.

Miles, S. W. (1951), "A Revaluation of the Old Copper Industry," *American Antiquity,* Vol. 16, No. 3, pp. 240–246, Salt Lake City.

Miles, S. W. (1962), "Sculpture of the Guatemala-Chiapas Highlands and Pacific Slopes, and Associated Hieroglyphs," MS., to be published in *The Handbook of Middle American Indians,* R. Wauchope, ed., Vol. 2, University of Texas Press, Austin.

Millon, R. F. (1954), "Irrigation at Teotihuacán," *American Antiquity*, Vol. 20, pp. 177–180, Salt Lake City.

Millon, R. F. (1957 a), *New Data on Teotihuacán I in Teotihuacán*, Boletín del Centro de Investigaciones Antropologicas de Mexico, No. 4, pp. 12–18, Mexico, D.F.

Millon, R. F. (1957 b), "Irrigation Systems in the Valley of Teotihuacán," *American Antiquity*, Vol. 23, No. 2, Pt. 1, pp. 160–166, Salt Lake City.

Millon, R. F. (1960), "The Beginnings of Teotihuacán," *American Antiquity*, Vol. 26, No. 1, pp. 1–10, Salt Lake City.

Millon, R. F. (1961), "The Northwestern Boundary of Teotihuacán: A Major Urban Zone," in *Homenaje a Pablo Martínez del Río*, pp. 311–319, Instituto Nacional de Antropología e Historia, Mexico, D.F.

Millon, R. F. (1964), "The Teotihuacán Mapping Project," *American Antiquity*, Vol. 29, No. 3, pp. 345–352, Salt Lake City.

Millon, R. F. and J. A. Bennyhoff (1961), "A Long Architectural Sequence at Teotihuacán," *American Antiquity*, Vol. 26, pp. 516–523, Salt Lake City.

Millon, R. F. and Bruce Drewitt (1961), "Earlier Structures within the Pyramid of the Sun at Teotihuacán," *American Antiquity*, Vol. 26, No. 3, pp. 371–380, Salt Lake City.

Mills, W. C. (1907), *The Explorations of the Edwin Harness Mound*, Ohio Archaeological and Historical Publications, Vol. 20, pp. 113–193, Columbus.

Mills, W. C. (1909), "Explorations of the Seip Mound," *Ohio Archaeological and Historical Quarterly*, Vol. 18, pp. 268–321, Columbus.

Moedano, Hugo (1941), "Estudio Preliminar de la Cerámica de Tzintzuntzan, Temporada III," *Revista Mexicana de Estudios Antropológicos*, Vol. 5, No. 1, Mexico, D.F.

Monzon, A. (1949), *El Calpulli en la Organización Social de Los Tenochca*, Publicaciones del Instituto de Historia, No. 14, Mexico, D.F.

Moore, C. B. (1903), "Certain Aboriginal Mounds of the Florida Central West Coast," *Journal Academy of Natural Sciences*, Vol. 12, Philadelphia.

Moore, C. B. (1905), "Aboriginal Remains of Black Warrior River, Lower Tombigbee River, Mobile Bay and Mississippi Sound, and Miscellaneous Investigations in Florida," *Journal of Academy of Natural Sciences*, Vol. 13, Philadelphia.

Moore, C. B. (1907 a), "Crystal River Revisited," *Journal of Academy of Natural Sciences*, Vol. 13, Pt. 3, Philadelphia.

Moore, C. B. (1907 b), "Moundville Revisited," *Journal of Academy of Natural Sciences*, Vol. 13, Pt. 2, Philadelphia.

Moorehead, W. K. (1922), *The Hopewell Mound Group of Ohio*, Field Museum of Natural History, Publications 211, Anthropological Series, Vol. 6, No. 5, Chicago Natural History Museum, Chicago.

Moorehead, W. K. (1928), *The Cahokia Mounds*, Bulletin, Vol. 26, No. 4, University of Illinois, Urbana.

Moorehead, W. K. (1932), "Exploration of the Etowah Site in Georgia," in *Etowah Papers*, Yale University Press, New Haven, for Phillips Academy, Andover.

Morgan, R. G. (1952), "Outline of Cultures in the Ohio Region," in *Archaeology of Eastern United States*, J. B. Griffin, ed., pp. 83–98, University of Chicago Press, Chicago.

Morley, S. G. (1915), *An Introduction to the Study of Maya Hieroglyphs*, Bureau of American Archaeology, Bulletin 57, Smithsonian Institution, Washington, D.C.

Morley, S. G. (1920), *The Inscriptions at Copan*, Publication No. 219, Carnegie Institution of Washington, Washington, D.C.

Morley, S. G. (1946), *The Ancient Maya*, Stanford University Press, Palo Alto.

Morley, S. G. and G. W. Brainerd (1956), *The Ancient Maya*, 3rd ed., Stanford University Press, Palo Alto.

Morris, E. H. (1927), *The Beginnings of Pottery Making in the San Juan Area, Unfired Prototypes and the Wares of the Earliest Ceramic Period*, Anthropological Papers, Vol. 28, Pt. 2, American Museum of Natural History, New York.

Morris, E. H. and R. F. Burgh (1954), *Basket Maker II Sites near Durango, Colorado*, Publication No. 604, Carnegie Institution of Washington, Washington, D.C.

Morse, Dan and Phyllis (1960), "A Preliminary Report on 9-Go-507, The Williams Site, Gordon County, Georgia," *The Florida Anthropologist*, Vol. 13, No. 4, pp. 81–99, Gainesville.

Morss, Noel (1927), *Archaeological Explorations on the Middle Chinlee, 1925*, Memoir, No. 34, American Anthropological Association, Menasha, Wisconsin.

Mulloy, William (1954), "The McKean Site in Northeastern Wyoming," *Southwestern Journal of Anthropology*, Vol. 10, pp. 432–460, Albuquerque.

Murdock, G. P. (1938), *Our Primitive Contemporaries*, The MacMillan Company, New York.

Neill, W. T. (1958), "A Stratified Early Site at Silver Springs, Florida," *The Florida Anthropologist*, Vol. 11, pp. 33–52, Gainesville.

Nesbitt, P. H. (1938), *Starkweather*

Ruin; A Mogollon Pueblo Site in the Upper Gila Area of New Mexico, Publications in Anthropology, Bulletin No. 6, Logan Museum, Beloit, Wisconsin.

Neumann, G. K. (1952), "Archaeology and Race in the American Indians," in *Archaeology of Eastern United States,* J. B. Griffin, ed., pp. 13–34, University of Chicago Press, Chicago.

Newell, H. P. and A. D. Krieger (1949), *The George C. Davis Site, Cherokee County, Texas,* Memoir No. 5, Society for American Archaeology, Menasha, Wisconsin.

Newman, M. T. (1951), "The Sequence of Indian Physical Types in South America," in *Papers on the Physical Anthropology of the American Indian,* W. S. Laughlin, ed., pp. 69–97, Viking Fund, New York.

Newman, M. T. (1953), "The Application of Ecological Rules to the Racial Anthropology of the Aboriginal New World," *American Anthropologist,* Vol. 55, pp. 311–327, Menasha, Wisconsin.

Newman, M. T. (1958), "A Trial Formulation Presenting Evidence from Physical Anthropology for Migrations from Mexico to South America," in *Migrations in New World Culture History,* R. H. Thompson, ed., Social Science Bulletin No. 27, pp. 33–40, University of Arizona, Tucson.

Newman, M. T. (1962), "Evolutionary Changes in Body Size and Head Form in American Indians," *American Anthropologist,* Vol. 64, pp. 237–257, Menasha, Wisconsin.

Newman, T. M. (1959), *Tillamook Prehistory and Its Relation to the Northwest Coast Culture Area,* Department of Anthropology, University of Oregon, Eugene.

Nicholson, H. B. and Frederic Hicks (1961), "A Brief Progress

Report on the Excavantions at Cerro Portezuelo, Valley of Mexico," *American Antiquity,* Vol. 27, No. 1, pp. 106–107, Salt Lake City.

Noguera, Eduardo (1939), "Exploraciónes en el 'Opeño,' Michoacan," *Proceedings,* 27th *International Congress of Americanists,* pp. 574–586, Mexico, D.F.

Noguera, Eduardo (1940), "Excavations at Tehuacan," in *The Maya and Their Neighbors,* C. L. Hay, *et al.,* eds., Appleton-Century, New York.

Noguera, Eduardo (1941), "La Cerámica de Cholula y Sus Relaciónes con Otras Culturas," *Revista Mexicana de Estudios Antropológicos,* Vol. 5, pp. 151–161, Mexico, D.F.

Noguera, Eduardo (1945), "Excavaciónes en el Estado de Puebla." *Anales,* Vol. 1, Instituto Nacional de Antropología e Historia, Mexico, D.F.

Noguera, Eduardo (1946), "Cultura Mixteca," in *Mexico Prehispanico, Antología de "Esta Semana," 1935–46,* Emma Hurtado, ed., Loera y Chavez, Mexico, D.F.

Nordenskiold, Erland (1912), "Une Contribution à la Connaissance de l'anthropogeographie de l'Amérique," *Journal, Societé des Américanistes de Paris,* Vol. 9, No. 1, pp. 19–26, Paris.

Nordenskiold, Erland (1921), *Comparative Ethnographical Studies: IV: The Copper and Bronze Ages in South America,* Ethnographic Museum Goteborg.

Nordenskiold, Erland (1931), *Comparative Ethnographical Studies: IX: Origin of the Indian Civilizations in South America,* Ethnographic Museum Goteborg.

Norweb, A. H. (1964), "Ceramic Stratigraphy in Southwestern Nicaragua," *Proceedings,* 35th *International Congress of Americanists,* Vol. I, pp. 551–563, Mexico, D.F.

Nusbaum, J. L. (1922), *A Basket-Maker Cave in Kane County, Utah, with Notes on the Artifacts* by A. V. Kidder and S. J. Guernsey, Indian Notes and Monographs, No. 29, Museum of the American Indian, Heye Foundation, New York.

Oregon Archaeological Society (1959), *Wakemap Mound, A Stratified Site on the Lower Columbia River,* Oregon Archaeological Society, Portland.

Orr, K. G. (1952), "Survey of Caddoan Archaeology," in *Archaeology of Eastern United States,* J. B. Griffin, ed., pp. 239–255, University of Chicago Press.

Orr, P. C. (1956), *Radiocarbon Dates from Santa Rosa Island, I,* Anthropological Bulletin, No. 2, Santa Barbara Museum of Natural History, Santa Barbara.

Osbourne, Douglas (1957), *Excavations in the McNary Reservoir Basin near Umatilla, Oregon,* River Basin Survey Papers, No. 8, Bureau of American Ethnology, Bulletin 166, Smithsonian Institution, Washington, D.C.

Osbourne, Douglas, W. W. Caldwell, and R. H. Crabtree (1956), "The Problem of Northwest Coastal Interior Relationships as Seen from Seattle," *American Antiquity,* Vol. 22, No. 2, pp. 117–127, Salt Lake City.

Osgood, Cornelius (1937), *The Ethnography of the Tanaina,* Yale University Publications in Anthropology, No. 16, New Haven.

Osgood, Cornelius (1940), *Ingalik Material Culture,* Yale University Publications in Anthropology, No. 22, New Haven.

Over, W. H. and E. E. Meleen (1941), *A Report on the Investigation of the Brandon Village Site and the Split Rock Creek Mounds,* Archaeological Studies, Circular, No. 3, University of South Dakota Museum, Vermillion.

Parsons, E. C. (1930), *Isleta,* Annual Report, Bureau of American Ethnology, Vol. 47, pp. 193–466, Smithsonian Institution, Washington, D.C.

Parsons, E. C. (1939), *Pueblo Indian Religion,* 2 Vols., University of Chicago Press, Chicago.

Patterson, J. H. (1960), *North America,* Oxford University Press, New York.

Patterson, T. C. and E. P. Lanning (1964), "Changing Settlement Patterns on the Central Peruvian Coast," *Ñawpa Pacha,* No. 2, pp. 113–123, Institute of Andean Studies, Berkeley.

Peterson, F. A. (1959), *Ancient Mexico,* Putnam's, New York.

Phillips, Philip (1940), "Middle American Influence on the Archaeology of the Southeastern United States," in *The Maya and Their Neighbors,* C. L. Hay, *et al.,* eds., pp. 349–367, Appleton-Century, New York.

Phillips, Philip, J. A. Ford, and J. B. Griffin (1951), *Archaeological Survey in the Lower Mississippi Alluvial Valley, 1940–47.* Peabody Museum Papers, Vol. 25, Harvard University, Cambridge.

Piña Chán, Román (1955), *Las Culturas Preclásicas de la Cuenca de Mexico, Mexico,* Fondo de Cultura Economica, Mexico, D.F.

Piña Chán, Román (1958), Tlatilco, Investigaciones, Nos. 1–2, Instituto Nacional de Antropología e Historia, Mexico, D.F.

Piña Chán, Román (1963), "Cultural Development in Central Mesoamerica," in *Aboriginal Cultural Development in Latin America: An Interpretative Review,* B. J. Meggers and C. Evans, eds., Smithsonian Miscellaneous Collections, Vol. 146, No. 1, pp. 17–26, Smithsonian Institution, Washington, D.C.

Pollock, H. E. D., R. L. Roys, Tatiana Proskouriakoff, and A. L. Smith (1962), *Mayapan, Yucatan, Mexico,* Publication No. 619, Carnegie Institution of Washington, Washington, D.C.

Porter, M. N. (1953), *Tlatilco and the Pre-Classic Cultures of the New World,* Viking Fund Publications in Anthropology, No. 19, New York.

Porter, M. N. (1956), *Excavation at Chupicuaro, Guanajuato, Mexico.* Transactions, Vol. 46, Pt. 5, American Philosophical Society, Philadelphia.

Powell, J. W. (1891), *Indian Linguistic Families North of Mexico,* Annual Report, Bureau American Ethnology, Vol. 7, Smithsonian Institution, Washington, D.C.

Prescott, W. H. (1843), *The Conquest of Mexico,* Modern Library edition, New York.

Proskouriakoff, Tatiana (1946), *An Album of Maya Architecture,* Publication No. 558, Carnegie Institution of Washington, Washington, D.C.

Proskouriakoff, Tatiana (1954), *Varieties of Classic Central Veracruz Sculpture,* Contributions to American Anthropology and History, No. 58, Publication 606, pp. 61–121, Carnegie Institution of Washington, Washington, D.C.

Proskouriakoff, Tatiana (1960), "Historical Implications of a Pattern of Dates at Piedras Negras, Guatemala," *American Antiquity,* Vol. 25, No. 4, pp. 454–475, Salt Lake City.

Proskouriakoff, Tatiana (1961), "Portraits of Women in Maya Art," in *Essays in Precolumbian Art and Archaeology,* S. K. Lothrop, *et al.,* eds., pp. 81–99, Harvard University Press, Cambridge.

Prufer, Olaf, *et al.* (1965), *The McGraw Site, A Study in Hopewellian Dynamics,* Scientific Publications, Vol. 4, No. 1, Cleveland Museum of Natural History.

Quimby, G. I. (1941), *The Goodall Focus: An Analysis of Ten Hopewellian Components in Michigan and Indiana,* Indiana Historical Society, Prehistory Research Series, Vol. 9, No. 1, Indianapolis.

Quimby, G. I. (1942), "The Natchezan Culture Type," *American Antiquity,* Vol. 7, pp. 255–275, Menasha, Wisconsin.

Quimby, G. I. (1951), *The Medora Site, West Baton Rouge Parish, Louisiana,* Anthropological Series, Vol. 24, No. 2, Field Museum of Natural History, Chicago.

Quimby, G. I. (1952), "The Archaeology of the Upper Great Lakes Area," in *Archaeology of Eastern United States,* J. B. Griffin, ed., pp. 99–107, University of Chicago Press, Chicago.

Quimby, G. I. (1960), *Indian Life in the Upper Great Lakes, 11,000* B.C. *to* A.D. *1800,* University of Chicago Press, Chicago.

Rainey, F. G. (1939), *Archaeology in Central Alaska,* Anthropological Papers, Vol. 36, Pt. 4, pp. 351–405, American Museum of Natural History, New York.

Ray, V. F. (1939), *Cultural Relations in the Plateau of Northwestern America,* Publications of the F. W. Hodge Anniversary Publication Fund, No. 3, Southwest Museum, Los Angeles.

Reed, E. K. (1954), "Transition to History in the Pueblo Southwest," *American Anthropologist,* Vol. 56, No. 4, pp. 592–597, Menasha, Wisconsin.

Reed, E. K. (1956), "Types of Village-Plan Layouts in the Southwest," in *Prehistoric Settlement Patterns in the New World,* G. R. Willey, ed., pp. 11–17, Viking Fund Publications in Anthropology, No. 23, New York.

Reed, E. K. (1962), "Cultural Continuity from Pre-Spanish Archaeological Groups to Modern Indian Tribes in the Southwestern United States," *Proceedings,*

34th International Congress of Americanists, pp. 298–300, Vienna.

Reed, E. K. (1963), "Tepehuan and Hohokam," *Regional Research Abstract*, No. 302, mimeographed, National Park Service. Santa Fe, New Mexico.

Reed, E. K. (1964), "The Greater Southwest," in *Prehistoric Man in the New World*, J. D. Jennings and E. Norbeck, eds., pp. 175–192, University of Chicago Press, Chicago.

Reichel-Dolmatoff, Gerardo (1961), "Puerto Hormiga: Un Complejo Prehistórico Marginal de Colombia," *Revista Colombiana de Antropología*, Vol. 10, pp. 349–354, Bogota.

Reinsford, R. C. (1940), *Archaic Sites in the Lower Southeast*, Papers in History and Science, No. 10, The Bringer Foundation, St. Louis.

Renaud, E. B. (1938), "The Black Forks Culture of Southwest Wyoming," *The Archaeological Survey of the Western High Plains, 10th Report*, University of Denver.

Renaud, E. B. (1940), "Further Research in the Black Forks Basin Southwest Wyoming, 1938–1939," *The Archaeological Survey of the Western High Plains, 12th Report*, University of Denver.

Ricketson, O. G., Jr. and E. B. Ricketson (1937), *Uaxactún, Guatemala, Group E-1926-1931*, Publication No. 477, Carnegie Institution of Washington, Washington, D.C.

Riley, C. L. and H. D. Winters (1963), "The Prehistoric Tepehuan of Northern Mexico," *Southwestern Journal of Anthropology*, Vol. 19, No. 2, pp. 177–185, Albuquerque.

Ritchie, W. A. (1932), *The Lamoka Lake Site; The Type Station of the Archaic Algonkin Period in New York*, Researches and Transactions, Vol. 7, No. 4, New York State Archaeological Association, Rochester.

Ritchie, W. A. (1936), *New Evidence Relating to the Archaic Occupation of New York*, Researches and Transactions, Vol. 8, No. 1, New York State Archaeological Association, Rochester.

Ritchie, W. A. (1938), "A Perspective of Northeastern Archaeology," *American Antiquity*, Vol. 4, No. 2, pp. 94–112, Menasha.

Ritchie, W. A. (1940), *Two Prehistoric Village Sites at Brewerton, New York: Type Components of the Brewerton Focus, Laurentian Aspect*, Researches and Transactions, Vol. 9, No. 1, New York State Archaeological Association, Rochester.

Ritchie, W. A. (1944), *The Pre-Iroquoian Occupations of New York State*, Memoir No. 1, Rochester Museum of Arts and Sciences.

Ritchie, W. A. (1946), *A Stratified Prehistoric Site at Brewerton, New York*, Researches and Transactions, Vol. 11, No. 1, New York State Archaeological Association, Rochester.

Ritchie, W. A. (1951), "Ground Slates: Eskimo or Indian?" *Pennsylvania Archaeological Bulletin*, Vol. 21, Nos. 3–4, pp. 46–52, Philadelphia.

Ritchie, W. A. (1953), "A Probable Paleo-Indian Site in Vermont," *American Antiquity*, Vol. 18, pp. 249–258, Salt Lake City.

Ritchie, W. A. (1961), "Iroquois Archaeology and Settlement Patterns," in *Symposium on Cherokee and Iroquois Culture*, W. A. Ritchie and John Gulick, eds., Bureau American Ethnology, Bulletin 180, pp. 27–38, Smithsonian Institution.

Ritchie, W. A. (1962 a), "Northeastern Cross-Ties with the Arctic," in *Prehistoric Cultural Relations Between the Arctic and Temperate Zones of North America*, J. M. Campbell, ed., Technical Paper No. 11, pp. 96–99, Arctic Institute of North America, Montreal.

Ritchie, W. A. (1962 b), "The Antiquity of Pottery in the Northeast," *American Antiquity*, Vol. 27, No. 4, pp. 583–584, Salt Lake City.

Ritchie, W. A. and R. S. McNeish (1949), "The Pre-Iroquoian Pottery of New York State," *American Antiquity* Vol. 15, No. 2, pp. 97–124, Menasha.

Ritzenthaler, Robert (1946), "The Osceola Site—An 'Old Copper' Site near Potosi, Wisconsin," *The Wisconsin Archaeologist*, Vol. 27, No. 3, pp. 53–70, Milwaukee.

Ritzenthaler, Robert and W. L. Wittry (1952), "The Oconto Site: An Old Copper Manifestation," *The Wisconsin Archaeologist*, Vol. 33, No. 4, pp. 199–222, Milwaukee.

Roberts, F. H. H., Jr. (1929), *Shabik'eschee Village, A Late Basketmaker Site in the Chaco Canyon, New Mexico*, Bureau of American Ethnology, Bulletin 92, Smithsonian Institution, Washington, D.C.

Roberts, F. H. H., Jr. (1930), *Early Pueblo Ruins in the Piedra District, Southwestern Colorado*, Bureau of American Ethnology, Bulletin 96, Smithsonian Institution, Washington, D.C.

Roberts, F. H. H., Jr. (1931), *The Ruins of Kiatuthlanna, Eastern Arizona*, Bureau of American Ethnology, Bulletin 100, Smithsonian Institution, Washington, D.C.

Roberts, F. H. H., Jr. (1935 a), *A Folsom Complex*, Smithsonian Miscellaneous Collections, Vol. 94, No. 4, Smithsonian Institution, Washington, D.C.

Roberts, F. H. H., Jr. (1935 b), "A Survey of Southwestern Archaeology," *American Anthropologist*, Vol. 37, pp. 1–33, Menasha, Wisconsin.

Roberts, F. H. H., Jr. (1936), *Additional Information on the Folsom Complex*. Smithsonian Miscellaneous Collections, Vol. 95, No. 10, Smithsonian Institution.

Roberts, F. H. H., Jr. (1937), "Archaeology in the Southwest," *American Antiquity*, Vol. 3, pp.

3–33, Menasha, Wisconsin.

Roberts, F. H. H., Jr. (1939), "The Folsom Problem in American Archaeology," *Smithsonian Institution Report for 1938*, pp. 531–546, Washington, D.C.

Roberts, F. H. H., Jr. (1940), *Developments in the Problem of the North American Paleo-Indian*, Smithsonian Miscellaneous Collections, Vol. 100, pp. 51–116, Smithsonian Institution, Washington, D.C.

Rogers, D. B. (1929), *Prehistoric Man of the Santa Barbara Coast*, Santa Barbara Museum of Natural History, Santa Barbara.

Rogers, M. J. (1929), *Report of an Archaeological Reconnaissance in the Mohave Sink Region*, Archaeological Series, Vol. 1, No. 1, San Diego Museum, San Diego.

Rogers, M. J. (1939), *Early Lithic Industries of the Lower Basin of the Colorado River and Adjacent Desert Areas*, No. 3, San Diego Museum Papers, San Diego.

Rogers, M. J. (1945), "An Outline of Yuman Prehistory," *Southwestern Journal of Anthropology*, Vol. 1, pp. 167–198, Albuquerque.

Rogers, M. J. (1958), "San Dieguito Implements from the Terraces of the Rincon-Pantano and Rillito Drainage System," *Kiva*, Vol. 24, No. 1, pp. 1–23, University of Arizona, Tucson.

Roosa, W. B. (1956), "The Lucy Site in Central New Mexico," *American Antiquity*, Vol. 21, No. 3, pp. 280–281, Salt Lake City.

Rouse, Irving (1954), "On the Use of the Concept of Area Co-Tradition," *American Antiquity*, Vol. 19, pp. 221–225, Salt Lake City.

Rouse, Irving (1955), "On the Correlation of Phases of Culture," *American Anthropologist*, Vol. 57, No. 4, pp. 713–722, Menasha, Wisconsin.

Rowe, C. W. (1952), "Woodland Cultures of Eastern Tennessee," in *Archaeology of Eastern United States*, J. B. Griffin, ed., pp.

199–206, University of Chicago Press, Chicago.

Rowe, J. H. (1962), "Stages and Periods in Archaeological Interpretation," *Southwestern Journal of Anthropology*, Vol. 18, pp. 40–54, Albuquerque.

Rowley, Graham (1940), "The Dorset Culture of the Eastern Arctic," *American Anthropologist*, Vol. 42, pp. 490–499, Menasha.

Royo y Gomez, Jose (1960), "Venezuela Note," *Society of Vertebrate Paleontology News Bulletin*, No. 58, pp. 31–32, Cambridge.

Rubin de la Borbolla, D.F. (1948), "Arqueología Tarasca," in *El Occidente de Mexico*, pp. 29–33, Mesa Redonda, Sociedad Mexicana de Antropología, Mexico, D.F.

Rudenko, S. I. (1961), "The Ust'-Kanskaia Paleolithic Cave Site, Siberia," *American Antiquity*, Vol. 27, No. 2, pp. 203–215, Salt Lake City.

Russell, F. (1908), *The Pima Indians*. Annual Report, Bureau of American Ethnology, Vol. 26, pp. 3–390, Smithsonian Institution, Washington, D.C.

Russell, J. C. (1927), *North America*, Oxford University Press, New York.

Ruz, Alberto (1962), "Chichén Itzá y Tula: Commentarios a un ensayo," *Estudios Cultura Maya*, Vol. 2, pp. 205–221, Seminario Cultura Maya, Universidad Nacional Autonoma de Mexico, Mexico, D.F.

Sahagún, Bernadino de (1829–1830), *Historia General de Las Cosas de Nueva España*, Bustamente Edition, Valdés, Mexico, D.F.

Sander, Dan (1959). "Fluted Points from Madden Lake," *Panama Archaeologist*, Vol. 2, No. 1, pp. 39–51, Archaeological Society of Panama, Balboa.

Sanders, W. T. (1955), *An archaeological reconnaissance of northern Quintana Roo*, Current Report, No. 24, Department of Archaeology, Carnegie Institution of

Washington, Washington, D.C.

Sanders, W. T. (1960), *Prehistoric Ceramics and Settlement Patterns in Quintana Roo, Mexico*, Contribution to American Anthropology and History, No. 60, Publication No. 606, pp. 155–264, Carnegie Institution of Washington, Washington, D.C.

Satterthwaite, Linton, Jr. and E. K. Ralph, (1960), "New Radiocarbon Dates and the Maya Correlation Problem," *American Antiquity*, Vol. 26, pp. 165–184, Salt Lake City.

Sauer, C. O. (1950), "Geography of South America," in *Handbook of South American Indians*, J. H. Steward, ed., Vol. 5, pp. 319–344, Bureau of American Ethnology, Bulletin 143, Smithsonian Institution, Washington, D.C.

Sauer, C. O. (1952), *American Agricultural Origins and Dispersals*, American Geographical Society, New York.

Sauer, C. O. (1959), "Age and Area of American Cultural Plants," *Proceedings, 33rd International Congress of Americanists*, Vol. 1, pp. 215–229, San Jose, Costa Rica.

Sauer, C. O. and Donald Brand (1932), "Aztatlan, Prehistoric Mexican Frontier on the Pacific Coast," *Ibero-Americana*, No. 1, University of California.

Sayles, E. B. (1935), *An Archaeological Survey of Texas*, Gila Pueblo Medallion Papers, No. 17, Globe, Arizona.

Sayles, E. B. (1945), *The San Simon Branch: Excavations at Cave Creek and in the San Simon Valley: I: Material Culture*, Gila Pueblo Medallion Papers, No. 34, Globe, Arizona.

Sayles, E. B. and Ernst Antevs (1941), *The Cochise Culture*, Gila Pueblo Medallion Papers, No. 29. Globe, Arizona.

Sayles, E. B. and Ernst Antevs (1955), "Report Given at the 1955 Great Basin Archaeological

Conference," *American Antiquity,* Vol. 20, No. 3, p. 311, Menasha, Wisconsin. (Cited from Wormington, 1957.)

Schellhas, Paul (1904), *Representations of Deities of the Maya Manuscripts,* Peabody Museum Papers, Vol. 4, No. 1, Harvard University, Cambridge.

Schenck, W. E. (1926), *The Emeryville Shell Mound (Final Report),* Publications in American Archaeology and Ethnology, Vol. 23, pp, 123–146, University of California, Berkeley.

Schmitt, Karl (1952), "Archaeological Chronology of the Middle Atlantic States," in *Archaeology of Eastern United States,* J. B. Griffin, ed., pp. 59–70, University of Chicago Press, Chicago.

Schroeder, A. H. (1947), "Did the Sinagua of the Verde Valley Settle in the Salt River Valley," *Southwestern Journal of Anthropology,* Vol. 3, No. 3, pp. 230–246, Albuquerque.

Schroeder, A. H. (1957), "The Hakataya Cultural Tradition," *American Antiquity,* Vol. 23, No. 2, pp. 176–178, Salt Lake City.

Schroeder, A. H. (1963 a), "Hakataya, Patayan, and Hohokam," mimeographed, *Regional Research Abstract* No. 308, National Park Service, Santa Fe.

Schroeder, A. H. (1963 b), "The Sinagua Branch," mimeographed, *Regional Research Abstract,* No. 309, National Park Service. Santa Fe.

Schroeder, A. H. (1964), "Comments on Johnson's 'The Trincheras Culture of Northern Sonora'," *American Antiquity,* Vol. 30, No. 1, pp. 104–106, Salt Lake City.

Schroeder, A. H. (1965), "Unregulated Diffusion from Mexico into the Southwest Prior to A.D. 700," *American Antiquity,* Vol. 30, No. 3, pp. 297–309, Salt Lake City.

Schultz, C. B. (1932), *Association of Artifacts and Extinct Mammals in Nebraska,* Bulletin 33, Vol. 1, pp. 171–183, Nebraska Museum, Lincoln.

Schultz, C. B. and W. D. Frankforter, (1948), *Preliminary Report on the Lime Creek Sites; New Evidence of Early Man in Southwestern Nebraska,* Bulletin, Vol. 3, No. 4, Pt. 2, pp. 43–62, University of Nebraska State Museum, Lincoln.

Schwartz, D. W. (1956), "Demographic Changes in the Early Periods of Cohonina Prehistory," in *Prehistoric Settlement Patterns in the New World,* G. R. Willey, ed., pp. 26–34, Publications in Anthropology, No. 23, Viking Fund, New York.

Sears, W. H. (1948), "What is the Archaic?" *American Antiquity,* Vol. 14, No. 2, pp. 122–124, Mehasha, Wisconsin.

Sears, W. H. (1953), *Excavations at Kolomoki: Seasons III and IV, Mound D,* University of Georgia Series in Anthropology, No. 4, University of Georgia Press, Athens.

Sears, W. H. (1956, *Excavations at Kolomoki (Final Report),* University of Georgia Series in Anthropology, No. 5, University of Georgia Press, Athens.

Sears, W. H. (1964), "The Southeastern United States," in *Prehistoric Man in the New World,* J. D. Jennings and E. Norbeck, eds., pp. 259–290, University of Chicago Press, Chicago.

Sellards, E. H. (1952), *Early Man in America,* University of Texas Press, Austin.

Sellards, E. H., G. L. Evans, and G. E. Meade (1947), *Fossil Bison and Associated Artifacts from Plainview, Texas,* Bulletin, Vol. 58, pp. 927–954, Geological Society of America, New York.

Seltzer, C. C. (1944), *Racial Prehistory in the Southwest and the Hawikuh Zuñis,* Peabody Museum Papers, Vol. 23, No. 1, Harvard University, Cambridge.

Setzler, F. M. (1933), "Pottery of the Hopewell Type from Louisiana," *Proceedings, United States National Museum,* Vol. 82, Article 22, pp. 1–21, Smithsonian Institution, Washington, D.C.

Shepard, Anna O. (1948), *Plumbate, A Mesoamerican Trade Ware,* Publication 573, Carnegie Institution of Washington, Washington, D.C.

Shetrone, H. C. (1926), "Explorations of the Hopewell Group of Prehistoric Earthworks," *Ohio Archaeological and Historical Quarterly,* Vol. 35, No. 1, Columbus.

Shetrone, H. C. (1930), *The Mound-Builders,* Appleton-Century, New York.

Shetrone, H. C. and E. F. Greenman (1931), "Explorations of the Seip Group of Prehistoric Earthworks," *Ohio Archaeological and Historical Quarterly,* Vol. 40, No. 3, Columbus.

Shiner, Joel L. (1961), *The McNary Reservoir: A Study in Plateau Archaeology,* Bureau American Ethnology, Bulletin 179, pp. 149–259, Smithsonian Institution.

Shook, E. M. and A. V. Kidder (1952), *Mound E-III-3, Kaminaljuyú, Guatemala,* Contributions to American Anthropology and History, Vol. 11, No. 53, Carnegie Institution of Washington, Washington D.C.

Shook, E. M. and Tatiana Proskouriakoff (1956), "Settlement Patterns in Mesoamerica and the Sequence in the Guatemalan Highlands," in *Prehistoric Settlement Patterns in the New World,* G. R. Willey, ed., Publications in Anthropology, No. 23, pp. 93–100, Viking Fund, New York.

Shumway, G., C. L. Hubbs, and J. R. Moriarty (1961), *Scripps Estate Site, San Diego, California: A La Jolla Site Dated 5460 to 7370 Years Before the Present,* Annals, Vol. 93, pp. 37–132. New York Academy of Science, New York. (Cited from Heizer, 1964.)

Shutler, Richard (1965), "Tule Springs Expedition," *Current Anthropology,* Vol. 6, No. 1, pp. 110–111, Utrecht.

Simpson, R. D. (1958), "The Lake Manix Archaeological Survey," *The Masterkey,* Vol. 32, No. 1, pp. 4–10, Los Angeles.

Simpson, R. D. (1960), "Archaeological Survey of the Eastern Calico Mountains," The *Masterkey,* Vol. 34, No. 1, pp. 25–35, Los Angeles.

Simpson, R. D. (1961), *Coyote Gulch: Archaeological Investigations of an Early Lithic Locality in the Mojave Desert of San Bernardino County,* Archaeological Survey Association of Southern California, Paper No. 5, Los Angeles.

Simpson, R. D. (1964), "The Archaeological Survey of Pleistocene Manix Lake (An Early Lithic Horizon)," *Proceedings, 35th International Congress of Americanists,* Vol. 1, pp. 5–9, Mexico, D.F.

Smith, A. G. (1957), "Suggested Change in Nomenclature of Major American Time Periods," *American Antiquity,* Vol. 23, No. 2, pp. 169, Salt Lake City.

Smith, A. L. (1950), *Uaxactún, Guatemala: Excavations of 1931–37,* Publication 588, Carnegie Institution of Washington, Washington, D.C.

Smith, A. L. (1955), *Archaeological Reconnaissance in Central Guatemala,* Publication 608, Carnegie Institution of Washington.

Smith, C. E., Jr. (1950), *Prehistoric Plant Remains from Bat Cave,* Botanical Museum Leaflet, Vol. 14, No. 7, Harvard University, Cambridge.

Smith, C. E., Jr. and R. S. MacNeish (1964), "Antiquity of American Polyploid Cotton," *Science,* Vol. 143, Lancaster.

Smith, E. R. (1941), *Archaeology of Deadman Cave, Utah,* Bulletin, Vol. 32, No. 4, University of Utah, Salt Lake City.

Smith, E. R. (1952), *The Archaeology of Deadman Cave: A Revision,* Anthropological Papers, No. 10, University of Utah, Salt Lake City.

Smith, H. G. (1948), "Two Historical Archaeological Periods in Florida," *American Antiquity,* Vol. 13, No. 4, pp. 313–319, Menasha, Wisconsin.

Smith, H. I. (1903), *Shell Heaps of the Lower Fraser River,* B.C., Memoirs, Vol. 3, No. 4, American Museum of Natural History, New York.

Smith, H. I. (1907), *Archaeology of the Gulf of Georgia and Puget Sound,* Memoir 4, pp. 301–441, American Museum of Natural History, New York.

Smith, H. I. (1909), *Shell-Heaps of the Lower Fraser,* Memoir 4, pp. 133–191, American Museum of Natural History, New York.

Smith, M. W. (1950), *Archaeology of the Columbia-Fraser Region,* Memoir No. 6, Society for American Archaeology, Menasha, Wisconsin.

Smith, M. W. (1956), "The Cultural Development of the Northwest Coast," *Southwestern Journal of Anthropology,* Vol. 12, Albuquerque.

Snow, C. E. and W. T. Sanders (1954), "The Durango Skeletons," in *Basket Maker II Sites near Durango, Colorado,* E. H. Morris and R. F. Burgh, eds., Publication No. 604, pp. 89–92, Carnegie Institution of Washington, Washington, D.C.

Soday, F. J. (1954), "The Quad Site: A Paleo-Indian Village in Northern Alabama," *The Tennessee Archaeologist,* Vol. 10, No. 1, pp. 1–20, Knoxville.

Solecki, R. S. (1950), "New Data on the Inland Eskimo of Northern Alaska," *Journal of Washington Academy of Sciences,* Vol. 40, pp. 137–157, Washington, D.C.

Solecki, R. S. (1951), "Notes on Two Archaeological Discoveries in Alaska, 1950," *American Antiquity,* Vol. 17, No. 1, pp. 55–57, Salt Lake City.

Spaulding, A. C. (1946), "Northeastern Archaeology and General Trends in the Northern Forest Zone," in *Man in Northeastern North America,* F. Johnson, ed., pp. 143–167, Papers, R. S. Peabody Foundation for Archaeology, Andover.

Spaulding, A. C. (1952), "The Origin of the Adena Culture of the Ohio Valley," *Southwestern Journal of Anthropology,* Vol. 8, pp. 260–268, Albuquerque.

Spaulding, A. C. (1956), *The Arzberger Site, Hughes County, South Dakota,* Occasional Contributions, No. 16, Museum of Anthropology, University of Michigan, Ann Arbor.

Spaulding, A. C. (1962), *Archaeological Investigations on Agattu, Aleutian Islands,* Anthropological Papers, No. 18, Museum of Anthropology, University of Michigan, Ann Arbor.

Spier, Leslie (1936), *Cultural Relations of the Gila River and Lower Colorado Tribes,* Yale University Publications in Anthropology, No. 3, New Haven.

Spinden, E. S. (1933), "The Place of Tajín in Totonac Archaeology," *American Anthropologist,* Vol. 35, pp. 271–286, Menasha, Wisconsin.

Spinden, H. J. (1928), *Ancient Civilizations of Mexico and Central America,* Handbook Series, No. 3, American Museum of Natural History, New York.

Staub, Walther (1920), "Neue Funde und Ausgrabungen in der Huaxteca (Ost-Mexico)," *Beilage zum Jahresbericht über dei Ethnographische Sammlung,* Bern.

Steen, C. R. (1953), *Two Early Historic Sites on the Southern Plains,* Bulletin Vol. 24, pp. 177–188, Texas Archaeological Society, Abilene.

Steen, C. R. (1959), "The Pigeon

Cliffs Site, Union County, New Mexico," *Abstract of paper presented at 24th annual meeting,* Society for American Archaeology, Salt Lake City.

Stevenson, M. C. (1904), *The Zuñi Indians.* Annual Report, Vol. 23, pp. 13–608, Bureau of American Ethnology, Smithsonian Institution, Washington, D.C.

Steward, J. H. (1937), *Ancient Caves of the Great Lake Region,* Bulletin 116, Bureau of American Ethnology, Smithsonian Institution, Washington, D.C.

Steward, J. H. (1948), "A functional-Developmental Classification of American High Cultures," in *A Reappraisal of Peruvian Archaeology,* W. C. Bennett, ed., Memoir No. 4, pp. 103–104, Society for American Archaeology, Menasha, Wisconsin.

Steward, J. H. (1955), *Theory of Culture Change,* University of Illinois Press, Urbana.

Steward, J. H. and L. C. Faron (1959), *Native Peoples of South America,* McGraw-Hill, New York.

Stewart, T. D. (1953), "Amériques," in *Catalogue des Hommes Fossiles,* Fascicule V des Comptes Rendus de la XIX Session des Congrès Geologique International, pp. 354–364, Algiers.

Stewart, T. D. (1960), "A Physical Anthropologist's View of the Peopling of the New World," *Southwestern Journal of Anthropology,* Vol. 16, pp. 259–273, Albuquerque.

Stirling, M. W. (1940), *An Initial Series from Tres Zapotes, Vera Cruz, Mexico,* Contributed Technical Papers, Mexican Archaeology Series, Vol. 1, No. 1, National Geographic Society, Washington, D.C.

Stirling, M. W. (1943), *Stone Monuments of Southern Mexico,* Bulletin 138, Bureau of American Ethnology, Smithsonian Institution, Washington, D.C.

Stone, Doris, Z. (1941), *Archaeology of the North Coast of Honduras,* Memoir, Vol. 9, No. 1, Peabody Museum, Harvard University, Cambridge.

Stone, Doris Z. (1957), *The Archaeology of Central and Southern Honduras,* Peabody Museum Papers, Vol. 29, No. 3, Harvard University, Cambridge.

Stonor, C. R. and E. Anderson (1949), *Maize Among the Hill Peoples of Assam,* Annals, No. 36, pp. 355–404, Missouri Botanical Gardens, St. Louis.

Strebel, Hermann (1885–1889), *Alt-Mexico: Archaeologische Beiträge zur Kulturgeschichte Seiner Bewohner,* Vols. 1–2, Hamburg.

Strong, W. D. (1930), "A Stone Culture from Northern Labrador and Its Relation to the Eskimo-like Cultures of the Northeast," *American Anthropologist,* Vol. 32, No. 1, Menasha, Wisconsin.

Strong, W. D. (1935), *An Introduction to Nebraska Archaeology,* Smithsonian Miscellaneous Collections, Vol. 93, No. 10, Smithsonian Institution, Washington, D.C.

Strong, W. D. (1948), "The Archaeology of Honduras." *Handbook of South American Indians,* J. H. Steward, ed., Vol. 4, pp. 71–120, Bureau of American Ethnology, Bulletin 143, Smithsonian Institution, Washington, D.C.

Strong, W. D., Alfred Kidder, II, and A. J. Drexel Paul, Jr. (1938), *Preliminary Report on the Smithsonian Institution-Harvard University Archaeological Expedition to Northwestern Honduras,* Smithsonian Miscellaneous Collections, Vol. 97, No. 1, Smithsonian Institution, Washington, D.C.

Strong, W. D., W. E. Schenck, and J. H. Steward, (1930), *Archaeology of the Dalles-Deschutes Region,* Publications in American Archaeology and Ethnology, Vol. 29, No. 1, University of California, Berkeley.

Struever, Stuart (1962), "Implication of Vegetal Remains from an Illinois Hopewell Site," *American Antiquity,* Vol. 27, No. 4, pp. 584–87, Salt Lake City.

Sturtevant, W. C. (1960), *The Significance of Ethnological Similarities Between Southeastern North America and the Antilles,* Publications in Anthropology, No. 64, Yale University, New Haven.

Suhm, D. A., A. D. Krieger, and E. B. Jelks (1954), *An Introductory Handbook of Texas Archaeology,* Bulletin, Vol. 25, Texas Archaeological Society, Austin.

Swadesh, Morris (1960), *La Linguística como Instrumento de la Prehistória,* Instituto Nacional de Antropología e Historia, Dirección de Prehistoria, Pub. 9, Mexico, D.F.

Swadesh, Morris (1964) "Linguistic Overview," in *Prehistoric Man in the New World,* J. D. Jennings and E. Norbeck, eds., pp 527–558, University of Chicago Press, Chicago.

Swadesh, Morris, et al. (1954), "Symposium: Time Depths of American Linguistic Groupings," *American Anthropologist,* Vol. 56, pp. 387–394, Menasha, Wisconsin.

Swanson, E. H., Jr. (1961), "Approach to Culture History in the Pacific Northwest," *Southwestern Journal of Anthropology,* Vol. 17, pp. 140–145, Albuquerque.

Swanson, E. H., Jr. (1962 a), "Early Cultures in Northwestern America," *American Antiquity,* Vol. 28, No. 2, pp. 151–158, Albuquerque.

Swanson, E. H., Jr. (1962 b), *The Emergence of Plateau Culture,* Occasional Papers, No. 8, Idaho State College Museum, Pocatello.

Swanton, J. R. (1911), *Indian Tribes of the Lower Mississippi Valley,* Bulletin 43, Bureau of American Ethnology, Smithsonian Institution, Washington, D.C.

Swauger, J. L. and W. J. Mayer-Oakes (1952), "A Fluted Point from Costa Rica," *American Antiquity,* Vol. 17, pp, 264–265, Salt Lake City.

Tauber, H. (1960), "Copenhagen Radiocarbon Dates IV," Radiocarbon Supplement, Vol. 2, pp. 12–25, *American Journal of Science,* New Haven.

Taylor, W. E., Jr. (1964), "Archaeology of the McCormick Inlet Site, Melville Island, N.W.T.," *Arctic,* Journal of the Arctic Institute of North America, Vol. 17, No. 2, pp. 126–129, Montreal.

Taylor, W. W. (1956), *Some Implications of the Carbon-14 Dates from a Cave in Coahuila, Mexico,* Bulletin, Vol. 27, pp. 215–234, Texas Archaeological Society, Abilene.

Taylor, W. W. (1961), "Archaeology and Language in Western North America," *American Antiquity,* Vol. 27, No. 1, pp. 71–81, Salt Lake City.

Thomas, Cyrus (1894), *Report on the Mound Explorations of the Bureau of American Ethnology,* Annual Report, Vol. 12, pp. 3–730, Bureau of American Ethnology, Smithsonian Institution, Washington, D.C.

Thompson, J. E. S. (1935), *Maya Chronology: The Correlation Question,* Contribution No. 14, Publication No. 456, Carnegie Institution of Washington, Washington, D.C.

Thompson, J. E. S. (1941), *Dating of Certain Inscriptions of non-Maya Origin,* Theoretical Approaches to Problems, No. 1, Division of Historical Research, Carnegie Institution of Washington, Washington, D.C.

Thompson, J. E. S. (1945), "A Survey of the Northern Maya Area," *American Antiquity,* Vol. 11, pp. 2–24, Menasha, Wisconsin.

Thompson, J. E. S. (1948), *An Archaeological Reconnaissance in the Cotzumalhuapa Region, Escuintla, Guatemala,* Contributions to American Archaeology and History, No. 44, Publication No. 574, Carnegie Institution of Washington, Washington, D.C.

Thompson, J. E. S. (1950), *Maya Hieroglyphic Writing: Introduction,* Publication No. 589, Carnegie Institution of Washington, Washington, D.C.

Thompson, J. E. S. (1954), *The Rise and Fall of Maya Civilization,* University of Oklahoma Press, Norman.

Thompson, R. H. (1956), "The Subjective Element in Archaeological Inference," *Southwestern Journal of Anthropology,* Vol. 12, No. 3. pp. 327–332, Albuquerque.

Thompson, R. H. (1958), *Modern Yucatecan Maya Pottery-Making,* Memoir No. 15, Society for American Archaeology, Salt Lake City.

Tolstoy, Paul (1958 a), "The Archaeology of the Lena Basin and Its New World Relationships, Part I," *American Antiquity,* Vol. 23, No. 4, pp. 397–418, Salt Lake City.

Tolstoy, Paul (1958 b), "The Archaeology of the Lena Basin and its New World Relationships, Part II," *American Antiquity,* Vol. 24, pp. 63–81, Salt Lake City.

Tolstoy, Paul (1958 c), *Surface Survey of the Northern Valley of Mexico: The Classic and Post-Classic Periods,* Transactions Vol. 48, Pt. 5, American Philosophical Society, Philadelphia.

Tozzer, A. M. (1957), *Chichén Itzá and Its Cenote of Sacrifice: A Comparative Study of Contemporaneous Maya and Toltec,* Memoirs, Vols. 11–12, Peabody Museum, Harvard University, Cambridge.

Tozzer, A. M., ed. (1941), *Landa's Relación de Las Cosas de Yucatán,* a translation, Peabody Museum Papers, Vol. 18, Harvard University, Cambridge.

Treganza, A. E. (1942), "An Archaeological Reconnaissance of Northeastern Baja California and Southeastern California," *American Antiquity,* Vol. 8, No. 2, pp. 152–163, Menasha, Wisconsin.

Treganza, A. E. (1952), *Archaeological Investigations in the Farmington Reservoir Area, Stainislaus County, California,* Reports of the University of California Archaeological Survey, No. 14, Berkeley.

Treganza, A. E. and A. Bierman (1958), *The Topanga Culture: Final Report on Excavations, 1948,* University of California Anthropological Records, Vol. 2, No. 2, Berkeley.

Treganza, A. E. and R. F. Heizer (1953), *Additional Data on the Farmington Complex: A Stone Implement Assemblage of Probable Early Postglacial Date from Central California,* Reports of the University of California, Archaeological Survey, No. 22, Berkeley.

Treganza, A. E. and C. G. Malamud (1950), *The Topanga Culture: First Season's Excavation of the Tank Site, 1947,* Report of University of California Anthropological Records, Vol. 12, No. 4, Los Angeles.

Trewartha, G. T. (1954), *An Introduction to Climate,* McGraw-Hill, New York.

Underhill, R. M. (1939), *Social Organization of the Papago Indians,* Contributions to Anthropology, No. 30, Columbia University, New York.

Vaillant, G. C. (1930), *Excavations at Zacatenco,* Anthropological Papers, Vol. 32, Pt. 1, American Museum of Natural History, New York.

Vaillant, G. C. (1935), *Excavations at El Arbolillo,* Anthropological Papers, Vol. 35, Pt. 2, American Museum of Natural History, New York.

Vaillant, G. C. (1938), "A Correlation of Archaeological and Historical Sequences in the Valley of Mexico," *American Anthropolo-*

gist, Vol. 40, pp. 535–573, New York.

Vaillant, G. C. (1941), *Aztecs of Mexico,* Doubleday, New York.

Vignati, M. A. (1927), "Arqueología y Antropología de los Conchales Fueginos," *Revista del Museo de la Plata,* Vol. 30, pp. 79–143, Buenos Aires.

Vogt, E. Z. (1961), "Navaho," in *Perspectives in American Indian Culture Change,* E. H. Spicer, ed., pp. 278–336, University of Chicago Press, Chicago.

Von Eickstedt, Egon (1933–1934), *Rassenkunde und Rassengeschichte der Menschheit,* Ferdinand Enke Verlag, Stuttgart.

Walker, E. F. (1951), *Five Prehistoric Archaeological Sites in Los Angeles County, California,* Publications, F. W. Hodge Anniversary Fund, No. 6, Southwest Museum, Los Angeles.

Wallace, W. J. (1954), "The Little Sycamore Site and the Early Milling Stone Cultures of Southern California," *American Antiquity,* Vol. 20, pp. 112–123, Salt Lake City.

Wallace, W. J. (1955), "A Suggested Chronology for Southern California Coastal Archaeology," *Southwestern Journal of Anthropology,* Vol. 11, pp. 214–230, Albuquerque.

Wallace, W. J. (1962), "Prehistoric Cultural Development in the Southern California Deserts," *American Antiquity,* Vol. 28, No. 2, pp. 172–180, Salt Lake City.

Walter, H. V. (1948), *The Pre-History of the Lagoa Santa Region.* Minas Gerais, Belo Horizonte, Brazil.

Waring, A. J., Jr. and Preston Holder (1945), "A Prehistoric Ceremonial Complex in the Southeastern United States," *American Anthropologist,* Vol. 47, No. 1, pp. 1–34, Menasha, Wisconsin.

Warren, C. N. and D. L. True (1961), *The San Dieguito Complex and Its Place in California Prehistory,* Archaeological Survey, Annual Report for 1960–61, pp. 246–291, Department of Anthropology and Sociology, University of California, Los Angeles.

Wasley, W. W. (1960), "A Hohokam Platform Mound at the Gatlin Site," *American Antiquity,* Vol. 26, pp. 244–262, Salt Lake City.

Wauchope, Robert (1948), *Excavations at Zacualpa, Guatemala,* Publication No. 14, Middle American Research Institute, Tulane University, New Orleans.

Wauchope, Robert (1950), "A Tentative Sequence of Pre-Classic Ceramics in Middle America," *Middle American Research Records,* Vol. 1, No. 14, Middle American Research Institute, Tulane University, New Orleans.

Wauchope, Robert (1964), "Southern Mesoamerica," in *Prehistoric Man in the New World,* J. D. Jennings and E. Norbeck, eds., pp. 331–388, University of Chicago Press, Chicago.

Webb, C. H. (1948), "Evidence of Pre-Pottery Cultures in Louisiana," *American Antiquity,* Vol. 13, No. 3, pp. 227–231, Menasha, Wisconsin.

Webb, W. S. and R. S. Baby (1957), *The Adena People, No. 2,* Ohio State University Press, Columbus.

Webb, W. S. and D. L. De Jarnette (1942), *An Archaeological Survey of Pickwick Basin in the Adjacent Portions of the States of Alabama, Mississippi, and Tennessee.* Bulletin No. 129, Bureau of American Ethnology, Smithsonian Institution, Washington, D.C.

Webb, W. S. and D. L. De Jarnette (1948), *The Flint River Site, Ma-o-48,* Geological Survey of Alabama, Museum Paper No. 23, University Alabama, University.

Webb, W. S. and W. D. Funkhouser (1936), *Rock Shelters in Menifee County, Kentucky,* Reports in Anthropology, Vol. 3, No. 4, University of Kentucky, Lexington.

Webb, W. S. and C. E. Snow, (1945), *The Adena People,* Reports in Anthropology and Archaeology, Vol. 6, University of Kentucky, Lexington.

Wedel, W. R. (1938), *The Direct-Historical Approach in Pawnee Archaeology,* Smithsonian Miscellaneous Collections, Vol. 97, No. 7, Smithsonian Institution, Washington, D.C.

Wedel, W. R. (1941), *Environment and Native Subsistence Economies in the Central Great Plains,* Smithsonian Miscellaneous Collections, Vol. 101, No. 3, Smithsonian Institution, Washington, D.C.

Wedel, W. R. (1942), *Archaeological Remains in Central Kansas and Their Possible Bearing on the Location of Quivira,* Smithsonian Miscellaneous Collections, Vol. 101, No. 7, Smithsonian Institution, Washington, D.C.

Wedel, W. R. (1943), *Archaeological Investigations in Platte and Clay Counties, Missouri,* United States National Museum Bulletin 183, Smithsonian Institution, Washington, D.C.

Wedel, W. R. (1953), "Some Aspects of Human Ecology in the Central Plains," *American Anthropologist,* Vol. 55, pp. 499–514, Menasha, Wisconsin.

Wedel, W. R. (1959), *An Introduction to Kansas Archaeology,* Bureau American Ethnology, Bulletin 174, Smithsonian Institution, Washington, D.C.

Wedel, W. R. (1961), *Prehistoric Man on the Great Plains,* University of Oklahoma Press, Norman.

Wedel, W. R. (1964), "The Great Plains," in *Prehistoric Man in the New World,* J. D. Jennings and E. Norbeck, eds., pp. 193–222, University of Chicago Press, Chicago.

Wendorf, Fred (1956), "Some Distributions of Settlement Patterns in the Pueblo Southwest," in *Prehistoric Settlement Patterns in the New World,* G. R. Willey, ed., pp. 18–25, Publications in Anthropology, No. 23, Viking Fund, New York.

Wendorf, Fred and J. J. Hester (1962), "Early Man's Utilization of the Great Plains Environment," *American Antiquity,* Vol. 28, No. 2, pp. 159–171, Salt Lake City.

Wendorf, Fred and A. D. Krieger (1959), "New Light on the Midland Discovery," *American Antiquity,* Vol. 25, pp. 66–78, Salt Lake City.

Wendorf, Fred, A. D. Krieger, C. C. Albritton, and T. D. Stewart (1955), *The Midland Discovery,* University of Texas Press, Austin.

Wheat, J. B. (1953), *An Archaeological Survey of the Addicks Dam Basin, Southeast Texas,* River Basin Surveys Papers, Bureau of American Ethnology, Bulletin 154, Smithsonian Institution, Washington, D.C.

Wheat, J. B. (1954 a), "Southwestern Cultural Interrelationships and the Question of Area Co-Tradition," *American Anthropologist,* Vol. 56, pp. 576–585, Menasha, Wisconsin.

Wheat, J. B. (1954 b), *Crooked Ridge Village, Arizona W:10:15,* Bulletin, Vol. 25, No. 3, University of Arizona, Tucson.

Wheat, J. B. (1955), *Mogollon Culture Prior to* A.D. *1000,* Memoir No. 82, American Anthropological Association, Menasha, Wisconsin.

Wheeler, R. P. (1954), *Selected Projectile Point Types of the United States: II,* Bulletin, Vol. 2, pp. 1–6, Oklahoma Anthropological Society, Norman.

Willey, G. R. (1949 a), *Archaeology of the Florida Gulf Coast,* Smithsonian Miscellaneous Collections, Vol. 113, Smithsonian Institution, Washington, D.C.

Willey, G. R. (1949 b), "The Southeastern United States and South America: A Comparative Statement," in *The Florida Indian and His Neighbors,* J. W. Griffin, ed., pp. 101–116, Rollins College, Winter Park, Florida.

Willey, G. R. (1953), "Archaeological Theories and Interpretation: New World," in *Anthropology Today,* A. L. Kroeber, *et al.,* eds., pp. 361–385, University of Chicago Press, Chicago.

Willey, G. R. (1958), "An Archaeological Perspective on Algonkian-Gulf Relationships," *Southwestern Journal of Anthropology,* Vol. 14, No. 3, pp. 265–272, Albuquerque.

Willey, G. R. (1960 a), "New World Prehistory," *Science,* Vol. 131, No. 3393, pp. 73–83, Lancaster.

Willey, G. R. (1960 b), "Historical Patterns and Evolution in Native New World Cultures," in *Evolution After Darwin,* Vol. 2, *The Evolution of Man,* S. Tax, ed., pp. 111–141, University of Chicago Press, Chicago.

Willey, G. R. (1962 a), "The Early Great Styles and the Rise of the Pre-Columbian Civilizations," *American Anthropologist,* Vol. 64, No. 1, pp. 1–14, Menasha, Wisconsin.

Willey, G. R. (1962 b), "Mesoamerica," in *Courses Towards Urban Life: Archaeological Considerations of Some Cultural Alternates,* R. J. Braidwood and G. R. Willey, eds., Publications in Anthropology, No. 32, pp. 84–105, Viking Fund, New York.

Willey, G. R., W. R. Bullard, J. B. Glass, and J. C. Gifford (1965), *Prehistoric Maya Settlements in the Belize Valley,* Peabody Museum Papers, Vol. 54, Harvard University, Cambridge.

Willey, G. R., G. F. Ekholm, and R. F. Millon (1964), "Patterns of Mesoamerican Farming Life and Civilization," in *Handbook of Middle American Indians,* Vol. 1, R. Wauchope ed., University of Texas Press, Austin.

Willey, G. R. and C. R. McGimsey (1954), *The Monagrillo Culture of Panama,* Peabody Museum Papers, Vol. 49, No. 2, Harvard University, Cambridge.

Willey, G. R. and Philip Phillips (1955), "Method and Theory in American Archaeology II: Historical-Developmental Interpretation," *American Anthropologist,* Vol. 57, No. 4, Menasha, Wisconsin.

Willey, G. R. and Philip Phillips (1958), *Method and Theory in American Archaeology,* University of Chicago Press, Chicago.

Willey, G. R. and A. L. Smith (1963), "New Discoveries at Altar de Sacrificios, Guatemala," *Archaeology,* Vol. 16, No. 2, pp. 83–89, Cambridge.

Willey, G. R., A. L. Smith, W. R. Bullard, Jr., and J. A. Graham (1960), "Altar de Sacrificios, a Prehistoric Maya Crossroads," *Archaeology,* Vol. 13, pp. 110–117, Cambridge.

Williams, Stephen (1957), "The Island 35 Mastodon: Its Bearing on the Age of Archaic Cultures in the East," *American Antiquity,* Vol. 22, pp. 359–372, Salt Lake City.

Wilmsen, E. N. (1964), "Flake Tools in the American Arctic: Some Speculations," *American Antiquity,* Vol. 29, No. 3, pp. 338–344, Salt Lake City.

Willoughby, C. C. and E. A. Hooton (1922), *The Turner Group of Earthworks, Hamilton County, Ohio,* Peabody Museum Papers, Vol. 8, No. 3, Harvard University, Cambridge.

Wissler, Clark (1922), *The American Indian,* 2nd ed., Oxford University Press, New York.

Wissler, Clark (1938), *The American Indian,* 3rd ed., Oxford University Press, New York.

Witthoft, John (1952), "A Paleo-Indian Site in Eastern Pennsylvania, An Early Hunting Culture," *Proceedings of the American Philosophical Society,* Vol. 96, No. 4, pp. 464–495, Philadelphia.

Witthoft, John (1956), "Paleo-Indian Cultures in Eastern and Southeastern North America," mimeographed, in *Chronology and Development of Early Cultures in North America,* F. Johnson, ed., Andover.

Witthoft, John (1959), "Notes on the Archaic of the Appalachian Region," *American Antiquity,* Vol. 25, pp. 79–85, Salt Lake City.

Wolf, E. R. (1959), *Sons of the Shaking Earth,* University of Chicago Press, Chicago.

Wolf, E. R. and Angel Palerm (1955), "Investigation in the Old Acolhua Domain, Mexico," *Southwestern Journal of Anthropol-ogy,* Vol. 11, No. 3, pp. 265–281, Albuquerque.

Woodbury, R. B. (1961), *Prehistoric Agriculture at Point of Pines, Arizona,* Memoir No. 17, Society for American Archaeology, Salt Lake City.

Wormington, H. M. (1955), *A Reappraisal of the Fremont Culture,* Proceedings, No. 1, Denver Museum of Natural History, Denver.

Wormington, H. M. (1957), *Ancient Man in North America,* 4th ed., Popular Series No. 4, Denver Museum of Natural History, Denver.

Wormington, H. M. (1961 a), "Prehistoric Cultural Stages of Alberta, Canada," in *Homenaje a Pablo Martínez del Rio,* 25 Anniversario de la edición de Los Origenes Americanos, pp. 163–171, Mexico, D.F.

Wormington, H. M. (1961 b), *Prehistoric Indians of the Southwest,* 5th ed., Popular Series, No. 7, Denver Museum of Natural History, Denver.

Wray, D. E. (1952), "Archaeology of the Illinois Valley: 1950," in *Archaeology of Eastern United States,* J. B. Griffin, ed., pp. 152–164, University of Chicago Press, Chicago.

Wyman, Jeffries (1875), *Fresh-water Shell Mounds of the St. Johns River, Florida,* Memoirs, Vol. 1, No. 4, Peabody Academy of Science, Salem.

Yarnell, R. A. (1964), *Aboriginal Relationships Between Culture and Plant Life in the Upper Great Lakes Region,* Anthropological Papers, No. 23, Museum of Anthropology, University of Michigan, Ann Arbor.

Maps

Chronological Charts

Index

A

Abnakis, 252
Adena, 268–272
Afontova Gora site, 70
Agate Basin complex, 40, 44, 46–47
Agate Basin point, 71
Agriculture, cultural stage in, 477–478
Ahtena tribe, 413
Ainus, 13
Ajuereado site, 31, 66, 67
Alberta points, 47
Aleutian Core and Blade industry, 71, 419
Aleuts, 412, 419
Algonquian-speaking Indians, 252, 413–414
Alkali Ridge, 206, 207–208, 213
Alma pottery, 184–185
Alta Vista de Chalchuites, 174
Altar de Sacrificios, 117, 141
Amargosa, 183, 230
Americas, 7–8
  adaptations in, 14–16
  Archaic tradition in (*see* Archaic tradition)
  Arctic and (*see* Arctic)
  area chronologies, 469–473
  Asia and, 33–37
  Big-Game Hunting tradition in (*see* Big-Game Hunting tradition)

Americas (*cont.*)
  California Coast and Valley tradition in (*see* California Coast and Valley tradition)
  climate of, 10–12
  cultural traditions, 454–469
  culture origins, 19–24
  culture stages in, 476–478
  Desert tradition in (*see* Desert tradition)
  languages of, 16–19
  major periods in, 473–476
  Mesoamerica (*see* Mesoamerica)
  Mississippian tradition in (*see* Mississippian tradition)
  natural setting of, 8–12
  Northwest Coast (*see* Northwest Coast)
  Northwest Riverine tradition in (*see* Northwest Riverine tradition)
  Old Cordilleran tradition in (*see* Old Cordilleran tradition)
  people of, 12–16, 29–37
  physiography of, 8–10
  Plains Village tradition in (*see* Plains Village tradition)
  Pleistocene glaciation and, 26–29
  South America (*see* South America)
  Southwest (*see* Southwest)
  Subarctic and (*see* Subarctic)
  sub-races in, 13–14
  Woodland tradition in (*see* Woodland tradition)
Ampajango site, 32, 33